Richard Gough, Thomas Payne

Sepulchral monuments in Great Britain

applied to illustrate the history of families, manners, habits and arts, at the different periods

from the Norman conquest to the seventeenth century

Richard Gough, Thomas Payne

Sepulchral monuments in Great Britain
applied to illustrate the history of families, manners, habits and arts, at the different periods from the Norman conquest to the seventeenth century

ISBN/EAN: 9783743335059

Manufactured in Europe, USA, Canada, Australia, Japa

Cover: Foto ©ninafisch / pixelio.de

Manufactured and distributed by brebook publishing software (www.brebook.com)

Richard Gough, Thomas Payne

Sepulchral monuments in Great Britain

P R E F A C E.

WHEN Pere MONTFAUCON firft undertook his inimitable Work, "Les Monumens de la Monarchie Françoife," he profeffed to give the Monuments of the refpective reigns detached and unconnected. But apprehending there would be too many vacant intervals to pafs over, and more books to be confulted by his readers to fill them up, he was induced to take on himfelf the trouble of fupplying this void. His intimate acquaintance with the hiftory of his country enabled him to do this properly. The innumerable monuments either actually exifting or preferved in drawings in the cabinets of the curious demanded fuch connection.

His work contains, in five volumes folio, the Hiftory of France, with all the monuments relative to her fovereigns, princes of the blood, nobility, the king's houfhold, and the great officers of the crown. He intended to add four more volumes: two of ecclefiaftical monuments, and two of private life, coinage, military matters, and *funerals*, on the fame plan; with a fupplement at the end, of all that had efcaped his obfervation, or been difcovered fince.

Such was the extent of this learned Antiquary's views. Whether his life or his encouragement proved unequal to the complete execution of them does not appear. His defign has been in part refumed by Monf. le Grand Auffy; who has fo fully illuftrated the hiftory of the private life of the French, from the earlieft period to the prefent time. The three volumes already publifhed in octavo comprize a very fmall portion of his extenfive plan, only what concerns the *table*, and its various appendages and pleafures; in which hufbandry, gardening, hunting, &c. are included; but he promifes, from his valuable collection of drawings, copied from tombs, painted windows and fronts of churches, and other antient monuments, a complete hiftory of dreffes and fafhions in all parts, and among all orders and ranks in Franks. And it is only from thefe fources that we can deduce fuch parts of the hiftory of paft times, and our acquaintance with thofe who lived before us.

The plan of thefe two writers includes the whole of what among us has been divided into different parts, and attempted by different perfons.

How much muſt we regret the failure of that well-concerted plan, which would, under the direction of its firſt promoter, have furniſhed a body of monuments of Engliſh Monarchy. Mr. Walpole cannot be diſpleaſed at the circulation of his own moſt laudable intention, as I find it in a letter addreſſed by him to the late Mr. Cole of Milton, in 1769.

" With regard to an Hiſtory of Gothic Architecture, in which Mr. Eſſex deſires my advice, the plan I think ſhould be in a very ſimple compaſs. Was I to execute it, it ſhould be thus: I would give a ſeries of plates, even from the concluſion of Saxon architecture, beginning with the round *Roman arch*, and going on to ſhew how they plaiſtered and zigzaged it, and then how better ornaments crept in, till the beautiful Gothic was arrived at its perfection; then how it declined in Henry VIII's reign; archbiſhop *Warham's* tomb at Canterbury being, I believe, the laſt example of unbaſtardized Gothic. A very few plates more would demonſtrate its change. Hans Holbein embroidered it with ſome morſels of true architecture; in queen Elizabeth's reign there was ſcarce any architecture at all; I mean no pillars, or ſeldom; buildings then becoming quite plain. Under James a barbarous compoſition ſucceeded. A ſingle plate of ſomething of Inigo Jones in his heavieſt and worſt ſtyle ſhould terminate the work; for he ſoon ſtepped into the true and perfect Grecian.

" The next part Mr. Eſſex can do better than any body, and is perhaps the only man that can do it. This ſhould conſiſt of obſervations on the art, proportion, and method of building, and the reaſons obſerved by the Gothic Architects for what they did. This would ſhew what great men they were, and how they raiſed ſuch aerial and ſtupendous maſſes, though unaſſiſted by half the lights now enjoyed by their ſucceſſors.

" The prices and the wages of workmen, and the comparative value of money at the ſeveral periods, ſhould be ſtated, as far as it is poſſible to get materials.

" The laſt part (I don't know whether it ſhould not be the firſt part) nobody can do ſo well as yourſelf. This muſt be to aſcertain the chronologic part of each building; and not only of each building, but of each *tomb* that ſhall be exhibited; for you know the great delicacy and richneſs of Gothic ornaments was exhibited on ſmall chapels, oratories, and tombs. For my own part, I ſhould have wiſhed to have added detached ſamples of the various patterns of ornaments, which would not be a great many, as, excepting pinnacles, there is ſcarce one which does not branch from the trefoil, quatrefoil, and cinqfoil, being but various modifications of it. I believe almoſt all the ramifications of windows are ſo, and of them there ſhould be ſome ſamples too. This work you ſee could not be executed by one hand. Mr. Tyſon could give great aſſiſtance. I wiſh the plan was drawn out and better digeſted. This is a very rude ſketch, and firſt thought. I ſhould be very glad to contribute what little I knew, and to the expence too, which would be conſiderable; but I am ſure fure we could get affiftance, and it had better not be undertaken than executed fuperficially.

" Mr. Tyfon's Hiftory of fafhions and dreffes would make a valuable part of the work, as in elder times efpecially much muft be depended on Tombs for dreffes. Pray talk this over with Mr. Tyfon and Mr. Effex. It is an idea worth purfuing."

Mr. STRUTT firft among us attempted any thing like refuming Pere Montfaucon's plan, and, with little affiftance but his own application, gave us, from our antient MSS. a curious felection of portraits, habits, manners, and hiftoric facts. He has fucceeded beft in his " Regal and Ecclefiaftical Antiquities ;" but has not, in his " Ƿopða Angel-cynnan," fufficiently difcriminated the fubjects of the different periods, nor the correct and original one of each.

Mr. GRANGER has difcriminated ftill lefs, and has tranfgreffed the very argument he alledges [a] for a collection of portraits " that is principally ufeful, as the more " important direction and fettlement of the ideas upon the true form and fea- " tures of any worthy and famous perfon reprefented." For he has thrown together every picture of every perfon that deferved or pretended to any connection with Great Britain, and has omitted the beft collection of fuch pictures, the original portraits themfelves, which he might have traced in their galleries, from whence many of them are now for ever disjoined. We fmile when he refers us for the improvement in the knowledge of *perfonal* hiftory to the coins engraved in Speed's Chronicle, or in moft books of coins. To fuch perfonification, even if it could be depended on, few collectors or engravers have attended.

It would not be altogether impoffible to draw up a lift of pictures, including thofe enumerated by Mr. Walpole, in his Anecdotes of Painting, relating to the Hiftory and Antiquities of England, in the manner of Montfaucon, from the Conqueft to the prefent time, beginning with the Tapeftry at Bayeux, of which it is a reproach to us, as a nation, that we have not procured moft accurate drawings and illuftrations, but have left the latter to Monf. Lancelot, and are content with the former on the fmall fcale in which he has given them, for the larger in Montfaucon take in a very fmall part ; nor is it clear to me, that the whole has been copied. The late Smart Lethieullier drew up a long account of this tapeftry different from Lancelot's, which was in the hands of Mr. Tindal of Doctors Commons, and printed at the end of Dr. Ducarel's " Norman Antiquities." The difficulty of completing fuch a lift has been confiderably increafed by the difperfion of fo many private collections, and by the inattention of our Antiquaries in tracing what remains : fo that in a few years more we fhall

[a] Mr. Granger, I. 10. gives a whole length of Philippa by Faber, which he fays was engraved from a painting at Queen's College, Oxford, and the face of an *antient* ftone head of her over the back gate of that College. My copy of the print fays it is *e cenotaph. in monaft. Weftmon.* It is curious to hear Hearne obferve, that the ftatuaries made Edward the Third's queen, *Philippa*, and the moft beautiful lady models for the Virgin Mary. Gloff. to P. Langtoft, p. 549, 550. Warton, Hift. of Eng. Poetr. I. p. 255. He fhould have faid, Henry III's queen *Eleanor*, of whom fee Langtoft, I. 213.

have

have no foundation left for fuch a work. The two ftatues of Henry I. and his queen, on the Weft door of Rochefter cathedral, are crumbling away without having been drawn. The picture fuppofed of the Crufades in Canterbury cathedral has been whited over, and the arras in the antechamber of the Houfe of Lords has never been examined with fufficient care to determine whether its fubject be the fame [1].

But without appearing to leffen the merit of preceding attempts to fill up the great Plan of National Hiftory, let me explain the defign of the prefent work, which concerns that part of it relative to Sepulchral Monuments, from which Montfaucon derived fo much affiftance.

Shall I then borrow the lively pen of the author beforementioned, who is engaged in the fame undertaking at this time in France, and fay: It is not an History of England that is here prefented to the public. After the number of hiftories already in print, what profpect of finding readers of a new one? I have neither the object, the plan, nor the method of an Hiftorian. Our materials are different, and my plan adopts only what his excludes. Great events, great perfonages, great characters, good or bad, are all that he brings upon his ftage.

I talk of graves, of worms, of epitaphs,
And that fmall portion of the barren earth
That ferves as pafte and cover to our bones!

Here is a ftay
That fhakes the rotten carcafe of old death
Out of his rags.

Mine are fubjects rejected by the hiftorian to the end of each reign, among the prodigies that diftinguifh it. Yet is this detail not uninterefting. It is a picture of private mixed with public life; a fubject in which my countrymen have been anticipated by their neighbours; and if it is here treated without the patronage of religious or literary focieties, it wanted not the encouragement of friends who have left the fcene before the completion of a work which they fome years ago pointed out and would have affifted. I avail myfelf of their friendfhip and their hints, as well as of what has been already publifhed abroad on a fimilar fubject.

A feries of excurfions to gratify an innate curiofity after our national Antiquities furnifhed the variety of obfervations and materials, which yielded renewed fatisfaction in reducing them to order, and thus travelling the ground twice over, when memory was relieved and refrefhed by the obfervations of others, and my library fupplied what a folitary traveller had wanted on the fpot.

[1] Henry III. ordered this Hiftory to be painted in the garden-chamber or fummer-houfe at his palace at Weftminfter, near what in the writ is called the King's Jewry, perhaps his treafury for receiving the fums levied on the Jews, and which room he ordered to be thenceforward called the *Antioch Chamber*, originally, probably, what is now ftyled the Jerufalem Chamber. Walp. I. 11.

As opportunity offered I have travelled the ground over actually a third time: and what wonder if I have feen with different eyes! At an interval of that leifure which is my inheritance, I formed the bold defign of a new edition of CAMDEN'S BRITANNIA; in the progrefs of which unexpected affiftances have arifen. Coæval with this prefented itfelf the idea of illuftrating the SEPULCHRAL MONUMENTS of this kingdom from the occafional minutes of my excurfions. I foon found thefe outlines were to be filled up from books; and the obfervations of others. What a bufinefs is that of a compiler! His induftry is eftimated at little; but he deferves better fate than he often meets with. I took courage, and in time brought my materials into fome regular arrangement. Under this diftribution new matter was eafily introduced in the additions, improvements, and new difpofitions which every day fuggefted. The drynefs of the fubject and the fcantinefs of the materials required decoration and anecdote to fet them off. A trait of hiftory, a pertinent digreffion, due comparifon of one age with another, and of antient with modern times, are all required to compofe one general and pleafing picture. Thefe are the difficulties to be furmounted. In endeavouring to furmount them I have the fatisfaction of reflecting that I have defcribed little befide what my own eyes, or thofe of judicious friends have examined, or what has been brought home to all by faithful reprefentations. Perhaps after traverfing more ground, prying into more churches, and engraving more monuments, curiofity once awakened would have been inquifitive for more. Unbounded as the plan is, I claim the merit of having executed it within certain limits.

Should the fcantinefs of materials be objected, I muft apply to myfelf, with due alteration, the anfwer of Pere Montfaucon, in the preface to his third volume: "The monuments of England are fo few in the eleventh and twelfth centuries, and even in the thirteenth, that after the moft diligent fearch there are periods which do not furnifh any. The reigns of Henry III. and the two firft Edwards afford no fmall number, but it was under Edward III. and Richard II. that they multiplied fo faft that new ones are continually prefenting themfelves, and the number increafes as we come nearer our own times."

Notwithftanding the diffolution of the religious houfes when fo many feries of family monuments were involved in the deftruction of the monaftic church which their family had founded; notwithftanding the devaftation of falfe zeal and fanaticifm[1] in the two laft centuries; the depredations of time, caprice, ignorance, intereft, and falfe tafte, and a variety of accidents for above a century fince; we have a fufficiency of monuments left to illuftrate our hiftory on the plan here propofed. It is perhaps too weak a hope that this defign may induce more attention in future to preferve what remains from immediate ruin, the defacement of the whitewafher's brufh, the rude hands of fchool-boys and the vulgar, and various other unfavourable circumftances; or that this work fhould be

[1] Whoever requires a fpecimen of thefe ravages let them read the atchievements of Dowfing, in the county of Suffolk, juft publifhed.

taken

taken up and improved by abler hands. It may be enough if it furvives the national tafte for fuch purfuits. Then indeed might one fay with the poet:

Exegi monumentum ære perennius,
Regalique fitu pyramidum altius;
Quod non imber edax, non Aquilo impotens
Poffit diruere, aut innumerabilis
Annorum feries, et fuga temporum.

Since the tombs affigned by every fexton, and, on no better credit, by fome antiquaries and defcribers of counties, to *Lucius*, *Ethelward*, *Ofric*, *Ina*, *Guthrum*, *Aldhelm*, *Aldred*, *Alfred king of Northumberland*, *Redowald*, *Anna* and his fon *Firminus*, *a daughter of Canute*, *Harold*, and more that might be named, if really belonging to them, are certainly not of their age, and the number of fuch whofe genuinefs we may depend upon is fo fmall in the preceding centuries; one may date the æra of authentic fepulchral monuments in Great Britain at the NORMAN CONQUEST, and from thence to the SEVENTEENTH CENTURY deduce a feries from whence may be derived to the knowledge of the Antiquities of this kingdom no mean acceffion to the labor of Genealogifts and Epitaph collectors, no little degree of light on our manners, habits, arts, national tafte, and ftyle of Architecture, no contemptible catalogue of Britifh worthies.

It is not forgotten how many fpecimens of monuments have been drawn by different perfons on the feveral vifitation-books in the Heralds' College, and others engraved by our country hiftorians, many of them by the mafterly hand of HOLLAR. Of the former I cannot praife many for fidelity, and it will be no reproach to Hollar that the drawings which he engraved are extremely incorrect. He worked as modern engravers for publifhers, and was obliged to take up with fuch draughts as were put into his hands: Suffice it to compare thofe in Sandford with fome in this work. Neither likenefs, proportion, nor any kind of truth, has been obferved in many of them. Hollar was more excufable than *Schynvoet*, who has erred unpardonably in the monuments of Canterbury, which he drew to be engraved by *Cole*, who has not been more faithful in thofe at Weftminfter. Thofe at Ely are not on a fcale favourable to exactnefs. If we look at the foreign monuments that have been engraved, not one of them which has come under my obfervation has fo good a title to xactnefs. Thefe in Montfaucon, where fo much was to be expected, are very inferior. Thofe in the "Theatre facre de Brabant" are worfe. Reyher's "Monumenta Landgraviorum Thuringiæ et Marchionum Mifniæ;" the "Nobilitas Daniæ ex monumentis curante T. de Klevenfeld," as well as thofe of the "Vitruve Suede," are not more faithful. Thofe in Lobineau's "Hiftoire de Bretagne," and a few other topical works publifhed in France, muft be excepted. And it is to be remembered, that I am fpeaking of the monuments properly called Gothic, which reach nearly to the reign of Elizabeth. I fhould pay a very indifferent compliment to Mr. BASIRE if I gave fuch foils to his engravings, which may ferve as models for thefe works, and as incitements to patronage,

while

while the times are ſavourable; beſore the caprice, or the avarice, or the indifference, or falſe taſte[4] of Deans and Chapters, ſuffers and authorizes a havock, leſs rapid it may be, but not leſs ruinous, than that which with the axes and hammers of Reformation brake down the carved work of antient art[5], and before a variety of other circumſtances conſpire to leſſen the number of theſe valuable records of antient ſtory.

But as ſome may think indifferent repreſentations, even thoſe in the Hiſtory of Northumberland and the Antiquarian Repertory, better than none at all (though I muſt ever beg leave to hold a different opinion), and they may not be diſpleaſed with verbal deſcriptions, it may be worth while to ſupply the great deficiency of ſuch deſcriptions, and to ſuggeſt certain rules and examples for this method of preſerving monuments[6]. Not to guard againſt the romantic anachroniſm of honeſt Lydgate, who repreſents *Hector* buried in a *Gothic cathedral* in a chapel and tomb of the 12th century; or the inexperience of one modern author[7], who miſtook two angels at a lady's feet for *two cherub like babes*; or the barbariſm[8] of another, who chriſtened a pilgrim *Jupiter Tonitruans* or *Silenus*; and a lion at a knight's feet *a water curled dog*[9]; or the miſtaken fancy of a third[10], who ſpeaks of two ſiſters kneeling *hand in hand* before a croſs; or that of a fourth[11], who talks of monkiſh *pleureurs*, as the pariſh clerk of St. Mary's church at Warwick does of *weepers*, at the ſides of tombs; or of Dr. Salmon, who did not diſtinguiſh *cenſers* in the hands of angels from *fiſhing nets*[12]; or a leopard and hedgehog from a *cat* and a *rat*[13]; or the tradition of the good people of Kirkby Stephen miſtaking the Wharton creſt for a *vanquiſhed devil*[14]: errors leſs pardonable than that of Dr. Plot[15], who, in the laſt age, miſtook a cairn of ſtone for a natural production; or the German[16], who made the ſame blunder about urns; or the Scot in the Weſtern Iſles, who thought ſand hills could be fixed by art. Such inaccuracy alſo leaves the *habit of the times* and a *knight of the holy voyage* without further light. But to point out the general cha-

[4] Witneſs the choirs of Weſtminſter and Saliſbury, and let the practice of antiquity be pleaded——if it can.

[5] The act of 3 and 4 Edw. VI. c. 10. was probably the ruin of many of our ſepulchral as well as other eccleſiaſtical monuments, though the former were expreſsly excepted, where the parties had not been *reputed ſaints*. All images and paintings taken out of or ſtanding in churches and chapels, as well as Popiſh ſervice books (which many perſons doubtleſs would extend to the MS records of religious houſes) are ſtrictly enjoined to be deſtroyed, under penalty of 10s. for the firſt; £. 4. for the ſecond; and for the third offence impriſonment at the king's will. Hence the inſcription under a Bible placed by biſhop Beauchamp in a niche in St. George's Chapel at Windſor for public reading was eagerly defaced, with the ſame eagerneſs, as the painting of the laſt judgement on the oppoſite pillar; and *orate pro anima* hatcht out of braſſes as the name of a *Pope* or *Becket* was eraſed out of Miſſals and Primers.

[6] So inattentive are the *reſident* deſcribers of our monuments that archdeacon Batteley miſtook for archbiſhop Iſlip's in the nave at Canterbury an altar tomb or ſlab, robbed of its braſſes, which repreſented a *man and wife*. Goſtling, p. 205.

Maitland ſays, the duke of Exeter's monument at St. Katherine's, near the Tower, is one of the antienteſt in London, except thoſe in the Temple-church; forgetting that that of Rahere in St. Bartholomew's church by Smithfield is much older; unleſs he diſputes the date of its erection.

[7] Antiquities of Northumberland, II. 335. [8] View of Northumberland, I. 97. [9] Ib. II. 313.

[10] Margate Sketches. [11] Tour in Wales, I. 286. [12] Hertfordſhire, p. 47. [13] Ib. 108.

[14] Burn's Weſtmorland, I. 540.

Montfaucon (Diar. It. c. 21.) mentions, in the chapel of St. Eraſmus at Gaieta a figure under whoſe head is an eagle, at the feet a dog, and at the ſame place a ſnake rolled up, as they commonly repreſent Æſculapius. I have my doubts if this be not a *Gothic* monument, perhaps like that at Pelham in Hertfordſhire, mentioned p. lxxxviii. and as much miſunderſtood by Chauncy and Salmon. Mabillon himſelf was miſled, by not diſtinguiſhing the right or left hand, or the *epiſtle and goſpel ſide* of a church or altar. Deſcr. de la haute Normandie, II. 259.

[15] Staffordſhire, p. 402. [16] Munſter Coſmogr. III. c. 49. p. 698.

racter

racter of figures as to expreffion, attitude, and habit; or of tombs, as to ftyle and ornament; or of epitaphs, as to turn and language; or of letters, as to cut and form; or of heraldry, as to fhields or bearings; whereby to form a common ftandard, approaching fomewhat nearer to accuracy and comprehenfion that feems to have been yet unattended to, and to fix certain criteria that may prevent us from confounding the æras and owners of our fepulchral monuments, and falling into the abfurdities of that marvellous collection of family monuments made by Mr. Camden's friend John lord Lumley, from Liulphus, the founder of the family, to John the third lord in the reign of Elizabeth.

I have elfewhere obferved, that "fepulchral monuments have their feveral æras from the coffin-fafhioned tomb, with no figure at all, or only a crofier, and feldom infcribed, to the moft ornamented canopy or chapel, which ended at the Reformation, and funk in the next reign into the univerfal difguife of architecture [17]." Mr. Tate wrote, or intended to write, of the Antiquity of tombs in England [18]." What he left unfinifhed was done by Maurice Johnfon the founder of the Spalding Society, whofe memoir is here inferted at large, and more flightly by Smart Lethieullier, whofe notes are alfo borrowed from the Archæologia.

The learned Montfaucon, though he has given the monuments, affigned them their dates, and detailed the hiftory of their proprietors, has not made fo material ufe of them for illuftrating national manners or modes, as might have been expected, or as he probably would have done, had he completed his defign: nor has he entered into any comparifon of one monument or figure with another, or thofe of one age with thofe of another; nor laid down any rules for judging by. Not that the fafhion of one age does not in this, as well as in other points, extend itfelf into the fucceeding, fo as frequently to create a difficulty in the inquiry; or the ftyle of the 8th or 9th centuries may be borrowed by the 13th or 14th, to give an air of antiquity for a particular purpofe. But ftill the chance is that the copy betrays its originality, and difcovers fome internal marks of premeditation and fraud. Such are our monuments of Saxon times, and the Lumley feries beforementioned, and among our neighbours the fucceffion of regal monuments before St. Louis.

The age of Henry VIII. and Elizabeth was the æra of the reftoration of the polite arts in Europe. Italy began to be decorated with a fpecies of funeral monuments unknown to Heathen or Chriftian Rome before the houfe of Medici gave a candidate for St. Peter's chair. From that time one may date the influx of fepulchral vanity which contrived monuments without appropriating maufolea, and crouded our churches without regard to proportion or propriety, lavifhing the wealth of commerce on pofthumous pride, thrufting out filent merit and

[17] Preface to Britifh Topography, p. xxxv.

[18] His Hiftory of Heads and Collections were in Mr. Anftis' hands. See Hearne's Preface to Curious Difcourfes, p. 114.

fimple

ſimple taſte for opulent elegance and falſe panegyric: memorials rather of ſurviving pride than of departed merit. A ſingle monument was now equal to a family chapel: a laboured cenotaph of more value than a grave. Hence the coſtly funeral chapels of biſhops Weſt and Alcock at Ely, and of their ſovereign at Weſtminſter, compared to which the Mauſoleum of Auguſtus, the Moles Adriani, the Pyramid of Ceſtius, the tower-like tomb of Metella, and many more in antient Rome were maſſive piles built for immortality, while the more modern monuments can hardly find an artiſt capable of repairing the ſmalleſt fracture, or by replacing a key ſtone, ſaving the whole from inſtant ruin. Hence we find the Cecil monuments executed by Florentines, as thoſe of our ſovereigns had been ages before, and we may trace the vanity or ſkill of foreign artiſts far back in ſome of the more accompliſhed performances of their kind.

After the impeachment here brought againſt moſt of the *draughts* of monuments now exiſting, which may be extended to moſt copies of inſcriptions, whether by fac ſimile or otherwiſe, the public will not be diſpleaſed to have a ſet of prints, epitaphs, and deſcriptions, intirely new laid before them. Where it is abſolutely neceſſary to touch on others, the ſubjects already publiſhed and engraved are referred to. But the greater part of the monuments and epitaphs are ſuch as it is believed have not been generally, if at all, noticed before; and of which I have procured or been favoured with faithful copies. The loweſt merit ſuch a work can pretend to is, to be deemed a ſupplement to Weever.

Far am I from being inſenſible of the difficulty of procuring accurate drawings of monuments at a diſtance from the capital. This I have experienced too often when I have been obliged to borrow an inferior pencil, and have frequently been left without any help at all: where, had a *Vertue*, a *Grimm*, a *Carter*, or a *Baſire*, aſſiſted, the monuments of diſtant cathedrals might have been rendered as familiar as thoſe of Weſtminſter. Nor is it only the diſtance of draughtſmen from the ſpot, but the little practice of the ſubject. The walk of fame for modern artiſts is not ſufficiently enlarged. Emulous of excelling in Hiſtory, Portrait, or Landſcape, they overlook the unprofitable, though not leſs taſteful, walk of Antiquity, or, in Grecian and Roman forget Gothic and more domeſtic monuments. The unfrequency of the purſuit enhances the price. I muſt except from this reproach my friend BASIRE, whoſe praiſe it is to be faithful in his tranſcripts and modeſt in his prices, though it is almoſt a perverſion of his burin, which ſhines ſo much in living portraits, to employ it on Gothic ones.

Nor muſt I forget how many ſpecimens are contributed to this collection by Mr. JOHN CARTER, whoſe riſing talents I had hailed with predictive applauſe, and to whoſe merit I am always ready to do juſtice.

It would be the higheſt ingratitude not to acknowledge what obligations this work is under to the hand of friendſhip. To Mr. TYSON I am indebted for ſeveral drawings, and had he lived to enjoy his long wiſhed for retreat, I ſhould have received many more. To the exertions of CRAVEN ORD, eſq. are owing the impreſſions of ſome of the fineſt braſſes, as well as many valuable deſcriptive hints. I am happy alſo in teſtifying my acknowledgements to Mr. KERRICH for ſeveral highly-finiſhed drawings; and for many uſeful particulars to the late Sir JOHN CULLUM *(O ſi fata aſpera rumpas!)* who lived not to ſee the ſucceſs of his labours and thoſe of his excellent coadjutor in my behalf. The hon. HORACE WALPOLE, with that readineſs of communication which marks his character, indulged me with the free uſe of a number of drawings by Mr. Vertue or Sir Charles Frederick, which he purchaſed among a vaſt fund of others at Mr. Lethieullier's ſale. And ſhould this work attract the notice of the curious enough to induce any perſon of taſte and liberality to communicate correct drawings of ſuch monuments in this period as have eſcaped or been omitted by me, I ſhall be ready to engrave them for a new edition or a ſupplement.

Since I firſt conceived the preſent deſign ſome events have happened which render the candour of the public of very ſerious concern to me. The Society of Antiquaries have publiſhed engravings of five monuments in Weſtminſter abbey, with an accurate deſcription by the Montfaucon of England, the late Sir JOSEPH AYLOFFE. When I reflect on his intimate acquaintance with every part of that venerable ſtructure, and the opportunities he had for purſuing his enquiries there, I am at a loſs whether to lament his reluctance to continue what he had ſo happily begun, or my own preſumption in attempting to ſupply his knowledge by vague conjectures. He cloſed a life devoted to the ſtudy of our national antiquities before three ſheets of this work had paſſed the preſs; and it can only pay a tribute to his abilities. Had my ingenious friend Mr. Tyſon been living, his taſte in drawing, and his knowledge of theſe ſubjects, would have corrected innumerable errors which now obtrude themſelves. It is enough for me to bewail my loſs by his death, and to add to it, and the inſtances of mortality I am here contemplating, thoſe of our common friend Mr. James Eſſex, and the Rev. Sir John Cullum, bart. Deprived of theſe aids,

Ferimur per opaca locorum,
Et me quem dudum non ulla injecta movebant
Tela, neque adverſo glomerati ex agmine Graium,
Nunc omnes terrent auræ; ſonus excitat omnis,
Suſpenſum, et pariter comitique onerique timentem.

LIST

LIST OF PLATES.

[1] Should be 36.

Small Plates in Letter Press.

CON-

CONTENTS OF THE INTRODUCTION.

INTRODUCTION.

Tombes upon tabernacles, tylde opon lofte,
Houſed in hornes harde ſet abouten
Of armed alabauſtre, clad for the nones,
Maad opon marbel in many manner wyſe,
Knyghtes in ther coniſance clad for the nones,
Alle it ſemed ſeyntes yſacred opon erthe
And lovely ladies ywrought leyen by her ſydes
In many gay garnemens that weren gold beten.

PIERS PLOWMAN'S CREDE.

THE ſepulchral memorials erected to eminent men in every age and nation have made no inconſiderable objects of curioſity and inquiry. Taſte and Vanity have been competitors for perpetuating their votaries in the Temple of Fame—from the Druid tumulus on the Wiltſhire downs to the lateſt tenant of Weſtminſter abbey or a village church-yard. Dr. Stukeley's diſcovery of a ſkeleton on the top of *Silbury* hill [1] proves that we have our pyramids as well as our Iriſh neighbours at *New Grange*; and ſuch is every barrow in the world—whether of PATROCLUS at *Troy*, of HALYATES in *Ionia*, of the SCYTHIANS on the *Boryſthenes* [2], or the TARTARS their ſucceſſors in their great deſerts [3], or the many unknown chiefs and bards in *Sweden*, *Denmark*, and *Britain* [4].

BARROWS are the moſt antient ſepulchral monuments in the world: but their contents are as various as the different people that occupied the globe, or the different circumſtances of thoſe people.

Homer is very particular in deſcribing that of Patroclus. It was firſt marked out with a circle; the foundations were then laid round the very ſpot where the pile was ſtill ſmoaking, and earth was thrown up over them:

> Τορνωσαντο δε σημα, θειμελια τε προβαλοντο
> Αμφι πυρην· ειθαρ δε χυταν επι γαιαν εχευαν.
> Χευαντες δε το σημα, παλιν κιον. Ιλ. Ψ. 255—257.

The remains of the body were collected in a golden urn, which was not lodged under this barrow.

Among the diſtinguiſhed barrows of Greece may be ranked that of Epytus in Arcadia, which Pauſanias deſcribes as not very large, and ſurrounded by a margin of ſtone: Γης χωμα ȣ μεγα, λιθȣ κρηπιδι εν κυκλω περιεχομενον [5]. which Homer admired, as not having ſeen a finer [6]. That of Icarus was a ſmall one, on a headland where he was caſt away [7]. That of Achilles was in a ſimilar ſituation:

> Αμφ' αυτοις δ' επειτα μεγαν και αμυμονα τυμβον
> Αχτη επι προχυση επει πλατει Ελλησποντω
> Ως κεν τηλεφανης εκ ποντοφιν ανδρασιν ειη,
> Τοις οι νυν γεγαασι και οι μετοπισθεν εσονται [8].

The brothers Amphion and Zethus lay under one common barrow, εν κοινῳ γης χωματι ȣ μεγα [9].

[1] John Fowler told him, that in digging there he found at top bucks' horns, a human jaw and teeth, all very rotten; Roman coins, an iron knife with an handle. Stukeley, MS. pen. me.
[2] Herodot. Melpomene, 71.
[3] See Archæol. II. 225. Memoires de Tott, P. II. p. 50.
[4] Mr. Forſter (Obſervations, p. 569.) met with but one tumulus in the South Seas. This was in New Caledonia, on the ſea-ſhore, four feet high, ſurrounded by an incloſure of ſticks, and on it other ſticks with turbings on them. Dr. Sparrman (II. 164.) deſcribes innumerable heaps of ſtones of the ſepulcral kind in the uncultivated plains to the North of the Hottentots' country.
[5] Arcad. c. 16.
[6] Il. B. 603. yet Il. Ω. 349. he celebrates the μεγα σημα of Ilus near Troy.
[7] Pauſan. Bœot. c. 11.
[8] Odyſ. Ω. 36.
[9] Pauſan. Bœot. c. 17.

Memnon's

Memnon's tomb ſeems to have been a great barrow; for Pauſanias ſays the birds Memnonides ſwept and watered with their wings that part of it on which no buſhes or graſs grew; *οποσον τυ μνηματος δενδρων εςιν η πιας ψιλον* [1].

It was an antient cuſtom at Athens from the time of Cecrops to ſow the ſpot where the body was buried with corn [2].

The lovers of Hippodamia, who loſt their lives with their race, had a high barrow (*χωμα γης υψηλον*) near the ruins of Harpinia, and afterwards Pelops erected a monument (*μνημα*) to them, on which he ſolemnized yearly [3].

The Meſſenian pentathlete Lycus had a tomb of earth; *χωμα γης* [4]; ſuch alſo was that of Lycurgus the father of Opheltes [5].

Dr. Chandler, p. 24. miſrepreſents the tomb of Euripides on the road from the port of Phalerum to Athens, as a *barrow of earth*; for Pauſanias expreſsly calls it only *μνημα* [6]. Pauſanias carefully diſtinguiſhes between *χωμα* a barrow, *ταφος* a tomb, and *μνημα* a monument. That of Euripides was of the latter kind, and it was without his aſhes; *κενον μνημα*, a cenotaph. Mr. Chandler, by the ſame miſapprehenſion, points out a large barrow by the ſide of this road, as the cenotaph of Euripides. *Ξεςος ταφος* in Euripides as cited by Mr. Williams, Phil. Tranſ. 458. p. 471, may be an altar tomb; alſo *τυμβος ξεςος*. What the Greeks called *τυμβος* Cicero [7] explains *buſtum*.

The ſlain in ſome battles were buried under cairns, *σωροι λιθων*; which had no inſcriptions to diſtinguiſh them [8]. Theſe are the *λαινοισι τεξαγωμασι* of Euripides, as cited by Mr. Williams [9]. The altars by barrows or tombs, not in temples, were ſo many cromlechs.

Laius and his ſervant were buried under cairns, *λιθοι λογαδες σεσωρευομενοι* [10].

That of the ſons of Iphitus, at Anticyra, ſeems to have been of the ſame kind, *ωκοδομημενον λιθοις τοις επιτυχουσι μνημα* [11].

And ſuch was Amphion's, ſaid to have had a *circle of ſtones* round it, rough hewn; *παρα Αμφιονος μνημα λιθοι καλωδεν υποβεβληται, μητε αλλως ειργασμενοι προς το ακριβεςατον*, ſaid to have been drawn thither by his lyre [12]. Such alſo was Hector's:

> *Αιψα δ' αρ' ες κοιλην καπετον θεσαν αυταρ υπερθε*
> *Πυκνοισιν λαεσσι κατεςορεσαν μεγαλοισι*
> *Χευαντες δε το σημα παλιν κιον.* Il. Ω. 797. 801.

Homer makes Priam call this *τυμβος*. Ib. 666.

Under this were depoſited the burnt bones in a golden caſe, *χρυσειη λαρναξ*.

Jacob ſet a pillar on Rachel's grave [13].

Three great ſtones marked the grave of Tydeus [14].

Pittacus forbad the placing on the tumulus any thing but a little pillar, three cubits high, or a table (*menſa*) or a little veſſel (*clabellum* [15].)

Solon forbad adorning graves *opere tectorio*, or ſetting *Hermæ* on them [16]. Dr. Potter [17] underſtands this properly enough of the ſtatues of Hermes; but Mr. D'Ancarville [18] ſtrangely of *heaps* of *ſtones*. As Solon further decreed, that no tomb ſhould be made of more work than ten men could do in three days, he had reſpect to ſimplicity, that monuments ſhould not be ſet off with arched roofs, like buildings or incloſures, or with figures of Mercury, like way poſts.

The roads to Athens were lined with tombs of heroes and illuſtrious perſons intermixed with temples. Pauſanias [19] enumerates a long liſt, including thoſe of Thraſybulus, Pericles, Chabrias, Phormio, and other citizens who had fallen in battle for their country, eminent artiſts, &c. with inſcriptions on pillars, ſetting forth their name and tribe. This was the Weſtminſter abbey of Athens; but violence and the plough have levelled all diſtinction.

[1] Pauſan. Phoc. 31. [2] Cic. de Legib. II. 175. Ed. Davies. [3] Pauſan. Eliac. II. 21. [4] Corinth. 7. [5] Corinth. 15. Chandler's Travels in Greece, p. 233. [6] Attic. 2. [7] Ubi ſup. p. 176. [8] Pauſan. Arc. 13. [9] Ubi ſup. [10] Phoc. 5. [11] Phoc. 36. [12] Bœot. 17. [13] Gen. xxxv. 20. [14] Pauſan. Bœot. 18. [15] Cic. de Leg. II. 26. [16] Cicero, ib. [17] II. 224. [18] Recherches, II. 160. [19] Att. I. 29.

The

The monument of Mardonius was ſhewn by the road ſide near Platea, and near the entrance of that city the tombs of theſe who fell fighting againſt the Perſians; the reſt of the Greeks had a common monument, but the Lacedemonians and Athenians diſtinct ones, inſcribed with elegies by Simonides [1].

" In gentili Domitiorum monumento ſolium porphyretici marmoris ſuperſtante " Lunenſi ara circumſeptum eſt lapide Thaſio :" ſays Suetonius, ſpeaking of the ſepulchre of Nero [2]. Is this an altar tomb?

Trajan's pillar was the only inſtance of a ſepulchral monument within the walls of the city before the enlargement of Rome by Aurelian. " Soluſque intra " urbem ſepultus eſt [3]."

The work on ſarcophagi is ſeldom or ever good, becauſe the uſe of them was diſcontinued at Sylla, and not revived till after the Antonines. During this interval was the riſe and fall of fine ſculpture. Alexander Severus and Julia Mammæa are ſaid to have been among the firſt exceptions to the cuſtom of burning. They were buried in a ſarcophagus, which remains to this day in the capitol [4]. How can this be, when the Barberini vaſe was ſuppoſed to contain the Emperor's aſhes? But D'Ancarville calls it the tomb of his father Varius.

The connexion between ſepulchres and places of worſhip is of the remoteſt antiquity in three quarters of the globe. The Aſiatics ſeem to have adopted the Jewiſh mode of burying.

Inſtances of tombs near and in temples are not unfrequent among the Greeks.

The tomb of the ſons of Medea was not far from the temple of Minerva Chalinuns at Corinth [5].

That of Arcas, near Juno's altar, at Mantinea, on a ſpot called the altars of the ſun [6].

That of Trygon, the nurſe of Eſculapius, was in his temple [7].

The two daughters of Antipœnus were buried in Diana's temple at Thebes, becauſe they died for their country [8].

That of Cecrops was *near*, and Erectheus was buried *in*, the temple of Minerva Polias in the citadel at Athens [9].

That of Epimenides was *before* a temple of Minerva at Argos [10].

That of Hypermneſtra and her husband Lynceus had an altar near it [11].

Pauſanias mentions one *before* the gate of a temple; another juſt on coming out of a temple [12].

That of Epopeus was *before the altar in the temple* of Minerva at Corinth [13].

That of Eacus *under an altar* in a ſquare incloſure called Eaceum at Egina, and the barrow of Phocus near it [14]. It was ſurrounded by a fence, and had on it a rough ſtone. Dr. Chandler thinks he ſaw it on the coaſt of Egina [15].

The bones of Pyrrhus king of Epirus, after his body was burnt, were buried in the temple of Ceres, at Argos [16].

That of Demoſthenes *in the court* of the temple of Neptune at Calaurea [17].

That of Tyndarus *before* the temple of Jupiter at Sparta [18].

That of Anchiſes *near* the temple of Venus near mount Anchiſes in Arcadia [19].

Hyacinthus was buried *in the pedeſtal* of Apollo's ſtatue at Amyclæ [20].

Agamemnon's monument was ſaid to be *in* the temple of Alexandria or Caſſandra there [21].

Certain beautiful pillars in the temple of Ceres, στηλαι περιφανεις επι Δημητρος, to which they turned as they ſung the praiſes of Aras, were ſuppoſed to be his children's tomb [22].

[1] Pauſan. Bœot. 2. [2] Nero, c. 53. [3] Eutrop. in Traj. Viaggiana, p. 63.
[4] See Nieuport de rit. Rom. 376. Viaggiana 71.
" Un tombeau qu'on decouvrit dans Herculanium etoit decoré exterieurement de piedeſtaux d'un bon genre; l'interieur etoit un caveau de briques ayant 12 pieds ſur 9 de large, avec des urnes funeraires; tout etoit reſté ſen plane au point que la brique meme poſée ſur chaque urne n'etoit pas derangée: la cendre y avoit cependant penetré & tout rempli." Voyage en Italie, 1765-6. VII. 106.
[5] Pauſanias, Cor. 4. [6] Arcad. 9. [7] Ib. 25. [8] Bœot. 7. [9] Chandler's Greece, p. 53.
[10] Pauſan. Cor. 21. [11] Ib. [12] Ib. 22. [13] Ib. 11. [14] Ib. 29. [15] P. 15. [16] Pauſ. Ib. 21.
[17] Ib. 33. [18] Lac. 17. [19] Arc. 13. [20] Ib. 19. [21] Ib. [22] Cor. 12.

What

What are these but so many prototypes of the disposition of monuments in Christian churches? As Christians had family chapels, so the pagans (ἡρωα μνημαῖα) heroic monuments had altars, where they paid honours to the memory of the deceased [1]. So Pausanias describes the *heroic monument* (ἡρωον) of Aratus [2], of Perseus [3], and even of women, as of Hymetho [4]; Andromache [5]; Iphigenia, at Megara [6]. The tomb of Opheltes, at Nemea, stood in an inclosure of stone, θριγκος λιθων, with several altars [7].

Epaminondas was buried on the field of the battle of Mantinea, and a pillar (κιων) with a shield, bearing a dragon, denoting him to be of the family of the Spartæ, was immediately set over his grave. There were also remaining on it in Pausanias's time two pillars (στηλαι) one antient with an inscription in the Bœotian dialect, the other with an inscription set up by the emperor Adrian [8].

The ταφος of Thyestes had *on* it a marble ram [9].

One of white marble, with *paintings* on it, by Minas, just without Tritia [10].

The monument of the slain in the battle of Marathon was a ταφος, terminated with pillars (στηλα) inscribed with their names and tribes; another for the Platæans, and a third for the slaves, who were inlisted on this critical occasion. Miltiades had a monument (μνημα) alone [11], which Count Caylus had engraved [12] from a monastery at Athens, VI. xlviii. 3. A trophy of white marble was erected on the spot. The Persians were also carefully buried, but Pausanias could find no ταφοι for them; no χωμα, nor any other token (σημειον); whence he concludes they were cast into the first pit [13]. After this minute description of a traveller on the spot fifteen centuries nearer the event, how is one to account for Dr. Chandler translating Pausanias's ταφος a *barrow*; and adding, that "it is likely "it still towers above the level of the plain, being of light fine earth, and having "a bush or two growing on it? At a small distance Northward is a square base of "white marble, perhaps part of the trophy." The other *barrows* mentioned by Pausanias are probably among those extant near *Brauron* now *Vraona*, where are one large and three smaller, and another a little out of the line, opened for a furnace or lime kiln: a lofty barrow, nearer the sea, was in view [14]. The barrow of Iphigenia which Dr. Chandler surmised here was an ἡρωον at Megara [15].

BEFORE we enter upon the monumental appendages of our ancestors, it may not be amiss to premise a few words on the modes of sepulture, which have prevailed among them.

Barrows were also *their* oldest tombs. But their contents in this island differ at different periods.

Urn burial was a druidical and antient British fashion; but not universally: for we find many skeletons under barrows, without urns; and in many instances both. In this last case the parties were probably slain in battle; or were Danes or Saxons. See Borlase's Antiquities of Cornwall, 2d edit. p. 220. 234, 235. Wright's Louthiana, b. III. p. 12. though the Doctor inclines to refer the skeletons to the Saxons and Danes, p. 221. as Camden [16] does the barrows round Dorchester. See also Hutchins's Dorset, II. 499. additions; where the human bones are probably remains of some battle. A skeleton and urn were found together with a spear-head under a barrow, at Durnford near Salisbury, 1732 [17]. By the road side near Breech-down, Kent, lay several skeletons, one of which had round the neck a string of beads of various forms and

[1] Gedoyn's Pausanias, vol. I. p. 53. n. [2] Cor. 8. [3] Ib. 18. [4] Ib. 28. [5] Attic. 11.
[6] Att. 43. [7] Cor. 15. [8] Bœot. c. 2.
[9] Cor. 18. [10] Ach. 22. [11] Attic. 32.
[12] And another Grecian *cippus* (as he calls it) in a more finished style, Ib. Pl. lix. 1.
[13] Att. 32. [14] 161—256. [15] P. 43. [16] Dorset.
[17] Minutes of the Society of Antiquaries.

fizes

fizes, from a pigeon's egg to a pea; and by his fide a fword, dagger, and fpear; the reft lay in good order, without any thing to diftinguifh them [1]. In a barrow opened at Muckleford was found a fkeleton that had been interred in an erect pofture [2]. In thofe a mile from Bradford Peverel are found urns, afhes, burnt bones and leather money [3]. Five urns were found under a barrow in Kemacs, in the laft century [4]. Some human bones were found near Abury temple without a barrow [5]. Seventeen urns, with bones and afhes, in one barrow, on Farnham down, Dorfet, were in a cell of flints, perhaps the principal [6]. Bodies often lay on the furface, and not under the level of barrows, at High-crofs, Leicefterfhire [7].

Thofe opened at Stevenage have been found to contain only bits of wood and gravel, and therefore are concluded to be rather boundary marks. The feven hills, as they are called, on the road from Bury to Thetford, about fix miles from the former, may be of the fame kind, though the number of barrows about Bury befpeaks them fepulchral [8]: "monticuli illi ex egefta terra conglobati," as Leland elegantly defcribes the barrow on Salifbury plain [9]. Hubba the Dane was buried in Devonfhire, under a *cumulus*, called *Hubbelowe* [10].

In a round barrow removed to erect fort George at Ardefiroon point in Scotland, 1750, was found a fkeleton, and a brafs fpear head 14 inches by 3. One near a camp in Dorfetfhire contained four human fkeletons [11]. A large one on Charborough-down, in the fame county, had two fculls, and other human bones, not burnt [12].

The great number of barrows on the Downs near Woodyates led Mr. Aubrey to a fingular conjecture, that Weftward of the rampart and ditch near Weft Woodyates had been a terrible fight. There are but a little within the line nineteen barrows, and fome of them very large. Here are alfo two or three circular trenches, with a tump or two, which, in all probability, were places *pro combuftione cadaverum*. There are many barrows between this and Pentridge, and in the chace is a coppice, called Barrow-coppice. One may plainly fee here the chace of the victory was Weftward. He obferved at leaft 100 barrows *fparfim* on the downs and in the enclofures from Woodyates towards Blandford, and thence to Dorchefter feveral [13].

Still lefs will the form of the barrow afcertain to which people it belongs. It is either long and ridged, or flat, campaniform, pyriform, or round; with or without a cavity at top: of different heights; fingle or furrounded by a ditch; or fet round with ftones; or difpofed in rows, in groupes, or feveral within one common ditch [14]. Some have a fmall circle of ftones at the top, others round the bafe [15].

One of the double barrows fouth of Stonehenge being opened 1722, was found to be compofed of good earth quite through, except a coat of chalk, of about two feet thick, covering it quite over under the turf. At the top or centre, not above three feet below the furface, was the fkeleton, perfect, of a reafonable fize, the head lying toward Stonehenge, or Northward. Another double barrow North of Stonehenge, confifted of a layer of chalk, as before, under the turf, then fine garden mould, then a layer of flints about a foot thick on a layer of foft mould another foot in thicknefs, in which was in-

[1] Gent. Mag. 1758. p. 552. [2] Hutchins's Dorfet, I. 445. [3] Ib. [4] Lloyd, in Pembrokefhire.
[5] Stukeley's Abury 33. [6] Hutchins, ubi fup. I. 527. [7] Stukeley, It. Cur. I. 104.
[8] Blomfield, I. 3. Salmon's New Survey, p. 161. [9] De Script. v. Merlin. [10] Bromton, p. 809. A. D. 875.
[11] Hutchins, II. 499. [12] Ib. 185. [13] Aubrey's Mon. Brit. Hutchins, II. 221.
[14] They are fuppofed to be the Saxon cnoubclas, of which three are mentioned in the charters of Wilton monaftery Mon. Ang. II. 861. though the word is not in the Dictionary. See Hutchins's Dorfet, I. 115.
[15] Williams, Phil. Tranf. N° 458. Three ditcht barrows by the camp on Warren-hill, by Ickingham.

 clofed

closed an urn full of bones, made of unbaked clay, of a dark reddish colour crumbled to pieces. It had been rudely wrought with small mouldings round the verge, and other circular channels on the outside, with several indentures between made with a pointed tool. The bones had been burnt, and crowded all together in a little heap, not so much as a hat-crown would contain; and, by the female ornaments, appeared to have belonged to a young girl of fourteen years old. There were beads of all sorts, and in great numbers, of glass of divers colours, most yellow, one black. Many single, many in long pieces, notched between, so as to resemble a string of beads, and these were generally of a blue colour. There were many of amber, of all shapes and sizes, flat square, long square, round, oblong, great and little. Many of earth, many large and flattish like a button, others like a pulley. But all had holes to run a string through, either through their diameter or sides. Many of the button sort seem to have been covered with metal, there being a rim worked in them wherein to turn the edge of the covering. One of these was covered with a thin film of pure gold. All had undergone the fire, so that what would easily consume fell to pieces as soon as handled. Much of the amber was burnt half through. If this person was a female she was a heroine; for there was a brass spear head, having at bottom two holes for the pins that fastened it to the staff. There was also a sharp bodkin, round at one end, square at the other, where it went into a handle. The next barrow to this, within the same ditch, contained, at fourteen inches deep of mould, mixed with chalk, the entire skeleton of a man, lying North and South, the skull and all the bones exceedingly rotten and perished; this Dr. Stukeley supposed the husband or father of the former, and the barrow of the latest sort [1]. Westward, among a groupe of barrows, whence Stonehenge bears E. N. E. was a large barrow, ditched about, but of an antient make. On the side next Stonehenge are ten lesser, small, and as it were crowded together. East of the great one another larger than those in the groupe, but not equaling the first. It would seem that a man and his wife were buried in the two larger, and that the rest were of their children or dependents. In one of the small ones a child's body appeared to have been burnt, and covered up in the centre, where was a little hole cut. From three feet deep they found much wood ashes, soft and black, some little bits of an urn, and black and red earth, very rotten, some small lumps of earth, red as vermilion, and some flints burnt through. Towards the bottom a great quantity of ashes and burnt bones. From this place could be counted 148 barrows in sight. One of those, which Dr. Stukeley calls Druid's barrows, being opened, he found in the centre a squarish hole cut in the solid chalk, three feet and a half by two feet, pointing directly to Stonehenge, covered with artificial earth, not above a foot thick from the surface, containing all the burnt bones of a man, but no signs of an urn. The bank of the circular ditch was on the outside. In another barrow of like dimensions was found a burnt body in a hole in the chalk. In some others large burnt bones of horses and dogs along with human; also, as seemed, of other animals, as fowl, hares, boars, deer, goats, &c. In a great and very flat old fashioned barrow West from Stonehenge, among such matters, bits of red and blue marble, chippings of the stones of the temple, from which the Doctor concluded the deceased was one of the builders. Homer tells us Achilles slew horses and dogs at the funeral of his friend Patroclus [2].

Dr. Stukeley [3] describes the barrows of *kings* as of different shapes, and some set round with stones. The long barrows he refers to the *arch-druids*

[1] Stonehenge, p. 44, 45. [2] Ib. 45, 46. [3] Abury, 5.

from their paucity [1]. Wormius seems to give the long barrows, like ships reverst, to kings. Such are Shipton hill, Dorset, 749 feet long, 150 which is more than Silbury; Shipley hill, in Leicestershire [2]. Others in Sussex, on the Downs near Aldriston. One near Pimpern, c. Dorset, called *Long Barrow* is 224 feet in length, and 10 feet perpendicular [3]. Perhaps that described by Mr. Pennant in Denbighshire, called *The Giant's Grave*, may be another instance [4].

A great tumulus 63 paces from the Roman camp at Oldborough 42 feet high and 14 perpendicular, and 250 in circumference, called the *King's Burial Place*, consisted of different strata of clay and clods, with roots of fern and heath, and at the bottom bones of an ox, and wood ashes, but neither urns, burnt bones, nor coins [5].

At the bottom of one at Otterbourne, Northumberland, 1729, they found a rude stone, like a grave stone, and several smaller wedged in where there were any interstices. Under this a grave, six feet by four, and near four deep. At the top lay fine mould for two feet, and then some ashes laid on fine white sand for above two feet, and with them mixed what were taken for small pieces of burnt bone, very black, and burnt wood like charcoal [6].

In a low or barrow near Elford in Staffordshire, opened 1680, was found level with the surface of the ground about it a moist blackish sort of earth, without any mixture of gravel or stones, about two yards diameter, and a foot and a half deep in the middle, lying much in the same form with the tumulus itself, on the edge whereof were ashes and charcoal in their true colours, and in the middle of it several pieces of bones so friable that they would crumble betwixt the fingers. The low itself, which covered these ashes and black earth, being made with gravel mixed with pebbles, as the soil itself thereabouts is, and so it was also under the black earth [7].

In cutting through the largest of those on Sandford-moor, Westmoreland, 1766, at a considerable depth below the surface they found a short broad sword, fragments of another, and a helmet, two spear heads, umbo of a shield, bones, charcoal, and a mass of such moss as grew on the outside of the stones laid over the above articles [8].

In some cases the body lay near the top as at Silbury, where Dr. Stukeley was beforehand, and the late discoveries produced only some rotten wood and a rusty knife or sword.

Bishop Lyttelton shewed the Society of Antiquaries, 1768, a piece of network, composed of ringlets of iron scarce $\frac{4}{10}$ths of an inch diameter, each ring rivetted and soldered, and seemingly whitened with tin: to these were affixed here and there several other ringlets of brass of the same size, supposed for ornament, being fastened to the other net work by their bases, as triangles. It was found in a barrow in Dorsetshire, and is perhaps the only instance of the kind [9].

Under Bartlow hills were found a stone coffin, containing two bodies, one lying with the head to the others feet; two other stone coffins, with pieces of bones in them, and many chains of iron, like those of horses bits, or perhaps links of mail [10].

In the largest of the barrows on Winstre common, c. Derby, were found two glass vessels, eight or ten inches high, with wide round mouths, and containing

[1] Stukeley, Abury, p. 44. [2] Stukeley, Itin. I. 102. [3] Hutchins, in Gent. Mag. 1768. p. 113.
[4] Wales, I. 384. [5] Arch. II. 56.
[6] Horsley to R. Gale, A. S. min. and among Gale's Letters, p. 259.
[7] Plot's Staffordshire, p. 405. [8] A. S. min. [9] A. S. Min. X. 566.
[10] Hollinshed, p. 176. Letter to the compiler of Magna Britannia, I. 670. Morant, Essex, II. 539.

about

about a pint of clear greenish water; a silver bracelet, about two inches in breadth, and an ornament of filigrain work, gold or silver gilt, with red glass beads, and remains of a wooden box, and clasps and hinges [1].

In the Gentleman's Magazine, September, 1752, p. 408. is an account of a bas relief in alabaster, of the Virgin Mary, Trinity, and angels, found in a barrow on Salisbury plain, and fixed over an alehouse-chimney at Shrawton; which is more likely to have come from the religious house at Ambresbury.

One of the tumuli on the side of the Icening-street leading over Hogmagog-hills being levelled in the summer of 1778, there were found in it several bodies laid from N. to S. and one perpendicular to them, like a T, with six tops [2]. These Mr. West of Furness conjectured to be Roman, differing from the others as that of the Megarensians from the Athenians, by which Solon determined the island of Salamis to have belonged to the latter *ab origine* [3].

In the parish of Llanarmon are abundance of tumuli. Mr. Pennant was present at opening one, which was composed of loose stones and earth, covered with a layer of soil about two feet thick, and over that a coat of turf. In the middle were several urns of a sun-burnt clay, of a reddish colour on the outside, black within, being stained by the ashes they contained. Each was placed with the mouth downwards, on a flat stone, another lying on it, to keep off the weight above. Mixed with the loose stones were numerous fragments of bones of the thigh and arm, and even a scull [4].

Mr. Freebairn, who discovered two Roman forts not hitherto noticed in the country from Duntocher Westward, saw an unusual mode of burying. On opening a tumulus for the high road they found on the level of the surface of the ground 12 urns, six and six, parallel to each other, made of unburnt clay, 13 inches deep, and part of a frustrated cone, seven inches diameter, at the mouth, four and a half at the bottom, full of burnt bones and pieces of the native stone of the country, about two inches long, one inch broad, half an inch thick, with a notch thus,

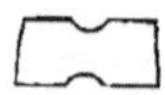

as if for tying a string round the middle; the notch was the only semblance of art in them. The urns were all inverted, upon a flat stone of the same kind, being a greyish freestone, full of talc, not hard. Immediately under these urns was a stone chest, of the same sort of flaggs, constructed for a person in a sitting posture, on opening which a human skeleton appeared in that posture, whose bones were exceeding large; but he saw none entire, except the Os Ischium, which indeed seemed double the size of any skeleton he ever saw, and none of the bones appeared to have suffered fire. It was said the workmen found a piece of gold; but it could not be traced [5].

The downs about Aldfriston, c. Sussex, are covered with barrows: the chief part are of a bell fashion, some single, some double, and others treble, and a few of the long kind. One at Aldfriston is fifty-five yards long, with three sinks, one at each end, and one in the middle, with a deep ditch on each side. with another added of another nation, whose sepulchral position differed as much On opening one of the circular barrows, 1763, the skeleton of a man was found lying on its side in a contracted form with the head to the west, the

[1] Arch. III. p. 174. [2] Ex inform. M. Tyson. [3] Plutarch in Solone. Wales, I. 381. See more, Ib. 383. [5] Letter to Mr. G. Paton, dated Freeport, in Ib, May 18, 1778.

bones very hard and firm, owing to the nature of the ground on which they lay, which was a bed of chalk. During the courfe of digging were found ten knives of different make, iron fpikes, charcoal, a thin piece of yellow metal, bones of beafts, &c. In the middle, under a pyramid of flints, an urn, of unbaked clay, the verge rudely adorned, holding about a gallon, full of burnt bones and afhes, carefully placed in the chalk rock, with about four feet of earth over it [1].

Dr. Knight, in a letter to the Society of Antiquaries, defcribed barrows on a heath bordering Eaft of Ipfwich, three or four miles off, in Walton, a member of Clare-priory; one larger in the middle, the reft in a circle round it: Here are ruins of an abbey, and an old crofs, with a date, 612, cut on it, but fufpicious. Some diftance Eaft of the town are ruins of a round wall on the ridge of a cliff next the fea, between Landguard fort and Woodbridge river, or Bawdfey-haven. It is 100 yards long, five feet high above ground, twelve broad at each end, turned with an angle, and compofed of pebbles and red bricks, in three courfes: fuppofed to be one of the Roman fortifications built on the coaft againft the Saxons in the time of the lower empire. All round are footfteps of buildings, and feveral large pieces of wall caft down on the ftrand, by the fea's undermining the cliff, all which have red brick at low water mark. Very much of the like is vifible at fome diftance in the fea. There are two entire pillars with balls; the cliff is 100 feet high.

Mr. Pownal mentioned a glafs urn found in a barrow Eaft of Lincoln, on the Roman road, which was in the poffeffion of the late Dr. Primrofe, after-in his, and given to Mr. Folkes. Another of curious make, of red earth, with letters, and a ftag on it.

Many tumuli are fcattered all over the ifle of Purbeck. The nine barrows near Corfe are probably Britifh. Thofe round Pool and Studland-bay Danifh. Some in other parts of the ifland may be Roman. They are generally fome round, fome fingle, fome in groups; moftly on hills, rifing ground, or long ridges on the heath [2]. On the downs to the N. E. of Bincomb are a great number, of different dimenfions, fome in groups, and fome fingle; fo that here feems to have been the fcene of fome remarkable action [3].

Barrows lie by dozens and fcores all the way between Everly and Ambrefbury. Above this laft are feven, and feven on Mendip hill, feven in Burghclere parifh. In three in Winterhurn-ftoke Mr. Holland found nothing: the biggeft thereabouts had eighteen inches under the furface a fingle body. They are compofed of pure earth, or chalk, without ftones; but fome have ftones. Some are 100 feet diameter. Lord Winchelfea on opening fome Roman burying places found fometimes an urn by the neck of the body. In the very old barrow faid to be Ambrofius's grave on the left hand, was found a large brafs weapon of near 20 pound weight, like a pole-ax. In another a brafs fword; and in a third a celt [4].

In moft parts of Wales and the Highlands, and fometimes in Cornwall, Northumberland, and Scotland, the barrows are heaps of ftones of all fizes thrown together in a round form. Thefe are called *Karneu, Karnedheu, Cairns.* Though often applied to cover the bodies of malefactors as a mark of contempt and notoriety, they are generally the burial places of the country, of the remoteft antiquity: for Mr. Llwyd fays Hector had a Cairn for his tomb. He adds

[1] Gent. Mag. vol. XXXIII. p. 396. [2] Hutchins, I. 172. [3] Ib. 336.
[4] Stukeley, Stonehenge, p. 46.

one or two inſtances, in which theſe contained near their ſummit a rude ſtone coffin or cheſt [1]. The great barrow at New Grange is made of pebbles or cogle ſtones [2].

The heaps of ſtones were often ſurmounted by croſſes, to which they ſerved as a baſe, and conſequently were rather ſacred than infamous. See Llwyd in Gibſon's Camden, Glamorganſhire, Margam: one at Lilford, c. Northumberland.

I reckon among Cairns certain concentric circles in the Orkneys deſcribed by Mr. Lowe [3], compoſed of an outer ring of looſe ſtones, and three within it of earth, ſurrounding a nucleus, or mound raiſed of earth, ſometimes ſurrounded by ſtones; and the whole diameter from 20 to 50 feet. Tradition indeed aſſigns no uſe to theſe monuments; but it is hard to form any other conjecture than that they were ſepulchral.

An entire ſkeleton was found between flags of proportionable ſize, near Llanarmon pariſh; as was another in one of the Orknies, and others in the ſhire of Murray; and with one of the laſt an urn, with aſhes, and ſeveral pieces of charcoal [4].

A barrow opened by Mr. Williams, on St. Auſtle Downs, had a ſmall circle of ſtones on the top, four feet high and fifteen broad at bottom; the body was compoſed of adventitious earth, and near the centre was a pit a foot deep and wide, dug out of the natural ſoil, and having two flat ſtones on it. In another ſimilar one was a cylindrical pit, two feet broad and one and a half deep, covered with three ſtones ſet edgeways. In the centre of another barrow was a layer of flat ſtones covering a large heap of others, as thoſe did more laid in a conical form, and covering a cylindrical pit two feet broad and two and a half deep, whoſe ſides were lined with flat ſtones, under which was black unctuous matter about an inch thick. A fourth, ſurrounded by two inches of ſtones, had in its centre an oblong ſquare pit one foot and a half deep, two broad, and five long, whoſe bottom had the ſame black greaſy matter. The outermoſt circle, or heap of ſtones, concealed an urn ſtanding in a pit on a flat ſtone, and covered by two other flat ſtones, and wedged in by many ſmall ſtones. This urn was thirteen inches high, diameter eleven inches, of hard burnt earth, half an inch thick, very black within, having four little ears or handles, and containing ſeven quarts of burnt bones and aſhes [5]. See an urn in a barrow in Angleſea [6]. Dr. Stukeley [7] has indulged a ſtrange chimæra, from Dr. Plot [8], about a tumulus of earth converted into a heap of ſtones, and of fortifications become ſolid cliff on St. Vincent's rock near Briſtol. This is of a piece with his conjectures, that a quarry of ſtone in Lincolnſhire and Norfolk, where many Britiſh ſkeletons were found, was once mould.

Barrows continued in uſe to the 12th century. The plain about Fornham in Suffolk is covered with thoſe thrown up over the Flemings ſlain under Robert earl of Leiceſter, 19 Henry II. Seven of them being larger than the reſt, and probably covering the bodies of officers, are ſtill known by the name of the *Seven Hills*, on the road from Thetford to Bury [9].

I might add, that the officers and private men ſlain at the battle of Culloden are laid under two ſeparate and ſimilar barrows, near the Frith of Forth river. Yet I doubt if the many that overſpread the field of battle fought at Otterburne in 1488, are of that late date.

[1] Britannia, Radnorſhire.
[2] MS. Hiſt. of Orkney.
[3] Phil. Tranſ. 458.
[4] Oxfordſhire.
[5] Archæol. II. 150.
[6] Rowland, p. 49. 2d edit.
[7] Pennant's Wales, I. 387, 388. Mr. Lowe, ubi ſup.
[8] Phil. Tranſ. N° 360. p. 966.
[9] Blomefield's Norfolk, I. p. 3.

In one layer of the barrows near Kingsgate the skeletons were found doubled together in graves cut in the solid chalk, together with urns, ashes, and bones. These two barrows are supposed to contain only the officers, most of the common men having been cast into the sea from the cliffs, either in the battle or when slain.

Mr. Davis of Anglesea described to Mr. Barrington a Kistvaen he saw in Llangaed parish, discovered by the plow. It was in the clear two feet nine inches by one foot nine, and three feet deep, composed of four rude slabs of grey marble or lime stone, and covered by a fifth, three feet nine inches by three feet five inches. It lay near North and South, the scull at the North end. The body being so disproportioned to the coffin, it was questioned how it could be laid strait in it, unless it was put in some time after death, at the period when the limbs recover their flexibility again. He sent him another account of a very extraordinary catacomb discovered in the neighbourhood of Sir N. Bayley. In a vault on Muckleford Down, Dorset, was opened a barrow, containing a skeleton, that appeared to be interred erect [1].

In one of the tumuli opened close by Stromness was found the entire body of a man inclosed in a stone coffin, about four feet and a half long. The body had been placed in a sitting posture, and when the chest was found was fallen down between the thigh bones; the other bones supported each other, so as to shew the original position. In another coffin discovered in the same hillock the body had been laid on its side, the knees to the breast, and the hands to the cheeks. At a small distance another hillock was opened, in which was first discovered a small stone chest about a foot square, containing a small quantity of discoloured earth. Nearer the centre a large coffin in which was an urn wrapt up in leather with a small stone cover containing ashes and bits of bones. The urn was made of a very gritty clay much discoloured, and split from near the top to the bottom. This, with all its contents, is now in the possession of my good friend Mr. George Paton of Edinburgh.

In the island of Sherness, or Saila, without the dykes of Hamna, is the *Giant's Grave*, a monument of standing stones, originally three, one now much shortened of its original dimensions, another broken short off at the ground. Tradition is quite silent about it. The stones have been brought from the neighbouring sea rocks.

Mr. Lowe [2] imagines the range of stones and ditch marked the sacred ground, and the hillocks nearly corresponding with the four points might be for the altars, as the neighbouring stones might have supported a table, though this is now gone, for preparing the sacrifice; all particulars necessary about a heathen temple. Probably their shape may be of use in pointing out their intention, and give us to understand that in the circle was performed the worship in honour of the Sun confessedly an idol of the Germans [3]; while the semicircle was dedicated to the moon. If this is the case, and it is very probable, as they are both excellently situated in the openest and plainest spot in the mainland, where the fullest view of these bodies could be had from their rising to their setting, these certainly are the circles of Loda, and the mossy stones of power mentioned by Ossian in his Carricthura; but alas the echoing woods "bending along the coast," are now no more. Near the circle is a series of tumuli of a much less size than the four abovementioned, being entirely sepulchral; many of them have been searched into, and possibly it has been here Wallace's fibulæ were found.

[1] Hutchins, I. 445. [2] MS. Hist. of Orkney. [3] Verstegan, p. 75, 76.

Near

Near Termifton is a vaft tumulus, probably fepulchral; but this is not afcertained; for though Lord Morton caufed feveral people to dig in it, they gave over too foon, before they came within a great way of the centre or the bottom. Among the arable land of Ireland in this parifh, we obferve a circular fpace, furrounded by a deep ditch, but without ftones; the like is to be feen at Weftbufter in Sandwich parifh. Thefe perhaps may have been the places of juftice in antient times; and if they have ever been furrounded with ftones, thefe muft have been fmall, and carried off for building.

In the mofs of Kennefs numbers of corpfes are dug up, fuppofed to be Cathneffmen, killed at the battle of Summerdale, which was fought between the earl of Cathnefs and lord Sinclair on the one fide, and Edward Sinclair of Strome, who commanded the Orkneymen, on the other.

In the links of Skail the tumuli are compofed either of ftones furrounding the coffins, and covered with fand, or of entire fand; fome of them contain one, fome more coffins, even to fix placed in rows, one above another. The bodies are all naked, though in fome which Mr. Lowe had feen opened, coarfe bags full of bones were found placed at the feet of the principal fkeleton. Beads of ftone and a fpecies of Lithanthrax were found in one, with feveral other little particulars, but no arms; which may hint to us that there were the graves of thofe who died at home. In one was found the body of a child of about feven years of age, as the fecond crop of teeth were beginning to make their appearance. In another an old man with the teeth worn down to the gums, the ftumps full of tartar, with a woman's bones put up in a bag at his feet. On the hard and dry brakes we fee numbers of tumuli placed for the moft part either clofe by the highways or common ftiles. In the conftruction of thefe the coffin was firft fet upon the live earth, and heaped round with ftones and earth to the bulk they defigned it; and as fome of them are very large, Mr. Lowe imagines the whole community might join, as we know in time of war the whole army did, to make up the hills raifed over the flain. If at any time they had occafion to bury in the fame tumulus, they opened the fide of it, and placed a leffer coffin, in which are laid bones or leffer bodies. They feem never to have ftretched their corpfes to their full length, as we never fee any of the coffins above four feet and an half long, and many lefs; the body with the knees to the breaft, and the legs along the thighs. We fee yet another fpecies of tumulus in this parifh, which is entirely without a coffin or urn. Here however the body has been burnt, and that in a very fierce fire, and the whole almoft vitrified, fomething like the clamps thrown out of forges. In one which Mr. Lowe opened, the whole cover of the tumulus was compofed of fuch clamps, with pieces of human bones unburnt, and fticking in them, the matter hard congealed about them. In one lump was half a jawbone, in others bones of horfes [1], and dogs, which had been confumed in the funeral pile, together with their mafter. The tumulus here, he imagines, has been raifed immediately over the funeral pile, as many of the lumps that are hollow are much difcoloured, as if they had been covered while yet fmoaking. In many of thefe ftone coffins we obferve a pretty large quantity of animal *humus*, efpecially about the bones of the thighs. The bags for enclofing the bones before taken notice of feem to have been made of rufhes. One of thefe was full of a fmall beetle, called Dermeftes, both the bag and beetles intirely black and rotten. Some of thefe tumuli on the moors are furrounded with ftones; others, and by far the greater part plain.

Mr. Lowe, in his way over the hills of South Ronaldsha, faw feveral tumuli, which the old men call *Ern Couligs*, but which they could not explain.

[1] So Balder was buried; Saxo Gram. 43. A. See alfo Northern Antiquities, p. 344.

A few

A few tumuli have been dug up in Forfar parish in Kirkwall, and some plain urns found in them, made of a very sandy kind of clay, rather dried than burnt.

Several circles without stones, or with very low ones in the Orkney isles, may have been *tings* or courts of antient times. Several tumuli are scattered up and down Rendale, to which tradition has handed down names, which is seldom the case. One is called *Enerow*, another *Disherow*, both no doubt corrupted from the original words.

In one of the tumuli opened close by Stromness, was found the entire body of a man inclosed in a stone coffin.

In Birsa, at the East end of the hill called Revè, near some large tumuli, are three upright stones at unequal distances, in a strait line. Tumuli are scattered all over the moors, which plainly shew this side of the country to have been well inhabited from the earliest time. In one of them, called *Stone Randy*, are stones set upright on the top, which is uncommon, and shews that *Randy*, or perhaps *Randolf*, was a person of no mean note among his countrymen. This tumulus had been dug up long ago.

Sanda on every sandy point discovers antient graves, all of them stone coffins under tumuli. In the sandy grounds of Stronza where they are blown, particularly about Rousholm links, graves have been discovered. These are all tumuli, and contain stone coffins, wherein are deposited the bodies entire.

In Dunrosness parish in the mainland of Shetland the blowing of the sand discovers tumuli, which are very rare in Shetland. Mr. Lowe opened one [1], in which he found no less than nine sculls, or their remains, but the corpses had not been laid in any order, but thrown together as chance directed, which seems to confirm the tradition of Foula, that they are the *Lewismen's* graves.

The shifting of the sands in Westram has laid open antient burying places, which in some places were above twenty feet under ground, and are either of stones and rubbish, or the grave simply set round with a tire of small stones on end. The last are generally in clusters, and even with the sand. In examining the latter we find, besides the bones of men, those of cows, horses, dogs, and sheep, besides warlike instruments of all kinds then in use, as battle-axes, two handed swords, broadswords, helmets, swords made of the jawbone of a whale, daggers, &c. knives, combs, beads, broches, and chains, a round flat piece of marble about two inches and half diameter, several stones shaped like whetstones, but no marks of such use, a very small iron vessel like a headpiece, only four inches and a half in the hollow, much wounded, as if by a sword or ax. In one was a metal spoon, and a neat glass cup, so rusted that it now appears of a pearl colour, and may contain about two gills Scots, or half a pint English. In another a great number of stones formed into such whirls as in Scotland were formerly used to turn a spindle. In another a gold ring encircling a thigh bone. Q. How put on. Whence arise such differences in the tumuli of the same nation, and in the same island? The Welsh Highlanders, at a certain æra, used the tumulus, but it seems to have been after the Norwegians settled among them; for in Ossian's poems we find four stones rising on the grave of Cathbar. We find them buried with their arms, dogs, and deers' horns, as symbols of a hunter. The tumuli may be memorials of the many battles between the Orkneymen and the Highlanders, and may be graves of invaders in very early æras from the Western isles. A stratum of clay covers the bones, as the translator of Ossian observes, that "the bottom of the grave was lined with fine clay, whereon they laid the deceased, if a warrior, with his sword and the heads of arrows by his side; if a hunter, a deer's horn; covering the whole with fine mould, and four stones on end, to mark the extent of the grave." As to the number of

[1] Mr. Lowe ubi sup.

ftones they do not feem to be fixed, as we fee the graves marked fometimes with one, fometimes with two, and oftimes, no doubt, with more than four grey ftones. I fhould be very far from placing the æra of thefe graves fo far back as Offian's time, though we learn that his father made fome vifits to Initore; but if we confider the pertinacioufnefs of the Weftern Highlanders to old cuftoms, we need not wonder to fee them adhering to thefe.

"The dead were interred at fome diftance from the houfes called Pictifh in Caithnefs fhire. The cemiteries were of two kinds. In fome the deceafed were placed within great circles of ftones of 100 feet diameter, and the corpfes covered with gravel. In others they were interred in cairns of a fugar loaf form. Sometimes bones have been found in them, fometimes urns with afhes. Sometimes the corroded remains of iron weapons, and in one a brafs fpear nine inches long [1].

Dr. Stukeley, perhaps too haftily, concluded that a piece of ground juft without the old city wall at Cirencefter, which goes by the name of the *Querns* or *Kairns*, full of heaps of ftones now by length of time covered with herbage, among which large monumental ftones have certainly been dug up, was the comman burying place of the antient *Corinium*. Mr. Rudder rather inclines to think them heaps of rubbifh made by digging of ftone for the purpofe of building [2].

Pillars (στηλαι, *cippi)* were fometimes contemporary with barrows. Jacob fet a pillar on Rachel's grave; and we have feen fome inftances among the Greeks in Paufanias. Thefe were either rude ftones, or infcribed with fret work, figures of men and beafts, or croffes. This laft circumftance befpeaks them Chriftian, which their being in churchyards alone would imply. But they are not confined to churchyards. They ferved on fields of battle, both as trophies and tombftones; as at *Forres*, and elfewhere in Scotland.

On a monument called Mikneint, in Merionethfhire, Mr. Llwyd defcribes 30 graves, about two yards long, and each diftinguifht by four fquare pillars, about two or three feet high, and nine inches broad at the corners, fuppofed to be erected after a battle [3]. One Mr. Vaughan opened one of them, but found no marks of human interment [4].

At Chedworth, c. Gloucefter, on a hill a little above the fite of a Roman hypocauft, about a mile on the North Weft of the Foffway, is a large tumulus, which had a huge rough ftone fet upright on its top, fuppofed to have been raifed by the Britons or Saxons. Not long fince fome of the farmers removed the ftone with a double team of oxen, and fo expofed great quantities of human bones lying near the top of the barrow [5].

On the top of Silbury-hill Dr. Stukely found a fkeleton, with the fragments of a bridle.

The pyramid of earth at New Grange contained two human fkeletons, as Molyneux, or, as major Vallancy, one, laid on a large ftone in the middle, and black afhes in three cells.

At Chatteris, in the ifle of Ely, 1757, was found, two feet and half under the turf, a fkeleton, with a fword at the right fide, fpear at left, and umbo of fhield on breaft; at the head a large urn of black earth unbaked, containing probably the wife's afhes, and a glafs vafe of fingular pipe-like projections [6].

On Barham downs was found, 1759, a fkeleton with a fword and fpear, and round the neck a ftring of glafs beads [7]. Dr. Stukeley pronounces all thefe Britifh.

[1] Pennant's 2d tour, App. p. 29.
[2] Gibfon's Camden, 791.
[3] Rudder, p. 334.
[4] Rudder's Hift. of Gloucefterfhire, p. 349.
[5] Wyndham's Tour in Wales, p. 131.
[6] Gent. Mag. March, 1766.
[7] Ib.

Lord

Lord Harley digging a canal at Wimple, near the Ermine-ſtreet, found ſixteen bodies, moſtly laid in heaps on each other, but ſome ſingle: near them were ſeveral pieces of ruſty iron, which ſeemed to have been fragments of ſwords, or other weapons [1].

At Holkham in Norfolk, on digging one ſide of a hill, 1722, were found many corpſes, with many beads, like amber, as big as a haſel nut, more of the ſize of a pea, pierced through in order to be ſtrung; ſome iron ſpear-heads, ſome pieces of braſs, &c. Theſe were thought Britiſh. Mr. Hare brought to the Society of Antiquaries that year ſeveral braſs fibulæ, curiouſly wrought, waſhed with gold, found at Holkham, ſuppoſed Daniſh [2].

Dr. Knight gave the Society of Antiquaries an account of a large ſkeleton found near Chippenham, c. Cambridge, with maſſy chains and fetters dug up near him 171$\frac{1}{2}$ [3]. Mr. Henry Johnſon ſhewed them, 1750, a large ſpear-head a foot long, with the rivets that faſtened it to the ſtaff, found at Weſt Mead, Hants, within a ſtone circular wall, on the eſtate of Henry Foxcroft, eſq. within which circle fifty yards diameter were found ſeveral bones of men and horſes, and adjoining are three hillocks of earth, ſuppoſed Daniſh burying places [4].

A copper ring was found round the arm of a human ſkeleton at Druton, near Cave, in the Eaſt Riding of Yorkſhire. It was quite black and bright, and not in the leaſt corroded except a little in the inſide where it touched the arm.

At Lidden, near Canterbury, two men, July, 1760, grubbed up a very large aſh, above fifty feet round at the root. In the centre were two ſkeletons almoſt entire, of large proportions, and by them lay a dagger. Their heads lay very near together, but the bodies one to the Eaſt and the other to the S.E. and each had a head-ſtone [5].

Some labourers digging chalk in a bank thirty feet high, near the N. E. corner of the glebe and yard of St. John's church at Lewes, which had formerly been a fort againſt the Danes, and is ſurrounded with natural banks and ditches, the former here loweſt and moſt acceſſible from the water; which formerly brought up the Daniſh boats cloſe under this fort at every ſpring tide, though now dry, except in land-floods, found a braſs fibula, of a circular form, which had been gilt and ſtudded. It was compoſed of two thin plates of braſs ſomewhat more than $\frac{1}{10}$ths of an inch broad, united by a ſmall concave hoop, the upper circular plate leſs than the under, which is $1\frac{1}{15}$ths diameter. The ſtuds were cut off to come at the inſcription, which is in old Engliſh characters, on the upper circle, and appears to be "Ave Maria gracia plen." About 15 feet to the right of the ſpot where the fibula was found, but within five feet of the top of the bank, was found a human ſkeleton, whoſe ſcull the labourers carried away, and it is now in the hands of Mr. Puxty of Brighthelmſtone [6].

In digging a vault or cellar near Gold court, in Wareham, 1753, were dug up above 30 ſculls, but other bones ſcarce proportionable to three or four bodies. Theſe ſculls, except three or four, were placed with the face downwerds, the top of the head to the Eaſt, and incloſed between flat ſtones ſet on edge. Theſe might be Danes, perhaps thus diſtinguiſhed from Chriſtians, as St. Ambroſe diſtinguiſhed the Arians from the Orthodox, after a battle at Milan [7].

At Ripatranſona, the antient Cupra of the Picentes, was found 1727, an antient monument, containing the bodies of two ſoldiers, and round about them various earthen lamps, and other veſſels: they had bracelets on their arms,

[1] Stukely, A. S. Min. [2] A. S. Min. [3] Ib. [4] Ib.
[5] Newberry's Deſcription of England, V. 75.
[6] A. S. Min. XV. 217.
[7] Hutchins, Hiſt. of Dorſet, I. 36. See another inſtance in the ſame volume, p. 574. Keyſler's Travels, I. 346.

little

little chains or links, phaleræ, bullæ, fibulæ, helmets, and fpearheads [1]. The author of this account underftands Virgil's defcription of Mifenus's tomb [2], that the arms, oar, and trumpet were put *into*, and not *upon* it: and mentions a fword and other fingular weapons found in an antient fepulcre at Fiefole.

There were found fkeletons in the Pavillia vault at Cumæ [3].

"At Northburne, Kent, was the palace of Edbald, Ethelbert's fon, and a few "years fyns in brakng the wall of the hall were found two children's bones that "had been mured up as yn buriall yn tyme of Paganite of the Saxons. Among "one of the children's bones was found a ftiff pin of laten [4]."

"A glaffe with bones in a fepulchre found by Dodington churche in the "high way. Potes exceeding fine nelid and floryfhed in the Romanes tyme "diggid out of groundes in the fields of Dodington. A yerthen pot with Ro-"mayne coines found in Dodington felde [5]."

The cuftom of burning the dead obtained among the Northern nations from the remoteft period [6]. The Danes diftinguifhed by this a particular period, called *Roifold* or *Brende tiide*, which feems to have ceafed with Paganifm. Of courfe the Danes, being lateft converted, retained it longeft. Among us, when the Britons laid it afide the Saxons took it up. The *Hoigold* or *Hoilfe tiid* was the Danifh æra of barrows, under which the corpfe was placed entire, with all its ornaments, arms, horfe, and even wealth and plunder [7]. The laft period of interment in Denmark was called *Chriftendom's old*, when Chriftianity introduced the prefent mode.

Yet on rebuilding, 1747, Fairwell church, in Staffordfhire, fuppofed to be the chapel of the nunnery founded there by Roger Clinton, bifhop of Litchfield, 1142, they found in the South wall, about fix feet from the ground, three ranges of coarfe earthen veffels of different fizes, and unglazed, the largeft capable of containing two, the fmaller one quart: the larger were four inches and a half over at the mouth, twenty-four round, and near a foot high: the fmall ones three inches one-eighth at the mouth, fixteen and a quarter round, and fix and a quarter high. They lay on the fides, in one direction, their mouths placed towards the inner fide of the church, and ftopped with a thin coat of plaifter [8].

At Yoxall, c. Staffordfhire, were found, near Mr. Wright's houfe, near forty urns of coarfe brown foft earth, almoft full of afhes, and fragments of human bones [9].

The Kiftvaen, or coffin compofed of rough ftones fet edgeways at the fides and ends, and covered with one or more flat ftones, was another receptacle of the dead antiently ufed in Britain, and may be called the early altar monument. Thefe are frequent in Wales; but feldom found to contain fkeletons, or remains of bodies in them. See Dr. Stukeley's Abury, p. 13, of one on a barrow at Rowldrich; another, p. 49, fimilar in Monkton-field, near Abury. Two that were found in Purbeck, on making a turnpike road to Corfe, had fkeletons in them [10]. Thefe one may venture to pronounce Britifh. Thofe

[1] Saggi di Differtationi di Cortona, tom. I. diff. V. p. 56, tav. I. 11.
[2] Aen. VI. 233.
[3] Phil. Tranf. XLIX. art. 66. Gent. Mag. 1756. 555.
[4] Leland. It. VII. 127. [5] Leland. It. VI. 75.
[6] Tac. de mor. Germ. c. 27. Mela III. 2.
[7] Mela, Ib. Wormius Mon. Dan. 40. Bartholin. Antiq. Dan. 438.
[8] Mr. Green, Gent. Mag. Feb. 1771. p. 53. Bp. Lyttelton, in A. S. Min. 1747.
[9] Gent. Mag. Aug. 1774. p. 358.
[10] Mr. Hutchins's Letter to bishop Lyttelton, 1768.

ftone

ftone cells which gave name to *Kerig y Druidhion*, in Denbighfhire, but are now removed, were of the fame kind. Some of thefe rude fepulchral receptacles Mr. Pegge has feen in Derbyfhire, and others may be found defcribed in Camden [1].

Of this earlier kind and date were the rude ftone chefts under barrows in Orkney, which contained entire bodies [2]. In one of thefe Mr. Lowe found with the body a bag of fome coarfe vegetable ftuff laid at the feet and containing the bones of a younger perfon, which feemed to have been a woman [3]. This bag might be the *bulga*, which Lucilius defcribes as the *all* of the perfon he fatirizes [4],

> " Cum bulga coenat, dormit, lavit; omnis in una
> " Spes hominis bulga."——

and hence Macaulay [5] derives the name of *Firbolg*, the old Irifh having fcarce any thing more defirable than their bag.

On the field of Loncarty, where the Hays beat the Danes, are feveral tumuli, wherein are found bones depofited in loofe ftones in form of a coffin [6].

On a farm called *Hondre*, in Miline parifh, Pembrokefhire, fome labourers hedging came to a number of ftones of different fizes, fome thrown together promifcuoufly, but the uppermoft lying over one another, like tiles on a roof. At about nine feet depth they came to a very large ftone, about feven feet long, four or five broad, and twenty inches thick. At its Eaft and Weft end were placed two ftones on edge, and others under the fides and in the middle was a cavity of about two, or two feet and a half high, and of the length of the ftone, containing only a little black earth. Over the whole the foil had been fomewhat raifed in a circular form as a barrow; but the field having been in conftant tillage had much reduced its height. In the fame or neighbouring parifh, on a high mountain, called, from its fugar-loaf form, *Voel dri garn*, are three cairns of loofe ftones, very near each other, and on the fame mountain veftiges of a camp double ditched, and the fites of the tents hollowed out very vifible [7].

On Eglwys Ilan common, two miles from Caerphyli, feveral tumuli were opened 1753, when burnt bones were found in urns, inclofed in a fquare cavity of flat ftones [8].

Kryg y Dern in Trelech parifh, c. Caernarvon, is a Karned of ftones, covered with turf, circular at bottom about fixty paces, height about fix yards, rifing with an eafy afcent, and a hollow at top. In the centre of this cavity was a vaft flat oval ftone, three yards long, five feet over where broadeft, and about ten or twelve inches thick. Mr. William Lewis of Lhwyn Dern having caufed it to be opened, found, after removing a large quantity of ftones, that it covered a kiftvaen, or ftone cheft, about four feet and a half long, and three broad, narroweft at the Eaft end, compofed of feven ftones, viz. the cover, two at each fide and end, and one behind each of the end ftones to keep them up, all equally rude, and about the fame thicknefs, except the two laft, which were very confiderably thicker. They found both within and without the cheft fome rude pieces of brick or burnt ftone, and wrought pieces of ftone; and fome pieces of bones, which they imagined had been brought thither by foxes, but they did not go to the bottom of the cheft. Confidering the labor and ftrength employed about this rude monument Mr. Lluyd thinks it belonged to fome

[1] Camden, col. 707. 750. 751. 753. 773.
[2] The Tartarian barrows have abfolute ftone vaults under them. Archaeol. II. 222.
[3] Archaeol. III. 277.
[4] Sat. VI.
[5] Voyage to St. Kilda, p. 52.
[6] Mr. Pennant, 1ft Tour, p. 79.
[7] Rev. Mr. Howel's letter to me, Sept. 6, 1777.
[8] Mr. Harris, Arch. II. p. 10.

 British

British prince before the Roman conqueſt, deriving the name *Dyrn* from *Tyern*, originally the ſame with *Tyrannus*[1]. Dr. Stukeley[2] mentions ſeveral barrows as containing coffins formed of ſeveral ſtones, and ſome arched, and Aubrey mentions one of three ſtones eleven feet long. The monument called *le Pierre couverte*, near Saumier, in Bretagne, engraved by Count Caylus, VI. Pl. cxvii. ſeems rather like the above than a Cromlech. In Pl. cxx he gives tombs of ſingle or ſeveral ſtones, cairns, and cromlehs intermixt at *Locbmariaker*, the antient *Dariorigum*.

In Bamffſhire Mr. Pennant deſcribes a large cairn of ſtones, which covered a coffin of flags, containing a perfect human ſkeleton, and a deer's horn; in two other ſuch coffins an urn and charcoal; in a fourth coffin were three urns, and one of them contained a fourth, beſides flint arrowheads; and all theſe near two circles of ſtones[3].

Near a farm houſe at Weſt Matfen, in Northumberland, was a tumulus of earth and coarſe rag ſtone, in the centre of which were found two ſtone coffins, formed of flags, ſet on edge with a ſtone bottom and cover containing aſhes like white duſt[4]. Near it, a ſtone nine feet high, three by one and half ſquare.

At Otterburne was a large cairn of ſtones under which was a large rough ſtone like a grave ſtone, with ſmaller ſtones wedged in between it and the ground, and under it in the ground a cavity in form of a grave, two yards long and four feet broad. About one feet and half deep was ſome very fine mould, then ſome aſhes laid in fine white ſand, above two feet thick, the whole cavity of the grave being near four feet. With the aſhes were mixed what they took for ſmall pieces of burnt bones, very black, but none entire, and ſome pieces of burnt wood like charcoal[5].

How can Mr. Hutchinſon take the numerous tumuli round this place for memorials of the battle fought there 1388.

In a tumulus at Over, in the pariſh of Almondſbury, c. Glouceſter, were dug up, 1650, two ſkeletons. One of them was of uncommon ſize, exceeding the uſual proportion by above three feet, incloſed in a ſtone coffin, ſo artificially cemented together that the joints were not diſcernable. The ſtone that covered the coffin was very ponderous, of a greyiſh colour without, but reddiſh and ſtudded with a ſhining ſparry ſubſtance within. In the coffin were found two coins, one of which bore the impreſſion of a falcon[6], as the writer among Mr. Wantner's MS. papers expreſſes himſelf. And on the other was a head, which he ſuppoſed that of Claudius Cæſar, but no inſcription is mentioned. The corpſe was buried *ſitting*, of which we have given an inſtance before, p. xi. and which Drexelius ſays was the cuſtomary manner of burying kings and princes, as an emblem of eternity. This poſture is not eaſily accounted for in the depth commonly given to ſtone coffins. Tradition makes this tumulus the burying place of king Offa, to whom it aſcribes the adjoining camp on the brow of a hill over-hanging the Severn: but it is more generally believed, on the authority of Matthew of Weſtminſter, and other monkiſh writers, that he was buried near Bedford[7].

About the ſame time ſeveral ſtone coffins containing human bones were dug out of the barrows near a circular camp called Old Abbey, in Alveſton pariſh, in the ſame county, overhanging the Severn[8].

At Leyterton, in Boxwell pariſh, in the ſame county, in a large tumulus, called Weſt barrow, were found three vaults, arched over like ovens, and at the entrance of each an earthen urn, wherein were many aſhes and burnt bones, the ſkulls and thigh bones whole[9].

[1] Gibſon's Camden, Caermarthenſhire. [2] Abury, 45. [3] Tour, 1769. p. 139, 140.
[4] Wallis's Northumberland, II. 141. Hutchinſon, I. 136.
[5] Horſley's Letter to Roger Gale, 1729 in Hutchinſon's Northumberland, p. 196.
[6] Probably an eagle. [7] Rudder's Glouc. p. 222. [8] Ib. 220. [9] Ib. 222. 306.

About

About the year 1772 ſome perſons employed to dig materials for repairing the roads in Titherington pariſh, in the ſame county, found a large ſtone like a ſtep not far below the ſurface of the ground, and then another ſuch ſtone, and ſearching further diſcovered two perfect ſkeletons, incloſed in ſtone coffins, lying North and South: whence ſome perſons have concluded, that theſe corpſes were placed here before the general eſtabliſhment of Chriſtianity in this country. One of the ſkeletons was ſix feet and a half long, as a gentleman who meaſured it aſſured Mr. Rudder, but they both fell to pieces on being ſlightly touched, and no coin, armour, or any thing that could determine the time of interment, or the people to whom the bodies belonged were found [1].

An imitation of theſe rude coffins in Chriſtian times may be found in the *Giant's grave*, as called in *Penrith* church-yard, four ſimilar ſtones, miſtaken for *boars*, for no other reaſon than that their ridges are round, and notcht like briſtles, and becauſe tradition ſays Sir *Owen Cæſarius* ſlew a monſtrous boar. Others, with as little pretence, have found on them ſculptures of horſemen, like the Scotch monuments. I call them *Chriſtian*, becauſe the croſs has been on the pillars, and becauſe they are in a churchyard, which I ſuppoſe to be coæval with them. This is conceived by ſome to have been the tomb of Ervain king of Cumberland, defeated by Athelſtan A. D. 928 [2]. Mr. Pennant [3] diſtinguiſhes the æra of the tumuli round Maen Achwynfan in Flintſhire, from that of the ſtone, referring the one to pagan, the other to Chriſtian times. May we not ſuppoſe the croſs had an after-reference to the tumuli, and its name from the field of battle?

The three ſtone coffins found at Chriſtchurch, in Hampſhire, 1777, which are ſomewhat more artificial, appear to be a degree of improvement on the former; and there is a circumſtance or two attending them, which make them highly worthy of notice. They are compoſed not of one block, formed by excavation, as the ſtone coffins often, and very antiently, were, but of various, not fewer than ten or eleven pieces; and there does not appear to have been any ſtone underneath for the body interred to lie upon.

As to the firſt particular, it may be doubted whether the parties concerned could find any ſtones for their ſervice in the neighbourhood of Chriſtchurch, ſo they had recourſe to Normandy for them (for the ſtones are apparently French from about Caen), where they either could not obtain a ſingle ſtone of a competent ſize, or were not then poſſeſſed of the idea of making uſe of ſuch an one, and ſo tranſported a number of ſmaller ones. And this may be an argument of the antiquity of theſe coffins, ſince, in later ages, the ſtone coffins have always been found compoſed of one piece, with a lid or cover. I know not whether this might not have been in imitation of the Romans, for though this people at laſt applied the ſingle ſtone, as we ſhall ſee hereafter, yet Mr. Thoreſby tells us, "There was digged up in the Roman burying ground "at York a ſort of coffin made of clay; I have by me, ſays he, part of the "bottom, which (for the convenience of baking I preſume) was divided into "ſeveral ſuch parts; this is entire as firſt moulded by the Romans, is 14½ inches "long, and almoſt 11 broad at the narrower end, and nigh 12½ at the broader, "&c [4]." He adds, that there were in his Muſeum "fragments alſo of ſuch a "coffin found at Burgdurum." All which ſeems to ſhew, that at firſt the ſtone coffins, both among the Britons and Romans, conſiſted of a number of parts, and that the cutting them out of a ſingle block was a later improvement; thoſe at Chriſtchurch are conſequently of the more antique kind.

[1] Rudder, ubi ſup. 766.
[2] Hutchinſon's Northumberland, I. 261.
[3] Wales I. 10.
[4] Thoreſby, Muſ. p. 561.

The

The next and laſt improvement of the ſtone coffin, was by forming them of a ſingle ſtone with mallet and tool; and this Mr. Pegge aſcribes to the Romans; for he apprehends that during the general prevalency of the cuſtoms of cremation and urn-burial among the Romans, they had not always recourſe to the funeral pile, but that bodies were ſometimes interred whole, and in their natural ſtate. He has the ſuffrages of Kirchman [1], Ainſworth [2], and Drake [3]; and this is agreeable alſo to appearances here. Mr. Thomas Beckwith of York informed him, that hearing of two ſtone coffins, diſcovered anno 1776, in the new incloſures at Acomb near York, he had the curioſity to go and view them, and ſaw them lying in the very place where they were found. He thinks they are Roman; and the obſervations on which he grounds his opinion are ſo juſt and forcible that I ſhall give the ſubſtance of them here.

"The coffins were of the coarſe grit, the ſame as that at Plumpton, near Knareſborough, which the Romans appear to have been fond of, as many of their works in York are of that ſtone. The coffins were $2\frac{1}{2}$ inches thick on the ſides, and the lids (which had a fillet, raiſed about $\frac{3}{4}$ of an inch, running down the middle) ſomething thicker.

"They lay, one for a youth of 12 or 14 years of age, with the feet pointing nearly South; and the other, for a grown perſon, to the South-Weſt; directions and poſitions ſo unuſual in Chriſtian burial, that one muſt conclude the coffins belonged to Pagans, and were more ancient than the converſion of the Romans and Britons in theſe parts.

"There is no account of any church, or religious houſe, either at, or near, this place; no foundations of any buildings found in plowing. It is about a mile N. W. from Acomb, where it is ſaid the body of the emperor Severus was burnt: and when the lids were on the coffins they could not be more than one quarter of a yard beneath the ſurface of the earth." The man who found the coffins told Mr. Beckwith, that on their being firſt opened there appeared ſomething like an human body; but as ſoon as it was touched it loſt its form, falling down and mixing with the water at the bottom of the coffins.

Theſe reaſons taken together may ſeem ſufficient to inforce a belief, that theſe bodies were interred during the Pagan government here. "Quae cum ita "ſint," ſays Mr. Ainſworth, "non compertum videtur omnes illas arcas, quae "multis locis effoſſae apud nos fuerunt, eſſe Anglo-Saxonum, ut vulgo perhiben- "tur. Sunt enim, quas etſi populi iſtius eſſe non abnegaverim, Romanis tamen "abjudicare non auſim." He concludes, "Haec obiter dicenda judicavimus, ne "quis cremationem unicam et perpetuam ſepulturae fuiſſe conſuetudinem apud "Romanos putaret [4]."

Of the ſtone coffins of the Etruſcans ſee Adami (Storia de Volſena, I. 30.) who, ſpeaking of the uſe of Greek characters by that people, has this paſſage: "Molte iſcrizioni in queſto carattere per la Toſcana tutta ſi ritrovano; ma par- "ticolariſſima, cred' io, che ſia quella che appreſſo di me ſi vede in marmo "ſcolpita, e guari non è che diſſepolta fu in Volſeno mia patria, la quale frap- "poſta era tra due ſepolcri in piana terra coperti colle tegole dè creta cotta, "ove eran ſeppelliti due corpi, come ſpeſſeſiate ſi legge in alcune lapidi ſe- "polcrali con queſta parolo BISOMATOS, chè viene dal Greco, anzi è puro "Greco, e vuol dir *di due corpi*, ſe pero dice ΔI e non BI."

Numa directed his body, contrary to the general cuſtom of his time, to be buried in a ſtone coffin, and his books in another. Both were diſcovered after a violent rain 400 years after; but the firſt contained no remains of the corpſe [5]. He was laid near the altar, which he had erected to the nymph Egeria; for ſo I underſtand *ad fontis aras* of Cicero de Legib. II. 22.

[1] P. [illegible]. [2] Mon. Kemp. p. 170. [3] Eborac. p. 63.
[4] Mon. Kemp. p. 171. [5] Plut. in Numa.

In

In regard to the circumſtance of the corps in the Chriſt-church coffins lying on the ground without any ſtones under them, bodies were depoſited much in the ſame manner in the kiſtvaens; and from this circumſtance theſe coffins appear to be the production of a rude and very unpoliſhed age. They muſt be of the 4th century at leaſt, and amount to a ſtrong additional proof that Twynham was a place very antiently ſettled, of which Mr. Pegge conceived the diſcovering of the birds bones in a grave under a large marble ſlab was no inconſiderable argument.

In ſummer, 1782, in making Mr. Brander's hothouſe, at Chriſtchurch, they dug up two ſtone coffins, compoſed of ſeveral ſtones, with a niche for the head, in which was found a ſcull, with fine light long hair[1], completely attired, and highly dreſſed. The boys coming at the inſtant out of the free-ſchool pulled it preſently to pieces, and the ſcull bone was replaced in the coffin, and both buried again in the ſame place.

In clearing the foundation of old St. Paul's Sir Chriſtopher Wren found that the North ſide had been antiently a great burying place: for under the graves of theſe latter ages he found in a row the graves of the Saxons, who caſed their dead in chalk ſtones, though perſons of great eminence were buried in ſtone coffins: below theſe were the graves of the antient Britons, as was manifeſt from the great number of ivory and wooden pins among the mouldered duſt; for it was their method only to pin the corpſe in woollen ſhrouds, and lay them in the ground, and this covering being conſumed the pins remained entire. At a ſtill greater depth he found Roman potſherds and coins[2].

That the Romans made their coffins of ſeveral ſtones appears from the following circumſtance. In 1731, ſome labourers digging for ſtone in a quarry at a field about half a mile eaſt from the cathedral diſcovered lying north by weſt and ſouth by eaſt an antient ſepulchre covered by two rough ſtones about one foot and an half or two feet below the ſurface, about four feet by five each, laid one at the end of the other. Four more ſet edgeways at the ſides were nine feet two inches long by three feet one; the end ſtones of the ſame width; all ſet together without mortar. In the north end a very thick ſcull (the teeth gone) and ſome pieces of thigh bones, and many iron ſpikes full ſix inches long, thick as the little finger, but conſumed by ruſt, broken at the ends. Probably the corps was caſed in a thick cheſt, of which were no remains except what ſtuck to the nail heads. About the middle towards the weſt was a fine red clay urn broken among the nails and mouldy earth with a little ſcroll round it: it was five inches deep, and might have held a quart. Near a yard ſouth from the feet of the tomb and at the ſame depth a heap of black ſtrong ſmelling aſhes. Next day they found a ſimilar ſtone coffin, the cover of one ſtone, and the inſide of the eaſt ſide ſtone hewn ſmooth not ſo long as the other, and in it only a piece of ſcull and bones. Many bones have been dug up in different parts of the hill as if thrown in from a field of battle: and in this quarry was found the braſs armilla mentioned by Dr. Stukeley[3] in the poſſeſſion of Mr. Pownall[4].

In 1766 a coffin hewn out of a rock was diſcovered in digging near the Roman ſtation at Rutcheſter, about 12 feet by four feet two inches deep; a hole cloſe to the bottom at one end: many decayed bones, teeth, and vertebræ in it, ſuppoſed by their ſhape and ſize to be the remains of ſome animal, ſacrificed perhaps to Hercules[5]. I ſhould doubt the bones belonging to beaſts.

[1] Some of this hair, in my poſſeſſion, beſpeaks it to belong to a young lady.
[2] Parentalia. [3] It. I. p. 86.
[4] Mr. Pownall's letter to Mr. Gale. Gale's letters, p. 165.
[5] Wallis, Northumberland, II. 168.

The Romans feem to have ufed ftone coffins for interment, as well as for cenotaphs.

Near Glanton pike have been difcovered feveral ftone chefts, three feet long and two broad, with urns of ordinary pottery, containing afhes, charcoal, and remains of fcorched human bones, and not far diftant was lately found a celt [1].

In a place called the Deerftreet, by Glanton Weftfield, a mafon digging for ftone 1716 found a ftone cheft upwards of three feet long and two broad, with a ftone cover, and empty; but as his fon, now living, was working down an uneven piece of ground, he difcovered three more fuch chefts, with covers, containing fine earth, and two urns in each, with fome charcoal and burnt bones, carrying the marks of fire. Near them were two more urns, one large, the other very fmall. On being expofed to the air they all fell to pieces. They were of very ordinary patterns [2].

Leland defcribes fepulchres *ex fećto lapide*, found at Cirencefter; in one a round leaden veffel, with afhes and bones [3].

" Deux tombeaux, ce font des auges de pierres, dont un de 6 pieds de longueur, et 2 de largeur a la tête: il a 18 pouces de hauteur a la tête et 15 aux pieds, ce qui forme un pyramidal tronquè, dont deux faces font plus larges que les deux autres. L'autre de 5½ pieds eft plus foible dans fes dimenfions. Ils font creufés de façon que le corps du tombeau n'a que deux pouces d'épaiffeur; le fond eft percé fous la tête d'un trou de deux pouces pour écouler la liqueur putride provenant de la diffolution du cadavre. Ces tombeaux étoient recouverts, l'un d'une pierre creufée de deux à trois pouces en deffous, l'autre d'une pierre plate ayant pour toute infcription M. Q. *manibus diis*. Les lettres font groffiérement gravées, même le D eft formé à contrefens. L'on doit obferver que la coupe du côté de la tête de ces tombeaux eft coupée fur un arc, dont le rayon eft formé par la longeur totale du creux, et la côté des pieds eft taillé fur une ligne perpendiculaire; ce qui feroit croire que l'on prenoit la mefure jufte du mort pour qu'il n'y ait point d'efpace vuide entre les furfaces intérieures du tombeau et les extremités du cadavre. Dans le plus grand tombeau étoient renfermés deux cadavres, l'un d'un homme pofé au fond, et l'autre d'un adulte de 13 à 14 ans, dont la tête étoit fur la poitrine de celui de deffous. Il y a lieu de préfumer que ces deux cadavres étoient ceux du pere et de fon fils. Il s'eft trouvé dans ce tombeau plufieurs médailles de Conftantin le Grand, & un couteau à deux mains très court et fort arqué. Comme c'étoit la coutume des Romains de graver fur les tombeaux la figure des inftruments de la profeffion du défunt, ou d'inhumer avec lui les outils de fon métier, ce couteau défigne ici la fépulture d'un charron enterré fous Conftantin [4]."

Two Roman tombs were found by the quarries half a mile out of Lincoln, on the Horncaftle road; four great ftones fet together like a coffin, and one on the top. There were in them the bones of a man, with urns, lacrymatories, and coins [5].

A brafs fpear head was found in a ftone coffin at Chute: a horfe buried about three yards from it. Mens bones found in Bloodfield there. Harodon-hill, a beacon-hill, juft by. Roman coins found thereabout in great plenty [6].

[1] Hutchinfon's Northumberland, p. 234.
[2] Wallis, ubi fup. II. 491.
[3] It. V. 65.
[4] Defcription de la haute Normandie.
[5] Stukeley Itin. I. p. 81. 2d edit.
[6] Stukeley, MS. pen. me.

In a ground called Wolcomb, in Tincham parifh, Dorfet, was found, 1769, a large marble coffin, containing a large fkeleton, the bones of an infant, and a long fword [1].

Three very antient ftone coffins (one infcribed with four or five Latin words in uncial letters) were found in the churchyard of St. Germain's, at Rouen, fuppofed to have been the common burial place of the city from the Roman times [2].

In 1725 they found an archt vault, fourteen feet deep, in St. Botolph's churchyard, Bifhopfgate, paved with large equilateral Roman bricks, in it two fkeletons, perfect. Dr. Stukeley proved this a Roman burial place after Chriftianity was eftablifhed. He faw there, 1726, a Roman grave, made of great tiles, or bricks, twenty-one inches long, which kept the earth from the body [3].

In digging near the fide of the high road, near Chefterton, c. Hunt. 1754, was found a coffin of a yellowifh hard ftone, fix feet two inches long, covered with a flat lid, which had on the under fide an edging let quite down about one inch and a half or two inches deep, coinciding with the edges of the cheft, and containing an entire fkeleton near fix feet long, the teeth found and firm, the ribs fallen from the back bone, the right leg broken in the middle and repaired by a callus: alfo three glafs lacrymatories, of which that which was entire contained a corrupted fungous fubftance, mixed with water, and of an aromatic fmell on firft opening) a fmall brafs feal with this mark 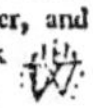

three or four pins like ebony or agate, one of brafs; feveral defaced coins, one of Fauftina, and one filver of Gordian, and fcraps of white wood, infcribed,

AAUITT VTERE TA ⊕ FELIX.

The fubftance of nine or ten other fkeletons was found near the cheft, and all of them only at the depth of one foot [4].

Caylus mentions feveral fkeletons found lying on their faces, juft below the furface of the earth, and one of a child in a brick tomb, at the village of Anieres, on the Seine. Moft of thefe fkeletons had between their legs empty earthen urns. It feemed that the fpot had ferved as a burying place for a long period of time. Many of the articles found here he thinks of different ages. The few medals turned up could not be made out. The moft confiderable articles were two perfect bronze fibulæ; one infcribed DOMINE MARTI VIVAS; the other VTERE. FELEX. The title of *Dominus* belongs to the fourth or fifth century. Tradition fays, that one of the Dagoberts, kings of France of the firft race, had a country houfe here. Several tombs of ftone, difcovered in the clofe of the year 1760, at Gourvieux, a village not far from Chantilli, contained fkeletons, medals, fword-hilts, lamps, and earthen veffels of different fhapes, the latter placed between the legs of the bodies, contrary to the moft ufual cuftom of placing them, either at the heads or feet [5].

In 1748 were found, in making the kitchen garden at Choifi, two ftone tombs without any infcription; and in 1751 a third fimilar near them, four feet feven inches long, lying like the others; and with it were dug up fome thin copper rings, fome glafs beads *(boutons)* of various fhapes and fizes, white, black, and blue, fome yellow, others not pierced, fome ftudded, other bits of glafs, and fome pieces of glafs like nails without heads, two wooden pins, furmounted

[1] Hutchins, I. 211.
[2] Voyage liturgique de France, p. 417.
[3] Stukeley, MS. pen me.
[4] Mr. Manning, in A. S. Min.
[5] Recueil d'Antiq. I. 257, 258.

by

by rude busts, a small club, pin, and hatchet, all of bronze, each about three inches long, and a small earthen patera. These several trinkets are supposed by Count Caylus [1] to belong to some child here buried. Near the same tomb were found a quantity of bones, and in the middle of them a little glass vessel like a lacrymatory.

A stone coffin five feet long, and not very wide, found in the parish of Vigneux, on the banks of the Seine, 1746, contained to appearance only an urn of earth, three inches high and four wide; all the rest being turned to dirt [2].

In Barking parish was found, about $172\frac{4}{5}$, a great stone coffin, with the body of a man entire: at the feet a heap of glass, probably a lacrymatory [3]. Another containing ashes, and a lacrymatory, dug up in the porch of St. Martin's in the Fields, $172\frac{4}{5}$, four feet under ground; the urn was in Sir H. Sloane's collection [4].

In the year 1768, the workmen employed to enlarge the fortifications at Strasburg, found near the White Tower gate twenty stone coffins, in which were a number of vessels of earth and glass of various sizes; the glass containing a liquor like water, together with urns and pateræ of hard earth, like stone; the urns contained ashes. One of the coffins had by it a stone broken, inscribed,

L. LICINIVS L. F. CLAVD. MAXIMVS. AEQVO. F. CV [5].

contained two urns filled with ashes, two busts of stone, two pateræ of red earth, two glass vessels filled with clean water, having a small quantity of oil floating on its surface, and two earthen lamps. The various vessels are supposed by Mr. Schœpflin [6] to have contained the wine and milk poured on the bones after burning, or as offerings to the dii manes, in allusion to which last custom the Romans annually, in February, the last month of the year, celebrated the Feralia or Parentalia.

In a corn field near Ongar was found in land-ditching, August, 1767, three feet under ground, a large white free stone chest, six feet four inches long, twenty-two inches wide, three inches and a half thick, thirteen inches three quarters deep, in which was one human skeleton of the common proportion, the head and feet lying East and West. The lid of the chest strongly cemented to it had a kind of ridge in the middle, where it was six inches thick, in other parts four. After numbers of people had satisfied their curiosity, Mr. King the tenant caused it to be re-buried a foot deeper. It was again uncovered Sept. 26, at the desire of Dr. Gower, Mr. Bramston, and myself, when the bones were found broken, and in great confusion, and much earth fallen in among them. The lid rotten and broken. At the time of the first discovering, in digging a ditch at the lower end of the field, they had opened another burying place, which they followed into the next field, in an oblique direction, and found five intire skeletons lying at the feet of each other, and covered with such kind of tiles as Thoresby describes to have been found at Bootham bar, and which he had in his museum. They have a ledge at the sides to receive the tiles which formed the sides of the coffin, and this ledge ceases about an inch from the end, to admit the next tile to lie on the other, to which it was probably fastened by a pin; for one found here had a hole as for that purpose, like our present plain tiles, and another had half an 8, like those at York [7]. The field was covered with fragments of urns and bones: some of the urns had ornaments, striated or indented: one peice had near the top these lines 

[1] Recueil d'Antiq. I. p. 197.
[2] Ib. p. 198.
[3] Mr. Lethieullier, in A. S. Min.
[4] Id. Ib.
[5] i. e. L. Licinius L. F. Claudia tribu, Maximus, Aequo *oppido ortus*, *fieri vel faciendum curavit*. Aequum was a town of Dalmatia, and Licinius a common name at Strasburg.
[6] Alsatia Illustrata, p. 508.
[7] Thoresby, p. 561.

of

of a black colour, burnt in: most of them were of a dirty flinty sand. There was one large brick eleven inches wide, the length imperfect, thickness one inch and a half. The field where the stone chest lay is called *Great Stockling*; the next to it, of five or six acres, *Little Stockling*, q. d. the *Station* or *Place mead*; that above them has the name of *Sheepling wood*. There seems little doubt that this was the cemetery of the Roman station whose earthworks are so visible round Ongar.

Such coffins have been found without the walls of York, 1761, containing skeletons firm and entire, and laid in lime [1].

This tile sepulchre was another mode of burial used by the Romans, and introduced into their provinces, of which Dr. Burton describes an instance discovered at York, 1768, on a piece of ground between that city and Severus's hills, about 250 yards from the walls, North of the present road to Burroughbridge and Aldborough, near Severus's hill. This tomb was in form of an oblong room, with a ridged roof, covered with hollow Roman tiles, like our ridge tiles. Each side consisted of three large tiles, if they may be so called, of a beautiful red, each 1 foot, 8½ inches long, 14¼ inches broad, 1½ inch thick. The projection of the edges of each tile 2 inches $\frac{4}{10}$ths, not quite flat, but bent a little forward, the curve being from about the middle toward the top, by which the upper end of these tiles were nearer to each other at the top than at the bottom. From the top of these the roof was covered in form of a ridge with hollow tiles. Each end of the sepulchre was enclosed with a tile of the same dimensions as those of the sides, and on each of the end tiles was towards the top this inscription, LEG. IX. HIS. very fair, made with a stamp. The edges of these side and end tiles were turned square, near two inches broad, and projecting forward, to make them close the nearer. Over these were also ridge tiles, to keep out the water. Sideways they were narrower than on the ridge. This tomb was about three feet and a half long within, and contained several urns, wherein were some ashes and earth, all standing on a tiled pavement. Part of the Os humeri and the lower jaw-bone, with all its teeth perfect, were likewise found. At a little distance from this tomb, on the same piece of ground, was found a coin of Vespasian; rev. PAX. AVG. S. C. and another of Domitian, rev. FIDEI PVBLICAE. S. C. Dr. Burton supposed this tomb belonged to some person of consequence, perhaps of the *Legio nona Hispanica*, which was in Britain before Hadrian's, and perhaps from Julius Cæsar's time [2]. Several such tombs were found 1703, 1721 and 1763, at Strasburgh, formed of four and six tiles, each 1 foot 9¼ inches, by 16¼ inches, and one inch thick, with a ridge at their two extremes, and each inscribed LEG. VIII. AVG. inclosing an urn with bones, some glass and earthen lacrymatories and lamps: one of the glass vessels had on the foot a figure of Victory holding a palm branch and crown of laurel between V. P. with the legend, VICTORIA AUGUSTORVM. Mr. Schœpflin understands these *Augusti* to be Marcus Aurelius and Aurelius Verus, to whose time he fixes these tombs belonging to the VIII Legio Augusta, which, according to Ptolomy, gave its name to *Argentoratum* or Strasburg. He supposes this the mode of burying the common soldiers of the legions. In two of these tombs were found the bodies. The ends do not appear to have been closed up at all [3]. These kind of tombs are in some inscriptions called *Obrendaria* [4], or,

[1] F. Drake, in A. S. Min. [2] Archæol. II. p. 177—180.
[3] Schœpflin Alsatia Illust. p. 510, 511. 513. Mem. de l'acad. des Insc. X. p. 457. 410.
[4] Fabretti Insc. p. 15. Gruter, p. 607. Gutherius de jure manium, II. 24. p. 338.

as Rigaltius [1] and Gori [2] conjecture, *Obruendaria* [3], thus mentioned in an inscription in Gruter [4].

D. M.
L. POMPONIVS. CLADVS.
ET CLAVDIA PARHESIA.
FECERVNT
SIBI ET SVIS POSTERISQVE
EORVM ET
M. QVINTINO CLAVDIANO
OLLARVM N̄ XII AB IMO.
IN SVMMO CVM
OBRENDARIO.

That the Romans used brick coffins, or sarcophagi, in their earliest periods, will appear by the following passage of Pliny, N. H. XXXV. c. 46. "Quin "& defuncti sese multi fictilibus soliis condi maluere; sicut M. Varro Pythago-"rico more in myrti & oleæ atque populi nigri foliis." F. Hardouin explains *solia* mobiles arces sive sarcophagi in quibus corpus integrum condebatur. See Florus IV. c. 11. of Cleopatra's death. Curtius X. c. 1 & 10. Suet. Ner. 50. An inscription in Gruter DCVII. 1. contains a singular petition from one man to another about the disposition of himself and family after death. CUM. ANTE. HOS. DIES. CONJUGEM. ET. FILIUM. AMISERIM. ET. PRESSUS. NECESSITATE. CORPORA. EORUM. FICTILI. SARCOPHAGO. COMMENDAVERIM. DONECUM. LOCUS. QUEM. EMERAM. AEDIFICARETUR.—— ROGO. DOMINE. PERMITTAS. MIHI. IN. EODEM. LOCO. IN. MARMOREO. SARCOPHAGO. QUEM. MIHI. MODO. COMPARAVI. EA. CORPORA. COLLIGERE. UT. QUANDONE. EGO. ESSE. DESIER. PARITER. CUM. EIS. PONAR. Another inscription in the same collection, DCCCCIII. 12. runs, OSSA. L. BACCHII. L. F. FICTILIARII. SARCOPHI. HEIC. POSITA. SVNT. Liberti epist. ad Elium Severum ap Schœpflin. Alsatia. Illust. p. 11. "cum "corpora eorum fictili sarcophago commendaverim."

In the celebrated family vault of the freedmen of Augustus and Livia, discovered by the side of the Appian way, about a mile out of Rome, 1725, among a few marble sarcophagi were two of *baked earth*, made to contain the body whole. These are thus described by Bianchini [5], "Cassa di creta "cotta, lunga piedi 6½, larga 1 e once 7, senza inscrizione. La forma interiore "di questa cassa, che in altre ancora d'altri sepolcri ho veduta, è stata osservata "avere da una parte un relievo della istessa materia di terra cotta, come si dovesse "al defonto servire di guanciale, non piu alto pero ne piu largo di once 6 con "pertugi che sembiano fatti per ricevere qualche liquore come se putrefacen-"dosi il celabro dovesse in quei buchi scolare l'acqui che ne deriva. L'uso pero de "questo guanciale e de quei forami non si comprende sin'ora." This exactly corresponds with the stone coffins among us used by Christians. Gori describes one of these earthen coffins as covered with tiles laid on its flat edge, whereas another had an inner ledge, on which the tiles were laid. These tiles he supposes are the *munitura sarcophagi* in an inscription in Gruter [6], and the names of the deceased were frequently inscribed on them. Three more brick tombs were worked up into the walls of this vault, in order, as Gori imagines, to be at some future time replaced with marble ones [7].

[1] Not. ad Auct. Rei Agrar. p. 296.
[2] Gori, Columbarium libert. & servor. Liviæ. Flor. 1727. p. 40.
[3] So Seneca: "Alios terra obruit; alios flamma consumsit; alios lapis ossa redditurus inclusit." De remed. For-tuit. And again, "At tu combustus, at tu obrutus, at tu inclusus,—at tu traditus lapidi qui te paulatim edat & "exsiccat."
[4] DCCCLXXXIV. 16. See also Fabretti, I. 15. who gives an inscription with "*hic obritus est.*"
[5] Camera ed inscriz. sep. de' liberti, &c. d'Augusto, p. 10.
[6] DXC. 7.
[7] Ubi sup. p. 38, 39. Tab. VIII.

6

Another of thefe earthen coffins in this vault was covered with two tiles inlaid with mofaic, reprefenting two great fifh, and two birds picking at fruit. Gori has engraved them, Pl. XIX. A. B. but calls them pieces of teffelated pavement [1].

Without Bootham bar at York was digged up a fort of coffin made of clay, of which Mr. Thorefby had part of the bottom, which, for the convenience of baking, he fuppofed was divided into feveral fuch parts. This was entire, as juft moulded by the Romans, fourteen inches and a half long, and almoft eleven broad at the narrower end, and was twelve and a half at the broader. This was the loweft part, for the feet; the reft were proportionably broader to the fhoulder. It was an inch thick, befides the ledges, which were two inches in thicknefs and one in breadth, and extended from the narrower edge to within three inches of the broader, where it was flat from edge to edge, and fomewhat thinner, for the next to lie upon it. The feveral parts feemed to have been joined together by a pin; for at the end of each tile is a hole that would receive a common flate pin. The ledges were wrought a little hollow, to receive the fides, and at the feet were two contrary notches to faften the end piece This bottom Mr. Thorefby would have concluded to have confifted of eight fuch parts from a character like 8 impreft on the clay before baking, but that he doubted the introduction of Arabic numerals fo early [2].

I come now to the ftone-coffin as ufed by Chriftians. After cremation ceafed, on the introduction of Chriftianity fuppofe [3], the believing Romans would generally betake themfelves to the ufe of farcophagi, and of various kinds, ftone, marble, lead, &c. The Romanized and Converted Britons would naturally do the fame, and place the bodies Eaft and Weft. As for the Saxons, they, as fucceffors of the Britons, would incline from the firft to adopt their practices; and then, after that important event, the arrival of Auguftine the monk, A. D. 596, and the converfion of the nation thereupon, coffins would univerfally take place, as likewife the mode of placing the body with the feet to the Eaft. Thus very foon after this we find St. Etheldreda of Ely tranflated from a wooden into a marble coffin; for Sexburga, abbefs of Ely, intending to remove the body of her fifter Etheldreda into the church, directed fome of the brethren to feek for a ftone "*de quo locellum in hoc facere poffent.*" They, finding no ftone proper for the purpofe in the ifle, came to Grantaceſter, "et "mox invenerunt juxta muros civitatis *locellum de marmore albo pulcherrime* "*factum*, operculo quoque fimilis lapidis aptiffime tectum [4]." The Saxons were now greatly improved in ftone-cutting, and as this receptacle was found ready prepared [5], one is obliged to conclude, that the cuftom of making ftone-coffins had prevailed there fome time before. A circumftance which would lead us to afcribe this to the Saxons, though it feems to have efcaped Mr. Pegge, is thus expreffed in Bede, "Mirum in modum ita aptum corpori virginis farcophagum "inventum eft ac fi ei fpecialiter præparatum fuiffet, & *locus* quoque *capiti fcor-* "*fum fabrefactus* ad incifuram capitis illius aptiffime figuratus apparuit." The place for the head might feem to be peculiar to the ftone coffins of Chriftians were it not for the infcription D. M. on fuch a coffin before defcribed, p. xxii. This is the oldeft inftance Mr. Pegge met with amongft the Saxons [6]; however, from this time downward, ftone-coffins have been difcovered all over England.

[1] Ubi fup. p. 5.
[2] P. 561. [3] Ainfworth, Monum. Kemp. p. 175. Thorefby, Muf. p. 560. Kirchman, p. 13.
[4] Bede, lib. iv. c. 19.
[5] Bede would have it underftood as a miracle; but be this as it will, a ftone we fee was to be fought to make a coffin of.
[6] It was A. D. 695. Etheldreda died 679, and this was 169 years after. Bede, l. c.

Mr.

Mr. Pegge traces them among us from the ninth century to the reign of Henry III. and in some cases to that of Henry VIII [1]. The patron saints at Arles were buried in Roman sarcophagi finely carved [2]. Dart says, stone coffins were rarely used in the 14th century.

Repton abbey, in Derbyshire, on the Trent, founded before A. D. 666, was the burial place of the royal family of Mercia, whose chief seat was at Tamworth in Staffordshire. In the close of the last century Thomas Walker a labourer cutting hillocks near the surface met with an old stone wall, which, on clearing further, he found to be a square enclosure of fifteen feet. It had been covered, but the top was decayed and fallen-in, being only supported by wooden joists. In this he found a stone coffin; and with difficulty removing the cover, saw a human skeleton nine feet long. Round it lay 100 human skeletons, with their feet pointing to the stone coffin. They seemed to be of the ordinary size. The head of the great skeleton he gave to Mr. Bowers, master of the freeschool, whose son, one of the masters in 1728, remembered it in his father's closet, though since lost, and had often heard his father mention this gigantic corps, and believed the skull was in proportion to a body of that stature. The bottom of this dormitory was paved with broad flat stones, and in the wall was a door case, with steps to go down to it, whose entrance was 40 yards off, near the church and river. The steps were stone, and much worn. It was in a close, on the North side of the church, and over this repository grows a sycamore, planted by the old man, when he filled on the earth. The owner, when Mr. Degge, who gave this account to the Royal Society, 1726, saw it, would not suffer it to be opened, the lady of the manor having forbidden it. This was attested by several old people, who had likewise seen and measured the skeleton [3].

In the Norman times it was the custom to bury monks in the bare ground. Warin, twentieth abbot of St. Albans, who died 1195, ordered that they should be buried in stone coffins, as more decent. M. Paris charges him with innovations in established customs to please the multitude [4].

In 1759, in making a turnpike road through *Wardlow* village, near *Ashford*, on opening a heap of stones 32 yards diameter, and about five feet high, was found a monument to the memory of seventeen persons who had been there interred. The bodies appeared to have been laid on the surface of the ground, on long flat stones seven feet and a half long, and their heads and breasts protected from the incumbent weight of stone by small walls [or rather chests] made round them, with a flat stone on the top, excepting the two principal ones, which were completely inclosed in two stone chests, about two feet high and seven feet long. On removing the rubbish many jaw bones and teeth were found undecayed, but none of the larger bones. The stones of which these coffins were composed appeared plainly to have been taken from a quarry about a quarter of an inch distance. Near half the circle was vacant, which might be owing to accidental disturbance, by laying near the road, or inattention on the first opening. The Rev. Mr. Evatt of Ashford, who communicated the account and drawing to the Royal Society, 1761, supposed the circle later than the fence wall above, which interfered with part of it, and therefore referred it to the slain in the wars between the houses of York and Lancaster; but it is much more probable that it was a family burial place of the same kind with that

[1] Gent. Mag. 1759. p. 66. [2] Thicknesse. [3] Phil. Trans. N° 400. p. 363.

[4] [illegible] consuetudines ab antiquo conservatas volens multis placere idem abbas Garinus in nova statuta commutavit, quod [illegible] videbatur temerarium, multis utile, honestum, & commendabile. Inter quæ constituit ([illegible] possessiuncula ampliasset) ut corpora monachorum defunctorum quæ antea cunctis temporibus sub [illegible] solebant sepeliri omnibus temporibus sequentibus, quod ei videbatur honestius, reconderentur in lapideis sepulchris. M. Paris, v. ab. Alb. p. 95.

before

before described at Repton, in the same county [c]. Mr. Bray thinks it more likely that they would carry the wall strait (especially as the stones removed furnished materials for it) than that the monument should be thrown up on both sides of such a wall, and be intersected by it [a].

Some labourers digging in a quarry between Kaer Leon and Christchurch, near a place called Porth Sini Crân, discovered a large freestone coffin, in which was a sheet of lead wrapt about an iron frame, curiously wrought and in it a skeleton. Near the coffin lay a gilded alabaster statue, in a coat of mail, holding in the right hand a short sword, and in the left a balance. In the right scale was a female bust, outweighing a globe in the left scale. Capt. Mathias Bird, who was on the spot, gave the statue to the Ashmolean Museum. The feet, right arm, and scales, have been since broken off; but the rest is in tolerable preservation, and some of the gilding remains in the interstices of the armor. Bishop Gibson thought it represented Astrea [d]. It is rather St. Michael weighing the devil against a soul, as on Glastonbury tower, and may have belonged to a Christian tomb, and been found on the site of an antient church. See it in the Marmora Oxoniensia, Pl. CXXVIII.

In the churchyard at Deerness, in the Mainland of Orkney, is a coffin-fashioned stone, en dos d'ane, six feet long; one side plain, the other adorned with what the heralds call Vairé in five rows. Such another in Rendale church-yard, twenty miles from Deerness, is called *the Queen of Morocco's gravestone*; and they tell a long legend about her arrival and death here [e].

In digging a cellar in an outhouse belonging to the chanter at Lincoln, fronting the West end of the Minster, they found two or three stone coffins, probably laid there since the dissolution of the antient parish church of St. Mary Magdalen to make way for the cathedral, and ten or twelve feet lower was found a Roman Hypocaust.

Two bodies were found deposited in coffin-shaped cavities in the live rock in the Anchoritage, near St. John's church yard at Chester [e], by which it should seem hermits were frequently buried in their retirements. A hermit had a chapel on the site of Red Castle, an oval camp near Thetford, and Mr. Martin digging found a very fine stone coffin, with bones in it, just where it is supposed the hermit's chapel stood, at the North East corner [e]. And the coffin lid with a cross in relief on it lying opposite or near to St. Robert's cave on the bank of the Nid at Knaresborough confirms this. The antient hermits dug their own coffins in the rocks where they past their lives [f].

Coffin-fashioned stones were always covers to coffins of the same materials, and thus answered the double purpose of receptacle and memorial.

It is worth enquiry whether stone coffins were always confined to persons of eminence, or allowed to the religious and laity of every rank. I think instances may be produced of both. In religious houses they were probably for the principal religious and nobility; but in parish churches for the incumbents or patrons. Perhaps in both cases they were for all who would go to the expence. Thus to give a few examples out of many, the stone coffin now lying in the vestry at Stone in Kent, and at Soame in Cambridgeshire, in the latter instance, and in the former those of St. Albans, where, in digging a vault, 1782, for alderman Nichols, below the steps within the great West door, they found a stone coffin, covered up, but filled with dirt and gravel. It now stands empty by the spot. They discovered the feet of another, which they did not disturb. A third has long stood behind the high altar.

[c] Phil. Transf. vol. LII. part II. p. 544.
[d] Gibson's Camden, Monmouthshire, p. 715.
[e] Pennant, Wales, I. 187.
[e] Blomfield, I. 378. Martin's Hist. of Thetford, p. 10.
[f] Vitæ Patrum, c. 20. L. de S. Leobardo recluso.

[a] Tour, p. 185. 2d edit.
[e] Mr. Lowe's MS.

In finking a well by the townhall and by the Fifh ftone at Spalding, where probably had ftood the church of Holycrofs, at four feet deep was taken up a ftone coffin in which was a corpfe looking frefh, and another corpfe covered with a plank [1].

Empty ftone coffins have been dug up in the fite of the now entirely demolifhed chapel of the Wake family adjoining to the North fide of the chancel of Market Deping church.

In St. Mary's church yard, Thetford, have been found ftone coffins of different fizes, fuppofed for a father, mother, and two children. Two lids in the chancel floor are afcribed to the larger, which were found under the pavement without lids; and one of them, which rings like a bell, lies in the tower. The lid of a fmaller makes a headftone in the churchyard, near the original fpot: the other larger, by the veftry, reverft, covers Edward Clarke late clerk, by his own defire [2]. This makes it probable that originally thefe coffins lay level with the pavement, of which the lid, fometimes infcribed, made part. Such may have been the *fepulchrum parvulum fuper terram fitum e rufticiori formatum lapide*, defcribed by Gregory of Tours [3], in the church of St. Venerand, at Clarmont, in Auvergne, among a number of fplendid tombs of Parian marble.

A ftone coffin found in the chancel of Purton, Wilts, had a piece of board at bottom, covered by the earth, which might have been a cover, or part of a wooden coffin [4], or have been thrown in on fome former opening.

At St. Mary's, the priory church at Wareham, are fome ftone coffins, in which the priors might have been interred; for Mr. Wood fays, that in Durham cathedral moft of the priors were buried in coffins of ftone or marble covered with another large ftone which lay level with the pavement, it being an antient cuftom to bury perfons of note no deeper. Not long ago was dug up in the churchyard a flat ftone which covered a ftone coffin: on it is carved a long narrow fhield which takes up the whole length, and is divided in the middle by an emboifed line as efcutcheons are ufually parted per fefs: on the upper part is a lion rampant, and on the lower fix fleurs de lis. It is thought to be two coats impaled, this being a very antient manner of empalement [5].

On the North fide of the altar in Abbotfbury church was a very antient coffin of coarfe black marble, with a cover of the fame. It is fuppofed to have contained the bones of Orcus, fteward to king Canute, and his wife, who founded this abbey, and to have been removed hither at the diffolution out of the conventual church; but, as prefent tradition fays, out of the vicarage houfe. It was four feet and half long, by two broad, and one and a half deep; and in 1750 was depofited under ground near the place where it once ftood, there being no convenient place to receive it [6]. "The bones of the founder Orcus, "inclofed in a daintie marbill coffin, which I have often feene, were removed to "the adjoining parifh church [7]."

A large ftone coffin, fmaller at the feet than at the head, forms the ground fill of the large Weft door of Dunftaple church, on which the very door cafe is founded. But who was here interred no infcription doth certify [8]. The fite of the Eaft end of the church was dug in for ftone, and coffins with bones were found and buried again, by the late Mr. Crawley, who owned it about 35 years ago. Mr. Willis informed the Society of Antiquaries, 1745, that about two feet under ground, and above three feet from a fide wall of this part, and

[1] Spalding Society's Minutes.
[2] Hift. of Thetford, p. 73.
[3] De Gloria Confeff. c. 36.
[4] Ib. I. 539.
[5] Hutchins's Dorfet, I. 36.
[6] Gent. Mag. March, 1761, p. 125.
[7] Coker's Dorfet, p. 31.
[8] Hift. of Dunftaple, p. 107.

7 the

the feet close to a crofs wall was found a ftone coffin, the lid compofed of four ftones, the piece at the foot a feparate one; the head, fides, and bottom, of one ftone; under the head an eminence inftead of a pillow, in a hollow or niche correfponding to the head. The fkeleton was intire, except the ribs, which had fallen in; the head inclined to the left. Between the upper bone of the left arm and the back bone was a glafs urn fallen down, and the lid off; ftained with deep brown on the inner fide of that part which lay over the ftone. About the feet were pieces of leather, very rotten, which by the holes appeared to have been fewed together [1].

On removing the ftone covers in the upper North tranfept of Lincoln minfter, July 10, 1783, I found nothing but earth; a very few fragments of human bones in one, as if they had been filled up originally, or on the diffolution, or fome repair or new laying of the pavement. One of thefe was the blue flab covered with the very rude relief in the North tranfept under the paintings of the four firft bifhops of this fee, one of whom it may be fuppofed to have covered, as the three others might have been covered by the three contiguous blueifh coffin-fafhioned flabs. The coffin under the carved ftone here mentioned confifted of more pieces than one, which is an argument of its antiquity. A blue ftab coffin-fafhioned, with a femi-circular ftone at the head, on which the epitaph, now worn out, was infcribed in old capitals, prefented the fame appearance in the upper South tranfept.

Mr. Blomfield, 1754, digging acrofs the choir at Caftle Acre, at more than twenty feet from the Eaft wall found the pavement whole and untouched, compofed of tiles of fine hard red earth, glazed, and not above half an inch thick, five inches fquare, laid in a chequer, white, black, yellow, green, and other colours, laid right in the middle, and exactly twenty feet from the Eaft wall, at the laft ftep to the altar. About fix inches below the pavement lay a ftone coffin, four inches thick, fix feet one inch long within, nineteen inches wide at the fhoulders, and only feven at the feet, the hollow for the head being nine inches over; had a hole through the middle at bottom, to drain the body when laid in. The coffin was full of mould, the free ftone with which it was covered having been broken by the fall of the walls had let in the rubbifh. In it were the bones of a man complete; and at the feet of the coffin was another fcull, and feven or eight leg bones laid in a heap; which led Mr. Blomfield to conjecture that at the reformation, before the demolition of this church, they pulled away the ftone or monument that was over it, and it lying uncovered they put in what bones they happened on elfewhere, and filled it with mould, and then pulled down the walls: fo that Mr. Blomfield dug a good depth through the rubbifh before he came to it. He fuppofed it the tomb of Philip de Mortemer, who was prior 1203, and is faid to be buried *ante majus altare*. He caufed the bones to be put into the coffin at the head, and filled it up again, leaving it in the fame place, not having ftirred the coffin at all. The fides were much broken, probably by the fall of the walls [2].

France affords a moft extraordinary inftance of the general and extenfive ufe of ftone coffins. In the village of Civaux, on the river Vienne, fix leagues from Poitiers, by the fide of the high road from that city, at the entrance of the village is a fpace of 3071 toifes fquare, full of ftone coffins, moft of them level with the furface, fome a little below it, and a few above it. This fpot is divided into two, and the fmaller half is inclofed for a yard to the parifh church with a fence made of the lids of thefe coffins: the other remains open, level with the road and the furrounding fields. By the fide of this churchyard is a down 504

[1] Hift. of Dunftaple, p. 183, 184.

[2] MS. Hift. of Norfolk, penes me.

of

toises square, where they formerly buried, and where still remain about twenty tombs. Forty or fifty more are to be seen in a little spot, in the centre of the village, surrounding the church, to which it served as a burying ground, till forbidden to be used by the then bishop of Poitiers about fifty years ago. Close to this, behind the presbytery, is a little open space, and by the side of it a spacious field hedged in. In the former spot are about twenty tombs. Though there are said to have been some in the latter, none are now to be found at the depth of three or four feet. Towards the centre of a great ploughed field of six acres by the side of the high road to Lussac and Lemoges, 200 paces from the village, were found, in two days search, at considerable distances, about twenty-five coffins, most of them empty, and without lids Some have pretended to find these coffins in the river; but it appears that the stones in its bed had been mistaken for them, though it is not improbable that the water might have washed away the earth which covered some, or by other accidents they might have found their way into it. The general shape of these coffins is that of our modern wooden ones, some few excepted, which are less contracted at one end, and approach nearer a long square. Two in particular were like cradles, little shallow niches, hollowed for children in the level surface of a plane convex block, three feet by fifteen or eighteen inches. The rest were of all sizes, from three feet to six feet two or three inches. The general size is six feet by two or three at the larger end, and one and a half or 20 inches deep: a very few were broader and deeper. Each was covered with a large stone, commonly flat, sometimes convex on the upper side, two feet five or six inches broad, by six feet six or seven inches long, and about two inches thick at the edges, always overhanging the coffin. One third of these lids had no mark: but by far the greater number had a cross reaching the whole length and breadth of the surface. These crosses were not raised above three or four lines: their slender shaft was crossed by three broad transverse pieces, one at each end, and the third in the middle, somewhat like those commonly called the *Lorrain Cross*. All these tombs were of rough coarse workmanship; not one exhibited the smallest sign of sculpture or taste: not an inscription or figure to shew that the dead whom they contained were at all above the common rank. On one of these lids were some characters half effaced, on which the only letters that could be made out seemed to form the word *Dominus*. On the inside of another lid was carved, in a tolerable style and relief, a workman with his hammer, probably a representation of one of the workmen in the neighbouring quarries, carved by himself, or some of his partners. Of about 150 of these coffins which lay in ground not used for cemetries, some were found empty, others full of earth and bones mixed together, others under the earth which filled them up had a complete skeleton in its natural order, of a yellow colour, and ready to fall in pieces on the first touch. In several were two skeletons, lying side by side, and in some larger than the rest were three. In several under the skeletons were sculls, whole and broken bones mixed with the earth, with which they seemed always to have filled up the coffin after depositing the body in it. The longest skeletons were of the common proportion, five feet nine or ten inches; and of these not more than three or four were found, the majority being under six feet and a half. At the bottom of one of these coffins were found, wrapt up in a sort of paper, and stuck together by rust, a dozen double tournois, one of 1636, half a wooden comb, with a row of close and another of open teeth, and two or three pieces of a kind of dark brown serge. In another was found a silver filegrain ring, with a collet of the same. In another a piece of base silver, not so large or thick as a French sol, stampt on one side with a shield surmounted by a crown, the figures indistinct, and round it an imperfect

imperfect date, 159 . Some perſons of credit affirmed, that in ſome of theſe coffins ſtone bottles were found by the ſide of the deceaſed; and it has been ſaid, that antient medals have been diſcovered among them. A little before the laſt ſearch the curate of the place ſent M. le Nain governor of Poitiers, by whoſe order the ſearch was made, ſeven medals, which he aſſured him were taken out of different tombs. They were middle braſs, of Claudius; Nero. rev. an altar, under which, ARA PACIS; a large braſs, too much defaced to be known; ſmall braſs of Gallienus, rev. AETERNITAS AVG. of Aurelian, rev. VICTORIA AVG. two of Conſtantinus Criſpus and junior. Beyond the river Vienne, half a quarter of a league higher up than Civaux, is an immenſe quarry, in which may be diſtinguiſhed the beds whence many of theſe coffins have been cut, being of the ſame grain.

Theſe particulars are extracted from the account given by the jeſuit Ruth of the grand ſearch into this collection of ſtone coffins made about 1738. The father has thoroughly canvaſt the ſubject, and has determined them indiſputably to belong to Chriſtians, and the ſpot where they are found to have been a public Chriſtian burying ground. Perhaps the croſſes were the ſtrongeſt evidence of this; for we have produced a variety of inſtances that make againſt the concluſion, that "monuments where the corpſe is preſerved entire are neceſſarily "Chriſtian works."

The quarter of St. Hilary at Poitiers is full of ſtone coffins, which chance brings to light continually in cellars and gardens. The abbé d'Armagnac, treaſurer to the chapter of St. Hilary, digging in his garden in the winter 1736 found twelve or fifteen; one of them was ſeven feet long, and contained bones of very large proportions. He has diſcovered them in his cellar under the foundations of old thick walls: and he is not the only perſon who has made theſe diſcoveries in this quarter. In enlarging and completing the high road from Poitiers to Chauvigny, about 1730, they found in the riſing ground which commands the city on the ſide of St. Cyprian and the gate of Pont-a-Joubert, a large ſtone coffin, which was left on the lands by the road ſide. Boucher, who was born before 1480, obſerves, in his Hiſtory of Poitou, that in this quarter, above the abbey of St. Cyprian, was an old burying ground, named the Burying ground of St. Gregory. The cuſtom of burying out of cities ſubſiſted a long while after the Romans, who firſt enacted it as a law. The towns and villages near the Vienne from St. Gervais two leagues, below Chatellerault to Luſſac four leagues above Chauvignè, at St. Gervais, Ingrandle, Cenon, Bonimatour, Vouneuil, Archigny, Chauvignè, Civaux, Queaux, Luſſac, are all full of the ſame kind of tombs. We find at all theſe different places fields not quite ſo large as that at Civaux full of ſtone coffins and covers marked with croſſes, and ſome of rough ſtone without any marks. Theſe circumſtances, the vicinity of theſe burying grounds to churches, and the Gothic ſtone croſſes ſet up at the entrance, or in the centre of theſe places, denote that they are Chriſtian; and the quarries before mentioned, or others near the ſame river, furniſhed the materials. Montmorillon, a little town of Poitou, on the Gartempe, four or five leagues from Civaux, where is now the church of the Auguſtines, contains a great number of theſe coffins, which have been taken up to make doors and chimney pieces to the monaſtery. The ſpot was walled round for near a century, and is uſed as a burial ground. Saulgè, a village on the Gartempe, has a great many. Journet, four leagues from the river, ſtill more. Benet, a village near the head of the Glain, is full of them, and moſt of the houſes there are built of them. One is to be ſeen in a lone houſe near Tranquart: and it is no uncommon ſight in many other parts of Poitou, where there are now no traces of these antient burial grounds. Twenty were found in digging in a garden of a priory-cure two leagues from Leccon. A considerable quantity are to be seen at the priory of St. John de Loudun. Lower Poitou abounds with them, and there are few parts of the rest of Poitou where they are not talked of. But these singularities are not confined to this province. The abbey of Notre Dame de la Tenaille, at Saintonge, seven leagues above Saintes, towards Blaye, standing alone in the midst of a wood, has a kind of burial ground almost as considerable as that of Civaux, full of the same kind of stone coffins, which have been found to contain entire skeletons, as there; and in some of them stone bottles placed by the side of the bodies. The like may be seen in Touraine, at Baleme near la Haye, at Brayes near Richelieu, and many other places in the same parts. About 1728 the canons of the castle at Bruges opening a road near their church discovered a great number of stone coffins. M. Dodart, governor of Berry, says they are very common in that province, that the curates of many parishes used them for horse-troughs; and he had seen many at the abbey of Foncombaud, in the diocese of Bruges, near Blanc. M. Catherinot, well known for his researches into the antiquities of Bourges and Berry, in his "Bourges souterrain," tells us, that the Capuchins of Bourges trenching their garden in 1640, found several stone coffins, which the antients properly called *bieres*, from the Latin *petra*; and in 1684 another at the foot of a tree which they had cut down in their great walk. This house is near the canons of the castle, and both are out of the town; circumstances which serve to prove this to have been an antient burial ground. Traces of this antient custom have been found in the provinces most distant from Poitou. Near a Benedictine abbey out of Arles is a large field full of tombs of the same shape, and disposed in the same manner as at Civaux. The conclusion is obvious, that all these were the burial grounds of the Christians of Gaul.

If the number of coffins, or of bodies in them, when the dimensions scarce allow of more than one, or the rank of the parties buried, and the finding of heathen coin in Christian graves be objected; the answer to the first is, we are not to expect a calculation correspondent to extent of ground to people the burial ground of a village of only 600 persons. Public burial grounds do not seem to have been forbidden to Christians in the most furious persecutions, and Christians affected common places of burial. The use of stone coffins may be carried back in Poitou to the third century, and probably continued to the end of the 13th; consequently the burial ground of such a village as Civaux was ten centuries at least in filling. Allowing sixteen deaths, one year with another, this period would give 16,000 dead bodies, and an equal number of tombs. The strictest allowance of coffins to the ground all round the town would not produce the whole number; and all the accidents of plague, famine, and war, will never bring the number of tombs to 13,000.

Civaux was certainly however a very antient parish, and as there were for several centuries but two cemeteries at Poitiers, it is not unlikely numbers would be carried to a spot so convenient for this heavy mode of interment. The traces of such a mode would sooner disappear in populous cities, where stone was wanted for buildings both public and private. Many towers and battlements of the walls of Poitiers are lined with such stones. One in particular is charged with a cross, an inscription in Gothic characters at top; on the right of the cross is a chalice well cut, and to the left an E. opposite to and on the same level with it. When the coffins contained more than one corpse which was in some instances less than the other, they may have been those of husband and wife, children or friends, or corpses of different periods, or which sunk under

some

I

fome epidemical diforder; or, laftly, were buried in later periods, after this mode of inhumation ceaft, as feems probable from the coins of 1636, and the remains of clothes. This is confirmed by the recollection, that where there were more bodies than one in a coffin, fome were reduced to a fkull or a few bones: not to infift on anatomical difquifitions, whether the corpfe of a peafant occupies lefs room than that of a rich citizen. The Roman medals found here are few and doubtful. As to the objection drawn from the expence of thefe ftone coffins, it fhould be confidered, that as they were near at hand, and would ferve more than once [1], the mode was more frugal than at firft fight appears [2].

I have been the more full in this extract, as the inftances here produced are conclufive in favour of the promifcuous ufe of ftone coffins, and as I believe the book whence it is taken is not in every body's hands.

" Dans le nef de l'eglife de St. Martin a Angers il y a trois anciens cercueils de pierre dans lequels ont etè mis trois perfonnes, & non en terre [3]."

" Il y a dans le nef de l'eglife de St. Pierre dans la meme ville deux cercueils de pierre fort anciens, enchaffez dans le mur a la hauteur de trois pieds audeffus du terre [4]."

" Au bas du collateral dans la derniere chapelle du cotè de l'Evangile paroit un cercueil de pierre en dos d'ane & a fleur de terre, qui eft peutetre la fepulture de Geoffroi premier abbe de cette maifon." Valmont abbey, founded about 1169 [5].

The like ftone coffin in the North wall of the nave (which is all that remains) of the abbey church at Dunmow, and is afcribed to Juga Baynard the foundrefs, may be only of an abbot [6]. Leland defcribes fuch a crofs on the tomb of Henry Doilli, fon of the foundrefs at Ofeney [7].

Coffins of this form are fuppofed to be the oldeft of the fort, a coffin and a monument united. That they were not always confined to religious perfons even though the ridge be charged with a crofs, may be prefumed, if I am right in my application of that in the Temple church to William Plantagenet fifth fon of Henry II. in the XIIIth century. Niger bifhop of London, who died 1241, had one in old St. Paul's [8]. Somewhat fimilar coffins, and both alike ornamented with arches, and therefore moft probably made at the fame period together contained the remains of kings Sebba and Etheldred there. Such were alfo thofe that are afcribed to archbifhop Theobald at Canterbury, and to bifhop Glanville at Rochefter. The conformity of thefe ftone monuments to the general form of our antient fhrines would incline me to believe the two in Kent were depofitories of reliques (the latter perhaps of thofe of St. Paulinus) as well as the two in London. In the floor of the nave of St. Alban's abbey church are two plain ftones, with a rounder ridge [9].

Croffes were very antiently fixed or carved on monuments and graveftones. Among the laws of Kenneth king of Scotland, about 840, we meet with this, " Efteem every fepulchre or graveftone facred, and adorn it with the fign of the " crofs, which take care you do not fo much as tread on." But the fathers, for that very reafon, forbid it to be placed on any graveftones [10].

[1] The Salic laws, however, of the antient Franks forbid burying twice in the fame coffin, either of wood or ftone, under a heavy penalty. " Si quis mortuum hominem aut in *naufo* aut in *petra* (quæ vafa ex ufu farcophagi dicuntur) *fuper* " *alium miferit*, MMD denarios qui faciunt folidos LXII & dimidium culpabilis judicatur."

[2] Recherches fur la maniere d'inhumer les anciens a l'occafion des tombeaux de Civaux en Poitou. Par le R. Pere B. R. Pretr. de la Compagnie de Jefus. Poitiers. 1738. 12mo.

[3] Moleon, Voyage liturgique de France, p. 81. [4] Ib. p. 105.

[5] Defcrip. de la haute Norm. I. 162.

[6] See it in the head piece to Century XII. fig. 2: Graveftones have been hewn in this form in later times. There is one in the South chancel at Gillingham church, near Rochefter, dated 1637. [7] Itin. II. 22.

[8] Dugdale's St. Paul's. Montfaucon mentions a large tomb in St. Lawrence's church at Milan, which by its fhape he judged to be of the firft ages of the church, but he gives no defcription of it. Diar. Ital. c. 2.

[9] " Des tombes de pierre *en boffe* ou des tombes plates" are mentioned for perfons " qui ne font morts qu'au quatorzieme fiecle." Defc. de la haute Normandie, II. 334.

[10] Blomf. Norf. I. 483.

Hearne

Hearne derives both the stone coffin and the crosses on it from the Holy Land, at the crusades [1]. He seems to appropriate the coffin-fashioned lids to abbots [2], which may be doubted.

In the church of Weting All Saints, c. Norfolk, lies an old grave stone with a cross flory in a circle on the summit of a staff, in memory, most likely, of some rector; and near the South wall at the East end of the chancel is another old gravestone, with a cross patee cut on the head of a staff, probably in memory (it being the insignia) of a knight templar [3].

At the West end of the nave at Narford lies a gravestone having a cross patee carved on the summit of a staff, the *insignia* of some *knight templar* [4].

In the chancel under the North wall, with an arch raised over it, lies a marble stone, with a large cross *floral* carved on it, in memory of the *founder*, no doubt some religious, probably some *rector* or *vicar* of the church [5].

In the middle of the chancel of Great Carbrook lie two very antient coffin stones, with a cross patee on each, to shew they belonged to the Templars, and two imperfect circumscriptions on them in capitals, which seem to be added long since they were first laid, and most probably when they were replaced after the rebuilding the church. Mr. Blomfield [6] took that most North to be the sepulchre of Maud countess of Clare, their foundress; and the other on her right hand, or most South, to be one of her younger sons, that might probably be the first commander of this house. They lie exactly in the place where he says the founders of religious places were generally buried; as Herbert founder of Norwich cathedral. By the crosses they were of the order; by their place of interment persons of distinction; by the remains of the inscription, mother and son, and of the *Clare* family. Now though, adds he, I do not meet with their names, Vincent on Brook [7] says she had by Roger de Clare her husband, Richard earl of Clare and Hertford, and others. Dugdale [8], telling us where he was buried, shews plainly this was not his sepulchre, else I should have thought so, by reason of his confirming of his father's and mother's benefactions to this house, to which he was also a benefator. It is plain from the inscription that he was a knight of the order, and had been at Jerusalem, and so was qualified to be a commander of the house, and must be of great note, his name being not mentioned.

On the First,

MATER. CLARENSIS. GENEROSO. MILITE. CLARA.
MA . . . . HIC. TUM. . . VE. .

On the Second.

A. DEXTRIS. NATUS. REQUIESCIT. MATRIS. HUMATUS.
HUNC. PETIT. PORTUM. PROPRIUM. REVOLUTUS. IN. ORTUM.

I must beg leave to differ from Mr. Blomefield, both as to the *date* of the inscriptions, their import, and the lady. I suppose the inscriptions are cut in the Saxon capitals, and shew that *she* was a *Clare* rather by *birth* than *marriage*, and that *he* might be a younger son of earl Roger.

1 Pref. to G. Neubrig. p. lxviii.
2 Roper's Life of More.
3 Blom. Norf. I. 483.
4 Ib. III. 514.
5 Ib.
6 Ib. I. 602.
7 P. 110.
8 I. 210.

"In

"In the churchyard at Balsham, c. Cambridge, at the East end of the chancel, are four freestone coffin monuments, very old, and much alike, each having three crosses florè on their tops. That most North was opened some years ago, and a stone coffin with a skeleton found in it; and in 1744, when the gentlemen of the Charter-house were on their circuit, Dr. Basset had that most South opened, which was found filled with gravel, being bricked on the sides and bottom, where lay a skeleton of a person who had never been in a coffin. I find this was a common way of burial for persons of distinction in the time of Edward II. and III. when some chose rather to have their bodies committed to the earth without a stone coffin than with it. At Thorndon in Suffolk the rector opened for me a monument of this kind, which had also a cross florè on the top of an escalop shell, to denote his having been a pilgrimage to St. James at Compostella. By its being joined to the South chancel wall on the churchyard side it appears to have been the monument of the builder of the church, supposed to be Nicholas de Bokland rector there, who was instituted Aug. 1333, at the presentation of John of Cornwall, second son to Edward II. The grave was fitted up with a stone slab on each side, and one at each end. The body was laid at bottom with nothing but the common earth under the coffin, which was of very thick oak. It was filled up with earth and gravel, and then large flint stones, and so one above another to the surface of the earth, and the whole monument above was solid mason's work. I mention this as in some measure shewing about what time these antient monuments that now remain in many places, were likely to be placed there [1]."

In opening a grave, covered with glazed tiles, on the right hand of the choir by the vestry door at Tewksbury, 1776, was found a stone coffin without a lid, and in it a skeleton, whose teeth were entire, also the spurs and part of the leather, in which it had been wrapt.

In repairing the foundations of the garden wall at the North East corner of the site of St. Catherine's Priory, Lincoln, the workmen opened a stone coffin, in which lay a human skeleton without a scull [2].

The instances of stone coffins, after the introduction of Christianity, in our religious houses are too numerous to be recited. There is hardly a site of such foundation in which there does not appear one or more desecrated for water troughs or worse uses.

In the South aile of Pelham Furneux church, Herts, just where it opens into the chapel, Dr. Salmon [3] describes an altar-tomb of cemented stone, which was hollow, and a stone coffin, with its lid even with the floor. This was smooth at the top, and had no brass upon it, but probably an inscription below, because Weever [4] has preserved a part of it, ". . . . Johannes de Lee, & Johannes "uxor . . . . . ." which the Doctor took for a daughter of Sir Simon Furneus and Sir John de la Lee, temp. Edward I. The tomb is now so covered with pews that I could barely (Sept. 30, 1783) see that both it and its lid had several mouldings, like that in Eastwick church in the same county, on which lies a beautiful figure of a cross-legged knight. On the floor of the chapel are two old stones which are but lids to stone coffins, the coffins remaining below the surface. The inscription remaining on one in Gothic capitals,

"Simon de Furneus filius."

[1] Blomf. Collect. Cantab. p. 199.
[2] Mr. Sympson's MS. collection.
[3] Salmon's Herts. p. 287.
[4] Fun. Mon. p. 548.

is remarkable for not reaching to the end of the ſtone, as in general ſuch inſcriptions do.

Theſe coffins were ſuppoſed older than the chapel, or indeed the church, and to have been replaced there on rebuilding. The bones were entire. In one of them, on taking it up to build a vault, were found ſome beads, of what uſe is hard to ſay, for the method of praying by them is hardly ſo antient.

The tomb of archbiſhop Langton, at Canterbury, 1228, is a large ſtone cheſt, with a croſs carved on its lid, *encbaſſe dans le muraille*, as the French would call it.

In taking down the decayed South chapel at Weſt Harling in the ſame county, the body of the founder, Sir Nicholas de Beauſo, who died in the beginning of the 13th century, appeared to be laid in a ſtone coffin incloſed in the ſouth wall, which, by order of the patron, Sir Baſil Gawdy, was preſerved as it was found, and being covered with bricks, now lies undiſturbed. Mr. Blomfield was told a ſmall thing like a candle-ſtick was found in the coffin, but rather thought it to have been a crucifix [1]. I am ſurpriſed he did not ſuſpect it was the ſhaft of a chalice, or perhaps an entire chalice, and this the coffin of ſome religious.

The coffin in which Lewellin the laſt prince of Wales was buried in Conway-abbey, and on the diſſolution removed into Llanrwſt church, is a cheſt of granite, four inches and a half thick, ſeven feet in the clear, the outſide carved with quatrefoils in relief. It has, like the Roman one before deſcribed at Cheſterton, p. xxiii, a ledge within, to receive the thickneſs of the lid, which is now wanting [2].

Weever ſays [3], the alabaſter effigies of Richard Lucy Lord Chief Juſtice of England lay on a flat marble ſtone, that ſtone on a trough or coffin of white aſhler ſtone, when it was dug up in the ruins of Leſnes abbey, which he founded 1178. In like manner one ſees the figures of abbots, biſhops, knights, and other perſonages, carved on the very ſtone which ſerved as a lid to their coffin. A diſguſting imitation of this mode retained in the laſt century may be ſeen in the figure of William Curle, eſq. 1617, lying on his ſide in the South aile of Hatfield church, in Hertfordſhire.

There is an odd ſort of ſtone coffin lid formed en dos d'ane, where the upper half is charged with a half-figure, with its hands joined. Such are two tombs in the church-yard at Brandon, Suffolk, where the inſcriptions are almoſt worn out by weather: a lady of the Diſney family, at Norton Diſney, c. Lincoln, and a prieſt in Appleby church, c. Weſtmorland. In Kingſbury church, co. Warwick, is a coffin-faſhion lid, on which a female bead peeps out of a quatrefoil [4].

In many churchyards in Lincoln and Huntingdonſhires the grave ſtones are cut coffin-faſhioned, whether raiſed or laid flat, and when accompanied with ſomething like a ſhield for more than half their length, I have frequently been deceived by their firſt appearance to aſcribe antiquity to them. In the ruined nave of Croyland church ſtill uſed as a cemetery key ſtones of arches have been perverted to this uſe. In the church yard at Potton are two ſtone coffins of different ſizes, ſhaped nearly as our preſent wooden ones.

Sir William Dugdale and his lady were buried in ſtone coffins, each made in two parts [5].

Mr. Ames, 1759, was buried eight feet deep, in virgin earth, in the church of St. George, Leiceſter, in a ſtone coffin, on whoſe lid his epitaph was inſcribed, as alſo on both ſides of a flat ſtone.

[1] Norf. I. 209.
[2] See it in Mr. Pennant's Supplementary Plates, Pl. IV.
[3] Fun. Mon. p. 777.
[4] Dugdale's Warwickſh. 1061. 2d edit.
[5] Ib. 1046. Ath. Ox. II. 690.

I

The

The uſe of *leaden* coffins was not unknown to the Romans. "When Chriſtianity encreaſed the cuſtom of burning the dead began to ceaſe, and was little practiſed by any in the later times of the Antonines, though the ſame place without Boutham bar, at York, was continued for their ſepulture; as appears by human bones that have never paſſed the fire digged up there. Theſe were interred at the depth of nine feet, whereof ſix were ſtiff clay, and three a black earth. The lead coffin, which was about ſeven feet long, was encloſed in a prodigious ſtrong one made of oak planks two inches and a half thick, which, beſides the rivetings, were tacked together with brags or great iron nails four inches long, the heads not die-wiſe, as the large nails now are, but perfectly flat, and an inch broad, except one, which was half an inch broad, and theſe ſomewhat in the form of a wedge, and the head not round, as the other, but ſomewhat like the modern draw nails; but the reſt of the old ones are ſquare, the four ſides of equal breadth. Many of them were almoſt conſumed with ruſt, and ſo was the outſide of the planks, but the heart of oak was firm, and the lead freſh and pliable; whereas one found in 1701 was brittle, and almoſt wholly conſumed, having no planks to guard it. The bones were very light, though entire; but the double coffins required a team of horſes to draw them out[1]."

The Romans buried both in wood and lead[2].

Morant deſcribes a leaden coffin found out of Colcheſter near a Roman urn[3]. Narſes' leaden coffin was robbed of a vaſt quantity of treaſure by the emperor Tiberius[4].

On plowing in Water Newton Lane, c. Lincoln, 1732, they found a large leaden coffin, containing an entire ſkeleton, and ſeveral ſmall urns and ſmall coins, ſilver and braſs, of Veſpaſian and Severus; alſo a ſtone coffin, in which was another ſkeleton, very perfect, and in order, which plainly appeared to have been a woman with child, there being within it the ſmall bones of a fœtus in regular order, but fallen together, and near this an urn with aſhes[5].

A leaden coffin ſix feet long, full of bones, was found at Padua, in the ſame place where was found the inſcription uſually aſcribed to Livy, but by Orſati[6] to Lucius Halys freedman of Livia, fourth daughter of Titus Livius. This coffin is ſtill preſerved in the hall of Juſtice there[7].

An antient chronicle cited by Du Cheſne, vol. III. p. 641. ſays, that 1054 was found at Marſeilles a human body entire and embalmed, in a leaden coffin, encloſed in a white marble tomb, which being ſuppoſed the corps of the emperor Maximinian, one of the perſecutors of the Chriſtians, who died A. D. 310. Rainchild, archbiſhop of Arles, cauſed it, with both its coffins, to be toſſed into the ſea[8]. It is much more probable that it belonged to ſome Chriſtian prince or prelate of a later age.

At Sturry, near Canterbury, 1755, was found, five feet deep in the earth, a large broad ſtone, covering a ſtone coffin, ſix feet four inches, incloſing a leaden one, five feet eight inches, in which was a human body almoſt decayed, though the teeth were perfect in the jaws. The lead, which was much waſted, as well as the ſtone coffin, ſeemed to be put together in ſix pieces without ſolder, and each piece ſuppoſed to weigh thirty pounds. An earthen quart jug near it crumbled to pieces on handling[9].

[1] Thoreſby, Ducatus Leod. p. 560.
[2] Kirkman, 441. Thoreſby, 419.
[3] Hiſt. of Colcheſter, p. 183.
[4] P. Diac. ap. Kirkman, p. 389.
[5] A. S. Min. XV. 23. See p. 81.
[6] Monumi. Antiq. ſ. 141.
[7] Mem. de Petrarque, III. 110.
[8] Univ. Hiſt. XV. p. 527. Le Beau Hiſt. du Bas Empire, I. 96.
[9] Newbery's Deſcription of England, V. 75.

Near

Near Ilchefter was found fome bones in a leaden cafe as big as a band box in a hollowed ftone, and near it, under a tree, was a vault of ftone, where a body was found lying at full length [1].

Carew fpeaks of Orgar, he means Cadoc, being found in a leaden coffin, in St. Stephen's church, near Trematons, Cornwall [2].

Hearne mentions a body in a leaden coffin in Cornwall, which had continued there from the Saxon times, and when touched fell to pieces [3].

" Many yeres fince men fought for treafor at a place called the Dungen [at " Canterbury] wher Barnhale's houfe now is, and ther yn digging thei fownd a " coarfe clofed in lead [4]."

St. Alban's relics were found, 1257, in repairing his church, in leaden fheets, with an infcription on a leaden plate [5].

Eadburga abbefs of Repton, c. Derby, daughter of Adulph, king of the Eaft Angles, who died A. D. 714, fent Guthlac a leaden coffin, *farcophagum plumbeum* [6]. This was the beft prefent that could be made by an abbefs who lived in the centre of fome of the principal and perhaps oldeft lead mines in the kingdom.

St. Dunftan, who died A. D. 988, was buried in linen, in a double coffin of lead, the outermoft more ornamented [7]. Mr. Somner [8] gives the account of the difcovery as " a pretty relation, and worth reading." It is fo long and circumftantial that I fhall content myfelf with an abftract of it. April 10, 1508, by order of the archbifhop and prior, three or four of the fraternity, men of diftinguifhed abilities and of more fervent zeal [9] for the work, went about it in the evening, after the church doors were fhut up, that none of the laity might interfere, and before day-light difcovered in the ftonework of the fhrine on the South fide of the high altar a wooden cheft, equal in length to the ftonework of the fhrine, which was feven feet, and about one foot and a half broad, lined and covered with lead faftened with nails, diftant about a hand's breadth from each other, and ftrongly bound round with iron bands. They got no further the firft night; but the next returning to their fearch, fix of the brethren, with other affiftance, had much difficulty to lift the coffin out of the ftone work. They then, with no lefs difficulty, got open the front of the coffin [10], by breaking part of a board on the upper part [11]. This difcovered to their view a leaden coffin, not made of fmooth lead, but wrought in folds in a moft beautiful manner [12], containing another leaden coffin almoft perifhed, which was fuppofed to be that in which he was firft buried. Between thefe two leaden coffins they found a fmall leaden plate lying on the breaft of the body, infcribed with thefe words in Roman letters [13]:

HIC REQUIESCIT SANCTUS DUNSTANUS ARCHIEPISCOPUS.

They next found a fair linen cloth, perfectly found, laid over the body. On removing this the faint appeared in his pontifical habit, for the moft part

[1] Stukeley, It. Cur. I. 147.
[2] P. 112.
[3] Hearne Spicil. ad Gul. Neubrig. p. 790.
[4] Leland. It. VII. 144.
[5] M. Paris, p. 942. Uffer. Ant. Eccl. Brit. 77.
[6] Lel. Coll. II. 590. It. IV. 131. and Pegge, Archæolog V. 373.
[7] See the certificate of the difcovery of his body, Ang. Sac. II. 228, 229.
[8] Antiq. of Cantab. Appendix, N° 38.
[9] *Ad ejufmodi opus aptiores & ferventiores.*
[10] *Anteriorem partem arcæ.*
[11] *Poftea afferis quo in fuperiori parte arca claudebatur effringerent.*
[12] *Talia non ex plano plumbo fed arte quadam pulcherrime fabricata & plicata.*
[13] *Literis Romanis.*

confumed

confumed by time. They faw his bald crown [1], and all his bones in order, with pieces of his flefh. They took part of his crown, which they lodged among their reliques, and then clofed up all the feveral coffins in the ftrongeft manner.

The duft of St. John of Beverly was found, 1664, under a thick marble flab, in the middle of Beverley choir, near the entrance into the choir, in a fheet of lead four feet long, in a vault of fquared free ftone five feet long, two feet broad at the head, and one and a half at the feet. A leaden box lay acrofs it containing fome of his bones mixed with duft. With it were fix beads, three of which were cornelian, the other crumbled to duft. There were in it alfo three great brafs pins, and four iron nails. Upon this fheet of lead was fixed a plate of lead, with this infcription:

" Anno ab incarnatione domini MCLXXXVIII combufta fuit hæc ecclefia in " menfe Sept. in fequenti nocte poft feftum fancti Mathæi apoftoli & in anno " MCXCVII. VI. id. Martii facta fuit inquifitio reliquiarum beati Johannis in hoc " loco, & inventa funt hæc offa in orientali parte fepulchri, & hic recondita, & " pulvis cemento mixtus ibidem inventus & reconditus."

Thefe had been fo depofited after the chapel was burnt, 1188 [2]; but this leaden box was rather for his fhrine and bones, being but three quarters of a yard long, and marked with a crofs in a ftone coffin fix feet and a half long.

The remains of St. William, who died archbifhop of York, 1154, were lodged in a fquare leaden box three quarters of a yard long, about eight inches diameter at top, and gradually decreafing at bottom clofely foldered up. They were depofited thus on his canonization in the reign of Edward I. by archbifhop Wickwane, who removed them from the place where they firft lay into the nave of his cathedral, and built a moft coftly fhrine over them. On laying the new pavement, 1732, Mr. Drake fearcht for them, and difcovered them about a yard below the furface, under a long flab of fpotted marble, which had been inverted, and by the mouldings round the edge was fuppofed to have been an altar ftone. The leaden box, much decayed, and having on its top a fmall plain crofs, made of two pieces of lead of equal bignefs, and at the end a piece of ftuff which mouldered upon touching, lay within a ftone coffin fix feet fix inches long, the lid arched, on which was a crofs the length of the coffins. There was no infcription, either within or without the box, or on the altar ftone. But all circumftances put together, the matter feemed to Mr. Drake indifputable. The fmaller bones, and thofe of the fcull, which were broken, were wrapt in a piece of farcenet double, which had acquired the colour of the bones it contained, and fome of which, for curiofity fake, was taken out. The larger bones were put down to the bottom of the box, and by meafuring a thigh bone entire our prelate appears to have been about five feet fix inches high. The remains of this once famous prelate were carefully repofited in the coffin, that clofed, and the grave filled up. Mr. Drake has given a print of the coffin and box [3].

Geoffry Magnaville, who died under fentence of excommunication in the habit of the Templars, was carried by them to the Old Temple in London, where putting him into a pipe of lead (*canaliculo*) they hanged him on a tree [4]. They would not be wanting in refpect to a founder and endower of monafteries. They durft not bury him for fear of the pope; fo they wrapped him in lead, and depofited him like Mahomet, between heaven and earth. The dangling pofture was

[1] *Tefta capitis.*
[2] Life of Wood, 192. 2d. edit.
[3] Ebor. p. 470.
[4] Mon. Ang. I. 448.

not over decent. If this had been done by an enemy or indifferent person it had looked like spite or contempt [1].

"Rosamunde's tumbe, at Godestowe nunnery, was taken up a late; it is a "stone with this inscription: Tumba Rosamundæ. Her bones were closid in lede, "and withyn that the bones were closed in lether. When it was opened there "was a very swete smell cam owt of it [2]." This account, given by the accurate Leland is sufficient to prove, that the double stone coffin shewn in the ruins of Godstow nunnery for Rosamund's [3] did not belong to her. This is however a single instance I believe of coffins thus divided into two compartments, and seems to be now destroyed [4]. Hearne, in his account of some antiquities in and about Oxford, at the end of Leland's Itinerary II. 132. does not describe it as divided, but as two stone coffins, reported to have belonged to Rosamond, and her keeper, which destination he laughs at as a vulgar notion, and refers the coffins to two nuns, or two other persons here buried. The imperfect inscription given by Hentzner as on Rosamond's tomb of stone, was really, as we learn from Leland, on a cross near Godstow. It was a precatory form for her soul, and not, as Mr. Grose conceived, an address to her as a saint [5].

Roger archbishop of York, who died 1281, was buried in the wall of his church, where his leaden coffin may be knocked against with a stick, through the openings of the fret work [6]. His successor Melton was interred in a leaden coffin, within a very strong one of oak [7].

King John is supposed to lie in a leaden coffin, which was discovered, but not opened, under his monument [8].

Prince Henry, son of Henry I. was done up in lead and bull's hides [9].

Fitzpiers buried at Winborn minster five hundred years ago was found in lead [10], by the sexton, who cut part of it in digging a grave close by it.

Bishop Bitton, at Exeter, who died 1307, appears to have been been buried in a leaden coffin of modern shape, with rings to it [11].

Bishop Dalderby, who died 1319, lay at Lincoln in a kind of stone vault lined with lead [12].

Bishop Grosthead, in the same cathedral, had only a sheet of lead laid over the top of his stone coffin on three iron bars [13].

The Black Prince was embalmed, and done up in lead, 1376 [14].

The Duke of Exeter was buried at St. Edmund's Bury, 1426, in lead and pickle.

The Delapoles at Hull were so buried in the Carthusian monastery at Hull; and at the suppressing of it were found diverse troughs of lead with bones in a vault under the high altar there [15].

So the Hungerfords at Farley. Sir Joseph Ayloffe told me he cut one with a couteau, and let out a horrid stench.

[1] Salmon, Herts, p. 99.
[2] Leland in Mon. Angl. I. 528.
[3] Mr. Grose's account under his view of it.
[4] It is not mentioned in the account of Godstow nunnery, Gent. Mag. vol. LIII. p. 462. 1783.
[5] —— Adorent;
Utque tibi detur requies, Rosamunda, precamur.
Or, as Leland,
Qui meat huc oret, signum salutis adoret,
Utque tibi detur requies, Rosamunda, precetur.
St. Hugh bishop of Lincoln caused her body to be digged up in the conventual church, and laid in the public burying ground, *plebeio more*, 1191. Walter Coventrensis in Lel. Coll. I. 357. says, "Rosamunda translata e celebri "tumulo ad incelebrem per Hugonem episcopum Lincoln." Hoveden (Chron. p. 495.) adds, her tomb stood in the midst of the choir, and was covered with silk, and surrounded with lamps and tapers before this removal. It was again disturbed, as above, at the Reformation.
[6] Drake, Ebor. p. 410.
[7] Ib. p. 433.
[8] See p. 37.
[9] Hoveden, p. 354.
[10] Hutchins, Dorset, II. 94.
[11] See p. 81.
[12] See p. 84.
[13] See p. 47.
[14] Sandford, p. 187.
[15] Lel. It. I. 57.

So the Ratcliffes at Boreham, 1583. 1593. This was fitted to the body like a cerecloth, and ſhewed the features of the face, and had the name, title, and date in Roman letters.

Thomas Grey marquis of Dorſet, who died 1532, was found on pulling down his chapel at Aſtley, c. Warwick, done up in cerecloth and lead, and quite perfect and ſound, after 78 years interment, in a large and long wooden coffin [1].

Sir Gerard Braybroke's bones lying in a coffin of lead covered with wood were digged up at the Eaſt end of the South aile of the choir at St. Paul's, in the reign of Edward VI [2].

Prince Henry, 1612, was wrapped in lead, according to the proportion of his body; his heart incloſed in lead upon his breaſt, in the form thereof, under which are the figures 1612, and under that the prince's device and motto, with a roſe and a thiſtle, ſubſcribed with the letters H. P. all emboſſed [3].

In the South aile of Lichfield cathedral was found, 1751, a ſtrong leaden coffin, with ſeveral large iron rings faſtened to the ſides: the lid, which was banded acroſs with ſtrong leaded ribs, lay looſe on the coffin, which was very much corroded. In it was a ſkeleton, with a dry friable ſubſtance, which ſparkled by candlelight, and like ſalt mixed with earth, ſcattered among the bones, as alſo ſeveral folds of fine linen ſticking cloſely together, and ſome pieces of broad lace, ſuppoſed ſilver, by their blackneſs, which probably made part of ſome pontificalia [4].

A ſkeleton, wrapt in red leather, covered with lead, and a ſort of coronet on its head, was found a foot under ground, in Moulton church, Lincolnſhire, on new paving the choir [5].

Mr. Vertue, Dr. Rawlinſon, and Mr. Umfreville, ſaw at the end of Hoſier lane, Weſt Smithfield, where they were digging deep for a ſewer, in freſh clayiſh gravel, a leaden cheſt, much decayed, four feet by twenty-one inches, and eighteen inches deep, lying towards the antient timber houſes behind St Sepulchre's church, and containing bones and ſculls, the ſize uncertain. It might have been a receptacle for many bones, a few lay looſe near it; the lead much decayed, adorned with a croſs on greeces, and four leaves at the margin in low emboſt work, but no date or inſcription. The old inhabitants ſaid St. Sepulchre's churchyard reached further this way. About the ſame place human bones were dug up [6].

A leaden coffin was dug up in the Black Friars, Oxford, about 40 years before 1658. When it was opened they found the ſkeleton of a man with a *candel* in his hand, and a ſilver penny hanging about his neck, and five gold rings upon his finger. About 30 years ago another leaden coffin was dug up at the upper end of Robinſon's lane in St. Ebb's pariſh without the town wall [7].

In October, 1783, ſome perſons digging for gravel in a yard in Humberſtone-gate at Leiceſter, at the depth of about two yards came to a leaden coffin, a parallelogram, five feet four inches long, eighteen inches broad on the outſide, half an inch thick, and weighing an hundred weight. The lid was ſupported on the inſide by iron reſts acroſs, about an inch broad, and of a competent thickneſs, but through ruſt eaſily broken, forked and bent at the

[1] Burton's Leiceſterſhire, p. 51, Dugdale's Warwickſhire, p. 113. Dugdale adds the *lead*, which is not mentioned by Burton, an eye-witneſs.
[2] Dugdale, St. Pauls, p. 45.
[3] Sandford, p. 562. Dart. II. 50.
[4] Mr. Green, Gent. Mag. 1751. p. 398.
[5] Spalding Society's Minutes.
[6] A. S. Min. VI. 1749.
[7] Wood's Notes about Oxford, Liber Niger, II. 573.

extremities

extremities so as strongly to sustain the lid and under part. Within the coffin was a complete skeleton, the bones in their natural order, the head lying East, inclining to the left shoulder, the teeth perfect, the under jaw fallen on the breast. On the right side near the middle of the coffin within were several dark balls lying together as if strung, which might have been held by the right hand; none an inch diameter, and all to appearance of equal size. On the outside toward the feet stood an earthen vase: there were also six or seven small urns, all plain, and of red clay, not glazed. In the same yard have been found human and other bones, and many ox horns [1].

Sir Robert Cotton told Weever of a chest of lead found in Radcliffe-field, in Stepney parish: the upper part garnished with scallop shells and a crotister border. At the head and foot of the coffin stood two jars three feet long, and on the sides a number of bottles of glistering red earth, some painted, and many great phials of glass, some six, some eight square, having a whitish liquor in them. Within the chest was the body of a woman, as the surgeons judged by the scull. On either side of her were two sceptres of ivory, eighteen inches long, and on her breast a little figure of Cupid neatly cut in white stone. And among the bones were two pointed pieces of jet with round heads in form of nails three inches long [2].

About the year 1720, in the grounds of the widow Giles, near Clifton, was found a leaden coffin, with the dust and bones of a corpse in it: as also another of oak two inches and a half thick, covered with lead, in which were the remains of mortality. Whether this might have been a place of interment to St. Magdalen's chapel we cannot say, though we may reasonably conjecture, that before York was encompassed with walls it reached to a much greater extent in the suburbs; and being then more populous, might have different burial places. In December, 1729, were likewise found, in another part of the ground, several urns, containing bones and dust, as also Roman coins, promiscuously buried in the earth. The like about the same time were found in Mr. Roberts's ground, which is contiguous to the said widow's [3].

Mrs. Babington, who died under sentence of excommunication in the reign of Charles II. was buried in a cave hewn in the rocks of Harnham, below the foundations of the castle, where her remains now lie in a leaden coffin [4].

Alexander the Great was buried at Alexandria, by his successor Ptolomey, in a coffin of *gold*, which, before the time of Augustus, had been changed for one of *glass* [5]. In this that Emperor viewed his body, after causing it to be brought out of the vault. Caligula took his breast-plate out of his vault, and wore it [6], or at least pretended to do so [7].

Some labourers employed in repairing the road between Walnsford and King's-cliff, Northampton, about a mile West of the former, within thirty yards of a large wood, in Rockingham forest, struck upon a *glass* coffin, about two feet three inches long, containing the bones of a child much decayed. It was shaped like the present coffins, was of fine transparent glass, of a beautiful aquamarine colour, clear, and ornamented with five concentric raised circles, the diameter of the outermost five inches three quarters. There was no appearance of a place of sepulture hereabouts; but on diligent search several human bones were found

[1] Gent. Mag. Vol. LIII. p. 910. [2] Weever, Fun. Mon. p. 30. [3] Gent's Hist. of York. Additions.
[4] Hutchinson's Northumb. I. 219.
[5] [illegible] Strabo, XVII. p. 546. Sueton. Aug. 18. The spot where Alexander was buried and probably had a mausoleum was called *Soma*, Σωμα, or *Sema*, Σημα. Achilles Tatius V. init. Suetonius says the corps was brought out of a vault, *penetrale*, and in Calig. c. 52. he calls it *conditorium*. Strabo's word Πυελος is any kind of trough.
[6] Sueton. Calig. c. 52. [7] Dio LIX. p. 653.

between

between the road and the wood, but all without coffins. It was fuppofed that this coffin contained the body in pickle, as none of the bones in it or in the field appeared to have been burnt. Mr. Wills gave the Society of Antiquaries a piece of the glafs containing the five circles, Nov. 14, 1776, and conjectured, that this interment happened in the reign of Henry VI. at which time an idea prevailed that human bodies might be preferved by fome liquid preparation. Another piece of plate glafs was fent me from the Roman ftation of Duntocher, in Scotland, which I exhibited to the fame fociety. I have fince feen, in the hands of Mr. Sheppard of Chefterford, c. Effex, two pieces of thick glafs, which may have been fepulchral. The late Dr. Barnard of Wethersfield gave the Society a drawing of a large glafs urn found there.

The oldeft inftance of *wooden* coffins on record among us is that of king Arthur, which was an intire trunk of oak hollowed, *quercus cavata* [1], which the monk of Glaftenbury calls *farcophagus ligneus*, and Leland will have to be an alder (*alnus*) as fitteft to laft in wet [2]. This example was imitated by Sir Edward Deering, who died in Ireland, and was brought over and buried at Pluckley in Kent.

Between Wormleighton and Stanton, c. Warwick, was found in a pit a trunk of a tree hewn into a coffin with bones in it, and many coins particularly of Conftantine [3].

The body found under Kingbarrow, near Wareham, 1767, was depofited in an oak trunk, whofe outer diameter was four feet, and its inner three feet. The body was wrapt in pieces of deer-fkins, with the hair on, curioufly ftitched together, and appeared to have been paffed feveral times round the body, and in fome parts adhered to the wood. In the middle of the wrapper the bones were compreffed together in a lump, and cemented together with a glutinous matter, perhaps the moifture of the body and fkins, and on opening yielded a vault-like fmell. A piece of what was thought gold lace, four inches long and two and a half broad, very much decayed, ftuck on the infide of the wrapper. Bits of wire plainly appeared on it. The bones found were one arm, two thigh and blade-bones, the head of the humerus, part of the pelvis, and feveral of the ribs. Thefe laft would twift round the finger; but no figns of the fcull. Near the South Eaft end was found a fmall wooden veffel, much broken and compreft, hatcht with irregular lines, three inches by two diameter, two deep, and two tenths of an inch thick [4].

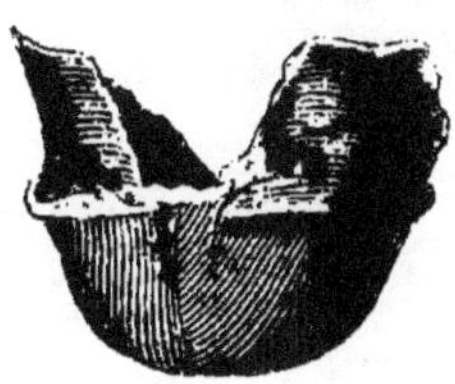

[1] Giraldus Cambr. in Speculo ecclefiaftico. [2] Affert. Artur. p. 45.

[3] Stukeley. Itin. II. 21.

[4] Hutchins's Dorfet, I. 25. One of Sir Chriftopher Wren's anceftors found in an old wall at Blachefter, the Roman ftation, an earthen urn, incloling a wooden one. *Pref.* to Parentalia.

m This,

This, with a large portion of the wrapper, is in my possession. There is no pretence for this having been the body of Edward the martyr, A. D. 978. but it is highly probable that it belonged to some petty prince or chieftain of the Saxon or Danish times.

King Edmund the martyr was found fresh in a wooden coffin many years after his death, and a fragment of it kept at Thetford [1]. This however he might get by some prior translation.

Osana sister of king Osred had, in Hoveden church, Yorkshire, a tomb of wood, *tumba lignea in sedis modum super aram eminens* [2].

We have already seen that archbishop Dunstan was found in a wooden coffin covered with lead within and without, and within this two leaden ones, the innermost supposed the original almost perished. He died about 988.

Erasmus describes Becket's shrine as a coffin of wood covering one of gold. He must mean gilt plateing [3].

Mr. Strutt describes two wooden chests, carved with female figures on the lids, in the niches of the wall of Little Baddow church, Essex, which through age are so much decayed, that the bones and remains of the bodies are to be seen under the covers [4].

Geoffrey de Magnaville, who died suddenly at Chester 1165, was salted and done up in leather, then put up in a strong fir coffin, and so conveyed on a carriage to Walden [5].

Edward I. was found in a wooden coffin inclosed in a stone one besides the outer stone tomb.

Alice Hackney, who died in the reign of Edward II. or III. and of whose extraordinary preservation by and by, was found in a coffin of rotten timber.

The marquis of Dorset, before mentioned, p. xliii, was buried in a wooden coffin, 1532.

In a moist spungy ground, about two furlongs off West Toftes in Grimshoe hundred, Norfolk, was found, in 1720, in making a ditch to drain the grounds, an oak coffin lying S. E. & N. W. filled with water, and containing many bones, among which were the rude representation of a face cut either in jet or Lancashire coal; a blue cypher which looked as if it had been set in a ring, some blue irregular beads, and a broken gold ferril, which the workmen said had slipt off a small piece of wood like a small knitting sheath, probably a cross, but broken and bent outright before Mr. Blomfield saw it. Near this place is a piece of ground moated round, the scite of the chapel belonging to the mansion house of Caston-hall [6].

In digging, 1737, in the churchyard of Little Carbrook, in the same county, which had been long desecrated, there were found a cross, here represented, fig. 1. laid over the coffin of some religious person buried here, most likely one of the knights of St. John of Jerusalem, to whom the place belonged. There were two chains, on which hung two jewels, that on one side being lost.

It is to be supposed, by the marks of the brass bosses on the cross, that there were formerly relics under them, and that it was buried with him on that account, and possibly might have been fetched by the party himself from the Holy Sepulchre. The stem of it was of oak [7]. I have copied Mr. Blomfield's print, though I rather incline to believe this cross was *within* the coffin.

[1] Blomfield's Norfolk, I. 450.
[2] Gerald. Camb. Itin. Camb. I. c. 1. p. 824.
[3] Gostling's Walk, 2d edit.
[4] Horda Angleyynnan, I. 109.
[5] Reg. Walden. Mon. Ang. I. 451.
[6] Blomf. Norf. I. 547.
[7] Blomf. I. 600.

The

The other figure repreſented in this plate is a circular plate found on a coffin in York minſter: the figure gilded, engraved on copper; the ground enamelled blue edged with white; with ſome dots of red and gold, referred by Mr. North to the time of Edward I. or II. when ſeveral Greek workmen came over and taught our workmen; and perhaps executed this among other pieces. It was in the poſſeſſion of Dr. Rawlinſon in 1741, who exhibited it to the Society of Antiquaries.

Mr. Le Neve ſhewed the ſame Society, 1724-5, a wooden croſs plated with tin, and adorned with fictitious ſtones, found in pulling down Biſhopſgate-church, and ſuppoſed to have belonged to a coffin.

The date, 1026, ſaid to have been found on a coffin-plate among ſome human bones, in digging the foundations of ſome houſes in Camomile-ſtreet, London, is an eaſy miſtake for 1626 [1].

Mr. Llwyd, in Gibſon's Camden, p. 793, mentions a wooden coffin, gilt, found in 1684, in a turbary, called Mwnog y ſtrat gwyn near Maes y Pandy, in Merionethſhire, ſo well preſerved that the gilding remained very freſh, and ſaid to have contained an extraordinary large ſkeleton. This is the only inſtance he knew of burying in ſuch places, and yet, ſays he, they who placed this coffin here might have regard to the perpetual preſervation of it. The circumſtances of the *gilding* ſtrikes me as more extraordinary.

At Aſh, in a field near Richborough, to which ſtation it ſeems to have been the burying place, were found 1762, ſeveral bodies in diſtinct wooden caſes, with a ſword on the right ſide, a ſpear on the left, a necklace of glaſs and amber beads round the neck, a fibula on the ſhoulder, and the iron umbo of the ſhield directly over the face. Several Roman medals of the upper and lower empire were found in the graves.

It is ſuppoſed by Dr. Chiflet, who gives a particular account of the diſcovery of his tomb, that Childeric king of the Franks, who died A. D. 481, was buried in a wooden coffin bound round with iron, pieces of which were found adhering ſo cloſe to the wood that it was difficult to ſeparate them [2]. Montfaucon [3] adds, they were ſo eaten with ruſt that it fell to pieces.

[1] Gent. Mag. 1765. p. 394.
[2] Anaſtaſis Childerici.
[3] Mon. de la Mon. Franc. I.

The

The old term for a wooden coffin is ſuppoſed to be *Noſſus* or *Nauſus*, from its reſemblance to a ſhip, called by the Franks *Nau* [1]. An ordinance of the Salic law [2] forbids laying two bodies one upon another in ſuch a receptacle: *aut in noſſo* [3], *aut in petra, quæ vaſa ex uſu ſarcophagi dicuntur.* The laws of our king Henry I. c. 83. forbid the digging up a body laid "*in terra, vel* noſſo, *vel* "petra, *ſub petra vel pyramide, vel ſtructura qualibet.*" And Gregory of Tours [4] ſpeaks of the bodies of the ſaints as being "*palliis ac* nauſis *exornata.*"

It is no uncommon thing to ſee in old pariſh churches in the country a wooden box, with one or two lids, with hinges, and ſometimes a haſp, *en dos d'ane*, in the form of Florence wine caſes, which were uſed as biers to carry out the poor dead who had no coffin but their winding ſheet. There is one, with a frame as of a table and four legs, in the old chapel or cloiſter at the South end of St. Alban's South tranſept. Dr. Kaye ſaw another in ſome vault at Durham, called St. Dunſtan's coffin, meaning probably St. Cuthbert's.

The Duke of York's coffin at Monaco was of a ſingular form, like an oblong cheſt.

From the ſeveral materials in which bodies were antiently depoſited, I proceed to take a view of thoſe in which they were wrapt or ſhrouded.

Edward the Confeſſor's body being diſturbed thirty-ſix years after its interment, on a diſpute in the convent about the *incorruptibility of the virgin* [5] King, was found in perfect preſervation. This tranſaction may be compared to the view which certain curious Antiquaries took of his nameſake 700 years after, on a different motive. We may be ſure the Monks were to be gainers by the examination, and to make the moſt of the miracle. Our modern examiners were animated by the more laudable motive of deciding a point of hiſtorical record, and inquiring into the mode of interment that then prevailed. On a ſet day the abbot, with the whole convent and the biſhop of Rocheſter, having taken off the ſtone, were agreeably entertained with a fragrant odour of ſpices. After removing the mantle [6] which inveloped the holy limbs, they proceeded to examine the other ornaments and veſtments, and found every thing ſolid and in perfect preſervation, the limbs capable of being extended, the fingers flexible, the joints diſtinguiſhable, and every part ſound and in its original vigour, the fleſh intire and white as at firſt; and the biſhop, who alone ventured to handle his beard, found it retained its original whiteneſs and adherence to the face, ſo that he could not carry off a ſingle hair. Having ſatisfied their curioſity, they wrapt up the corpſe in a new mantle (for the old one was too precious to be parted with), and placed him again ſafely in his old apartment [7]. Abbot Laurence made three copes of the three wrappers of his body [8], and it was re-wrapt in *veſtimento boloſerico*, in a wainſcot cheſt. Accordingly Taylor, in 1688, drew out pieces of gold-coloured and flowered ſilk.

[1] Du Cange in voc. If the true original name of the *One night's work*, or monument in form of a ſhip, in the county of Louth, could be aſcertained, and derived from *Navi*, which ſignifies a *ſhip* in Iriſh, one might ſuppoſe it ſepulchral. See Major Vallancey's conjectures on it in Collectanea Hibernica, Vol. III. N° X. p. 208.

[2] Tit. 17. § 1.

[3] Heroldus § 4 reads *in oſſo*, but tit. 57, § 4, we have *nauſo*. Muratori, Script. Ital. I. part 2, ſays, a copy of theſe laws at Eſte reads tuſus, which Charpentier thinks ſuits better with ſarcophagus. But the other inſtances are againſt this alteration whether *noſſus* refers to wood or not.

[4] De gloria confeſſorum.

[5] Bromton, p. 909, tells a pleaſant ſtory of Canute's incredulity about the ſanctity of St. Editha at Wilton, the daughter of ſuch an amorous father as Edgar. Archbiſhop Ethelnoth, to confute him, opened her tomb, and the deceaſed virgin ſtarting up, flew in the King's face. "Cingulo tenus ſe erigens in contumacem regem impetum facere "viſa eſt." I ſuppoſe ſhe was dried, and flew up on a touch.

[6] *Pallium.*

[7] *Triclinum.* Alured Rieval inter X Scriptores, p. 408.

[8] *Tres capas brudatas de tribus panni in quibus S. Edwardus requievit.* Flete in Dart I. 53.

Constance wife of Alan Fergant, 1090, was found buried in leather, on opening her tomb at Melaine, 1672 [1].

Hugh de Grentmesnel, 1094, was salted, and wrapt up in a hide, and buried at St. Ebrull [2].

Hugh Lupus, who died 1101, was found in his stone coffin in Chester chapterhouse, 1724; his bones bare of flesh, but wrapt up in gilt leather, and his ancles tied together with a string. The stone in form of a T with his crest and device, which served to distinguish the place of his interment is now fixed over the door within [3].

The Empress Maud, daughter of Henry I. was buried in Bec abbey, where her corpse was found wrapt up in an ox's hide [4].

Henry I. 1135, was gashed and salted, and sewed up in a bull's skin [5], after his bowels, tongue, heart, eyes, and brains, were taken out [6]. How awkwardly, see Matthew Paris [7].

" Corpus Henrici I. allatum est Rothomagum, & ibi viscera ejus & cerebrum " & oculi consepulta sunt: reliquum autem corpus cultellis circumquaque dissecatum, & sic multo sale aspersum coriis taurinis reconditum est & consutum, " causa fœtoris evitandi, qui multus & infinitus jam circumstantes inficiebat, " unde & medicus ipse qui magno pretio conductus securi caput ejus diffiderat " ut fœtidissimum cerebrum extraheret, quamvis linteaminibus caput suum obvolvisset mortuus tamen ea causa pretio male gavisus est. Inde vero corpus regium Cadomum sui deportaverunt, ubi dum diu in ecclesia positum in qua pater " ejus sepultus erat, quamvis multo sale repletum esset, & multis coriis reconditum, tamen continue ex corpore niger humor & horribilis coria pertransiens decurrebat, & vasis subpositis sub feretro susceptus a ministris horrore " fatiscentibus abjiciebatur [8]."

Prince Henry, son of Henry I. was done up in lead and bulls' hides [9].

Leland [10] mentions " a corpse wrapt up in a bull's hide, lately taken up in Gloucester cathedral, which a monk told him was a Countess of Pembroke. It lay at the head of Edward II. under an arch where Malverne, alias Parker, late abbot, made himself a chapel to be buried in."

Robert de Ferrars, founder of Merivale abbey, c. Warwick, was buried there in an ox-hide, in the reign of Henry II. [11].

Geoffry de Magnaville, who died suddenly 1165, at Chester, was salted and done up in leather; then put up in a strong fir coffin covered with tapestry, and so conveyed on a carriage to Walden [12].

On digging a grave at the West end of Lincoln minster, 1741, they found a corpse sewed up in a strong tanned leather hide, the seam running up the middle of the breast. Maurice Johnson, who gave an account of it to the Society of Antiquaries, supposed it that of Walter Deincourt, or his son William, buried here in the 11th century, whose epitaph on a plate of lead was found 1670 [13]. This church was built about the time of the Norman conquest by Remigius,

[1] Lobineau, t. I. l. 3. c. 120. p. 104.
[2] Ordericus Vitalis, p. 716. Dugd. Bar. I. 425.
[3] Pennant's Wales, I. 178.
[4] Ducarell Ang. Norm. Ant. p. 89. Hist. of Bec. p. 99.
[5] Polychr. VII. f. 282.
[6] Robert of Glocester, p. 419. in Sandf. 27.
[7] P. 73, 74.
[8] Hoveden, p. 276.
[9] Ib. p. 354.
[10] It. IV. 172. 2.
[11] Camden. Brit. Warw. Dugd. Warw. 1090. Bar. I. 259.
[12] Reg. Walden. Mon. Ang. I. 452.
[13] See Dugd. Bar. I. 386.

Who, in obedience to a canon of 1076, removed his epiſcopal ſee from Dorcheſter hither, and here laid the foundation of his cathedral, under the protection of the caſtle, and in the capital city of his dioceſe, in 1088. He had a near relation, Walter lord Deincourt, who had a large eſtate in this part of England, and ſeventeen lordſhips in Lindſey, whereof Blankney (afterwards lord Widdrington's) was one, and his chief ſeat, not far from Lincoln. This might be the ſepulchre either of him, or of his ſon William, who, from the inſcription beforementioned, which was taken out of his ſepulchre, near, if not in, this tomb about 1670, and is ſtill to be ſeen in the dean and chapter's library at Lincoln, appears to have been buried there. Gilbert de Grant, earl of Lincoln, and conſtable of Lincoln caſtle, and his iſſue, were buried at Bardney abbey, which he refounded or reſtored, not far from Lincoln, and whereof they were patrons [1].

The beauteous Roſamond Clifford was cloſed up in leather [2]. Wood ſays, after the removal of her corpſe from the church at Godſtow into the churchyard or chapterhouſe, by order of Hugh biſhop of Lincoln, "her fleſh being quite pe-" riſhed, the chaſt ſiſters put all her bones in a perfumed lether bagge, which " bagg they encloſed in lead, and laid them againe, with her ſtone coffin, in the " church, under a large grave ſtone, on which ſtone, as it is ſaid, was engraven, " *Hic jacet, &c* [3]."

The corpſe of the lady of Sir William Truſſel, founder of Shotteſbrook college, 1337, was to be ſeen there done up in leather through the wall of the North tranſept [4].

In the South aile of the choir of Ely minſter, in the late repairs, were found, as Mr. Eſſex informed me, ſeveral leather fragments about a body which may have been that of Edward Tiptoft earl of Worceſter, buried here 3 Richard III.

The body of James III. of Scotland, who was ſlain at the ſiege of Roxburgh, was ſaid to be found wrapt in a bull's hide, in the caſtle of Roxburgh, in Cromwell's time [5].

A ſkeleton, wrapt in red leather, covered with lead, and a ſort of coronet on its head, was found a foot under ground, in Moulton church, Lincolnſhire, on new paving the choir [6].

Apollonius Rhodius III. 206. & Ælian Var. Hiſt. IV. c. 1. mention, that the Colchians ſew the corps of their deceaſed relations in the raw hides of oxen, and hang them up by a chain in the air.

In a tomb opened on clearing the ſite of Tyntern abbey was found a body intire, with leather buſkins and buttons on his coat, which all crumbled away on touching, as I was told, 1761. See a like inſtance at Tewkſbury, p. xxxvii.

On digging the foundation of a new room at Mr. Strut's ſeat at Hortonpriory large quantities of human bones were found, and ſeveral bodies buried in boots and ſpurs [7].

Mr. Peck [8] gives an account of a body found in a ſtone coffin, in the South aile of Southwell minſter, 1717, dreſt in cloth of ſilver tiſſue, with leather boots, a wand by his ſide, and on his breaſt ſomething like the cover of a ſilver cup, with an acorn or bunch of leaves on its top. He ſuppoſed this one of the

[1] Extract of a letter from M. Johnſon, eſq. to William Bogdani, Eſq. concerning an extraordinary interment : read at the Society of Antiquaries, Oct. 8, 1741. Printed in Archæologia, I. p. 31.
[2] See before, p. xlii.
[3] Wood's MS. notes on Godſtow, in Aſhmolean Muſeum.
[4] Hearne's Letter on Antiquities between Windſor and Oxford, p. 14.
[5] Abercrombie's Martial Achievements, II. 537.
[6] Spalding Society Minutes.
[7] Hutchins' Dorſet, II. 88.
[8] Deſid. Cur. book VI. N° 17.

family

family of Cauz, referring to that family in Dugdale's Baronage. It rather ſeems to have been ſome religious, with the chalice and croſier.

On making a vault for Mr. Calcraft in 176 . in St. Mary's church, at Warham, which had been the priory church, a great number of bones were found under the altar, and a body in a coffin with gloves on its hands and a belt round its waiſt, ſuppoſed a woman, but more probably a prior. Theſe were all buried in the yard, but many bones wheeled with the gravel to Stowborough cauſeway.

The following account of the funeral of WILLIAM twenty-ſecond abbot of St. Alban's, who died 1235, taken from Matthew Paris (vit. ab. S. Alb. 133), may ſerve to ſhew the practice on thoſe occaſions, before the council of Lateran. "Corpus "equidem cum in camera abbatis ubi obiit examinaretur exutum eſt & lotum; & "niſi die antecedente proxima raſus non extitiſſet utique raderetur corona & barba "ejus. Deinde intromiſſis non utique omnibus ſed maturis & diſcretis fratribus "& uno ſolo miniſtro ſeculari, viz. miniſtro ſacriſtæ qui officium anatomiæ perac- "turus erat, inciſione corpus apertum eſt a trachia uſque ad occiduam corporis "partem, & quicquid in corpore repertum eſt in quadam cuna repoſitum eſt ſale "conſperſum, et in cœmiterio non procul ab altare S. Stephani veneranter cum "benedictionibus & pſalmorum devotione eſt humatum; ubi proceſſu temporis "tumbula marmorea extitit adaptata. Corpus autem interius aceto lotum & "imbutum & multo ſale reſperſum & refutum. Et hoc ſic factum eſt circum- "ſpecte & prudenter ne corpus per triduum & amplius reſervandum tetrum "aliquem odorem olfacientibus generaret, & corpus tumulandum contrectantibus "aliquod offendiculum preſentaret. Portabatur corpus a camera quæ dicitur "abbatis ubi expiraverat in infirmariam; & ibidem pontificalibus eſt indutum: "mitra capiti appoſitum, manibus chirothecæ cum annulo & dextro ſub bra- "chio baculus conſuetus, manibus cancellatis, ſandalia in pedibus decenter "aptata. Et depoſito cooperculo a feretro, poſitum eſt corpus ſuper illud, & faſ- "ciis cautè ligatum ne caderet cum portaretur evolutum; prolatum eſt a lavatorio "ubi hæc parabantur ante oſtium infirmariæ, & demiſſum eſt ſicut corpora ali- "orum mortuorum, & loco in eodem, donec pro eo ſicut pro alio fratre defuncto "conſuetæ collectæ dicerentur cum prædictis vii pſalmis pœnitentialibus & om- "nibus quæ ſecundum conſuetudinem dici debuit dum corpus ornaretur. Pulſato "igitur ſollemni claſſico deportatum eſt corpus in eccleſiam ſequente conventu, "& pſallente conſueta, & illico vidente toto conventu & quolibet introducto con- "fractum eſt ſigillum abbatis uno martello ſuper unum graduum lapideorum "ante majus altare, ita ut tota celatura imaginis ſcil. & literarum deleretur. Ex- "inde non defuit pſalmodia die ac nocte ſolemnis & aſſidua & ad majus altare "cotidie miſſa ſolemnis ſicut ſolet fieri pro fratre mortuo prima exiſtente in albis; "& qui chorum tenebant in capis, accenſis cereis quamplurimis; & ſic uſque "in diem venerabiles exequiæ continuabantur. Fratres intima devotione pro "tanti paſtoris anima & pſallebant & miſſas quotidie corpore adhuc inhumato "celebrabant. Vocavimus igitur amicum noſtrum ſpecialem, abbatem ſcil. de "Waltham, Henricum nomine, ut ſanctus ad ſancti corpus tumulandum venire "charitatis & vicinitatis intuitu non omitteret. Et ipſe abbas pontificalibus redi- "mitus, corpus pontificalibus ſimiliter adornatum, baculo alterato, ſolemniter "valde toto aſſiſtente conventu veſtito in medio capitulo tumulavit."

A ſimilar account is given of the burial of John Wodnyſburgh, prior of Chriſt Church, Canterbury, Feb. 29, 1428. "Mortuo igitur predicto vene- "rabili patre corpus ejus per cuſtodes camere ſue ex integro lotum & mundatum "eſt, & barba ejus raſa. Deinde ſtamino familiari, botis, caligis, & cuculla ex "integro totaliter novus veſtitus & indutus eſt. Poſtea amictu, alba, cingulo,

"dal-

"dalmatica, ſandaliis & planeta reveſtitus, & mitratus, tenens in manu bacu-"lum paſtorale, in capella prioris, ſic infulatus, aperta facie de mane decenter "collocatum eſt, ubi exequie mortuorum & miſſa de requiem pro eo [1]."

When the workmen were erecting the new ſcreen at Glouceſter choir, 1741, they found in the paſſage three abbats, buried near the ſurface of the ground, in ſtone coffins, *in pontificalibus*, part of their gloves and apparel remaining. Another ſtone coffin, with a ſword, a little pewter chalice, and a ſtaff; two ſculls in it, which I ſuppoſe belonged to Sir Richard Gamage and wife, buried near his brother, abbot Gamage, who was laid near the door opening to the cloiſters, and probably was one of the three then found, and all buried again where they were found. Before this alteration there were five other large graveſtones found, robbed of their braſſes, three of which belonged to ſome of the abbots [2].

Abbot Crokeſley, buried in Weſtminſter abbey, 1258, was diſcovered, in the time of Henry VI. firm and freſh, in his maſs habit [3].

Abbot Eſtney, who died 1498, and was buried in the South ſide of St. John's chapel there, was found, in digging near his tomb 1702, intire, cloathed in crimſon ſilk, in a large coffin lined with lead, the lid of which was carefully cloſed again, and the body left untouched [4].

St. Dunſtan, in his pontificals; ſee before, p. xl.

In ranſacking St. Paul's cathedral, ſeveral biſhops of London were found lying in their proper habits, with mitres on their heads and croſiers in their hands [5].

In new paving the great North tranſept of Lincoln minſter, 1782, a body was found wrapt in a dreſs which came no lower than the knees, where it ended in a ſort of roll like that of a roll-up ſtocking, and was wrapt about the thighs ſo as to leave the ſpace between them open. The hands and head were wrapt up in it. It appeared to be made of ſattin, or a ſtuff like corderoy. The face, or at leaſt part of it, was covered by it, though by the fall or ſhrinking of the neck from the raiſed part of the ſtone coffin, on which the head originally lay about three inches higher than the bottom of the other part of the coffin, which was a foot deep, the lower part of the jaw, &c. appeared to have been diſplaced, and the dreſs perhaps removed by the ſame means; or it may have formed a ſort of ruff, or falling collar, or cape, from the inner part of the dreſs, as it appeared of a different and fine ſpecies of ſtuff. There was beſides a kind of ſtanding up collar or border, viſible in part of the drawing, round the upper part of which appears to be a different part of the dreſs, over which this other ſpread. The grain of the ſtuff was fine, and on a nearer view there ſeemed a difference between the two ſides, the threads being bare and more viſible on one ſide than the other, as if the materials had been of the velvet kind. The plate annexed repreſents it very accurately in this reſpect. The ſtone that formed the cover, though nine inches thick, the croſs and lines or ribs of which are here repreſented, had been broken towards the bottom, and the duſt, &c. had got in there, and covered the remaining bones of the legs, except ſo far as marked in the print of the left leg. The head was entirely reduced to that ſort of appearance which a decayed pyrites has, a purple kind of aſhes, with a white efflorescence in it, and when it was firſt laid open there was a ſtrong pitchy or bituminous ſmell from it. There was little appearance of moiſture in the coffin, though it lay in a part which has occaſionally been overflowed in

[1] Reg. Moloſh. 6 Hen. VI. in Peck's Deſid. Cur. VII. IV. p. 245. ex exempl. MS. P. Le Neve Norroy, penes editorem.
[2] Rudder's Gloc. p. 175.
[3] Dart's Weſtminſter abbey, II. xxiv.
[4] Widmore, p. 119. ex Batteley's Coll. MSS.
[5] Dugdale's St. Paul's, p. 48.

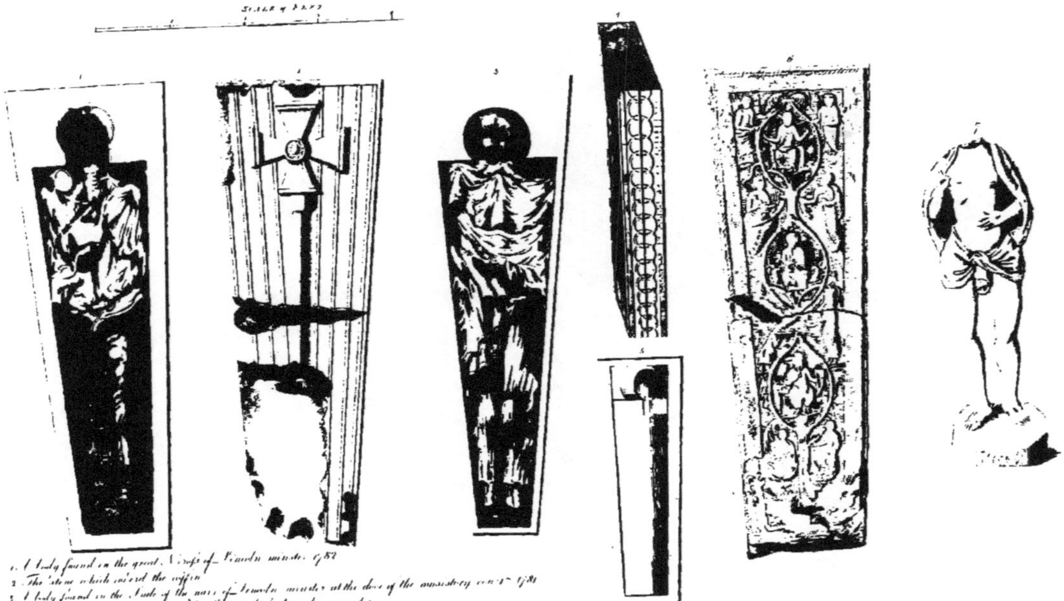

1. A body found in the great Cross of Lincoln minster 1782
2. The stone which covered the coffin
3. A body found in the Aisle of the nave of Lincoln minster at the door of the consistory court 1781
4. A coffin found on the outside of the East end of Lincoln minster
5. Another found in the same church
6. A coffin lid in the Aisle of Lincoln minster.
7. The statue of the crucified child formerly in the Aisle of the choir of Lincoln minster see p 15 n 31

hafty and violent fhowers of rain. The cover had formerly made part of the common floor, as the crofs, &c. carried evident marks of being worn, and there was now only a very thin ftone, or rather layer of common ftones over it, to make it level with the late pavement. The chalice and patin were either common pewter or that fort of mixture which the workmen call latten, and were decayed on that fide where they toucht the body. There was not the leaft trace of infcription, that Dr. Gordon could difcover, nor had he conjectured to whom it belonged. The oldeft and almoft only monument mentioned here in Dugdale and Willis's plans of this church, is that of Dean Lexington, who died 1272, but he had an infcription given by Willis. We know of no Bifhop buried in this tranfept, though Bifhop Dalderby lay in the oppofite or South one. But from an attentive examination of all the particulars with which the præcentor favoured me, together with a piece of the wrapper itfelf, which was of a dingy yellow colour, I am inclined to conjecture this was fome dignitary of the church buried in his cope. Inftances of this fort are not wanting at Peterborough, where the copes taken out of the graves are ftill fhewn in the library.

In new paving the South aile of the nave of the fame cathedral, 1781, a ftone coffin was opened in prefence of the fub-dean and precentor. On removing the cover the intire figure of a man was found lying in it in full robes, with very little appearance of decay, except that the under jaw had fallen down and perifhed. In the upper jaw was a tooth remaining very white and perfect. The drefs was very full and flowing, and had the refemblance of being plaited, or done into ribs, or narrow folds, down the leg and thigh, which feemed to retain their full fize and juft proportion. On opening fome of the folds of the drapery there was a degree of moifture, if it might not be called a kind of liquid, of the colour of coffee grounds; but it evaporated almoft inftantly. On the infide of the robe, where it had touched the body, there adhered a kind of pitchy or waxy fubftance, as if the body had been covered over with fomething of that fort before the drefs had been put on. The outer part of the drefs might feem to have been a cape, and probably befides that there was an inner garment of the caffock form: as the cuffs where the hands croft were clearly of a different ftuff and make from the other. There did not appear to have been any thing on the head; but there were fhoes or flippers of leather on the feet, with a part of the robe, like a flounce, fpread over them, almoft to the toes. Under the right arm, or at leaft under the drefs of it, towards the fhoulder, was laid a fmall chalice of latten. The coffin was placed very near the furface, with three large rough ftones, about four or five inches thick, to cover it, and immediately on them, with only the neceffary fand between them was laid the common floor of the church. There was no other graveftone, or the leaft trace of infcription, to afcertain either the name of the perfon buried, or the date of his interment. It was probably one of the prebendaries or dignitaries of the church. By the ill ufe that was made of the permiffion given to view the body the robe was almoft intirely pulled to pieces and carried away, and the fubftitute for the flefh, whatever it was that filled and fupported it, on being uncovered and expofed to the air, mouldered away in the manner and with much the fame appearance as a decayed piece of pyrites or charcoal afhes. The infide of the head alfo, where it was vifible from the falling of the under jaw, had the fame appearance of being burnt [*].

[*] Letter from Dr. Gordon to Sir Jofeph Banks, Bart. dated April 27, 1781.

The body of Thomas Thirlby, bishop of Ely, who was deprived of his see by act of parliament, 1559, and dying in confinement at Lambeth, 1570, was buried in the middle of the chancel of the parish church there, was found on making a grave for the late archbishop Cornwallis. His leaden coffin had all the appearance of having never been covered with wood, the earth around it being perfectly dry and crumbly. It was six feet four inches long, eighteen inches broad, and eight inches and a half deep. The corpse was wrapt in fine linen, was moist, and had evidently been preserved in some sort of pickle, which still retained a volatile smell, not unlike that of hartshorn. The flesh was preserved and had the appearance of a mummy, the face was perfect, and the limbs flexible, the beard of a remarkable length, and beautifully white. The linen and woollen garments were all well preserved. The cap, which was of silk, adorned with point lace, had probably been black, but the colour was discharged. It was in fashion like that represented in the pictures of archbishop Juxon. The hat a slouched one, with strings to it, which was under the left arm, was of the same materials as are used at present, but the crown was sewed in. It lay by the side of the body, as did the stockings, made of white worsted with green feet. Great care was taken that every thing was properly replaced in the coffin, and the remains of archbishop Cornwallis were deposited in the same vault [1].

Ralph Thoresby had a sort of mummy found at or near Chester, given him by Henry Prescot, esq. Whether from the nature of the soil where it was found or by embalming he had not heard: but some ground he observes is of such a nature, and particularly a sandy desert in Africa, that human bodies laid in the same, do not in the least corrupt, but become like mummies [2].

When St. John's church at Dunwich was taken down, on raising and taking up a plain fair gravestone in the chancel, next under it was a great hollow stone, hollowed after the fashion of a man, for a man to lie in, and therein a man lying, with a pair of boots on his legs, the fore part of them picked after a strange fashion, and a pair of chalices [3], of coarse metal, lying on his breast; which was thought to be one of the bishops of Dunwich; but when they touched and stirred the same dead body it fell, and went all to powder and dust [4].

King John was, by his own desire, buried in a monk's cowl, and is supposed to lie in a leaden coffin, which was discovered, but not opened, under his monument [5].

Richard Peche bishop of Coventry and Litchfield was buried 1182, in the habit of a canon regular, in the convent of St. Thomas at Stratford [6].

In the chancel at Ickleford, c. Herts, was taken up, about the beginning of this century, a stone coffin, in which some person had been buried in his habit, probably a monk. The soles of his shoes were remaining, and a piece of leather about eight inches long, with gilding on one side, perhaps one of the insignia of his order or his family [7].

On repairing Worcester cathedral, 1752, on taking off the top of a tomb, the inscription of which was obliterated, except the date, 1296, the bones were found firm, most of them adhering together in the same posture as when interred, and about the scull and shoulders appeared something like a coarse sacking or sack-cloth, very fresh [8].

[1] Gent. Mag. LIII. p. 179.
[2] Duc. Leod. p. 430.
[3] Or rather a chalice and patten.
[4] Weever. p. 720.
[5] See p. 37.
[6] Mon. Ang. III. p. 220.
[7] Salmon, Herts. p. 174.
[8] Newberry, Description of England, X. 94.

In 1653, in making a grave near the altar in Sherborne church, a grave ſtone was removed, and under it was found, in a ſtone coffin, a body cloathed in robes of purple coloured cloth, with a croſier lying by it: the robes and croſier were taken away, and the corpſe reinterred. The inſcription on the grave ſtone was illegible [1]. It probably belonged to ſome abbot of this houſe.

The ſame year produced the remarkable diſcovery of Childeric's remains at Tournay, of which hereafter.

In 1674 was found deep under ground in the iſle of Athelney, a tomb wherein was a ſcull, ſome bones, earth, and duſt, and ſome cloathing, of which Mr. Paſchal ſent a fragment to Mr. Aubrey [2]. This was probably ſome abbot of this Monaſtery.

On making a vault for Mr. Calcraft, in 176 , in St. Mary's church, at Warham, which had been the priory church, a great number of bones were found under the altar, and a body in a coffin with gloves on its hands and a belt round its waiſt; ſuppoſed a woman, but more probably a prior. Theſe were all buried in the yard, but many bones wheeled with the gravel to Stowborough cauſeway.

King Ethelbert's body, on its removal from the river Lugg, into which his murderers had thrown it, was wrapt in royal fine linen, and conveyed to Fernley, in a ſmall carriage. *Sindone regali involutum in quodam curriculo extulerunt* [3].

The body of Sebba, one of our Saxon kings, was found in St. Paul's, curiouſly embalmed with ſweet odours, and clothed in rich robes [4].

On lifting up the lid of Edward the Firſt's coffin the royal corpſe was found wrapped up within a large ſquare mantle, of ſtrong, coarſe, and thick linen cloth, diaper'd, of a dull, pale, yellowiſh brown colour, and waxed on its under ſide.

The head and face were entirely covered with a *ſudarium*, or face-cloth, of crimſon ſarcenet, the ſubſtance whereof was ſo much periſhed as to have a cobweb-like feel, and the appearance of fine lint. This *ſudarium* was formed into three folds, probably in imitation of the napkin wherewith our Saviour is ſaid to have wiped his face when led to his crucifixion, and which the Romiſh church poſitively aſſures us conſiſted of the like number of folds, on each of which the reſemblance of his countenance was then inſtantly impreſſed.

When the folds of the external wrapper were thrown back, and the *ſudarium* removed, the corpſe was diſcovered richly habited, adorned with enſigns of royalty, and almoſt intire, notwithſtanding the length of time that it had been entombed.

Its innermoſt covering ſeemed to have been a very fine linen cerecloth, dreſſed cloſe to every part of the body, and ſuperinduced with ſuch accuracy and exactneſs, that the fingers and thumbs of both the hands had each of them a ſeparate and diſtinct envelope of that material. The face, which had a ſimilar covering cloſely fitted thereto, retained its exact form, although part of the fleſh appeared to be ſomewhat waſted.

Next above the before-mentioned cerecloth was a dalmatic, or tunic, of red ſilk damaſk; upon which lay a ſtole of thick white tiſſue, about three inches in breadth, croſſed over the breaſt, and extending on each ſide downwards, nearly as low as the wriſt, where both ends were brought to croſs each other. On this ſtole were placed, at about the diſtance of ſix inches from each other, quatrefoils of philligree-work in metal gilt with gold, elegantly chaſed in

[1] Hutchins' Dorſet, II. 381.
[2] Aubrey's Miſcellanies, 1714, p. 54.
[3] Brompton, p. 753.
[4] Dugdale's St. Paul's, p. 48.

figure,

figure, and ornamented with five pieces of beautiful tranſparent glaſs, or paſte, ſome cut, and others rough, ſet in raiſed ſockets. The largeſt of theſe pieces is in the centre of the quatrefoil; and each of the other four is fixed near to the angle: ſo that all of them together form the figure of a quincunx. The falſe ſtones differ in colour. Some are ruby; others a deep amethyſt: ſome again are ſapphire; others white; and ſome a ſky-blue.

The intervals between the quatrefoils on the ſtole are powdered with an immenſe quantity of very ſmall white beads, reſembling pearls [1], drilled, and tacked down very near each other, ſo as to compoſe an embroidery of moſt elegant form, and not much unlike that which is commonly called, The True-lover's Knot. Theſe beads, or pearls, are all of the ſame ſize, and equal to that of the largeſt pin's head. They are of a ſhining, ſilver-white hue; but not ſo pellucid as necklace-beads and mock-pearls uſually are.

Over theſe habits is the royal mantle, or pall, of rich crimſon ſattin, faſtened on the left ſhoulder with a magnificent *fibula* of metal gilt with gold, and compoſed of two joints pinned together by a moveable *acus*, and reſembling a croſs-garnet hinge. This *fibula* is four inches in length, richly chaſed, and ornamented with four pieces of red, and four of blue tranſparent paſte, ſimilar to thoſe on the quatrefoils, and twenty-two beads or mock-pearls. Each of theſe paſtes and mock-pearls is ſet in a raiſed and chaſed ſocket. The head of the *acus* is formed by a long piece of uncut tranſparent blue paſte, ſhaped like an acorn, and fixed in a chaſed ſocket.

The lower joint of this *fibula* appears to be connected with the ſtole, as well as with the chlamys; ſo that the upper part of each of the lappets or ſtraps of the ſtole being thereby brought nearly into contact with the edge of the royal mantle, thoſe ſtraps form, in appearance, a guard or border thereto.

The corpſe, from the waiſt downward, is covered with a large piece of rich figured cloth of gold, which lies looſe over the lower part of the tunic, thighs, legs, and feet, and is tucked down behind the ſoles of the latter. There did not remain any appearance of gloves: but on the back of each hand, and juſt below the knuckle of the middle finger, lies a quatrefoil, of the ſame metal as thoſe on the ſtole, and like them ornamented with five pieces of tranſparent paſte; with this difference, however, that the centre-piece in each quatrefoil is larger, and ſeemingly of a more beautiful blue, than thoſe on any of the quatrefoils on the ſtole.

The feet, with the toes, ſoles, and heels, ſeemed to be perfectly intire; but whether they have ſandals on them is uncertain, as the cloth tucked over them was not removed [1].

The princeſs Joan, wife of Edward the Black Prince, dying at Wallingford, 9 Richard II. was wrapt in cerecloth, and being put in lead, was kept till the king her ſon's return from Scotland, when ſhe was buried at the Grey-friars, Stamford [2].

Elizabeth Tudor, ſecond daughter of Henry VII. was cered by the *wax-chandler* [4].

The corpſe of prince Arthur was *coyled*, well cered, and conveniently dreſſed with ſpices, and other ſweet ſtuff. This was ſo ſufficiently done that it needed not lead, but was cheſted [5].

[1] Several of the gentlemen preſent at opening the coffin thought them to be real ſeed pearls; but all of them being exactly of the ſame ſize, hue, and ſhape, militates againſt that opinion.
[2] Walſingham, Hiſt. Ang. p. 316.
[3] Archæol. III. 380—385.
[4] Dart's Weſtm. Abb. vol. II. p. 28.
[5] Interment of prince Arthur, printed at the end of Leland's Collectanea, 1770. V. 374.

The

In a MS. ceremonial of the funeral of queen Mary, daughter of Henry VIII. in the College of Arms[1] we are told that, after her departure she was *perussed* by the lords of the council and ladyes of the realme, and after opened, *cered*, and *tramelled* in this manner. First her Grace's physician, with the surgeons, did open her, and take out all her bowels, with her heart; then the clerk *of the spicery*, with the *officers of the chaundry*, came and *cered* the said royal corpse with linen cloth waxed, and with a number of spices very costly. After which the corpse was coffened, and then the serjeant plumber inclosed the same in lead.

Archbishop Parker allowed £. 23. for cering and dressing his body[2].

The following charges in the accounts of the chaplain of Cecilia widow of William Talmache of Hawsted, c. Suffolk, 1281, shew that no small cost was bestowed on the lady's own person. To the chandler *(candelario)* of Bury St. Edmund's in part, ix*s.* ij*d.* To John Sencle of the same, for wax and divers spices, iiij*l.* iiij*s.* ij*d.* To Alexander Westlee of the same, for fine linen and silk, and other necessaries for attiring the lady's body *(pro sindone et serico et aliis necessariis pro corpore domine attiliando[3])* xxxij*s*[4].

The *chandler* was the person who made and applied the cerecloth.

The examples alledged will illustrate the meaning and design of the last three articles. The silk was probably designed as an envelope for the corpse after it was embalmed.

The directions for the burial of Edward IV. say, that the body must, on its first laying out, be *bamed* (embalmed) wrapped in laun, or *raynes*, if it may be gotten, an hosyn, cherte, and a perer of shone of red leather, his surcote of cloth, his cap of estate on his head. "And when he may not godeley longer "endure, take him away, and bowel him, and then estsones bame him, wrappe "him in *raynes* wele tramelled with cords of silk, then in *garteryn tramelled*, "then in cloth of gold, and so in velvet well tramelled, and then led him, and "coffen him[5]."

The whole external covering of an Egyptian mummy dissected by Dr. Hadley, 1763, consisted of several folds of broad pieces of linen cloth, made to adhere together by some viscous matter, which had not yet lost its property, and the whole had received an additional degree of strength and substance from the coat of paint laid on. There were not the least remains of hair or integuments on any part of the head. Some parts of the scull were quite bare, particularly about the temporal bones, which had the natural polish and appeared in every respect like the bones of an ordinary scull. To other parts of the scull adhered several folds of pitched linen, which together were near half an inch thick. On removing them they were found to have been in actual contact with the bones, so that the integuments must have been taken away before the wrappers were at first applied.

The outward painted covering being removed, nothing but linen fillets were to be seen, which inclosed the whole mummy. These fillets were of different breadths; the greater part about an inch and half, those about the feet much broader. They were torn longitudinally; those few that had a selvage having it on one side only. The uppermost fillets were of a degree of fineness nearly equal to what is now sold in the shops for two shillings and four pence per yard;

1 Printed at the end of Leland's Collect. 1770. V. 309.

2 Appendix to the supplement to Somner's Canterbury, p. 19.

3 Du Cange has attilium and attilamentum for the attelage, equipage, or harnois of horses, and other beasts of draught, and of ships. The verb does not occur. I know not how to translate it better.

4 Hist. of Hawsted, by Sir J. Cullum, Bart.

5 Archæol. I. 348.

under the name of long lawn, and were woven ſomething after the manner of Ruſſia ſheeting. The fillets were of a brown colour, and in ſome meaſure rotten. Theſe outward fillets ſeemed to owe their colour to having been ſteeped in ſome gummy ſolution, as the inner ones were in pitch. The fillets immediately under the painted covering lay in a tranſverſe direction. Under theſe, which were many double, they lay oblique diagonally from the ſhoulders to the *ilia*. Under theſe the fillets were broader, ſome nearly three inches, and lay longitudinally from the neck to the feet, and alſo from the ſhoulders down the ſides; on which there was a remarkable thickneſs of theſe longitudinal fillets: under theſe they were again tranſverſe, and under theſe again oblique. The fillets in general externally did not adhere to each other: but though pieces of a conſiderable length could be taken off entire, yet from the age ſo tender was the texture of the cloth that it was impoſſible regularly to unroll them. As the outward fillets were removed, thoſe that next preſented themſelves had been evidently ſteeped in pitch, and were in general coarſer in folds, and more irregularly laid on, as they were more diſtant from the ſurface. The inner filleting of all was ſo impregnated with pitch as to form with it one hard black brittle maſs, and had been burned nearly to a coal. On breaking this it appeared in many places as if filled with a white efflorescence, like that obſervable on the outſide of pyrites which have been expoſed to the air. This efflorescence however had nothing ſaline to the taſte, and did not diſſolve in water; but inſtantly diſappeared on bringing it near enough to the fire to be ſlightly heated, and was ſoluble in ſpirit of wine.

The lower extremities were wrapped ſeparately in fillets to nearly their natural ſize, and then bound together, the interſtices being rammed full of pitched rags. On cutting through the fillets on the thighs the bones were found inveſted with a thin coat of pitch, and the filleting was bound immediately on this. The tibia and fibula of each leg were found alſo wrapt in the ſame manner, and the bones in actual contact with the pitch, except in one or two places, where the pitch was ſo very thin that the cloth appeared to adhere to the bone itſelf. The feet were filleted in the ſame manner, being firſt bound ſeparately, and then wrapt together. On cutting into the filleting of the left foot they were found to encloſe a *bulbous root*, the appearance of which was very freſh, and part of the ſhining ſkin came off with a flake of the dry brittle filleting, with which it had been bound down. It ſeemed to have been in contact with the fleſh: the baſe of the root lay toward the heel.

If the fleſh of this mummy had not been previouſly removed, though its appearance would have been entirely changed, yet the filleting could never have been found in contact with the bones. From this laſt circumſtance it is moſt likely that the body, excepting the feet, had been reduced to a ſkeleton before it was laid up. It is alſo pretty certain that it muſt have been kept ſome time in boiling pitch, both before and after ſome of the larger of the innermoſt filletings were laid on. The feet ſeem to have been ſwathed, at leaſt in part, before they were committed to the hot pitch, and this ſeems to have pervaded the bandages, the fleſh, and the bones.

A great variety of experiments were made on this pitchy matter. The reſult of them all tended to prove that it had not the leaſt reſemblance to *aſphaltus*, but was certainly a vegetable reſinous ſubſtance.

From this examination, and the relation of various authors, it appears that the Egyptians uſed different materials for this purpoſe; and though Herodotus and Diodorus Siculus have given us reaſon to expect to find the bodies in a much more perfect ſtate than we ever do meet with them; yet, on the other hand, it

it

is evident from the foot of this mummy, and from the accounts which Monf. Henelle [1] and Count Caylus [2] have given us, that all the flefhy parts were not always previoufly deftroyed [3].

This account has a wonderful conformity with the defcription of the mummy examined by Gryfius, at Wratiflaw, near a century before. It appears, that under the upper painted cover of plaifter or clay from the chin to the bottom of the belly was a number of bandages of brown unwhitened linen, bound on with hempen cords, which being cut, the bandages were unfwathed, and found to confift of different lengths of from two to three *cubits*, and in breadth four or five fingers. Thefe were held together, and fometimes croft by others thinner fcarce a finger's breadth. Both feemed to be rather torn according to the grain of the cloth than cut. The texture was not inferior to our modern weaving, and the thread what we call the *middle* fort. The warp refifted when attempted to be torn; but the woof yielded. After unrolling twenty folds, which lay one on another, an intire piece of linen prefented itfelf reaching from the neck to the feet. Under this were thin bandages fcarce one third of an inch broad croft over each other, fwathing the arms and feet tight; but the breaft and back more loofely. On removing thefe all the lower part of the belly fell to a brownifh duft. The falfe ribs and lower vertebræ were loofe: the upper part of the leg bones bare, but the thorax, belly to the navel, thighs, and legs, remained firm: the feet, though feparated from the ancles, retained the mufcles and nails. Under the middle of the right foot was found a *flower* of the lotus, betony, or leek, the broad leaves at the bottom, and the narrower at the point, clofed like thofe of an hop flower or artichoke. No fuch thing occurred under the left foot; but under each fide, at the loins, was a large ftout palm leaf, which, except fome alterations in colour, appeared as frefh as if gathered the day before; and near the groin lay a little ftick or cane, longer than a man's little finger [4]. The arms were doubled up at the elbow, fo that each hand could touch the chin. The left hand was clencht, the right open. The head was covered with a ftuff of thicker grain, and in all refpects different. This being cut open, difcovered the face covered with a new coat of bitumen like glazing or white of eggs. The hair was inclofed in a net of finer linen, and was black, curled, greafy, without ornament, difficult to be pulled up, and not exceeding half a finger's length. The forehead rather low: there were traces of the eyelids and eyelafhes; the eyes prominent, the nofe depreft, the noftrils ftopt with cotton and the fame kind of ointment as the thorax and belly; the mouth very wide, the lips having been removed, and the cavity filled with fweet fcented duft; the teeth, thirty-two in number, complete, white, and perfectly beautiful; the ears not at all wafted, nor the cheeks fallen, but the whole face kept firm by a mixture of pitch and afphaltus [5]. The body, without the wrappers, weighed ten pounds and a half, and meafured three feet eight inches, the arms to the wrift one foot two inches and a half, and to the extremity of the fingers one foot eight inches and a half. It was fuppofed the body of a young woman [6].

[1] Mem. of the Royal Academy of Sciences for 1750.
[2] Hift. de l'Acad. des Infc. & Belles Lettres, vol. XXIII. p. 120, &c.
[3] Phil. Tranf. vol. LIV. p. 1—14.
[4] So Frofper Alpinus defcribes branches of rofemary found in the cheft of a mummy. Rerum Ægyptiacarum, &c. cum notis Weffelingii, 1735, p. 36.
[5] *Piffafphalto folidata.*
[6] Mumiæ Wratiflavienfes. Wratiflav. 1662, 12°. p. 17—51.

 From

From the foregoing accounts of the Egyptian mummy I extract in this place merely what relates to the *Envelope*; leaving the discussion of the composition of the embalming matter as foreign to my present purpose.

Statius says, the corpse of Alexander the Great was done up in *honey*[1]. So were Agesipolis[2] and Agesilaus[3], kings of Sparta; but Plutarch[4] says, the latter, for want of honey, was done up in *wax*. The Ptolomies, and Antony and Cleopatra were all embalmed[5].

Isaac Casaubon, in some MS collections cited by Hearne[6], mentions the discovery of a female body in the Via Latina at Rome in the 16th century, lying embalmed in a marble chest, the shape and colour so pliant and well preserved that it seemed but lately buried. The flesh pitted at the touch, and if pulled up resumed its place. The joints were flexible, and there was no other smell but that of the ingredients used to embalm it. The hair was on the head, and nothing but the brain and intrails wanting. After it had been viewed by a great resort of people in the capitol, and was on the point of ministring an occasion of superstition, the Pope (Innocent VIII.) ordered it to be taken away, and no one knew where it was deposited.

Mr. Valtravers informed the Society of Antiquaries, 1772, that in some tombs opened in Saxony a few years before the corpses were found enveloped in a brown clay, in which their skin and bones were preserved very fresh, though buried in the time of the antient Saxons, who could not be subdued by the Romans. That clay formed into a paste round the body, near half an inch thick, is now full of iron ore, and hard as stone, of which he brought over and exhibited a specimen.

Human skeletons deposited in red clay and covered over with thin slabs of stone, on which were heaped larger stones and clay, have been found in the Roman station at Wroxeter, co. Salop.

Lydgate, with the chymical ideas of his time, anachronically describes Hector's body embalmed and exhibited to view, in a chapel in the high church at Troy, with the resemblance of real life, by means of a precious liquor circulating through every part in golden tubes, artificially disposed, and operating on the principles of vegetation. Before the body were four inextinguishable lamps in golden sockets[7].

Thomas Grey marquis of Dorset, who died 17 Henry VII. was buried in the middle of the chancel at Astley, c. Warwick, where, on the repair of that church, about 1607, his body was found embalmed and wrapt in cerecloth many double, in a large and long coffin of wood, which, at the desire of some, and earnest motion of others, being burst open, was, at the cutting open of the cerecloth, viewed perfect and sound, nothing corrupted, the flesh of the body nothing perished or hardened, but in colour, proportion, and softness, like any ordinary corpse newly interred; his body large of length, six feet wanting four inches; his hair yellow, his face broad, which might seem to be thus preserved by the strong embalming thereof. Mr. Burton, the Leicestershire Antiquary, was present, and saw this[8].

1 Duc & ad Emathios manes ubi belliger orbis
Conditur *Hyblaeo* perfusus *nectare* durat. Sylv. III. 2.
2 Xenophon, Hist. Graec. l. IV.
3 Diod. Sic. L. XV.
4 In Agesilao. 5 Dio. LI.
6 Spicilegium ad Gul. Neubrig. p. 796.
7 Warton's Hist. of English Poetry, II 98.
8 Burton's Leicestershire, p. 51. Dugd. Warw. p. 115.

Gertrude

Gertrude marchioness of Exeter, who died 1558, was found wrapt in cere-cloth, in her tomb at Wimborn minster, when it was opened some years since out of curiosity, and repaired [1].

Sir Lewys Clifford, in the beginning of the 15th century, ordered by his will, "yt on his stinking careyne be nether laid clothe of golde ne of sylke; but "a blake cloth; & a taper at his head & another at his feet; ne stone ne other "thing, wherby eny man may witt where my stinking carene leyyeth [2]."

Dr. Bathurst Dean of Wells, and President of Trinity College, Oxford, who died 1704, directed "his mouth and nostrils to be finely closed up with a plais-"ter of diachylon, and his whole head wrapt in cerecloth, and no cover to his "coffin, but a black pall of woollen stuff, loosely nailed on, and hanging loose "down [3]."

Hearne says, it was the custom so late as Elizabeth's time to bury only in windingsheets in the ground [4].

That it was customary to bury royal personages with crowns on appears from the drawings of the funeral of the Offas, in a MS of Matthew Paris, Cotton Library, Nero, D. 1. engraved by Mr. Strutt, I. pl. 45 and 66. or it may be only put to denote a royal funeral.

In digging the foundations of a new house for the governor of the isle of Rè, 1731, was found a crown of copper set with precious stones, and ornamented with four fleurs de lis, and four triangles alternately. Part of the scull adhered to the rim of the crown. It was supposed to have belonged to Eudes duke of Aquitaine, who founded a monastery here, and dying A. D. 735, was there buried with his wife Valtrude. Chilperic II. and Rainfroi his mair de palais sent this duke a crown among other presents, to engage him to join them against Charles Martel [5].

The famous horn of Orlando, or Roland, was buried with him, at his feet, as was his sword at his head. *Mucronem ipsius ad caput & tubam eburneam ad pedes*, says his Romance. The figure of a horn at the right side of the head of one of the statues over the great West door of the church of the royal abbey of St. Magdalen at Chateaudun was commonly supposed to point out this hero, though Monf. Lancelot, who shewed drawings of the several statues there to the Academy of Inscriptions, 1733 [6], inclines to refer it to Charlemagne, expressive of his passion for hunting. It may be doubted if this be not too far fetched, especially in this place, where the different statues certainly have attributes more expressive. The horn on funeral monuments generally points out the office of forester, as the stone figure in Glenton churchyard, c. Northampton, and the brass figure in Baldock south aile.

The discovery in May, 1653, of the remains of Childeric king of the Franks, who died A. D. 481, and was buried at Tournay, affords so many interesting particulars in the history of antient inhumation, that I cannot forbear giving an abstract of the copious book published on the subject by Dr. Chiflet first physician to the archduke Leopold, who, as soon as he was informed of the discovery, directed him to draw up an account of it. Some workmen digging to the depth of seven or eight feet to the solid rock, to rebuild certain ruinous houses adjoining to the churchyard of St. Brice's church at Tournay, threw out a gold fibula, and a rotten leathern bag [7], probably fastened to the

[1] Hutchins' Dorset. II. 92.
[2] Burn's Westmorland.
[3] His Life, by Warton, p. 191.
[4] Spicilegium ad Gul. Neubrig. p. 796.
[5] See Mem. de L'Acad. des Inscr. vol. V. p. 176. 12mo.
[6] Mem. de l'Acad. des Inscr. V. 285.
[7] *Nidus ex aluta* putri.

king's belt, containing near an hundred gold medals of the emperors Theodosius, Valentinian, Marcian, Leo, Zeno, Julianus Nepos, Basiliscus, and his son Marcus, and Theodorus; near 200 silver Roman coins, too much defaced to be made out, and therefore thrown away; many pieces of iron rusted by the moisture of the ground; two human sculls, one larger than the other, and the bones of a human skeleton lying at its length. In the space of five feet they discovered a variety of other articles; a sword of two feet and a half long, of such well tempered steel that at the first touch it fell all to pieces; its hilt, grasp, and the gold plate of its scabbard; the point of the belt gold, studded with jewels; a stylus, an ox's head, which had served as an ornament to his horse's bridle (not, as Chiflet hastily conjectured, as an object of worship[1], and made two calves heads on the hilt of the sword for the same reason[2]); above three hundred figures of bees, out of a great number carried away in the rubbish, one needle, several fibulae, hooks of different sizes, nails, studs, threads, bullae; all of gold, set with a number of carbuncles[3]; and as if intended to ascertain the whole, the king's gold seal, with his bust in flowing hair and breast plate, and holding a spear in his right hand, and circumscribed CHILDIRICI REGIS; and another circular ring of solid gold, which Chiflet supposed his wedding ring. They also found his horse's scull, part of his shoe, and some gold studs of his belt, part of a rusty lance, and a battle ax of the kind known by the name of *Francisca*[4], and some gold threads as of his garment.

Dr. Chiflet conceives, that Childeric was buried in a *wooden* coffin bound round with iron, pieces of which were found adhering so close to the wood that it was difficult to separate them[5], and that a barrow was thrown up over him. Thus, says an old genealogy at Brussels cited by him, the four earlier kings of the Franks, Pharamond, Clodion, Merovæus, and Childeric, died pagans, and were buried after the fashion of the barbarians. So Tacitus, speaking of Poppæa, says, her corpse was not burnt after the Roman fashion, but opened[6] and embalmed, after the manner of foreign princes[7], and laid in the tomb of the Julian family. It was the opinion of Wendelin, one of the canons of Tournay, that Childeric's tomb was 150 feet to the north on the left hand of the Roman road leading from that city to the river Scheld, the area between it and the road being now occupied by the parish church and churchyard of St. Brice[8].

The Roman laws seem to have discountenanced the depositing of *ornaments* with the dead: "*Si quid ad corpus custodiendum vel etiam* commendandum *factum* "*sit, vel si quid in* marmor *vel* vestem *collocandum*, hoc funeris est. *Non au-* "*tem oportet* ornamenta *cum corporibus* condi, *nec quid aliud hujusmodi quod* "*homines simplicioris faciunt*," says Ulpian[9]. But Servius says, "*In antiquis* "*disciplinis relatum est quæ quisque* ornamenta *consecutus esset ut ea mortuum cum* "*condecorarent*[10]."

The fathers condemn in the strongest terms the wrapping up the dead in garments of silk and gold[11].

But to come nearer the time of Childeric. Chilperic buried his brother Sigebert king of Austrasia in the village of Lambros *vestitum*, as Gregory of Tours calls it[12]; or, as the Gesta regum Francorum express it[13], *vestitum vestibus*

[1] P. 142. [2] P. 202. [3] *Pyropi*.
[4] Isidor. Orig. xviii. 6. Montfaucon says it was *so eaten with rust* that it fell to pieces.
[5] Anast. Child. p. 80, 81. In like manner our Edward the Confessor is now lodged in a wood coffin iron-bound.
[6] *differtum odoribus conditur.*
[7] *Regum externorum consuetudine.* Ann. xvi. c. 6.
[8] Anast. Child. p. 88.
[9] *L. Medico* 40 § *mulier* ff. de auro & argento legato, L. 14. ff. de religione & sumptib. funer.
[10] In Aeneid. XI. 194.
[11] Hieron. Lib. 1. Epistol. Ambros. L. de Nabuthe. Lactant. Inst. Div. II. c. 4.
[12] Lib. IV. c. 46. [13] C. 32.

ornatis.

ornatis. Chilperic himself was buried in his best clothes [1]; his son Theodebert *dignis vestibus indutus* [2]; and Charlemagne in his imperial robes, and his face covered *sudamine* under his diadem [3]. From being *burnt* with them among the Romans [4], they came to be *buried* with them.

The custom of burying treasure with princes is more early than the time of Childeric [5]. If we believe Josephus [6], Solomon filled the sepulchre of his father David with treasure, of which it was plundered by Hyrcanus. Strabo says the Albanians buried much treasure with them in their coffins [7]. With such an hope the emperor Alexius Angelus is said to have broken open the tombs of his predecessors, and particularly of Constantine the Great, but found himself disappointed [8], as Herodotus tell us happened to Darius at the tomb of Nitocris [9]. Curtius [10] relates, that the Persians believed the tomb of Cyrus to be full of gold and silver; but that when Alexander the Great opened it he found in it only his shield, rotten, two Scythian bows, and a scymeter. Bagoas the eunuch attending told him he had not seen the tomb opened before, but that his late master Darius assured him 3000 talents were laid up in it with the body. Most likely Darius had made free with the treasure for the necessary defence of his kingdom, or other purposes. That gold and silver was buried with the Eastern princes is confirmed by the example of the Tartars their successors, in their monuments opened in the vast desarts [11], and Tavernier relates the same of the kings of Tonquin. The Tartar corpses are not unfrequently found shrouded in sheets or thin plates of gold. Alexander paid Cyrus's coffin *(solium)* the compliment of covering it with a gold crown and his own robe.

Alaric king of the Goths was buried with a quantity of treasure, in the bed of the river Busentia, near Cosenza, which was laid bare for that purpose, and then the river turned back again into its channel, and all the labourers concerned put to death [12]; and Attila was interred in three coffins, one of gold, the second of silver, and the other of iron, with a variety of weapons taken from his enemies, trappings set with jewels, and other insignia of state [13].

Narses' leaden coffin was robbed by the emperor Tiberius II. of vast quantities of treasure [14]. One of Charlemagne's biographers gives the like description of his sepulchre at Aix-la-chapelle [15].

The numerous golden figures on which Chiflet [16] spends so much time to prove that they were neither *toads*, nor *crescents*, nor *crowns*, nor *lilies*, nor the flower called *iris*, nor the *plant* usually put into the hand of Hope on coins, nor *spear heads*; and at last determines them to be *bees*, from whence the *fleur de lis* in the arms of France were afterwards derived, Montfaucon [17] determines at once to have been nothing more than ornaments of the horse-furniture. What the Doctor [18] calls his *stylus*, the Father pronounces a *fibula*, which being adorned on one side with crosses, may have been among some Christian spoils. Chiflet having found a stylus, proceeds to find the gold setting of an ivory table book [19].

[1] *Vestimentis melioribus indutus.* Greg. Tur. VI. c. 46. *Vestitus cum vestimentis regalibus.* Gesta reg. Franc. c. 35.
[2] Greg. Tur. IV. c. 45. [3] Monach. Engolism. vit. Caroli Magni, c. 14. [4] Stat. V. 315.
[5] Phaedrus alludes to it as a common practice. *Humana* effodiens *ossa thesaurum* canis invenit. Fab. I. 27.
[6] De Bell. Jud. I. 2. 711. [7] XII. 348.
[8] Erasm. Francis. Schaub. p. 2. p. 196. [9] L. c. 187 [10] X. 5.
[11] Archaeol. II. p. 222—226. See also Quenstedt de sepult. vet. p. 361, &c. [12] Jornandes.
[13] Et diversi generis *insignia* quibus colitur *aulicum decus.* Ib. Among instances of stone coffins in the bed of rivers Mr. Grundy the Surveyor clearing the bed of the river Glen in Lincolnshire, found one some feet under the bed containing a human scull and shoulder blade. (Spalding Society Minutes). See also the coffin found at Temple Mills in Hackney marsh, 1783. Gent. Mag. vol. LIII. p. 900.
[14] Paul. Diac. par. ii. p. 64. Fredegarius Scholastic. c. 80.
[15] Monachus Engolismensis S. Eparchii vit. Car. Magni, c. 24.
[16] P. 164—181. [17] Mon. de la Monarchie Franc. I. p. 12. [18] P. 182—193. [19] P. 194—195.

Weapons

Weapons were buried with the dead from the remoteſt antiquity. Where cremation obtained they were firſt thrown into the funeral pile [1]. The Carians were known by the kind of weapons buried with them [2], which were a ſmall ſhield and a creſt to their helmets [3].

Servius [4] ſays, it was an Indian cuſtom to bury the horſes with their maſters; and among the Gerri, a Scythian people, the grooms and other ſervants were added [5]. The ſame cuſtom obtained among the Tartars [6]. The ſcull, and part of the iron ſhoe of Charlemagne's horſe were found, which laſt circumſtance proves the antiquity of that mode of guarding the feet of that uſeful animal if we had not remoter evidence in the claſſical authors [7]; but this is ſuppoſed the earlieſt inſtance of *nailing on* the ſhoe [8]. The next inſtance in France is in 832, when the cavalry of Louis le Debonnaire could not be ſhod on account of the froſt that followed a heavy rain [9]. In England they ſeem to have begun ſoon after the Conqueſt. William the Conqueror gave to Simon St. Liz, a noble Norman, the town of Northampton, and the whole hundred of Fawſley then valued at £. 40. *per ann* to provide ſhoes for his horſes [10]. Henry de Averyng held the manor of Morton, c. Eſſex, of the king, in capite, by ſervice of a man, and an horſe worth 10 *s.* and four horſeſhoes [11], &c. for the Welſh expedition [12]. Henry de Ferrars, who came over with the Conqueror, took his name and arms (ſix horſeſhoes) from being ſome horſe-officer [13]. At Battleflats, ſix miles Eaſt from York, the ſcene of the battle between Harold and the Norwegian invaders, A. D. 1066, are frequently found in plowing a very ſmall ſort of horſeſhoes, which could only fit an aſs, or the leaſt breed of Northern horſes [14]. The arms of Glouceſter in a ſeal of Edward III's time ſtill uſed for recognizances are on each ſide of the king's head an horſeſhoe, near it a horſe-nail, three above and three below it, two and one; and in Crypt ſchool gate, built 1529, is the city ſword ſided by an horſeſhoe, and three horſe nails erect in baſe, alluding to the iron manufacturers here at the Conqueſt [15]; and a record of Clent, c. Worceſter, 37 Edward III. has "*Solvit receptori d'ni* "*per tallia* VI *l.* III *s. in* ferratura *equi ſeneſcalli* [16]." A ſilver horſe-ſhoe was found in Camalet caſtle, c. Somerſet, ſaid to have been a favourite reſidence of king Arthur, and afterwards belonging to the Hungerfords [17].

The rich decorations of horſe-furniture are deſcribed by Virgil [18], Ovid [19], that of the emperor Julian by Ammianus Marcellinus [20], that of the emperor Honorius by Claudian [21], and that of prince Sigiſmere, by Sidonius Apollinaris [22]. To this furniture, or to Childeric's garments, belong moſt of the fibulæ, boſſes, ſtuds, and other ornaments, which were of ſolid pure gold, and perhaps the gold threads might be part of the apparel both of the horſe and his rider. The needle might be part of a fibula.

[1] Virg. Æn. XI. 194, 195. Stat. Theb. V. 314. Ælian. Var. Hiſt. VII. c. 8.
[2] Thucyd. I. c. 8.
[3] [illegible] Schol. in loc.
[4] In Æn. V.
[5] Herodot. IV. c. 71. See alſo Chryſoſtom Homil. 3. ad pop. Antioch.
[6] Archæol. II. 223, 224.
[7] See Rogers and Pegge, in Archæol. III. 35—52.
[8] Ib. p. 38.
[9] Daniel Hiſt. de France, I. p. 566.
[10] Dugdale, Bar. I. 58. ex Chron. Bromtoni, p. 974, 975. Blount's Tenures, p. 50.
[11] *Ferres equorum.*
[12] Blount's Tenures, p. 16. Morant's Eſſex, I. 144. ex plac. cor. 13. E. I.
[13] Pegge in Archæol. III. 51.
[14] Drake's Eboracum, p. 81.
[15] Rudder, Hiſt. of Glouceſterſh. p. 134.
[16] Comput. Rot. 37 Edw. III. Naſh's Worceſterſh. in Clent, Append. p. xiii.
[17] Leland, II. ll. 47.
[18] Æn. vii. 277.
[19] Metam. vi. 118, 123.
[20] XXIII. c. 3.
[21] IV. Conſ. Honorii, 548—552.
[22] Epigram. and in Paneg. de 410 ejus conſul. lib. IV. ep. 20.

It is not so easy to determine the use of a little globe of chrystal an inch and an half in diameter. Montfaucon parallels it with twenty similar ones found with a gold ring, an hair pin, an ivory comb, and some little gold threads in an urn at Rome at the close of the 16th century; but he does not assign the use of them. From the company they were in I should suppose them female ornaments, like the beads found in our barrows. Mr. Pennant [1] imagines the globe in question had a magical use.

Besides the coins of the lower empire there were found one consular denarius, and the following silver coins of the upper empire: 1 Nero. 2 Trajan. 5 Hadrian. 9 Antoninus Pius. 3 Faustina. 7 Antoninus Philosophus. 3 Faustina jun. 6 Aurelius Verus. 2 Commodus. 1 Julia Severi. 1. Caracalla. 1 Constantine jun. Four of them had a hole in each, as if to hang them by, as amulets or ornaments [2], like the rude figures on gems engraved by Chiflet, p. 267. to illustrate his idea of these perforated coins; but by Montfaucon pleasantly mistaken, as if found in Childeric's tomb.

Part of these curiosities are now in the king of France's library [3]. They were given to the archduke Leopold, and after his death John Philip Schonborn obtained them of the Emperor, and having great obligations to Louis XIV. presented them to him by Monf. Du Fresne, 1665. They were first lodged in the cabinet of medals at the Louvre, and afterwards in the king's library.

The tomb of Childeric II. was accidentally discovered 1646, in the abbey of St. Germain des Prez, in a repair of the church. It consisted of two great stone coffins, whose stone lid being removed, discovered the bodies of the King and Queen Blicheldis, habited in their royal robes, not totally decayed, with a little stone coffin containing the young prince Dagobert their son, who was murdered with them by Bodilon and his adherents, whom the king had ordered to be beaten. None of the religious being present, it was suspected that the workmen secreted some of the spoils of these tombs. All that could be got out of them was part of the king's diadem woven with gold. But ten years after, on removing these tombs, with those of some other kings in the same church, they found in the king's tomb the remains of his sword, his belt, and a clasp or buckle of fine gold, weighing about eight ounces, exactly like that of Childeric I. with pieces of a staff, supposed his royal sceptre, a glass vessel filled with perfume which retained some smell, and several square pieces of silver with the figure of an amphisbæna, which was probably this prince's device. In the Queen's coffin were found only her bones, with her robes, which fell to dust on opening it. After having cleaned the bottom of the King's coffin they discovered his name and title written in uncial letters.

CHILDR REX.

Which left no doubt that it belonged to Childeric II. son of Clovis II. and St. Bathildis, whose stone coffin is still to be seen at Chelles, whether she retired on the death of her husband [4].

In the same abbey of St. Germain were found, 1643, in the cloister, two stone coffins, on one of which was inscribed in uncial Roman letters interlaced,

TEMPORE NVLLO VOLO HINC
TOLLANTVR OSSA HILPERICI

[1] Tour in Scotl. 1776. p. 27.
[2] I have a bronze sword hilt studded with four coins of Trajan of the same metal.
[3] Velley, Hist. de France, I. 51. Montfaucon's Description of the tombs of the French Kings. Mem. de l'Acad. des Insc. vol III. p. 411. 12°.
[4] Montfaucon, Mem. de l'Acad. des Inscr. III. 414. 12°.

And within, theſe words written with vermillion,

PRECOR EGO ILPERICVS NON
AVFERANTVR HINC OSSA MEA.

The feet of this Chilperic were turned to the Eaſt, and within the tomb was a little croſs, with a crucifix of copper, and a little lamp of the ſame metal. The other tomb, which had no inſcription, probably contained his wife. Monſ. Valois conceived this to be the tomb of Chilperic I. huſband of Fredegonde; but beſides that this inſcription does not give the party the title of king, nor was any mark of royalty found in the coffin, it is certain that king Chilperic I. was buried with his wife in the church which they had rebuilt, where their tombs, with their figures, were formerly to be ſeen near the altar of St. Germain [1].

It appears by this that the mode of burying the kings of France of the firſt race was very ſimple yet with dignity. All the magnificence was indeed within; for there was no want of precious clothes, gold, nor ſilver. And the concealing theſe from being plundered may have been the reaſon why they put no inſcription on their tombs.

Guinever, queen of Arthur, was interred in a far more coſtly manner than her royal conſort, if we may credit the relation of thoſe who ſaw her tomb opened in the beginning of the 16th century, in the ruins of the monaſtery at Ambreſbury. "There was a ſepulchre found hewn out of a ſtone, and placed in the middle of a wall, by the deſtruction of which it was diſcovered. On its coverture it had in rude letters of maſſy gold R. G. A. C. 600. and was ſuppoſed to be the tomb of the famous Guinever, queen to king Arthur. The bones within this ſepulchre were all firm, fair yellow coloured hair about the ſcull, and a piece of the *liver*, about the ſize of a walnut, very dry and hard. Therein were found ſeveral royal habiliments, as jewels, vails, ſcarves, and the like, retaining even *till then their proper colour*, all which were afterwards very choicely kept in the collection of the right honourable the earl of Hertford, and of the aforeſaid gold divers rings were made and worn by his Lordſhip's principal officers [2]."

I confeſs myſelf ſtrongly tempted to ſuſpect, that this might have been the body of queen Eleanor mother of Edward I. who is known to have been buried in this monaſtery [3]. She died 1290, and the letters may have been miſread for R E G I N A A L I O N O R A, &c. as on the tomb of her ſon's wife, her nameſake. We have no authentic evidence that the monaſtry of Ambresbery ſubſiſted before the cloſe of the 10th century. Biſhop Tanner [4] aſcribes its foundation to Alfrida or Ethelfrida queen of Edgar, A. D. 980. and Henry II. refounded it 1177. Guinever hardly ſurvived her conſort 50 years. The original inſcription Mr. Jones ſays he could not procure, but inſerted the relation on the credit of thoſe perſons of quality from whom he received it.

The body of Charlemagne was embalmed, and placed under a vault, ſitting on a chair of gold, dreſt in his imperial robes, and under them the hair cloth which he uſually wore, having at his ſide a ſword whoſe hilt and the furniture of the ſcabbard were of gold, and a pilgrim's purſe which he uſed to wear when he went to Rome. He held in his hands the book of the Goſpels written in letters of gold. His head was adorned with a gold chain in form of a diadem, in which was ſet a piece of the true croſs, and his face was covered with a *ſudarium*. His

[1] Montfaucon, Ib. p. 418.
[2] Jones' Stoneheng reſtored, p. 17. folio. Mr. Ray, 1662, was ſhewn what was ſuppoſed her graveſtone. Itin. p. 102.
[3] See p. lx. To what is there ſaid let me add, that Biſhop Tanner, Not. Mon. p. 589. cites Pat. 25 Henry III. "De amovendo corpore Alienoræ conſanguineæ regis a Briſtol ad monaſterium de Ambreſbury." which muſt relate to ſome other lady of the name.
[4] Notit. Mon. p. 589.

ſcymeter

ſcymeter and his ſhield, which were all of gold, and had been bleſt by Pope Leo III. were hung up before him. His tomb was then cloſed up, and even ſealed, after it had been filled with much treaſure and all ſorts of perfumes, and a gilded arch was erected over it, with this inſcription in Roman capitals recited by Eginhard his ſecretary:

SUB HOC CONDITORIO SITUM EST CORPUS
KAROLI MAGNI ATQUE ORTHODOXI
IMPERATORIS, QUI REGNUM FRANCO-
RUM NOBILITER AMPLIAVIT, ET PER
ANNOS XLVII FELICITER REXIT. DE-
CESSIT SEPTUAGENARIUS, ANNO AB IN-
CARNATIONE DOMINI
DCCCXIV, INDICTIONE VII,
V KAL. FEBRUARIAS.

This, ſays P. Montfaucon [1], is the firſt epitaph of the Kings of France.

In ſcouring ſome ditches in the fields round Jutrebog on the borders of Saxony and Lower Luſatia, in the ſummer of 1721, was found a large heavy ſteel ſword, with a pummel of the ſize of a man's fiſt, and inſcribed on one ſide,

DIM Aō ATINVS DIX RGō FERVS DIX IERGNR.

And on the other,

IERC. VIINIVS C. S. DIM Aō ATINVS DXC. E.

The letters engraved deep, and filled up with ſilver, the R larger than the reſt. Eckhard referred it to ſome general of the Emperor Henry II. who had cauſed the names of his fellow ſoldiers to be here inſcribed, with other words as a charm, in ſome expedition againſt the Sclavonians, then invading Germany, and that the ſword falling into the enemy's hand might be buried with the conqueror as a trophy. He read it thus:

Domini Chriſti milleſimo anno Atinus (tribunus) *Domini Jeſu Chriſti* [2]. *R. Goſerus (tribunus*, ſome other officer) *Domini Jeſu Chriſti in exercitu Romani Cæſaris Henrici.*

And on the other ſide,

In exercitu Romani Cæſaris Vicinus (an officer) *Chriſtianus Saxo D. Jeſu milleſimo anno Atinus duxit Chriſtianor. exercitum* [3].

With the twenty ſkeletons diſcovered in the tomb or cell, thirty feet long and ſeven wide, formed of five large rude ſtones on the lordſhip of Cocherel between Evreux and Vernon, 1685, which ſhould properly have been noticed under the article of ſtone coffins, were found ſeveral coloured ſtones and black flints, cut in oval ſhapes, pointed at both ends, or blunt at one, from three to four inches long, like arrow heads, and a grey flint five inches long, three broad at the ſharp end, and one at the ſmaller end, ſhaped like a battle ax, and fixed on a piece of ſtag's horn; three or four baked earthen pots filled with charcoal aſhes, ſome fragments of burnt bones, and a circular maſs of free ſtone, whereon three flat ſtones were placed. It was the opinion of the French anti-

[1] Mem. de l'Acad. des Inſcr. III. 413—415. [2] Or perhaps DVX.
[3] Eckhard duo perantiqua monumenta ex agro Jutteboccenſi eruta, &c. Vitembergæ, 1734. 4°.

2 quaries

quaries of that time that these were the skeletons of the prisoners of some barbarous invaders taken by the Gauls, and sacrificed to the manes of their own countrymen, whom they burnt, and interred in the same tomb [1]. But as two of these skeletons were separated from the rest by a large stone laid over them, why might not the whole have been the burial place of a considerable family, of which these two skeletons were the chiefs, and the ashes have belonged to servants or inferior persons of the same household.

In 1732, in the borders of *Cinna*, a village scarce a quarter of a mile from Jutrchog, were found two sepulchres, containing 12 urns and ashes and a silver coin, having on one side the figure of the Slavonian Deity *Prono* or *Prove*, with a sword and shield, and on the reverse a spear head between two heater shields [2]. This coin and others frequently found in graves are supposed to have a reference to the fare for the passage over the Styx, or to the wants of the deceased in the other world [3]. The urns, of which the middlemost of nine in one grave was largest, might contain the ashes of a family, or of a great man and his dependants, as in Anhalt, 1719, was found a single urn inclosed in stones, and surrounded by many others on the outside of the inclosure [4].

Mr. Seyffert [5] has collected a variety of instances both of single pieces of money and of treasures being buried with the dead of various nations and ages. Bartholinus [6] had a silver coin found in a human scull near Neustadt, and Tenzelius [7] was shewn in another scull two *nummi bracteati* inscribed L A N D. In an old burying ground at Dresden were dug up three pieces of coin of later ages, in the mouths of as many corpses [8]. Whether any of these were fees for the Stygian ferry, the *δανακη* and *ναυλος* of the Greeks, the *naulus* and *portorium* of the Romans, imitated by the superstition of later ages; or, as Lambecius [9], with greater probability, conjectured, memoranda of the time of the party's decease, and in what reign he died, as in regard to two coins of the Antonines so found, or two of Caracalla, in 1662, in an old tomb at Vienna, and others in that of a Roman soldier at Strasburg, 1663 [10], is a question foreign to my purpose.

A copper ring was found round the arm of a human skeleton at Druton, near Cave, in the East Riding of Yorkshire. It was quite black and bright, and not in the least corroded, except a little in the inside where it touched the arm. We have here engraved it from a drawing by Mr. Thomas Beckwith of York, F.S.A. 1779.

[1] See Phil. Trans. N° 185, and abbe Cocherel's "Account of these skeletons," translated from the French, and printed 1760.
[2] Eckhard ubi supra, p. 26. [3] See Keysler, Antiq. Septentr. § II. c. 2. p. 114. [4] Eckhard, p. 35.
[5] De nummis in ore defunctorum repertis. Dresdæ, 1712, 12°.
[6] Lib. II. 9. 460. [7] Colloq. 1696. p. 919.
[8] Olearius in Parentat. B. Magen. 1699. [9] De Bibliotheca Col. P. I. p. 89.
[10] Bebelius, Antiq. Argentorat. p. 21.

Mr.

Patens & Chalices

"Mr. Le Bœuf dit qu'ayant fait fouiller il y a quelques années dans un ancien "cimitiere d'Auxerre il y decouvrit un chevalier sur la poitrine duquel etoient en-"core les restes du fil d'archal de la cage de son oiseau de proye & les os de "cet oiseau [1]."

An officer of the abbey of St. Alban's, whom hard study had driven beside himself, was interred in their cell at Binham in Norfolk, in the fetters wherewith he had been confined [2].

The paten and chalice were buried with ecclesiastical persons of common rank, as well as with prelates and presidents of religious societies. Patens and chalices of tin, latten, or pewter, must be very antient; for in the council of London, A. D. 475, we find a strict injunction to administer the sacrament only in gold and silver [3]. It is however probable the poverty of country parish churches made it necessary to dispense with this. In Landbeach chancel was found, 1711, within less than a foot under the surface, under a white stone, a stone coffin, without any lid to it, the stone covering only the upper part, with a pewter chalice, the bowl and foot very thin, but the shaft thick and heavy. In the coffin was also a piece of stone or cement, very heavy, which Mr. Cory, then rector, supposed a relique, brought by the party interred from some pilgrimage. He fancied he could see marks of the tonsure on a piece of the skull [4].

In Little Ilford church-yard at the North door of the church was found, 1724, two feet under ground, a stone coffin lid with a plain cross, and six feet below it a body: on the left side of the scull a leaden (pewter) cup and cover, or rather chalice and paten, the cup 4 inches diameter, the cover or paten $4\frac{1}{2}$ [5].

In Mr. Sturdy's garden at St. Nicholas at Carlisle, supposed the site of St. Nicholas' hospital, were found, 1765, a pewter chalice and paten, in a stone coffin, six feet four inches long, fifteen inches deep, five feet eight inches within, and one foot and a half broad at the shoulders, covered with three flag stones, and the middlemost carved with a quatrefoil in a circle[6], but no inscription: within was a skeleton. Near the same place was dug up another stone which covered a skeleton, and having a cross in relief, and at its sides carved a chalice and a square paten. See the plate, fig. 1 and 2.

In digging the vault for the last earl of Bristol of the Digby family at Sherborne were found four stone coffins covered with flat stones, in which the bodies appeared entire, but soon mouldered away when exposed to the air. Two of the coffins, which contained the bones of the four bodies, were re-interred under the vault. A silver chalice was in one of them, which had a niche designed to receive it. There was also a piece of money and a little cup in each of them. The two first coffins still remain in the chapel where Horsey's monument is. The stones that covered them were used for the pavement. It is probable that some of the abbots or monks of this abbey were interred in them [7].

In making a vault in the middle aile of Lichfield cathedral, about fourteen inches below the pavement was discovered a stone coffin covered with a large stone. Within the coffin were some few human bones, the upper leathers of a pair of shoes, a great many fragments of plain gold lace about an inch broad, and a pewter chalice, with its cover, but much decayed, particularly the cover, which is extremely brittle, and almost reduced to a calx. There was also found

[1] Mem. de l'Acad. des Inscriptions, XXVII. p. 154. 410.

[2] Mat. Paris, vit. abbat. S. Albani, p. 118.

[3] "Precipimus ne consecretur eucharistia nisi in calice aureo vel argenteo, & ne stanneum calicem aliquis episcopus a "modo benedicat interdicimus." Spelm. Concil. Brit. cited by Mr. Cory in Blomfield's MS. Coll. for Cambridgeshire, pen. me. I cannot find this reference in Spelman or Wilkins: but the Saxon canons promulgated in the reign of Edgar ordain that every chalice used for the eucharist shall be of *metal* (ȝeȝoten) and not of wood (treopenum) (Spelm. Conc. p. 453. Wilkins, I. 227.) and the council of Calchuth in the close of the 8th century forbids the use of horn (cornu bovinum) for chalices or patens. Ib. 295. Ib. I. 148.

[4] Blomfield, MS. Collections for Cambridgeshire, pen. me. The canons now in force direct, that the wine shall be brought to the Communion table in a clean and sweet standing pot or stoop of *pewter*, *if not of purer metal*.

[5] Stukeley. Lethieullier, in A. S. Min.

[6] Probably the head of a cross, as on the coffin-lid under-mentioned.

[7] Hutchins's Dorset, II. 381.

a capital

a capital Roman W cut out of the gilded leather [1]. Mr. Green possesses another nearly similar, found also in the same church. See the plate, fig. 10. At Peterborough they shew one of laten taken out of an abbot's grave, of the same form with that at Carlisle beforementioned, but the shaft longer, and more slender: fig. 7.

A stone coffin containing a skeleton intire, and near the head a pewter chalice, the metal almost destroyed, was found in digging a grave in Diss church for Mr. Taylor, 1773. About six feet south from this coffin and at the depth of about five feet they discovered two large urns of red earth, one holding fifteen pints, the other fourteen, containing only fœtid earth [2].

A chalice was found in the North transept of the abbey church of Bath, in a stone coffin, wherein were also leather soles of shoes, and what the sexton called short tobacco pipes.

The chalice and paten commonly went together, though the latter is sometimes described as the cover of the former, and in some graves is missing, being more liable to decay. In the coffins found in Lincoln minster, described p. lii. liii. the patens and chalices lay over the right shoulder or under the right arm. On brasses where the chalice surmounted by the wafer appears as a sacerdotal badge, the paten is presumed of course, or where the wafer rises out of the chalice the paten is implied as laid on its top. Both vessels, when found in graves, or with stone or brass figures, or with crosses, are most frequently of the simplest form: but on brasses we meet with a greater variety of chalices. In the 16th century they departed from the simple form, as in the hands of a priest, in St. Margaret's church, Rochester, 1540. and under the inscription of a rector of Stibert, in Walsingham church, Norfolk. See the plate, fig. 11. and 15. A priest in Effingdon church, Herts, holds a chalice shaped like a teacup, surmounted by a wafer inscribed ihs. See the Plate, fig. 14. where fig. 4. is from the brass of a priest in Hereford cathedral, 1524. Fig. 6. is carved on the fonts in Southfleet and Shorne churches, Kent. Fig. 9. is the chalice now in use in Wigmore church, c. Hereford; the date 1571, on the flat of the cover [3]; the form approaches nearest to those now in general use [4].

It is most probable that all these vessels so interred being rather emblematical of the profession of the party than his private property (for it is not to be supposed the parish could part with their communion-plate) were made of meaner metal, silvered over, as the rings interred with prelates were gilt [5]; and with this restriction we must understand Mr. Blomfield's account, that under a coffin-fashioned stone in Diss church, was found, 1705, an entire skeleton, with a *silver* chalice by its head [6]. So also that of the *silver* patten, thin and antient, with a fine radiated head of Christ found in the church at Kirkton in Holland [7]; and that found in the supposed tomb of William Rufus in the last century [8]. That found with Bishop Bitton at Exeter is called *base silver*, and it is remarkable that the consecrated wafer, covered with a linen cloth, was supposed to have been buried with his chalice and paten. Keysler [9] quotes a variety of authorities, to shew that this was no unfrequent practice. Mr. Drake [10] calls two

[1] Mr. Green, in Gent. Mag. 1772. vol XLII. p. 168. where the chalice is engraved.

[2] Gent. Mag. 1773 vol. XLIII. p. 459.

[3] That at St. Peter's Mancroft, Norwich, is dated 1569. Blomf. II. 623. Mr Green describes a rude silver chalice at Welch Bickner, c. Monmouth, dated 1176. Gent. Mag. XXVI. p. 239. 1756. Mr. Pennant, one of pure gold, at Wellspool. Wales, II. 379. See archbishop Sandys's private chalice, which he used abroad, in Dr. Nash's Worcest. II. 124.

[4] Three chalices O. on each a wafer A. occur in the windows of many churches in Norfolk, and on some brasses. Mr. Blomfield calls them the "emblems of the priesthood." I. 603. 648.

[5] See Bishops Grosthead and Bitton, in their respective articles. See also the chalice painted on the wall of the vault wherein Humphrey duke of Gloucester lies at St. Alban's, fig. 13. and another found in a stone coffin there, and preserved in the locker. Fig. 5.

[6] Blomf. Hist. of Norf. I. 14. but in his MS. penes me, he describes it as a man buried in leather, in a priest's habit, with a small silver cup on his breast.

[7] Spalding Society's Minutes. [8] See p. 15. [9] Antiquit. Septentr. p. 174.

[10] Eboracum, p. 472. See the plate fig. 8. 12. 16. Fig. 3. is from a shield in bishop Stainsbury's chapel, in Hereford cathedral: the chalice is surmounted by the dragon which St. John is said to have exorcised out of it.

that

that were found in the graves of two archbishops of York, and are still shewn in the vestry of the cathedral, *silver* ones: and adds, there are with them some others of lead, taken out of several graves on laying the new pavement. Sir William Dugdale says, that in the barbarous ransacking of the monuments in Old St. Paul's during the civil war, he could never hear that they found more than a ring or two, with rubies, and a chalice of no great value [1].

Mr. Carter, late verger at Salisbury, told me, the body of bishop Woodville, who died 1483, had been found in a stone coffin, with a candlestick.

In digging a grave at Lamport was found a stone coffin, not very deep in the ground, and seeming fastened to the wall, containing mould and bones decayed. At the head was a candlestick, supposed pewter, quite rotten: at the feet a large iron key. It may be doubted, if this supposed candlestick was not mistaken for the shaft of a chalice, as in the instance beforementioned. Mr. Bridges thought it probable that this person was Accolyte and Ostiarius, whose office was to take care of the church doors and candlesticks (somewhat like our sexton) and he was invested by delivery of a key by the bishop or minister; who, to prevent alteration of the keys, took a drawing or description of them. The same ceremony seems to have been practiced with regard to other orders in the church, and may account for the chalices found in antient graves, which Whitby [2] and Bingham [3] imagined contained the Eucharist in both kinds; but which seemed only intended to shew that the person there buried had been a bishop or priest, like the frequent portraits of religious holding chalices on their breasts or in their hands [4]. The chalice, though found in the coffins of bishops, never appears on their monuments.

In digging in the choir of the parish church of Chartenay sous Baigneux, near Sceaux they found ten or twelve tombs of plaster [5], in each of which was at least one pot of grey earth with little red stripes, full of ashes and coals, in some three or four, and sometimes also a little phial. The like pots were found in other coffins in the old churchyard of the parish above half a quarter of a league from the town. A plate of copper, with a buckle, was also found on a bone of the arm, which it had eaten [6], and coloured with rust. John Beleth, who lived in the 12th Century, in a treatise on the ceremonial of the church, says, it was customary to put holy water, coals, and incense [7] into tombs: the first to drive away the devil, the second to keep off the ill smell, and the third to shew that the ground was not to be applied to any other uses. This custom was falling into disuse about 1286. He adds, that in his time none but the bodies of saints were to be buried within the church, which Durand [8] confines to the chancel. Such pots, to whatever uses they served, were found in the tomb of Philip, son of Lewis le Gros, who died 1161, and was buried in the church of Notre Dame, and in the tomb at Cocherell, already described, p. lxvii [9].

In the lockers at St. Alban's abbey church they shew two pots so different from the generality of Roman urns, and found, as several more have since been within the nave of the church, among and near stone coffins, that I am tempted to suspect they were intended to receive the bowels of the parties deposited in the coffins. Of the two still shewn there one is broken, of a light pale red earth, unglazed, terminating in a point like one engraved by Count Caylus in his Recueil VI. pl. II. 1. which its inscription

ΦΙΛΙΠΠΟΣ ΧΑΡΙ:
ΛΕΥΚΟΝΟΕΥΣ.

proves to have been sepulchral. The other glazed like our common Dutch

[1] St. Paul's, p. 48. [2] Idolatry of Host Worship, speaking of chalices dug out of graves of ecclesiastics in the church of Sarum, of which he was precentor. [3] Antiq. XV. c. 4. § 20.
[4] Hist. of Northamptonshire, II. 116. where is given a pleasant tradition of such a figure in Geddington church, that the party died as he was *celebrating the Eucharist*.
[5] *Platre.* [6] *carie.* [7] *aqua benedicta & pruinæ cum thure.*
[8] Lib. I. c. 5. n. 12. [9] Hist de l'Acad. des Inscr. V. 281. 12°.

ware,

ware, resembling a fruit pan, with a cover, and two ansæ, and a scallopt border round its upper rim. Both were found filled with dust or white mould, and such I am informed by Mr. Kent the present sexton are now not unfrequently found, but rarely taken up whole.

Such was probably the use of the numerous earthen vessels found in Fairwell and Yoxall church, before mentioned, p. xvi. to which should have been added twenty two others, two feet under the floor, in Charborough church, Dorset, having under them the bones of eleven skeletons [1].

In the family vault of the Hungerfords at Farley castle, the bowels of the last branches of that family, who died so late as the middle of the last century, were enclosed in glazed earthen pots or jars covered with white leather, one of which being lately by accident broken to pieces discovered the heart, &c. preserved in liquor. There still remains in the vault a large cylindrical vase of lead, inclosing the like contents.

HEARTS and BOWELS were not unfrequently, if not generally, lodged separately from their bodies.

We have already seen that the bowels, tongue, heart, eyes, and brains, of Henry I. were buried together, separate from his body, in the church of St. Mary de Pré, at Rouen [2].

The body of Richard I. was buried at Fontevraud; his heart at Roan, in memory of the hearty love that city always bore him; and his bowels at Chaluz, at the siege of which he was killed, for a disgrace of their unthankfulness [3].

King John's bowels were buried at Croxden abbey [4].

Henry III's at Font Evraud [5].

Queen Eleanor's at Lincoln, where she had a monument, the counterpart of that at Westminster; see p. 66.

The bowels of Ranulph de Blundvile, sixth earl of Chester, were buried at Wallingford, where he died 1232, his heart at Dieulacres abbey, which he had founded, and his body, with those of the other earls, in Chester chapter-house [6].

Those of Gilbert Marshall earl of Pembroke, 1241, before the high altar of St. Mary's church, Hertford [7].

The mangled limbs of Simon de Montfort and Hugh Despencer were disposed of among different religious houses [8].

The heart of William de Estouteville archbishop of Rouen was buried in the choir of his cathedral, in the tomb of his predecessor St. Maurile, who died 1067 [9].

That of Stephen brother of Alan the Black and Red was buried at St. Mary's abbey, York, and his body in the monastry of Begar in Bretagne, 1104 [10].

The heart of Giffard bishop of Winchester, who died 1129, was found not the least decayed, in digging down a wall at the North West end of Waverley abbey, in a stone loculus, in two leaden dishes soldered together, and filled with spirits, now in the hands of Mr. Martyr of Guilford.

The heart of Richard Poore bishop of Durham, 1237, was buried at Tarrant Monkton nunnery, which he founded [11].

The heart of one of the Ralph Scophams, lords of the manor of Brianston, c. Dorset, in the reign of Henry III. and Edward I. was buried near the font there, as appears by the inscription: *Hic jacet cor Radulphi de*
. . . . ham [12].

That of Matilda de Hastings, first wife of Gilbert de Peche lord of Barnwell, was buried *in plumbeo locello*, before the high altar of that priory, near her children: the reason assigned for which is, that her body could not be brought from St. Mary Overey, where she died, to be buried there, as she desired, because of the then troubles, by which must be meant the barons wars [13].

[1] Hutchins' Dorset, II. 185. [2] Hoveden, 276, a. At Rennes; Rob. of Gloc. p. 446. [3] Mat. Paris, p. 196. [4] Mat. Paris, 288 [5] Ib. 1006. [6] Dugdale, Baron. I. 45. ex Chron. Tewkfbury, MS. in Bib. Cotton. [7] See p. 51. [8] See p. 55 & 90. [9] Molcon, Voyage literaire de France, p. 274. [10] Blomf. Norf. I. 655. [11] Hutchins, I. 88. [12] See p. 43. [13] Hist. of Barnwell abbey, p. 18. ex Reg. f. 16.

That of Ethelmare bishop of Winchester, who died 1261, was found in a vase, and buried by the South wall of the choir there, with an inscription [1].

Stephen Longespee's at Bradenstoke; but his body at Lacock; the heart of his brother Nicholas, bishop of Sarum, at Lacock, his bowels at Ramsbury, his body at Sarum [2].

That of Peter de Aquablanc, bishop of Hereford, who died 1268, was buried at a monastery of his founding at Aigues belles in Savoy, of which place he seems to have been a native.

The heart of Richard earl of Cornwall was deposited under a sumptuous pyramid, in the Grey Friars, Oxford, 1272 [3].

His wife Isabel was buried at Beaulieu, her heart in a silver cup at Tewksbury, and her bowels at Missenden abbey [4].

The heart of Henry son to Richard king of the Romans murdered 1296, was buried in the coffin with St. Edward, at Westminster [5].

Robert earl of Mellent's in salt and lead [6]. "Cor Roberti de Mellento adhuc in "hospitalitate de Bracleye integrum in plumbo sale servatum habetur [7]."

The heart of Robert Bruce king of Scotland, who died 1329, was conveyed to Jerusalem, and buried near the holy sepulchre, by James 8th lord of Douglas, whose family had the addition of a heart G. imperially crowned, in a field A [8]. Our Edward I. directed his heart to be carried to the same place.

The heart of Charles V. king of France, [1380] benefactor to the cathedral of Rouen is buried in the choir there, under a tomb of black marble, whereon is his effigy holding his heart in his hand [9].

The heart of the Emperor Leopold, who died 1705, was put into a silver box, and with great ceremony deposited in the chapel of Loretto behind the high altar of the church of the barefooted Augustines at Vienna; his bowels, with like ceremony, in the cathedral church of St. Stephen, and his body in the church of the Capuchins in the same city [10].

Instances of this practice were very common in France, and it still obtains so universally abroad that the walls of the principal conventual churches are covered with sumptuous memorials of the several hearts sent from different countries and deposited under them.

Prince Arthur's heart was buried in the chancel of the church at Ludlow, but the inscription against the North wall has been washed over and forgotten. The heart was taken up in a silver box, and found to be double, or as they call it there *twinney*, and the box embezzled by the sexton, who was dismissed from his place. I persuaded myself I had discovered the memorial of this interment when I revisited this church, June 7, 1784, and observed against the wall of the North transept a heart carved in stone; but the inscription on it was for "Simon Williams of Merioneth, c. Caernarvon, 1620." There is another stone of the same form, but blank; and a third in the chapel of the South aile, inscribed to "Robert Vaughan of Merionethshire, 1642."

The bowels of Walter Skirlaw bishop of Durham, who died 1405, were buried at Howden, in Yorkshire, where remains a slab, with a cross, and this inscription:

Hic requiescunt viscera Walteri Skirlaw, quæ
sepeliuntur sub hoc saxo. An'o D'ni 1405.

[1] Gale's Hist. of Winchester, p. 24. [2] Sandford, p. 116. [3] Dugdale, Bar. I. 764.
[4] Ther after in Jenver Isabel is wife
Contesse of Gloucestre let at Bercounstade yt lise
Ibured heo was at Beulu, & ir harte ibured is
At Teukesburi & ir guttes at Messendene iwis. Robert of Gloc. p. 528, 529. See p. 41.
[5] Stowe's Lond. 1618. p. 866. [6] Hist. of Northampton, I. 145. [7] Knighton, col. 2346.
[8] Fordun XIII. 20. Buchanan, VIII. c. 58. Douglas Peerage, 183.
[9] Molean. Voy. Liter. de Fr. p. 274. [10] Sandford, p. 819.

The heart and bowels of Miles Salley bishop of Landaff, who died 1516, were, by his will, buried before the high altar of the church at Mathern, where his episcopal palace was; his body in the Gaunt's, or St. Mark's chapel, Bristol [1].

The heart of Thomas Skevington bishop of Bangor, who died 1534, was buried under a common stone, close by the North wall, within the rails of the altar of his cathedral, which he rebuilt 1532. It was inclosed in a small leaden coffin, made in form of a heart. When bishop Humphreys was at school at Bangor, 1665, it lay under a loose stone of the pavement: he had seen it often taken up, and had it in his hands. After he came to Oxford one of the school-boys opened the coffin, and the heart was very intire, but upon the letting in the air it began to turn to dust. Bishop Morgan hearing of this, ordered the little heart coffin to be immediately soldered up again, and buried deep, and the stones well fastened on it, and there it rests [2].

"About 1644 there was a heart dug up at the Friars Preachers, Oxon. It was closed in lead, as big as the bole of a man's hat; and when it was opened the heart looked as fresh as if it had been buried but a week. What else was in the lead Wood had not heard; but Mr. Smith of Brasen-nose College had the lead; some thought there was a crucifix in it. Mr. Wrench the gardener told Wood there was such a thing found at the Black Friars, with the date on it [3].

Mr. Masters repairing his chancel at Landbeach, 1759, found in a cavity of a pillar a human heart, wrapt up in something fibrous, like hair or wool, perhaps spikenard, and inclosed between two dishes or bowls of sycamore, or some soft wood cemented together by linnen. The cavity of the pillar was covered by a square stone carved with a rose, behind which was another stone, four inches and a quarter by three inches three quarters, and one inch thick, cemented to the first with pitch. He supposed this heart belonged to some crusader, or founder, or to Chamberlayn, or Bray, lords of manors here. It is now in the British Museum.

In affixing a mural monument to a pillar of Kirkwall cathedral the workman struck his tool into a square hollow containing a quantity of human bones, tied up with ribband, in all probability the relics of St. Magnus, part of whose bones are said to have been deposited here, and perhaps never disturbed before [4].

In St. Nicholas' chapel, in Westminster Abbey, is a pyramid, supporting a cup, in which is inclosed the heart of Anne Sophia Harley, an infant of a year old, who was daughter of the Hon. Christopher Harley, ambassador from the French King, and died 1600.

In a chapel on the side of Henry VIIth's, in the same church, is another pyramid of black and white marble supporting a small urn, in which is contained the heart of Esme Stuart, son of the duke of Richmond and Lenox, who died in France at the age of ten years, 1660.

The heart of Arthur Capel earl of Essex, who was found murdered in the Tower 1683, is inclosed in a marble case in form of an heart, and kept in the family seat at Cashiobury, where I have seen it lying in the hall window.

Dr. Richard Rawlinson's heart was buried in the chapel of St. John's College, Oxford. His body in St. Giles's church there, having in his right-hand the head of Counsellor Layer, which he purchased of Mr. John Pearce, the nonjuring attorney, after it was blown down from Temple-bar.

Sir William Temple's heart was buried by his own desire in a silver box, under the dial in his garden at More Park, Surrey.

[1] Willis' Landaff, p. 61.
[2] Bp. Humphrey's Additions to Wood's Athenæ Ox. in Hearne's Caius, II. 674.
[3] Wood's Memoranda, at the end of Hearne's Liber Niger Scaccarii, p. 583. 2d. edit.
[4] Lowe's MS.

Archbishop

Archbishop Sudbury's HEAD is shewn inclosed within a grate at St. Gregory's church, at Sudbury, where that prelate and his brother founded a college on the site of their father's house. The skin and the ears are dried on, and the jaw is fallen, as they pretend from the blows he received from the rebels in dying. Godwyn [1] however affirms, that both the body and head were carried to Canterbury, and there buried in the cathedral.

Margaret the beloved daughter of Sir Thomas More caused his head to be placed on her coffin, or in her hands within it, in the vault of the Roper family in St. Dunstan's church at Canterbury. She caused it to be taken from London-bridge, and kept it by her in a leaden-box for some time [2].

Tradition says, Carew Raleigh, youngest son of Sir Walter, kept his father's head to be buried with him. A scull was found in a small niche of the chalk rock by his coffin at West Horsly, Surrey [3].

Among the most extraordinary discoveries supposed of a sepulchral kind, and the least accounted for, are the bones of birds found in a grave at Christ-Church priory, c. Hants [4], and those of beasts, in a stone chest at Rutchester, the antient Vindobala. From the situation of the former near the refectory one would at first sight suppose these bones were neither more nor less than what the monks had pickt. I have a parcel of bones of fowls which I took with my own hands out of a vault just opened in or near St. Mary's Abbey, at York, about 1768. But though from this and other circumstances I am doubtful about my friend Mr. Pegge's mode of accounting for those at Christchurch, as reliques of Paganism, cautiously put out of the way on the introduction of Christianity (a caution which reformers are little apt to observe) I confess myself unable to substitute a more satisfactory hypothesis.

Near the Roman station at Rutchester, the ancient Vindobala, was found 1766, a coffin hewn out of a rock, about twelve feet long by four broad and two deep: a hole close to the bottom at one end; a transverse partition of stone and lime: many decayed bones, teeth, and vertebræ, supposed by their shape and size to be the remains of some animal sacrificed perhaps to Hercules [5]. Human bones have been so often confounded with those of beasts, and extravagant dimensions ascribed to them by superficial observers, that I beg leave to suspend my assent to this appropriation till better authenticated.

Under the old altar in King's College chapel at Cambridge, on fitting up the new one, close to the East end were found bones of oxen, sheep, chicken, &c. a human scull, the jaw having a long strong red beard. One would be tempted to suspect that these were thrown together accidentally among rubbish. Of the supposed foundation-stone, mentioned by Fuller, with an inscription, pointing out the precise spot: *Ex orientali si bis septem pedetentim, &c.* only the bed of mortar was found in the middle of the foundation of the old altar; whence it is with greater probability referred to Eton-college chapel.

[1] P. 120. Ed. Richardson.
[2] More's Life of More, p. 177. Wood, Ath. Ox. I. 39.
[3] Salmon's Surrey, 146. The bodies of chiefs at Otaheite are buried in three different places after their bowels have been cut out by the priests before the great altar. Cook's Voyage, II. 44.
[4] Archæologia, IV. 117. 414.
[5] Wallis's Northumb. II. 168. See before, p. xxi.

Having

Having thus difcuffed the feveral appendages of our interments, let us attend to a few inftances of extraordinary prefervation of bodies in their refpective graves.

The body of archbifhop Elphege, who was murdered by the Danes at Greenwich, 1012, and buried at London, was found ten years after *ab omni corruptionis labe immune*, and transferred to Canterbury [a].

The corpfe of Etheldritha, foundrefs of Ely monaftery, was feen through an hole which the Danes broke in her coffin; a prieft, more forward than the reft, prying too bufily, and endeavouring to pull the envelope out by a cleft ftick, the faint drew back the drapery fo haftily that fhe tript up his heels, and gave him fuch a fall as he never recovered, nor his fenfes, afterwards. Bifhop Athelwold ftopt up the hole, and fubftituted monks to the priefts. Abbot Brithnoth transferred hither the body of Withburga the foundrefs's fifter; and when afterwards, in the time of abbot Richard, fome doubts were entertained about the incorruptibility of the foundrefs, nobody prefumed to examine her body, but they contented themfelves with uncovering that of her fifter *ultra mammas*, who was found to be in fuch good prefervation that fhe feemed more like a perfon afleep than dead: a filk cufhion lay under her head, her veil and veftments all feemed as good as new, her complexion clear and rofy, her teeth white, her lips fomewhat fhrunk, and her breafts reduced [b].

"In the year 1497, in the moneth of April, as labourers digged for the foun-
"dation of a wall within the church of St. Mary Hill, nere unto Belinfgate, they
"found a coffin of rotten timber, and therein the corps of a woman whole of
"fkinne and of bones undiffevered, and the joynts of her arms plyable without
"breaking of the fkin, upon whofe fepulcher this was engraven:

"Here lye the bodies of Richard Hackney, fifhmonger, and
"Alice his wife, which Richard was fheriff in the 15th of Edward II.

"Her body was kept above ground three or four dayes without noyance; but
"then it waxed unfavory, and was again buried [c]."

In the curious and antient regifters of this parifh is the following entry, alluding to this fact: A receipt of feven fhillings and eight pence from John Halked, grocer, paid by Thomas Colyn, 1496, "for the obyt and fettyng up the tombe and buryenge of Richard Hakney and Alys his wyff, the xx day of Marche." And in another book a charge "for lyme, fand, and for the mafon's huyr and his laborer, making *ageyne* of their tombe, and their dyrge, and maffe, and maffe peny, and for the ryifkyng to the priefts, and to the parifhioners for al maner of charges."

The body of Robert Braybroke bifhop of London, who died 1404, and was buried in his cathedral, though he had exprefsly forbidden any perfons to be buried in it under pain of excommunication, being dug up after the fire, was found complete and compact from head to foot, except an accidental wound in the left fide of the fcull and left breaft, within which one might perceive the lungs and entrails dried up, without diffolution, or any kind of decay [d]. Notwithftanding it had been expofed to the air on the damp earth or ground floor of the chapter-houfe, and to the fight and handling of moft fpectators for two or three years together, the flefh kept firm on the neck, and the whole weight of the body, which was but nine pounds, was fupported on the tiptoes, the bones and

[a] Malmfb. de geft. reg. II. p. 35. a. [b] Ib. 167. b.
[c] Stowe, Lond. 117. Ed. 1633. From Fabian's Chronicle.
[d] See Lord Coleraine's account of it, Antiquarian Repertory, II. p. 57.

nerves

nerves continuing all as they were ftretched out after death, without having any Egyptian art ufed to make mummy of the carcafe, for on the clofeft examination it did not appear to have been embowelled or embalmed at all. On the right cheek was flefh and hair, very vifible, enough to give fome notice of his vifage and ftature, which was but ordinary, and fo eafy to be taken up, by reafon of the lightnefs of the whole body, that it could be held up with one hand, and all of it looked rather like finged bacon, as if it had been dried up in a hot place (according to the appearance of St. Charles at Milan, or St. Catharine at Bologna) than as if it had been cured by furgeons, or wrapt up in cerecloth, there being no part of the whole covered or put on by art, or taken off as aforefaid, as far as could be perceived.

The body of William Parr, marquis of Northampton, brother to Queen Catharine Parr, who died 1571, was found in making a common grave in the choir of St. Mary's church, Warwick, about 1620, perfect, and the fkin intire, dried to the bones, rofemary and bay lying in the coffin frefh and green, preferved by the drynefs of the ground, it being above the arches of the fair vault under the choir, and of fand mixt with lime rubbifh [1].

The body of Dr. Caius, who died 1573, was found intire and perfect when the chapel at his college was rebuilt and lengthened 1725, and his tomb raifed from the ground, and placed in the wall as it now ftands [2]. His beard was very long, and on comparing his picture with his vifage, it is faid there was a great refemblance [3].

The body of Humphrey duke of Gloucefter was found intire, in pickle, in a vault in the choir at St. Albans, 1747.

Some bodies of the Engayne family were not many years ago difcovered in the fame ftate in repairing the family vault near Upminfter.

In the South aile of the choir of the abbey church at Bath is a freeftone monument, a kind of farcophagus under a canopy fupported by fix pillars of the Ionic order. In the farcophagus are lodged two bodies, in flight oak coffins, one upon another. The man, who lies uppermoft, is reduced to a fkeleton, with the fkin completely dried on the breaft and belly, and the hair of his head, chin, and cheft, perfectly preferved, that on his head thin and red. His head reclines to the right, the jaw fallen, his arms ftretched by his fide, the right hand lies on his right thigh; the left arm pendant; the nails on the great toe and third toe of his left foot perfect and long, and the leader of the leg complete; the toes of the right foot lefs perfect. The body meafures five feet ten inches. Pieces of the wrapper remain between the thighs and legs. The woman, who, by being placed under the other coffin, was not difcovered till within the laft fix or feven years, is completely inveloped in a wrapper of linnen incrufted with wax, or fome preparation, which, when firft opened, was white, but is now turned to a yellow colour [4]. The outer fwathing is gone, but the webb of the linnen may be feen in that part which has been broken into, and which difcovers the left hand dried like the man's, and lying on the belly. This corpfe meafures five feet four inches, and the head reclines to the left. By the falling of the man's jaw it may be prefumed his corpfe was never fwathed. Tradition, fupported by fome printed account which I have not been able to meet with, afcribes this monument to one *Thomas Lychefield* (Lutanift to Queen Elizabeth) and Margaret his wife. The arms on the top are Barry or a fefs croft by a bend. Creft, an armed arm and hand holding a ring or garland. It is pretended that a fum of money was left to have the monument opened at

[1] Dugd. Bar. II. 381.
[2] Blomf. Norf. II. 211.
[3] Idem Collect. Cantab. p. 172. See a curious account of the embalment of a corpfe near Riom in Auvergne. Gent. Mag. XXVI. p. 311—314.

certain ftated times; but this depends intirely on the confent of the church-wardens, by whofe favour I was permitted to take a view this fummer [1784], and thereby enabled to give the above particulars.

About the year 1737 were found in St. Margaret's church yard, Weftminfter, in a dry gravelly foil, at the depth of about eighteen feet, or lefs, which had not been broken up for above fifty years before, three entire fir coffins, the two largeft clampt together with iron, as boxes fometimes are. In one was a fat broad faced man, the body perfect and foft, as if juft dead; the lid had been glewed together lengthwife, and the weight of the earth had preft down his nofe: his beard was about half an inch long, the winding fheet was crape, tied with black ribbons and the thumbs and toes with the like, the date was compofed of fmall nails, [1665], by which it appeared he had then been dead feventy-two years, as were alfo the figure of an hour glafs, death's head and crofs bones. In the fecond coffin was a female body, in the fame ftate, in a white crape winding fheet, date 1673. And in the third a male child, perfect and beautiful as wax work, the eyes open and clear, but no date on the coffin. In one of the larger coffins was a dry nofegay of bay and other leaves and flowers, which appeared like a nofegay that had lain a year among linnen. Thefe bodies changed within twelve hours after they were expofed [1].

A woman was found in the fame churchyard, 1758, in an old coffin. The body was four feet eleven inches long, the fkin and flefh intirely dried up, like old parchment, which it much refembled in colour. The features were perfect, except the nofe and part of the upper lip, the nails were all on the hands, and on the left foot fomething like a very thick thread ftocking [2].

A few years ago two dried bodies of men, who, by the infcriptions on the coffins, appeared to have been a drummer and trumpeter to king George I. were taken out of the vaults under St. Martin's church in the Fields, and made a fhew of, till Dr. Hamilton the rector ordered them to be reftored to their places.

To thefe may be added, the famous inftance of a poor parifh boy, fuppofed to have been fhut into a vault in St. Botolph's church, Aldgate, and ftarved to death, at the time of the plague, 1665, fince which time the vault was known not to have been opened, where he was found, 1742, with the fancied marks of having gnawed his fhoulder, only perhaps becaufe his head reclined towards it. The fkin, fibres, and inteftines were all dried, and very little of his bones appeared. The body weighed about eighteen pounds, and was as exact a counter part of Lichfield's as could be. No figns of any embalment appear, and the body is perfectly free from any fetid or other fmell [3].

In February, 1750, in a vault of the antient family of the Worths at Staverton near Totnefs, Devon, was found in a fingle wooden coffin the body of a man entire and uncorrupt; his flefh folid and not hard, his joints flexible as if juft dead, his fibres and flefh retained their natural elafticity, his beard was black, and about four inches long, and the flefh no where difcoloured, the lips found, and fome of the teeth loofe. The beard black, and four inches long. The body never was embalmed, as there was not the leaft fign of incifion, and the bowels feem to be ftill intire. It was wrapt in a linen fheet very white and dry, over which was a tar cloth. The coffin lay nine feet under water. By the regifter it appeared that the laft perfon buried in this vault was Simon Worth, 1669, and the tradition of the parifh was, that he died in France or Flanders, and was brought over to be buried [4].

[1] Kirkpatrick's Reflections on the caufes that may retard the putrefaction of dead bodies. 1751. 8vo. p. 25—27.
[2] Gent. Mag. 1758. 472.
[3] It was in the poffeffion of Mr. J. Rogers of Maiden-lane, Wood-ftreet, where a print of it, by R. Rogers, was fold for two fhillings.
[4] Kirkpatrick, ubi fup. p. viii.

Leland

Leland [1] fays, he faw in St. Peter's abbey church at Bath a fair great marble tomb of a bifhop of Bath, out of which they faid oil did diftil, and likely, for his body was baumed plentifully.

Antient Chymiftry made people fancy that bodies could be preferved with the refemblance of real life, by means of a precious liquor circulating through every part in golden tubes artificially difpofed, and operating on the principals of vegetation [2].

In the peatmoffes of Derbyfhire were found the bodies of a man and woman intire, twenty-eight years and nine months after their interment, having perifhed in the fnow, the joints flexible, and the flefh frefh and white [3].

On the moors of Amcotts, in the ifle of Axholme, was found about fix feet below the furface a female body lying on its fide; the head and feet almoft together, intire, foft, and pliable, the fkin of a tawny colour, ftrong as tanned leather, and ftretched like it. The hair frefh; the bones of the legs and arms fhook out of the fkin; the grifty part of the heel and the nails frefh; but both the hand and nails fhrunk on being expofed to the air. It had on fandals made of one piece of a raw hide, with a feam at the heel, and a thong of the fame, and tanned of the fame colour, with the corpfe by the moor water. Mr. Vertue referred the form of it to the time of Henry III. or Edward I. A body was taken up on the moors at Geel, and another in the great moor near Thorn, with the fkin like tanned leather, the hair, teeth, and nails quite frefh [4].

There was found in Locherby mofs in the Stewarty of Annandale the body of a man of gigantic ftature, his upper coat appeared to have been made of the fkins of beafts; his fhoes of the fame, and in the fafhion of rullions worn by the antient Scots, and at this day by fome of the Highlanders, and fewed together in a new and wonderful tafte. The corpfe was found four feet under the mofs, with a heap of ftones above it; the flefh feemed fomewhat frefh on the bones when firft difcovered, but being brought to the bank mouldered to afhes [5].

In the moffes of Saila or Stennefs ifland, Shetland, was found a female corpfe which had lain above eighty years. Every part was fo well preferved that the mufcles were difcernible, the hair of her head, and the gloves on her hands [6].

The tomb which once contained the famous national mummies is at the South Eaft corner of the ifland of Stroma, on a fmall neck of land, near the fea bank. Mr. Lowe was in full hopes of being gratified with a fight of them intire as formerly, but was highly difappointed when entering the tomb he faw only two bare fculls laid apart, and in the bottom of the vault, which is full of fheeps' dung, a few leg and thigh bones, with others; but all quite bare, and no appearance of what they had been, nor could one have judged from their look that they had been preferved above ground. He was informed by the inhabitants of the ifland that curiofity to fee the mummies had brought many idle people to Stroma, that fome out of wantonnefs had fhattered the door, and others the bodies; and the door not being repaired, fheep and cattle entered the vault and trampled them to pieces. There is little doubt but thefe bodies have been preferved without any farther preparation than excluding infects by the faltnefs of the air. Even the fituation of the tomb favours this, which is furrounded on three fides by the fea. It was a common cuftom in the ifles to preferve beef and mutton by hanging it in the caves of the fea, which effectually refifted putrefaction by the faltnefs of the air; and there is little doubt but this has been the

[1] Itin. II. fol. 39. [2] Warton's Hift. of Englifh Poetry, II. 98. [3] Balguy, in Phil. Tranf. N° 434. p. 431.

[4] Phil. Tranf. 484. p. 571—575. Dr. Shaw, in his edition of Bacon's works, III. 571. propofes an enquiry, whether tanning may not be applied to dead bodies.

[5] Caledonian Mercury, 20 July, 1742. See in Archaeologia, VII. 90—110. Lady Moira's account of a fkeleton and its habits, found in a peat-turbary at the foot of Mount Drumkeragh, in the county of Down, from whence fhe deduced a complete fyftem of Irifh apparel.

[6] Lowe's MS.

cafe with the bodies at Stroma, which were light and thin, the limbs flexible; certain figns of inartificial prefervation [1].

The corpfe brought from Teneriffe by Capt. Young of his Majefty's fhip Weazle, and prefented to Lord Sandwich, who gave it to Trinity College, Cambridge, is intire, and perfect in all its parts. The fkin is of a deep tawny brown, dry and hard, but many of the mufcular parts fo prominent as to be eafily defined. The body is laid out at full length, the hands brought together over the belly. The nails, except a few, remain on the fingers and toes, both which are connected and fecured by thongs, probably of goat's leather, continued round each finger and toe. It is five feet one inch long, and weighs only thirty pounds. The hair of the head, which has almoft all fallen off fince its expofure, is of a darkifh black colour and curled deeply, a few hairs on the chin fhort and ftiff. The face is the leaft perfect part, having fuffered by fome violence, and the upper jaw on the right fide beat in, fo as to be now nearly in the middle of the palate, and the parietal bone on that fide projects confiderably over, yet there is no apparent fracture, fo that it is perhaps owing to the refiftance made by the hardnefs of the fkin in that place. The bones of the nofe were gone, and the fkin, in this part, is fo flexible as to be capable of being fomewhat elevated, and here it feels like tanned leather. A probe paffes freely into the orbits of the eyes, and quite back into the cavity of the fcull, through which the optic nerves pafs, likewife perpendicularly into the fcull through a fmall hole in the top of the head. There appears to have been an incifion made horizontally on the right fide of the abdomen, which is fewed up again, by which probably the inteftines were extracted. There are likewife cuts about an inch long, one on the back part of each thigh, and one on the calf of each leg, through which a probe will eafily pafs down without any refiftance. As the neck has never been cut through, the mufcles and teguments being completely whole all round, and there is no mark of the cranium having been fawn through, and the fcalp is likewife nearly intire, the brain cannot have been extracted by the former opperation. May we not conjecture it was left in, and has wafted to duft. This at leaft is known to be the appearance of its remains when examined in fculls buried in common graves [2]. Captain Young accidentally difcovered the cave, which contained in its receffes a number of human corpfes, not lefs than thirty, laid horizontally on their backs on the rugged ftones, neatly fewed up in goatfkins with the hair on, and in many parts very perfect. The cave was in its natural ftate, without any offenfive fmell from the bodies, and yeilding a refrefhing coolnefs [3]. Some of thefe bodies were feven feet one inch long, and he had ordered one of thefe dimenfions to be brought off; but there was fome miftake, which prevented his orders being obeyed. He was informed there were many fuch caves fo filled in the ifland, and held in fuch reverence by the inhabitants, that it was deemed facrilege to remove any of the bodies, not to mention that in general their fituation is inacceffible. The goat-fkin is of a light brown colour, feemingly tanned, and retaining the hair, the feam remarkably ftrong and neat, and the thread of a fine tough animal fubftance like catgut. This account is alfo given by former travellers, by Mr. Nicholls in Hackluit's voyage [4], in Sprat's Hiftory of the Royal Society, and by Glafs in his account of the Canaries [5]. The latter adds, that after fwathing the body round with bandages of goatfkins, they fixed it upright in a cave, cloathed in the fame garments as the deceafed wore when alive.

[1] Low's MS.

[2] Account of this mummy by Dr. Collignon.

[3] See a curious paper on this fubject by the Rev. Dr. Lort, in the Minute-book of the Society of Antiquaries, vol. XIII. p. 368. 1774.

[4] Vol. II. 151. Copied in the Univerfal Hiftory, and the French Collection of Voyages.

[5] F. II. c. 4.

The practice of embalming bodies appears to be the most antient and universal, from the patriarchs and the kings of Judah and Israel, to the most barbarous nations, the Indians in South America, and the Incas of Peru. The subterraneous vaults at Kiow on the Dnieper, those at Catana in Sicily, at Toulouse, Bremen, and other parts of the continent, as well as in England, Scotland, and elsewhere, serve to shew, that the process is not very difficult or complicated, or the preservation to be always ascribed to any antiseptic quality in the soil or receptacle where the bodies were deposited.

Acosta [1] mentions the body of an Inca so whole and well preserved by a certain rosin that it seemed alive. Garcilasso de la Vega says, before he went to Spain [1578] he was allowed a sight of his deceased ancestors, whom he found intire, cloathed as when alive, in a sitting posture, their hands crost on their breasts, in which state they had continued two hundred years when the Spaniards ordered them to be removed out of their chapels, and oratories where they were worshipped. He supposed the method of preserving them was by carrying them into snow mountains, where, after they were well dried and congealed by the cold, they applied bituminous matter, which may plump up the flesh. Chardin says, that bodies in the sands of Chorassan became dry as if petrified.

The body of a chief at Otaheitè was found intire in every part, and though it had been dead above four months, and the climate one of the hottest, not the least disagreeable smell proceeded from it. The only remarkable alteration that had happened was a shrinking of the eyes and muscular parts, but the hair and nails were in their original state, and still adhered firmly; and the several joints were quite pliable, or in that kind of relaxed state which happens to persons who faint suddenly. Mr. Anderson, Capt. Cook's surgeon, was informed, that soon after death they are disembowelled, by drawing the intestines and other viscera out at the *anus*, and the whole cavity is then filled or stuffed with cloth, introduced through the same part; that when any moisture appeared on the skin it was carefully dried up, and the body afterwards rubbed all over with a large quantity of perfumed cocoa-nut oil, which being frequently repeated preserved them a great many months; but that at last they gradually mouldered away. Omai told Capt. Cook, that they made use of the juice of a plant that grew among the mountains, of cocoa-nut oil, and frequently washing with sea-water; and that the bodies of all their great men who died natural deaths are thus preserved, and exposed for a considerable time to public view every day, when it does not rain; till at last they are seldom to be seen [2].

In the city of *Kiow*, on the banks of the Dnieper, under a high mountain, are two spacious crypts, called by the names of Antony and Theodosius, and supposed to have been hollowed out about the beginning of the eleventh or end of the tenth century, when Wlodomir Swetoslaus was created first Czar of the Russias, and introduced Christianity into his dominions. They are cut in a clayey soil [3], and contain vast numbers of bodies in perfect preservation, whose incorruptibility the tradition of the place ascribes to their sanctity, and annually in Easter week they are visited by the priests of the place, who address them with informatiom of Christ's resurrection, and after incensing them well, return back again. In the Antonian crypt are deposited many Russian saints, bishops, monks, princes, and other eminent personages. The Theodosian is fuller of chapels than of bodies. All these bodies, placed in separate repositories, are swathed round tightly with clothes and bandages, and only the face appears, which retains the natural skin. The whole are perfectly dry and void of smell. There are some sculls lying in dishes, which exsude a kind of oil; and in other parts of the crypts are piles of bones. This oily matter may be no-

[1] Hist. of India, b. VI. c. 21. [2] Cook's Voyage, 1784. II. 52, 53. [3] *terra limosa.*

thing more nor lefs than the moifture or exhalation of the place, which is attracted by fuch porous matter as the human fcull, and drops or falls into the difh; for Herbinius fuppofes the Greek priefts too undefigning to befmear them with real oil, by which manœuvre nothing was to be got, nor is this a trick played even by the fculls of the three kings at Cologne, fo much reforted to [1].

"The burial place at the Capuchin Convent at Palermo is a vaft fubterraneous apartment, divided into large commodious galleries, the walls on each fide of which are hollowed into a variety of niches, as if intended for a very great collection of ftatues, inftead of which they are all filled with dead bodies, fet upright on their legs, and fixed by the back to the middle of the nich, in number about 300. They are all dreffed in the clothes they ufually wore, and form a moft venerable affembly. The fkin and mufcles, by a certain preparation, became as dry and hard as a piece of ftock fifh: and although many of them have been here upwards of 250 years, yet none are in any degree reduced to fkeletons; the mufcles indeed in fome appear to be a good deal more fhrunk than in others, probably becaufe thefe perfons had been more extenuated at the time of their death. The bodies of the princes and firft nobility are lodged in very handfome chefts or trunks, fome of them richly adorned; thefe are not in the fhape of coffins, but all of one width, and about one and a half or two feet deep. The keys are kept by the neareft relations of the family, who fometimes come and drop a tear over their deceafed friends [2]."

Such is Mr. Brydone's defcription of this catacomb, which Mr. Breval [3] reprefents as "a large fouterrain filled from top to bottom with the dried up carcaffes of the friars of the houfe from time immemorial, in the habits of their order, which is the Francifcan. This is caufed by depofiting them as foon as dead, in a peculiar ground that belongs to them, which, by a confuming property, turns the corpfe into a perfect mummy in a few weeks. I have feen, adds he, inftances of the fame deficcation at Touloufe in France, where there is a vault under the cloyfter of the Cordeliers, in which are preferved abundance of corpfes dried up by having lain fome time in a churchyard that has much the fame property with that of Palermo. Thefe bodies are expofed for three or four days to the open air, in their belfrey, before they are ranged in this manner. A celebrated beauty of Touloufe, known by the name of *Le belle Paule*, was for a long time one of thefe mummies; but is now almoft mouldered away [3]."

Sutton Cofield vaults are faid to have the contrary properties. In two of them, lately opened, bodies interred within the memory of man were found reduced to duft, together with their wooden coffins. This is fuppofed to be in part occafioned by the height of the church, and the fandinefs of the foil [4].

It has been fuppofed to be the nature of hair to acquire a yellowifh hue in the grave. As Arthur's queen Guinever (if it was her fepulchre) having been married in the beginning of the 6th century, could hardly efcape being greyhaired at the conclufion of it; neither was Humphry duke of Gloucefter a young man, and his hair was exactly of the fame colour with that found on the fcull of a fkeleton in a bog in the county of Down in Ireland, of which lady Moira gave an account to the Society of Antiquaries [5]. I may add, that I was told of golden coloured hair found on a fcull dug up in the cloifter of Chickfand nunnery, c. Bedford, though the hair which was given me from a ftone coffin dug up in the ruins of Chrift church nunnery, Hants, 1782, before-mentioned, was of a bright brown.

[1] Religiofæ Kijovienfes cryptæ per M. J. Herbinium. Jenæ, 1675. 12°.
[2] Brydone's Tour through Sicily, II. 66, 67. Of thofe at Naples fee Blainville's Travels, III. 357—359.
[3] Travels, I. 49. [4] Newbery's Defcription of England, IX. 100. [5] Archæolog. VII. p. I. p. 93. 100.

In

In illustrating the different fashions of sepulchral monuments I cannot do better than subjoin a learned memoire drawn up by the late Maurice Johnson, esq. founder of the literary society of Spalding, before whom it was read, and from whose Minutes I have been permitted to transcribe it. I shall occasionally enlarge it from my own observations. He divides our tombs into eight forms.

"Before the evil practice of burying in churches became general, and the arts of designing were restored, our ancestors, if of fortune sufficient to afford it, were interred in stone coffins, the bottom part being of one large stone sufficient to receive the corpse, and usually accommodated to that figure, in imitation of the more antient sarcophagi. The form of the lid or upper part varied with the times, as arts were retrieved. Perhaps, though of stone, they were called *coffins*, being destined to the like use, and much of the same shape, with those of Gopher or Cypress wood, used by the antients, and the term taken from Κοφινος, *cophinus*, *corbis*, which Pasor makes a primitive word[1]. The lid, or upper part, of the most antient of these we find was in the form of a prism, or triangular, and though they be now generally under ground, originally only the bottom part, or that which contained the corpse, was seen above ground; and that was the reason, I conceive, why it was made of that form, the better to shoot off the wet, and defend it and its depositum from the injuries of the weather; a very necessary caution towards what they wished to preserve so in the air of this island; and though they might be afterwards removed into churches, or even supposing they were originally there deposited, yet did they for some time retain their triangular form and plain superficies of the lid or cover, though they adorned the sides with carving, the inscription if any being about the basis of the lid or covering-stone, as in that of John of St. Yves prior, on the South side of Peterborough minster yard[2]; and the imagery, as on that within the same cathedral of the abbot and monks murdered by the Danes, being on the sides[3]; that of William Rufus in Winchester cathedral, and that rich shrine of St. Thomas Becket[4], and the stones in Spalding church-yard near the free-school commonly called *The Lambs*, by tradition that gentleman of that antient family in that town were thereunder interred." This Mr. Johnson calls the FIRST form, prismatic, and plain on the top.

To these instances add the stone coffin of Waldevus abbot of Mailros, and of prior Basing at Winchester.

"The first improvement of it may be so called from the distinguishing these covers with crosses, at first plain, afterwards fleury, in bas relief, which was soon converted into alto relievo, as on a like tomb of Theobald archbishop of Canterbury in the cathedral there, A. D. 1160[5]," supported by seven low round pilasters, with capitals fleury between the arches, the top, lid, or cover, divided into several compartments by circles and semicircles, and lozenges and heads, as it should seem by their coverings and tonsure, of princes, prelates, and persons eminent for piety in the monastic profession[6]."

This is the SECOND form, prismatic, and carved on the top.

To the instances of coffin lids adorned with crosses add the coffin ascribed to Juga Baynard, those of prior Basing, Stephen Langton archbishop of Canterbury, Alan abbot of Tewksbury, a monument among the figures in the Temple church, and that shewn in Bangor cathedral for Owen Glendwr's, but more probably Owen Gwenneth's, sovereign of North Wales.

[1] See Herodotus in Euterpe, and Pliny, N. H. XXIV. 5.

[2] Inscribed in Gothic capitals:

✠ Aĩa Johannis de Sco Yvone quondam
Prioris per miām dĩ in pace requiescat. MCXII.

[3] Gunton, p. 243. [4] Monast. Angl. I. 21. [5] Parker's Antiq. p. 195. Dart, p. 124. [6] Dart, p. 123.

That

That ascribed to bishop Glanville, on the South side of the choir near the altar at Rochester, is of the same form with archbishop Theobald's, and was adorned with similar heads in quatrefoils divided by angels, now almost defaced. The form and ornaments of this tomb give it an earlier date.

"And probably of as great age are the stones before Mr. Jackson's house, taken from the conventual church at Spalding. These are termed by the inaccurate writers of former ages *lapides et petræ pyramidales*, which, had they arisen from an equal basis, they might properly have been termed: and their first forms may be properly ascertained as one, and called the *prismatic* tombs.

"This I say for the general use. Not but some few very extraordinary persons, as princes, and those who had been invested with princely power, and mighty benefactors, might, as early as any of these, be honoured with having their entire effigies carved in a remarkable posture, lying, as it were, on their backs on the topstone.

"But it is commonly thought, that those monuments (though antient) were devised and made in honour of them some time after: such are those of AILWIN duke or earl of the East Angles, cousin to king Edgar and chief justice of all England, who died A. D. 993, at *Ramsay* abbey, which he founded [1]. ALGAR, earl of Holland, overcome and killed in battle by the Pagan invading Danes [2], A. D. 870. in *Alder*, alias *Algarkirk*, church-yard, in North Holland, Lincolnshire. These most antient are generally of a sort of granite, or the hardest black marble, or raggstone, which would bear a polish; and have all some animal, as a lion, dog, or such like, at their feet, against which they seem to rest: whence, perhaps, supporters might be taken.

The figure of ROBERT duke of Normandy, who died 1134, and was buried in the cathedral church of Gloucester [3], lies cross-legged, in his coat of mail, surtout, sword, spurs, and coronet, having vowed and performed a crusade, or voyage, to the Holy Land, for the purpose of recovering it from the Saracens. That of WILLIAM LONGESPEE earl of Salisbury, who died 1226, lies in the cathedral there [4]. Sir HENRY BATHE chief justice of all England, 1252 [5], and PHILIP prior of St. Fridefwide [6], both in the church of St. Frideswide, or Christ Church, Oxford. Some of the first abbots and priors of Peterborough [7]; and see in Drake's Eboracum, p. 491, the figures there called *Constantine*, and Prince *William of Hatfield* son of Edward III.

THIRD form: Tables, whereon effigies or sculpture.

But this manner of representing the effigies of the deceased lying on the back on the top-stone became the general practice for eminent personages, and priests with chalices in their hands on their breast, by which they were distinguished, as military men or knights were by their arms, spurs, and swords. So *William* earl of Flanders, son of the before-mentioned Robert, at St. Omer's [8]. He died 1127-8, but seems to have been sometime after honoured with that monument by the manner of its workmanship. Prelates were represented with their mitres, crosiers, great crosses, by being habited *in pontificalibus*; as *Hubert Walter* in Canterbury, whereof he was archbishop, and deceased 1205 [9]. And king *John*, at Worcester, 1213, with ouches or jewels on his gloves, collar, and sword hilt, with images of his tutelar saints, the bishops Oswald and Wulstan, with their mitres on and censers in their hands, and a lion at his feet [10]. Those of the lord *Rous* and others, in the Temple-church, in London [11]; of

[1] Stukeley, Itin. Cur. I. 77. Pl. 17.
[2] Ingulf. p. 20.
[3] Stebbing, p. 16. See p. 19.
[4] Stebbing, p. 115. See p. 41. Pl. XIII.
[5] See p. 45. Pl. XIV.
[6] See p. 36*. Pl. XII.
[7] Pl. III. p. 19. Add the abbots of Westminster, pl. I. p. 10. bishop Roger and the other bishop at Salisbury, pl. IV. p. 20.
[8] Stebbing, p. 17.
[9] Dart. p. 131.
[10] Stukeley, It. Cur. 18. Pl. 68. Stebbing, p. 85.
[11] See p. 42. Pl. V. Fig. 3.

the

the *Bonoworths*, at Sutterton; of a forefter of Rockingham and his wife, at Glinton, c. Northampton; of another lady at Stoke Doyley in that county; of *Thomas* lord *Burgh*, knight of the Garter, and his lady, in the church of Gainfborough, of alabafter and granite.

"About this time, I apprehend, if they did not place the effigies they left off raifing the upper ftone to a point, and only carried it up fome part of the way, with fome decoration on the plain top, as an old crofs fleury fhews of archbifhop *Langton* [1], made about 1233, and of this form were tables fet in pillars on feet, as archbifhop Sewal's, in York cathedral, A. D. 1258 [2].

Inftances of coffin ftones with heads or bodies emerging from them may be feen at Brandon in Suffolk, Appleby in Weftmorland, Kingfbury in Warwickfhire.

"Thefe were frequently placed for fafety (efpecially if they built churches) within the wall, and had an arch turned over them; as Sir   Mullendin, knight, at Soleby, and a lady at Rippingale; and then they frequently made them of alabafter, or fome foft chalky ftone, which cut eafily, and they were thick covered over with paint and gilding.

FOURTH form; tombs with teftoons or arches over them.

"In the beginning of the fourteenth century, according to Monier, the arts of defigning, with a good tafte of drawing and painting, emerged out of that ignorance and ill gufto the Goths and Barbarians had reduced them to, and kept them in. Our Henry III. a wife prince, who had experienced, and was equal to both fortunes, reigning long, and at length peaceably, much encouraged them; and his wife fon and fucceffor, Edward I. was trained up in them. Though his father had beftowed a cheft of gold for enfhrining the reliques of St. Edward the Confeffor, Edward did them greater honour in the ftately and fumptuous manfoleum compofed of all kinds of precious marbles, and other coftly ftones, even gems and pearls, wherein he placed them, at Weftminfter, raifed on columns diminifhing one ftage above another, as may be feen in Mr. George Vertue's fine print, done for the Society of Antiquaries, and in Dart's Antiquities of Weftminfter abbey. A tomb of like tafte and materials, of two ftages, he erected for his father, whofe effigies of copper gilt he caufed to be caft, and laid thereon, with a lion at his feet [3], with a teftoon [4], or covering over it, flat and in a ftrait line, to preferve it from duft or what might fall on and injure it. The like he erected there for Eleanor his beloved queen, who died 1298 [5]. And though they foon began to throw the teftoon or covering higher by arched work inftead of it, yet we find many of the nobleft made ftill with that ftrait line or flat covering, as that of queen *Philippa* wife of king Edward III. at Weftminfter [6]; and his own there [7]; the *Black Prince* at Canterbury [8]; king *Richard* II. and *Anne* his queen, at Weftminfter [9]; King *Henry* IV. and *Joan of Navarre* his queen, at Canterbury [10]; *Katharine Swynford*, dutchefs of Lancafter, in Lincoln cathedral; archbifhop *Chicheley's* at Canterbury [11]; and it feems as if fuch a teftoon had been intended, but not finifhed, for the beautiful alabafter tomb of *William of Waynfleet*, Lord High Chancellor of England and bifhop of Winchefter, 1459, in All Saints church in Waynfleet.

"Some tombs having been thus raifed with teftoons over them which were flat, gave rife to a much farther improvement, the raifing an arch over them, which being then oxeyed, or terminating in an obtufe point, was ufually deco-

1 Parker, p. 245. Dart. p. 134. fee p. 42.
2 Drake's Eboracum, 479 & 494.
3 Stebbing, 92. fee p. 17. Pl. xx. xxi. xxii.
4 Or, *tefter*. The tefters of Henry III. Eleanor, Philippa, Richard II. are of wood, painted with the Deity, faints, and angels, on their ceiling: that of Catharine Swynford has been fupplied with a later roof in a very different ftyle.
5 Stebbing, 131. fee p. 63.
6 Stebbing, p. 173.
7 Stebbing, p. 176.
8 Stebbing, p. 188.
9 Ib. p. 203.
10 Ib. p. 175. Dart. p. 15.
11 Ib. p. 153.

rated

rated at top with foliage work all the way up the fides, and a jeffe, or large fleur de foliage over the fummit, and images of the wife, children, relations of the party, faints or fovereigns and benefactors about the table, on the fides; and much painting and gilding was now beftowed on the fculpture, though of marble or copper. Thus in the monument of *Aveline* wife of Edmund earl of Lancafter, &c. at Weftminfter, who died 1269[1], and of that earl himfelf, who died 1296[2]; and in that of king *Edward* II. at Gloucefter cathedral, who died 1327[3]; of *John Peckham* archbifhop of Canterbury[4], and in that of *John of Eltham* earl of Cornwall, at Weftminfter, who died 1334[5]; *John of Gaunt* and his dutchefs Blanche, in St. Paul's cathedral, London[6]; Cardinal *Beaufort* bifhop of Winchefter, at Winchefter, who died 1447[7]; thofe of Lord *Henry Burgwash* bifhop of Lincoln, 1340, in the cathedral there; and of *Nicholas* lord *Cantalupe*, 1371; and *Robert* lord *Badlefmere*; thofe of archbifhops *Grey*, 1255; *Greenfield*, 1314; and *Bowet*, 1423, in York cathedral. The *Queen of Scots* and *Queen Elizabeth*, both at Weftminfter[8].

FIFTH form of tombs, in chapel burial places.

" Thefe arched monuments they much enlarged fo as to incumber and take up too much room, even in the moft fpacious cathedral and conventual churches; therefore they fell into a method for avoiding that inconvenience of annexing chapels to them, having doors out of the fide ailes of the churches, and being open to the church, only fecluded by iron work, of which great deformities the inftances are too frequent, having an extraordinary ill effect, and fpoiling the view on the outfide, and defigns of the artifts, which, though not true according to rules of the artifts, yet were grand, and looked awful. In fuch a chapel, at Weftminfter, lies king *Henry* V[9]; king *Edward* IV. at Windfor[10]; Bifhop *Ruffell* and archbifhop *Longland*, 1548, in Lincoln cathedral.

" But thofe great men avoided this error, and well confulted for and increafed the beauty of thefe venerable piles, who added fuch chapels for the reception of themfelves and their relations or friends at the Eaft end of them; that divifion from the crofs ifle being much too fhort for the nave and well admitting it. Thus king Henry VII's fumptuous chapel added to Weftminfter abbey greatly increafes the beauty of that pile[11]. Sometimes well enough when running parallel in the choir, as that of *Humphry* the Good duke of *Gloucefter* at St. Alban's; the fumptuous chapel of *Richard Beauchamp* earl of Warwick governor of Normandy 1439, wherein is his tomb, and his effigies of brafs gilt[12], and of *Arthur*, Prince of Wales, at Worcefter, who died 1502[13].

To thefe add the ellipfe of chapels round the choir at Tewksbury, that of bifhop Hatfield, on the South fide of the choir at Durham, that of abbot Ramridge, on the North fide of the choir at St. Albans: that of Walter lord Hungerford, on the North fide of the nave at Salisbury, now removed to the South fide of the aile. Additions to the outfide of the building are thofe of bifhop Audley at Salifbury on the South fide, and that of the Hungerford family on the North fide, of the choir there; bifhops Weft and Alcock, at Ely.

SIXTH form, inlaid with brafs.

" As to the infcription, the characters or letters were fometimes antiently exfculped, and in relcivo more frequently infculped, and appear to have been filled with lead, before the ufe of brafs and copper became frequent, after which, and what we may, I think reckon the 6th form, they, in the area of very broad coarfe, grey marbles cut out, or funk in, the form or figure of the images of the

[1] Stebbing p. 105. [2] Ib. p. 106. [3] Ib. p. 152. [4] Dart, p. 138.
[5] Stebbing. p. 154. [6] Ib. p. 255. Dugd. St. Paul's. [7] Stebbing. p. 260. [8] Ib. p. 535. 516.
[9] Ib. p. 159. [10] Ib. p. 413. [11] Ib. p. 472, 473. [12] Dugdale, Warwickfhire, p. 328.
[13] Stebbing. p. 476. [14] Ib. p. 318.

perfons,

persons, their escucheons, and of much arch and pinacle work, filled with foliage, and of saints in the niches. These they filled with thick plates of brass or copper gilt, and sometimes enamelled, fixt in with long pieces of the same metal, and curiously engraven, the legend or inscription being carried along by the edge in metal also. Some of the most elegant of these are that of *William Smith* bishop of Lincoln [1], who founded two colleges, and was the first president of Wales, which he governed long, and died 1513. That of *Margery* wife of Robert de *Wylughby* lord of Eresby, at Spilsby, 1391; that of *Thomas de Bramstone* constable or chastellan of Wisbeach, in the church there 1401. That of *Joan* niece and coheiress of *Ralph* lord *Cromwell* of Tattershale, wife of *Humphry Bourchier*, who bore that title in her right at *Tattershale*, who died 1480. Those of *Thomas* duke of *Gloucester*, 1397, surnamed of Woodstock, and *Eleanor*, 1399, his dutchess, at Westminster [2], of Dr. *Richard Waldby* archbishop of York, at Westminster, about 1397 [3]; and that of lady *Lambert*, in the chancel of Pinchbeck church." Instances of rich brasses are innumerable.

"The last sort were frequently elevated in a sort of oblong square tables, composed of the same sort of marble, or other materials, and called *altar* monuments, at which business has been frequently done by surrogates, and monies been made payable and paid, they being as convenient for those purposes as any other table. These might perhaps be called *altar* monuments from the altar which stood in the midst of the great North porch of St. Austin's abbey church at Canterbury, wherein solemn masses were said for the souls of the Saxon kings and first archbishop of that province, amidst the place of their interment, as archbishop Parker tells us, which might have taken rise from what we are told in the Chronicle of John abbot of Peterborough [4]. Godrick, his predecessor, did over the before-mentioned stone monument erect in the area before the East end of the abby church *omni anno super petram sanctum tentorium figens pro animabus ibidem sepultorum missas per biduum devotione continuo celebravit.*

Seventh form: against the walls.

"Another method has of late years been, chiefly since the Reformation (the pavements being either full, in the most conspicuous places, or rather to prevent their being worn with treading or defaced) to let them into, or fix them up against, the walls and pillars of churches; so that great part of the monument, with entire columns and statues on each side, projects.

"This ordinance and disposition in some stately sepulchres has a grand air, and the best effect of any, and is now most in use. The dead person being represented generally in a reclined posture, as in that of the duke of Beaufort, at Windsor, the dukes of Newcastle and Buckinghamshire, Sir Isaac Newton, Mr. Thynne, earl Stanhope, Dr. Chamberlain, Sir Cloudesly Shovel, at Westminster; the earl and countess of Exeter, at St. Martin's, Stamford; Mr. Deacon sheriff of Northamptonshire, in Peterborough cathedral; bishop Gunning, and other bishops, at Ely; that of Aylmeric de Courcy lord Kingsale baron of Ringrone, lord Cottington, Sir Christopher and lady Hatton, Sir Dudley Carlton, in Westminster abbey; the archbishops Sterne, Dolben, and Sharpe, in York cathedral. But sometimes the entire statue of the person erect, in a graceful posture, which is more noble, as Secretary Craggs, at Westminster, the late duke of Ancaster Lord Great Chamberlain, at Edenham, archbishop Lamplugh, and the earl and countess of Strafford, and the Hon. Mr. Wentworth, in York cathedral [5].

[1] Stukeley, Itin. Cur. I. pl. 16. p. 86.
[2] Stebbing, p. 230. 232. See the latter page.
[3] Drake's Eboracum, p. 436.
[4] P. 10. Edit. Sparke.
[5] Drake's Ebor. part II. p. 467. 512.

"And

EIGHTH form: detached buildings.

"And lastly the most sumptuous sepulchral monuments are detached buildings, erected to preserve the remains of the dead, or their memory: as domes, of which, perhaps, that of the emperor Hadrian [1] is the grandest, that of the duke of Tuscany of the Medici family at Florence the most sumptuous, the pyramid of Cestius at Rome, Porsena near Clusium, and those in Egypt. To these may be added obelisks, columns [2], and equestrian statues.

The late Smart Lethieullier, esq. has confined his observations on sepulchral monuments, printed in the second volume of the Archæologia, p. 291—300, chiefly to those in parochial churches, erected either in the chancel or in small chapels, or side ailes, which had been built by the lords of the manors, and patrons of the churches (which for the most part went together) and being designed for burying places for their families, were frequently endowed with chantries, to pray for the souls of the founder and his descendents.

It appears to me, that there is pretty good authority for referring those monuments whose situation within the substance of the walls of churches or chancels makes it highly probable that they must have been coæval in them, to founders or refounders of the several churches or parts of churches where they are found. Of this the churches in Hertfordshire and Essex within my own neighbourhood afford many instances. I cannot help particularizing one.

An old monument in the North wall of the nave of Brent Pelham church, c. Herts, which has furnished matter for vulgar tradition, and puzzled former Antiquaries, is, by Dr. Salmon, supposed a founder's tomb. Weever [3] describes it as "a most ancient monument stone, whereon is figured a man, and about him "an eagle, a lion, and a bull, having all wings, and a fourth of the shape of "an angel; as if they should represent the four Evangelists. Under the feet of "the man is the cross flourie, and under the cross a serpent. He is thought "to have been sometime the lord of an ancient decayed house, well moated, not "far from this place called, *O Piers Shoonkes*. He flourished ann. Conquestu *vicesimo primo*" This description is correct, except in the figure of the *man*, who is really an angel flying, and conveying up a soul in a shroud, or sheet, in the usual attitude. At his right hand is an angel sitting, holding in his lap an open book; at his left is a bull: the eagle and winged lion over his head complete the number of the symbols of the Evangelists. The serpent is really a two-footed dragon pierced by the cross, whose point is in his mouth; and so the sculpture conveys the idea of the destruction of Satan by the cross of Christ, securing immortality to all who die in the faith of his Gospel, as transmitted by the Evangelists. Over the lines is now written, *O Piers Shonks, who died A° 1086*. Salmon, by a train of "amusing conjectures" on the name of *Shonks*, makes him out to be either a founder of the church, or Gilbert *Sank*, on whom Simon de Furneuse, lord of the manor, levied a distress for his homage and service, 16 Edward I. which is 221 years from the Conquest, instead of 21, and so makes out the old farmer's tale, about a hero of Pelham defeating a giant of Barkway, and obliging the latter manor to pay a quitrent to the former ever since. A manor here retains the name of *Shonks*. Neither the English nor the Latin poetry, with their variations, over the monument, within the arch, attesting the legend, are worth recording. In almost every church a singular or unknown monument of any antiquity is given to a giant.

This monument, from its simplicity, may be of early date. I recollect another instance in the North wall of the church at Landbeach in Cambridgeshire, of

[1] *Moles Hadriani.*
[3] Fun. Mon. p. 549.
[2] The pillar of Pompey in Egypt.

the

the time of one of the Edwards, and probably enough afcribed by Mr. Malters its rector to one of the lords of the manor at that time. Where fuch monuments appear in the walls of chancels, and have on them a religious, inftead of a lay figure, we may prefume, that fome rector was the builder or rebuilder of the chancel. An inftance of this kind at St. Hippolyte's, in Hertfordfhire, is, by the vulgar, referred to the patron Saint, inftead of the lay patron, or officiating prieft.

Thefe monuments vary with the feveral periods in form and ornaments, and in having or wanting figures on them; and a little attention to the ftyle of the time, or the fucceffion of property, will enable us to afcertain them, when armorial and other diftinctions fail. It is not uncommon, when chapels were built for the fole ufe of a particular family, or fucceffive lords of the manor, to find the original founder or benefactor inclofed within their walls.

Mr. Lethieullier is of opinion, that "few or no funeral monuments were erected during the time of our Saxon anceftors; at leaft, being ufually placed in the churches belonging to the greater abbies, they felt the ftroke of the general diffolution, and fcarce any had fallen within his obfervation, or were, he believed, extant. Thofe we meet with for the kings of that race, fuch as Ina at Wells, Ofric at Gloucefter, Sebba and Ethelbert, which were in St. Paul's, or wherever elfe they occur, were undoubtedly cenotaphs erected in later ages, by the feveral abbies and convents of which they were founders, in gratitude to fuch generous benefactors [1]." On this fubject I fhall offer a few obfervations.

The fepulchral monuments before the Conqueft are certainly of dubious authority.

The tomb of king LUCIUS, at *Winchefter*, ought to be left undetermined till the reality of the king himfelf be fettled.

That of OSRIC, at *Gloucefter*, confeffedly favors of the eleventh or twelfth century, more than of the feventh.

GUTHRUM, at *Hadleigh* in Suffolk, lies under an arch terminating in a bouquet, to which his age had no more pretence than it had to the rich chapels of the fifteenth century.

The tombs of ANNA and his fon FIRMINUS, at *Blithburough*, whence their bones were removed Bury, have been covered with brafs figures, and more probably belong to Sir John Hopton, temp. Henry VI. and one of the Swillingtons. Gardiner [2] defcribes a black marble coffin, which may rather belong to Anna.

King INA, by fome accident or other, has not obtained fo modern a cenotaph, but is faid to lie under a plain whitifh coffin-fafhioned ftone in the centre of the nave at *Wells*, which church he founded about the beginning of the eighth century.

"In the new chapel at *Glaftenbury* a very faire toombe of king EDGAR, *copper gilt* [3]."

That of SEBBA king of the Eaft Saxons, 676, in old *St. Paul's*, like its companion ERKENWALD's 1017, their conformity proves to have been made when that church was rebuilt, about 1083 [4].

That of ETHELWERD, at *Winbornminfter*, the form of the letters on the brafs plate proves to be not older than the Reformation.

ALDHELM's, at *Malmefbury*, is in a ftyle very fuperior to the rudenefs of the feventh century; and fo is ALDRED, at *Gloucefter*, which Mr. Ray [5] calls king

[1] Archæol. II. 293. [2] Hift. of Dunwich, p. 124.
[3] Defcription of Glaftonbury, at the end of Hearne's Hemingford, p. 641.
[4] Dugdale's St. Paul's, p. 92. [5] Itinerary, p. 852.

Lucius, the firſt Chriſtian king. And Atkyns [1] ſays "he lies as if he had been *laid in a manger*: his freeſtone figure on a *ſhelf* tomb, which is only a beautiful and ſingular altar tomb arching forward on pillars. His figure holds a church.

Biſhop LEOFRIC's, at *Exeter*, is confeſſedly of Queen Elizabeth's reign.

What has been miſtaken for HAROLD's tomb at *Waltham* abbey is the ciſtern of a garden fountain in James the Firſt's time.

The current tradition of Waltham is, that the piece of dark grey marble, with a gaping head between two tritons in bold relief, formerly fixed at the further end of Mr. Jones's cellar at the abbey houſe, ſince the demolition of that houſe removed to that of ſome of the inhabitants, and now, by favour of Sir William Wake, baronet, in my poſſeſſion, belonged to HAROLD's tomb. Farmer has engraved a like head, then in his houſe, now fixed in the wall of a houſe on the bank, as it is called, formerly inhabited by him, and an inſcription under it, which ſays it was part of Harold's tomb. Both fragments are in a ſtyle too good for Harold's age. There is nothing in either face characteriſtic of a tomb. Nor is it likely, or ſcarce poſſible, that Harold, or any other perſon, ſhould have been buried in the place fixed upon by Fuller, which is at leaſt as far Eaſt as the whole length of the preſent church, and too far for the choir, or eaſtern chapel, of ſuch a church as Waltham church, however magnificent it appears to have been, to have extended. It is therefore moſt probable, that theſe fragments ſerved ſome other purpoſe, and may have been a baſon to a fountain, under which they are ſaid to have been found. Smith's deſcription of the tomb inſinuates, that it was unornamented. Fuller ſays it was plain, except the croſs fleury, the moſt uſual ornament of tombs in that age and later, though Arthur's had a croſs, if we believe Leland [2]. Fuller would hardly have omitted the two faces, had they been there. By his *pillorets* it ſhould ſeem this coffin-faſhioned monument was raiſed from the ground, a circumſtance not unuſual at that time, or had ſome arch work in relief at the ſides. Knighton expreſsly ſays [3] of Harold's tomb that it was "*tumulatio cum imagine.*" Mr. Morant ſays, Dr. Uvedale, of Enfield, was the laſt who ſaw the tomb at Waltham mill, which muſt have been about ſixty years ago. From that time to the preſent it has never been heard of; but the fragments here deſcribed exhibited inſtead of it. The account given by Sir Edward Denny of the diſcovery of Harold's body here on his clearing away the rubbiſh of the abbey, is no more than that his gardiner found a ſtone coffin, with a ſkeleton, which crumbled to pieces on touching. Fuller adds, that he was buried in the garden, under a leaden fountain, where, in his time, was a bowling green, which formerly belonged to the earl of Carliſle. Accordingly the fragments in queſtion were accompanied with a pedeſtal of the ſame marble, about fourteen inches ſquare and nineteen high, having on two of the ſides two lions rampant againſt a wheatſheaf, the creſt of Cecil, and other ornaments, on the other two ſides, and through one of the corners a hole, as for a pipe. From the particular of the croſs fleuri one might perhaps refer the coffin to an abbot. As to the epitaph, Fuller omits it, as not ſufficiently atteſted; perhaps only made by ſome rhyming monk, in the abbey-regiſter; a common practice.

Of the ſame legendary caſt is the tomb ſhewn againſt the South wall of the choir at *Cheſter*, for that of the *emperor* HENRY IV. who, after a diſtracted reign of fifty years, inſulted by that wretch pope Gregory VII. who, to ſupport an independent power of diſpoſing of eccleſiaſtical preferments in his dominions, ſtirred up his ſubjects and his own ſons againſt him, was at laſt formally dethroned, by his

[1] Hiſt. of Gloceſterſhire, p. 131. [2] Itin. III. 85. [3] II. 2343.

son Henry V. and being refused a lay-prebend's place in the church of Spires, ended his days at Liege, 1106, and was there buried; afterwards dug up, by order of pope Pascal II. and left above ground five years, till his son having in his turn quarrelled with the pope, caused him to be deposited in the imperial vault at Spires. Giraldus Cambrensis [1] is the first who tells us he was buried at Chester, and Camden copies him. But besides that Giraldus, or his informer, confounds this emperor with his son; he tells a story equally improbable and false of Harold, whom the people of Chester pretended to have escaped the battle of Hastings, and after leading the life of a hermit, ended his days and was buried among them. It is probable therefore those who copied the story from Giraldus are answerable for the confusion of persons, as those who informed him are for burying an emperor of Germany at Chester, under an altar tomb adorned with quatrefoils. Browne Willis describes his tomb as a "pyramid on an arch, towering six or seven yards above the roof of the cloister or side aile, having no other ornaments answering it, and seeming as antient as any part of the church." He adds, "a story goes, in a MS. of one Godeshal [2], a great man, dying in this monastry; and it is conjectured, this pyramid was erected over his grave [3]." This does not appear in the South view of the church in his cathedrals: but in a South view, by Smith, there is a kind of *stone bee-hive*, with a door, towering above the roof, but on the opposite side of the aile to the tomb.

Orc's, at *Abbotsbury*, is a cenotaph of any age; an antient coffin of black marble, with a cover of the same [4].

The figures called the Saxon kings at *Axminster* are some religious of later date; and the bones taken up here filled with lead, and preserved in the sexton's house, till it was burnt a few years ago, have as little pretensions to royalty as the supposed owners of them had to reality; for neither the field of battle, nor the heroes of it, are known.

"In the North aile at Hexham is a monument in the wall, in such a form as usually designed at the building of churches for founders or great benefactors: but to what personage this belongs is not known, no insignia or inscription remaining. It is supposed to be the tomb of ALFWOLD, king of Northumberland, who was assassinated at Cilchester by Sigga, a factious lord of his court, A. D. 788. I measured an effigy which lays near this tomb, and found it answering exactly in length. The tomb is formed in an aperture made through the wall, by an elegant piece of arched work. The effigy represents an ecclesiastic, with his hood thrown back to his forehead, his hand elevated, and robed to the feet; the folds of the drapery thrown into excellent order, easy, and elegant [5]."

In *Bosenham* church, Sussex, is an antient monument, with a female figure on it, supposed to be a daughter of king Canute [6]. They might as well suppose it a daughter of Harold.

AESCHWINE, or AESCHWY, twelfth bishop of Dorchester, from about 980 to about 1000, had "an image of freestone that lay on his tomb, as appeared by the inscription in Leland's time [7]. This may be the defaced figure in freestone of an archbishop, dug up some years since in the North aile, and now lying in the South aile.

[1] "Imperatorem Romanum Henricum se jactat hæc urbs habere sepultum. Qui quoniam suis diebus tam patrem "carnalem quam etiam spiritualem, summum pontificem scil. Pascalem incarceraverat, demum pœnitentia ductus & ultro- "neus exul effectus sanctam in eremo finibus suis vitam (ut fertur) consummavit." This double imprisonment of his spiritual and temporal father is true of Henry V. but Henry IV. was but six years old at the death of *his* father.

[2] Mr. Pennant, Wales, I. 183, says, the emperor Henry is said to have "resided in *Godstall-Lane*, in this city.

[3] Mitr. Ab. I. 250. [4] Hutchins's Dorset, I. 539.

[5] Hutchinson's View of Northumberland, 1778. vol. I. 98.

[6] Newbery's Description of England, IX. 173.

[7] It. II. 10.

Nothing

Nothing remains of king SEBERT, at *Westminster*, but the arch under which his stone coffin was probably deposited. The beautiful paintings over it are acknowledged to be coæval with the foundation of the abbey by Henry III. and by Vertue ascribed to Cavallini [1]. One cannot help lamenting the peculiar hard fate of these morceaux. Of the eight whole length figures, that of Becket, we may be assured, fell the first sacrifice. Another has perished by the pannel being taken out to make a passage to some of the royal family, who were seated on this tomb at coronations. The rest on the back of the choir have been the sport of idle boys, and are completely scratched out. The only two perfect ones came to light in the new modification of the choir, and happily furnished Sir Joseph Ayloffe with an opportunity of getting them engraved before they were shut up again for ever. These are as beautifully engraved as they were drawn, by Mr. Basire, at the expence of the Society of Antiquaries, for their Vetusta Monumenta.

A small whole length figure of a bishop or abbot, with crosier and mitre in the South wall of the nave at *Sherborne*, has, from its pure simplicity, a chance of being original.

The like figure of a bishop in the South wall of the chancel of the Temple church is ascribed in a MS. note of Browne Willis, in his history of that church, to Sylvester de Everdon, bishop of Carlisle, who died 1254, of a fall from a mettlesome horse.

The figure of AILWIN, who founded *Ramsey* abbey, A. D. 969, is one of the oldest genuine sepulchral monuments among us, and almost the only remains of that rich house, where it now lies neglected in a yard [2]. It is habited in a kind of mantle, buskins and pileus: the right hand holds two keys and a ragged staff, the left lies on the breast: over the top of the Gothic arch over him is a representation of two angels carrying off his soul as it rises from the tomb. Ailwin is styled duke or earl of the East Angles, and *alderman of all England*. The title of *Aldermannus* is shewn by Spelman [3] to be synonymous to that of *Dux* and *Comes*: and that of *Alderman of all England* to that of *Half King*, which his father Athelstan held on account of his great influence with the king of that name [4]. His epitaph calls him *Cousin* to king Edgar: I suppose because his mother Alswen was that prince's nurse. On his tomb was this epitaph:

> "*Hic requiescit Ailwinus incliti regis Edwini cognatus*
> "*totius Angliæ aldermanus, et hujus sacri cœnobii*
> "*miraculose fundator* [5]."

The Cromwells converted the abbey-house into a mansion-house, and this figure was dug out of a pond belonging to it, in the time of Charles II. when colonel Titus owned it. The head was broken off in the frost 1745.

BRITHNOTH, duke, earl, or alderman, of Northumberland, for so many different titles he bears in the Saxon Chronicle and Annals of Ramsey and Ely, who was slain in battle with the Danes, A. D. 991, was buried by the monks of Ely, to whom he had been a great benefactor, in their old conventual church, and thence removed to the new one, where his bones were lodged with those of their oldest benefactors, in the North wall of the choir built in the time of Edward the Third, with portraits of them on the face of each recess. On the removal of

[1] Archæol. I. 37.
[2] Stukeley, Itin. I. 77. Pl. xvii.
[3] Gloss. in voce.
[4] See Hist. Ramesiensis, c. iii. p. 387. Ed. Gale.
[5] Dugd. Bar I. 17.

the

the choir they were taken out, and repofited in niches over the tomb of bifhop Weft in his chapel. The bones of this nobleman had this peculiar circumftance attending them, that his head being carried away by the victorious Danes, the monks fupplied its place with a wax one, which was not found on the fecond removal [a]. By the meafure of his thigh bone he is fuppofed to have been fix feet and a half high [1].

ATHELSTAN bifhop of Elmham, who died 996, and EDNOTH bifhop of Dorchefter, flain by the Danes, 916: WULSTAN archbifhop of York, who died 1023; ALSWIN and ELFGAR, bifhops of Elmham, 1021.—1029; and OSMUND a Swedifh prelate, 1016, were of this party; and all men of large dimenfions, being rather more than fix feet high. A MS in Ely library [1] fays, on the firft removal of archbifhop Wulftan, "corpus diffolutum invenerunt; fed cafulam et "pallium auratis fpinulis affixum, cum ftola & manipula invenerunt, ut mirum "fuerit tanto temporis fpatio fub putredine corporis potuiffe illa faltem in aliqua "fua parte duraffe." The pin of brafs, once gilt, 5 7/10ths of an inch long, the head flat or lozengé, adorned on each fide with a different flourifh, was fhewn by Mr. Bentham to the Society of Antiquaries, June 2, 1777.

Giraldus' account of the finding of ARTHUR's body is in his "Speculum Ec- "clefiafticum," where he adds, that the bones were of gigantic proportion, the tibia being three fingers longer than that of the then abbot, the fpace between the eyes and forehead a hand's breadth, and in the head ten wounds, his death-wound larger than the reft. The leaden crofs (engraved in Camden's Britannia) was let into the ftone, the letters next to the ftone. The anonymous monk of Glaftonbury adds, that the tomb of his queen being opened at the fame time (1189), her yellow hair was found nicely braided, which fell to pieces on the touch. It does not appear that thefe corpfes lay *between* the pyramids mentioned by Malmsbury [4], or that they had any relation to them. Matthew Paris, indeed, in Leland's Affertio Arturi, p. 54. fays they ftood *circa* farcophagum; but query, if the names fo different in the printed copy and MSS of Malmesbury had any reference to Arthur, or were thofe of perfons buried in thefe pyramids, as Malmesbury thinks. William of Worcefter [5] defcribes the place of Arthur's burial between two hollow ftone croffes in the churchyard oppofite the fecond window of the South fide of St. Mary's chapel [which I take to be St. Jofeph's], at the Weft end of the church, and there lies Jofeph of Arimathea in *linea bifurcata*. Edward I. and Queen Eleanor opened the tombs of Arthur and his Queen, and removed them before the high altar, putting into them an account of this proceeding, with all the bones, except the fculls.

Leland [6] defcribes Arthur's tomb in the middle of the prefbytery at Glaftonbury between Edward the elder and Edward Ironfide. On it this epitaph by abbot Swanfey,

> *Hic jacet Arturus, flos regum, gloria regni,*
> *Quem mores, probitas, commendant laude perenni.*

Lower, at the feet of the tomb:

> *Arturi jacet hic conjux tumulata fecundo,*
> *Quæ meruit cœlos virtutum prole fecunda.*

[a] In the vault with archbifhop Rotheram's bones at York was found a *wooden* head, exactly refembling a barber's block, with a flick thruft through the neck to carry it on. This head is a piece of extraordinary fculpture for that age (the end of the fifteenth century); but whether it be a reprefentation of his own, or of fome titular faint, Mr. Drake could not determine. He thought it moft probable that it was a refemblance of his own; for dying of the plague his body being buried immediately an image was fubftituted inftead of it, for a more grand and folemn interment, of which this ferved for the head. Drake, p. 447. 480.

[1] Hift. of Ely, p. 85. Archæol. II. 364. [3] L. II. c. 57. [4] Gale, 306. [5] P. 294. [6] Itin. III. 85.

At

At the head this infcription,

Henricus abbas I fuppofe Swanfey, who might make the tomb.

a crucifix at the head, the figure of Arthur at the feet, a crofs on the tomb, two lions at the head and two at the feet of the tomb, touching the ground [1].

ALDHELM was buried under the high altar at Malmsbury, but the Eaft end and both the tranfepts being ruined at the diffolution, his monument is now fhewn on the South fide of the prefent altar. It is an altar-tomb of free-ftone, with a recumbent figure, habited in a mantle, with a clofe coat, and on his head a crown fomewhat refembling the naval crown of the Romans, his hair long and flowing, his beard curled, a cufhion with two angels under his head, and at it a canopy broken, as if made of plafter; his hands broken, a lion at his feet.

Mr. Lethieullier goes on to obferve, that "the period immediately after the Conqueft was not a time for people to think of fuch memorials for themfelves or friends. Few could then tell how long the lands they enjoyed would remain their own; and moft indeed were foon put into the hands of new poffeffors, who frequently, as we find in Domefday, &c. held thirty or forty manors at a time. All *then* above the rank of fervants were foldiers; the fword alone made the gentleman; and accordingly, on a ftrict enquiry, we fhall meet with few or no monuments of that age, except for the kings, royal family, or fome few of the chief nobility and leaders; among which thofe for the Veres earls of Oxford, at Earls Colne in Effex, are fome of the moft ancient. And thus I imagine it continued through the troublefome reign of Stephen, and during the confufion which prevailed while the Barons' wars fubfifted, and until the 9th of king Edward III."

From this opinion I muft beg leave to differ. The tombs of Gundreda countefs Warren, the Conqueror's neice, at Lewes; of William de Eincourt, at Lincoln, of Bifhop Roger, at Salisbury; of Ilbert de Chaz, at Monkton Farley, and many others hereafter defcribed, will ferve to refute it; and though a concurrence of various circumftances has thinned the memorials of the eleventh and twelfth centuries more than thofe of the fucceeding ones, there is no reafon to doubt that many more once exifted, perhaps in as great numbers as thofe that came after them.

"In the 9th of Edward III. Magna Charta being confirmed, and every man's fecurity better eftablifhed, property became more difperfed, manors were in more divided hands, and the lords of them began to fettle on their poffeffions in the country. In that age many parifh churches were built; and it is not improbable the care of a refting-place for their bodies, and monuments to preferve their memories, became more general and diffufed.

"The holy war, and vows of pilgrimage in the holy land, were then efteemed highly meritorious. Knights Templars were received, cherifhed, and enriched, throughout Europe; and they being ufually buried crofs-legged [2], in token of the banner they fought under, and compleatly armed, in regard to their being foldiers, this fort of monument grew much in fafhion: and though all which we meet with in that fhape are vulgarly called fo, yet I am certain many are not; and indeed I have rarely found any which I could be certain were for perfons who had been of that order.

"This religious order of laymen had its rife but in the year 1118. And in 1134, we find Robert duke of Normandy, fon to William the Conqueror,

[1] Vulgar tradition afcribes to Arthur and his Queen two mean altar tombs which have had each an ordinary brafs figure on each fide of the afcent to the altar in St. John's church, Glaftonbury. That on the fouth fide has had a woman in a mitred head-drefs, four fhields with G. a crofs A. between angels, and one fhield at the feet. The oppofite tomb [illegible] with this had the figure of a man.

[2] For this particular we feem to want authority.

reprefented in this fafhion on his tomb at Gloucefter [1]. Henry Lacy, earl of Lincoln, was reprefented thus on his fine tomb, which was in St. Paul's before the fire of London. And in the Temple church there ftill remain the crofs-legged effigies of William Marfhall earl of Pembroke, who died 1219, William his fon, who died 1231, and Gilbert, another fon, who died 1241; none of whom, I take for granted, were of the order of Templars. If thefe monuments were defigned to denote at leaft their having been in the Holy Land, yet all who had been there did not follow this fafhion; for Edmond Crouchback, earl of Lancafter, fecond fon to Henry III, had been there; and yet, as appears by his monument, ftill in being in Weftminfter abbey, is not reprefented crofs-legged. However, it feems to have been a prevailing fafhion till the 6th of Edward II. anno 1312; when, the order of Templars coming to deftruction, and into the higheft contempt, their fafhions of all kinds feem to have been totally abolifhed."

The queftion about crofs-legged figures on tombs is curious and interefting. Mr. Lethieullier miftakes in faying the legs of Edmond Crouchback are not croft, as his figure engraved in pl. XXVI. will evince. Among the many effigies of private lords of manors neglected and mutilated in our parochial churches, and not always afcertained, not a few in this attitude befpeak them to have been infected with that holy rage. To have taken the vow of croifading was enough to be fo commemorated, whether they actually went or not. Indeed, as we have fo much certainty about feveral, on what other principle, without actual evidence, or to whom but croifaders, can we refer the other figures, whofe legs are croffed? Mr. Lethieullier's objection to Robert de Walcran being a knight Templar, becaufe he abetted Henry III. in plundering the Templars at London is of little weight; he might be a tool of that prince, who was himfelf a croifader [2]. Pope Innocent had a trick of abfolving croifaders from their vows for a little money [3]. The crimes alledged as a reafon for fuppreffing the order of Templars may fairly enough be prefumed againft certain individuals of the order.

But it is by no means neceffary that thefe parties fo reprefented were of the Order of the Templars, whofe vow enjoined celibacy, and thefe figures have neither the habit nor badge of the order. Not any particular order therefore, but the vow of going to the holy land, either on a croifade or pilgrimage, is the object in queftion. And on this laft account only can we fuppofe a lady of the family of Mepham to be fo reprefented, as well as her husband, in a tomb in a chapel adjoining to the once collegiate church of Howden in Yorkfhire [4]. I do not recollect a church belonging to any place where there was a preceptory of this order now remaining with their monuments except in London. Dr. Salmon fays, "The Benfted at Bennington, c. Herts, is not to be fuppofed a *Knight Templar* from the pofture, for he has no fhield. Befide, though it be poffible his wife was dead when he entered into the order, there is I believe no inftance to be found of a woman in the fame monument. There are examples of crofs legged figures which are known not to have been either Templars nor Hofpitalars. In a niche of Tenbury church, in Shropfhire, lies a child crofslegged, fuppofed to be a fon of lord Arundel [5]." If the above arguments were well founded they would greatly favour what I take to be the moft probable hypothefis, that the croffing of the legs was a badge of a *croifader*, and not of either of the military orders. There is another inftance of a lady on the fame tomb with her crofs-legged husband in the monument of Sir Fulk Fitz Warin one of the Knights of the Garter, 34 Edward I. in the chancel at Wantage, c. Berks, which is determined by the arms and other circumftances though the infcription is gone. He died 23 Edward III [6].

[1] He was a leader in the firft cruifade, 1096. [2] Rapin, III. 379. [3] Ib. 381.
[4] Nafh' Worcefterfh. I. 31. [5] Herts, p. 196.
[6] Afhmole, II. 229. Mr. Afhmole does not exprefs the circumftance of croffing the legs, but his drawing in the Heralds college does.

Neither-

Neither does it follow, that perſons who had been of the order, or engaged in the holy war, would decline the diſtinction on their tombs, even after the ſuppreſſion of the order, or the ceſſation of the croiſades, which happened forty years before [1]. Sir Robert de Bois is repreſented croſs-legged [2], though he died within a year of the firſt of theſe events, which we cannot ſuppoſe him ignorant of, it having taken place in France before it happened in England, 1312. Aymer de Valence, who died 1323, eleven years after the ſuppreſſion, is repreſented croſs-legged [3]; ſo is one of the Benſteds, whom I ſuppoſed to have died at the ſame time [4]; and John Sturmy, who is croſs-legged at Tenbury, may have lived to as late a period [5]. John of Eltham, the ſon of the king who ſuppreſt the order, has his legs croſt on his monument erected 1334 [6]: ſo has Robert de Hungerford, 1354 [7], which is no proof of the monument being erected in his life-time; a practice of which no inſtance has occurred to me. So has one of the Huſſeys, at Flintham, c. Nottingham, where his family had not poſſeſſion before 8 Edward III [8]; and one in Cromhall church, c. Glouceſter, aſcribed to a Ligon, of which family George lived in the reign of Richard II. and Richard in that of Henry IV [9]. This has ſince been built into the wall. The croſs-legged figure in Cubberley church, c. Glouceſter, belongs to ſome of the Berkleys, of whom Sir Thomas held the manor 8 Edward III. 1335. and his ſon Thomas 6 Henry IV [10]. It ſeems more certain that the like figure in Downe Amney church, in the ſame county, bearing on his ſhield a croſs of St. George charged with five eſcallops belongs to Nicholas de Villers or Valers, who held the manor 15 Edward I. and was in the Holy War, 1268, when, Mr. Rudder ſays [11], he relinquiſhed his paternal coat, S. 3 cinqfoils A. for the other, which was the antient badge of the Croiſes [12]. Of this laſt figure Sir Robert Atkins [13] ſays, "the man lieth like a Knight Templar." This church belonged to the Knights Templars. The figure at Alvechurch, c. Worceſterſhire, may belong to either Thomas or John Blanchfront, the former of whom lived in the reign of Henry III. or Edward I. the latter is mentioned in a deed 21 Edward III [14]. In Aldworth church, Berks, are four croſs-legged figures of the Beches, of which family the firſt on record lived in the reign of Edward II. the laſt in that of his ſon [15].

Mr. Hutchins, ſuppoſing ſuch figures not to have exceeded the croiſades, imagines the two croſs-legged figures in St. Peter's church Dorcheſter older than the Chidiocks, who founded the priory there about 38 Edward III [16]. to whom Mr. Coker aſcribed them. One in the chancel of Winborn St. Giles belonged to the Malmaynes, lords there temp. Henry I. or the Pleceys, who held the manor during the reigns of Edward II. and III [17]. One at Stoke Gaylard, to Ingelram Walleys, temp. Edward I. the firſt known lord after the Conqueſt [18]. Mr. Blomefield aſcribes the figure in South Acre church, Norfolk, to Eudo Arſick, the firſt of the name, who lived in the reign of Henry I [19]. Of the three antient figures in the window ſills of Hitchin church [20], ſaid to be brought from Temple Dinſley Preceptory adjoining, only one has its legs croſt. Theſe are a few of the many inſtances that might be alledged of figures retaining the croſs-legged attitudes after the Croiſades, and ſuppreſſion of the order.

I doubt not more inſtances might be produced of croſs-legged figures on tombs during the remainder of the 14th century. There are but ſix ſuch figures in the whole county of Warwick; nor more in that of Nottingham; twelve in Glouceſterſhire, nine in Berks: but only one in Norfolk.

[1] No ſubſequent attempt to raiſe a croiſade ſucceeded. Sir Walter Malbyſſe of Acaſter Malbyſſe, c. York, mortgaged his eſtate there to William Fairfax of Scalton, 1366, to raiſe money for a croiſade, the eſtate to remain to Fairfax's ſon ... chaſed if he did not return. He died the ſame year.
[2] See p. 83. [3] Pl. xxix. xxx. [4] P. 91. [5] Naſh's Worceſterſh. II. 418. 420.
[6] Pl. xxxi. xxxiii. [7] P. 107. [8] Thoroton, p. 135. [9] Rudder, 397 Naſh's Worceſt. II. 118.
[10] Rudder, 399. [11] P. 416. [12] I doubt this is a miſtake for the ſingle eſcallop, that being the badge of pilgrims.
[13] Se p. 10. [14] Naſh's Worceſterſhire, I. 3.. [15] Dugd. Bar. II. 127.
[16] Dorſet, I. 389. [17] Ib. II. 219. [18] Ib. 250. [19] III. 316. [20] Salmon, Herts. p. 164.

In the North aile at Eaftwick is a fine figure, in dark grey marble, on a coffin-fafhioned ftone, with many mouldings; the pews conceal his legs, but Salmon [1] calls him a Templar, and he may be Richard de Thany, or his fon Richard, lords of this manor, in the reign of Henry III. or Edward I.

I obferve here *en paffant*, that feveral perfons went to the Croifade as *proxies* for others, and yet it fhould feem their conftituents are reprefented crofs legged. Such was Hugh Travers fon of Simon de Auvrington, who went for William Staunton of Staunton, c. Nottingham; and yet both probably are reprefented by the two figures in that attitude in Stanton church [2].

The crofs-legged figure is rarely met with on braffes. I recollect but three. One is a Trumpington, in Trumpington church, Cambridgefhire, whofe arms are in the window at Hilburgh, Norfolk [3]. The others, two knights at Gorlefton and Acton, Suffolk. If thefe are not admitted as late fpecimens of the attitude, they muft be early ones of the material.

"To thefe Mr. Lethieullier thinks fucceed the table tomb, with figures cumbent on it, with their hands joined in a praying pofture, fometimes with a rich canopy of ftone over them, fometimes without it; and again, the more plain without any figures. Round the edge of thefe for the moft part were infcriptions on brafs plates, which are now too frequently deftroyed."

Mr. Lethieullier is certainly miftaken in his date of the *table tomb with figures cumbent on it*, if he thinks it pofterior to the crofs-legged figures; for the inftances of thofe very figures before mentioned all lie on table-tombs, though all the tables are not raifed on altars. But the whole wording of the paffage is incorrect. Neither the praying pofture of the hands, nor the prefence or abfence of the ftone canopy or figures, or infcriptions on brafs plates, were peculiar to the æra here affigned them; but prior to it.

The figures emboft, or carved in low relief, on the lids of coffins, were the firft attempt at the cumbent figure. Such an one Mr. Blomefield [4] defcribes in the churchyard of Necton, Norfolk, the effigy of a lady in an antique drefs, without fhield or infcription. Such are the half-lengths in Brandon churchyard, Suffolk, and three in Notgrove churchyard, c. Gloucefter [5]. But thefe kind of partial figures are not always of the higheft antiquity. A lady of the Bracebridge family is reprefented only by a head in a quatrefoil, on a flab at Kingfbury, c. Warwick [6]. A knight and lady at Stoke Rochford, c. Lincoln, only to the middle. Such too are the monuments within the walls of Lichfield cathedral, "of a moft frugal nature, having no appearance of any part but the head and feet [7]."

A curious queftion arifes here how far the effigies on tombs are to be confidered as *portraits*. That this is the cafe on our regal monuments there feems no doubt. They difcover a fuperiority of ftyle which befpeaks refemblance. This may hold alfo with refpect to particular monuments of lords or prelates after the thirteenth century. Dr. Stukeley thought all the ftatues of Queen Eleanor copies of each other, and of her real features. The fame may be faid of many elegant ftatues on the fronts or fides of churches; and Hearne [8] affirms the Virgin Mary was copied from the queens of the time. But before that time the knights, the crufaders, the abbots, and the bifhops, are too uniform and rude to mean any thing more than a human figure.

[1] Herts, p. 255.
[2] Thoroton, p. 156. 165.
[3] Blomef. III. 439.
[4] III. 396.
[5] Rudder, 583.
[6] Dugdale's Warwickfh. p. 763.
[7] Pennant's Journey from Chefter, p. 108.
[8] Pref. to Gul. Neub. p. lxxx.

Among

Among Piranesi's "Vasi e Candelabri," is a curious sepulchral monument of an oblong form, with the figures of a man and woman half recumbent as on a seat in a triclinium, surrounded by a border or battlement; on the sides of the tomb in four and two compartments or arches, the labours of Hercules. This may be one of the oldest altar-tombs. The posture is not uncommon on the funeral monuments of the Greeks and Romans.

How much more natural is the old cumbent attitude representing the body as actually laid in a tomb below than the varied attitudes of modern times, which seem to suppose the party reanimated, or never dead!

The materials of these figures was stone, of various kinds; freestone, alabaster, Purbeck, Sussex, or other marbles. Abbé Winkelman observes of the antient statues that as alabaster was too hard to make the whole figures of, the extremities were generally of bronze. There is but one head (or rather one face of it, for the hinder part is wanting) at Rome, and that is a head of Adrian. Of whole figures we have only three Dianas and the fine Torso in armour, now at St. Ildefonso in Spain; the head and arms of this last are of bronze gilt. There are also some Hermes and some busts [1]. England abounds with statues of alabaster; those of various marbles seem to have grown into disuse after the thirteenth century; and as their substance was originally in many instances concealed by gorgeous paintings, in later times all is confounded by the plasterer's brush [2]. The figures of Sir John Davis, knight banneret, who died 1625, and his two wives, in Pangborn church, Berks, are all carved out of chalk. In the will of Sir William Manwaring, of Cheshire, knight, dated 1394, he orders a *picture* of alabaster to cover his tomb in Acton church [3]. By a like misnomer the statue of George I. in the High Street, Gloucester, is to this day called the king's *picture*. William Wilbraham applies this term to a brass plate on a slab, to be laid over him and his wife in the same church. That of William Tufton of Acton [4], at Northampton, is called in his will *his picture* [5]. Thomas Stanley earl of Derby, in his will, 1504, mentions the *personages* which he had caused to be made for his ancestors [6].

Figures in wood are of various ages, and not so uncommon as at first imagined. Perhaps one of the oldest was that of bishop Caducan in Dore abbey, c. Hereford. The next may be Robert Curthose, in Gloucester cathedral, 1134. though Leland [7] says his figure was made long since his death. Two at Danbury, c. Essex, referred by Mr. Morant [8] to the St. Cleres in the reign of Stephen; William de Messing founder of Messing church, in the same county; a knight in Buers church, Suffolk; Bois at Fersfield, Bardolph at Banham, Sir Roger Harsick, first of that surname, at South Acre [9], all in Norfolk. William Valence earl of Pembroke, at Westminster, has both a tomb and figure of wood, while the wooden figures of William Longespee earl of Salisbury at Salisbury, and archbishop Peckham at Canterbury, lie on stone tombs. There is one with a lady at Sparsholt, c. Berks [10], and a lady in Englefield church in the

[1] Hist. de l'Art.

[2] The occasional decoration of our parish churches, and, I am sorry to add, our cathedrals, is a terrible enemy to the remains of antiquity; though it must be confessed, whitewashing has preserved several valuable ones from the rage of fanaticism. In the autumn of 1784 Mr. Ord and myself rescued some of the finest reliefs on a font at Baddingham in Suffolk, and an inscription round the foot of another at Stradbrook, in the same county, from the plaster and stone which had covered and filled them up.

[3] Pennant's journey from Chester, p. 21. [4] Ib. p. 23.

[5] Collins's Peerage, II. 349. [6] Dugd. Bar. II. 249.

[7] It. IV. 171. [8] Mr. Morant too hastily concluded the statue of Robert Vere at Hatfield Broad Oak was of wood.

[9] Weever (p. 815) has confounded this Roger with his descendant and namesake who lived in the reigns of Henry V. and VI and was buried under an altar-tomb formerly adorned with brasses on the North side of the chancel at South Acre, whereas this wooden figure really lies under the South wall of the chancel. Hence Mr. Blomefield conjectures, that "his collection was not made by his own view, but taken on trust and as it was ignorantly communicated to him." Norf. III. 418.

[10] Aslim. II. 206.

ſame county [1]. William Delapole earl of Suffolk, 1389, and his lady, at Wingfield in Suffolk; and a knight and lady at Heveningham, in the ſame county, are all made of wood, and hollow as the figure of Bois: whence it is plain that wooden figures did not ſerve as covers to coffins, however ſtone ones might. Among croſs-legged figures of the ſame material we may reckon one at Abergavenny; one in St. Mary Overy's church, Southwark; one at Burfield, Berks [2]: It was not till the 14th century, I believe, that the whole monument, canopy, and figures, were made of oak, as of Sir   Culpeper and lady, at Godehurſt, Kent; and Henry Neville earl of Weſtmorland, who died 1564, 5 Elizabeth, with his two wives, at Staindrop, c. Durham. The maker of this laſt is recorded on the ledge, John Starbottom [3].

Bronze, or copper plain or gilt, was too coſtly a material for common uſe in ſtatues; and hence we find the wooden figure of William Valence earl of Pembroke only plated with it. Godwin deſcribes the tomb of biſhop Groſthead, who died 1254, as having an image of braſs *over* it [4]. Whether by this he means a ſtatue or inlaid figure (moſt probably the latter) cannot now be determined, for the ſlab which probably reſted on pillars, or an altar, is gone [5].

The firſt inſtance of a braſs ſtatue among us is that of Henry III. himſelf; the ſecond his daughter-in-law, queen Eleanor, who had two [6], one at Weſtminſter and one at Lincoln: whence it may be no improbable conjecture, that monumental braſſes among us owe their introduction to the improved ſtate of the arts at that time.

Peter de Dreux, duke of Bretagne and earl of Richmond, who died 1250, and was buried in the church of St. Yved de Braine, is there repreſented in relief, on his tomb of copper [7].

We are told that Henry III. cauſed a figure of his daughter Catharine, who died 1257, to be made of *ſilver*.

Gilbert Clare the firſt earl of Glouceſter, who died 14 Henry III. had an image of *ſilver* on his tomb in Tewkſbury choir [8].

Queen Katherine cauſed to be ſet up for her conſort, Henry V. a ſtatue covered all over with ſilver plate gilded, "the head whereof was all of maſſy ſilver [9]," and conſequently ſoon ſtolen.

It is not eaſy to account for ſeveral figures of ſmaller proportion than ordinary which one meets with in ſome churches. In the North wall of the church at Pirton, c. Herts, is a low ſmall arch, which may have been for the founder, as there is at Anſty in the ſame county, where he lies in a ſort of miniature, at half the bigneſs of a man [10]. In the South aile of this latter church is a very old ſtone with the effigies of a man in a very grave habit, leſs than the life, which is ſaid to be for Richard de Aneſtie, who built the church in the reign of Henry III [11]. To theſe add the three figures in the window ſills of Berkeley church, Glouceſterſhire [12]; whether intended for incumbents or younger branches of the Berkeley family. In the church of Mapowder, Dorſet, is another figure of almoſt infantine proportion [13]; and on the window frame at Botsford ſtands a lit-

[1] Aſhmole, I. 26. [2] Ib. I. 30.
[3] This monument is wretchedly engraved in the Antiquarian Repertory, I. 146.
[4] Engliſh ed. 1601. p. 240.
[5] See Pl. XVI. where it is repreſented agreeable to Mr. Eſſex's idea of its original ſtate, and thus it will reſemble that of Dean Langton at York.
[6] Richard I. had two ſtatues: one over his body at Fontevraud, the other over his heart at Rouen. Montfaucon, Mon. de la Mon. Fr. II. 114.
[7] *en boſſe ſur ſa tombe de cuivre*, Montfaucon, Mon. de la Mon. Franc. II. p. 164. pl. xxx. f. 1. He ſeems to diſtinguiſh braſs or copper figures from plates of the ſame metals, by calling the former "tombes *de cuivre*," and the latter only "figures *gravées*."
[8] Leland, It. VI. 98. [9] Weever, p. 474.
[10] Salmon, Herts, p. 172. [11] Ib. 291. [12] P. 114.
[13] Hutchins, II. 268.

tle figure of speckled marble, about eighteen inches high, of a knight in compleat mail and mantle: his hands joined, and his shield on his left arm; his legs broken off; under his head a cushion. Dr. Nash [1] describes another in the chancel at Tenbury, c. Worcester, the figure of a child in compleat armour and a surcoat; between his hands, which are raised on his breast, a large heart, his legs crossed, and at his feet a talbot. This may have been a son of John Sturmy the croisader, and have followed his father under age. In the South aile at Long Witton, Berks, is a cross-legged figure, three quarters fixed in the wall [2]. There is another such figure, but not cross-legged, in Frampton church, in the same county, which Mr. Hutchins [3] is for referring to the infant son of Mr. Coker, in the last century, under whose monument it is. But the situation alone proves it of higher antiquity. Among the monuments of the Veres at Earl's Coln priory, Weever [4] describes "a little monument of alabaster, on which is the image of one in a gown with a purse hanging at his girdle: he is in length about four feet."

The effigies of William of Windsor and Blanche de la Tour, children of Edward III. who died infants, are the only figures among us that bear any proportion to the small natural size. P. Montfaucon observes, that in France it was not uncommon to represent children as of full proportion [5].

"At the same time, continues Mr. Lethieullier, came in common use the humble grave-stone laid flat with the pavement, sometimes with an inscription cut round the border of the stone, sometimes enriched with costly plates of brass. But either avarice, or an over-zealous aversion to some words in the inscription, has robbed most of these stones of the brass which adorned them, and left the less room for certainty when this fashion began. Earlier than the 14th century I have seen or read of very few; and towards the beginning of that I am apt to think they were but scarce. One I think was produced at the Society of Antiquaries last year [1771], dated 1300; but of this I should be glad of a farther certainty. Weever mentions one in St. Paul's for Richard Newport, anno 1317, and gives another at Berkhamstead in Hertfordshire, which, by mistake, he dates 1306, the true date being 1356 [6]. Upon the whole, where we have not a positive date, I should hardly guess any brass plate I met with to be older than 1350, and few so old; but from about 1380 they grew in common use, and remained so even to king James the First's time. Only after the reign of Edward the Sixth, we find the old Gothic square letter changed into the Roman round hand, and the phrase *Orate pro anima* universally omitted."

The flat gravestone, with and without the inscription inlaid in brass, is also of higher antiquity than Mr. Lethieullier ascribes to it. We have instances of it in the 13th century. The capital letters, whether Saxon, or Gothic, or a mixture of both, occur about the close of that century, and continue through the reigns of the three Edwards at least. These letters were cut deep in the stone, and brass or lead poured into them, which having been picked or worn out, the cavities retain a bold and legible impression in many parish churches in Hertfordshire and elsewhere. Mr. Blomfield gives one in North Pickenham church, for Margaret Wanton, who died in the reign of Edward II [7]. The oldest inscription in York cathedral, for Dean Langton, who died 1279, is of this sort undated [8].

Simon de Beauchamp earl of Bedford, who compleated the foundation of Newenham abbey near Bedford, and died before 9 John, 1208 [9], was buried

[1] Worcestersh. II. 470. This is gone, with that mentioned before p. xcv. from Salmon, who places it in Shropshire, and calls it a son of lord Arundel.
[2] Ashm. I. 72. [3] I. 351. [4] P. 615.
[5] Mon. de la monarch. Fr. II. p. 160. 161. pl. xxvii 4. xxviii. 1.
[6] See another instance of his inaccuracies in Blomefield, II. 615.
[7] III. 497. [8] Drake, 494.
[9] Dugd. Bar. I. 223.

before

before the high altar in St. Paul's church at Bedford, "with this epitaphie *graven in brass*, and set on a flat marble stone.

De Bello campo jacet hic sub marmore Simon
. . . . *fundator de Newenham* [1].

which inscription seems to have remained in Leland's time. Richard de Berkyng abbot of Westminster, who died 1246, had a slab inlaid with his figure *in pontificalibus*, and an inscription on the ledge in brass, the traces of which are still to be seen on the stone now lying in the area at the foot of the steps of Henry VII's chapel [2].

I lay no stress on the *picture inlaid with brasse* of Gilbert Crispin abbot of Westminster, who died 1114, though seen and described by Weever [3], which I suspect to be of later manufacture. Nor on that which Mr. Bridges inaccurately ascribed to William Rowel, 1222, since there is every evidence to convince me it bears date 1351. Nor on the brass figure supposed to have represented Isabel countess of Cornwall and Gloucester, who died before 1243, and was buried in Beaulieu abbey, though I have engraved it pl. XIV. There has been a brass cross, &c. inlaid on the tomb of Robert Bingham bishop of Salisbury, who died 1247; and on the slab assigned by Mr. Dart to Roger de Wendover bishop of Rochester, who died 1250.

Whether the letters of bishop Gravesend's inscription, 1279, were inlaid with metal, or only cut as deep as Prior Basyng's at Winchester, 1284, is uncertain; but marks of such inlaying may be still seen on the slab of William de Luda, bishop of Ely, who died 1298. Elias de Bekingham, who died after 27 Edward I. had both his figure and inscription inlaid in brass in Boresham church. Mr. Lethieullier himself observes, that the pompous marble which lies over Nicholas Longespee, who died bishop of Salisbury [1297], and appears to have been richly plated, though the brass is now gone, is one of the most remarkable of that kind that he had met with.

"Ela countes of Warwick, a woman of a very great riches and nobilite, lyithe "buried at the hedde of the tumbe of Henry Oilley, undre a very fair flat mar-"ble, in the habit of a woves [*vowess* or nun] *graven yn a coper plate*," says Leland [4], who speaks as an eye-witness. She died 1300. This I had cited [5] as one of the earliest instances of brass plates, which I had added inadvertently were probably just introduced about this time. Mr. Rudder gives one in Badminton church for Ralph Botiler lord of Badminton, who died 3 Edward I. 1275, on a grey marble slab inlaid with brass the figure of two knights, a shield with a lion rampant, and round the edge *Ralph Botiler, miles, dominus* . . . [6]. Thomas de Corbridge, archbishop of York, who died 1303, had a brass figure on his slab at Southwell, long ago torn off [7]. Weever saw the brass epitaph on the tomb of Walter Wenlok abbot of Westminster, who died 1307 [8].

The authorities above recited assign an early date to brass figures, and by the beginning of the 14th century they were become so common that in 1308 a canon of Hereford could afford a very handsome one, though it is still the oldest sepulchral brass, now intire and well preserved, that I have seen. A bishop of Salisbury, whom I suppose Mortival, who died 1329, was content with a cross inlaid in brass [9]. If the vergers are right in giving this tomb to bishop Roger, brass inlaying will be 150 years older.

[1] Lel. It. II. 19. Dugd. Bar. I. 73.
[2] Dart, xxi.
[3] P. 487.
[4] Leland, It. I. 117. VIII. 71.
[5] See p. 100.
[6] P. 257.
[7] Drake, 431.
[8] P. 486.
[9] See p. 22.

The

The fecond archbifhop of York that had braffes was Melton, 1340 [1]. We have feen that of Curtlington, at Weftminfter, 1331, was not one of the oldeft abbatial braffes. How faft fuch memorials multiplied among all ranks from this period appears by innumerable inftances.

Thomas de Cailey, rector of Weft Bradenham, Norfolk, from 1318 to 1324, has a brafs in the chancel there: his head in a quatrefoil on a crofs with fomething at the feet of it. The infcription in capitals round the rim:

Continet. haec. foffa. Thome. nunc. corpus. et. offa.
Ecclefie. rector. hujus. extitit. atq. protector.
Gratia. quefo. Dei propitietur. ei [2].

William de Neuport, prebendary of Credington and Wells, and rector of Redenhale in Norfolk, had one, 1326, with his figure and an infcription in antient capitals [3].

William Ernald, rector of Carleton Rode in the fame county, has in the chancel there his effigies in brafs, in his prieft's habit, in his defk, with a book lying and a crofs ftanding before him [4].

Mr. Blomefield defcribes [5] a flab robbed of its braffes at Strandon for Sir Roger de Bourne, who died 1331. Sir William Bernak's death is dated 1334, on a brafs in Hetherfet church, Norfolk, and that of his lady 1341 [6]. That of Sir Hugh Haftings, at Elfyng in the fame county [7], is referred to about 1347: thofe of Robert Egglesfield, founder of Queen's college, Oxford [8], of Walter Stutelie, rector of Eaft Dereham, Norfolk [9], and of Margaret Torrington, at Great Berkhamfted [10], are but two years later, fuppofing the monuments to be coeval with their dates. As alfo that of Sir Edmund Illey, knight, who died 1349, and his wife, with a French infcription, in Holme Hale church, Norfolk [11]. One between 1349 and 1362, at Fouldon, Norfolk, has this fhort epitaph, like Venerable Bede's.

Hic funt in foffa
Caro Thome Palmer & offa [12].

The next to thefe is that of Sir Robert Buers at Acton in Suffolk, 1361; and from this period they multiplied fo faft that feveral at Lynne are in the higheft ftate of finifhing. Perhaps the intercourfe with the continent by this port peopled the county of Norfolk with fo many more and finer than one meets with in other counties. The fame reafon may be affigned for the coftly braffes among the clothiers in Gloucefterfhire.

In Great Hadham church, c. Herts, is a plain brafs plate infcribed,

Pryez pur l'alme Alban Pfone de Hadh'm.

No fuch perfon occurs in Newcourt's lift of rectors of this church, unlefs we fhould fuppofe *Alanus de Fen*, who was here from 1372 to 1382, to be meant by it. Simon Flambard, another rector, unknown to Newcourt, is commemorated on the verge of an old ftone in the fame chancel [13].

Mr. Lethieullier miftakes Weever's account of Richard Newport's monument in old St. Paul's. He calls it [14] "*a little monument*, not a brafs plate, and fays it belonged to *bifhop* Newport.

[1] Drake, p. 433. [2] Blomef. III. 242. [3] Blomef. III. 459.
[4] Blomef. III. p. 85. [5] II. 175. 148.
[6] The infcription was loft when Mr. Blomefield wrote; but he fays it was
"Obitus Domini Will'i de Bernak m° ccc° xxxiv vi° menfis Aprilis.
"Obitus Domine Alicie de Bernak m° ccc° xli° xii° die Aprilis III. 20.
[7] See p. 58.
[8] Pl. xxxvi. p. 102. [9] Blomef. V. 187. [10] Salmon, Herts, 116. [11] Blomef. III. 369.
[12] Ib. III. 352. [13] See p. 78. [14] P. 364.

Sir

Sir John Fastolfe wills for his mother in Attleburgh church a marble stone of convenient length, with an image of *laten* [brass] according to her degree, with a *scripture* of the day, and then of her obiit, with four escocheons, three of her husbands, Mortimer, Fastolf, and Farewell, and the fourth of her ancestors' arms [1].

Many of our old brasses bear the mark of rich enamelling in various colours: the traces remain strong on one laid on a raised tomb in Broxborn church, Herts, and more faintly on that of Sir Miles Stapleton in Ingham chancel, Norfolk.

On the floor of the Wynne vault at Llanrwst are three square brass plates, of the size of the paving stones, beautifully engraved by Sylvanus Crew and William Vaughan, in memory of Sir John Wynne, of Gwedir, knight and baronet, 1626, whose son Richard founded the chapel.

Lady Sidney Wynne wife of Sir John Wynne of Gwedir, knight and baronet, 1632.

Owen Wynne of Gwedir, their third son, 1660.

Against the East wall is a brass plate with a lady three quarters standing in a praying posture, representing Sarah wife of Sir Richard Wynne, who died 1671. This by Vaughan is celebrated by Mr. Pennant [2] as far the most beautiful piece of engraving he ever saw.

Opposite to this on the West wall is another brass plate, with a lady kneeling, for Mary Martyn, eldest daughter of Sir John Wynne, who died 1653; put up by his second son, 1658.

A sixth brass plate has a lady in a veil, half length, praying; Catharine Lewis, 1660. All these have inscriptions in Roman capitals; and arms.

Brass plates occur so late as 1702, for John Somers, at Cerne, c. Dorset. And even in this century, for the learned Jeremiah Markland, in Dorking church, 1776.

On the continent we meet with brasses bearing as early a date, or at least commemorating persons who died at as early a period, as in our own country [3].

The instances of figures cut in the slab, and not inlaid with metal, nor always blacked, are not uncommon: such are Adam Framton, in Wyberton church, Lincolnshire, 1325 [4]; lady Delamare, in Hereford library, 1421; John Gyse, 1479, at Elmore, c. Gloucester [5]; William de Tracy rector of Morthoe, Devon, 1322 [6]: or only the letters thus cut round the edge between a border of double lines, as frequently for rectors; e. g. at Dedham, c. Suffolk; or citizens, &c. as in the parochial and cathedral churches at Lincoln; John prior of Ranton, c. Stafford, and abbot of Dorchester, who died 1518, at Dorchester, c. Oxford; an abbot at St. Albans by duke Humphry's monument: a mutulated epitaph, dated 15 . . in the chancel at Little Wymondley, c. Herts.

[1] Blomef. V. 1550. [2] Wales, II. 144.

[3] A plate of copper enamelled, fixed against the second pillar, near the screen in the nave of the cathedral church of St. Julien at Mans, 2½ inches high by 1½ long, exhibits the figure of

Geofroi le bel Comte de Maine, fils de Foulques, Comte d'Anjou et du Maine, qui mourut le 7 Sept. 1150.

Over his head these lines,

Ense tuo princeps prædonum turba fugatur,
Ecclesiisque quies pace vigente datur

On his shield his arms, 8 lioncels rampant.

Engraved in Montfaucon's Monumens, vol. II. pl. XII. fig. 7. from Hist. des eveques de Mans per Courvaisier, Par. 1648. p. 444. 4° tiré du Cabinet de M. Clairambault.

A beautiful coloured drawing of this is in the Society of Antiquaries Library.

A second instance, and perhaps more coæval with the person whom it represents, is that of *Robert de Souave*, King at Arms, in the reign of St. Louis, who died 1260, and was buried in a chapel of the abbey of Mount St. Quintin. Montfaucon calls the epitaph one of the most curious to persons who are fond of such kind of antiquities, and has engraved it in his second volume, plate xxix.

Margaret, Queen of France, consort of St. Louis, who died 1295, has a tomb plated with brass in the choir of St. Denys. Felibien, Hist. de l'abbaie de St. Denys, p. 554 and plan.

[4] P. 89. [5] Rudder. p. 440. [6] P. 40.

Mr.

Mr. Lethieullier goes on:

"Towards the latter end of the fourteenth century a custom prevailed likewise of putting the inscriptions in French, and not Latin. Of these I have seen and read many; but they are generally from 1350 to 1400, and very rarely afterwards. John Stow has indeed preserved two, which were in St. Martin's in the Vintry, dated 1310 and 1311; but I have seen no others so early."

Here again I am sorry to differ from so respectable authority. The epitaph of Robert de Vere at Hatfield Broad Oak, 1221; of Henry III. 1272; Queen Eleanor, 1290; Urien de St. Pierre, 1295; John Warren earl of Surrey, 1304; Adam de Franton, 1325, are a few instances, produced in their several places, out of many more that might be found. At the same time it must be observed, that as the majority of these are for the laity, it is probable the clergy and religious preferred Latin, as their more familiar idiom.

Mr. Lethieullier seems to have mistaken Stowe's words; for he only says[1], "that Sir John Gisors, mayor of London 1311, lay buried in this church; and that in St. James, Garlickhithe, Robert Gabeter, esq. mayor of Newcastle-upon-Tyne, 1310, had a monument[2]."

Mr. Lethieullier adds, "The late editor of the Antiquities of Westminster [by whom I suppose Mr. Dart is meant] affirms (from what authority I know not) that stone coffins were never or rarely used after the thirteenth century. If this be true, we have an æra from whence to go upwards in search of any of those monuments, where the stone coffin appears, as it frequently does."

"As Grecian architecture had a little dawning in Edward the Sixth's time, and made a farther progress in the three succeeding reigns, we find in the great number of monuments which were then erected the small column introduced with its base and capital, sometimes supporting an arch, sometimes an architrave; but every where mixed with them you will observe a vast deal of the Gothick ornaments retained: as small spires, ill-carved images, small square roses, and other foliage painted and gilt; which sufficiently denote the age which made them, though no inscriptions are left."

The same sentiment is so happily expressed by Mr. Walpole that I cannot forbear transcribing his words.

"It is certain that the Gothic taste remained in vogue till towards the latter end of the reign of Henry VIII. His father's chapel at Westminster is entirely of that manner. So is Wolsey's tomb-house at Windsor. But soon after the Grecian style was introduced, and no wonder when so many Italians were entertained in the king's service. They had seen that architecture revived in their own country, in all its points; but whether they were not perfect masters of it or that it was necessary to introduce the innovation by degrees, it certainly did not at first obtain full possession. It was plastered upon Gothic, and made a barbarous mixture. Regular columns with ornaments neither Græcian nor Gothic, and half embroidered with foliage, were crammed over frontispieces, facades, and chimnies, and lost all grace by wanting simplicity. This mongrel species lasted till late in the reign of James I[3]."

This consideration induced me to close my work with the sixteenth century, after which period so little of the object proposed by it for the illustration of manners and habits is to be learnt from our monuments. The present century will teach us less, though it may amuse itself in handing down history in real or emblematical representations.

The monument of Margaret countess of Lenox, mother of lord Darnley, is the first complete deviation from the Gothic form of tombs; and a second in-

[1] Survey of London, 1633, p. 261. [2] Ib. p. 262.
[3] Anecd. of Painting, I. 121. 4to.

stance

stance of that motley taste which prevailed for the remainder of that century, to which it should seem so much more easy for draughtsmen and engravers to do justice than to the pure Gothic that there are many more specimens of it preserved even by the hand of Hollar than of the other, and later books abound with them.

Sepulchral chapels were not always additions to a building [1], as those of bishops West and Alcock, at Ely; bishop Audley, at Salisbury; bishop Langton, at Winchester; but distinct erections within the church, as bishop Wickham's at Winchester, abbot Ramridge's and Humphry duke of Gloucester, at St. Alban's; Richard Beauchamp earl of Warwick at Warwick; the two beautiful ones on each side the nave at Wells; and of Walter lord Hungerford at Salisbury, now removed to the chancel; the Black Prince at Canterbury; prince Arthur at Worcester; all those between the arches of the choir at Tewkibury, and St. George's chapel, Windsor: in all or most of which mass was celebrated in honour of a patron saint, whose image was placed at the head, over the tomb, and for the soul of the defunct. William Rokeley, archbishop of Dublin, who died 1521, ordered his bowels to be buried at Dublin; his heart at Halifax, where he was vicar; and his body at Kirk Sandal, whereof he had been minister; and a chapel to be erected over each. The memorial of him in the chapel on the North side of the chancel at Halifax is now removed, and his heart has been often dug up [2].

Mr. Lethieullier proceeds to observe, that "some knowledge in Heraldry is very necessary in searches of this nature. A coat of arms, device, or rebus, very often remains where not the least word of an inscription appears, and where indeed very probably there never was any; for I am apprehensive, that a vanity in surviving friends, who imagined a person eminent in their time could never be forgotten, induced them frequently not to put any on his monument. And it is not uncommon to find a pious ejaculation, or text of Scripture, by way of epitaph, without the least mention of the person who lies there interred.

"It may be useful likewise to remember the aeras when certain customs were introduced in the manner of bearings, &c. Thus, whenever supporters are found to a coat of arms, it must certainly be later than the time of king Richard the Second, that prince being the first who used any."

Mr. Edmondson says, arms were not used in England before the commencement of the tenth century. Mr. Gale [3], not before the year 1147, when the second croisade began.

Philip, 1159, is the first of the earls of Flanders who bore arms on his shield or helmet [4]. His successors bore them regularly.

The first instance of arms on a shield on monuments given by Montfaucon in France is 1109. The oldest I have met with in England is on the shield of Geffrey Magnaville earl of Essex in the Temple church.

In the sixteenth century, when armorial bearings multiplied so fast that the canopies of tombs were covered with them, it is not uncommon, both here and on the continent, to find the names written under them.

"Where the figure of a woman is found with arms both on her kirtle and mantle, those on the kirtle are always her own family's, and those on the mantle her husband's [5]. Byshe [6] says the arms on the inner garment are *maiden*,

[1] In Turkey the tombs of the emperors are for the most part built in little chapels, close by, but not adjoining to the mosques. In these Muezins and Dervises pray and read the Alcoran; lamps burn at the head and feet of the grave, over which is placed an empty coffin, covered with cloth or velvet, and on it is set a turban. Greaves on the Grand Seignor's Seraglio, II. 796. See also Chardin's account of the tombs of the Persian monarchs at Kom.

[2] Gibson's Camden, Yorkshire. Watson's Hist. of Halifax, p. 502.

[3] Pref. ad Reg. Richmond, p. xvi.

[4] Vredius, p. 14. pl. II.

[5] Lethieullier, ubi sup.

[6] Byshe on Upton's Aspilogia, p. 64.

and

and thofe on the outer *married* bearings; fo it is in the portrait of a Goddard married to a Rochford in St. Peter's church at Walpole; and on the lady in Worcefter cathedral, whom he makes a *Verdon* by birth, and a *Warren* by marriage [1]; whereas the only arms the latter bears are *outer* on her garment, and they are thofe of *Warren*, which fhe was by *marriage*. This diftinction is more frequently expreffed in windows than on tombs: Thus to mention two inftances; thofe on the fine feries of Beauchamps, in the windows of the choir at Warwick [2], and that of the Cloptons in the clereftory of Long Milford church. In Harwood church, Yorkfhire, are the portraits of Judge Gafcoigne and his two wives, having on their mantles his arms impaling their own, and over them their own arms [3].

On a feal of Elizabeth Lucy given by Byfhe on Upton, p. 72. fhe holds her hufband's arms in her right hand, and her own in her left. Yet Alice wife of Giles de Aftley bore in her left hand her own arms, and in her right thofe of Clinton, in the window of a chantry, which fhe founded at Wolvey [4].

Two ladies in the windows of Burton Pedwardine church, c. Lincoln, have alternately on their furcoat their husbands arms' and on a pennon in their hands their own [5]. On the other hand, the windows of the parlour at Newnham Padox, c. Warwick, furnifh an exception to this rule, by putting the woman's arms on the mantle, and none on the kirtle [6]; and at Merivale and Grendon in the fame county, the man's on the mantle and none on the kirtle [7]. The wife of Gerard D'Ewes, in the 16th century, has on her mantle her own coat impaled by her hufband's [8].

The ladies, fays Colombiere [9], bore their hufband's arms impaled with their own on their robes, petticoat, or mantle of ceremony, which they in their life wore on public occafions when they affifted with them.

The firft inftance of a fubject's quartering of arms is John Haftings earl of Pembroke, following the example of king Edward the Third.

"When there are only three fleurs de lis in the arms of France, and not femée, it is later than king Henry the Fifth.

"The number of princes of the blood royal of the houfes of York and Lancafter may eafily be diftinguifhed by the labels on their coats of arms, which are different for each, and very often their devices are added. Till the time of Henry the Third we find no coronets round the heads of peers. Thus William de Valence earl of Pembroke, half brother to king John, who died anno 1295 or 1296, and is buried in Weftminfter abbey, has only a plain fillet; but John of Eltham, fecond fon to king Edward the Second, who died anno 1334, and is buried in the fame place, has a coronet with leaves on; and is the moft ancient of this fort which is met with [10].

"As to monuments for the feveral degrees of churchmen, as bifhops, abbots, priors, monks, &c. or of religious women, they are eafily to be diftinguifhed from other perfons, but equally difficult to afcertain to their true owners. Among thefe, as among the forementioned monuments, for the moft part the ftone effigies are the oldeft, with the mitre, crofier, and other proper infignia; and very often wider at the head than feet, having indeed been the very cover to the ftone coffins in which the body was depofited.

"When brafs plates came in fafhion, they were likewife very much ufed by bifhops, &c. many of whofe grave-ftones remain at this day, very richly adorned; and in many the indented marble fhews that they have been fo. In

[1] "Paterno genere ex familia *Verdonorum* fuit & conjux cujufdam comitis Surreiæ è *Warrenis*. Veftis enim interior *Verdonorum* habet infignia, exterior *Warrenorum*. Per quem morem ortum & conjugia heroinæ olim exprimebant." Notæ ad Specim. p. 91. Le Neve, in a MS. note on this paffage thus explains it. "Veftis exterior familiam fœminæ, exterior viri denotat."

[2] Dugdale's Warwickfh. firft edit. p. 318. 320.
[3] Thorefby's Ducat. Leod. p. 177.
[4] Dugd. ib. 47.
[5] Saunderfon's MSS collections.
[6] Dugdale, ubi fup. p. 60.
[7] Dugd. ib. 781. 796.
[8] Weever, 629.
[9] Science heroique, p. 479.
[10] See p. 95. and pl. xxxiii.

Salifbury

Salifbury cathedral I found two very ancient ftone figures of bifhops, which were brought from Old Sarum, and are confequently older than the time of Henry the Third. In that church likewife the pompous marble which lies over Nicholas Longefpe bifhop of that fee, and fon to the earl of Salifbury, who died anno 1297, appears to have been richly plated, though the brafs is now quite gone, and is one of the moft early of that kind which I have met with. There are in Peterborough church many monuments for abbots of that convent [1]; as likewife at Tewksbury for nine [2]; and in Wells cathedral many, which were brought from Glaftonbury; and the like in many other places: but their names are intirely forgotten; and it is now impoffible to reftore them to their true owners. Frequently where there are no effigies, crofiers or croffes denote an ecclefiaftick. I think I have feen the latter, with little difference in their make, for every order from a bifhop to a parifh prieft."

Of Crosiers alone on tombs I faw an inftance on that of Henry abbot of Margam, c. Glamorgan, laid acrofs a drain [3]. There is fuch an one on the tomb of Waltman firft abbot of St. Michael's abbey at Antwerp, who died 1138 [4].

A crofier held by an arm is on the tomb of abbot John Sutton, at Dorchefter, c. Oxford. 1349. A crofs fo holden is on that of Urien de St. Pierre in Glamorganfhire.

The variety of Crosses in ftone or brafs is fo great, that it has coft no fmall pains to reduce them into claffes, in four plates, here fubjoined.

1. Plain. Pl. I. 1. 4. and next to thefe, Pl. I. 10, 11. Thofe numbered 6. 9. in the fame plate refemble the rude ftone croffes in our Weftern and Northern counties, whereon the circle alludes either to the *nimbus* or the *crown of thorns*, as the crofs on the coffin lid at Carlifle, in the plate of Chalices.
2. Lefs plain. Pl. I. 2. 3. 5. 8. 11. III. 13.
3. On the ridged coffin lid. Pl. III. 1, 2, 3, 5, 6, 7, 8.
4. Accompanied with a fword, bow, hunting horn, or other thing. Pl. II. 1. 2. 4. 6. 8. 12. III. 10. A hand holding a wafer. Pl. III. 9. A clothier's fheers. Pl. II. 12.
5. Accompanied with coats of arms. Pl. II. 3. 7. 10. 11. IV. 9. 11. or with fword and coat of arms, II. 5. 9. 10. IV. 3. or with arms and infcription, IV. 3. 9.
6. Ramified, and emblematic of the vine branch. Pl. II. 7. IV. 1. 6. 10. Pl. III. 11. or with a refemblance of the thunder bolt. Pl. III. 1, 2, 3, 4. Thofe numbered 2. & 5. Pl. I. have the vine bud at their extremities, as in Pl. III. 11.
7. With infcriptions on or round them. Pl. I. 12. II. 3. 4. IV. 3. 4. 5. 7. 10.
8. Refting on the holy lamb, or fome other animal, IV. 9, 10. 13.
9. With figures of Christ, the Virgin, or Saints, on the top. Pl. IV. 8. Such has been a fhort crofs in brafs on the flab of Giles Seymour in the chancel at Croydon, 1390.
   Or worfhippers kneeling to them at the fides, or under the fteps. Pl. IV. 7. 8.
10. furmounted with figures of the parties buried below. Pl. IV. 9. A half-prieft at Appleby, and whole ones in Hereford cathedral, Cobham and Stone churches, Kent.

[1] See Pl. III. p. 19.
[2] Thefe are now reduced to five, and none of thefe has, or ever had, a figure on it.
[3] Engraved in the new edition of Camden's Britannia, II. pl. xviii.
[4] Le Grand Theatre de Brabant, II. p. 94.

Plate

Plate I.

1. *Welbec* priory, c. Nottingham.
2. *Kirklees* park, belonging to Sir George Armitage, bart. in the Weſt Riding of Yorkſhire. The figure of the ſtone over the grave of Robin Hood, now broken and much defaced, the inſcription illegible. That printed in Thoresby Ducat. Leod. 576, from Dr. Gale's papers, was never on it. The late Sir Samuel Armitage, owner of the premiſes, cauſed the ground under it to be dug a yard deep, and found it had never been diſturbed; ſo that it was probably brought from ſome other place, and by vulgar tradition aſcribed to Robin Hood [1].
3. *Kirkby in Aſhfield*, c. Nottingham, freeſtone on South ſide of the church-yard.
4. *Winterborne* chapel, Berks, in the belfrey, imboſt on a plank of wood antiently uſed as a graveſtone [2].
5. *Kirklees* priory, dug out of the ruins in the antient cemetry, 1754, now placed on a raiſed tomb.
6. *Tankerſley*, Weſt Riding of Yorkſhire, freeſtone, South ſide of the church yard.
7. *Royſton*, Herts, inlaid with braſs on blue marble, within the rails.
8. *Buckland*, Berks, emboſt on a raiſed graveſtone, under the main arch on the North ſide of the chancel [3].
9. South ſide of *Ernley* church yard, in the Weſt Riding of Yorkſhire.
10. *Kirklees*, dug out of the ruins of the antient cemetery.
11. Eaſt end of *Ramſey* church yard, c. Huntingdon.
12. *Long Sutton*, in Holland, c. Linc. middle aile.

Plate II.

1. *Aldwick in the Street*, in the Weſt Riding of Yorkſhire, in the chancel.
2. *Bowes* church, ſtep into the nave; probably for one of the family of Bowes [4].
3. *Kirk Deighton*, Weſt Riding of Yorkſhire, on the North ſide of the chancel: for one of the family of Roſs, formerly of Ingmanthorpe in this pariſh, and lords of Kirk Deighton [5].
4. *Waſhington* church yard, c. Durham. This James Sanderſon, alias de Bedick, was ſecond ſon of Alexander de Bedick of Bedick, in the pariſh of Waſhington, who lived 1333, and alſo lies buried in the ſame church yard, with his effigy on his tomb [6]. From this James deſcended the Saunderſons viſcounts Caſtleton in the kingdom of Ireland [7].
5. *Bolam* church, Northumberland, South aile; ſuppoſed for one of the antient family of Carnaby there [8].
6. *Bowes* church, near the North door.
7. *Chetwynd* church, Shropſhire, now the eſtate of —— Pigot, eſq. for one of the family of Chetwynd, as appears by the arms [9]. In the middle of the chancel.
8. Middle aile of *Thornton* church in Craven, from the church yard.
9. *Catworth* church yard, c. Hunt. removed from the church when the floor was repaired.
10. *Leek* church, North Riding of Yorkſhire [10].
11. *Brecknock*, over one of the family of Price [11].
12. *Kirkby in Aſhfield*, c. Nottingham, free-ſtone, North ſide of the church.

[1] Mr. Watſon's Letter in Antiquary Society Minutes.
[2] Aſhmole's Berks Monuments. C. xii. p. 177. in Coll. Arm.
[3] Ib. C. xii. p. 98.
[4] See Lel. It. IV. 12.
[5] Dugd. Mon. Ebor. in Coll. Armor, 153. a.
[6] C. xxxii. f. 86. Coll. Arm.
[7] C. 41. Coll. Arm.
[8] Dugd. Mon Ebor. in Coll. Arm. f. 146. b.
[9] See Thoroton's Nott. 474.
[10] Harl. MS. 911. p. 26.
[11] Harl. MS. 911. p. 113.

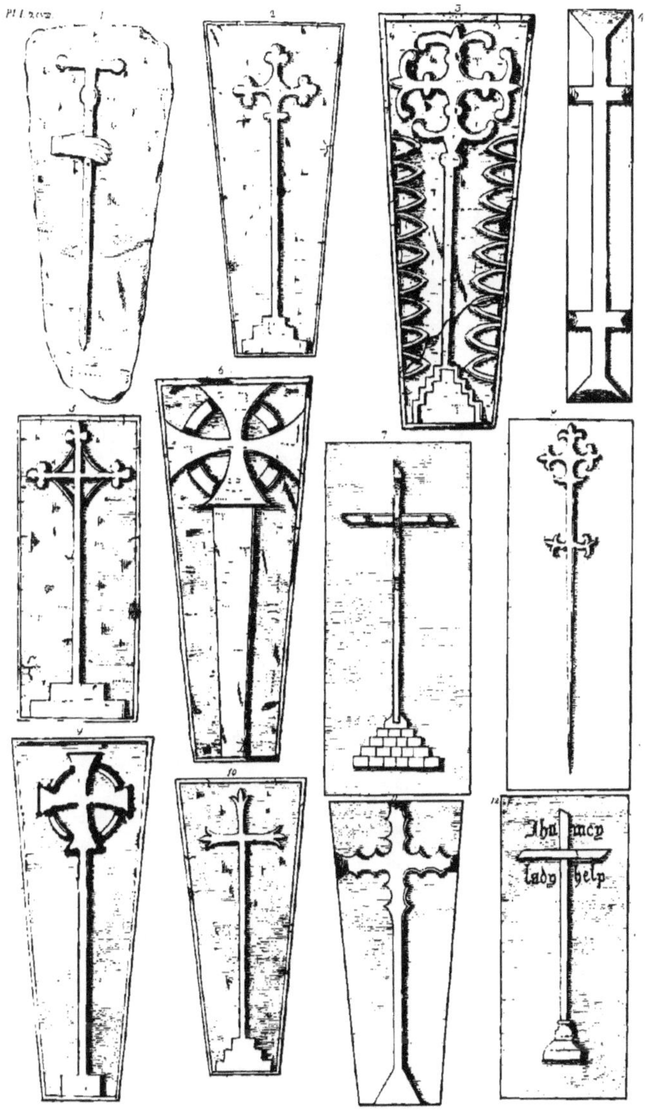
Ihu mcy
lady help

Pl. II

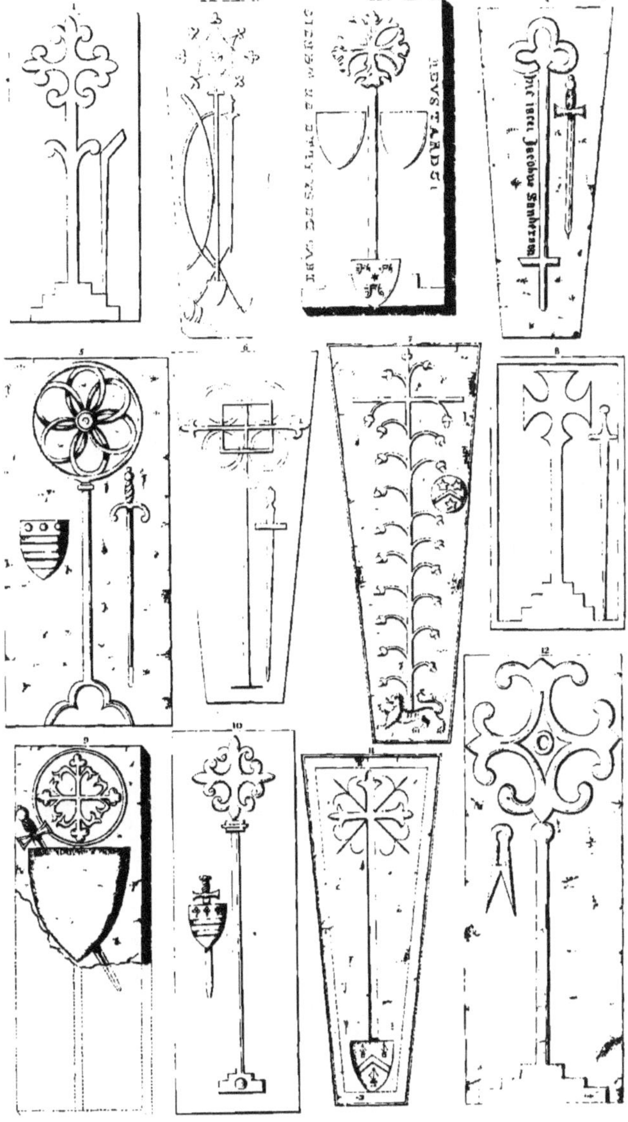

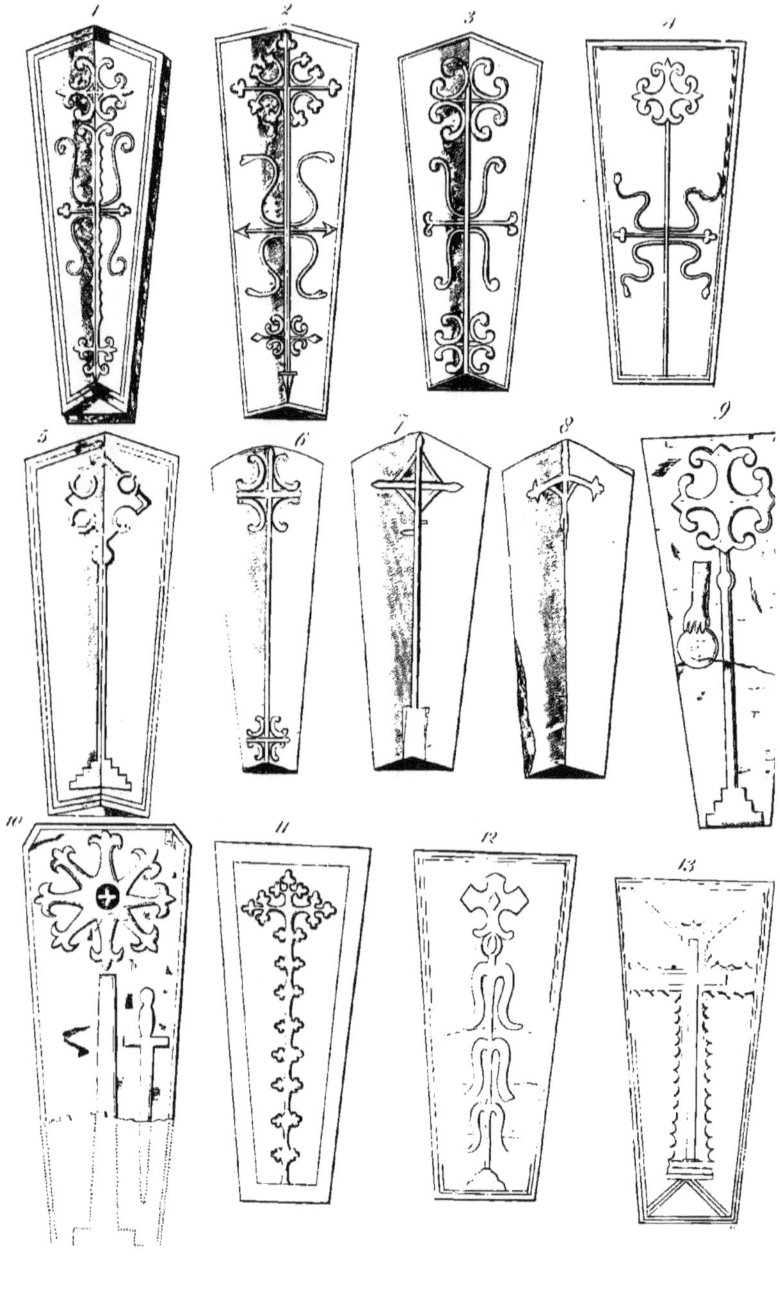
1
2
3
4
5
6
7
8
9
10
11
12
13

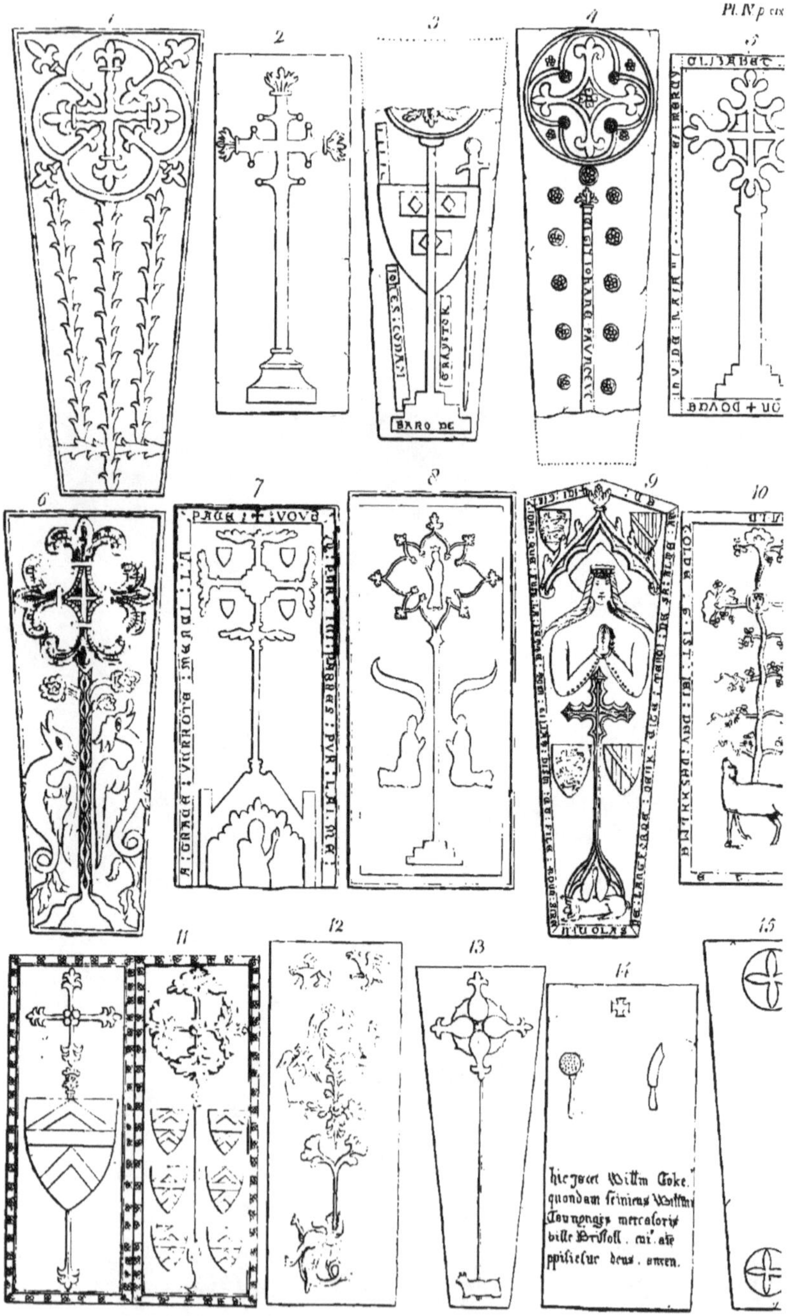
1
2
3
4
5
6
7
8
9
10
11
12
13
14
15
IOHES . CORANI
CRAYTOR
BARO DE
NICHOLAS
hic jacet Willm Coke.
quondam seruiens Willm
Caunyngis mercatoris
ville Bristoll . cui' aie
ppicietur deus . amen.

Plate III.

1. *Ramſey*, c. Hunt. Eaſt end of the church-yard. Such an one in Soham church.
2. *Landbeach* church, c. Cambridge.
3. *Steeple Gidding* church-yard, c. Hunt. See the firſt croſs in the Hiſtory of Thetford, Pl. III.
4. *Ramſey* church yard, as a fence in the wall.
5. *Dorcheſter*, c. Ox. A ſimilar one at *Malling* abbey, c. Kent.
6. 7. 8. On the wall of *Cheſterford* churchyard, c. Camb.
9. *Kirkby in Aſhfield*, c. Nottingham, South ſide of the churchyard.
10. *Dewſbury*, c. York, now placed againſt the vicarage houſe, but formerly in the South choir.
11. *Ramſey* church, North aile.
12. In the South ſide of the South aile of the choir of *Rocheſter* cathedral.
13. *Norwich* cathedral.

Plate IV.

1. In the chancel at *Fownhope*, c. Hereford; in which the vine branches and croſs are united.
2. *Home Lacy*, in ſame county, near the South porch, free-ſtone; ſuch another, but richer, inlaid in braſs, in the veſtry of St. Mary's church, Lincoln.
3. *Greyſtock*, c. Cumberland, within the rails of the altar, near the North wall: in freeſtone. This John lord Greyſtock was ſummoned to parliament from 23 to 34 Edward I. in which laſt year he died. The arms are G. three cuſhions A. taſſelled O.
4. *Aconbury*, c. Hereford, freeſtone laid looſe, near the Weſt end.
5. In the cemetery of the nunnery at *Kirklees*, Yorkſhire. *Douce Jeſu de Nazareth ei mercy a Elizabet de Stanton iadis priores de ceſt maiſon* [1].
6. *Dewſbury* church, Yorkſhire, now againſt the wall of the vicarage-houſe, but dug out of the South choir when the church was repaired a few years ago. It lay over one of the Soothills of Soothill in this pariſh, who bore G. an eagle diſplayed A. to which the animals on the ſtone are ſuppoſed to allude. This choir, with the manor of Soothill, belonged to the late Sir George Saville, of Thornhill and Rufford, bart. in right of the marriage of his anceſtor Sir Henry Saville, of Thornhill, knight of the Bath in the reign of Henry VIII. with Elizabeth daughter and heireſs of Thomas Soothill, of Soothill, eſq.
7. In the chancel of *Buckworth*, c. Hunt. ſuppoſed for an antient rector. In braſs, now reaved.
8. *Henly on Thames*, in the chancel: the braſs reaved.
9. *Norton Diſney*, c. Linc. North chancel. Inſcription: *Ici giſt Joan que fuſt la femme moun Gillam Diſni et file moun ſire Nicolas de Lancforte Deu eite merci de ſa alme. Amen.*
10. Found in digging the foundations of the Quaker's meeting-houſe at *Briſtol*, 1749, on the ſite of the Blackfriars. Inſcription round it, *Reynold: Tolde: giſt: ici: deu: de ſa alme eit merci.* It had been uſed as a chimney-piece, and was ſince broken to pieces.
11. *Dore* abbey, Herefordſhire, in the ruins of the nave, in free-ſtone.
12. In the North wall of the nave at *Burnt Pelham*, c. Herts. deſcribed p. lxxxviii.

[1] See a wretched copy of it in the Account of Antiquities in and about Oxford, annexed to Leland's Itin. II. 118. It is alſo incorrectly copied in Thoreſby's Duc. Leod. p. 91.

13. In *Much Hadham* church, Herts. on the ſlab of a ſtone circumſcribed in Gothic capitals, *Hic jacet Simon Flambard, quondam rector hujus eccleſiæ* [1].
14. In the South chancel of St. Mary Radcliffe, *Briſtol*, near Canninges' tomb, over William Coke his ſervant, and as it ſhould ſeem by the devices, a menial in the kitchen, unleſs they are a rebus of his name.
15. *Dore abbey*, c. Hereford, South ſide of the church-yard, free-ſtone.

The two laſt ſtones in this Plate have very ſmall croſſes, accompanied with other devices.

Theſe are ſo many proofs that the croſs was not confined to the monuments of religious. Mr. Strutt [1] gives one from a Saxon drawing on the lid of a royal coffin. I aſcribe one in the Temple-church to a ſon of Henry II. Mr. Blomefield gives one at Fersfield over Sir Robert Bois and another formè, in Titſal chancel, over a religious who built that part of the church. A long great croſs of braſs was on the ſlab of William ſon of Sir John Rochford conſtable of Wisbech-caſtle, in Walpole church, in the ſame county [3]. In Gent. Mag. 1749. p. 405. 551. one is deſcribed over a married woman at Carliſle. Leland [4] mentions one at Oſeney over Henry Doily, ſon of the foundreſs. Juga Baynard, foundreſs of Dunmow, is ſuppoſed to have one on her coffin in the wall of the church there [5]. The laws of Kenneth king of Scotland, in the eighth century, order a croſs to be put on every grave-ſtone.

One lies over archbiſhop Sudbury's father, in St. George's church at Sudbury: one over archbiſhop Chicheley's father, in Higham Ferrars church [6]: two older than theſe in the church-yard at Matherne, c. Monmouth, over Urien de St. Pierre and wife, 1295 [7]. In the Eaſt end of the South tranſept of Bangor cathedral is a croſs on an altar tomb ſaid to cover *Owen Glendwr*, or more probably *Owen Gwenneth*, Sovereign of North Wales, who died 1169, and was buried here with his brother Cadwallader, according to Giraldus Cambrenſis [8]. I have a drawing of one over a burgeſs and his wife, a plain croſs, the ſhaft and tranſverſes, pointed: on each ſide of it labels with **Jesu : mercy ! lady : helpe !** and at the foot, **memento !** and round the ledge,

> **Hic jacet Johannes Barker quondam Burgensis istius ville qui obiit xvi die mensis Aprilis anno d'ni millesimo cccclxxx° cuius anime propicietur deus. Amen. In d'no confido.**

Mr. Lethieullier concludes,

"I ſhall only mention one monument more, which is ſomewhat peculiar; I mean the repreſentation of a ſkeleton in a ſhroud, lying either under or on a table tomb. I have obſerved one of this make in almoſt all the cathedral and conventual churches throughout England, and ſcarcely ever more than one; but what age to attribute the unknown ones to, I can find no date to gueſs by, ſince there is one in York cathedral for Robert Claget, treaſurer of that cathedral, as ancient as 1241; and in Briſtol cathedral Paul Buſh, the firſt biſhop of that ſee, who died ſo late as 1558, is repreſented in the ſame manner, and I have obſerved ſome in every age between."

The leaſt degree of reflection would have ſhewn that the figure here alluded to, which has created an unneceſſary perplexity with ſeveral curious perſons, and given riſe to the fooliſh tales of vergers and ſextons, was nothing more than a ſtriking exemplification of the change of condition made by death contraſted

[1] See p. cii. & 178. [2] I. 57. 66. [3] Parkins' Continuation of Blomefield's Norfolk, IV. 718.
[4] It. II. 19. [5] See before, p. xxxv. [6] Engraved in the Stemmata Chicheleiana.
[7] See p. 68. Archæol. V. p. 76, 77. Pl. II. and the new edition of Camden's Britannia, II. pl. xvi.
[8] It. Cambr. in Willis's Bangor, p. 36.

with

with the appearance of the party on the upper ſtory of the tomb. Inſtances of this kind are, among others, biſhop Fleming at Lincoln, 1431. Archbiſhop Chichely at Canterbury, 1443. Biſhop Lacy at Exeter, 1455. Biſhop Beckington at Wells, 1465. Dean Heywood at Lichfield, 1492. John Barret, in St. Mary's church, at St. Edmundſbury, 1463. Edmund Cornwall, baron of Burford, at Burford, Shropſhire. Abbot Iſlip, at Weſtminſter, 1510, now gone. Archdeacon Aſheton in the antechapel of St. John's College Cambridge, 1522. Biſhops Fox, 1528, and Gardiner, 1555, at Wincheſter. Prior Weſton 1540, at Clerkenwell. Præcentor Bennet, 1558; and another at Saliſbury, miſcalled biſhop Fox, and now ſhut up in doors like a preſs. Edward Wakeman, eſq. in a chapel at Tewkſbury, 1634. Dean Colet's was the moſt complete ſkeleton of all theſe, carved in wood, and great part of it ſtill remains, with its matraſs highly finiſhed, in the vaults under St. Paul's. I ſuſpect the figure in Weſtbury church, c. Glouceſter, deſcribed as "a naked man, ill executed in ſtone [1]," and referred to Carpenter biſhop of Worceſter, 1476, is nothing more. Lay figures of the kind are not very common among us, except one of the counteſs of Suffolk, at Ewelme; one of the noble family at Arundel, c. Suſſex; Sir Marmaduke Conſtable 5 Edward IV. at Flamborough, in Yorkſhire, 15 . [2]. Henry lord Windſor, at Tarbic, c. Warwick, 1605 [3]; Sir John Colaſre, at Fyfield, Berks [4]; and Mr. Blount at Mamble, c. Worceſter, 5 Eliz. 1563 [5]. A writer in the Gentleman's Magazine ſays there are ſeveral in the royal abbey of St. Denis, near Paris [6]; and another correſpondent of Mr. Urban's deſcribes one of a duke de Croy, in the church of the Celeſtines at Heverle near Louvain [7], where the ſkeleton is repreſented with the worms preying upon it, as René of Anjou is ſaid to have painted his miſtreſs after he had opened her tomb at Avignon, as he found her at his return from a pilgrimage to Jeruſalem [8]. This I ſuppoſe is the figure of Charles firſt duke of Croy and fourth of Arſchot, who died 1612, having rebuilt the church of Heverlé, 1569, and erected on it a ſeries of monuments for his family and predeceſſors. He and his wife are repreſented in their ducal robes upon the tomb, and below as dead. At the entrance of the tomb is another figure of the duke on a copper plate, in the habit of a Capuchin, ducally crowned, and round it an inſcription compoſed by himſelf, on which are the words *nunc putredo terræ et cibus vermiculorum* [9]. Probably this figure is like that of Philip Dengelberge before the altar at Vilvorde abbey, near Bruſſels, 1645, a corpſe on a mat with worms preying on it [10]. A third correſpondent of Mr. Urban's [11] ſuppoſes the different figures repreſented the party in their ſepulchral dreſs, and in their emaciated ſtate before death. He muſt have conceived all of them lived to be emaciated, but in truth the direct contrary is the deſign of theſe figures [12], which were ſucceeded or imitated by corpſes in ſhrouds tyed at head and feet, not uncommon on braſſes, though I do not recollect an inſtance of this kind, where the contraſt abovementioned is obſerved, except it be on biſhop Fleming's tomb in Lincoln minſter. Dr. Donne's is a famous inſtance of the kind in ſtone, ſtill remaining intire in the vaults under St. Paul's. Aſhmole [13] mentions a man painted in a window praying in a winding ſheet. A later inſtance is a good figure in Sanderſted church, Surry, of Mary Bedell wife of Ralph Hautrey, and Ludolphus Audley, who died 1655. She is repreſented in white marble, lying on a mat and wrought cuſhion, in a ſhroud tied

[1] Rudder, 803.
[2] Gent. Mag. XXIII. 456.
[3] Dugd. Warw. p. 549.
[4] Aſhmole, I. 106.
[5] Naſh. II. 160.
[6] Gent. Mag. LIV. 486.
[7] Ib. 348.
[8] Breval's Travels, I. 138. A picture was made of the ſtate in which William the Conqueror's corpſe was found when the Hugonots broke open his tomb, 1512. Rech. de Normandie. Archæol. III. 391.
[9] Supplement au theatre de Brabant, I. 268. Sanderi Chorographia ſacra Brabantiæ, II. 173.
[10] See it engraved in Le Grand Theatre ſacrè de Brabant, I. p. 83.
[11] Gent. Mag. LIV. 32.
[12] Gent. Mag. LIV. 172. 348, 349. 409.
[13] Aſhm. Berks. II. 241.

at

at head and feet, her head bound with a chin-cloth, reclined to the right-hand, which lies acrofs her waift, her left hanging down; her left knee lifted up. Mr. Blomefield calls thefe figures in brafs "effigies looking out of their "winding fheets[1]." Salmon[2] fays of fuch at Hitchin, "that they are effigies "of men and women with part of their habits tied above their heads; the "woman's hair hanging down at each fide, like a long peruke." In Sabridge-worth church are a man and woman fo apparelled, holding each an heart. Others on braffes of the 15th, 16th, and 17th centuries, in St. Laurence's church, Norwich[3]. Others in Sedgefield church, co. Durham. The figure of lady Bruce on her monument in Exton church, c. Rutland, is fo habited, 1627[4].

The oldeft figure I recollect of Death reprefented as a fkeleton is on the brafs plate of archdeacon Ruding, 1471, in Biggleſwade church. There is a moft beautiful and well-preferved little one in alabafter againft the wall over the Morley tomb in the chancel at Little Hollingbury, Effex. There is a complete fkeleton, praying in the Eaft window of the Lennard chapel, at Weft Wickham, in Kent, probably of the middle of the fixteenth century. Petronius Arbiter fays, that Trimalcio introduced with his wine a filver figure fo contrived that the joints and vertebræ moved by fprings, and after it had performed fome gefticulations he repeated fome verfes on mortality[5]. In Spence's Polymetis, plate 41. death is reprefented by a human fkeleton. Count Caylus remarks, that the antients never reprefented death on their monuments, either in his proper figure or emblematically, and when they introduced fkeletons, they confidered them not as images of death, but of the ftructure of the body (*charpente du corps*[6]). This may be applied to all Chriftian monuments till Mr. Nightingal's: the fkeletons are only for contraft.

I do not recollect that any notice has been taken of the circumftance of the foul carried to heaven by angels from the head of the effigies. Yet this is not uncommon, and will be found here on the monuments of Aymer de Valence, pl. XXIX. and lord Burgherfh, pl. XXXV. It is alfo on the brafs of Sir Hugh Haftings at Elfying in Norfolk, and on that rich one of Roger Thornton and wife in Allhallow's church, Newcaftle; and in France, over the tomb of Dagobert at St. Dennis[7]; and over the dying St. Louis in the window of the fame church[8].

Mr. Blomefield[9] defcribes an altar-cloth in St. Gregory's church at Norwich, ufed when mafs for the dead was celebrated, having on it many angels holding fheets, thofe like men having a demi-man naked in each fheet; and thofe like women a demi-woman; to reprefent that by their miniftration the fouls of the righteous are conducted to heaven.

It reminds us of the idea that the foul efcapes with the laft breath, confequently out of the mouth. Hence Tavernier tells us, the Parfis make ufe of a dog to receive the laft breath of a perfon juft expiring. In the monument of lord Burgherfh, however, this groupe is at his feet.

Among the innumerable inftances of figures on tombs, very few variations of attitude occur. The recumbent attitude with the hands elevated in devotion is adopted by perfons of both fexes, and of all ranks. Croifaders are diftinguifhed by croffing their legs; and prelates by lifting up the right hand, and extending the two firft fingers to give the benediction; though they as frequently have their hands joined and elevated. Some religious, befides the crofiers and paftoral ftaff, which they hold in different attitudes, more or lefs elegant, have books or churches, which two laft are put into the hands of kings or nobles[10]. Abbot Ramridge, at St. Albans, has his hands croft, and hanging down.

[1] Norf. III. 129. [2] Herts, 165. [3] Blomf. II. 678. [4] Wright's Rutland, p. 59. [5] [illegible] Had[...]anidis, p. 115. [6] Recueil, III. 189. [7] Montf. I. xiv. [8] Ib. II. xxx. [9] II. 688.
[10] Lebeuf mentions in the Sainte chapelle du palais at Paris a prieft of the 14th or 15th century, who, inftead of a chalice, holds in his two hands a reliquary or fhrine in form of a Gothic pyramid. Can he have miftaken this for a church? Hift. de la ville & dioc. de Paris, I. 355.

The

The figure at Hatfield Peverel assigned to the foundress of the abbey, but which I rather incline to give to some superior or priest of the house, has in its elevated hands what may pass for a chalice or a heart. A lady of the Brian family, at Brampton Brian, Herefordshire, holds a heart in her hand; and, though the oldest of the family, has survived the devastations of the civil war, and is the best preserved figure of the kind. Leland describes at Oseney an image of the foundress (1125) "Edithe, of stone, in thabbite of a woves, holding an hart "in her right hond, in the North side of the high altare [1]." Agatha de Narborough, a half statue, holds an heart in her hands [2]. So does a man in a short coat reaching only to his knees, and his sleeves only to his elbows, in Hatford chancel, Berks [3]. The little figure in the chancel at Tenbury holds a large heart in its elevated hands, and so does a brass figure in Berkeley church, c. Gloucester, inscribed *mcy*, and bishop Wainfleet, at Winchester. Thomas Fisher and wife, in Warwick church, 1577, hold bibles [4]. Anne Grey, 1505, in Wotton Waveney church, has a very large string of beads [5].

Bishop Rainelm, Sir John de la Rivere, and Sir John Cobham, hold models of Hereford cathedral, and of Tormarton [6] and Cobham churches. John Wyrrall has his horn and falchion; a forester at Glinton his arrows and horn: an old cross-legged knight in mail, in Pershore church, has in his hand a horn fastened to his belt: on his left arm a shield, the end whereof a serpent bites, at his feet an hare [7]; William Malgeneste, one of the king of France's huntsmen, who died 1301, has on his brass plate his hunting horn hanging from his right side, and holds a dog fastened to a strap past over his right arm [8]. Another figure in brass, in Baldock church, has at his right side a hunting horn, and at his left a couteau de chasse, with something like a lesser couteau inserted on the same scabbard, and by the side of the larger one something like a skain of whipcord: John Ceysill a purse; as has another man at Baldock with a large rosary.

Some few attitudes are varied to a degree of greater lightness and elegance, as some of the knights in the Temple church and elsewhere, drawing their swords. So the defaced Beches, at Aldworth and the Bracebridges at Kingsbury, c. Warwick [9]. Edmund Crouchback turns his back to the aile, and looks behind him, lying on his right side; so does a prior in Normandy. "La tombe "de Thomas de la Queue-d'haie, prieur du monastere de Sausseuse, enterré dans "la chapelle de la vierge est remarquable en ceci qu'on l'y a representé comme "appuyee sur la coté droit, vetu en habit d'hyver, le rochet pendant jusqu' "aux talons comme une aube [10]."

In the sixteenth century they supported their heads in their right hand: an attitude taken from the Greek and Roman monuments.

It has been supposed unusual to place the lady at the right hand of the man, and Dr. Salmon refers it to her being an heiress [11], but there are many instances, as the Harsicks at South Acre, Norfolk; Delalee, at Albury, Herts; two knights and ladies at Beverly; the duke of Norfolk, at Framlingham. Richard the Second's queen, at Westminster, takes the right hand of her husband; so does Henry the Fourth's at Canterbury; as also the wife of lord Bardolf, at Donnington.

[1] Itin. II. 19. [2] Blomf. III. 470. [3] Ashmole, I. 175.
[4] Dugd. 351. [5] Ib. 603. [6] Rudder, 774.
[7] Nash's Worcester, I. 251. The lower part of this figure is now broken off.
[8] Montf. Mon. II. xxxix. 6.
[9] Dugd. Warw. p. 1061. Ed. Thomas.
[10] Descr. de la haute Normandie, II. 311.
[11] Herts. 113. 284. Survey, 575. Ashm. Berk. I. 31.

The uſual place for children on braſſes is under the feet of the reſpective parents; and thoſe of each group looking towards each other: but this rule is not without exception. Elizabeth wife of Thomas lord Scrope, who died 9 Henry VIII. directed her executors to lay a ſtone over her grave, with three images, the one of her lord and huſband, another of herſelf, and the third of her daughter, with their arms thereon, and an inſcription making mention who they were, and this to the value of ten pounds [1]. On a braſs at Welwyn there is a ſon fronting, in the middle, between his brother and ſiſters. Under the pews in the North aile of Orford church are a mother and ſon ſtanding together, in Grecian attitudes. The ſons of Sir Nicholas Hawberk and Reginald lord Braybrook, at Cobham, ſtand at their father's feet and left hand, on pedeſtals inſcribed with their names. The kneeling attitude for children was not, I believe, introduced till after the reformation [2], any more than that of parents or other figures on monuments (except to the croſs), nor the infant in ſwaddling clothes or cradle. There is indeed a figure of a lady at Bodenham in Herefordſhire who is folding an infant under her mantle.

Salmon [3] mentions the hair curled, and no defence about the head and face, as is uſual to find of thoſe buried ſince the Norman Conqueſt, as a peculiarity in the figure ſhewn for the emperor *Severus* in York Minſter. Sir John Ros in the Temple church is a like figure.

An attentive compariſon of the tombs of our princes and nobles of the thirteenth century will juſtify a conjecture, that foreign artiſts were employed about the ſtatues if not about the whole: and the idea ſuggeſted by Mr. Walpole that Cavallini was the principal artiſt ſo employed, receives no little confirmation from the conformity of the various pieces executed by order of Edward I. and during his reign: ſuch as the ſhrine of the Confeſſor, the tomb of his father Henry III. the pavement of the Confeſſor's chapel, and of the high altar in the ſame church, and the beautiful croſſes erected to his conſort, an unparalleled memorial of conjugal affection and art united. To borrow the words of an excellent judge of theſe matters, Sir Henry Engleſield, in his deſcription of the croſs at Geddington, read before the Society of Antiquaries, 1781, "The deſign of all the parts of this ſtructure is very elegant, and the execution ſuch as would not diſcredit any age. The roſes that cover the baſe, though too crowded, and therefore wanting in effect, are of an antique appearance, and carved with much delicacy and ſpirit. The ſtatues, though mannered, and rather ſtiff, have a great ſhare of merit. The air of the head is graceful; the drapery falls in natural though too minute folds, and the hands and feet are well drawn. On the whole, the ſtatues are thought to bear ſo great a reſemblance to the ſtyle of the antient Italian ſchool, that it is highly probable Edward had artiſts of that nation in his ſervice, if not ſent for purpoſely on the occaſion." Henry III. died 1272; Eleanor 1290. The tomb of the former was executed 8 Edward I [4], or 1280; the tomb and croſſes of the latter ten or fifteen years after. Aveline counteſs of Lancaſter was living 4 Edward I. 1276; and how much longer does not appear: her conſort Edmund Crouchback, died 1296. Sir Joſeph Ayloffe [5] was for aſcribing the memorials of all theſe great perſonages, as well as the embelliſhments of the ſhrine of Sebert, 1308, to Pietro Cavallini, as the deſigner, if not the executor,

[1] Dugd. Bar. I. 661.

[2] A counteſs of Eppendrein at Crucenaw, in the Palatinate, 1455, has however her two children kneeling on the ſame plane with herſelf at her feet. Hiſt. Acad. Theodoro-Palatinæ, I. 29.

[3] New Survey, 576.

[4] See p. 57.

[5] Account of the Weſtminſter Monuments.

as far as painting was concerned. I have indeed[1] dated the birth of that artiſt 1279, and his death 1364: but in the uncertainty under which the beſt writers labour as to dates, it is ſufficient to the preſent purpoſe if he can be proved to have been contemporary, or indeed that any artiſts were engaged from Rome about this period. This is known to have been done by Richard de Ware, who went to Rome 1267, in order to be confirmed abbot of this ſplendid monaſtery, whoſe church had been deſtined to the honour of ſerving as a Mauſoleum to our kings, and was then actually rebuilding by Henry III. Unfortunately for the artiſts of our own country, the known ſpecimens of their talents are now no more: the ſilver image of Henry the Third's daughter Catherine, in Weſtminſter abbey; and the monument of Henry II. at Fontevraud[2]. Let us not then aſcribe to them all the rude figures, and to foreigners all the more animated ones on our tombs: but candidly confeſs, that the Engliſh five centuries ago felt an emulation to excell in arts and ſciences proportionable to that of their deſcendents of the preſent age.

Sir Henry Englefield will forgive me if I tranſcribe from his memoir his obſervation, that "whatever the origin of the now Gothic architecture was, it can admit of no doubt that the commerce with the Eaſt in the time of the croiſades, brought into Europe a great ſhare of elegance in the polite arts, as the rapid improvements in ſculpture and ornamental architecture fully evince. Nothing could exceed the rudeneſs of the Saxon and early Norman attempts at the human form: yet at and about this period every thing had an elegant and pictureſque turn. In the ruins of Tintern abbey, founded in the year 1131, is a mutilated ſtatue of the Virgin, of very great beauty; and if it may be ſaid that the ſtatue is of a later date, no doubt can be entertained of the alto reliefs with which the Weſt front of the cathedral church of Wells, built during the long adminiſtration of biſhop Jocelyn, from 1206 to 1242, is covered, and which are many of them of no deſpicable workmanſhip. At this period the taſte of the carvers rather diminiſhed, though their neatneſs and delicacy in ornament runs to exceſs." Mr. Eſſex aſcribes the beautiful Weſt front of Croyland abbey church with its Grecian imagery to the reign of Henry III[3].

According to the rules for ſepulchral monuments, in Anſelme's "Palais de "l'Honneur, Par. 1663[4]," "kings and princes, in whatever part, or by what means ſoever they died, were repreſented on their tombs cloathed with their coats of arms, their ſhields, *bourlet* or pad, crown, creſt, ſupporters, lambrequins or mantlings, orders, and deviſes upon their effigies and about their tombs. Knights and Gentlemen might not be repreſented with their coats of arms, unleſs they had loſt their lives in ſome battle, ſingle combat, or rencontre with the prince himſelf, or in his ſervice, unleſs they died and were buried within their own manors and lordſhips; and then to ſhew that they died a natural death in their beds they were repreſented with their coat of armour ungirded, without a helmet, bareheaded, their eyes cloſed, their feet reſting againſt the back of a greyhound, and without any ſword. Thoſe who died on the day of battle, or in any mortal rencontre, on the victorious ſide, were to be repreſented with a drawn ſword in their right hand[5], and a ſhield in their left, their helmet on, which ſome think ought to be cloſed, and the viſor let down, in token that they fell fighting againſt their enemies, having their coat of arms girded over their armour, and at their feet a lion. Thoſe who

[1] P. 14. [2] P. 50. [3] Hiſt. of Croyland, p. 198.

[4] See alſo Colombiere, Science heroique, p. 447.

[5] The drawn ſword is in the right hand of ſeveral Saxon princes, in Reyner's Monumenta Landgravier Thuringæ, &c. 1662.

died

died in prison, or before they had paid their ransom, were represented on their tombs without spurs or helmet, without coat of arms or swords, only the scabbard girded to, and hanging at their sides. Those who fell in battle or rencontre on the side of the conquered were to be represented without coats of arms, the sword at their side and in the scabbard, the visor raised and open, their hands joined on their breasts, and their feet resting against the back of a dead and overthrown lion. The child of a governor or commander in chief, if born in a besieged city, or in the army, however young he died, was represented on his tomb armed at all points, his head on his helmet, and clad in a coat of mail of his size at the time of his death, as may be seen at St. Ouyn at Rouen [1]. The military man, who at the close of his life took on him a religious habit, and died in it, was represented completely armed, his sword by his side on the lower part; and on the upper the habit of the order which he had assumed, and under his feet the shield of his arms. The gentleman who has been conquered and slain in the lists in a combat of honour ought to be placed on his tomb armed at all points, his battle-ax lying by him, his left arm crost over the right. The gentleman victorious in the lists was exhibited on his tomb armed at all points, his battle-ax in his arms [2], his right arm crost over the left. If these rules are not of the same romantic cast with those said to be made by Charlemagne, and recited below [3], they are probably observed, or

[1] Query. If the armed figures of small proportion, before mentioned, p. xcix. are to be so explained.

[2] The only instance of a battle-ax among us I recollect is on Richard Corbet's rude figure at Malvern, engraved in Antiq. Repert. III. p. 17.

[3] "Ordinaunces made by Charles the Greate, who lived in the yeare of our Saviour Christe 700, appoyntinge in "what maner the image or representacion of every man of noble and vallerous courage should be formed, and "placed upon his sepulcher in armes, accordinge to the worthyness of theyr actions performed in theyr lyfe-tyme." From a MS. in the Scudamore Library, now the property of Charles Howard earl of Surrey, at Home Lacey, com. Hereford, compared with another in the cathedral library at Lichfield.

1st. If a man in his life-time hath encountered and fought with his enemy in close lists, and hath departed thence with honour, his effegy or representation shall be figured on his sepulchre in complete armour, fournished with all pieces *a cape a pe*, having his helmet upon his head, the beaver open, his hands conjoined and erected, with his horseman's battell-axe placed in the bowing of his arm: this sword girt unto him, and bestowed along by his side, adorned with gilt spurs, if he be Miles Auratus, otherwise his spurs shall not be gilt.

2. If it shall happen a man to coape or encountre with his adversary in close lysts, and to be therein anyways foiled, so that he come not out of the field with honour, in such a case he shall have his image or effigies insculped upon his tomb, completely armed throughout, as the former, saving that his beaver shall be shut, his hands conjoined and his horseman's battle-axe placed by his side.

3. If in case a knight or gentleman chaunce to be killed in single fight within the lists, then shall his image be formed upon his tomb, armed throughout, yet having his beaver close, his sword drawn in his right hand, advancing the point upwards towards his head, and his shield on his left arm, and his scabbard bestowed decently along by his side.

4. If by chance a General, Captain, or Lieutenant, be slain in a foughten fielde, on that part which was vanquished or discomfited, his representation shall be formed upon his sepulchre in complete armour, his sword in his scabbard, his beaver open, and his hands conjoined and erected as before.

5. If a man by chaunce do happen to be taken prisoner in a battayle, and to dye in prison before he hath paid his ransom, his image shall be made upon his sepulchre, armed, having his beaver open, but without either sword or spurs, holding an empty scabbard in his hand.

6. It is to be observed, that no man may have his effigies or image insculped upon his sepulchre, adorned with his coat of arms, unless he be interred in the church or chapel whereof himself is patron, either by descent or by purchase, as a dignity inseparablye annexed to the lordship or manor whereof he is lord, and to whom the right of patronage doth properly appertain; in such case both himself and his heirs after him may have their images or representations cut in armour, and invested with their coat of arms over their armour.

7. If a martial man happen to retier himselfe from the worlde, and betake hyme to a monasticall or other religious kind of life, in such a case his effigies shall be carved upon his tomb, in the habit of the order of religion whereof he was professed, having his sword placed along by his side, to signifie he was sometime a professed martial man, until being sore spent by reason of aged years, or of long following of militarye profession, debillitye, or some other occasion, he gave over the world, leavinge his active life, and taking upon him that contemplative, wherein he woulde end his dayes, so that he might be spending the remainder of his shorte tyme in the service of God and prayer. This retired man (I saye) shall have his sword placed along by his syde, and his shield at his feet, to signifie thereby his resolute determination to treade under his feete all pompe and glorye, &c.

8. If a martiall man having served in hostile warrs shall happen to be slayne in the battayle, he may have his effigies or representation compleatlye armed at all points, his head only unarmed, and no coat of armes upon him.

9. If at any tyme a gentlewoman chaunce to go to visit hir husbande lyeinge at the siege of some cittye, towne, or castelle, if shee be conceived with childe, and shall be delivered (the siege endueringe) of a man-childe, dyeing, his image or portraiture shall be insculped or graven upon his tomb, armed throughout, habited in his coat of armes, over his harnysse, his hands conjoined and elevated (as before is shewed) savinge only his head shall be unarmed, his helmet placed under his head, and his battayle-axe by his side.

10. Note, All these representations may be sett forthe in their coat of armes, so as they have served in the field, where the sovereigne or prince of the contrie was personally present, of whom they received neither paye nor wages, but have served freelye att theyr owne charge, otherwise none can be invested in coats of armes, but a Kinge, Prince, Duke, Marquesse, Earle, or Greate Barone.

 in-

intended to be obferved, only on the continent. Colombiere[1] exprefly fays, they were left to the difcretion of the parties themfelves, or their furvivors. It is believed they were never enforced among us. They are however a fpecimen of monumental punctilio.

The place for rectors or vicars was near and about the altar or in the chancel, as John Cowall rector of Stratton St. Michael, Norfolk, in the middle of the chancel, which he built, 1487[2]. John Wright, 1491, at Stratton[3]; Henry Herveys, 1460, at Blickling in the fame county[4]; as incumbents at prefent. Chaplains and chantry priefts were buried in their refpective chapels, churches, and religious houfes or colleges. Lords of manors, patrons and founders, were alfo interred in the chancel, and fometimes, though not fo frequently, within the rails. In the chancel of the collegiate church at Ingham, Norfolk, is a feries of the founder's family, who all refer themfelves to him in their feveral infcriptions[5]: fo do the Cobhams, at Cobham in Kent. In the South wall of Aldenham church, Herts, Weever[6] defcribes the figures of two fifters cut in ftone, the foundreffes of this church, and coheirs to the lordfhip, which at their death they gave to Weftminfter abbey. That of Torrington, founder of Great Berkhamfted church, he defcribes in the body of the church[7].

In the middle aile of Baldock church is a ftone with a crofs fleury, circumfcribed,

Reignald d'Argentein ci gift
Qui cette chapell foire fist
Preft chivaler Saint Marie
Chefcun pardon pour l'alme prie.

tranflated by Weever[8] as if he was a knight *of* St. Mary. What remained of this infcription, 1783, fhews that he was a knight, and that the Virgin is to be intreated for his foul. I read it thus:

Reynaud: de: Argenten: ci: gift:
. . . chapele: fere: fift:
Fu: chivaler; Seynt: . . . .
Prodom: ky: pur: alme: prie

Or it may be *Pru* chevaler; good knight.

On each fide of a crofs floré were two fhields. Salmon[9] fuppofes the church was rebuilt fince Stephen's time; for otherwife this ftone would have lain in a chapel. Who fhall fay it has not been removed from the chapel of his building? The ftyle of the infcription is about the reign of one of the three Edwards.

The figure afcribed to one of the abbots of St. Auftin, Briftol, on a raifed tomb in the North aile of Almondsbury church, c. Gloucefter, which belonged to that abbey, may reprefent a founder or early incumbent[10]. The founder of Dumbleton church, in the fame county, has the old French epitaph in Saxon capitals. Sometimes their only memorial was an arch in the wall[11]. The crofs-legged knight, in the North wall of the chancel at Hawfted, Suffolk, was probably the founder thereof, and fuppofed to be one of the Fitz Euftaces, lords there in the reigns of Henry III. and Edward I[12]. In the North wall of the chancel of Buckland, c. Berks, is an arch with a fair graveftone, and thereon a crofs em-

[1] Science heroique, p. 479.
[2] Blomf. III. 132.
[3] Ib. III. 595.
[4] Ib. III. 641.
[5] Parkins' contin. of Blomf. V. 873. See p. 119.
[6] P. 592.
[7] Ib. 592.
[8] P. 545.
[9] Herts, p. 181.
[10] Rudder, 214.
[11] Ib. 411.
[12] Hist. of Hawfted, p. 49.

bolfed,

boffed, and oppofite to it a like arch with a plain graveftone [1]. The tomb of Suger, abbot of St. Denys, and prime minifter to Louis le Jeune, who died 1151, is like thefe formed in the wall of the South tranfept of his church. Felibien fays it was generally thought to have been made by himfelf, when he rebuilt this church: but this is a miftake, fince his body was not removed into it till 1259, when abbot Matthew de Vendofme transferred hither under the two arches on the fide of the great door of the cloifter the bodies of Suger and five more of his predeceffors. Before the former is a ftone with fome ornaments cut on it, and this infcription,

Hic jacet Sugerius abbas.

which conveys more than all the long panegyrics offered up to his memory [2].

The tradition of Whittington, in Shropfhire, buries Fitz Warine, founder of the caftle, in the church *porch*, it being, fays Mr. Pennant [3], an action of devotion for all perfons on their entrance into churches and religious houfes to pray for the fouls of the founders and benefactors. Fulk Fitz Warine, feventh of the name, who had the greateft revenue of any of the family, by his will dated 15 Richard II. directed his body to be buried in the chancel. It is moft probable, the firft of the family was buried there. The porch was not an unufual place. The antient parochial churches dependent on abbies had commonly a cemetery near them, and the dead were buried there, even in the *parvis* or *atrium* of the church, whence it has been fuppofed *Atrium* came frequently to fignify a cemetery [4].

Leofric earl of Mercia and his countefs Godiva were buried in the porches of the abbey church at Coventry, which they had founded [5]. Three of the Tankervilles, father, fon, and grandfon, in the chapter-houfe of Kenilworth-priory [6].

Milo, earl of Gloucefter, who founded Lanthoni abbey, near Gloucefter, with his two daughters, and four of the Bohuns, earls of Hereford, allied to his family, were all buried in the *chapter-houfe* of that priory [7]. So were the earls of Chefter at Chefter.

We are not however to conclude, that every antient flab to be feen in a church porch is in its original fituation, fo many circumftances occafioning the removal of fuch monuments.

The abbots of St. Albans before Robert the 19th, who died 1166, were buried in the chapter-houfe, which he built. He depofited them there, *nimis abjecte et fine hominum difcretorum notitia*, by the advice of his mafon, who dying fuddenly, the memory of the fpot was loft [8]. *Polyandrium* was the name given to the common burying grounds of abbies, in which, as it feems from Matthew Paris [9], *the faithful under interdict* might be buried. It is of Greek extract, applied to the tomb of the Thebans who fell fighting againft Philip [10], to the Argives who accompanied the Athenians to the conqueft of Sicily [11], and who fell victorious over the Lacedæmonians at Hyfia [12]. The council of Tribur under Charlemagne ordaining that graves in churches be levelled with the pavement, that no footftep of a grave appear, adds, if this cannot be conveniently done on account of the multitude of corpfes, let the place be turned into a *polyandrium*, or cemetery [13].

[1] Adm. I. 104. [2] Felibien, Hift. de l'abbaie de St. Denys, p. 190. [3] Wales, I. 245.
[4] Lebeuf, Hift. du dioc. de Paris, II. 44. In the porch of St. Sulpice were found, in 1719, two ftone coffins, the feet turned to the Eaft, one about five or fix hundred, the other a thoufand years old. The proof of the latter being of the twelfth century, or thereabouts, was a plate of copper, enamelled, with the hiftory of Elijah and the widow of Sarepta, which proves it to have been Chriftian: the other was alfo the tomb of a Chriftian named Herluin, with this infcription in characters of the eighth century at lateft,

Hic jacet inclufus Tetopi de ftripe creatus,
Harluinus comitam vocatus nomine qui obiit. Lebeuf, ib. Merc. Franc. Mai, 1724.

[5] Dugdale, Warwickfh. p. 157. ed. Thomas, quoting Malmefbury, 165. a. but no fuch thing is there.
[6] Leland It. VI. 73. [7] Hift. Abb. Lanthoni, Mon. Angl. II. 66, 67. [8] Vit. Abb. S. Alb. p. 92.
[9] Ib. p. 119. In later times it was applied to the tomb of one perfon only. See Du Cange in voc.
[10] Paufan. Bœot. c. 42. [11] Paufan. Corinth. c. 12. [12] Ib. c. 24.
[13] Bingham, 23 c. 1. §. 7. So the parifh of Stepney lately ferved their cemetery.

Matthew

Matthew Paris has a remarkable ſtory about the privilege of being buried before the high altar granted to a woman. "Cecily Sanford a lady of condition, relict of William Goſham, governeſs of Joan ſiſter of Henry III. and widow of William Marſhall, junior, died 1251, about a mile from St. Albans. She had made a vow of perpetual widowhood, and with her wedding ring aſſumed the ruſſet habit, the uſual ſign of ſuch reſolution. Her ſcholar did the ſame; but preferring to be a mother, obtained a diſpenſation of the Pope for a ſecond marriage. Cecily, on her death-bed, having paſt through the uſual forms with her confeſſor, he obſerved a gold ring on her finger, which he ordered her attendants to take off. The lady juſt expiring, recovered herſelf enough to tell them that ſhe would never part with this ring, which ſhe intended to carry to heaven with her into the preſence of her celeſtial ſpouſe, in teſtimony of her conſtant obſervance of her vow, and to receive the promiſed reward. She had no ſooner ſaid this than ſhe expired; and this being atteſted by her confeſſor, ſhe was honourably interred in St. Alban's abbey-church, in a ſtone coffin, before the altar of St. Andrew, on account of her vow and her rank [1].

Archbiſhop Thoresby, who died 1353, was laid before the altar of the bleſſed Virgin Mary, in his new work of the choir. No ſtone or monument now marks the place of his interment; but ſo long as this part of the fabrick ſtands it cannot want a memorial [2].

Mr. Hackluit told Leland, that the body of Merewald king of Mercia was found *in* a wall of the old church of Wenlock where his daughter founded a nunnery [3].

Foſſa is the antient name of *a grave*, merely from its being an opening *dug* in the earth: ſo in Bede's epitaph, and that of Thomas de Cailey, rector of Bradenham in Norfolk [4], in imitation of it. So Lebeuf [5] ſpeaks of a man buried "dans une *foſſe* particuliere," in the preſent century; and Hall [6], ſpeaking of the ſpot whereon the French ſlain in the battle of Agincourt were buried, calls it a *grove*, converted afterwards into a churchyard.

There are few, if any, inſtances among us of tombs reverſt in ſituation, as has happened to an old coffin-faſhioned one in the church of Ville Taneuſe, near Paris, which Mr. Lebeuf mentions as having the head to the altar, in proof that it was removed from an older church [7].

"Among the monuments of antiquity now remaining none decline ſo faſt as the old ſtones with braſs plates. The plates fall a prey to petty church robbers,

[1] *Propter cœlibatus ejus privilegium & generis ſui nobilitatem in eccleſia ipſa ante altare beati Andreæ honorifice in lapideo ſarcophago ſepeliebatur.* Mat. Par. p. 818.

The following form of a vow of chaſtity made by a Counteſs of Suffolk, 1382, is taken from the regiſter of Fordham biſhop of Ely, fol. 59. b.

"Votum caſtitatis d'ne comitiſſe Suff'. M'd q'd nobilis d'na d'na Iſabella comitiſſa Suff. 21° die menſ. Martii coram ſummo altare prioratus predicte [*Campeſey* Norwic dioc.] in præſentia rev. patrum d'norum Thome ep'i Elienſ' miſſam tunc ib'm ſolempniter celebrantis & Henr' Norwicenſ. ep'i pontificalibus induti & alior' plurimorum abbatum & priorum eiſdem aſſiſtentium votum vovit ſolempniter prout ſequitur in hec verba: 'Jeo Iſabella jadys la femme William de Ufforde count de Suff. vowe a Dieu & a notre dame Seynte Marie & a toux ſeyntz en preſence de tres reverentz piers en Dieu eveſq. de Ely & de Norwiz qe jeo doi eſtre chaſt d'ors en avaunt ma vie durante.' Et d'ns Elienſ. vice & auctoritate dicti d'ni Norwic. votum hujuſmodi recepit & admiſit, & mantellum ſive clamidem ac annulum dicte voventis ſolempniter benedixit & impoſuit ſuper eam. Preſentibus etiam ib'm comite Warwic. d'no de Wyloweby, d'no de Scales, ac aliis militibus & armigeris & aliis in multitudine copioſa."

Compare this with that of Philippa counteſs of Warwick, 1360. Dugd. Bar. I. 235.

[2] Drake, 491.

[3] Itin. IV. 178. a. Francis lord Lovel, who fled after the battle of Stoke, and was ſaid to have lived long after in a cave or vault, (Bacon's Hiſt. of Henry VII. p. 31.) was ſuppoſed to have been found in a vault at Minſter Lovel houſe, c. Oxon. 1708. But the circumſtances of the diſcovery, as related in Peck's Appendix of Hiſtorical pieces to his Memoirs of Cromwell, p. 87. are not very probable. He tells, p. 66. another extraordinary ſtory of a ſkeleton found crammed into a cellar in Collyweſton houſe, c. Northampton, ſuppoſed of ſome perſon made away by Henry VIII's order. Immuring of ſtate priſoners ſhould ſeem to have been antiently no uncommon practice. In one of the towers of Thornton college, c. Lincoln, in a room whoſe door had been walled up, was found in the laſt century a ſkeleton, with a table, braſs candleſtic, and book. In the very ſubſtance of an old ſtone wall of Dublin caſtle was found a ſkeleton, with a ſtrange old pair of wooden clogs at the feet, and a ſeal with a prieſt praying to the Virgin and Child, circumſcribed *S. Henrici vicar. de Hoydla*. Gent. Mag. vol. xxv. p. 211. In the centre of a thick wall at Norham caſtle the ſkeleton of a man was found entire, in a recumbent poſture. Hutchinſon's Hiſt. of Durham, I. 150.

[4] Blomeſ. III. 241. See before, p. cii.

[5] Dioc. de Paris, II. 310.

[6] Fol. li. b.

[7] Hiſt. du dioc. de Par. II. 333.

whose behaviour is countenanced by the bad example of great ones, or the negligence of their superiors; so that in another century, unless greater care be taken, but very few of these will be found remaining [1]."

In the body of York cathedral, of an hundred and thirteen epitaphs not twenty were left at the time of new paving, 1734, and half of these were cut in stone, which plainly proves, that the poor lucre of the brass was the great motive to the defacing these venerable remains of antiquity. Of fifty-two epitaphs in the church, which Mr. Drake gives, near thirty were entire and legible before the above paving, being preserved by the doors being kept shut [2].

When Browne Willis [3] was at Lincoln, 1718, he counted about two hundred and seven grave stones that had been stript of their brasses; but the better half of them preserved in bishop Sanderson's MS. account of the monuments there, and printed in Peck's Desiderata Curiosa.

In some late essential repairs to the West front of Hereford cathedral several capital brasses, which I copied ten years before, were torn up by the rapacity of the workmen before the vergers could prevent them.

Browne Willis shewed the Society of Antiquaries, 1737, from the Augmentation Office, a particular of the dissolution of religious houses, 30 Henry VIII. which, because it shews how monuments and brasses were then disposed of, I shall subjoin from their Minutes.

"County of Warwick; Mirival, six gravestones, with brasses on them, 5*s.* four bells, by estimation £ 30.

County of Stafford; Brewood or Rywood [4], in the steeple three bells.

Littleshull, seven bells, weight 37 C. not sold, but valued at £66. 13*s.* 4*d.* Sir Thomas Stafford, Jun. four bells, val. £ 54.

Delacres, the paving of the church, with isles, *gravestones*, roof, &c. sold for £ 13. 6*s.* 8*d.* Six bells, weight 50 C. val. £ 37. 10*s.* Gilt plate 87 oz. white plate 30 oz.

Darley, the *tombs* and *gravestones*, with the *metal* on them, and roof of the church, isles, &c. sold for £ 20. roof, &c. of the cloisters, sold for £ 10. Gilt plate 98 oz. Six bells, sold for £. 45. 10*s.*

Dale. The clock sold for 6*s.* iron, glass, gravestones, &c. for £ 18. the cloisters for £ 6. six bells, weight 47 C.

Repton. The church sold for 50 *s.* the *gravestones* and paving remain unsold, with four bells. Mr. Thatchet put into possession of the late priory.

County of Leicester; Grace Dieu. The church sold for £ 15. the cloisters for £ 3. 6*s.* 8*d.* three bells, by estimation, weight 9 C.

County of Northampton; Pipewell. The church, valued at £ 16. 3 *s.* The whole goods sold for £ 121. 1 *s.* five bells, weight 56 C. Gilt plate 70 oz. white plate 271 oz.

County of Cambridge; Barnwell church, valued at £ 16. 11*s.* 4*d.* the whole building at £ 61. 15*s.* 2*d.* Six bells, weight 25 C."

The brasses in Thatcham church were stolen when it was broken open [5].

The bells at Mepham in Kent being to be new cast, some mischievous persons tore off the brasses to add to the metal [6].

When the late lord Colerane rebuilt Driffield church, c. Gloucester, the old monuments were not put up again [7]. On rebuilding Tarbick church, c. Worcester, in pulling down lord Plymouth's chancel the family monuments were so

[1] MS. account of Campden, communicated to Mr. Rudder, Gloucestersh. p. 324.
[2] Ubi supra, 592. Mr. Drake gives, p. 491, a plan of the old pavement, with all the inscriptions remaining in the time of Mr. Torre, by whom it was taken, which must be allowed a great curiosity, since the whole, except in the choir end, is now quite taken up and erased. Ib. p. 519. In the new edition of Camden's Britannia will be found a similar plan of the cathedral of Lincoln, before its new paving, 1783. The choir there has hitherto escaped alteration.
[3] Survey of Lincoln cathedral, p. 31. [4] Q. Brewood or Bywood, Shropshire. Tanner.
[5] Ashm. II. 325. [6] Hasted, I. 469. [7] Rudder, 420.

broken

hroken as not to be put up again [1]. They are however engraved in Dugdale's Warwickfhire [2]. I have heard of a church in Suffolk where all the monuments of former lords of the manor were facrificed to the vanity of the prefent proprietor, who having no train of anceftry to boaft of, could not bear the memorials of thofe who had. One brafs only efcaped, which I have engraved. The miferable ftate of the fine feries of the monuments of the Wingfield and Naunton families, at Letheringham in the fame county, is a fad memorial of controverted inheritance.

The churchwardens of Allhallows Stayning pulled down their monuments, and fwept them out of the church, for which they were forced to make a large account of twelve fhillings for brooms, &c. befides carrying away the ftones and brafs at their own expence [3]. Dr. Hanmer vicar of Shoreditch of late, fays Stowe [4], for covetoufnefs of the brafs, which he converted into coined filver, pluckt up many plates fixed on the graves.

In the appraifement of St. Andrew's church, Lincoln, 1551, when its materials were fold by the corporation for £ 32. 16 *s.* 8 *d.* "the *plate* in the chapel with the *plate* of other ftones in the church," was valued at 40 *s.* and "the *fellaring* over the tomb (which I fuppofe was a wooden or ftone canopy over fome particular tomb) at 12 *d* [5].

A brafs of Sir Adrian Fortefcue, 1653, from his tomb in Hodington church, c. Worcefter, is preferved in an alehoufe in the village [6].

1646, a brafs ftatue in Windfor was ordered by Parliament to be fold, and the money to go for pay of the garrifon [7].

A fine brafs of the Clifton family at Methwold was fold by the clerk to a tinker, from whom only a few uninterefting fragments could be recovered [8].

Braffes ftolen from Hilburgh church by a tinker, in the civil war, were found by the rector after the Reftoration at Swaffham [9].

Mr. Johnfon bought of a dealer in hardware, who was going to melt it down, a brafs plate, 20 inches by 16, on which was an elderly man bareheaded and bearded, in a ruff and fur gown, four fons behind him kneeling at a table and two books: a woman in a coif fet back and hood hanging down behind, a ruff round her neck and ruffles at her wrifts; five daughters kneeling behind. Arms, a chevron S. between three wolf's heads, impaling G. a chevron O. between three fleurs de lis O. under them *Love and Lyve*, in black letter, and the following infcription:

"Here within this chauncell on the North fide doth lye the corpeffis of "Thomas Lovell, efquire, and Margaret Pyckeringe his wyfe who was to him "full deare, they lyved together in the ftate of holy matrimonye 33 yeares and "11 dayes, and had iffue between them IX children, IIII fonnes and V daughters; viz. Thomas, William, John, and Dudley; Elizabeth and Elizabeth, Margaret, Ellenor, and Luce, whofe mother deceafed in the fayth of Chrifte the "fixthe daye of Julye, Ano Domini 1597, being of the age of lx yeares [10]."

The braffes of the younger branches of the Delapole family, at Wingfield in Suffolk, which had been carefully preferved in the church cheft as they came off, and were there feen and copied by me twenty years ago, have fince, on a late repair and beautifying of the church, been converted into money by one of the churchwardens.

[1] Nafh, II. 408.
[2] Ed. Thomas, p. 734, 735.
[3] Stow's Survey, p. 222.
[4] Ib. p. 474.
[5] Symonds's MS Collections, p. 140.
[6] Nafh, I. 491.
[7] Whitelock's Memor. p. 206.
[8] Blomefield's Norf. I. 509.
[9] Ib. III. 439.
[10] Spalding Society Minutes.

The monumental flabs with the braffes on them in the chancel at Attleborough church, Norfolk, were taken by Robert earl of Suffex, to whom Henry VIII. granted it at the diffolution of the college there, to pave his hall, kitchen, and larder [1]. Dean Whittingham and his widow, 1579, made the like application of many monumental flabs in Durham cathedral [2]. I have heard a fimilar charge brought againft the chapter at Worcefter fome years ago. A like ufe feems to have been made of the flabs with braffes in Stoke Courney church, c. Somerfet.

The flab which covers the tomb of Thomas Seckford in his chapel at Woodbridge has had on its now under-fide a brafs crofs, on which ftood two figures in niches; and at the fides of the crofs two fhields: but all the brafs is reaved. This flab feems to have ferved fome other family, and to be here out of its place. In the abbey church of Bridlington a large coffin-fafhioned flab of black marble, feven feet long, whofe under fide was adorned with reliefs, has been turned, and infcribed, in memory, I think, of Sir R. Prefton, 1587.

I cannot omit an inftance of frugality in making the brafs plate of one family ferve for another by turning it, were it only to exprefs my obligation to the Rev. Dr. Difney, who having engraved this memorial of his family in the church of Norton Difney, c. Lincoln, has permitted me to take a number of impreffions, and carried his politenefs fo far as to make me the offer of the plate itfelf. It commemorates William Difney, efq. fheriff of London, 1532. and Richard Difney, efq. his eldeft fon and heir, burgefs for Grantham, 1554, and fheriff of Lincolnfhire, 1557 and 1566, with their wives and iffue, to whofe memory it was put up, probably by Jane fecond wife and widow of the latter, about the middle of the reign of Elizabeth. At the back is a long infcription, in the German or Low Dutch language, recording the foundation of a chantry fomewhere on the Continent, which I fhall give at large in the Appendix.

The communion table at Stow Bardolf, Norfolk, is made of the flab of Sir Ralph Hare, knight of the Bath, who died 1623, taken down in erecting the monument of his grandfon Sir Thomas Hare, bart [3]. The reverfe has happened to an altar ftone at St. Edmund's Bury, converted into a flab for the tomb of Mary Queen of France, afterwards Dutchefs of Suffolk; to another which covers a tomb in the South aile of the abbey church at St. Albans; and to a third, which makes a part of the pavement of the church at Hawfted in Suffolk [4]. Thefe once confecrated ftones are known by a crofs cut in the centre and four at the corners, in allufion to the five wounds of CHRIST. A very fine one twelve feet long and three feet wide makes part of the pavement of the choir of Bridlington abbey church.

A MS. communicated to Mr. Rudder mentions the prefervation of a fine ftone monument in Campden church, Gloucefter, which would have fallen a facrifice to the lucre of an iron grate that encompaft it, the fale of which would have put a few pounds into the fpoiler's pocket [5].

Some curious infcriptions in Gothic capitals, four or five hundred years old, in the church of St. John Baptift lez St. Julian at Paris, were worn out by laying the ftones to make a wall round the outfide of the church [6].

The infcription round the tomb of Anfelm de Bercenay bifhop of Laudun, who died 1238, in the abbey church of Vauluifant, fets forth, that the monument was originally of copper, but that abbot Henry fold it, 1448, to repair the church, and made another in ftone.

[1] Blomef. I. 344. from the Parifh regifter.
[2] Antiq. of Durham Cathedral, p. 374—379.
[3] Parkin's Hift. of Norf. IV. 172.
[4] Hift. of Hawfted, p. 48.
[5] P. 344.
[6] Lebeuf, Hift. du diocefe de Paris, I. 175.

"Hic

Sufferance dothe ease
Willm Disney Esquier & Margaret Joiner
Sara: Ester: Judeth: Judeth and Susan:
Nele daughter of Sr Willm Huson knyght Richard Disney Janne daugr of Sr Willm Ayscoughe K.
The lyfe, conversacion, and Service, of the first above named Willm Disney and of Richard Disney his Sonne were comendable amongest ther Neigbours trewe and fathefull to ther prince and cuntre & acceptable to Thallmighty of whome we trust they are receved to Salvation accordinge to the Stedfast faythe which they had in it throughe the mercy and merit of christ or savior Thes truthes ar thus sett forthe that in all ages God may be thankfully glorified, for thes and suche lyke his gracius benifites

Engraved from a Brass Plate in the Parish Church of Norton Disney in the County of Lincoln

"Hic jacet Anselmus de Bricena natus quond' laudunens. ep's qui obiit Icio none Septēbris ano
"m° duceno XXXVIII. sed urgēte iōpia ano m° cccc° XLVIII°. XII° Novēbris hui' loci abbas Hen-
"ricus nōie cuperū tumulū vendt quō p'sat erex'at de cui vendicōe hāc celtā tūba ī cilice
"sculpsit & hinc ecclie que tūc ruinosa p'multū erat possetenus altissimo disponente subvēt
"pro eis orate."

A freestone in the wall of the chancel at South Acre, Norfolk, is thus inscribed: "Aug. 1725, the Rev. Mr. William Brocklebank, rector, new paved "this chancel with stone at his own charge, had the gravestones cleaned and "laid even; removed none that had any inscription; but gave three plain ones "to be laid in the body of the church [1]."

The monuments of the Freman family are all set up in Absden church, Herts, being rescued by major William Freman, from the hands of those who had stolen them from St. Michael's, Cornhill, in the fire of London [2].

Sir Hugh Calverley's tomb at Beeston is kept clean by legacy [3].

Mr. Hearne [4] explains the lions at the feet of effigies as emblems of vigilance, industry, and courage, and parallels them with the lion on the tomb of the Bœotians, who died fighting against Philip, and were buried in one common *polyandrum* [5]. I doubt this etymology, and rather incline to think the practice derived from the allusion to the words in Psalm xci. 13. "*Super aspidem & "basiliscum ambulabis, conculcabis leonem et draconem.*" "Thou shalt tread upon "the lion and the adder; the young lion and the dragon shalt thou trample "under feet." Nor should it be objected, that this relates only to the clergy; for the words are applicable to Christians in general [6]. Indeed there are not a few instances in which animals so placed are family supporters, as was the case perhaps universally after the reformation. Thus the buck at the feet of Bois, p. 82. 104. is the family crest. Such perhaps might be the meaning of the bear at the feet of bishop March, at Wells; the two rabbits at those of lady Tiptoft, at Ely [7]. At the feet of Thomas Cecil, earl of Exeter, in Westminster abbey, 1621, are his lions supporting the gerbe. Or they are rebuses of the name, as two hares at the feet of bishop Harewell at Wells, and at those of the knight at Pershore before mentioned, who is supposed to have borne the same name. Under those of one of the figures in the Temple church [8] are two human heads, perhaps alluding to the Infidels slain in the crusades; under the right foot of a knight in Ryther church, York, is a collared dog, under his left an old bearded head: between the feet of Thomas de Inglethorpe bishop of Rochester 1291, is a demon's head pierced by his crosier. Under the feet of archbishop Grey in York minster are two human figures writhing as if in pain, while a dragon bites the point of his crosier. Raymond Ragnier lord of Ourchy, 1421, in the church of the Celestines at Marcoussy, has a muzzled dog under his feet. A man in the choir of the church of Nanteuil stands on a naked child. Under a knight in Ardenne abbey in Normandy are two basilisks: under an abbess at Port royal des champs, two fish [9]; under a countess of Vendosme, 1305, in the Mathurines church, at Paris, an ass couchant; under the wife of Hervè de Neanville, in the Carthusian church there, 1413, two lambs. Under the figure of William Rufus painted on an abbey wall in France [10], under that of bishop Wermund de la Buissiere, 1272, in Noion cathedral, under an abbess of St.

[1] Blomef. III. 418.
[2] Salmon, Herts, p. 316.
[3] Pennant's Journey from Chester, p. 18.
[4] Roper's Life of More, p. 270.
[5] Pausan. Bœot. p. 606. Ed. Hanov. 1613.
[6] In the parish church of Ville Taneule, near Paris, Lifard the patron is represented with a black animal at his feet, the serpent or dragon mentioned in his life. Lebeuf, Hist. du Dioc. de Paris, II. 331. Q. If the figure did not give rise to the legend, instead of the legend to the figure.
[7] Bentham, pl. XXXVII.
[8] Pl. XIX. p. 50.
[9] Moleon, p. 134.
[10] Montf. I. pl. LV.

Saviour

Saviour at Evreux, 1298, and several others, is a double-bodied sphinx or griffin. Charles of Anjou, earl of Maine, 1472, in the cathedral of Mans, has only a helmet at his feet. At the feet of John lord Russel, who died 1584, and has a monument in Westminster abbey, is a small figure of his infant son Francis, who died in the same year. Under the feet of John Perient, in Digswell church, Herts, 1415, Salmon describes a creature like a cat, and under his wife's feet one like a rat; the former is really a leopard, the latter an hedge-hog: one of the Swinborns, at Little Horkesley, Essex, has a cat at his feet. "What the meaning "is of chusing such things I could never," says Salmon, "arrive at. They are "sometimes their crest, but frequently arbitrary, and with relation to their arms." Thus the lion of bronze gilt, large as life, on the tomb or mausoleum of the dukes of Brabant, restored by the archduke Albert, is the arms of the said duke, which he also holds in a shield, in the church of St. Michael and St. Jude, in Brussels. In this tomb rests the body of duke John II. who died 1312. and his consort Margaret, sixth daughter of our Edward I. who died 1318.

The learned antiquary Lebeuf, in a dissertation on the statue of queen Pedauque, or the *goosefooted*, whom he explains the Queen of the South or Sheba, *Regina Austri*, has a curious conjecture on lions in porches of churches, serving as supporters of the seats of ecclesiastical judges; whence the sentences of Officials, Deans, &c. have this formula. "*Datum* or *Actum inter duos "leones*[1]."

To account for *dogs*, one or more, at the feet of ladies, or even of knights, may not be so easy. They may only allude to their favourite lapdogs. Chaucer's prioress kept small houndes[2]. Judith daughter of the emperor Conrad is represented on her tomb, 1191, with one in her left hand[3]. Those at the feet of countess Aveline Sir Joseph Ayloffe[4] calls *talbot whelps*; they are couchant, the head of one lying over and resting on that of the other.

Lacombe[5] says, *Cocet* is "petit chien de bois qu'on mettoit au pied du lit:" Quære, if the dogs at feet of ladies, whose drapery is tuckt or gathered round their feet, as Matilda at Dunmow priory, lady Crosbie in St. Helen's, London, and other instances, allude to this; as also the instances of dogs holding up the robe at the feet. They are not unfrequent at the side of the feet looking up to the faces of their mistresses. Mary countess de St. Paul kneeling on her monument at Vendome has her dog on the skirts of her robe. Sir Bryan Stapleton, on his brass at Ingham, c. Norfolk, rests one foot on a lion, the other on a dog, whose name is recorded on a label, *Jakke*[6]. Round the collar of a dog at the feet of an old stone figure of a knight in Tolleshunt Knight's church, Essex, I traced five other capitals, somewhat like *Howgo*[7]. King Richard II. had a favourite greyhound, named *Matt*, whose transfer of attachment from him to the usurper of his crown is naturally told by Froissart. By this it should seem

[1] Histoire de l'Acad. des Inf. XI, 405. 12mo.
[2] Canterb. Tales, I. 146. [3] Reyner, ubi sup.
[4] Account of the Westminster monuments, p. 5.
[5] Dict. du vieux langue François.
[6] Pl. XLV. p. 119.
[7] Perhaps for *Huge* or *Hugh*.

Among Sir David Lindsay's poems is "the Complaint of the king's old hound called *Bags*, directed to *Bawty*, the king's best beloved dog."

The dog at the feet of Thomas II. lord of Savoy and count of Maurienne and Piedmont, who died 1233, on his tomb at Aoust, has on his collar inscribed in Gothic capitals the word FERT, and on his breast a shield, with the arms of Savoy, of which house this word was the antient device. Guichenon, who has given a print of this monument, Hist. de Savoye, p. 251.) confesses himself (p. 141.) unable to explain the meaning of the device, which he says is plainly a word, there being no stops between the letters. Notwithstanding this, Pere Hardouin (than whom no man was fonder of a conceit) in a dissertation professedly on the subject, takes no little pains to give each of these four letters a distinct meaning, in the same manner as he explained away the legends of antient coins. See his note on Pliny, N. H. VIII. c. 9.

Feijoo, in his Vulgar Errors, tells a wonderful story of a dog named *Gondolon*.

that

that our anceftors gave their Chriftian names to their dogs [1]. Knights and nobles may have them at their feet as the companions of their fports, or fymbols of their rank. The greyhound is introduced in pictures of ceremonials from the Bayeux tapeftry to the Champ de drap d'or [2].

Archbifhop Greenfield, 1317, in York minfter, has at his feet two dogs, one a prick-eared fhock, the other ftrait-haired and flap-eared; fo have the wives of Robert Braunche at Lynne, 1364 [3]. An abbot of L'Efpau near Mans, and another of Evron in Maine, have a greyhound under their feet.

On the French monuments one or both dogs are continually reprefented gnawing bones or eating acorns; and under the feet of Henry feigneur de Pary, in Jard church, is a dog running.

One of the lateft inftances in which ftatues have animals at their feet is that of Lionel Cranfield earl of Middlefex, 1645, and his countefs, in Weftminfter abbey. At thofe of Louis Stuart duke of Richmond and his duchefs there, 1639, they are on coronets in that fituation. They hold fhields of arms on the corners of the flab of the Duke of Norfolk, at Framlingham. In all thefe inftances they are known fupporters of the family arms. At the feet of Louis de la Tremouille, who was killed at the battle of Pavia, 1524, in the church of Notre Dame de Thouars, the dog lies as ufual, but has the arms on his fide.

Charles de Bourbon earl of Soiffons and his countefs have a lion and a dog at their feet, 1633–1643, in the Carthufian church of Gaillon.

The next difpofition in which we find animals is as fupporters of various memorials of the parties whofe arms or fupporters they are. Thus two elephants of white marble bear up the black marble farcophagus of Sir Henry Wood, knight and baronet, 1671, in the South aile of Ufford church, c. Suffolk; and two griffins the obelifk on the Marquis of Halifax's monument in Weftminfter-abbey, 1715.

Cumbent figures continued in fafhion as late as William Cavendifh Duke of Newcaftle, 1676, in Weftminfter abbey; and the beautiful ones of an alderman and his wife at Gloucefter, evidently wrought from a defign of Vandyck. Mr. Walpole calls it a taftelefs attitude. It is however the moft natural attitude, expreffing the laft act of a human being imploring mercy in the extremities of life. Either the whole or half cumbent pofture is a very common one on all the fepulchral monuments tranfmitted to us from the antient Greeks and Romans, and it certainly is the moft natural.

On the fronts of two fepulchres at Palmyra are cumbent figures, with the hands reclined on the belly, and under one of them, on two farcophagi, are bufts of other perfons of the fame family, with infcriptions below them [4]. Thus in our own country, on a flab of the Carew family, at Beddington church, we fee under their parents' feet the bufts of thirteen children, with their names fuperfcribed.

In Maffei's Verona Illuftrata, p. cxxxvii. is a cumbent figure, its left arm fupporting its head, at which is a Cupid or Genius with a Cornucopiæ.

[1] So the antients gave the names of men to dogs. Lyfimachus's dog, who leapt into the fire of his mafter's funeral pile, was called *Hircanus*. Pliny, N. H. VIII. 11. Solinus, c. 15. Ælian. Hift. Anim. VI. 25. Plutarch de folert. animal. p. 970. and that of Gelo the tyrant of Sicily was called *Pyrrhus*. Plin. ib. Ælian, H. An. VI. 62.

[2] See Sir Jofeph Ayloffe's defcription of the Windfor picture, Archæol. III. p. 109.

[3] Pl. XLV. p. 115.

[4] Ruins of Palmyra, Pl. LV. LVI.

The article of our ancient habits derives much light from ſepulchral monuments, which ſupplied the place of portraits before we had painters among us, which is indeed almoſt till the time of Holbein [1]. "In elder times much muſt be depended on tombs for dreſſes," was the opinion of an excellent judge in theſe matters, when he was promoting a deſign which, had the gentlemen to whom he aſſigned their ſeveral parts been living, would have done honour to this age and country; "*An Hiſtory of Gothic architecture in its various periods, with a hiſtory of faſhions and dreſſes in England.*" This obſervation is not to be entirely confined to female dreſs, becauſe almoſt all our male figures till the 15th century are clad in armour; for in that article very material varieties will be found from the prince to the various orders of his ſubjects.

None of our hiſtorians have attended to ſuch minutiæ. Facts, not manners or faſhions, were their object. Montfaucon was the firſt who thought of them in France. Mr. Strutt adopted his plan in England, and has ſucceeded in proportion to the extent of his obſervations.

It is amazing how ſuperficial is Mr. Granger on an article for enlarging on which he had ſuch advantage. For the piked ſhoes of Richard the Second, and a law made to limit them to two inches, he quotes Baker's Chronicle. Had not Mr. Granger read original authors? But he did not carry his views in this kind beyond the reign of Henry VII [2].

The induſtrious Hearne is not much more explicit, nor does he carry his views much further back. "'Tis alſo, ſays he, from old monuments that we learn the ſhape of the ſhoes and other habits of our countrymen in former times. The make of the ſhoes, 10 Henry VIII. we have in the church of Ewelme; and of thoſe in 31 Henry VIII. in the church of Eaſt Hakborn. The figure of thoſe 37 Henry VI. may be ſeen in the church of Lechlade in Glouceſterſhire, as thoſe of the reign of Henry V. may be found in John Dade's MS. treatiſe of arms in the Bodleian library. The habit of Prince Arthur's auditor may be ſeen in the church of Brightwell, in Berks: where may likewiſe be ſeen the habits of the women in the beginning of Henry the Eighth's reign. We have the habit of a bachelor of divinity, 9 Henry VIII. in the church of Evelme, where we have alſo the ſhape of the

[1] Some of the fineſt illuminations in our MSS. are the work of foreign Artiſts, particularly the Froiſſart in the Royal Library. The illuminated copy of Mat. Paris, in the Britiſh Muſeum, was certainly a preſentation book to Henry III. There is another very neatly illuminated with the hiſtories in outlines in Benet College Library. Mr. Walpole has comprized our painters, &c. from Henry III. to Henry VI. in thirty quarto pages. Our oldeſt drawings are in the Saxon MSS. of which Mr. Strutt has made good uſe. Probably the hiſtories of Alexander the Great, the Cruſade, the lives and other figures and hiſtories on the walls of the royal apartments in the reign of Henry III were of this kind. They certainly were not better than the ſeven champions painted on the walls of private houſes in the reigns of Henry VII. and VIII. as over the gatechamber of Nether-hall, Eſſex, over the cloiſter at Wenlock abbey, with mottoes; or the ſingle figures in compartments on the North ſide of the room adjoining to Selby abbey church, which is ſhewn for the chamber where Henry the Firſt was born, when an inſcription round the cornice expreſsly ſays it was built by abbot Deping juſt before the diſſolution. The Deity, or the Trinity, with angels, and the ſymbols of the Evangeliſts, were depicted on the ceilings of the wooden canopies over the royal and other monuments in Weſtminſter abbey; the Virgin and Child, or Saints with worſhipers, at the back of ſeveral monuments, as in Hereford library, &c. Inſtances of this ſort were more common in France than in England. St. Chriſtopher, on the wall of the North tranſept of Wincheſter cathedral, and on the doors of ſome pariſh churches in Norfolk, the ſaints, fathers, and apoſtles, on the ſcreens of Woodbridge and ſeveral other churches in Suffolk. The legends of St. Cuthbert and St. Auſtin on the back of the Weſtern ſtalls in the cathedral at Carliſle. The figures of ſaints, kings, queens, and prelates, on pannels over the door and on the roof of the chapter-houſe at York, of the time of archbiſhop Gray, in the beginning of the 13th century; thoſe on the ceiling of the nave of Peterborough minſter, of the 12th; thoſe on the ceilings of Saliſbury cathedral, St. Alban's abbey church, and innumerable others, which might be referred to one of theſe two centuries. The half-effaced legends of the Virgin Mary, in her chapel in Wincheſter cathedral, aſcribed to biſhop Langton, in the reign of Henry VII. The ſtars and blue ground in churches and apartments. The *geſta Antiochiæ*, or hiſtory of the Croiſade, ordered to be painted in a low chamber in the garden at Weſtminſter, probably a ſummer or banqueting houſe, might be in the ſtyle of the figures on the tomb of Edmond Crouchback at Weſtminſter, or the now effaced ſiege of Damietta (which turns out, however, to be only a repreſentation of the wiſe-mens' offering) in Canterbury cathedral. William of Florence was one of Henry III's artiſts. Walpole, I. 16.

If the *Antiochia* were the firſt hiſtorical piece in which we were intereſted, the coronation of Edward I. in the biſhop's palace at Lichfield was the ſecond. One may venture to affirm, there was more hiſtorical preciſion than in his grandſon's triumphs by Verrio, at Windſor. On the outſide of the choir next the South aile of St. George's chapel there are ſuppoſed portraits of three of our kings and prince Edward ſon of Henry VI. and on the oppoſite ſide of the choir in the chapel over the tomb of William lord Haſtings, the hiſtory of his patron St. Stephen, in four pannels.

Painting in glaſs is firſt mentioned in the Claus Roll 20 Henry III. Aubrey quotes Sir William Dugdale for its being firſt done in the reign of John. Walp. I. 5.

[2] See Granger, I. 86, 87.

bands

bands that were in ufe 13 Henry VII. And in the forefaid church of Brightwell is the habit of a Mafter of Arts, 23 Henry VII. which, as it varied at the different times, fo we meet with the figures of it fometimes in old printed books, as we do with the figures of a Mafter of Grammar in old grammatical tracts, the frontifpieces of which may be in fome meafure illuftrated from the old hieroglyphical figures in the quadrangle of Magdalen College, Oxford. And by the fame obfervations we may gather the forms of other habits from one age to another, as we may likewife the figures of the military inftruments; and the nature of the occupations in which they were engaged. We may know the figures of the fwords before Edward the Third's time from the monuments in Aldworth church, and the figures in Lechlade church do as naturally fhew that the perfons upon whofe monuments they are expreffed were woollmen, as if there had been no infcriptions to teftify the fame [1]."

Bifhop Nicolfon's cenfure of Hall for reciting the fafhions of each reign implies how little his lordfhip efteemed fuch matters.

He brings a charge againft that valuable hiftorian, that his principal merit confifts in defcribing "what fort of cloaths were worn in each king's reign, and how the fafhions altered." The fact is, as Hearne obferves in his defence, that he declines giving an account of cloaths and fafhions, excepting on fome folemn occafions in the reign of Henry VIII [2]. For the dreffes and entertainments at the receiving of Henry the Sixth's Queen, Margaret, he refers to the Chronicle of London, and Robert Fabian, who is not at all diffufe on the fubject. Except this and his defcription of an armed man preparing for a tournament, hereafter given, he fays nothing of thefe things in an earlier period than that in which he lived.

What few obfervations have been made on the fubject have not been carried higher than the 15th century, when monuments of every kind became more numerous. But though I feel myfelf here deferted by the affiftance of preceding Hiftorians and Antiquaries, and entering upon unexplored ground, in which I have no guide but my own experience and obfervation, I do not defpair of forming a tolerable collection for the preceding centuries, up to the Norman Conqueft.

The figures on the fides of the tombs of Aymer de Valence and John of Eltham at Weftminfter are good reprefentations of habits, and the latter well preferved; fo are thofe on the fides of the tombs of Thomas Beauchamp at Warwick, of Robert de Vere at Earl's Colne; not to mention others.

What can be faid of the wretched reprefentations of thofe on the fides of monuments in Bedal church in the Regiftrum Honoris de Richmond, p. 242. or of the monuments themfelves, as there drawn, which even after all the injuries of time make a better appearance?

The author of the Roman de la Rofe, who lived in the clofe of the thirteenth century, gives us the following inventory of a wardrobe in France.

Ja pour leur *manteaulx febelins*,
Ne pour *furcots*, ne pour *tonelles*,
Ne pour *guimples*, ne pour *cotelles*.
Ne pour *chemifes*, ne *pelices*,
Ne pour *joyaulx*, ne pour *delices*,
Ne pour leur *moes* defguifees,
Ne pour leur *hysans fuperfices* [3].
Qui bien les auroit advifées.
Dont ils ufent par artifices;
Ne pour *chapeaulx* de fleurs nouvelles,
Ne leur femblaffent eftre belles [4].

[1] Roper's Life of Moore, 271, 272.
[2] Appendix to Heming's Chartulary.
[3] Q. painted complexions.
[4] l. 9347—9357.

That

That chitchat historian Rofs of Warwick is the firft who gives a brief view of the fafhions of each reign.

"In the Confeffor's time the garments reached to the knees, the arms were loaded with golden bracelets, the head was fhaved, the beard let to grow on the upper lip, except of priefts, and the fkin disfigured with various marks. Their arms were ftaves and battle axes: thofe of the Normans fwords and arrows[1].

"After the Conqueft the Norman fafhion of fhaving the beard, and letting the hair flow to the fhoulders was adopted[2]. Malmfbury fays[3] the men's hair was fo long that they looked like women; and a young foldier letting his grow to his knees was fhamed out of it by a dream: he prefently cut his hair fhort, and all his comrades adopted his fafhion; but this did not obtain long, for within the year all who would be thought courtiers relapft into the former folly, letting their hair grow as long as that of the women, and fupplying the want of it by artificial hair. Henry I. rounded the hair to fhew the ears; and ordered that his foldiers fhould trim it round to a decent length[4].

"In William Rufus's time a great abufe of drefs, and luxury in wearing the hair, and a horrid fafhion of picked and turned up fhoes obtained, and men adopted a mincing gait and a loofer drefs[5].

"In the reign of John, as appears by the feals, the men wore tunics over their coats of mail; but not before; and the tunics reached down to their heels[6].

"In that of Henry III. they had, as ufual, on their feals, horfemen in armour, with their fwords, and firft introduced their coats of arms in fhields, at the back of their fhields, and the faces of images firft had *umbrelles*[7].

"After the taking of John King of France by Edward the Third, the Englifh, who till then had worn their beards and fhaved their heads, and worn tunics, *colobia*, and bracelets, firft came to wear long robes and hair, and fhaved their beards; and leaving out the figures of horfemen on their feals, put their arms into fmall fhields[8].

"In Richard the Second's time began the deteftable ufe of picked fhoes, faftened with filver, and fometimes gilt chains, to the knees. The ladies of quality then wore high head-dreffes, with horns and long mantles, with trains, and rode on fide-faddles; a fafhion firft introduced by the refpectable Queen Anne, who was daughter to the king of Bohemia[9]."

The monkifh writer of Richard the Second's life[10] fays, Queen Anne brought from Bohemia thofe curfed fafhions[11] of fhoes with long points, called in Englifh *Cracowys*, or *Pykys*, half a yard long; fo that the wearers were obliged to faften them to the leg with filver chains before they could walk. He adds[12], that

[1] His diebus Anglici veftibus folebant uti protenfis ad medium genu, brachiis oneratis annulis aureis. Tunc erant Anglici vefte fuperiori ad medium genu expediti, crines tonfi, barbis in fuperiore labro nunquam rafi exceptis folum presbiteris, armillis etiam aureis brachiis onerati, picturis (f. *punctis*) ftigmatibus cute infigniti—Pugnabant baculis et bipennibus, Normanni enfibus et fagittis. P. 99. Ed. Hearne.

[2] In Anglia qui more Trojanorum et aliorum Orientalium barbas nutrierunt, exemplo Normannorum eas raferunt, & crines ad humeros crefcere permittebant. Ib. 100. b. See Granger, I. 87.

[3] Hift. Novel. 99. b.

Criniti noftri obliti quid nati funt in muliebris fexus habitum capillorum longitudine feipfos transformant.—Vix anno elapfo cuncti qui fibi curiales effe videbantur in prius vitium reciderunt: longitudine capillorum cum feminis certabant, & ubi crines deficiunt involucra quædam innodabant. [4] Holinfhed, 341.

[5] Iftius regis tempore erat in ufu nova inventione abufio veftium, lux (l. *luxus*) crinium, et horribilis afperitas fotularium roftratorum, id eft, cum armatis aculeis. Solebant tunc homines *greffus frangere*, gefto foluto, et nudo latere incedere. Rofs, Ib. p. 101. b.

[6] His diebus in figillis dominorum erant tunicæ fuper loricas, antea non, & ipfæ tunicæ erant longæ ad talos. Ib. p. 162. b.

[7] Circa hæc tempora domini in figillis modo folito habebant equites armatos cum gladiis, & in dorfo figillorum de novo arma fua præfuerunt in fcutis, & facies ymaginum primo habuerunt *umbrelles*. Ib. 163. a.

[8] Poft captionem regis Franciæ Johannis Anglici prius barbati et capilli capitis tonfi etiam ad tunicas et colobia & armillanfes inceperunt uti (l. *uti*) togis et longis crinibus in capite, et radere barbas, ac domini et generofi relictis ymaginibus equitum in figillis impofuerunt arma fua parvis fcutis, P. 165. b.

[9] Diebus etiam fuis incepit deteftabilis ufus fotularium roftratorum cum ligaturis catenarum de argento & quandoque deaurato ad genu ligatorum. Etiam mulieres nobiles tunc utebantur thiaris altis et *cornutis* cum togis caudatis & fellis vel fedilibus *lateralibus* equorum, exemplo venerabilis Annæ reginæ filiæ regis Bohemorum, quæ hæc primum in regnum introduxit. Rofs, p. 166 a. Stowe, p. 295. See thefe fleeves in Strutt's Regal Antiquities, pl. xix. p. 15. In a drawing in Froiffart, Ifabel, Edward the Second's Queen, enters Paris, 1324, riding thus.

[10] P. 126. [11] *abufiones execrabiles*. [12] P. 156.

Richard had one garment [1] so richly adorned with beryls [2] and other precious stones and gold, of his own ordering [3], that it was valued at 3000 marks.

These picked cracows, as they were called, were common in the 14th century in France. See Montfaucon. Mr. Strutt says, Verstegan mistakes in making this a part of our dress before the Conquest; for it is not seen in any delineation whatever [4]. Something like them however we have before heard of in the reign of Rufus.

Of the extravagant fashions of his own time the reign of Henry VII. Ross gives this picture: "They let their hair grow so long that it hid their forehead, which bore the mark of the cross in baptism; they scarce concealed the parts which nature bids us conceal, and in walking shewed their backsides, by the shortness of their garments, or by having servants following to lift up their trains. The capes of their tunics and mantles were as short as if they were preparing to be beheaded. Formerly they were made high, that they might stand up to keep the cold out of their necks; but now they are short, as if intended to be out of the way of the executioner's ax. The women of the present time wear mourning hoods, as if in mourning for some near relation [5]."

In the fashion of beards and hair Harrison is ready to concur with Ross: "Our heads are sometimes polled, sometimes curled, or suffered to grow at length, like woman's locks, manie times cut off above or under the ears, round as by a wooden dish: our varietie of beards, of which some are shaven from the chin, like those of the Turks; not a few cut short, like to the beard of marquis Otto; some made round, like a rubbing brush, others with a *pique devant* (O fine fashion!) or now and then suffered to grow long; the barbers being growen to be so cunning in this behalf as the tailors. And therefore if a man have a leane and streighte face a marquesse Otton's cut will make it broad and large; if it be platter like, a long slender beard will make it seeme the narrower; if he be wesell becked, then much heere left on the cheekes will make the owner looke big like a bowdled hen and so grim as a goose, if Cornelis of Chelmeresford say true. Manie old men do weare no beards at all [6]."

To judge from the broad seals of our Norman Princes in Sandford, William the Conqueror wore short hair, large whiskers, and a short round beard. Rufus his hair a degree longer than his father, but no beard or whiskers. Henry I. and Stephen neither hair, beard, nor whiskers [7]. Henry II. short hair, no beard or whiskers on his first seal; but on his second large whiskers, and short double-pointed beard. Richard I. longish hair, without beard or whiskers. John, short hair, large whiskers, and short curled beard, and the same on his monument. Henry III. middling hair, no beard or whiskers on first seal; on second whiskers and short round beard; on his monument whiskers, and a broad long beard. Edward I and II. short hair, no beard or whiskers; John of Eltham, whiskers on his monument. Edward III. long hair, no beard or whiskers on first and second seal, shorter hair, large whiskers, and double pointed beard on third. Richard II. in his picture and monument at Westminster short curling hair, and a small two pointed curling beard. In his seal both longer. He has the same beard on the screen in York minster, which is said to have been brought from St. Mary's abbey there. The statue of Henry III. thereon has the same bifid beard; that of Edward III. has a very long one; Henry IV. and V. none.

Can one help admiring Hearne's [8] curious reasoning on the rude coins of the Conqueror and Rufus, that the ugly features, thin hair and beard, prove the

[1] *roba*. [2] *berillis*. [3] de propria sua *ordinatione*. [4] Dress, p. 47.

[5] Longitudine crinium faciem in baptismo sanctæ crucis signo signatum abscondunt, pudenda palam faciunt, de viciis non pudent, & in ambulando nates denudant aut togarum curtitudine aut famulorum sequentium juvamine & tortura sublevatione. Decollationi etiam se aptant colariorum tunicis et togis decurtatione. Olim erant alta ad frigus expellendum, sed nunc sunt curta, non quia impedientia nec resistentia securi percutientis manu proni ad decollandum. Mulieres etiam moderna utuntur *capuciis lacrymariis* quasi carorum suorum necem plangentes. P. 116. a.

[6] Description of England, c. 7. of apparel, p. 171.

[7] 1104. 4 Henry I. Serlo bishop of Seez preaching at Carenton before the King against long hair, caused him and all his courtiers to be immediately cropt.

[8] Praef. ad Gul. Neubrig. p. xviii.

corrupt

corrupt manners of the times, and the king to be a complete debauchee, as well as avaricious tyrant; and his son blood-thirsty and sacrilegious; as if any of our coins before the Edwards bore the impress of a human figure?

In France Charles de Blois, who was killed at the battle of Avrai, 1364, is represented with a beard, contrary, says Montfaucon [1], to the custom of that time. One might believe that Philip Augustus king of France, who died 1223, introduced the custom of shaving, because both he and his son Louis VIII. have beards on their seals. Thus much is certain, that neither St. Louis nor his successors to Francis I. wore them [2].

Thorn has thought it of importance to record in his Chronicle the æra when the monks of St. Austin's ceast to scrape off one another's beards; and he has remarked, that a pious commemoration was instituted for the soul of abbat Roger, who, with the concurrence of the convent, had ordained, that the brethren should be shaved by seculars—"propter læsuras et diversa pericula quæ frequenter contigerunt inter eos qui rudes & nescii erant in officio radendi [3]." This was about A. D. 1264. Mr. Tanner, in his preface to the Notitia Monastica [4], on the authority of Ingulphus, says, that it was within the province of the *Infirmiarius* to shave all in the convent, but by Lanfranc's constitution the monks were to shave one another. "Alter alterum radat, magistri pueros radant, & ipsi a pueris radantur:" with this proviso however, "si tamen hujusmodi scientiam habent [5]." This is a complete system of monastic pogonotomy.

Chaucer's monk's

> Hed was balled (bald) and shone as any glas,
> And eke his face as it had been anoin'd [6].

His Reve's beard was—"shave as neighe as ever he can [7]." The merchant and the sailor wore their beards [8].

To begin the varieties of dress, as Mr. Aubrey [9] does, with crowns: he observes, that "the first crowns used by the Roman emperors were only diadems with the addition of pointed spikes, which they afterwards adorned and tipt with pearls, and afterwards adorned the intervals with trefoils." The radiate crown seems to have been first assumed by the thirty tyrants, or by emperors about their time; before which the heads of emperors, on their coins, are bound with laurel. After the time of Constantine the fillet of pearls came into use. This the later Byzantine emperors turned into a kind of coronet, with a broader band in front, surmounted by a cross, as appears on the coins of Tiberius Constantius [10]; and on those of Maurice it seems to come over a helmet [11]. Phocas wears a plainer crown [12]; and later emperors varied its form according to their fancy. The Virgin Mary on a coin of the emperor Michael Ducas wears a radiate crown, whose spikes are tipt with pearls [13]; and when we come to the time of Manuel Palæologus, who was crowned 1363, he is represented wearing a close crown studded with pearls, and his queen with a very different one [14]. The trefoil is thought to have been of Gothic introduction. We find it on the crowns of Clovis and his sons, which has induced some antiquaries to call it the *fleur de lis* [15]; but the truth is, these trefoils were used on Constantinopolitan crowns before the time of the Franks [16], and afterwards on those of German

[1] II. 289. [2] Ib. p. 110.
[3] X Script. col. 1915. [4] XXX. not. d. d. [5] Wilkins Conc. I. 351.
[6] Canterb. Tales, I. 198, 199. [7] Ib. I. 590. [8] Ib. I. 272. 408.
[9] Monumenta Britannica, MS.
[10] Du Cange Hist. Byzant. p. 102. [11] Ib. 104. [12] Ib. 109.
[13] Ib. 159. [14] Ib. 242.
[15] Montf. Monum. de la Mon. Fr. I. p. xxviii. Disc. Prelim. On the tomb of Adelaid of Savoy, Queen of Louis le Gros, who died 1154. and was buried in Montmartre Abbey, her crown consists of four fleurons. Lebeuf, II. 107.
[16] Ib. xxxii.

princes

princes no way allied to Charlemagne [1]. This ornament was adopted by our Norman kings, and continued on their coins till the Restoration, when, except in a few instances of both, the laurel wreath took place, as it still continues to do, of the crown. Edward the Confessor wears the trefoil in the tapestry of Bayeux. It appears on the Great Seals of the Conqueror and his wife in Sandford, and it probably adorned the figures on his monument, as it does that of his son Robert Curthose, at Gloucester, and of all the kings his successors of whom we have any monuments in England; for those at Font Evraud are of modern workmanship. Mr. Aubrey [2], observed a like crown on the head of king Ethelred, in the windows of Kingston St. Michael, c. Wilts, and on the keystone of the North door there; as also on a grave-stone at Wimborn. The last of these instances is very modern, though it may be a copy of an older figure; the others are of better authority. He noticed a similar on the head of Ethelred's queen. Such crowns were worn by Edward II. and his queen, and are often found on borders of glass windows in churches both in England and France, and on the mouldings of porches of Suffolk churches. Aubrey remarks that "Edward the Confessor wore a barred crown: the former Saxon kings crowns of silver like our coronets: Canute, a coped helmet like a mitre. Then came in use the regal circle after the manner of the Greeks. The kings of England first wore the arched barred crown. In France Louis XII. wore a single bar arched over his crown, about 1500, before only a cap till he married Henry the Eighth's sister; see his coins. Till Francis I. an open flowery border, somewhat like our ducal coronet, was generally used. In Spain, Philip, after he had married Queen Mary, used a barred crown. In Germany Maximilian, grandfather of Charles V. first wore an arch over a ducal coronet. In Denmark Christian III. after he came into England, used the barred crown. James IV. on his marriage with Margaret daughter of Henry VII. introduced it in Scotland. John duke of Braganza was the first who wore it in Portugal."

The close or arched crown appears on the coins of our first Norman Princes, and of the Byzantine Emperors. This is properly called the *Imperial* crown, and was worn by Charlemagne, after he had been declared Emperor at Rome, on whose statue at Aix-la-Chapelle it was copied for Montfaucon [3]. If we may trust the seal of Dagobert, and the many figures on the porch of St. Denis, we may believe the kings of France, before Charlemagne's time, wore a crown closed at top. The Emperors of Constantinople were not in a condition to hinder their wearing the same kind of crown as themselves [4]. Mr. Evelyn indeed says [5], the monarchs of England were the first who pretended to the arched crown. Selden says Edward V. was the first of them. It appears in Scotland first on the groats of James III. Others say it was first worn in France by Charles VIII. 1485. Henry III. brought the closed crown into Poland, and was soon imitated by the Swedes.

"The crowns on our antientest coins are much different both from one another and from that Imperial crown of England (as it is styled) which is on the modern ones. The two Williams have the pearled diadem, having labels at each ear, and something like an arch that goes across the head." This is Selden's description of it [6]. Henry I. is crowned with an open crown of three fleurs de lis, without any rays between the fleurs, which are raised but little, and labels of pearls hanging at each ear [7]. Stephen's crown is much the same arch, the flowers are raised higher, like those of the empress Maud and Henry II. on their seals. The son of Henry I. who was crowned in his father's life-time, and John, have

[1] Montf. I. xxiii.
[2] Ubi sup.
[3] I. II. last crown on the 5th row.
[4] Montf. Ib. p. xxix.
[5] Numism. p. 34.
[6] Titles of Honour, p. 134.
[7] Ib.

the

the ſame on their ſeals; but the latter king's is only pointed with ſhort rays, inſtead of flowers. Henry III. wears on his ſeals a crown fleurie pointed or rayed, the points raiſed, but not high, between the flowers; in his ſecond ſeal the points are wanting, as on that on his tomb. But in Matthew Paris we read he was firſt crowned with a circle of gold[1]. Edward I. has a ſimilar crown on his coins and ſeals, and his queen on her tomb; ſo have his ſucceſſors Edward II. and III. Richard II. Henry IV. and V. Mr. Selden had read in a book of the inſtitution of the garter, written in the time of Henry VIII. that Henry VI. firſt made him an Imperial crown, and archbiſhop Sharpe found it firſt on his coins; and from Henry VII. downward the arched crown, with the globe and croſs, has been alſo uſed on coins. Francis Thinne, in a MS. on arms, attributed it to Edward III. But Henry the Sixth's crown differs not on his coins from that of Henry V. being both fleurie and arched, with a globe and croſs over the arch, almoſt like our preſent crown. That drawn in the illumination of the "Ordo Coronationis," written long before Henry VI. is fleury, not without an arch, having a globe and croſs on it. Edward V. and Richard III. have both crowns fleury. The old crowns with croſſes fleury, and without arches, may be ſeen on the ſtatues of kings within and on the front of Weſtminſter-hall.

The crown of Scotland, as deſcribed in the inſtrument upon lodging the regalia in Edinburgh caſtle, March 26, 1707, (the original of which, ſigned by the notaries and witneſſes, and curiouſly illuminated, was preſented by the preſent earl of Buchan to the Society of Antiquaries of London), is deſcribed as compoſed of a large broad circle or fillet, which goes round the head: above the great circle is another ſmall one: the upper circle is heightned with ten croſſes florè, interchanged with ten high fleurs de lis. This is ſaid to be the antient form of the crown of Scotland, ſince the league made betwixt Achaius king of Scots and Charlemagne. The ſpecific form of this crown differs from other Imperial crowns in that it is heightned with croſſes florè and fleurs de lis alternately: the crown of France is heightned only with fleurs de lis; and that of England with croſſes patee alternately with fleurs de lis. The Scottiſh crown ſince James VI. went to England has been ignorantly repreſented like the Engliſh crowns. From the upper circle proceed four arches which meet and cloſe at top, ſurmounted with a mound or globe of gold enamelled with a large croſs patèe, ſuch as tops the church of Holyrood-houſe, and cantoned with other four in the angles. At the foot of this croſs are theſe characters, J. R. V. by which it would appear that James V. was the firſt who cloſed this crown with arches, and topped it with a mound and croſs patee. But it is evident that the coins of James III. and IV. have a cloſe crown, and that the arches have been added to the antient regal crown[2].

King John's *name* is ſaid to have been inſcribed *within* his crown, on his monument at Worceſter; but no trace of it now remains.

Henry the Sixth's high cap of eſtate, called *Abococket*, was garniſhed with two rich crowns, and was taken at the battle of Hexham[3].

Moſt of the kings of England, to Edward I. have ſceptres on their coins, and ſome have two. From that time we meet with none till Henry the Eighth's pence and halfpence[4]. The oldeſt pattern of a ſceptre is on the coins of William the Conqueror, his ſon, Henry I. and Stephen, ſurmounted by the croſs patèe, or made of pellets, or by a trefoil formed of pointed leaves or pellets. The Conqueror and his wife had a trefoil ſceptre in their portraits[5]. The queen has a ſingular but

[1] *circulo aureo.* [2] Maitland's Hiſt. of Edinb. p. 161. See in Arnot's Hiſt. of Edinburgh, p. 191, a doubt what is become of theſe regalia. [3] Hall, fol. cxc, b.

[4] Archbiſhop Sharpe on Coins, in Ives's Select Papers; and ſecond edition in Bibl. Top. Brit. Nº XXXV. p. 12, 13.

[5] Montfaucon, I. pl. LV.

rude

rude imitation of it on her feal. Henry III. has fuch an one on his coins, being the laft prince with that mark on our coins; but on his great feal in Sandford he bears the fceptre with the dove, as ftill ufed. His Queen Eleanor on her feal bears both the fceptre with the crofs, and that with the dove, and fometimes that with the trefoil. The fceptre with the crofs was evidently borrowed from that borne by the Byzantine Emperors on their coins, and continued on our lateft great feals engraved by Sandford. This fceptre was found in the right hand of Edward I. and that with the dove in his left.

Henry I. fourth duke of Lorrain and Brabant, who died 1235, bears in his right hand a fceptre furmounted by a fleur-de-lis, on his tomb in St. Peter's church at Lorrain [1]. Alice countefs of Bretagne, wife of Peter de Dreux, who died 1221, has a flowered fceptre in her right hand on her tomb at St. Yvet de Braine.

Mr. Aubrey [2] fays the fleur de lis is really a fpear head adorned: no flower of that kind having the middle part folid.

Edward I. in his tomb, holds in his right hand the fceptre with the crofs, made of copper gilt, two feet fix inches long, and of moft elegant workmanfhip. Its upper part extends to and refts on the fhoulder. In his left hand he holds the rod or fceptre with the dove, which paffing over his left fhoulder reaches up as high as his ear. This rod is five inches and an half long, the ftalk is divided into two equal parts by a knob or fillet, and at bottom is a flat ferule [3].

Leland defcribing a Mohun effigy at Dunftar, c. Somerfet, fays, "it has a garland round the helmet, and fo were lordes of old time ufed to be buried [4]." He probably means, fo were they reprefented on their tombs. The fame attentive antiquary gives an inftance of one of the Bruces in Pickering church, Yorkfhire, who had a garland about his helmet [5]. Other examples might be adduced to fhew that this was no uncommon ornament.

The crown on the head of the ftatue of Philip king of Navarre over his heart in the Jacobines church at Paris is faid by Montfaucon to refemble the cap called *mortier* [6].

John of Eltham has a coronet on his head, the form whereof indeed is fleury, or as at this day a duke's is with us. But he died almoft two years before any duke was made in England, whence we may perhaps collect alfo that the coronet of our earls, before the creation of dukes, was of like form to thofe of dukes; and in the later ages an earl's is pointed and pearled on the top of the points as we fee it at this day. But alfo long before the death of this earl we have exact teftimony of an earl's coronet in Aymer de Valence [7]."

William de Hatfield fon of Edward III. at York, has a trefoil coronet.

The coronets of Agnes countefs of Dreux, and of other ladies, are fo various that P. Montfaucon could fix no ftandard [8].

Thofe of the countefs of Evreux wife of Louis of France brother of Philip the fair; of Mary wife of Charles count d'Alencon, 1379, in the Jacobins church at Paris; of Catharine wife of John de Bourbon earl of Vendofme, in the collegiate church of Vendofme, and that of the queen of René, king of Anjou, at the Celeftines at Paris, are abfolutely mural crowns. Francis II. duke of Bretagne and his wife, 1488, at Nantz, have coronets of fleur de lis: fo has the countefs d'Alencon, 1492, in the church of Alencon: Joan of France queen of Navarre, 1349, has one indented and ftudded on her tomb at St. Denis. Margaret

[1] Theatre facre de Brabant, I. 94.
[2] Archæol. III. 384.
[3] Ubi fup.
[4] Lel. It. I. 71.
[5] It. II. 61, 62.
[6] II. p. 288. L. 1.
[7] Selden's Titles of Honour, p. 562. Camden's Apology, fubjoined to his Britannia, 4to, p. 13.
[8] II. 71. Pl. xii. 6.

countefs of Evreux, 1311, has what Montfaucon[1] calls *crenelé*, on her tomb in the Jacobine church at Paris. Louis duke of Bourbon, 1341, at the Jacobines in Paris, has a very fmall one. That of Catharine wife of the Count de Maulevrier at Pavilly in Normandy is formed of pellets. Ifabel d'Artois daughter of John earl of Eu, 1379, and Charles earl of Eu and wife, 14 . . 1448, on their tombs in the abbey of Eu, all wear beautiful circles ftudded with ftones.

John Gower the poet, who died 1402, has a chaplet of flowers, with four rofes placed at equal diftances, on his monument in St. Saviour's, Southwark. Shall we fancy this has any reference to the chaplet of rofes which crowns Polyhymnia, in the collection of Pope Clement XIV.

The habits of our kings have been fo happily illuftrated in the defcription of thofe in which Edward the Firft's body was found arrayed, already given, p. lv. after Sir Jofeph Ayloffe's account, that I muft refer back to it.

Walfingham, in his account of the coronation of Richard II. mentions that the king was invefted with a ftole: firft with the tunic of *St. Edward*, and then with his dalmatic, and a ftole round his neck. The invefting with a white ftole, *in modum crucis in pectore*, is particularly mentioned in feveral foreign ceremonials.

The *fibula* on the right fhoulder of the image of Henry III. exactly refembles that of Edward the Firft, except that it has the fhape of a rofe, in the centre of which is the *acus*: and this, like the other, takes hold both of the pallium or chlamys and ftole. So it does on the great feal of Louis king of France[2]. That on the figure of John king of France is of a very different form[3].

Sir Jofeph Ayloffe obferves, that "the fhape and form of the crown, fceptres, and fibula, and the manner in which the latter is fixed to the mantle or chlamys, exactly correfpond with the reprefentations of thofe of the broad feal of this king in Sandford." It feems to me, however, that the *fibula* on the feals faftens the mantle acrofs the breaft, but on the great feal of Henry III. the mantle is faftened by the *fibula* on the right fhoulder, as alfo on the figure of Philip de Valois, king of France, who died 1300, on his tomb at St. Denis. The mantle in which king John's figure is habited on his tomb is more like a carter's frock or furplice, with a rich cape and wriftbands, ftudded with pearls, fomething like the cape on his and his fon Henry the Third's great feals. Richard I. and Henry I. have the like cape and wriftbands to their undergarments on their feals.

The *Paludamentum*, or *Chlamys (un habit de campagne)* was faftened generally on the right fhoulder, with a large button, and fell over the left fhoulder. The tunic under the chlamys was faftened with two belts or girdles[4]. The firft of thefe dreffes is the upper garment of Henry the Third's ftatue on his tomb, and of Edward the Firft's body on his tomb. The fecond is the furcoat of figures in armour, or otherwife habited.

"The feet of Edward I. with their toes, foles, and heels, feemed to be perfectly intire, but whether they have fandals on them or not is uncertain, as the cloth tuckt over them was not removed."

The feet and legs of Henry the Third's figure are covered with embroidered half-boots. Herein the figures differ from the bodies, that the latter, probably like this of Edward I. and the images of many ladies, have the feet tuckt up in the robe.

The apparelling the corpfe of this monarch in his royal veftments accompanied with the enfigns of regality as before defcribed, is not to be confidered as a peculiar mark of refpect paid to him in contradiftinction to preceding

[1] II. 213. Pl. xxxviii. 4. [2] Montf. II. 2. 4. [3] Ib. II. lv. 4.
[4] Fabroni fur les Statues de Niobe, p. 10.

kings,

kings, but as being done merely in conformity to usual and antient custom. He was on this occasion habited *more regio*, i. e. in the same manner that the corpses of all other kings his predecessors had been dressed in order to their sepulture, and similar, except in some few particulars only, to a mode or regulation established by authority, *de exequiis regalibus*. A copy of this regulation is entered in the *Liber Regalis*, immediately after the formulary for the coronation of our English monarchs. After the body has been washed and embalmed, follows the dressing.

"Deinde corpus induitur tunica usque ad talos longa, et desuper pallio regali adornabitur. Barba vero ipsius decenter componitur super pectus illius. Et postmodum caput cum facie ipsius sudario serico cooperatur. Ac deinda corona regia aut diadema capiti ejusdam apponetur. Postea induentur manus ejus cirothecis cum aurifragiis ornatis, et in medio digito dextræ manus imponetur annulus aureus aut deauratus. Et in dextra manu sua ponetur pila rotunda deaurata in qua virga deaurata erit fixa a manu ipsius usque ad pectus protensa, in cujus virgæ summitate erit signum dominicæ crucis, quod super pectus ejusdem principis honeste debet collocari. In sinistra vero manu sceptrum deauratum habebit usque ad aurem sinistram decenter protensum. Ac postremo tibiæ ac pedes ipsius caligis sericis et sandaliis inducntur [1]."

"A similar practice of arraying the dead in those habits of splendor, dignity, and ceremony, to which they were intitled in their life-time, antiently extended itself to those of inferior degree, as well clergy as laity; most of which were usually buried in the dress properly belonging to their respective qualities. Thus emperors were entombed in their imperial and kings in their royal robes; knights were interred in their military garments; bishops were laid in the grave in their pontifical habits; priests in their sacerdotal vestments; and monks in the dress of the particular order to which they belonged.

Constantine the Great was put into a chest of gold, clothed in the imperial purple, with a diadem of gold, and decorated with ensigns of royalty [2]. The Normans demolishing the tomb of king Clovis, in the church of St. Genevieve, found part of his royal robes, and several jewels, and other treasures [3]. We have already seen the contents of Childeric's tomb, and how Charlemagne was drest in his. On rebuilding the abbey church of Westminster, by Henry III. the sepulchre of Sebert king of the East Angles was opened, and part of his royal robes seen, with his thumb ring, in which was set a ruby of great value [4]. The like contents of the grave of Canute [5], Edward the Confessor, and William Rufus, have been already mentioned. The body of William the Conqueror was found royally cloathed, as perfect as when just buried, on the opening of his tomb at Caen, 1522 [6]; and his queen in like manner, 1562 [7]. The younger Henry was buried 1183, in the vestments that had been consecrated at his coronation [8]. Henry II. his father, was habited in like manner [9]. Richard II. directed, by his will, that his body should be clad in white sattin or velvet, *more regio*, and so interred, with the crown and sceptre, gilded, but without any stones, and on his finger a ring, *more regio*, with a precious stone of the value of twenty marcs English money [10].

[1] Archæol. III. ubi sup.
[2] Euseb. in Vita, IV. 66.
[3] Anglo-Norm. Ant. p. 53.
[4] Archæolog. III. 390.
[5] Or rather Henry de Blois bishop of that see. See p. 28.
[6] Antiquitez de Normandie.
[7] Rilenhert Antiquitez de la Province de Neustrie.
[8] Math. Paris, p. 141.
[9] Ib. p. 151.
[10] Rymer, Fœd. VIII. 75. Royal Wills, p. 194.

"On

"On a careful inspection of both hands of Edward I. no ring could be discovered. However, as it cannot be supposed that the corpse was deposited without that usual attendant ensign of royalty, we may with great probability conjecture, that on the shrinking of the fingers by length of time, the royal ring had slipt off and buried itself in some part of the robes [1]."

William of Windsor, son of Edward III. who died in his infancy, and is buried in Westminster-abbey, has the short coat buttoned quite to the bottom, and on the close sleeves from the elbow to the wrist, and girded round the waist with a rich girdle: over this is a mantle with a standing cape, having buttons, but let down and unbuttoned, the seams on the shoulders trimmed, and the edges of the mantle, as well as the plaits at the bottom, hatcht like a nobleman's gown in our universities; his hose are all of one piece [2].

William of Hatfield, in York minster, is drest in flowing hair with a coronet of trefoils, a mantle fringed with fur, fastened down the front of the shoulder with four roses, with which the neckband is also adorned; such also go above the back of his hands, and come down the front of his shirt; his surcoat or coat of mail, richly embroidered or enamelled; his stockings plain, his shoes reticulated with quatrefoils; no sword or dagger. Under his head are two tasseled cushions, and at his feet a lion. This elegant little alabaster figure of a royal infant has been removed from its neglected situation, and placed out of reach of injury, in a niche in the North wall of the church, by the care and good taste of the present Precentor.

Gloves are represented on the hands of kings and prelates on their monuments, and gauntlets on those of military men. The mother of Aymer de Valence earl of Pembroke, on the side of his tomb in Westminster abbey, 1323, holds hers in her hands [3]: so does a lady in Worcester cathedral. A king holds his in his left hand, on the tomb of John of Eltham. Montfaucon gives them on the hands of two lords of St. Louis' court [4]. Officers of state, and other noblemen, are represented with one at the right hand, for the purpose of supporting a hawk, while the other is off, and held in the left hand. In the abbey church of Barbeau in Brie a young man has his glove on his left hand, which holds the glove of the other hand; so Robert earl of Dreux, 1233, holds his right glove doubled in his right hand [5]. The last abbot of Evesham, 1557, in Worcester cathedral, has a glove on his left hand.

The jewels on the back of the gloves appear on the hands of king John's effigies at Worcester, and are appendages to most episcopal and many abbatial figures.

Pass we from kings to nobles, knights, and military men, almost the only persons of the laity who merited distinguished monuments, as they were the only class above the mechanics and peasantry. The profession of all this class being arms, their habit of course was military, and the distinguishing features of it the helme, surcoat, and coat of mail or armour.

Hall, in his Chronicle [6], speaking of the preparation for justs, in the first year of Henry IV. gives the following description of an armed man: "Some had the helme, the visere, the two baviers, and the two plachardes of the same curiously graven, and conningly costed: some had their collers fretted, and other had them sett with gilt bullions; one company had the plachard, the rest, the port, the burley, the tasses, the lamboys, the backpiece, the tapull, and the border of

[1] Archaeol. III. 15.
[2] Pl. XXXIV. p. 98.
[3] Pl. XXXII. p. 94.
[4] Monf. II. xxxiv. 1. 2.
[5] Monf. II. xxix. 1. [6] Fol. 12.

the curace, all gylte, and another bande had them all enamyled azure. One fort had the vambrafes, the pacegardes, the grandgardes, the poldren, the pollettes parted with gold and azure, and another flocke had them filver and fable; fome had the mainferres, the clofe gantlettes, the guiffettes, the flancardes, droped and gutted with red, and other had them fpeckled with grene. One fort had the quifhes, the greves, the furlettes, the fockettes on the right fide, and on the left fide filver. Some had the fpere, the burre, the cronet all yelowe, and other had them of diverfe colours. One band had the fcafferon, the cranet, the bard of the horfe all white, and other had them all gilt. Some had their armyng fweardes frefhly burnifhed, and fome had them conningley vernifhed. Some fpurres were whit, fome gylt, and fome cole blacke. One parte had their plumes all whyte, one had them all redde, and the third had them of feveral colours. One ware on his head-piece his lady's fleeve, and another bare on his helme the glove of his dearling. But to declare the coftlye bafes, the riche barde, the pleafaunt frappery, both of goldefmithes worke and embrauidery no leffe fumptuoufly than curioufly wrought it would afke a long time to declare; for every man after his appetite devifed, his fantafy verifying the old proverb, fo many heades, fo many wittes."

"The armour of a man at arms, till near the middle of the fourteenth century, confifted of the following particulars; a loofe garment ftuffed with cotton or wool, called a *gambefon*, over which was worn a coat of mail, formed of double rings or mafcles of iron interwoven like the meflies of a net, called a *hawberk*. To it were fixed a hood, fleeves, and hofe alfo of mail. The head was defended with a helmet, and by a leather thong round the neck hung a fhield. The heels of the knight were equipt with fpurs having rowels near three inches in length. Over all thefe men of confiderable family wore rich furcoats, like thofe of the heralds, charged with their armorial bearings [1]."

The oldeft form of the helmet was the *round*, though it muft be confeft the feals of our early Norman kings and the tapeftry of Bayeux exhibit them pointed alfo. The firft on monuments is that of Robert Curthofe, round, as is that of his fon William earl of Flanders at St. Omer, though on this earl's feals his helmet is pointed [2]. Henry I. wears one like a cap of maintenance on his great feal [3]. Richard I. both round and pointed. Thofe of Geoffrey Magnaville and the Marfhalls earls of Pembroke are round on their monuments in the Temple-church [4]. King John, in the thirteenth century, has a round helmet on his great feal [5]; fo has Edmund earl of Cornwall [6]. Edmund earl of Lancafter [7], and William Longefpe earl of Salifbury [8], on their tombs; thofe of Edward I. and his fons, on their feals [9], and Richard earl of Cornwall [10], are flat on the top. Philip earl of Boulogne, flain at a tournament at Corbie, 1223, is reprefented with a helmet flat at top, as were all the helmets of the age of St. Louis. He is alfo in mail from the helmet to the fole of his foot [11].

The earls of Flanders, in the twelfth century, have the flat helmet [12]. Raoul de Beaumont was painted in a chapel of the abbey of Eftival, which he founded 1210, armed in a fingular manner, with a helmet like a kettle reverft, flat at top, after the fafhion of the times. A piece of iron reaching from the top of the helmet to his chin is intended to parry a blow of the fword. He is in mail from head to foot and to his fingers' ends, and wears his fword in an

[1] Grofe's Additions to the Preface to his Antiquities.
[2] Sandford, 17, 18. Vredius doubts the arms on his fhield, p. 11.
[3] Sandford, 56.
[4] Pl. V. fig. 1.
[5] Sandf. 55.
[6] Ib. 94.
[7] Pl. XXVI.
[8] Pl. XIII.
[9] Sandf. 110—115.
[10] Ib. 94.
[11] Montf. II. 112. Pl. xiv. 4.
[12] Vredius.

extraordinary manner across his thighs from right to left [1]. Thibald count de Blois, who died 1218, has a helmet guarded in front with frame work or grates [2]: So has St. Louis himself [3]; Ferdinand king of Castille, who died 1252 [4]; Peter de Dreux duke of Bretagne, earl of Richmond, 1250 [5]; and other instances throughout this century [6]. Gilbert de Clare, 1295 [7]. Hugh Vidame of Chalon has one guarded by a cross fleury [8]. That of Susane the herald, 1260, is round, and of mail [9]. It continued to the reign of Edward III. See his seal to a deed in the possession of Mr. Astle, as also others of John earl Warren, 1254—1276, who has the flat helmet guarded with lattice work, or gratings, and the escarboucle of his arms on it.

These flat helmets have the nose-piece, or grating, or bar work, to the vizors both on the French and English monuments before cited; of which the first instance among us is on the figure of Geffrey Magnavile. The helmets given by Mr. Grose, with such defences, are many of them of late date. They illustrate, however, the lifting up and letting down these defences. The nose pieces, which he gives to Grecian helmets, in the British Museum, if genuine, may be paralleled with those in the tapestry de Bayeux, except that the latter are more prominent [10]. Nor does it follow that Pompey's troops at Pharsalia wanted this defence to their faces; for the Roman sword was of the stabbing or thrusting kind; and it is well known Cæsar directed his men to aim at the faces of their enemies, because they affected a too great tenderness of their persons. Fauchet says, that a lucky stroke on the nose-piece, *ventaille*, or *visiere*, would turn a helmet quite round on the head, as happened to a French knight at the battle of Bovines.

Of the helmets of the Warren family, that of William earl Warren 1089, in Philpot's Ebor. MS. Coll. Arm. is round with barrs to the eyes, and a mail apron from them. On Hameline's seal, 1202, square and pointed. A seal of earl John's has a pointed helmet with gratings. One of Waleran earl of Worcester, 1166, pointed with a pendant before the nose.

The mail helmets were always round [11]. The earls of Burgundy, in the 13th century, have flat helmets [12]. The round, or, as Mr. Grose calls them, conical, or cylindrical helmets, he distinguishes by the name of *chapelle de fer*; but P. Daniel, whose authority he quotes, describes them as the lightest of all helmets without visor or gorget; and like those afterwards called *Basinet* [13].

In the 14th century the helmets were both round and pointed. Of the first sort is that of John of Eltham, 1334 [14]; Philip de Valois, 1350 [15]. But in this century the helmets, like the armour, were hammered and plated. Fauchet says, when helmets better fitted the head, they were called *bourguinotes*, by which I understand that they were an improvement on the other.

One of the Sewals, from 4 Richard I. to 44 Henry III. or of the Shirleys, from 44 Henry III. to Dugdale's time, appears in complete armour, with a round helmet, in Eatendun church, c. Warwick [16].

Thomas earl of Lancaster, eldest son of Edmund Crouchback, is the first whose helmet is surmounted by a crest [17]. Radulph de Monthermer earl of Gloucester and Hereford, and John St. John, have them on their seals appendant to the barons' letter to the Pope, 1300.

We see them on the great seal of Edward III [18]. and Edward the Black Prince and his brothers [19]. and of Richard II [20]. The seals of the dukes of Burgundy,

[1] Montf. II. Pl. xiv. 7. [2] Ib. xvi. 3. [3] Ib. xxi. 3. [4] Ib. xxix. 2.
[5] Ib. xxx. 3. [6] Ib. xxxii. 5. xxxiii. 1, 2, 3. xxxvi. 5. See these helmets in Grose, Pl. VIII. 1. 2. 5. IX. 5, 6, 7. 9, 10, 11, 12, 13. 16. VIII. 1, 2. X. 1. 2. are of the beginning of the 13th century, 5. is of Henry the Eighth's time. [7] Sandf. 139. [8] Montf. II. xxxvi. [9] Ib. xxix. 3.
[10] See another in Grose, IX. 3. [11] Montf. II. xxxviii. 10. [12] Seaux de Bourgogne. Pl. I.
[13] Fauchet and Grose. They were worn in the time of Edward II. and III. and Richard II. *Salets* had *grates*.
[14] Ib. Pl. xxxi. [15] Montf. II. xlix. P. 1. [16] Dugd. 478.
[17] Sandf. 102. Ant. Soc. Seals. Pl. IV.
[18] Sandf. p. 124. [19] Ib. p. 125. [20] Ib. p. 190.

1315;

1315; and fome of the dukes afterwards kings of France, 1366, 1405; have crefts [1]. On monuments the creft is on the helmet that lies under the head of the figure.

The feals of Hugh V. duke of Burgundy, and Lewis of Burgundy, both 1315, have a kind of wings to the helmet [2].

Sometimes the part which covers the neck, and connects the helmet and hauberk or mail coat, is fixed to the former; fometimes it is feparated, and is called a *Gorget*, or throat-piece, and is generally of mail. In fome inftances there is no feparation between it and the helmet of mail, in which cafe it becomes the hood before defcribed, and is frequently feen on monuments, particularly in France, thrown off behind, and falling on the fhoulders, or it reaches to the chin, the ears, or even to the eyes, even when the helmet is not of mail. The *chaperon de mailles* continued in fafhion above two centuries [3].

What we call the *gorget* the French diftinguifh by the name of *chaperon*, or little cape. Charles I. king of Naples, and Robert earl of Clermont, and Peter de Dreux duke of Bretagne, all in the thirteenth century, have it on their tombs [4]. It falls down on the back and fhoulders, and was drawn up over the head in time of action. Gaucher de Chatillon conftable of France, 1329, has the fame "chaperon de mailles rebattu fur les epaules [5]," as the greater number of warriors on French monuments have. Louis I. duke of Bourbon, 1341 [6]. Lord Clifford letting it down, or putting it off, for heat or pain, at the battle of Ferrybridge, was fhot in the throat with an arrow. Ros has this to his furcoat in the Temple church.

This is what Matthew Paris calls the *collar*, when he fays that Ernald de Mounteney loft his life in a tournament at Walden, 1252, his throat being pierced for want of a collar to protect it by the lance of Roger de Leiburne, which was fharp, when on fuch an occafion it ought to have been blunt [7].

The mouth-piece, or the gorget, is up to the mouth of one of the figures in the Temple church, Pl. V. fig. 2. and one of the St. Cleres, at Danbury, Pl. VI. fig. 3. which is one of the ftrongeft arguments for the antiquity of wooden figures.

The facings of helmets are various over the forehead and down the fides of the face, which may be called frontlet and fide pieces: fome are ftudded in both parts; fome in the frontlets only: fome frontlets are enriched with flowers and foliage; fome, as that of a Vere at Earl's Coln, and a Neville at Staindrop, infcribed with letters, **Ihus Nazarenus.** This infcription is frequent on rings [8]. On the hinge of Munaffing church-door, in Effex, is this rude infcription, which has puzzled all antiquaries:

Jefus Nazarenus Rex Judeorum miferere meorum.

Alberic de Vere, 1215. Pl. IX. had round his helmet a fillet ftudded with ftones; fo have the Nevilles at Coverham, Pl. XIV. William de Valence earl of Pembroke, 1304, Pl. XXVII. That of Thomas Furnivall, at Wyrkfop, particularly noticed in the rhyming genealogy of his family [9]:

With his helme on his head well en quere
With precious ftones fometyme yt were fette there,
And a noble charbuncle on hit doth he bere
On his hedde to fee they may who fo will.

[1] Seaux de Bourgogne, Pl. I. IV. V. [2] Ib. Pl. IV. 3, 4.
[3] Montf. II. 289. [4] Ib. 111. 162, 163. [5] Ib. pl. LII. 1. [6] Ib. LI. 3.
[7] Rogerus fuam aptans lanceam, cujus mucro prout debuit non erat hebetatus, fub galea Heraldi guttur ejus cum trachea præcidit & arteriis. Erat enim ea parte difcoopertus & carens *collario*, M. Paris, 848.
[8] See Hutchins's Dorfet, I. 556. and Gent. Mag. LIV. 134. 817.
[9] Mon. Angl. II. 916.

The

The helmets of John of Eltham, and the Black Prince, and many others, have coronets or chaplets round them.

The beam, or vizor, of the helmet of Sir Hugh Haftings is exprefsly exhibited as lifted up; and fo are thofe of three knights at the fides of his canopy. The mail gorget of the earl of Pembroke there has above it a plated cape, and his fword has no tranfverfe bar.

The vizor was let down in time of action. Richard II. ftopt the combat between the dukes of Hereford and Norfolk, juft as the former had clofed his *bavier* [1]. In the old painting on the walls of part of Thanet-houfe, by Temple-bar, which being uncovered for rebuilding was copied for me by Mr. Bafire, and was of the time of Henry VII. or VIII. feveral figures had elevated over their helmets a kind of bar, which, when let down by rivets, would have guarded the eyes or nofe.

Upon comparing the Englifh with the French helmets on monuments, I find great variety in the former.

The various kinds of helmets enumerated by Mr. Grofe, in his fcientific treatife on our antient armour, by the names of *Chapelle de fer*, *Burgonet*, *Bafinet*, *Salet*, *Scull or Hufken*, *Caftle*, *Pot* and *Morion*, are too light to appear on monumental figures, where parade was principally confulted; for I do not conceive the firft of thefe helmets was of the heavy kind, or confined to cavalry.

The armour that covered the body and limbs was divided into two forts, mail and plated. I do not agree with Mr. Grofe's definition of chain and plate mail; as I conceive mail, from its derivation, to imply net or ring work of mefhes intirely diftinct from the fcales of plated armour, which were fewed together, or on a lining, while the mail mefhes were connected together like links of a chain without any other affiftance.

The figure of Sir Hugh Bardolph, engraved Pl. X. and XI. is the completeft fpecimen of an armed knight among us, and moft happily illuftrated by Mr. Kerrich's defcription of it, p. 36.

The hauberk was a complete covering of mail from head to foot. It confifted of a hood joined to a jacket with fleeves, breeches, ftockings, and fhoes of double chain mail, to which were added gauntlets of the fame. Fauchet defcribes a knight as arming himfelf with the breeches upwards to the *gobiffon* or *gambefon* [2]. This he defines a long garment reaching down to the knees, and

[1] Hollinfhed, p. 494.

[2] Le chevalier commence a s'armer par les chauffes, puis endoffert un gobiffon—c'estoit un veftement long jufques fus les cuiffes & contre-pointe. Ce monftre l'autheur et le peintre du livre intitule " Le Pelerinage de l'ame" ancien.

> Et tout ainfi comme faict eft
> Des pontures le *Gambifon* al. *Gambeffon*.
> Pourquoi pourpoint les appelle on, &c.

Et encore le mefme autheur dit que c'eftoit la premiere piece du harnois.

> Car defous vale Gambefon
> Qui armer fe veult par raifon.

Par la peinture que j'en ai il femble long jufques au deffoubs des genoux: et le mefme autheur monftre que les femmes en portoient fus leur chair: mais il eft croyable qu'ils eftoient legerement contre pointez, je croi, comme encore elles font aujourdhui pour fe monftrer avoir le corps droit ou cacher leur defauts de nature: car il dit.

> Et fa campagne au Gambefon
> Chantoit une telle chanfon;
> Je chanterny faire le doi
> Rien je ne porte avec moi
> Au petit guichet retenue
> Ne ferai pas, car je fuis nue.

Deffus ce Gambefon ils avoient une chemife de mailles longues jufques au deffous des genouils appellee *Aubir* ou *Hauber*, je crois du mot *albus*, car *Albumen* ce tourne en François Aubin, *Alburnum* Aubier, qui eft le blanc de tout bois, *Alba* aube, et autres femblables, et celui-ci en Auber, pource que les mailles de fer bien polies, forbies, et reluifantes en fembloient plus blanches.

A ces chemifes eftoient coufues les chauffes: ce difent les annales de France parlant de Regnault comte de Dammartin combatant en la bataille de Bovines. Un capuchon ou coeffe auffi de maille y tenoit pour mettre la tefte dedans; lequel capuchon fe rejettoit derriere apres que le chevalier s'eftoit ote le heaulme, et quand ils vouloient fe refraichir fans ofter tout leur harnois; *ainfi que l'on void en plufieurs fepultures*.

Le *Hauber* ou *Brugne*, ceints d'une ceinture ou large courroye appellee jadis *Baltheus* et des ancient François Baudrier, pource qu'il eftoit fait de cuir fec et manié par un Baudroyeur, qui eft un ouvrier qui baudroye et endurcit les peaux en les maniant." II. 2 i. p. 107, 108.

counter

counter pointed or fringed, not unlike what the women wore by way of boddice to regulate their ſhapes.

Over this Gambeſon they had a ſhirt of mail, reaching below their knees, called *Auber* or *Hauber*, q. d. from *Albus*, from the whiteneſs or glittering of its ſcales or plates[1].

We ſee here the *ſhirt* of mail diſtinguiſhed from the *coat* of mail, as plainly in our monuments. The outer coat was afterwards made of plated armour, of which Mr. Groſe gives many varieties, but I think none of great antiquity. He ſeems to miſtake when he ſays the mail ſhirt was *without ſleeves*. Sometimes the mail ſhirt was covered with a ſurcoat of linen or woollen, like a tabard on which the family arms were embroidered; but this was laid aſide when plated armour came into general uſe.

The variety of faſtenings of the mail-ſhirt are numerous; ſometimes like the plated armour it ſeems to be tied on the arms or at the elbows, by thongs in a bow, ſometimes differently[2]. Neville at Goverham has it faſtened at his ears by a bow ſtrap. One of the Ryther's, at Ryther, at his elbows: one of the knights at Harwood, in plated armour, on his elbows and ſhoulders. A Middleton in Ilkley chancel at his wriſts. It is a faſtening common on our Northern monuments. Sir Richard Harcourt, 1470, has the plated armour, with bows at the elbows and wriſt. James lord Berkeley, 1463, and the figure by his ſide, at Berkeley, have two bows on and above each elbow.

To this ſhirt were faſtened the breeches, and a hood of mail, to put the head into, which hood the cavalier threw back when he put off the helmet, or would refreſh himſelf without totally diſarming as appears on many ſepulchral monuments.

The Hauber was girt round with a belt or long ſtrap called *Balteus*, and by the French *Baudrier*[3], from its being of tanned leather.

In France only perſons poſſeſſed of a certain eſtate, called "un fief de hauber," were permitted to wear an hauberk, which was the armour of a knight; eſquires might only wear a ſimple coat of mail without the hood and hoſe[4].

The *Haubergeon* was a coat compoſed either of plate or chain mail without ſleeves.

The *Jazerant* ſeems to have been another name for a *coat of mail*, or rather for mail itſelf. Thus in the inventory of Louis le Gros, 1316, cited by Du Cange are three "coleretes pizaines de *jazeran* d'acier et une couverture de *jazeran* de fer." And ſo Du Gange deſcribes it as a garment of woollen or cotton ſtuff, quilted and fitted to the body, to preſerve it from the injury of the armour, or as the ſtatutes of the armourers and *couſtre pointiers* of Paris direct, "que elles ſoient couchées deuement ſur neufes eſtoffes & pointees enfermées, "faites a deux fois, bien & nettement emplies des bonnes eſtoffes ſoient de "cotton ou d'autres eſtoffes," &c. No man was to make "cote gamboiſiee ou "il noit trois livrés de coton tout net, ſi elles ne ſont faites en ſremes & au "deſſous ſoient faites entremains & que il y ait un ply de viel linge emprez l'en-"droit de demie aulne & demy quartier devant & autant derriere." Thus alſo P. Daniel[5] calls it a kind of long pourpoint waiſtcoat of taffety or leather and wadding of wool, tow, or hair, to break the ſtroke of the lance. In an inventory cited by Du Gange, *Alberis* and *Contræpointes* are expreſsly diſtinguiſhed.

[1] Under the Hauberk was ſometimes worn a breaſtplate of iron, for the greater ſecurity in tilting. P. Daniel Mil. Fr. I. 388. This is well expreſſed by a citation from William le Breton's deſcription of a tilting match.

> Utraque per clipeos ad corpora fraxinus ibat,
> Gambeſumque audax forat, et thoraca trilicem
> Disjicit; ardenti nimium prorumpere tandem
> Vix obſtat ferro fabricata *patena* recocto.

[2] See the ſtraps and knots in the armour of Arthur duke of Bretagne, Lobineau, I. 665.

[3] Whence our *Bauldrick*.

[4] Groſe, p. 15.

[5] Mil. Fr. I. 387.

The

The German name *Wambasium* is nothing more than a corruption of *Gambeson*, and is explained, "Tunica spissa ex lino & stuppa vel veteribus pannis consuta "& desuper camissia ferrea." It is the *Thorax* of the antients, the *Jupas* of the Spaniards, the *Guipon* of the Italians, the *Pourpoint* of the French, and the *Doublet* of the English. The *Jack*, or *Jaque*, was of the same materials, and the *Jacket* or *Jaquette* of deerskin:

> Un pourpoint de chamois
> Farci de boure sus & sous. *Coquillart.*

The *Haqueton*, or *Aketon*, was another name for the same habit, and a MS. Chronicle of Bertrand Guesclin describes it as resisting the blows which broke the shield and good jazerant, because it was made of buckram:

> L'escu li derompi & le bon jazerant:
> Mais le Hauqueton fut fort, qui fut de bouquerant

The coat of armour was lined, or had a jacket under it. So Chaucer's knight

> Of fustian wered a *gipon*
> Alle besmotred with his habergeon.

Baldwin de Betencourt, in Orcamp abbey, in France, has the mail and surcoat without any side armour.

The suit of mail armour in the possession of Mr. Green of Lichfield, engraved by Mr. Grose, pl. XXI. will give a perfect idea of that antient kind of casing of the body: the rings at the extremities of the arms and shirts are smaller than those of the body and head, every ring being drilled and rivetted. On many of our monuments the mail has the appearance of SS, or such links as forms a jack chain. The large suit in Mr. Grose's plate weighs altogether thirty-nine pounds. On the breast and back are a set of plates, on those on the breast are clasps to make them fast by a leather strap, the whole coat being open before.

Over the coat of armour was the surcoat of stuff, of which some of our first examples are the Temple figures. On this the arms were embroidered, but on the breast of the plated armour they were enamelled or relieved. One of the first examples of the first sort on the plated armour among us is William de Valence earl of Pembroke, 1296[1]. Of the latter, Thomas second lord Berkeley, at Bristol[2]. In France, of the surcoat, Thibald earl of Blois, who died 1218[3], in the windows of the cathedral of Chartres, where he is represented "*revetu de son blason,*" according to the antient mode of expressing it; see also Peter de Dreux, surnamed Mauclerc, duke of Bretagne, and earl of Richmond, 1250, twice in the windows of Notre Dame de Chartres[4], and others there; but not on tombs till 1279, on that of Hugh vidame of Chalon at Chalon[5]. Before that they seem in France to have been on small painted shields, as if fastened to the belt; which was a very general mode in that kingdom, though, according to the general opinion, blazonry and coats of arms were first introduced in the reign of Louis le jeune, in the end of the twelfth century. Montfaucon doubts[6] if they were worn on garments so early, or before the reign of St. Louis, which was near an hundred years later, at which time they were also, he thinks, put into lozenges. Peter de Dreux, before mentioned, duke of Bretagne, 1250, in the abbey of St. Ived de Braine, has his arms enamelled on the pomel of his sword. Henry Spanheim at Hemmenrode has a long surcoat over all his armour, and nothing but his

[1] Pl. XXVII. [2] Pl. XIV. [3] Montf. II. 114. xvi. 3. [4] Ib. xxx. 2. 3.
[5] Ib. XXXVI. 5. [6] II. 70.

sword,

ſword, ſhield of arms, and ſpurs, beſpeak him a knight [1]. The ſame may be ſaid of Simon de Thouars count de Dreux, 1365 [2].

John count de Roucy and Braine, "the luſty earl of Rouſſi," as our Shakſpeare calls him, killed at Agincourt, 1415, on the day of St. Criſpin and St. Criſpinian, is habited on his monument at Yved de Braine, in a mail gorget and a furcoat, which intirely covers his armour, except the lower joint of the arm. His coat of arms is at the back of his head.

The Black Prince is repreſented in black armour emboſt with gold, and with a golden lion on his breaſt, a hat with a white feather, and a large ruby exactly in the ſhape of the rough ruby ſtill in the crown. Mr. Walpole [3] has ſtampt originality on this portrait, and Mr. Godfrey has engraved it [4]. It was in the hands of the Speaker Onſlow; now of his ſon George, and came out of Betchworth-caſtle, Surry. I know not how to controvert ſuch authorities; but the lion *rampant*, as here, is neither the Black Prince's coat nor creſt. What Mr. Walpole calls *armour*, the engraver repreſents as a furcoat with a plated gorget and mail ſleeves; the ruby ſtill in the crown would hardly have ever been in the Prince of Wales's bonet.

The arms of Robert du Bois, at Fersfield, 1311, are painted alternately with thoſe of his lady on the *folds* of his furcoat [5]. Sir John Say, at Broxborne, about 1473, bears his on the breaſt-plate, and ſkirts, as well as the arm plates of his plated armour. In the braſs figure of Trumpington they are on his ſhield and ſcabbard, and on two ſtanding ſhoulder pieces or pennons behind him [6].

Theſe pennons or gonfannons are extremely common on French monuments: Thus Sir Jerre de Bleneu, 1285, at Senlis and Herevil de Cheriſy, in Longpont abbey, Robert fifth earl of Dreux, 1329, at Dreux, with arms. Plain and in front are thoſe of St. Peter ſire de Candoire, 1297, at Orcamp abbey, Guy lord of Plaiſier Brioun, Flament, John de Bretigni, 1315. In front with arms thoſe of Sir Oudart Huart, 1261. John ſire de Candoirre, 1265. Jehans, 1300, and two other knights, all in Orcamp abbey. We have one more inſtance among us in a braſs knight at Gorleſton, c. Suffolk.

The furcoat of Sir Robert de Buers, 1361 [7], falls lightly in handſome plaits, gathered round his waiſt by a kind of cord, and fringed at the bottom and ſides. His belt, in every part of it, is alſo more ornamented.

That of Simon de Thouars count de Dreux, killed in a tilting match on his wedding day, 1365, on his tomb in the abbey of Notre Dame d'Eu, is plaited in the waiſt, and cloſe girt at the waiſtband. That of Louis of France earl of Evreux, 1319, in the Jacobines church at Paris, is hemmed with furr.

Mail armour maintained its ground from the Norman invaſion to the fifteenth century. Henry IV. is the laſt of our kings who appears in it on his great ſeal [8].

The tranſition from mail to plated armour is ſtrongly marked on the braſs of Creyk. Montfaucon gives no inſtance of it in France after the thirteenth century [9]. Chalo de St. Mars appears in plated armour, in the reign of Philip the Fourth [10],

[1] Acta Acad. Theod. Pal. III. 49.
[2] Montf. II. xv. 2.
[3] Anecdotes of Painting, I. 26.
[4] Antiq. Repert.
[5] P. 87.
[6] See it engraved in the Antiq. Rep. II. 225. from the drawing by Mr. Tyſon. As my late friend inclined to fix the date of this *croſs-legged* figure prior to the year 1312, I ſhall here add, to what has been already obſerved, p. civ. as a confirmation of what is there advanced, the circumſtances which he thought intitled other perſons beſides Knights Templars to be ſo repreſented: 1. Having ſerved perſonally, though for hire, in the Holy Land. 2. Having made a vow to go thither, though prevented by ſickneſs or death. 3. Having contributed to the fitting out ſoldiers or veſſels for the ſervice. 4. Having been born with the army in Paleſtine. Laſtly, having been a conſiderable benefactor to the order of Knights Templars perſons were rendered partakers of the merits and honour of that fraternity, and buried with their diſtinctions, an idea which has been more recently adopted abroad by many great perſonages who have been interred in the habits of capuchins." Antiq. Rep. II. 226. The fourth of theſe reaſons accounts for the croſs-legged figures of ſmall proportion.
[7] Pl. XLII.
[8] Sandf. 144.
[9] Pl. LVI.
[10] Montf. II. 218. pl. xli.

but

but Montfaucon refers the painting which represents him to the reign of Francis I. Mail occurs on the Burgundian ſeals, 1405; and on thoſe of the earls of Flanders, 1349[1], and mixt with plated, 1366, and as late as 1460[2]. The gorgets are mail, while the leg and thigh pieces are plated, on the ſoldiers of the duke of Lancaſter, temp. Richard II. in the drawings of that time, engraved by Mr. Strutt, pl. 29. 31. See alſo Robert Chamberlayne, in the ſervice of Henry V. at Agincourt, 1417[3], which is a compleat example of an armed knight. Fauchet, from Froiſſart, ſays, armour made of plates of iron was not in common uſe till 1330. The genouailles, or knee-pieces, of Bardolph, 1203, are plated; ſo are thoſe of the Coverham knights; of John lord Montacute, at Saliſbury in the 13th century. Thomas lord Berkeley, 1361, has the mail coat and gorget. Sir John Beauchamp, in Old St. Paul's, 1361, had the mail coat and gorget, and round helmet.

Sir Humphry Littlebury, at Holbeach[4], and Sir Hugh Haſtings, 1347, has armour *mi-partie*, plated and mail; as have alſo the figures at the ſides of the latter's canopy. John lord Montacute has the mail gorget and ſkirt. Thomas de Vere earl of Oxford, 1371, has plated armour, with mail gorget, arm-piece, ſkirts, and ſhoes. Edward lord Deſpenſer, 1375, has the mail-gorget. Sir Guy de Brian, 1391, has a mail-gorget, his ſurcoat richly diapered. Sir John de Creke, in the reign of Edward III. has the ſame mi-partie armour, gorget, and mail coat, finiſhing in a point, over which is an embroidered apron and a ſurcoat, ſhort and plaited, and an helmet elegantly adorned and incircled by a fanciful fillet, a ſword plain, the knee-pieces ornamented, and the rowels roſes.

Sir John Croſby, 1475, has the plated armour, ſtrapt at the elbows, and buckled at the waiſtband; mail appears between the thighs. Over the ſhoulders is a falling mantle, with a ſtanding cape, and round his neck a collar. His helmet is round, and under his head a helmet and torſe without creſt. He is "clad in complete ſteel[5]," armed from head to foot, or *cap a pee*, q. d. *a capite ad pedem*.

Sir Richard Harcourt, 1470, has the plated armour ſtrapped on the elbows and wriſt, mail at his gorget and between his thighs, and a kind of ruffle turned back at his wriſts. A mantle of the garter, with a rich cape and a cordon, his belt charged with oakleaves, his head bare, and hair flowing; the garter round his left knee. Grey, at St. Albans, 1490, has plated armour buckled at the waiſtband, mail under his gorget or cape, his hands covered to the fingers ends with one plate; at his elbows a trefoil ornament. The Bardolfs, at Wotton, 1438, have the plated armour, with pointed ſhoulder-pieces, mail between the thighs, and the hair cut cloſe above the ears. John Vere earl of Oxford, 1513, at Earl's Colne, had plated armour buckled at the waiſt, a ſtiff ſtanding cape, flowing hair, bareheaded, and over all the mantle of the garter.

John Borel, at Broxborn, 1531, has plated armour, with mail ſkirts, gauntlets in ſcales, cloſe at the back of his hands, in his left hand a large mace; his helmet and gorget under it; the vizor up.

In France Charles earl of Alencon, 1348, in the Jacobines church at Paris has mail mixt with plated armour. Peter I. duke of Bourbon, 1357, in the ſame church, ſhows mail at his neck, ſhoulders, arms, ſkirt, knees and inſtep.

Edward Tiptoft earl of Worceſter, at Ely, though in full armour, has his head and hair bare; ſo has Fitz Walter at Dunmow, but his hair is cropt like a roundhead, as by a bowl, ſo are Grey, the Bardolfs, the earl of Lancaſter on Sir Hugh Haſtings' braſs, and two knights at Harwood.

[1] Vredius, 47. Pl. 26.
[2] Ib. 56. Pl. xl.
[3] Strutt, pl. lix.
[4] P. 97. Stukeley It. Cur. I.
[5] Comus, 410.

When

When plated armour came into fashion [1] it was composed of different pieces for the back, breast, shoulders, arms, hands, thighs, legs, and feet, under the several names of *Cuirass*, consisting of a back and breast-piece, *Pouldrons*, *Brassart*, or *Gondebras*, or *Avant bras* (corruptly in English *Vambraces*) *Gauntlets*, *Cuissarts*, with *Genouillieres*, *Greaves*, and iron shoes.

The Vambraces included all the defence of the arms from the shoulder to the wrist. At the joint or bend of the arm they were cut obliquely, and the vacancies on the inside, when the arms were extended, were covered by plates called *Goussets*, of various forms, as hearts, rounds, ovals, irregular triangles and squares, &c. more or less adorned. Sometimes these arm pieces, in the upper division, or from, the elbow to the shoulder, left the mail shirt partially bare, or only covered the outer half of the arms. Sometimes the shoulder pieces were divided into several scales or folds, at a greater or less distance from each other.

The older Gauntlets were of mail: afterwards they were made of small plates of iron or steel rivetted together in imitation of a lobster's tail, so as to yield to every motion of the hand; some inclosed the whole hand in one case, others were divided into fingers, each finger consisting of eight or ten joints, lined with buff leather like a glove: in general they reached no higher than to the wrist. The gauntlets, if of mail, were really divided into fingers, though apparently the division is not shewn. The plated ones were fingered: and the brass of Sir John Harsyck exhibits a singular pattern of gauntlets reaching only to the second joint, like cut fingered gloves. Those of Gaucher de Chatillon constable of France 1329, reach only to the knuckles [2]. So do those of one of the Rythers in Ryther church, c. York.

The gauntlets of John of Eltham are of a new pattern about the wrists.

Those of Robert de Dreux baron Esneval, in the Jacobines church at Rouen, 1478, hang to the hilt of his sword.

To the back part of the Cuirass was affixed a piece of armour called *Garde des reins* or *Culettes*, but in the older armour this was supplied by *tassets*, or skirts, hooked or otherwise fastened on, resembling the finish of the Roman and Grecian coats of armour [3].

Mr. Pennant describes a Pollard at St. Andrew's Auckland, cross-legged, armed in mail to his finger's ends, with a *skirt formed of stripes* reaching to his knees. Is not this the common plaited surcoat? The strange figure of Sir Stephen Hatfield, Antiq. Repert. IV. 116. is the same kind.

The Cuisses were composed either of stripes of iron plate laid horizontally over each other, and rivetted together, or of an intire upper and under casing, and sometimes only an under, leaving the part next the horse bare. They were made flexible at the knees by joints or kneepieces.

The cuisses of Peletot, Pl. XLI. are studded; as are the gauntlets of a knight in Kent.

The cuisses of Charles earl of Alencon, 1346, in the Jacobine church at Paris are adorned with double rows of flowers. Those of Robert de Dreux baron Esneval, at the Jacobines in Rouen, 1478, as well as his greaves have the holly leaf.

[1] Mr. Grose (p. 74.) says, plated armour was completely introduced, both here and in France, about the middle of the fourteenth century. Painel de Chaworth held the manor of East Gareston, c. Berks, by service of finding a knight, armed with *plated armour*, in the king's army, when it should be in the territory of Kidwelly in Wales. (Esc. 11 Ed. I. n. 35. Blount's Tenures, p. 14.) Blount gives (p. 38.) and Mr. Beckwith (p. 75.) an original record, Plac. Cor. 12 Edward I. wherein Patric Chaworth holds this manor for finding "armigerum armatum" for the Welsh wars. I do not here see the distinction of the kind of armour; nor was it probably in the original of the record before cited.

[2] Montf. II. iii. 2. [3] Grose, p. 21. 23.

The mail on Robert de Vere's cuiffes, Pl. VIII. is the moſt laboured and neat I recollect.

The knee-pieces of Sir Hugh Haſtings have pointed boſſes, and alſo thoſe of king Edward on the ſame braſs. Thoſe of Robert de Buers, Pl. XLII. are highly ornamented.

Below the knees of William Marſhall, in the Temple, and Brian Fitz Alan, temp. Henry III. at Bedal, are bands or garters, as if to ſeperate the cuiſſes from the greaves. John of Eltham, 1334, has the like, but ornamented. Such appear double at the bend of the arms of William de Valence, at Weſtminſter, Pl. XXVII. who has alſo wriſtbands, and both theſe and the arm-pieces are flowered. Theſe bands, when perpendicular on the greaves, whether of mail or plated armour, denote the ſeparation of the plates, or mark the ſhin.

The Greaves were either of iron plates, or caſes, covering only the front of the leg, or of two parts incloſing the whole. They had pointed or ſquare broad toed iron ſhoes, with joints at the ankle reaching to the toes, and ſometimes they had *Sabatons* of mail.

The moſt antient armour for the foot was long pointed; the plated armour grew ſhorter, and was jointed.

Two ſorts of ſpurs ſeem to have been in uſe about the time of the Conqueror, the *pryck* or ſingle point, and the *rouelle* or wheel. The firſt obtained on the croſs-legged figures and others to the time of Edward III. and ſo do the other occaſionally, and both are uſed by the ſame perſon on different monuments. Montfaucon noticed it on the figure of Louis earl of Evreux youngeſt ſon of Philip le Hardi, who died 1319, in the windows of Notre Dame the Evreux. It is not ſtrait, but waving, as on the Temple knights. The rowel with points like ſtars appears on William Longeſpee, at Saliſbury, 1226; others like roſes, on Sir Hugh Haſtings. See alſo the figure of Robert Chamberlain, before referred to. As it is not eaſy to conceive of what uſe the wheel-ſpur could be, we may ſuppoſe its circle was ſoon left off, though the name is retained to this day.

Of the great variety of *Shields*, ſome reach from the ſhoulder to the ground, incloſing half the body in a ſemicircular defence; others are of a middle ſize; and others do not exceed the firſt bone of the arm. That of Sir Hugh Haſtings is barely of the ſize of an eſcocheon of arms. The Norman and thoſe of the croſs-legged knights are triangular, vulgarly called by the modern name of *Heater* ſhields, of great length, generally a little convex, and very rarely flat. This is the general form on our antient tombs, only varying the length. Thoſe in the tapeſtry of Bayeux have the upper extremities circular, if this be not an error in the deſigning. In France the pendant ſhield, a mere eſcocheon of arms, is the prevailing faſhion, though not to the total excluſion of the other. I have ſeen but one inſtance of the pendant ſhield among us, and that is on a mutilated neglected figure of a lady reſting each hand on ſuch a ſhield on the North ſide of the nave of Selby abbey-church. That of Sir Hugh Haſtings is not of a larger proportion. Some of our longeſt ſhields, if not ſo contracted at the point, would almoſt have ſerved the purpoſe of the *Pavache*, a large ſhield, or rather a portable mantlet, uſed as the Teſtudo of the ancients to cover the ſap of walls, as when the earl of Derby took the fortreſs of Roche Milan in France[1]. Edward the Third's ſhield of ſtate in Weſtminſter abbey is three feet long, with a boſs or umbo.

[1] Froiſſart, I. c. 109.

Before

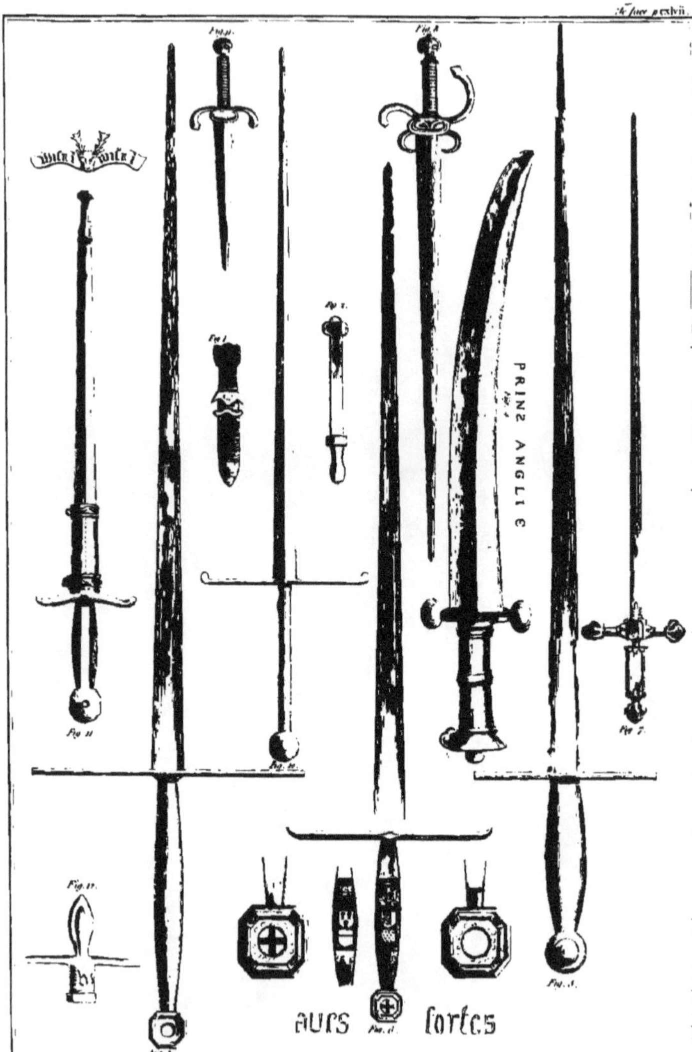
PRINZ ANGLIE
aurs
fortes

Before and after arms were put on shields they were adorned with a beautiful work called *diapering*; such is the shield of Robert Vere at Hatfield Broad Oak, and such probably was that of Richard de Lucy at Lesnes abbey, ill described by Weever [1]. Such the shield of Conan duke of Bretagne, 1171, on his seal [2]. This diaper work is a ground of painting on glass.

The *Sword*, universally of the stabbing and long kind, is worn either perpendicularly by the side, as in the Temple figures and William Longespe, or across the thighs and legs in front, as Raoul de Beaumont beforementioned. This Montfaucon calls, *l'epee en bande brochant* [3].

Peter de Navarre earl of Mortaigne, 1412, in the Carthusian church at Paris, has one end of his hilt bent down and not the other.

Grandeson, at St. Mary Ottery, has his sword drawn in his crossed hands [4]; or it is in the act of drawing, as by William Marshall earl of Pembroke, Pl. V. fig. 3. and Robert de Vere, Pl. VIII. Another Templar, Pl. XIX. draws the exact *Parazonium* [5] on Roman coins [6]. It is also worn by one of the Nevilles at Coverham, Berkeley at Bristol, and Sir Hugh Bardolph. This on the tomb of John count of Spanheim, 1399, at Hemenrod in the Palatinate, is turned with the point up [7].

In the annexed plate, fig. 3. is the sword of Edward III. in Westminster abbey, described hereafter, p. 140.

N° 4. at Armathwaite castle, c. Cumberland, is a falchion with a basket hilt, and on the blade,

on one side, EDWARDVS

on the other, PRINS ANGLIE.

supposed to have belonged to Edward II. probably left by him when his father's head quarters were at Lanercost. It is mentioned by Mr. Machel in his MS Collections for Cumberland and Westmoreland, VI. 679. and in Dugdale's visitation of Cumberland, 1665, when the castle belonged to the Skeltons, but now to William Milburn, esq [8].

Mr. Watson, Feb. 8, 1781, sent a drawing of a sword belonging to Mr. Thomas Barritt of Manchester, who said that sixty or seventy years ago it was used by a park keeper at Garsewood-hall, in Lancashire, the seat of the Gerards. Its whole length was twenty-eight inches and an half, the blade twenty-two inches and a quarter; the handle stag's horn, and the cap at the pommel, the guard and ring on the handle iron, once gilt. On one side of the blade is written *Edwardus*, and after it some animal: on the other *Prins Anglie*; the letters puncht with a tool, and filled with gold wire. The style of the inscription would refer it to the Black Prince, who had the title of *Princeps Anglie*, till he was thirteen, when 1343 he was created Prince of Wales. The inverted S and inscriptions on coins would prove it of higher date, and perhaps to have been the property of Edward son of Henry III. who was many years *Princeps Anglie*, during the reign of his father.

N° 5. is Edward the Third's sword of state, preserved in the chapter-house at Windsor, both edges sharp. It is six feet long, 8 inches of the point broken off; the handle of wood, one foot four inches; the cross bar iron, one foot four inches.

[1] See p. 18. [2] Reg. Hon. Richmond.
[3] II. 214. [4] P. 95. [5] See the plate of swords, fig. 1. and 2.
[6] Count Caylus (Recueil, II. p. 323. pl. xciii. 1.) supposes the *parazonium* to have been the short Spanish sword, not unlike those blades found in England and Ireland, and worn on the right side, like our dagger. See also Lipsius de milit. Rom. III. 3. 175. Josephus says it was twelve fingers or inches long.
[7] Act. Acad. Theod Pal. III. 49.
[8] Burn's Westm. II. 343.

N° 6.

N° 6. The ſword of ſtate of Edward prince of Wales, duke of Cornwall, Mortimer and Ulſter, earl of Cheſter, &c. eldeſt ſon of king Edward IV. It is ſix feet long from pomel to point, the blade near five feet, both edges ſharp, three inches broad at the hilt, the croſs bar ſixteen inches long, the handle fifteen inches; ſingle letters in the angles of the pomel, making together the words **ales fortes**: the croſs and two ſides of the hilt were alſo charged with Dutch rhyming inſcriptions, defaced; on one ſide of the hilt, which is braſs, are theſe coats of copper enamelled; O 3 lions paſſant guardant G. *Kings of Wales*. S. bezanté, *Cornwall*. *England* and *France* under a label of 3, crowned and borne up by angels. On the other ſide *Mortimer* quartering *Ulſter*. *Cheſter*. Arg. a chief Az. In a round in the middle of the pomel A. a croſs G. *St. George*. This prince was born 1470, and next year after the death of the ſon of Henry VI. was created Prince of Wales, 1475, duke of Cornwall, earl of Cheſter, and cuſtos of the realm of England during his abode beyond the ſea in France and Flanders. But the Prince of Wales was at Ludlow when the king his father died, living in ſtate as Prince of Wales, and being then about thirteen years old, he proceeded to London to be crowned, and was murdered in the Tower. For him it is moſt probable this great ſword of ſtate was uſed. It may have been made in the Low Countries, and afterwards brought to England, and the coats of arms added.

Fig. 7. was ſaid to have been ſent as a preſent to Henry VIII. and a cap of Maintenance, with the title of *Defender of the Faith*: ſome parts of the handle are made of rock chryſtal, and that mounted in ſilver, chaſed, and gilt with gold. To this time when the king ſits in parliament on his throne the cap is ſupported by a nobleman on one ſide, and a great ſword on the other.

Fig. 8 is the ſword, and fig. 9 the dagger, taken from James IV. king of Scotland, when he was ſlain at the battle of Flodden. The blade of the ſword is three feet and half an inch, and the handle ſix inches and an half: the blade of the dagger fourteen inches, the handle five inches long. The hilt of this ſword may be accounted the firſt advance to the baſket or cloſe hilt of the 17th century.

Fig. 10. is the ſword of Sir William Bruce, temp. Elizabeth, preſerved at Handal abbey, c. York (where it is alſo carved in ſtone) but now in the poſſeſſion of Mr. Beckwith, of York, F. S. A.; the blade three feet nine inches long, the handle and croſs bar each fifteen inches.

Fig. 11 is an antient ſword found in the Thames, about eight feet below the bed of the river, by Mr. Smith, who contracted for drawing ballaſt out of the river for the roads, 1745.

Fig. 12. is the handle of a ſword on the monument of one of the knights at Harwood, c. York, with the word **ihs** inſcribed on it. Arms are not unfrequent on the pomels of ſwords.

Mr. Brereton ſhewed the Society of Antiquaries, 1764, a ſword in form of a tuck, which has been in his family above an hundred years. The blade is damaſkt with gold to within two inches of the point, and the twelve apoſtles, with their names engraved thereon and gilt. It is likely to have received papal benediction, or to have been employed in the cruſades. The handle is of agate, with a ſilver ſcallop on one ſide of the hilt. Whether the mounting is of the ſame antiquity with the blade is not very clear, moſt probably not.

Mr. Henry Baker ſhewed another very like it, with the twelve apoſtles engraven on the blade, the mounting quite modern, and nothing ſingular in it, and its age unknown.

The varieties of older ſwords may be ſeen in the ſeveral monuments here engraved.

The

The hilt and ſcabbard, as well as the belt, are varioſly ſhaped and ſtudded. One ſees many belts in Montfaucon adorned like thoſe of the three Templars, Pl. XIX. Some ſcabbards have the coat of arms on them, as one of the Markenfields at Ripon, p. 143.

Henry III. in his thirty-ſixth year, orders an elegant ſword, with a ſcabbard [1] well covered with ſilk, and a pomel [2] with ſilver, and a handſome belt, to be got ready for him to knight the king of Scots at York the enſuing Chriſtmas [3]. The ſcabbard of Robert de Buers, 1361, Pl. XLII. is highly ornamented.

The ſword of horſemen, frequently on ſeals, appears to be faſtened on by a chain.

The dagger was worn on the right ſide. This was called the *miſericorde*. " Pour ce que de ce *ferrement* volontiers etoient occis les chevaliers abbatus, et " leſquels voyans telles armes en la main de leurs ennemis demandoient *miſeri-* " *corde* s'ils deſiroient etre repitez de la mort [4]."

It ſeems by Fauchet as if this weapon firſt came in uſe in the reign of Philip Auguſtus. Pity, in the Roman de la Roſe, is repreſented holding, inſtead of a ſword, a *miſericorde*, ſharp enough to pierce a diamond. Fauchet compares them to the Scotch daggers, called *dagues à roelles*, becauſe they had at the ends of the croſs-bar two rounds to protect the hand completely.

Knyghton [5] deſcribes Wat Tyler " cultellum evaginatum quem *dagger* vul- " gus vocat in manu gerens," and ſlain by Walworth " arrepto *baſilardo*." Stowe calls this latter weapon *baſilard*; Froiſſart [6], " grand *badelaire* qu'il portait." Charpentier explains it *Coutelas* olim *Bazelaire*, and cites records where it is called *Baſalardum* ſive *cultellum*; petit *couſtel* portatif appellé *Baudelaire*.

Mr. Warton [7] explains *Curtle-ax* in Shakſpeare [8] a kind of ſhew-dagger worn on the kirtle or ſurcoat.

Of the *anelace* and *pavade* ſee hereafter.

The reſt for the ſpear on the right breaſt is well expreſſed in the portrait of Arthur ſecond duke of Bretagne and Conſtable of France 1457, in Lobineau, I. 665. John V. duke of Bretagne, who died 1399, and has a monument in the middle of the choir of the cathedral at Nantz, has two projections from the armour on his breaſts that reſemble reſts. His helmet under his head, like that on it, has a flowered frontlet, and over his mail gorget he has the collar of Ermines. His armour is plated: the lion under his feet holds in his mouth a label, with his motto, *A ma vie*.

Another inſtrument in the hands of ſome figures is the mace, as in that of one of Philip the Fair's attendants, when Jehan de Meun preſented his tranſlation of Boetius de Conſolatione [9], and of our Henry V. when John de Galopes preſented his tranſlation of Bonaventure's Life of Chriſt [10]. I recollect but one inſtance of a mace on monuments, and that is on the braſs of John Borrel at Broxbourn, 1531.

The rich capariſon of horſes may be ſeen in the pediments of the tombs of Edmund earl of Lancaſter and Aymer de Valence at Weſtminſter, and of Sir Hugh Haſtyngs at Elſing.

[1] *ſcauberg*. [2] *pomellum*.

[3] Quod cum feſtinatione perquirat quendam pulchrum gladium et ſcauberg ejuſd. de ſerico, et pomellum de argento bene et ornate cooperiri, et quamdam pulchram zonam eidem appendi faciat, de quo rex Alexandrum regem Scociæ cingulo militari decorare poſſet. Rot. Clauſ. 6 Hen. III. m. 31.

[4] III. 341.

[5] Col. 2636.

[6] II. c. 77. p. 130.

[7] On Milton, p. 279.

[8] As you like it, Act I. Sc. III.

[9] Montf. II. x.

[10] Archæol III. 194.

The clerical habit of the times may be learnt from various monuments both of dignified and inferior clergy. Prelates and abbats add to the common pontificalia only the mitre, crosier, and gloves, and a more costly fashion of trimming the robes.

Mr. Lewis[1] has thus described the habit of a priest illustrated with an example of a brass figure of Thomas Cardiff, 1515, in St. John's church, Margate.

The upper vestment was a close *Cope* like a surplice without sleeves, with a standing cape. Under that was the *Chasuble* or *Chesible*, a sort of cope open only on the sides, and worn at mass both by the priest, who has it round at bottom, and by his assistants and the subdeacon, who have it square. As he lifts up his hands from under the close cape are seen the sleeves of the *Alb* (on which are two flaps) which he wears under the *Chesible*. On his left side, just under the Alb, is seen the end of the flannen, or *maniple*, as it is called, which the priest wears round his left arm when he celebrates mass. It was first worn in imitation of the Jewish or Pagan priests, who used a towel or napkin when offering burnt sacrifices. It is embroidered round with crosses, and fringed at the bottom. At each side of the border of the Chesible (which is likewise embroidered with crosses) appear the two ends of the *Stole*, which the priests wore about their necks over the Alb. This also is embroidered with a cross and fringed at the bottom. In the middle of the border of the Alb is another flap embroidered with a cross, with which is interwoven the Greek X.

One of the richest figures of what seems to be a private priest is that of alabaster in the North transept of Beverley minster. His Alb is fringed, as well as his Maniple, and over his Chesible falls in front a rich pall or scarf. On the hem of the Alb are these shields; a chevron between three escallops, and semé de lis a saltire impaling three lions passant guardant. At his feet a lion, and under his head, which is covered with a cowl, two angels hold a cushion.

In the porch at the door of the church of the abbey of Port Royal in France is the tomb of a priest habited in his sacerdotal vestments, a *chasuble* round on all sides, and not scollopt[2], raised up on his arms, so as to form a point before and behind; his *maniple* no broader at bottom than top, as well as the *stole*, which is not crost on the breast, but worn as at present by bishops, Carthusians, and the antient monks of Cluny, who in this instance have adopted no new mode: His *albe* at bottom has ornaments conformable to the other ornaments such as is called in briefs *Alba parata*, and still used in cathedrals and antient abbies[3].

As a matter of curiosity merely, it may be mentioned there is still remaining in the MS library at Lambeth[4] the habit of a priest, consisting of a stole, maniple, chasuble, cord, two bands marked with the letter P. and the corporal, together with a crucifix of base metal, with a string of beads, and a box of relics.

In the church of St. Andrew at Paris is a tomb with a figure in relief of a priest in his sacerdotal habits and chesible, after the antient fashion, with an amice on his head, falsely ascribed to Anthony de Montholon lord of la Plesse, who died 1694, and was only an Auditor of Accounts. But both the date and the dress contradict this supposition, and it is more probably the tomb of one of his ancestors, perhaps Jacques de Montholon canon and great archdeacon of Chartres, son of the keeper of the seals of that name[5].

[1] See Lewis's Hist. of the Isle of Thanet, p. 141. second Edit. Peter de Lacy, rector of Northfleet, 1375. John Grenhull, rector of [illegible]; Radulf Wolfe, rector of Tunstall, 1525; and John Seys, rector of West Hanny, c. Berks, 15[illegible] are more such instances.

[2] [illegible] [3] Moleon, Voyage Lit. p. 236.

[4] Dr. Du[illegible], in MS History of Lambeth Palace.

[5] Le Beuf, Hist. du dioc. de Paris, II. 461.

The

The amice *(aumusse)* was the antient covering of the head among religious men, as the veil of the women; but in 1682 the Augustine nuns of Chaillot had the amice black spotted with white, which Du Moulinet remarks as a new custom [1].

Milton's morning "came forth, with pilgrim-steps in amice *gray* [2]." This, says Mr. Warton [3], is what is called *graius amictus* in the Roman ritual; so the *gray hooded* evening in Comus [4].

A priest in Magdalen chapel, Oxford, has the tonsure, the hood down from his head over his shoulders, short sleeves, and an upper tunic over the other.

A priest vested for the altar, holding the chalice in both hands, has been engraved by Mr. Thorpe.

Mr. Pennant [5] describing the figure of Oswald Dykes, in his priestly vestments, with his chalice in his hand, in Wensley church, Yorkshire, who, his epitaph says, had been rector of the parish, and died 1607, presumes "by his habit he was only *nominal* rector." What can this mean?

William Bois rector of Fersfield, 1352, had his gown painted black, cassock red, gilt all over in imitation of embroidery, and powdered with ermine the field of his arms, and fastened round with a green girdle buckled on his breast [6]. From the neck to the girdle was the complete arms of Bois, a circumstance rather unusual on a priest's habit. One may presume this to have been the original painting. On each side of him, as of Rahere, in St. Bartholomew's, Smithfield, kneel two priests in surplices, which on the prior's tomb are black gowns, or at least painted so now.

If one could trust the representation of the priest at Bedal [7] he holds a book with a crucifix on it; but as plainly as I could distinguish it, 1785, it was a chalice on a book. The variety of chalices on monuments has been already treated of. This sacred vessel was both buried with the priests and inscribed on their tombs, where they sometimes hold it in their elevated hands, and sometimes we see it carved on one or both sides of a cross.

Philip prior of St. Frideswide has a plain habit, short hair and beard. But the greatest peculiarity is on the figure of Patteshul bishop of Lichfield and Coventry, 1243, that though he is pontifically habited, he is said to have the wounds of CHRIST painted on his hands and feet.

In the will of Edmund earl of March [8], and other wills, these various dresses are enumerated as parts of the complete furniture of a chapel, *amytes, estoles, ceyntres, chesible, tonicles, chapes, frounteles, towaille,* avec un *frontell.*

The *pallium,* or *pall,* was the peculiar vestment of the monks [9], insomuch that pope Celestine reproved the Gallican bishops for using it. We see it inscribed with letters on bishop Roger, and richly adorned on the officiating parochial priests in Kent, &c. The prior of St. Swithin's at Winchester gave to the church of Dorchester for two books a pall, on which was embroidered in silver the history of St. Birinus [10].

The maniple is not often part of the abbatial or episcopal dress on monuments, as it was not the constant habit of abbots or bishops. Compare the Peterborough abbots, pl. III. who all hold bibles in their left hands; so do two figures on the wall of St. Leonard's hospital chapel at York, and one dug out of the ruins of St. Mary's abbey there, which I saw soon after it was found, but which was gone 1785: all which bear marks of great antiquity.

[1] P. 144. Lebeuf, Hist. du dioc. de Paris, II. 58.
[2] Par. Regained, IV. 426. [3] Milton's Poems, p. 155. [4] I. 188.
[5] Tour in Scotland, 1772, p. 348.
[6] P. 102. [7] Reg. Hon. de Richm., p. 155.
[8] Royal Wills, p. 105. [9] Monachorum vestis propria fuit. Du Cange.
[10] Reg. prior. S. Swithini, in Warton's second Dissertat. prefixt to Hist. of Poetry, vol. I.

The

The habit of monks, if we wanted examples, may be ſeen on the ſides of the tomb of biſhop Burgherſh at Lincoln.

Prior Rahere has the ſame habit on his tomb; and ſo have the two monks who kneel on each ſide of him; but they are miſrepreſented in flowing hair, whereas they really are ſhorne.

The old Saliſbury biſhops, and one coeval diſcovered at Glaſtonbury, 1783, now fixt up in the abbat's kitchen, are habited as prieſts, the maniple excepted; and Roger, as I ſuppoſe him, has down his breaſt in addition to his habit a pall, whereon is the inſcription which ſo pointedly marks him in my eyes. See Pl. IV.

Robert Waldeby archbiſhop of Dublin and York, 1397, has the complete habit with maniple, pall, and fringe.

Biſhop Burgherſh, at Lincoln, is richly habited and fringed, but his mitre gone.

Archbiſhop Langham and biſhop Goodrich have a double fringe.

Archbiſhop Wolſtan, buried in Ely cathedral, when removed by biſhop Nigel into the North Weſt of the choir, was found in his caſula and pallium faſtened together with gilt pins [1].

Biſhop Inglethorp, at Rocheſter, 1291, appears to have the maniple. He and biſhop St. Martin there, 1273, are copies of the Margate prieſt, as is the braſs figure of biſhop Goodrich at Ely, 1554, on which he bears the great ſeal as chancellor [2]. Biſhop Heaton at Ely, has the pontifical robe without the mitre [3].

Luxemburgh biſhop of Ely, 1443, is the only inſtance of a cardinal's figure and habit among us [4]. Archbiſhops Langham and Courtney, and biſhop Beaufort, the only prelates raiſed to that dignity who have monuments with figures on them among us, are content to wear their mitres. Kemp and Wolſey's hats appear only on the gates erected by them at Cawood and Chriſtchurch.

The copes of many of our prelates, both in ſtone and braſs, are thick ſet with ſaints and apoſtles. Biſhop Waltham, in the Confeſſor's chapel, has them down his pall in front, where biſhop Roger has an inſcription. The copes of Thomas Eyre and John Newcourt, deans of St. Pauls, 1400 and 1485. William Rythyn minor canon, 1400, in the ſame cathedral, are richly embroidered with ſuch figures, and even ſcripture hiſtory.

Biſhop Fitz Hugh has a rich embroidered rochet. Biſhop Braybrook, Thomas Okeford, Richard Lichfield, Roger Brabaſon, canons: Dean Worſley, Dr. Grene, have rich embroidered facings to theirs.

. Biſhop Heaton, 1609, at Ely, is a ſingular inſtance of a biſhop *after the Reformation* having ſaints embroidered on his cope.

I am told, biſhop Wykeham's robe, kept at New college, is faced with ſilk and the buttons are rubies.

The jewels on the back of their gloves are not confined to archbiſhops, as appears on thoſe of Betun, Melun, Foliot, and Bruſe, biſhops of Hereford; biſhop Ruthall of Durham, archbiſhop Grey at York, Peckham and Langton at Canterbury; abbot Ramridge, at St. Albans; Hawford abbot of Eveſham, at Worceſter; alſo abbot Colcheſter of Weſtminſter, in Dart's print, but not at preſent.

Archbiſhop Kemp's gloves are yellow, and well repreſented in the marriage of Henry VI [5].

Langton biſhop of Lichfield and Coventry, 1321, has gloves more ſtrongly expreſſed. He has a jewel en croix on his breaſt: ſo has the figure called Conſtantine the Great in York minſter. Dean Aquablanc has a lozenge.

[1] Auratis ſpinis affixum.
[2] See Bentham, pl. XXV. [3] Ib. Pl. XXVI. [4] Ib. Pl. XIX.
[5] Walp. Anecd. of Painting, I. 37.

The

The usual posture of prelates' right hands is to be lifted up, with the two fore-fingers extended, giving the benediction.

The mitres of Christian prelates were borrowed from the *Apex* or *Tutulus* of the Flamen Dialis[1].

In the collegiate church of St. Marcel at Paris is the tomb of the celebrated Peter Lombard, who died bishop of Paris, 1160. His figure and inscription are not of that time; but above an hundred years later, as is thought from the *height of the mitre*[2].

The mitres of abbots differed a little from those of bishops, who carried their crosiers in their left hand, but the abbots in the right[3]. In the procession roll, 3 Henry VIII. the abbots are drawn with barons' caps, not mitres, as MS Ashmole, but in the parliament house, 15 Henry VIII. they are drawn with mitres on their heads, as Fiddes' Life of Wolsey, p. 303. Mitred abbots had episcopal authority within their own limits, and were exempted from the jurisdiction of the diocesan, but were not always summoned to parliament nor necessarily so in consequence of being mitred[4].

Mr. Bridges[5] describes in Wapenham church, near Towcester, in the middle aile, under the pulpit, part of the brass pourtraiture of a religious person, mitred, with a label out of his mouth, inscribed *Ihu, mercy!* and four shields, torn from the corners of the slab.

The rules before mentioned from Anselm's "Palais de l'Honneur," say, "As to what concerns ecclesiastics it is usual to represent them clothed in their sacerdotal habits, the canons with the surplice, square cap, and aumasse or amice; abbots with their mitres and crosiers turned to the left; bishops with their great copes, their gloves on their hands, holding their crosiers with their left hands, and seeming to give the benediction with the right; their mitres on their heads, and their armorial bearings round their tombs, supported by angels. Popes, Cardinals, Patriarchs, and Archbishops, are likewise all represented in their official habits."

The varieties of crosier heads are infinite from the plain one in bishop Grosted's coffin to the highly finished one of bishop Wickham at New College, Oxford. The holy Lamb is usually placed within the circle of the crosier, but in Wykeham's his own figure on his knees.

The abbatial staff was a pastoral crook of the simplest form, barely curled like those of the two antient bishops, and bishop Poore[6], at Salisbury, and the abbots at Peterborough. That of Philip Hawford last abbot of Evesham, in Worcester cathedral, is more like a beadle's staff, without any curve at top; such an one is in bishop Bridport's hands at Salisbury, 1263, and there is no appearance of its having been longer. Bishop Fauconberg, 1228, in Old St. Paul's, has such another, more like a mace than a crosier[7]. An abbess at Elnstow, c. Bedford, has a more ornamented one of the usual form.

"The pastoral staff of the archbishops of Rouen any more than that of antient bishops and abbots, is not bent, as we see it on their tombs, for the last 300 years. It has only on the top a kind of nob *(pomme)* on the top of a cane. In later times it has been represented like a shepherd's crook; and afterwards the end was turned up, as we see at present[8].

There seems no ground for Mr. Gostling's conjecture, that the pastoral staff was derived from the *lituus*[9], the rudest representation approaching nearer to the shepherd's crook.

[1] Falser, II. 7. Patin Sueton. init. Pancirol. Thesaur. Var. Lect. I. 85. Landini Numism. p. 26.
[2] Lebeuf, Hist. de ville & dioc. de Paris, I. 97.
[3] Austis in Appendix to Fiddes' Life of Wolsey, p. 113.
[4] Tan. Not. Mon. Pref. xxvi. n. f.
[5] Northamptonsh. I. 214.
[6] Pl. XII. [7] Dugd. p. 80.
[8] Moleon, Voyage liturgique de France, p. 371. [9] Antiq. Repert. II. 164.

The

The Peterborough abbots, all but one, tread on double or single headed dragons, whom they pierce with their staves, expressive of the triumphs of Christianity over the old serpent; so does the old bishop at Salisbury, and others.

"All the archbishops in Rouen cathedral have their faces turned to the East, like all those that I have seen in other places made before the 16th century, which shews that the contrary custom of burying bishops and priests at present with their face to the West, is altogether modern. The new ritual of Rheims, Sens, Mets, and the Ambrosian, order that they should be buried with their faces to the East, like the laity [1]."

"The new ritual of Rheims, 1677, ordains, that, according to the antient custom, the priests should be buried in the same manner as the laity, so as to have their heads towards the door or bottom of the church, and their feet to the altar; and we see the bishops, abbots, and priests, on the antient tombs so placed [2]."

"Lewis de Bellamonte bishop of Durham, who died 1317, had, before the high altar in the choir a most curious and sumptuous marble stone, which he prepared for himself before he died, being adorned with most excellent workmanship of brass, whereon he was most excellently and lively pictured as he was accustomed to sing or say mass, with his mitre on his head and his crosier staff in his hand, with two angels finely pictured, one on the one side of his head, and the other on the other side, with censers in their hands censing him, and containing also most exquisite pictures and images of the twelve apostles divided and bordered on either side of him; and next them are bordered on each side of the twelve apostles, in another border the pictures of his ancestors in their coats of arms being of the blood royal of France, being a white lion placed upon the breast of his vestment, underneath the *verses* [3] of his breast with flower de luces about the lion, and two lions pictured, one under one foot of him and the other under his other foot, supporting and holding up his crosier staff, his feet adjoining and standing upon the said lions and other two lions beneath them, the nethermost border of all being most artfully wrought and set forth all in brass, manifestly beautifying the said *trough* [4] of marble, wherein was graven in brass such divine sayings of scripture which he had peculiarly selected for his spiritual consolation, at such time as it should please God to call him out of this mortal life; as the following

Epitaphium:

In Gallia natus,
De Bellamonte jacet hic Ludovicus humatus
Nobilis ex fonte regum comitumq' creatus,
Præsul in hac sede cœli lætetur in æde
Præteriens siste, memorans quantus fuit iste,
Cœlo quam dignus, justus, pius, atque benignus,
Dapsilis ac hilaris, inimicus semper avaris.

Super caput:
Credo quod redemptor meus vivit, &c. &c. [5]

In pectore:
Reposita est hæc spes mea in sinu meo.
Domine miserere.

Ad dextram:
Consors sit sanctis Ludovicus in arce Tonantis.

Ad sinistram:
Spiritus ad Christum qui sanguine liberat istum [6]."

[1] Moleon, Voy. lit. p. 173. [2] Ib. [3] Q. *folds?*
[4] Q. *coffin*, or altar tomb, not unfrequently called so in the North of England.
[5] As on bishop Gravesend's, at Lincoln, p. 60. John Hetor, rector of Beaifield and Lufwick, c. Northampton. Bridge, II. 247. and others; also issuing from a scroll on a brass plate of a vicar of St. John's church, Margate. Lewis's Tanet, p. 78. and on the tomb of Thomas Knyghtley, esq. 1516. in Fawsley church, c. Northampton. Bridges, I. 68.
[6] Antiquities of Durham, p. 19, 20.

I the

I the rather insert this at length as, not being now remaining, it could not be mentioned in its proper place, and may serve as no bad specimen of prelatical magnificence: another instance of which may be the larger size of the slabs used to cover their graves. That over bishop Bubwith at Wells, 1309, is called by Godwin *Marmor ingens*. Bishop Longespee's, at Salisbury, 1291, is sixteen feet eight inches by seven feet eight inches. Bishop Gravesend's, at Lincoln, 1279, twelve feet.

"The custom of burying bishops in old times was to bury them with their Alb, Stole, and *Phannel*[1], and their other vestments wherein they used to say mass, a mitre on the head, and a crosier staff in the hand, and so laid in the coffin, with a little chalice of silver, other metal, or *wax*, which wax chalice was gilt finely about the edge, and the knobs in the midst of the shank of the chalice, and about the edge of the patten or cover, and the foot of it also was gilded: which chalice was set upon his breast in the coffin, and its cover nailed down[2]."

Censing angels are not peculiar to bishops: an attitude so grossly misunderstood by some antiquaries that Dr. Salmon mistook their censers for fishing nets in the windows of Stapleford church, Herts. King John has two bishops to do him that kind office, that his evil deeds might acquire a better odour.

These angels are much more common in France, occuring almost in every monument, and on that of archbishop Cherney at Sens two single hands hold the censers.

The conveyance of the soul to heaven in a sheet, by angels, is not unfrequent on the monuments of religious in France from the twelfth to the sixteenth century[3].

Sometimes there, and with us on the pediment of the fine monument on the North side of Beverley choir, the Deity himself places the soul thus on his knees. At the head of a lady at Nanteuil two bishops carry off her soul. The souls of two abbots of Herivaulx, whose figures are on the same stone, are conveyed by angels in one sheet together; so are those of two men and their wives in the Jacobines church at Chalons; and a widow and her two daughters all three together. That of George lord de Preaux in the church of Notre Dame in the castle of Loches is held at his head by a mitred saint, perhaps his patron. The souls of Ansculph and Josceline de Vierey bishops of Soissons in Longport abbey are *pontifically habited* and *mitred*.

It is not unusual on French monuments to see a hand pointing down from heaven over the head of the party, either altogether expanded or with two of the fingers closed, as in the act of benediction: but I do not recollect this in England.

Abbots Eastney, 1438, and Kirton, 1466, are both pontifically habited on their brasses at Westminster. Q. If a mitred abbot drest more pontifically? The last abbot of Pershore is as much undressed, appearing only as a simple monk on his tomb, in the chapel, now the school-house, at Pershore.

Paul, fourteenth abbot of St. Albans, who died 1093, 5 Rufi, and was buried in the chapter house there, was the first that wore the pontifical habit, as his figure on his marble tomb shewed; *primus pontificalibus redimitus (prout in sarcofago suo marmoreo testatur ipsius imago) dignoscitur in hac ecclesia*[4].

"Thomas de Merleberg abbas Evesham primo sculpsit super duas tumbas
"prædecessorum suorum ad honorem et ostensionem dignitatis ecclesiæ imagines
"*episcopales*, et sibi ipsi cum eisdem fecit mausoleum, et incidit in lapide mar-
"moreo superposito imaginem episcopalem ad honorem ecclesiæ. Obiit. A. D.
"1236[5]." The mitre had been obtained by abbot Roger, who died 1160.

[1] Q. Maniple.

[2] Antiquities of Durham abbey, p. 74.

[3] In an old print of a dying man, by C. de Mallory, after Stradun, this conveyance is beautifully touched.

[4] Matt. Par. v. Ab. S. Alb. p. 90

[5] Tanner, Not. Mon. pref. xxv. note (e) ex Histor. Evesham. Bib. Cott. Vesp. B. xxiv. Nash, Worc. I. 399.

The

The oldest original paintings of bishops in their habits of ceremony may be supposed those in the North wall of the old choir at Ely, built in the reign of Edward III. which, before the removal of the choir to its present situation, were copied by Mr. Tyson, 1769, who gave them, 1778, to Mr. Cole. From the last of these gentlemen I received them, for the purpose of having them engraved for this work. The account of them in the old MS *Liber Eliensis* now in the hands of the Dean and Chapter, is in these words: "Isti sunt con-"fessores Christi quorum corpora jacent ex parte aquilonari chori ecclesie Eliensis "in loculis separatim in pariete lapideo. *Wlstanus* Eboracensis archiepiscopus, "*Osmundus* epus Swetheda regione, *Helfwinus* Helmamensis epus, *Elfgarus* Hel-"mamensis epus, *Ednodus* abbas Ramysiensis epus Lincolniensis, *Adthelstanus* "Helmamensis epus, *Brithnodus* dux Northanimbrorum strenuissimus." They were brought thither from the old conventual church in the reign of Stephen by Nigellus bishop of Ely, and their names were legible over their painted effigies [1]. They were found on taking down the wall. The manner of their disposition was exactly conformable to the above account, the bones of each being placed in separate cells, each cell twenty-two inches long, seven broad, and eighteen deep, within the wall, under their several names and painted effigies, each figure two feet five inches and three quarters high. They were put, 1771, into distinct cases, and deposited under the arch of bishop West's tomb in his chapel, with their names and dates painted on the front [2], over a row of small Gothic niches of stone corresponding with the cells, and an inscription over all.

Over fig.

1. Wlstanus epus Helmamensis.
2. Osmundus ep's [in Suetheda regione]
3. Alwin' epus Helmamensis.
4. Elfgar epus Helmamensis.
5. Ednodus ep's Lyncolniensis.
6. Athelstanus ep's Helmam'sis.
7. Brythnodus dux Northanymphrorum.

Among the monuments of Danish nobility [3], published by Klerenfeld, is a brass one of an archbishop, 1497, at Lunden, pontifically habited, with a double fringe to his stole, like archbishop Langton, and on his albe a flower as on that of Cardiff. His arms and hands are crost, in his right a cross; and at his right elbow a crosier. The helmets on his arms are surmounted by a crosier. The inscription round the tomb is in our common black letter, between a double border of vine branches, and at the corners the symbols of the evangelists with labels.

> Hic. jacet. reverendiss'. i. x'. pater. dn̄s. dn̄s. Joh̄'s. brostroup. di. grā. quondā. arep' lūde. suecie. p'mas. et. aplice. sed'. legat'. vo. decretoru. bacal ". cui'. a'a. requiescat. i. pace ij. d. ā. dn̄i. m' c d 97.

A brass figure of a priest in Great Adington church, c. Northampton [4], has on his breast IHC, perhaps the host. Another so early as 1286, at Higham Ferrars in the same county [5], **Fili Dei miserere mei.**

John Grothurst rector of Horsmanden church in Kent has behind his elevated hands a scroll reciting his gift to Beyham abbey.

> **Qui dedit mancrium de Leveshothe abbati et conventui de Beghamme ad inveniendum unum perpetuum capellanum celebrantem in ecclesia de Horsmondenne et capella de Loveshothe** [6].

[1] Bentham's Ely, 85. [2] Ib. 285, 286. Archaeol. II. 365.
[3] "Nobilitas Daniae ex monumentis curante T. de Klerenfeld." 15 fol. plates.
[4] Bridges, II. 205. [5] Ib. 175. [6] Thorpe, Reg. Roff. p. 881.

Chaucer

Fig. 1.
Fig. 2.
Fig. 3.
Fig. 4.
Fig. 5.
Fig. 6.
Fig. 7.

Figures of priests in stone are not unfrequent under arches in the walls of village-churches. They are supposed founders or rebuilders, and they may have been incumbents or chantry priests, or perhaps relations of the lords of the manor, or otherwise connected with the place. They seldom have any inscriptions. Such a figure in the wall of the South aile of St. Hippolyt's church near Hitchen is vulgarly called *St. Hippolyt* himself. Salmon conjectures he was the founder [1].

On the North side of the chancel at Lilford, c. Northampton, is such an antique freestone figure who, from his habit and tonsure of his head, appears to have been a priest [2].

Next to the ecclesiastics rank the students or graduates of our universities, whose habits may be seen on their monuments in the several college chapels. Perhaps the largest collection of them is in the outer chapel at New College, Oxford. I have engraved one specimen in the brass ascribed to Robert Egglesfield, founder of Queen's college there, 1349, which represents a priest in a cap and rich rochet, powdered with fleurs de lis and lozenges, and faced and hemmed with a different border, and fastened on his breast with a jewel: the sleeves of his black gown are faced with fur [3]. In Dowdeswell church, c. Gloucester, Mr. Rudder describes a figure in a long robe semée with mullets and fleurs de lis, but which is the exact counterpart of Eglesfield only smaller. A Kentish priest, engraved by Mr. Thorpe, has exactly such a habit, except the cap and the different ornament on the breast. Indeed priests are oftener thus represented and distinguished by the tonsure, than vested for the altar, as is the phrase of our describers from Aubrey to the present time.

Hacomblen in King's College Chapel has the like habit, with a furred cape, reaching down to his elbows, his head bare, and crown shaved.

John Perch, A. M. M. B. in Queen's College, Oxford, has his gown fastened by a buckle with the St. Suaire, and faced with ornaments like fleurs de lis, sleeves to his wrist under very long ones almost to his feet, and a kind of long tippet over all. Another brass figure in the antechapel has the like habit, the inner sleeves longer, the gown faced with sprigs of roses, fastened by a rich studded broche, the fur tippet round his neck and pendant, a sizar's cap on his cropt hair.

The poor Oxford scholar's *overest courtesy*, or uppermost short cloke, of coarse cloth, was "thred bare [4]."

At the installation feast of Richard Clifford bishop of London, 1407, was a subtylte of a doctor in a pulpit, in a clothynge of *grene* taberde and hode with a rolle on his hede, and thereon written, *In Deo salutari meo* [5].

Chaucer's spruce parish clerk Absolom had

> Poules windows corven on his shoes [6].

i. e. They were reticulated or laced with fret work.

> In hosen red he went ful fetisly.
> Yclad he was ful smal and properly,
> All in a kertle of a light waget [7],
> Ful faire & thick ben the pointis set,
> And therupon he had a gay surplice,
> As white as is the blome upon the rise [8].

[1] Herts, p. 182.
[2] Bridges II. 243.
[3] Pl. XXXVI. p. 102.
[4] Canterb. Tales, l. 292.
[5] Noble boke of Cookery.
[6] Ubi sup. 3315—23.
[7] *watchet*, blue.
[8] Millar's Tale, l. 3318.

 The

The only clafs of laymen, except the military, feem to have been *Burgeffes* and *Merchants of the Staple*. Thefe are chiefly to be found in borough towns, or the parochial churches of large commercial counties where the woollen manufacture flourifhed. What a profufion of workmanfhip was difplayed on their monuments appears by thofe of the mayor or burgefs of Lynne, the clothiers of Campden and North Leach, and other inftances in the wealthy counties of Norfolk, Suffolk, and Gloucefter.

The firft inftance I have to give of a lay habit of a burgefs is that of Sir William Delapole father of the firft earl of Suffolk of that name [1], who, on his tomb at Hull, is habited in a cloak with a ftanding cape and buttons in equi-diftant fets of three, over a clofe coat open at the knees, and buttoned at the waift with the fame arrangement, and with a full row on the clofe fleeves, which before they reached the wrifts had fome kind of plait or ornament. At an ornaméntcd girdle hangs by a plain belt a couteau. He wears his hair, forked beard, whifkers, and fhoes. His wife over her tunic has a gown buttoned to the waift, and from thence open below; the fleeves clofe and buttoned to the back of the hands, and over her fhoulders, paffing under her arms, a loofe cloak; over her head a veil headdrefs.

The next is the burgefs of Lynne, with a more fplendid monument of brafs [2], habited in a plain clofe coat flit and turned back from the knees downwards, and laced on the flit and hem, with long clofe fleeves buttoned from the elbows to the wrift, and long hanging fleeves from the elbows; ftanding cape open in front fallen down; ftockings dark and coarfe; his pointed fhoes faftened on the inftep with a lace or latchet. The five men at the fide of the canopy are habited one in a fhort coat buttoned in front with long hanging fleeves, piked fhoes, one with the hofe, a hat faftened as an hood under the chin: the fecond in a like fhort coat girt with a belt, and a fhort cloak over the fhoulders; a hooded cap on the head; the third a long cloak buttoned on the breaft whence the hands juft iffue: the fourth a fhort cloak buttoned on the breaft, and plaited at the fkirts, which do not reach to the knees; the fifth is in a coat, and cloak only over the left fhoulder, and held up to the waift: thefe two laft have the hooded hat, and all have the piked fhoes and hofe of one piece.

John chatelain of Thorote and his wife, 1325 and 1353, in Orcamp abbey, very much refemble this burgefs and his two wives.

The principal figures of the men at the feaft below are habited in long cloaks over clofe coats with fleeves, hooded hats or caps [3].

It has been fuggefted to me by an ingenious friend, that the muficians, who are two men blowing trumpets, and a little boy with a pipe, appear as if fewn up clofe in leather dreffes, to fhew the fhape of the bodies; a circumftance he has heard or read, not unufual in great entertainments.

Robert Attelathe, another burgefs of this wealthy corporation, is my third example [4]. He is habited in a cloak with a ftanding cape, falling off his right fhoulder and over his left arm, covering a clofe coat girt round the waift, and buttoned from a little above the girdle down to the inftep, with buttons in pairs. The fleeves of this coat are buttoned at the wrift, and on the back of the hands is a half-glove of a rich flowered pattern. His fhoes are piked, and faftened on the inftep, with a buckle. He wears his hair in buckles, fhort whifkers, and a fhort divided beard.

John Fountain, who died 1403, is reprefented on his brafs at Narford in a long plaited coat girt about his waift, with a broad belt, a ftanding cape, and on his head a round cap like a bowl. His three wives have the long plaited gown

[1] Pl. XLVI p. 121.   [2] Pl. XLV. p. 115.

[3] So Chaucer defcribes his merchant, "And on his hed he wore a *Flaundrifh bever* hat." Ubi fup. 371.

[4] Pl. XXXVI. p. 101.

with

with a broad belt at the waist, and standing capes, and two have on their head the latest imitation of the mitred headdress with the falling veil, and the third has the veil only.

The first of these instances was the very *Frankelein* of Chaucer [1]:

> An *anelace* and a *gipciere* all of silk
> Hung at his girdle white as morwe milk;
> A shereve had he ben and a contour;
> Was no where swich a worthy vavasour.
> At sessions ther was he lord and sire,
> Ful often time he was knight of the shire.

The *anelace* was a knife or dagger usually worn at the girdle. Matthew Paris [2] describes Peter de Rivaulx as "gestans *anelacium ad lumbare quod clericum non decebat*." The five city mechanics in Chaucer [3] are described as wearing knives, and probably at their girdles.

> Hir knives were *ychaped not with bras*,
> But all with silver wrought full clene and wel;
> Hir girdeles and hir pouches every del.

See a very good representation of one at the left side of the girdle of William Grevel at Campden.

This at the side of a brass figure in Baldock church before described has a lesser knife inserted in its scabbard.

Occleve's picture of Chaucer represents him with a knife hanging from a button on his breast, probably a *Sheffield whittle*.

The ship-man had

> A dagger hanging by a *las* [lace]
> About his neck under his arm adoune [4].

On such a weapon we may suppose the king-making earl of Warwick's roast beef was carried away by his guests. With such an one the earl Marshall was stabbed in the back by an Irishman, who lifted up his coat of mail [5] and plunged his anelace up to the hilt [6].

The *gipciere*, Fr. *Gibeciere*, was a purse; of which hereafter.

Chaucer's character of his tradesmen in their livery-men's gowns, is, that they were fit to make aldermen;

> Wel semed eche of hem a fayre burgeis
> To sitten in a gild halle on the deis [7].

i. e. at the upper end of the hall on the hustings or raised floor, as now at the Guildhall of the city of London, and in college halls, and formerly in all halls.

The Knight's son the Squire in Chaucer [8] was,

> a lusty bachelor
> With lockes *crull as they were laide in presse*,
> Short was his gowne with sleves long and wide.

The Physician in Chaucer,

> In sanguin and in perse he clad was alle
> Lined with taffata and with sendalle [9].

[1] Ubi sup. l. 357—362.
[2] P. 405.
[3] Ubi sup. l. 367—370.
[4] Ib. l. 393.
[5] *loricam sublevando*.
[6] Mat. Paris, p. 400.
[7] Ubi sup l. 371.
[8] Ib. l. 80, 81. 93.
[9] Ib. l. 441.

The

The habit of a Judge may be feen on the monument of Gafcoigne, at Harwood, c. York. He appears in a robe or mantle, with long puffed fleeves edged with ermine, and under them ftrait fleeves buttoned to the wrift, over a tunic girt with a belt ftudded with rofes, whereat hangs his *anelace* or dagger, and under his left elbow his purfe. On his head and fhoulders is a coif covering his ears, which appears through, and falling in a flap at the fides of his face, his hair juft feen under it.

Chaucer's Sergeant of the Law ware and wife,

> He rode but homely, in a medlee cote,
> Girt with a *feint* [1] of filk, with barres fmall [2].

The Alderman's robes occur on the brafs figure of Jeffrey Qwynfy, 1461, in the church of St. Clement the Martyr, at Norwich [3].

The habit of a Sheriff of London, 1381, fee in John Lions, p. 137.

Stowe [4], fpeaking of the proceedings of the infurgents under Wat Tyler in the reign of Richard II. fays, "They took in hand to behead all men of law, as well apprentices as utter barrifters and old juftices, with all the jurors of the country whom they might get into their hands. They fpared none whom they thought to be learned, efpecially if they found any to *have a pen and inkhorne about him*: they pulled off his hood, and all with one voyce crying, Hale him out, and cut off his head." A tomb in the North tranfept at Chrift Church, Oxford, of the 16th century, has an inkhorn and pen-cafe in compartments at the front and fides, and nothing elfe remaining to afcertain it.

Chaucer's Millar (who was alfo a thief),

> A white cote & a blew hode wered he [5],
> A fwerd & bokeler bare he by his fide [6].

and the Reve got his mafter's thanks,

> and yet a cote and hood.
> A long furcote of perfe upon he hade,
> And by his fide he bare a rufty blade;
> Tucked he was, as is a frere about [7].

Of the Millar of Trumpington Chaucer fays,

> Ay by his belt he bare a long pavade,
> And of a fwerd ful trenchant was the blade;
> A joly popper bare he in his pouche,
> Ther as no man for peril dare him touch;
> A Shefeld thwitel bare he in his hofe [8].

Pavade is a dagger, *popper* a bodkin, *thwitel* a knife. They are all ranged together as the Miller's defenfive weapons, and whoever affronted or attacked him,

> he wold be flain of Simkin
> With *pavade*, or with *knife*, or with *bodkin* [9].

Thus the poet explains himfelf.

[1] *Ceinture*, girdle. [2] Canterb. Tales, l. 330. [3] Blomef. II. 818.
[4] Lond. p. 48. [5] Ubi fup. l. 566. [6] Ib. l. 560. [7] Ib. l. 614. 619, 620. 623.
[8] Reve's Tale, l. 3917–31. [9] Ib. l. 3957—9.

On

On holidays the miller wore "his tipet ybounde about his hed" & *red* stock-"ings. His wife's *gite* or gown was of the same colour[1]; so was the wife of Bathe's[2].

Chaucer's friar's tippet was,

ay farsed full of knyves
And pinnes for to given fayre wives[3].
For there was he not like a cloisterere,
With thredbare cope as is a poure scolore;
But he was like a maister or a pope;
Of *double worsted* was his *semicope*
That round was as a belle out of the presse[4].

Chaucer's knight's yeoman

Was cladde in cote and hode of grene,
A shefe of *peacock* arwes bright & kene
Under his belt he bare full thriftily.
Wel coude he dresse his takel yemanly.
His arwes drouped not with fetheres lowe,
And in his hond he bare a mighty bowe.
A not-hedde had he with a broun visage;
Of wood-craft coude he well alle the usage.
Upon his arm he bare a gaie bracer,
And by his side a swerd and bokeler,
And on that other side a gaie daggere,
Harneised well and sharpe as point of spere;
A cristofre on his brest of silver shene
An horne he bare, the baudrick was of grene,
A forster was he sothely, as I gesse[5].

A figure cumbent on a gravestone in the churchyard at Glinton, c. Northampton, might serve as an illustration of this description:

His gay yeman under a forest ride,
A bow he bare, and arwes bright and kene
He had upon a courtepy of grene.
An hat upon his head, with frenges blacke[6].

They had also about that time, says Camden[7], a gown called a *git*, a jacket without sleeves called a *baketon*, a loose jacket like a *tabard*, a short *gabbardin* called a *court pie*, a *gorget* called a *chevesail*, for as yet they used not bands about their neck, a pouch called a *gipser*.

The *Gite* was a woman's gown. See Chaucer's Canterbury Tales, l. 3952. 6141.

The *Haketon* was part of a military habit, and as such worn by the dainty Sir Thopas:

He didde next his white lere
Of cloth of lake fin & clere
A breche and eke a sherte,
And next his shirt an haketon,
And over that an habergeon,
For percing of his herte,
And over that a fin hauberk
Was all ywrought of jewel work;

[1] Chaucer, Ib. l. 3950—1—2.
[2] Ib. l. 261.
[3] Ib. l. 6141.
[4] Ubi sup. l. 103—118.
[5] Canterb. Tales, l. 233, 234.
[6] Ib. 6562.
[7] Rem. p. 234.

The

Ful ſtrong it was of plate :
And over that his cote-armoure,
(As white as is the lily floure)
In which he wold debate [1].

Mr. Tyrwhitt obſerves, it is difficult to ſay what ſort of cloth is meant by *lake* here. *Laccken*, Belg. ſignifies both *linen* and *woollen* cloth. Kilian.

The *Tabard* was worn by the nobility and gentry in the reigns of Henry IV. and V. It was a ſhort coat, without ſleeves, as ſtill worn by the heralds, on which their arms were embroidered : whence the term, a *coat of arms*; Fr. *cotte d'armes*. The coat having the creſt in profile was the ſleeve or ſide coat. It is often found in portraitures in old glaſs-windows [2]. In Queen's College, Oxford, are ſcholars called *Taberders*, who wore ſuch an habit. Before the civil war the ſcholars of New College were obliged to wear a black tabbard of ſtuff and a ruff when they went abroad. Scholars of other houſes wore them, as alſo pilgrims anticntly [3]. Chaucer's plowman rode in a tabard, and perhaps our ploughmen's ſhort coats ſtill keep up the reſemblance.

The *Courtepy* was the ſhort cloke before mentioned worn by the Oxford ſcholar and by the gay yeoman [4]. It is a Teutonic word, from *kort*, curtus, and *piie*, penula coactilis ex villis craſſioribus. Kilian, Tyrrwhit.

The *Chevesail* is a necklace in the Roman de la Roſe, l. 2189, faſtened by two gold claſps ; and ſo tranſlated in Chaucer's verſion of it, l. 1082. Camden ſeems to have imagined it a cape.

The *Gipſer*, or, as Chaucer calls it, by its French name, *Gipciere*; DuCange, *Gibaſſarius*, and Charpentier *Gibacaria*, was a purſe; of which we have various inſtances on our monuments. Perhaps judge Gaſcoigne's is the faireſt. Montfaucon has engraved in his Monuments [5] a ſplendid one of the princes of Dreux and Britany, embroidered with their arms, from the collection of M. de Gagnieres, who ſays it was appropriated to reliques. The chimney piece of the principal room in Tatterſal tower is adorned with purſes, in alluſion to the poſt of lord high treaſurer held by Ralph lord Cromwell, who died 1455. " Bagges or purſes" remained in Leland's time [6], in the chapel and other places of the houſe at Collyweſton, which belonged to the ſame nobleman.

At the foot of Vitaille de Query, knight, ſerjeant, 1400, and his wife, on their tomb, in Froidmont abbey, are five figures of men ; two are religious, with hoods fallen ; two of them have the purſes, and hoods on their heads, not unlike Chaucer's : the others are laymen, in coats girt with belts. The ſerjeant himſelf is in a furred gown ſlit up to the knee in front, girt round with a belt on which is the arms of France and a crowned ſhield, pouch ſleeves furred at the wriſts, and under them a buttoned ſleeve ; his cape fallen diſcovers ſomething like a ruff, or plaited collar : his half-boots are laced on the inſide of his legs.

Simonet, ſon of the vicomte du Bois, 1354, on his tomb at Bonport abbey, Normandy, has a ſhort coat to his knees, long waiſted, and full buttoned, long ſleeves buttoned to wriſt, and ſleeves pendant, a falling cape edged with an embattlement, and at his belt a pouch with four buttons and a lock.

John Hannetay, merchant, 1479, in Vauluiſant abbey, has a purſe wider than long, with two taſſels at the ends and one in the middle.

John Clerk, prieſt, at Baſildon, Berks, 1496, has a pouch at his right ſide, and a roſary at his left ; a furred gown and cap [7].

A man at Nanteuil has a very ſmall purſe.

[1] Ubi ſup. l. 137. 90. [2] Aubrey. [3] Ib. [4] Canterb. Tales, 6964. [5] II. pl. xxxi. [6] It. I. 25. [7] Aubrey.

A man

A man in Brunoy church in the Isle de France has a long coat with buttoned sleeves, and five buttons like a lapell on the left shoulder.

Such is also appendant to the figure of Henry I. fourth duke of Lorrain and Brabant on his tomb in St. Peter's church at Lovain. A great chamberlain of France of this time has one of the same kind at his girdle. The custom of wearing the purse at the girdle came from the Eastern nations, where it still obtains, and did in Europe till pockets were invented, which seem a consequence of short skirts of tighter bodied garments. These purses were of leather, or more costly materials.

Some judgement may be formed of the first *coats* from the pictures of Chaucer, and one of Nyte, in the chancel window of Kington St. Michael, as well as from the monuments of burgesses before described. They were loose down to the calf of the leg, with wide sleeves, and succeeded gowns gathered at the girdle [1].

The coat, long as the oldest fashioned ones of the present century, with buttons down to the toes, appears on the figures at the sides of lady Montacute's tomb at Christ Church, Oxford; of that of Thomas Vere earl of Oxford, at Earl's Colne; of Thomas Beauchamp earl of Warwick; of Edward III. &c. On the brass of Braunch, and on the tomb of Edward III. we have both the long and the short coat.

The tomb of Thomas Beauchamp earl of Warwick furnishes the greatest varieties of habits for both sexes of any that I know of. With this view I got Mr. Carter to make the separate drawings of each figure in Pl. LI. though I could have wished he had succeeded better with them. There are the mantle, flowing, buttoned on the breast, or on the shoulder, with one or more buttons, or thrown across like the Roman Paludamentum, and with or without the hood; the long coat buttoned to the waist; the short coat united with the hose, and the buttons continued below the waist, the cape standing or fallen, the hood, hat, or bonnet; the shoe of different lengths.

Alan Fleming at Newark, 1373, is drest in a close coat with a standing cape, and slits for pocket holes: his sleeves are long and close, and his mantle faced with miniver.

If we can depend on the portrait of Charles the Good, thirteenth count of Flanders, in Montfaucon, II. pl. XI. the close coat with buttons and the standing cape will have been in fashion so early as 1127, in which year that prince was murdered.

The coat of Thibans Plante Oignum, bourgeois de Biauves, in Chaalis abbey cloister, is slit at the sides and in front, and faced with miniver.

In Barbeau abbey is a figure of Peter le Maire, 1353, in a coat with long buttoned sleeves issuing from others at the elbows, and pocket holes: his wife has a pointed hood, and her mantle is faced like it, with miniver, long buttoned sleeves and pocket holes.

"In the beginning of Henry the Fourth's reign the fashions of dress were extravagant, especially of gowns with deep wide sleeves, commonly called *Pokys*, shaped like *bagpipes*, and worn indifferently both by servants and masters. They may rightly be called "the devil's receptacles: for whatever could be stolen was popt into them: some of them were so large and wide that they reacht down to the feet, or at least to the knees, full of slits and devils. When the servants were bringing up pottage, sauces, or any other liquors, these sleeves went into the dishes, and had the first taste: and all that was given them, or that they could get, was spent to clothe their uncurable carcases with these *pokys* or sleeves, while the rest of the habit was cut short [2].

[1] Aubrey.

[2] Vita Rich. II. 172. In primordio hujus regis excrescebat nimis insolentia indumentorum in *regno* & maxime togatorum cum profundis & latis manicis vocatis vulgariter *pokys* ad modum *bagpipe* formatis adeo ut eis tam a servis quam dominis indifferenter utebatur. Quæ quidem receptacula dæmoniorum recte dici &c.

The

The long pocketting ſleeves, as Camden calls them [1], continued in uſe in the reign of Henry IV. which Occleve ſays "pennileſſe groomes" might clear the ſtreets of their dirt. Such were in vogue in Edward the Firſt's reign, as appears by the figures on the ſide of John of Eltham's tomb, both men and women.

The monk's ſleeves in Chaucer [2]:

> Purſiled at the hond
> With *gris*, and that the fineſt of the lond.

Gris was a ſpecies of furr; of which and of miniver hereafter.

Richard de Boſco abbot of Eſtrees in Normandy has his arms croſt, hanging down in his ſleeves, which come over his hands. One of the ſuite of Louis de Bruges, in the reign of Charles VIII. in Montfaucon IV. Pl. IV. has ſuch a ſleeve over his left hand.

Our hat is derived by Skinner from the Teutonic and Dutch *Hoed* and *Hat*, and that from *Hoeden* and *Hatten*, to preſerve; as if no other part of dreſs was a defence. It was a ſuccedaneum to the *Hood*, and the Saxon ꝥæt was a covering of the head from the tiara and mitre to the modern round hat, which is but a diminitive of the cardinal's red hat on Luxemburg's tomb and Wolſey's college. The Malays and Chineſe, and all Aſiatics who wear hats, have them round; ſuch is even the *turban*. Varro derives the Roman *Galerus*, which Iſidore calls a ſhepherd's bonet, from *Galea*. In Juvenal [3], and other writers, it is equivalent to a wig or falſe hair. Chaucer wears on his head a hood falling down behind. His monk's

> For to faſten his hood under his chinne,
> He hadde of gold ywrought a curious pin [4].

The bonets of Peter count d'Alençon and Robert count de Clermont, in Montfaucon [5], are of different forms: that of St. Louis [6] is very like a modern hat: thoſe of Louis XI. and Philip le Hardi duke of Burgundy [7] are bonets of particular orders. See alſo thoſe of the orders of St. Michael, inſtituted by Louis XII [8]. That of the order of the Creſcent, inſtituted by Rene king of Sicily, is an abſolute hat [9]; ſo is alſo that of Charles VII [10].

John Edwards, *apprenticiatus in lege*, 1461, in Rodmerton church, c. Glouceſter, has a cap like that of the Preſident *au mortier*. Rudder [11] ſays he is habited in the antient dreſs of a lawyer.

The form of the half-boot may be ſeen on a braſs figure in Copel church, c. Bedford. The boot ſeems to have been faſtened at the ſide with claſps, like our ſpatterdaſhes. The merchant's in Chaucer were

> "—— clapſed fayre and fetiſly [12]."

Somewhat like the ſhoes beforementioned, p. clvii. were the *Campaga* and *Reticuli* of the Roman emperors and nobility mentioned by Trebellius Pollio and Julius Capitolinus, and deſcribed by Salmaſius as ſo called from the flexibility of the ſtraps that faſtened them, and from the net-work which they formed on the leg. The *Reticulum*, or ſhoe, of the Roman ladies was ſet with emeralds [13]: "Patriciorum calcei et imperatorum ita vocabantur a corrigiarum flexuris et implicaturis quibus circumligabantur. Hinc campacos *reticulos* appellare ſolebat Gallienus, quod reticulaturis decuſſaturiſque multis circum crura flexuris aliis ſuper alias ſcandentibus connecterentur. Hinc Latinis *campacus* ejuſmodi calceus appellatus qui multas *καμπας* et decuſſes in calceanda faceret ex corrigiarum alligaturis [14]."

[1] Rem. 235. [2] Ubi ſup. 191. [3] VI. 120. [4] Canterb. Tales, l. 195. [5] II. xxvii. 8. 9. [6] Ib. II. [7] Ib. III. lxii. 1, 2, 4. [8] Ib. lxi. [9] Ib. xlviii. [10] Ib. xlvi. [11] P. 635. [12] Ubi ſup. l. 275. [13] Maximin. jun. c. 1. [14] Salmaſius in Capitolini vita Maximini jun. c. 2.

I have

I have met with no fatisfactory reafon why the Conqueror's eldeft fon, Robert, had the name of *Curthofe*; or Henry II. that of *Court mantel*. Camden [1] fays, the former ufed the fhort hofe, or, as Trevifa, in one part of his tranflation of the Polychronicon, has it, *Short boot*, though in another he writes *Short hofes*. But as the Saxon drawings prove thefe were antiently ufed by the Englifh, Mr. Strutt thinks it more likely Robert fet the fafhion to his Normans; and in the fame manner he accounts for Henry the Second's fobriquet, that he was the firft Norman prince who adopted the Saxon fhort cloak.

The drefs of young perfons may be reprefented on the monument of Edward the Firft's infant children in Weftminfter-abbey. The boy has his flowing locks bound with a fillet, a mantle faftened by four ftuds on his right fhoulder, a doublet, a richly ftudded belt, breeches and ftockings of one piece, and fhoes feparate. The girl has a horned headdrefs, boddice ftudded in front, and a petticoat, a mantle tied by a cordon, with a rofe and two quatrefoils ftudded [2].

See alfo the drefs of William of Hatfield fecond fon of Edward III. on his monument in York minfter before defcribed p. cxxxvi.

Henry Prince of Wales, afterwards Henry V. when he went to make his peace with his father, was apparalled, fays Holinfhed [3], in a gown of blue fattin full of fmall oeillet holes, at every hole the needle hanging by a filk thread, with which it was worked; about his arms he wore an hound's collar fet ful of SS of gold, and the tyrrets likewife of the fame metal.

Henry VI. at his wedding is reprefented in a rich flowered robe with long cuffed fleeves, through which his arms come out; his hair long and lank, in his right hand a cap, not unlike that of Philip de Valois, before mentioned. His bride has a mantle faftened on the breaft by a cordon and jewels, a robe, on whofe hem in a frame of jewels are letters embroidered, her fleeves long, the cuffs drawn over the fingers of the left, but the right hand clear; her hair flowing, a coronet on her head. Mr. Walpole thinks the painter has conveyed a reflection on her virginity inconfiftent with the long hair [4]. The nimbus fignifies the king's fanctity at his death.

Edward earl of Rutland, the lord Spencer, earl of Arundel, and others, the lords appellants who impeached the duke of Gloucefter before Richard II. at Nottingham, were clad in red gowns of filk, garded and bordered with white filk, and *embroidered with letters of gold* [5]. Round the hem of the Queen's robe in the picture of Henry the Sixth's marriage in Mr. Walpole's poffeffion, are fome letters, which are far from being fo intelligible as the other before mentioned. The words are involved in the folds; what appears are, *Vol. falv. Regin.* On the abbefs's girdle is *Vel ave*, as little to be decyphered as the other. There is a third inftance of letters on garments on the robe of the Emperor Charles IV. on his interview with Charles V. of France, 1378 [6]. Charles VI. of France, 1422. has the hem of his robe, on his tomb at St. Denis, charged with *Jamais* repeatedly. An Etrufcan ftatue in bronze in Dempfter's Etruria Regalis [7], has three lines of infcription on the hem of his robe. There are traces of letters down the front of a lady's garment, on a monument at Weft Tanfield in Yorkfhire. Thofe on the pall of bifhop Roger at Salifbury are rather part of his epitaph. The Grand Falconer of Charles VIII. of France has his initials on his fword hilt [8].

[1] P. 132. [2] Pl. XXXIV. [3] P. 1160.
[4] Anecdotes of Painting, I. 38.
[5] Chron. 316. in Parl. Hift. I. 495. Peck's Annals of Stamford, 11. 59. Walp. Anec. of Paint. I. 38, 4to. In the reign of Edward III. fays an old chronicle in Mr. Ives's poffeffion, cited by Mr. Strutt, the Englifhe men were clothede all in cootes and hodes peynted with lettres and with floures." Ποµπα Angelcynnan, II. 83.
[6] Montf. Mon. III. x. p. 40. [7] I. 281. [8] Montfaucon IV. Pl. iv.

Henry VI. according to Stow [1], usually wore a cap or hood of red velvet, which was afterwards preserved a long time on his tomb. His high cap of astete, called *Abococket*, or *Abococke*, was garnished with two rich crowns [2].

The beau of Edward the Third's time was a party-coloured animal. He wore hose of one colour on one leg, and of another on the other; short breeches which did not reach half way down his thighs; a coat half white, half black or blue; a long beard; a silk hood, buttoned under his chin; and embroidered with grotesque figures of armorial dancing men, &c. and sometimes ornamented with gold, silver, and precious stones [3].

When the rioters plundered and burnt the duke of Lancaster's palace at the Savoy they took his most precious garment, such, says Walsingham [4], as we call a *Jacke*, and stuck it on a spear, as a mark for their arrows, and when they found they could not damage it sufficiently by shooting at it, they chopped it in pieces with swords and hatchets.

The showy luxurious habit of a Gascon Knight, to whom Francis de la Marque, a French gentleman, presents his history of the latter part of the reign of Richard II. [5] deserves attention. When the knights were not clad in armour they wore a dress that seems to have more than Asiatic softness and effeminacy [6]. In the same MS the long pointed shoes of that reign, before described, are particularly expressed [7]; and it is remarkable, that in the drawing of Rutland's resignation to Henry IV. from a MS of Froissart in the royal library, (xviii E. II.) the fashion is altered, and the toes shortned [8]. Joan countess of Kent, mother of Richard II. wears them [9]; and they appear to have been revived in the reign of Edward IV [10]. Those of Edward III. and his two royal prisoners, David king of Scotland, and John king of France, are broad, but picked, and embroidered with net work [11].

We may suppose the figure painted in Hungerford's chapel at Salisbury represents a beau or gallant of the reign of Henry VI.

In the year 1369, 44 Edward III. "as the book of Worcester reported, they began to use caps of divers colours, especially red, with costly linings: and 1372, 47 Edward III. they first began to wanton it in a new round curtall weed, which they called a cloak, and in Latin *armilausa*, as only covering the shoulders; and this notwithstanding the king had endeavored to restrain all these inordinances and expences in clothing by act of parliament in his 36th year, forbidding the use of gold and silver, and other ornaments, to all who could not afford to spend £10 a year; and all furr and precious costly apparel to all who could not spend £100 a year [12]".

The author of the Eulogium cited by Camden [13] says, "the commons were besotted in excess of apparell, in wide surcoates reaching to their loines, some in a garment reaching to their heeles, close before, and strutting out on the sides, so that on the back they make men seem women; and this they called by a ridiculous name *gowne*; their hoods are little, tied under the chin, and buttoned like the women's, but set with gold, silver, and precious stones; their *lirripoppes* [14] reach to their heeles, all jagged. They have

[1] Chron. p 421. [2] Grafton, p. 662. Hollinsh. 1312. See Spelman in voce.
[3] Camden's Rem. p. 194.
[4] Ibid. p 249.
[5] MS. Harl 1319. [6] Strut, pl. xx. p. 16. [7] Ib. pl. xix. [8] Ib. pl. xxxii.
[9] Ib. pl. xxxv. from a Register of Benefactors to St. Alban's abbey. Nero, D. VII.
[10] Ib. pl. xlvi. [11] Ib. pl. lxii. liv.
[12] Omne ornamentum aureum sive argenteum erat damnatum nisi in talibus qui possint per annum expendere 10 libras, et ut nulli pannis pretiosis aut pilleis uterentur nisi qui possent expendere per annum 100 libras. Walsingh. v. E. III. p. 171. The continuation of Adam of Murimuth's hist. says 40 lib. which is most likely. Strutt II. 84.
[13] Remains, p. 233.
[14] A tippet round the neck, hanging down before. See Harl. MS. 219.

another

another weed of filk, which they call a *paltock*[1]: their hofe are of two colours, or pied with more[2], with white lachets, which they called *beclots*, they tie to their paltocks, without any breeches. Their girdles are of gold and filver, fome worth twenty marks: their fhoes and pattens are fnowted and piked more than a finger long, crooking upwards, which they call *crackowes*, refembling the devil's claws, and faftened to the knees with chains of gold and filver."

Chaucer[3] alfo makes the fame complaint cenfuring "the coft of enbrouding, the difguyfing, endenting, or barring, ounding, paling, wynding, or bending, and femblable wafte of clothe in vanitie: the coftlewe furringe in hir gounes fo much pounfoing of *chefel* to make holes, fo much dagging of fheres, with the fuperfluite in length of the forefed gounes trailing in the dong and myre on hors and eke on foot, as well of man as of woman, that all thilke trayling is verely as in effect wafted, confumed, thred bare, and rotten with dong.— Upon the other fide, to fpeak of the horible difordinate fcantynefs of clothing as bene thefe cutted *floppes* or *hanfelines*[4], that thro their fhortnes cover not the fhameful membres of men." He proceeds to inveigh againft the party-coloured hofe departed in white and red.

Petrarch, in his letter to the Pope, 1366[5], expreffes the fame indignation at the monftrous fantaftical fafhions which his contemporaries had invented to deform, rather than adorn, their perfons: the long pointed fhoes, the caps with feathers, the hair twifted and hanging down with tails, the foreheads of the young men, as well as women, formed into furrows, with ivory headed pins, their bellies fqueezed with cords, and the indecent parts of their drefs offenfive to every modeft eye.

Harding, in his Chronicle, c. 193. f. 194. rebukes, in as ftrong terms, the wafte of materials in the expenfive fafhions of this reign.

> Ther was great pride among the officers,
> And of all men furpaffyng their compiers,
> Of riche aray, and much more coftious
> Then was before or fith, and more pretious.
> Yomen and gromes in cloth of filke arayed,
> Sattyn and damafke in the oublettes and gounes
> In cloth of grene and fcarlet for unpayed
> Cut werke was great bothe in court and tounes,
> Bothe in mens hodes and alfo in their gounes.
> Brouder and furres, and goldfmith werke ay newe
> In many a wyfe eche day they did renewe.

Fabian[6] fays, in the reign of William Rufus "preiftes ufed buſhed and "breyded hedes, long tayled gownes, and blafyng clothes, fhinyng and golden "girdelles, and road with guilt fpurres with ufyng of dyverfe other enormities." All which Anfelm would have corrected, but was not fupported by his brethren the bifhops. Henry I. enacted that priefts fhould wear apparel of one manner of colour, and fhoes after a comely fafhion[7].

[1] A clofe jacket like a waiftcoat. Camden calls a jacket without fleeves a *haketon*. *Hequeton* was alfo a cloak.

[2] This was not confined to thofe, but we meet with figures habited in garments divided in the middle ftrait down, one fide of one colour, and another quite different. In a Cotton MS. Nero D. VI. John of Gaunt, as High Steward of England is fo reprefented. Strutt, Reg. Ant. Pl. xvi. where fee others, pl. xxxix. A famous inftance of this party-coloured fafhion is in the portrait of Sir Anthony Browne, at Cowdry, who in fuch a motley drefs is faid to have efpoufed Anne of Cleves by proxy.

[3] Parfon's Tale, f. 103. 1598. Urry, p. 198. Tyrwhitt, III. 183.

[4] *Trouffers*, fo fhort that tying at the hips could not reach below the thigh at moft, and the hofe were drawn up ftrait, and rolled up under them; which hanging loofe round about muft have been very indecent when a man ftooped to the ground. Strutt, II. 85.

[5] Opera, ed. Bafil. p. 812.

[6] Caxton, II. c. 234. p. 9.

[7] Holinfh. p. 340.

Richard

Richard II. was so sumptuous in his apparel that Holinshed says he had, among other gorgeous suits, one coat of gold and precious stones valued at 3000 marks; and Sir John Arundel's wardrobe exceeded his master's, for he had a change of no less than fifty-two new suits of cloth of gold tissue [1].

Chaucer thus describes the luxuriant dress of the prelates of his time:

They hie on horse willeth to ride,
In glitterande golde of grete arai,
Painted and portrid all in pride;
No common knight maie goe so gaie:
Chaunge of clothing every daie;
With golden girdels grete and small.

Miters they werin mo than two,
Iperlid as the Quen'is hedde;
A staff of gold & pirrie lo!
As heivie as it were made of ledde,
With clothe of golde both newe & redde [2].

We are not to lay all the stress that some do on the satirical representation which the Scots make of the fashions of Edward the Third's time. He learnt French fashions by his conquests; they adopted them by their alliances. While they represented us as if,

Long beerds hesteles,
Peyntede whoods witles,
Gay cotes graceles,
Maketh Englonde thristeles.

Walsingham [3] seems to date the introduction of French fashions among us from the taking of Calais, 1347.

Of the same kind are the reproaches cast by a monk of Glastenbury on the fashions that prevailed at the time of the institution of the round table at Windsor, 19 Edward III. "The Englishmen hawnted so moche unto the folye "of strawngers that every yere thir clamyed em in diverse shappes and disgi-"singges of clothengge; now longe, now large, now wide, now straite, and "every day clothingges newe, and destitute and deserte from alle honeste oft "old array and gode usage: and another tyme to shorte clothes and so streite "waisted, with full sleves and tapetes of surcotes and hodes over longge and "large, all to naggede [4] and knet on every side, and alle to slatteredde, and "also botenedde that if yweth shalle say they weren more lyke to turmentours "and develes in ther clothyng, and also in their schoyng and other array "than thei semed to be like menne. And their wymmene weren more nycely "arraiedde and passed the menne in alle maner of araies and curious clothing; "for thei weredde such streite clothes that they had long fortailes sewede "withynne their garments to hold them forthe for to hede their posteriors [5]."

[1] Chron. p. 1119. See also Vita R. II. p. 156, before cited.
[2] Works by Urry, p. 179, in Henry's Hist. of England, IV. 587.
[3] Hist. Angl. p. 168. Tunc superbire ceperunt matronæ Anglicanæ in apparatibus matronarum Galliæ celticem (*f. Celticensis*)
[4] *jagged.*
[5] Douglas, Monk of Glastenb. Harl. MS. 4690. f. 81. Strutt, II. 83.

As the heads of military men recline on helmets, with or without their crests, so those of kings and queens, ladies, ecclesiastics, &c. rest on single or double cushions, laid flat or anglewise on each other. The double cushion is called in the Lincolnshire church-notes of 1629, MS. in the British Museum, "a pillow and bolster." The supporters of these cushions are generally angels; but an old knight in Royston church, and the figure called *Severus* in York minster, have two lions.

To cushions in the 16th century succeeded the mat or matrass, as under dean Colet; William Thynne, esq. 1584; Sir Francis Vere, 1608, at Westminster; though this was not unfrequent before, and the cushion is retained in some monuments of the later ages; as Sir Francis Norris in the time of Elizabeth at Westminster.

In Burford church, c. Oxon. under the figure of Sir Laurence Tanfield, baron of the Exchequer 1625, is his skeleton lying on a mat, exquisitely carved in marble.

The first instance of the *Garter* that has occurred to me on tombs is that of Sir Richard Pembridge, at Hereford [1]. The next is Richard Vere earl of Oxford, at Earl's Colne, 4 Henry VI. Le Neve mentions it on Sir William Chamberlain, 1463, at East Harling [2]. On all these it is round the left knee; and on the first round *both* knees. John Vere earl of Oxford, 1512, at Earl's Colne, has it on his mantle on the left shoulder; and so it is worn on the brass figures of the officers of the Order in St. George's chapel at Windsor. John de Vere earl of Oxford, who died 1539, on his monument in Castle Hedingham church, has it on the left shoulder of his mantle. We shall see it also worn by ladies.

Mr. Blomefield [3] describes the habit of Sir Thomas Shardelow founder of Thompson college, c. Norfolk, on a stone before the college chapel in the parish church there as *like a priest's*. In the Cordeliers church at Senlis is a monument of Janico du Halde *archer des ordonance du roy notre seigneur de la compagnie de monsieur le duc de Lorraine soubz le capitaine monsieur de Bajart, lequel trespassa a Senlis et fut enterre en habit de St. Francois le* III *jour de Juing*, MVXIIII. He is represented in the monkish habit, with a cowl and cord, and holds in his hands a scroll inscribed, *Libera me domine de morte eterna.*

Guy de Dampierre, a monk in the Cordeliers church of Champagne, near the priory of Souvigny in Bourbonnois, has his habit and cowl and a knotted cord hanging down before him. John de Bassing, 1482, another monk in the cloister at St. Denys, has his hood over his eyes. A daughter of the good St. Louis wears the habit of St. Francis.

An article of dress common to both sexes was the *Ring:* worn among the Romans from the highest ranks to the lowest—of gold and iron. Pliny has a curious disquisition on the antiquity of this ornament, of which he finds no mention in Homer or the Trojan times. Whoever, says he, first introduced it, did it with hesitation, on the left hand, where it would not be seen, whereas if it had been deemed a mark of honour it would have been exhibited on the right [4]. Against the use of gold rings he thus exclaims, "Pessimum vitæ scelus fecit qui "id primus induit digitis," and he takes every opportunity of inveighing against it. He says, the Gauls and Britans wore the ring on the middle finger [5], but the Romans antiently on the third finger only [6], for which he refers to the statues of Numa and Servius Tullius: then on the forefinger, as on the statues of the Gods: then on the little finger, and at last on several, some wearing on the little finger three rings, and some only the seal ring. Our figures on monuments, both of stone and brass, have it on all fingers.

[1] Pl. LIV. p. 135. [2] Blomef. II. 224. [3] II. 637.
[4] Quisquis primus instituit cunctanter id fecit, laevisque manibus latentibus, cum si honos securus fuisset dextra fuerat ostentandus. N. H. XXXIII. 1. [5] Galliae Britanniaeque in medio [digito] dicuntur usae. Ib.
[6] For the physical reason of this, see Macrob. Sat. VII. 13. Gellius, x. 10.

 by

The number and ſituation of rings on antient ſtatues are various. Biſhops and abbots wear their rings on various fingers; either of a circular or oval form: the former principally appears on monuments: the latter has been dug up in the ruins of their palaces. A gold ring ſuppoſed to have been worn by Richard duke of York, becauſe dug up on the ſpot where he was ſaid to have been killed, and fenced round ever ſince, was bought out of Ralph Thoreſby's Collection by Mr. Benj. Bartlett, who permitted it to be engraved in the new edition of Camden's Britannia, is of gold, circular, adorned with figures of ſaints, and this inſcription within: **Pour bon amour.** I have ſeen ſuch another found in the ruins of St. Alban's abbey, plain on the outſide, and inſcribed within. I have a third, with the inſcription in relief on the outſide, and ſet with a blue ſtone.

Our ſerjeants rings may be taken from thoſe worn by the Roman judges[1]. Juvenal[2] ſhews they were worn by pleaders in his time, and that they ſometimes made part of their fee.

Among the varieties of inſcriptions on rings the following ſeem intended for wedding rings:

On an old ſilver ring adorned with two hands conjoined, **eu vou ar.**

On another gilt and broad, like a ſerjeant's, found at Calne, **Amour chef et.**

Within a braſs one, with a heart, **Poun ceoz le veut**: on the outſide, **que voſtre en ſoiet.**

On a gold one found in Eſſex, ✠ AMI AMES AMIE AVES. and on another found in Sir John Webb's garden at Canford, Dorſet, AMIC AVCZ AMI AVEZ.

On an old braſs ring flat ſerrated on the outſide, **Love ledit me to mi lemen.** On the other ſide, **Jolie e't qi me porte.**

On a thick gold ring, within, DYE. DONA. A. QVI. LV. PLEAT.

A gold ring found in Suffolk, 1755, had on the outer circuit ten knobs, on the firſt a croſs, on the reſt characters which were read **Pour ſouvenir.**

One ploughed up near Caſtle Hedingham, Eſſex, had **en luze loiall.**

Mr. Drake has engraved, in his Eboracum, p. cii. a ring with Runic characters, like one found at Harwood in Yorkſhire, and ſhewn to the Society of Antiquaries 1737. 1740. Mr. Drake's was found on Bramham-moor, about 1734, and was quite plain, with ſquare edges; the letters cut, raiſed, and filled up with enamel to a ſmooth ſurface. It might be the ring of ſome chieftain of the Danes, who ſtormed York, 1066, and were defeated by Harold at Stamfordbridge or Battleflatts, where many relics of the battle are ſtill found[3]. This ring weighed near five guineas, or one ounce ſix pennyweights, and was ſold in London, among other like curioſities, by Whiſton Briſtow, 1765, for £.15.

Of the abbatial kind was a gold ring with a great alloy of ſilver, weight five pennyweights, found at Kirkſtall abbey; ſhewn to the Society of Antiquaries by Dr. Byron. On it a crucifix, the Virgin and St. John: farther on St. Anthony's croſs, a Tau, and within this inſcription, **nul autre.**

A gold ring, or fibula, found at Canterbury, had on the outſide, **Penſez li par riſviei.** Within, **Je ſui ici en liu.**

Another, ſilver, **Jeſus nazarenus r.**

Another, ſilver, the middle made up of two hands conjoined, had the ſame inſcription.

Another, ſilver, IHESVS NAZARENVS REX.

The ſame inſcription ſeems to have been on a gold ring dug up at Alva, in the county of Sterling, 1766. diameter five eighths of an inch, weight twenty-ſeven grains.

Mr. Peck had a large ſilver ring, ſuppoſed of an abbot, with a capital **R.**

[1] Plin. xxxiii. 1. [2] Sat. vii. 140. 147. [3] Ebor. p. 83, 84.

A gold

Seals of arms and devises were worn on rings. The valuable antique gems which frequently discover themselves among our monastic seals, were set in rings that were worn. Charles I. had a ring dial which he highly prized [1]. George III. had the first ring watch. Demosthenes and Annibal carried poison in their rings.

A gold ring found at Durham-yard was oval, heavy, and set with a small blue stone carved with a star: a thinner of the like form, with a plain blue stone, found at Llandilo in Glamorganshire, 1760, and shewn to the Society of Antiquaries 1762, may have been episcopal; and a third of the same sort, of a substance between both these, was found in bishop Grosted's coffin. Archbishop Langham at Westminster has on the middle and left finger a seal ring, on the first of the same hand a plain one.

Andrew Richer bishop of Chalcedon, 1555, wears his rings over his gloves on his monument in Vauluisant abbey.

A lady in Harwood church has rings on the second, third, and fourth fingers of each hand.

A knight there has a ring on each third finger, and the half-handed gauntlets.

But no lady is so charged with them as the fair Matilda at Dunmow [2], who has on her left little finger two together, on the third one, on the second two, separate, on both thumbs one square, and one on the middle, third, and little finger of her right hand.

On the beautiful monument in Methley church, c. York, with figures of Sir Robert Waterton and lady, in the time of Henry IV. she has rings on every finger, and several on some, and on every joint; also the same collar of SS as her husband. Dr. Nash, from Abingdon's MS collections, describes a lady at Dudley with the same collar [3].

A mantle and ring were given to ladies who took on them the vow of chastity. See an admission of this kind 1393.

"15 Mar. 1393. Dña Blanchia relicta dni Nichi Styvecle, milit' allegans ipam esse pchiān. dm Joh' epi Elien' eid' epo humiliter supplicans q̄d votum suum castitatis admittere et eidem *mantellum* et *annulum* intuitu caritatis conferre dignaretur, &c. et postea dca dña Blanchia in capella maūii de Dodyngton Elien' dioc' coram summo altari in presencia dci rev' patris missam tunc ibidm solempniter celebrantis votum vovit solempniter castitatis prout sequitur in hec verba.

"Je Blanche jadys femme de Monsr Nicholas de Styvecle, chevaler, vow a Dieu et a notre dame seinte Marie et a touz seinz en p̄sence de vous reverent pere en Dieu John per la grace de Dieu evesque d'Ely qe je seray chaste desoresnavant ma vie durante.

"Et dictus rev. pater votum hujus recepit et admisit, et *mantellum* et *annulum* ilce voventis solempniter benedixit et imposuit super eam præsentib' ibm dnis Johe Wynteperic rectore de Kertlynge, Rob' Orum rectore de Gransden, Johe Fendour p̄bito et Rob' Flat, notario publico."

Reg. Fordham epi Elien f. 181. b.

Henry III. in his picture over the shrine of Sebba in Westminster abbey has a ring on each little finger over his gloves.

Of the physical reasons for appropriating a particular finger to the wedding ring [4], see Mr. Brand's edition of Bourne's Antiquities of the common people [5]; but he does not recollect the antiquity of this ring; that the Romans applied it so [6], and their widding ring was of *iron*, and without a *gem*, so late as Pliny's time [7]. In this application as a pledge of love and fidelity it came to be worn by kings and sovereigns of all ranks [8], as also by prelates and abbots, and the inscriptions before given are to be understood in this sense. It was considered as an earnest by the Goths [9]. Yet Pliny seems to think rings were at first worn rather as seals.

[1] Walpole, II. 49. [2] Pl. VII. [3] Worcestersh. I. 361.

[4] *quia in medio est quedam vena procedens usque ad cor*, says the rubrick of the Salisbury manual, 1542, which directs, "that the man is to put the ring on the woman's thumb, saying, *In nomine patris*; on the forefinger, *et filii*; on the middle finger, *et spiritus sancti*; and on the third, *Amen*. [5] P. 333, 334.

[6] Et *digito pignus* fortasse dedisti. Juvenal, sat. vi. 27. Tertullian calls it *annulus pronubus*. [7] Ubi sup.

[8] So the Doge of Venice *weds* the Adriatic, over whom he is sovereign, by throwing a ring into it annually.

[9] Du Cange in voce.

THE

THE hardest task yet remains—to describe the varied fashions of female apparel: fashions more varied than any held forth on the cloak of Asmodeus, whether the waists of my fair countrywomen were confined in the stiff boddice or surcoat and their aubern tresses in the reticulated headdress of the fourteenth century; or nature left in her more graceful proportions in flowing robes of blazonry and embroidery, and female coeffeure more bedeckt with drapery and flowing tresses in the fifteenth century. Dr. Henry thinks it would be *ungraceful* to dwell on this subject, and therefore gives but one specimen, the high headdress. How much must Antiquaries regret the want of Newspapers, to record the fashions of the twelfth and fifteenth centuries, which require some industry to pick them out of Glossaries! The grave recitals of historians shew however that fashions were not so changeable as in the eighteenth.

The Norman Queen Matilda is attired like a matron on her great seal in Sandford; while the consort of Edward I. unbinds her tresses, lets her mantle fall about her shoulders, or fastens it by a cordon on her breast, and then folds it gracefully near her feet. So this fair example of conjugal affection is attired on her monument in Westminster abbey [1], her tresses falling gracefully on her shoulders. The attitude of Isabel of Arragon, first wife of Philip the Hardy king of France, who died 1271, is the same on her tomb at St. Denys [2]. Her grandaughter the German Philippa is vested in nearly the same manner which she less becomes, and her hair is confined in the stiff reticulated full dress. Montfaucon gives the first instance of this stiff hair-dressing in the effigy of Beatrix countess of Clermont daughter-in-law of St. Louis, and calls it and her coronet *extraordinary*; her shoes also are long and pointed [3]. Richard the Second's consort, perhaps *à la Bohemienne*, is without the mantle, her hair dishevelled, her sleeves lengthened below her wrists. Eleanor of Woodstock appears in the habit of a nun, which she assumed at Barking on the untimely death of her lord. Joan of Navarre, queen of Henry IV. is habited in looser and richer garments, perhaps after the fashion of her own country, her neck and breasts barer and decked with jewels; but her headdress reticulated. The next royal female is the venerable Margaret countess of Richmond, in her ermine robes, with a veil falling back. The queen of Scots and Elizabeth her rival scarcely come within our plan.

The first instance in this work is the lady of Alberic de Vere earl of Oxford 1215, formerly in wood, at Earl's Colne [4]. She is habited in a close mantle with precious stones. Her headdress gathered close under her chin, and bound in part by a fillet studded in like manner; a cordon hangs from her shoulders on her breast.

The next specimen is about thirty years later, of Jane wife of Thomas lord Berkeley, who died 1243, and is buried in Bristol cathedral [5]; she has the mantle gathered over her arms, and falling first to her knees, and then to her feet: on her head an hood fastened under her chin, and falling over her ears on her shoulders.

From hence an interval of about fifty years more carries us to Queen Eleanor, 1290, who has the mantle close round the neck, open in front till below the knees, and on her flowing hair a coronet [6].

Between the two last should come in Aveline countess of Lancaster, whose dress on her monument in Westminster abbey, as described by Sir Joseph Ayloffe, is a loose robe, over that a mantle in elegant foldings reaches down to her feet.

[1] Pl. XXIII. p. 61.
[2] Montf. II. p. 163. Pl. xxviii. 15.
[3] Pl. XIV *.
[4] Montf. II. xxxv. 5.
[5] Pl. IX. f. 4.
[6] Pl. XXIII.

On her head is a *coif*, which a little below her temples joins to a *barbe* that paſſes over the lower part of her chin and covers her neck [1].

Theſe are all my authorities in the thirteenth century. In the fourteenth we have the lady in Worceſter cathedral, p. 80. and another there, who both have the ſame mantle gathered up ſhorter, before it falls to the feet, a deeper barbe and plainer coif. Lady Warren, as called, at Worceſter has the wimple very deep, and reaching almoſt to her mouth. The mutilated ſtatues on the ſides of Aymer de Valence and John of Eltham's monuments [2] are inſtances of the ſame kind.

To particularize a little the ſeveral parts of dreſs here mentioned:

In the earlier periods the treſſes were left to their natural flow, as thoſe of queen Matilda beforementioned. The coeffure of the 13th century concealed the hair intirely. In the middle of the 14th century, as cloſer headdreſs was introduced, the hair was ſhewn only in curls on the forehead, and covered with a veil, as on Joan de Cobham, 1354 [3].

What objection the ladies had to the diſplay of the hair (the greateſt ornament of the human face) is hard to ſay: it was certainly more becoming, however formal, than either the faſhions which ſoon ſucceeded, or perhaps obtained at the ſame time (the end of the fourteenth century) of muffling up the whole head and almoſt the face in drapery, or of purſing up the hair in protuberant nets, which covered the ears, or, which was ſtill more ugly, was raiſed above them. This latter faſhion appears at the beginning of the fifteenth century.

The *reticulated headdreſs* appears firſt on our monuments and thoſe on the continent about the middle of the fourteenth century. Perhaps it was introduced into England by queen Philippa, who died 1369, and has it on her monument [4].

Lady Berkeley at Berkeley, 1360, has the long cloſe headdreſs, adorned with net work of quatrefoils, a ſtrait robe reaching up to her chin, and parting juſt below it; a border with a cordon [5]. It continued with us as late as the beginning of the 15th century, as appears on the braſs of Joan wife of Richard ſon of Robert lord Poynings, in St. Helen's church, Biſhopſgate, 1420, whoſe veil folds over it in front of the head in form of a ſurbaſt arch, like that of the lady of Judge Gaſcoigne, near the ſame time, in Harwood church, Yorkſhire, who has alſo the reticulation. John of Gaunt's ducheſs in Old St. Paul's had the reticulation with the pediment.

The queen of Rene of Anjou, and Joan de Dreux lady of Seirant, 1356, have the cloſe reticulated headdreſs. The latter, with her huſband, are repreſented kneeling on a monument of the 16th century, in St. George's abbey, near Angers.

It is not faithfully repreſented in the engravings of Mary wife of Frank van Halen lord of Lillo 1415, in the metropolitan church of Malines in the Theatre de Brabant [6]; and Matilda counteſs of Spanheim, at Hemenrode, 1357, who has alſo the long buttoned ſleeves [7].

The hair of Cecilia Kerdeſton [8] is richly dreſt in three rows. That of Maud de Cobham, in the ſame plate, fig. 2. in one maſs of zigzag work, in five rows, which appears again at the bottom of the treſſes. She has a ſingle row of jewelry on her forehead. That of Catherine wife of Sir John Harſick, who died 1384, has the plaited or braided hair only at the ſides of the face, it being left *à la nature* on the crown, and a ſtudded fillet on the forehead. Joan dutcheſs of Burgundy firſt wife of Philip de Valois, who died 1348, has the ſame headdreſs [9]. The wife of Sir Miles Stapleton ſhews the ſame plaiting at the ears, while her hair on her forehead curling naturally is incircled by a ſtudded fillet. Sir

[1] Sir Joſeph Ayloffe, p. 5. [2] Pl. XXXII. [3] Pl. XXXIX. [4] Pl. XLIX. [5] Pl. XLIV. [6] I. 48. [7] Acta Theod. Palat. III. p. 49. [8] Pl XXXIX. 3.

[9] Monf. II. XLIX. 3. Les cheveux treſſez d'une maniere particuliere.

Thomas

Thomas Chaucer's lady at Ewelme wears a veil covering the whole of her head. In all or most of these cases I doubt whether the hair be inclosed in net work, as the Spaniards of both sexes do up theirs in silken *redenillas*, over which the women throw a veil, or gathered up in some kind of cloth as seems to be the case on lady Beauchamp's figure at Warwick [1], in which such plaits as these evidently appear to come round and finish in a facing of that sort; and on that of Isabel duches of Clarence, about 1477, at Tewksbury, it is more strongly markt. These were the antient *couverchefs*, in after times called *kerchiefs*.

One of the Marmion ladies at Tanfield, about the reign of Henry III. or Edward I. has a close short cap shewing her ears, but no hair.

Later ladies dressed their hair closer, with a narrow studded fillet: the gown plaited, large loose sleeves, mittens, and girdle. A little figure in Cheshunt church age unknown has close braided hair, with this close headdress and fillet, her ears left uncovered: she wears a kind of loose gown or frock, with bag sleeves close at the wrist, a standing cape or collar, and mittens on her hands.

We see the headdresses of the 14th century trickt and frounced in proportion as much as in Drayton's time [2].

With dressing, braiding, frouncing, flowering,
All your jewels on me pouring.

Or as Spenser describes [3],

Some frounce [4] their curled hair in courtly guise,
Some praunche their ruffes——.

The female headdress of the 14th century appears by the picture of Isabel queen of Edward II. before cited, in a MS of Froissart, in the king of France's library [5], to have been of the sugar-loaf or conical form, very high, with lace floating in the air: a fashion which Montfaucon observes continued in France near two centuries, to the end of the fifteenth. A lady in Mr. Walpole's picture of Henry VI. whom he takes for Jaquelina duchess of Bedford, in a *widow's* habit, has the same headdress.

So have several ladies in Montfaucon, who calls it a *conic* ornament, which continued in fashion near two centuries, and on Mary of Burgundy, wife of the Emperor Maximilian, appears of an extraordinary length, having fastened on the top a very long gauze, which hangs down on both sides to the ground [6]. This is the origin of our lappets. Isabel de Bourbon wife of Charles duke of Burgundy has the same headdress, which Montfaucon there calls a *sugarloaf*, from the form, whence falls a gauze so fine and loose that though it covers her eyes and the greatest part of her face, her features are seen distinctly through [7]. Isabel de Maille wife of John de Brie wears that great pointed headdress which continued near two centuries, and lasted till near the end of the fifteenth [8]. See also Margaret of Scotland, who married the Dauphin of France, son of Charles VII. 1436 [9].

When Isabel of Bavaria, the vain voluptuous consort of Charles VI. of France, kept her court at Vincennes, 1416, it was found necessary to make all the doors of the palace both higher and wider, to admit the headdresses of the queen and her ladies [10]. Her rich dress and train may be seen in Montfaucon, who adds, we have not yet seen a queen so set off as she [11].

The high headdress was however in fashion fifty years before; as we see by the dutchess of Bretagne, 1341 [12].

[1] Pl. L. [2] Nov. Elys. Nymph. II. vol. IV. p. 146. [3] F. Q. I. IV. 14.
[4] from froncer, Fr. to curl. [5] Montf. II. xlii. p. 233.
[6] Montf. IV. vi. p. 59. [7] III, lxiv. 2. [8] Ib. III. p. 166. Pl. liv. [9] Ib. III. xxxviii.
[10] Jouvenal des Ursins gives this curious account of them: "Et quelque guerre qu'il y eut, tempêtes et tribulations, "les dames et damoiselles menoient grands & excessifs etats, et cornes merveilleuses, hautes et longues, et avoient de "chacun coté, en lieu de bourlees, deux grandes oreilles si longes que quand ils vouloient passer l'huis d'une chambre "il falloit qu'elles se tournassent de coté et baissassent, ou elles n'eussent pu passer." Brantome says, "On donne le "los a la reyne Isabelle de Baviere, femme de roi Charles VI. d'avoir apporté en France les pompes & les gorgiasetez "pour bien habiller superbement et gorgiasement les dames." Hist. de la Reine Marguerite.
Villaret, XIII. 123. Monstrelet, f. 39. col. 2. Pasquier, p. 578. Henry's Hist. of England, V. 557.
[11] III. xxv. p. 108. [12] II. xlv. p. 156.

To ſupport the breadth of theſe dreſſes they had a kind of artificial horn on each ſide of the head, bending upwards, on which many folds of ribbands and other ornaments were ſuſpended. From the top of the horn on the right ſide a ſtreamer of ſilk, or ſome other light fabrick, was hung, which was ſometimes allowed to fly looſe, and ſometimes brought over the boſom, and wrapt about the left arm [1]. Theſe horned headdreſſes, imperfectly repreſented by Mr. Strutt [2] from illuminated MSS. are what are otherwiſe called *mitred*, and ſeem to have been introduced about the reign of Richard II.

The headdreſs deſcribed by Roſs as before cited as "tiara alta et *cornuta*," and known to antiquaries by the name of *mitred*, is not ſo common on foreign as on Engliſh monuments, though frequent in illuminations in Montfaucon's tome III. Mr. Pennant [3] calls it a remarkable *mitre-ſhaped cap*, deſcribing the monument of Sir Thomas and lady Boteler, in Warrington church, about the time of Edward the Firſt. I am led to diſtruſt my own conjecture on the monuments aſſigned to the Fitz Walter family at Dunmow, where the knight has *plated* armour, and the lady the *mitred* headdreſs; both which were not introduced till two centuries later. I can only plead the tradition of the place, ſupported by the regiſter of the houſe, and ſuppoſe the monuments made ſo long after the time of the perſons' death that no regard was paid to the dreſs of the time when they lived. Compare my print of this monument with that in Antiq. Repert. III. p. 17. Matilda has what Montfaucon would call the *Mortier*, the mantle, the ſtrait-bodied long-ſleeved tunic, a collar of SS. and a profuſion of jewels and rings. No figure like hers is to be found in the Monumens de la Monarchie Françoiſe.

The headdreſs of lady Say, 1473, in Broxborn church, reſembles a cylinder with hoops, having wires at the end to buoy out the flowing veil. She has a kind of falling double cape of fur and lace, and a jacket under her ſurcot reaching to the knee. Joan de Bokenham, in Great Livermore church, Suffolk, and a lady at Long Melford in the ſame county, about 1425, has ſuch an headdreſs.

The headdreſs was ſometimes pointed at top like a pediment. So Aubrey deſcribes the wife of one of the Mortimers earl of March, in the time of Edward III. in Maule church, c. Hereford. He ſays it was made of velvet or cloth embroidered. Henry the Seventh's Queen, in a picture by Holbein, at Whitehall, is ſuch. Such is Anne Bulleyn's reputed portrait at Hever Caſtle, at Knoll, &c.

Margaret counteſs of Saliſbury, daughter of the king-maker earl of Warwick, beheaded 1541, has this kind of headdreſs like ſo many on tombs [4]. It came in about the reign of Henry VII. and is very common on ſtone figures, braſſes, and pictures. I have not found one inſtance of it out of this country.

Inſtances of this divided headdreſs not ſo high are to be found among the houſe of Bourbon in the middle of the 15th century, on Mary wife of Peter d'Orgemont, 1470 [5], and two other ladies of the reign of Louis XII [6]. on which laſt Montfaucon obſerves [7], that they are dreſt in the habit of the times, and their headdreſs is extraordinary, and both dreſt alike. See alſo two ladies about the middle of the 14th century [8]; and the two peaks gradually diminiſhed almoſt to a concave form in the monuments of the ſucceeding age. On the ladies of the Funtayne family at Narford, c. Norfolk, 1453. [9] theſe peaks appear to the veil, which on one of the wives is flat, as on lady Harcourt about 1470.

The *barbe* or *wimple* was a kind of chin-cloth of fine linen, worn by mourners. No lady under the degree of a baroneſs was permitted to wear it *on* her chin. Knights wives were to wear it *under* their chins; and eſquires' wives and

[1] Montf. II. pl. VI. [2] II. xlv. [3] Voyage to the Hebrides, p. 10.
[4] See Ant. Repert. IV. 169. [5] Montf. IV. ii. 5. [6] Ib. Pl. after xxviii. 2, 3.
[7] IV. p. 146 [8] III. liv. 8, 9. [9] Blomef. III. 522.

gentlewomen

gentlewomen of note wore them beneath their throats [1]. This is the obfervation of Sir Jofeph Ayloffe, in defcribing that of Aveline, but we have no authority for it.

Mr. Pennant [2] defcribes a figure in an arch in the wall of Warrington church in a long robe muffled up to the chin; a ghaftly figure; the head wrapt in a fort of cap, and bound with a neat fillet. What idea does this defcription convey? or is the ghaftly figure a prieft or a lady in a wimple?

Gymple and *furcot* are female habits in the Roman de la Rofe, l. 8916. 9349.

> D'ung chapperon en lieu de voile.
> Sur la *Guimple* euft couverte fa tefte. l. 1343

The wife of Bath was *ywimpled* well [3].

It appears to perfection on the brafs figures of Joan wife of John Cobham, and the lady at Worcefter, in the 14th, and on the figure of countefs Aveline in the 13th century; and remarkably well plaited on one of abbeffes at Elnftow. It is alfo plaited on the wife of Sir Thomas Chaucer at Ewelme, 1436.

Amelia wife of Lewis Elector of Bavaria, 1502, has the wimple over her mouth [4]; and fo has Margaret wife of Henry III. duke of Brunfwic, 1528. On a buft in the ceiling of Lincoln cloifter it affumes a different form, as if pinned up under the chin to the coif [5].

In France we fee the wimple on Ifabel d'Alencon, Mary de Bretagne, and Ifabel d'Artois, nuns of St. Louis de Poiffy, about 1350, 1344, 1371, very ftiff, like a chin-cloth, with a ftrait gorget, on Margaret countefs of Evreux, 1311, in the Jacobines church at Paris, and Alice countefs of Bretagne, 1221, at Ived de Brain; and with the gorget plaited on Joan queen of Navarre, 1349, over her heart in the fame church, and on the ftatue over her corpfe at St. Denis. Catherine duchefs Alencon, in the Carthufian church at Paris, 14 . . Thiephaine la Magine wet nurfe of Mary of Anjou and her brother René king of Sicily has the wimple and divided headdrefs on her tomb at Notre Dame de Saumur, 1458. Her figure holds the children fwaddled in her hands, and over her is this tender epitaph:

> Cy gift la nourice Thiephaine
> La magine qui ot grant paine
> A nourir de let en enfance
> Marie d'Anjou Royne de France
> Et apres fon frere Rene
> Duc d'Anjou et depuis nome
> Comme encor et roy de Sicille
> Qui a voulu en cefte ville
> Pour grant amour de nouriture
> Faire fa fepulture
> de l'un a lautre du devoir faquicte
> pour avoir grace et tout deduit
> Mil CCCC cinquante et huit
> du moys de mars xiij jour.
> Je vous prie tous par bon amour
> affin quelle aut un pou du V're
> donnez luy un patre noftre.

[1] Sir J. Ayloffe ub. fup. note.
[2] Voy. to the Hebrides, p. 10.
[3] Chaucer, l. 471.
[4] Ryner, Monumenta Landgraviorum Thuringiæ, &c.
[5] Carter, N. 2.

Helen

Helen de Melun countess of Eu, 1472, in the abbey church of St. Anthony at Paris, has the like dress.

It appears slit in front on Joan countess of Dreux, 1375, in the abbey of Eu, whose husband was killed at a tournament on his wedding-day, 1365.

Isabel lady of Noion sur Andele, 1209, has it on her tomb at Joyenval abbey.

On Aveline's coif is a long *Paris hood*, which falls down in easy folds to the front part of her shoulders [1]. This I call the veil.

On the head of Philippa duchess of York, in Westminster, 1474, it is finely plaited; as also of lady Montacute at Christ Church, Oxford, 1354, where it is blended with the reticulated headdress.

Eleanor duchess of Gloucester has a plaited headdress; under it her wimple is also plaited. She is a complete pattern of female dress, and her cordon terminates in tassels.

As the wimple, muffler, or neckerchief, gathered up to the chin appears first among us on Aveline countess of Lancaster, who was dead before 4 Edward I. so in France on Joan wife of Alfonso brother of St. Louis, who died 1261, and on Isabel a daughter of the same king, who died 1269, and is represented in the habit of the order of St. Francis, with his cord round her waist [2]; and though another religious lady has it [3], it is not confined to the religious habit, but worn by others in the following century [4].

Margaret queen of St. Louis wears the same neckerchief on his tomb at St. Denys [5]. Joan d'Evreux, third wife of Charles the Fair, 1370 [6]; and Joan of Navarre, queen of Philip the Fair, on her statue at the gate of the college of Navarre [7]. Joan has the buttons on her long close sleeves, and two dogs at her feet. Eleanor duchess of Gloucester has the same close long buttoned sleeves.

The veil is either *pendant* or gathered up over the head as a part of the mantle, and tied under the chin; the first is the more usual fashion: the last appears on the figure of Yoland de Montaign in Montfaucon [8].

Montfaucon makes the veil a mark of widowhood in the 14th century [9]; as the antient stole or veil covering the head and shoulders was worn only by such of the Roman matrons as were distinguished for the strictness of their modesty.

The Carpenter's wife in Chaucer wore a white *volupere*, or cap, tied with tapes of the same suit of here colore, with a fillet brode of silk, and set full high. The volupere worn by men was a night cap [10].

Mr. Brydges [11] mistakes the habit of a married woman, 1437, in Wollaston church, for that of a *nun*, probably only from her veil; but why he gives her husband a *religious* habit I cannot guess.

The garment called the *Surcot* appears of different lengths. It is explained by Du Cange [12] *Robe à femme, superhumerale,* and the longer kind is thus described in the MS Gesta Erminæ cujusdam puellæ Remis, an. 1396, in St. Victor's library at Paris. "Il me vint deux femmes qui portoient *seurcos* plus longs qu'elles "n'estoient environ une aulne, et falloit qu'elles portassent en leurs bras ce qui "estoit bas ou il trainnast a terre, et avoient aussi poingnes en leur seurcos pendans "aus coudes & leurs tetins troussés en hault." By this last circumstance it should seem to have been of the stay or boddice kind. It was forbidden to nuns and abbesses by the council of Treves, 1227. [13] Monks were also forbid-

[1] Sir Joseph Ayloffe's Account.
[2] Montf. II. xix. 1. 2.
[3] Ib. xxvi. 4.
[4] II. xxxiv. 3.
[5] Ib. xxxvi. 1.
[6] II. xliii. 6.
[7] Ib. xxxviii. 4. 6. 9.
[8] Ib. xxxvii. 4.
[9] III. 20. Pl. iv.
[10] I. 4301.
[11] II. p. 199.
[12] In voce.
[13] Du Cange, v. *furcolatus.*

den to wear it[1]. Such an habit was worn by soldiers at home, but not permitted on service[2]. In a MS. cited by Charpentier in voc. *Surcotium*, the long and short surcot are expresly distinguished, and the latter has sleeves to it. "Un "*surcot lonc* de *mabre* fourrè de gros ver, un *surcot* de *mabre* fourrè de gros ver, "a manches fourrees delcasses." So also Phil. Mouskes in Carolo M.

> A tousjours en ivier si ot
> A *mances* un noviel *surcot*
> Fourre de vair & de goupis
> Pour garder son corps & son pis.

And in Vitæ patrum MSS among female apparel are enumerated,

> Lor *seurcors* at lors cortes botes,
> Et font faire les *longes cotes*
> Ou a sept aunes et demie.

The materials of which the short surcot was composed, here called *mabre*, were cloth or stuff of various colours, or, as we should now say, *marbled* pattern. *Mabre* or *maubre*, or the Latin *marbrinus*, *marbretus*, or *mebretus*, being all derived from the French *marbre*, and explained *pannus ex filis diversi et varii coloris textus*, or *draps tixus de diverses laines* comme *marbres* ou *camelins*. A MS cited by Charpentier has "*supertunicale de marbreto* fourratum de bougre." Another mentions "une *cote de marbre* nuefve *a femme*[3]. The several colours of this *marbre* are recited in an antient account book, 1351[4], *verdelet*, *vermeillet*, *brousequin*, *caignez*, *acole*, *de graine*, *dosien*.

As a *long boddice* or gown open at the arms like it, and of a piece with it, the surcot appears on Joan queen of Navarre, at St. Denis, 1349[5]; Joan queen of Charles V.[6] and three princesses of that reign[7]; Mary daughter of Charles IV. 1341[8]; Blanche de Navarre, 1349[9]; Blanche de France, 1392[10]; also on Philip and John sons of Louis VIII. who died young, before their father, who died 1226[11]; and on Catharine countess of Vendosme, 1412.[12]

The surcot and gown and mantle appear united with the mitred headdress in the portraits of a family in the windows of the abbey church of St. Pere at Chartres. Margaret de Feireres wife of John lord de Flonguy and Pomerel, 1414, in Estree abbey, Normandy, has the reticulated headdress and surcot, and her arms are horse-shoes.

Margaret de Pasi a jolly dame in the church of Chartrees near Melun, 1357, has a plain full surcot and petticoat, and buttoned long sleeves, mantle and wimple, and reticulated headdress, shewing very little hair. Agnes d'Autun, in the same church, is habited in the same style, but without a mantle, and has a little coronet.

Of this form it appears on Isabel duchess of Clarence at Tewksbury[13].

In its shorter form, Montfaucon first gives it the name of *surcot*, when he describes it on Mary of Burgundy wife of the Emperor Maximilian, who died 1481,[14] and on whom it appears intirely of furr. *Elle porte*, says he, *un* surcot *d'hermines*. It continued to the middle of the 16th century, and he gives on Susanne de Coesmes wife of Louis lord of Rouille and Granville, "*sur le haut de sa juppe elle* "*port un* surcot a la maniere ancienne[15]." *Surcot* is also mentioned in the list

[1] Stat. Conradi archiepi Coloniensis. [2] Du Cange, v. Syrcotum, ex constitutionibus Frederici regis Siciliæ, c. 96.

[3] The *tunica audax*, or *hardiata*, or *cote ardie*, a garment common to both sexes, but expresly distinguished from the *supertunicale* or *surcot*, was also made of *marbre*, and faced with furr. Charpentier, v. *Hardiata tunica*.

[4] Comput. Steph. de Font. argent. reg. Charpent. v. *Marbretus*.

[5] Montf. II. L. 3. [6] Ib. III. xii. 5. [7] III. xiii. 1. 3. 4.

[8] II. xlix. 6. [9] Ib. 4. [10] Ib. 5.

[11] Ib. II. xviii. [12] Ib. III. xxxiv. 2. [13] IV. vi. p. 59.

[14] In Rous's life of Richard Beauchamp earl of Warwick, Bib. Cot. Jul. E. IV. engraved in Strutt, II. xli. the empress of Germany has it; but her attendants and the English ladies, pl. xlix. at the beginning of the 15th century, have it like a modern stay. [15] IV. xlix. 4. p. 365.

of apparel before cited from the Roman de la Rose, l. 9348. and in Chaucer's Flower and Leaf, l. 141. The first instance of it in France I find in the figure of Isabel of Bavaria queen of Charles VI.[1] It appears in four different sorts of dresses: first, open like a mere border, on Gillette de la Fontaine wife of Hamon Raguier, treasurer to Charles VI.[2] and on Joan de Sancere, in the fourteenth century, who has a stomacher in front over it[3]; also on the queen of Charles V[4]. and on Joan wife of John duke of Berri son of Charles VI. about 1389, and her two daughters[5]. Secondly, the like open border with a stomacher over it in front on Jaqueline de Montagu[6]. Thirdly, the border and stomacher of one piece; as on Joan de Bouchard[7] and Agnes de Bourgogne[8]; in which last instance it ends in a strait line; and on Valentina daughter of John Galeazzo Visconti duke of Milan and wife of Louis duke of Orleans, 1408[9]; and on Blanche de Couci wife of Hugh count de Rouci, 1395[10], it assumes a different form. On the wife of Oliver de Clisson constable of France, who has also the reticulated headdress, it is of fur[11], as on Valentina before mentioned; and on Margaret of Orleans, 1466[12]; on Joan daughter of king John[13]; and on Frances d'Amboise. On Agnes de Bourgogne wife of Charles I. duke of Bourbon, in the middle of the 15th century[14], the stomacher and surcot are of one piece; Montfaucon says her dress has nothing uncommon[15]. Lastly, the wife of Denis de Chailly of the same date, has surcot, jacket, and sleeves, all of one piece[16]. Isabel wife of John de Brie lord of Serrant has a close jacket or boddice with sleeves, but no border[17]. The stomacher is also varied. On Mary daughter of Charles IV. 1341. it is divided and square[18]; and on Margaret de Beaujieu, 1336[19], divided and pointed; on Joan queen of Navarre, 1349[20], and Mary countess of Evreux, 1379[21], single, and rounded off at the point. It has frequently a fillet of jewels running down the middle[22].

The surcot is also worn by Joan daughter of Louis Hutin and her daughter Blanche of Navarre[23].

The countess of Roucy, 1410, at Yved de Braine, has the surcot studded in front, the gown with long sleeves powdered with spread eagles, and the skirt emblazoned, a coeffeure of jewels and lappets loose at the sides; her head on a blazoned cushion. Another countess of Roucy, 1396, has the wimple and veil, mantle blazoned, lined with ermine, which appears in an elegant fall, a strait gown, with bag sleeves, and under them within her cushion, blazoned at the ends, but plain under her head.

Catharine d'Alenson duchess in Bavaria countess Mortaign wife of Yesme de St. Silvaing and du Thuit in Normandy, who died 1462, has on her monument in the church of St. Genevieve du Mont, the veil, wimple, mantle, gown, mitten sleeves, surcot faced with precious stones. So has Catharine d'Alenson wife of Peter de Navarre earl of Mortayn, 1412, in the Carthusian church at Paris; but her surcot is *over* her mantle, and her headdress stiffer. Catharine countess of Vendosme, in St. George's church at Vendosme, has a cordon fastened like an escutcheon before her surcot; her sleeves end in wristbands. The same cordon is on Mary of Spain countess d'Evreux wife of Charles d'Alencon[24]. Isabel d'Artois, 1379, at the abbey of Eu, has the surcot over the mantle, which falls back, and mitten sleeves; so has Helen de Melun wife of Charles d'Artois count of Eu, 1472, in the abbey of St. Anthoine at Paris. Joan de Sau-

[1] Montf. III. xxv.
[2] Ib. III. xxxvi. 9.
[3] Ib. II. lii. 3.
[4] III. ix.
[5] III. xxviii. 5.
[6] III. xxxvi. 4.
[7] Ib. xiv. 4. 6.
[8] Ib. l. 5.
[9] III. xxvii. 2.
[10] Ib. xxxv. 5.
[11] Lobineau, I. 678.
[12] Montf. III. lxi. 1.
[13] Ib. xlii. 2.
[14] Ib. III. l. 5. p. 361.
[15] n'a rien que d'ordinaire.
[16] Montf. III. liv. 6.
[17] Ib. liv. 4.
[18] II. xlix. 6.
[19] lii. 4.
[20] Ib. II. 288. pl. l. 4.
[21] li. 2.
[22] III. l. 7. 9. li. 4. li. liv. 8.
[23] II. pl. xlix. 4.
[24] li. 8.

veuse

veuſe wife of Charles d'Artois count of Eu, who died 1448, has the ſame ſurcot and wriſtband-ſleeves, but no mantle, on her tomb in Eu abbey church.

Blanche of Navarre, ſecond wife of Philip de Valois, who died 1398; Blanche counteſs of Beaumont, daughter of Charles the Fair, 1392; Mary daughter of Charles IV. 1341; and Joan daughter of Louis Hutin and wife of Philip count d'Evreux, 1349; and other ladies of this period [1], have ſome habit like a bib and apron or long ſtomacher, under their mantles and over their gowns. The ſtatue of the latter lady, on the tomb which contains her heart in the Dominican church at Paris [2], has on its head, inſtead of a coronet, only a circle, or a kind of mortier, like her husband; and Mary counteſs d'Alencon, 1379 [3], has a ſtudded ſtrap that hangs down over her long ſurcot in front.

With us it is firſt ſeen on Edward the Third's infant daughter Blaunch de la Tour, who has a plain border over her ſurcot, which is buttoned in front; alſo the long cloſe buttoned ſleeves and mantle, faſtened acroſs the breaſt, but no cordon. See alſo the portrait of Joan wife of the Black Prince, in Strutt, pl. xxxv. A Marmion at Tanfield, ſuppoſed of the reign of Henry III. or Edward I. has it.

Margaret wife of John de Vere earl of Oxford, who died 1513, had the ſurcot and apron, the former faced with ermine, with long cloſe ſleeves: a triangular cordon confines her mantle: round her neck a necklace, and on her head a ſtudded morter or filleted coronet.

The mantle of Maud de Cobham [4] is faſtened below the neck with a double cord to two roſes. Her juſtaucorps has a petticoat with a long fringe.

The wife of Richard Poynings, 1420, before mentioned, has the ſame juſtaucorps, but terminated in folds: the upper part of it above the cordon is inſcribed **ihu, mcy!** Lady Croſby has a juſtaucorps exactly fitted to her ſhape.

The dreſs of Margaret de Beaujeu wife of Charles de Montmorenci, who died 1336, a mantle letting her arms through the ſlits, Montfaucon notes as very remarkable [5].

The lady of Sir Richard Harcourt, who was ſlain 1470, has a ſurcot and apron, and cloſe robe, the ſleeves buttoned to the wriſt; over it a looſe mantle, gathered over and under her feet: a falling veil covers her head, and conceals her hair. The garter is round her left arm juſt above the elbow. This is the third inſtance of a lady with the garter; the counteſs of Suffolk at Ewelme is the ſecond, and has the ſame dreſs, with a double cordon, the mantle folded over and under her feet, the garter round her left wriſt, the veil and wimple to her chin, and a coronet on her head.

The wife of Oudart Huart, at Orcamp, 1259, has her mantle powdered in front with ſhields of her arms. Her arms come out as from a horſeman's great coat, leaving the mantle cloſe in front.

In Eſtoile abbey is a figure of a lady in a mantle, long buttoned ſleeves, wimple, and veil. At the ſides of the tomb ſix figures, two or three religious, a woman in a pointed bonet, a man in hood and doublet, a woman reclining on right arm, which reſts on left hand; the ſixth may alſo be a religious.

The cape of the mantle is unbuttoned in front, and falling down, on the figure of Mary wife of John de Bretigni, undated, in Orcamp abbey.

Joan de St. Verain, 1297, has a large cape with buttons to her mantle, like that of a horſeman's great coat [6]. Such appears on the figure of judge Gaſcoigne's lady at Harwood; her waiſt is remarkably ſhort, and the juſtaucorps plaited and girt round it with a broad belt faſtened with a large buckle. The ladies of John Funtayn's family at Narford in Norfolk, 1453, have the ſame kind of belt almoſt

[1] Montf. II. xlix. 4, 5, 6. [2] Ib. li. 2. [3] A third inſtance of double ſtatues, to be added to thoſe before mentioned. [4] Pl. XLIV. [5] II. lii. 4. [6] II. xxxix. 2.

up

up to their breaſts over plaited gowns. So alſo Joan Bokenham, at Great Livermore, 1425.

The contemporary varieties of female dreſſes in France will be found to correſpond with theſe abovementioned. Conſtance ſecond wife of Louis the younger is girt round her waiſt with a belt, on her tomb in the church of Barbeau [1].

The Queens of Henry the Second, John, and Richard the Firſt, have the ſame belt on their tombs at Fontevraud and l'Eſpan. The firſt and laſt have the veil falling back, and the wimple under the chin [2]. Blanche queen of Louis VIII. has the ſame belt, and in one inſtance her robe is faced with what P. Montfaucon calls *vair* and *vair renverſé*, and which is the ſame with miniver, (of which hereafter), with which the mantles of ladies are faced and lined in innumerable French monuments. So Alice wife of Peter de Dreux, 1221, on her ſeal in Reg. Hon. Richmond, and Joan wife of Dreux de Trainel, 1297 [3].

Agnes ducheſs of Dreux, who was living 1202, has the ſame kind of buckled belt on her tomb [4]; but on her ſeal is ſwathed round the waiſt by a different bandage, and wears long hanging ſleeves [5]; as does lady Stapleton, 1365 [6]. Agnes has at her girdle a purſe [7], like our modern work bags. So Petronilla, wife of Relude Marcelles, on a coffin-faſhioned ſtone in Royaumont abbey. A lady in the choir at Nanteuil has a very ſmall one.

The Carpenter's wife in Chaucer had

> —by hir girdle hung a purſe of lether,
> Taſſeled with ſilk and perled with latoun [8].

Jane wife of Robert Thornton, in the South chancel of Stonegrave church, in the North Riding of Yorkſhire, about the reign of Edward IV. has a belt buckled round her waiſt. Her garment, like a carter's frock, with a ſtanding cape, is buttoned in front to the waiſt.

The long buttoned ſleeves came moſtly into uſe in the 14th century. They appear firſt among us on the princeſs Blanche before cited. Thoſe of lady Montacute, 1354, in Chriſt Church, Oxford, are embroidered with roſes and fleurs de lis alternately in rondeaux. Thoſe of Joan Cobham are buttoned a little below the elbow, and cloſe buttoned at the wriſt. Maud de Cobham ſhews only the cloſe buttoned part of her mitten ſleeves out of her mantle.

Joan de Senlis wife of Adam Vicomte de Melun, 1306, in the abbey church of St. Anthony des Champs at Paris, and Margaret d'Artois, wife of Louis of France, count of Evreux, 1311, have the buttoned ſleeve on their tomb in the Jacobines church at Paris [9], not unlike Joan Cobham.

The ſleeve of Gabrielle de Bourbon wife of Louis de Tremouille, who was killed at the battle of Pavia, has a falling cuff, beſides one buttoned behind it on her monument at Thouars. She died 1516. Catharine de Dreux, at Pavilly, has the looſe ſleeve and cloſe gown of later date. The figure over the heart of Mary de Bourbon wife of John firſt of the name earl of Dreux, at St. Ived de Brain, 1274, has a falling cape and long ſleeves, or a ſhort mantle. The ſleeves of Margaret de Foix ducheſs of Bretagne, 1487, at Nantz, are buttoned to the wriſt, and continued to the knuckles.

The wife of René duke of Anjou king of Sicily, on their tomb in the cathedral at Angiers, has a looſe ſleeve over the tighter on her left arm, and buttons to both ſleeves.

Peter de Bretagne, duke of Bretagne, 1457, has the ſame dreſs on his left arm, on his tomb at Nantz.

[1] Montf. II. xii. 3.
[2] Ib. II. xv.
[3] II. xvii. 2, 3. p. 119.
[4] Ib. xiv. 6.
[5] Ib. 5.
[6] Pl. xlv.
[7] *gibeciere*.
[8] Millar's Tale, l. 3250.
[9] Montf. II. xxxvii. 4, 9.

The wife of John de Rocquemont, about 1327, in the abbey church of Chartris, has the long buttoned fleeves iffuing from others which reach only to her elbows.

In Barbeau abbey Mary de Caunefle, 1321, has the wimple and the maniple hung acrofs her left arm, like the nuns of Port Royal. Emeline de Montier, in the fame church, 1302, has a plaited mantle and fallen cape of miniver.

This lady, and another in the fame place, wear a fingle jewel on the tunic under the mantle, not intended as a faftening, but an ornament: and the like is on the breaft of the tunic of Tebald de Montmorence.

Lady Crofby has a very clofe gown, with a kind of flat tucker at her neck, the fleeves long and clofe, covering over the back of the hand; a belt girt obliquely round her waift; the cordon falling at her right fide: the feet of the gown gathered up clofe: a ftiff open mantle over her fhoulders down to her heels, and on her head a clofe ftiff cap with lappets at her ears, and flat on the top, and a veil flying behind.

Mary of Hainault daughter of John II. count of Hainault, wife of Louis I. duke of Bourbon, aunt to our queen Philippa, wears in a drawing engraved by Montfaucon [1], the fame long fleeves as her niece on her tomb at Weftminfter. So does the wife of Jakemes Loucart [2], Ifabel countefs of Clermont, who died 1385 [3], though Montfaucon [4] dates them of the fifteenth Century, when the MS where this is painted was written. They appear however on the ladies of Charles V's court [5].

The firft article on the figure of countefs Aveline is a loofe robe; over that a mantle in elegant foldings reaches down to her feet [6].

One of the moft elegantly dreft female figures in this collection is that of the wife of Sir John de Creyk in the reign of Edward I. Her veil falls in graceful folds; her tunic has long clofe plain fleeves, her mantle with a fcallopt hem, and faftened at the breaft with a plain cordon, folds about her *à la Grecque.*

Mahaut countefs of Bologne has a long clofe gown with long clofe fleeves like a fhift, and on her head a fillet adorned with pearls [7], faftened under her chin by ribbands. Joan, a fucceeding countefs, has the fame robe girt with a belt, and three diftinct fringes or broad hems at the bottom of it [8], and the like fillet on her flowing treffes.

The cordon on one of the figures at the fide of lady Montacute's tomb in Chrift Church, Oxford, feems to hang from the waift only, from the point of the waiftcoat, which is buttoned in front. The habit of another female figure there refembles a modern gown gathered back.

Margaret wife of Jakemes Loucart, 'fquire to the king of France, and founder of Magdalen chapel at Orcamp, has a pointed neckerchief of ermine, or rather the cape of her mantle turned out in that fhape, long buttoned fleeve, the wimple and veil [9]. Joan de St. Verain in Vauluifant abbey has the like, but fhorter [10]; and Joan queen of Navarre [11].

The wife of John Chaftelain of Thoroti and lord of Hovrecourt, 1353, has a like neckerchief, floped off at bottom, her gown flowered, and ftudded wriftbands, and her mantle blazoned, her headdrefs reticulated, and her veil brought clofe to her eyes. This is the monument I compared with that of Braunch.

Mary of France, daughter of Charles VI. has it fquare, and more like a ftomacher [12].

A lady of the name of Agnes, in Jovay abbey, 1270, has a mantle of miniver, wimple, belt, and long purfe, and paned fhoes. The wife of Pierre la Ragne,

[1] II. li. 5. [5] Ib. xxxviii. 8. [7] lvi, 4. [4] P. 316.
[2] II. xii. 5. [6] Sir J. Ayloffe's account.
[3] Montf. II. xiv. 5. [8] Ib. 6.
[9] Ib. xxxviii. 8. [10] Ib. xxxix. 2. [11] Ib. xxxvii. 3.
[12] Ib. xlix. 6.

in

in Lagny abbey, 1384, has her coeffeure drawn forward towards her forehead and fillet, like the creſt of an antient helmet.

The wife of Sir Anthony de Fay lord of Farcourt, in Cauvigny church, 1521, has a rich ſtudded ſurcot and gown emblazoned without a mantle: the wife of Sir Gilles de Fay lord of Richecourt, 1485, is habited in the ſame manner, but in a plainer ſurcot.

Judge Gaſcoigne's lady is habited in a cloſe gown, buttoned on her breaſt, and belted round her waiſt with a ſquare buckle ſet with ſtones: the ſleeves long, cloſe, and buttoned over her gown as a mantle, with a falling cape. Her headdreſs is reticulated, but ſpread wider at the ears than any other inſtance I have ſeen. The dog at her feet ſeems wrapt up in the mantle which reaches below him.

"Within the rails of the altar at Horton church, on a large marble lying on the ground, are three figures in braſs: in the midſt is a man in armour, with a ſword hanging down before him, and on each ſide of him a woman in the habit of the times [1], viz. in ſtrait boddices with ſleeves coming down and covering the back of their hands to their fingers; their gowns long and covering their feet, and laced one third part from the bottom upwards; their headdreſſes falling back upon their ſhoulders like a ſhort hood with a cap behind like the crown of an hat, with a girdle buckled at the waiſt, and the end of it falling down to the ground." This is for Roger Saliſbury, eſq. 1492, and his two wives. Mary wife of Sir William Par lord Par of Houghton, 1555, has a marble figure in the ſame church, in "a reſembling habit with thoſe of the preceding monument, having a mantle claſped with a buckle hanging down behind to her feet, and a bracelet round her neck [2].

Among the Daniſh monuments before referred to is one in braſs of a man in flowing hair, long coat with long ſleeves and falling cape, and pointed ſhoes, and at his left hand two wives: the firſt in a veil, wimple, and mantle; the other in the jacket and petticoat, collar, and reticulated headdreſs; all three under ſeparate arches; round the tomb this inſcription in black letter:

anno. dñi. mccclxb. in. die. franciscis. dña. heñigus. molteke. miles. ribi'. die. amicia.
cois. marcie. e. dña. elcebe. uxor. suar. ribii'. ɛ dña. cristina. uxor. dñi. [illegible]

The two wives of the burgeſs of Lynne [3] are habited alike, in hoods or coifs, the wimple or neckerchief gathered under and round the chin, their gowns cloſe about their arms and waiſts, but falling thence in elegant folds and gathered and held up on the right arm of one and left arm of the other, the long cloſe ſleeves richly embroidered in nearly the ſame patterns on both ladies, from a little above the elbow, where they are divided by a kind of border; the long ſleeves fall down open from the elbows; the wriſtbands cloſe and double banded: the hems and linings of their gowns are likewiſe richly flowered, but with more variety of patterns. The three women at the feaſt below have the cloſe boddice, and their hair unconfined. The two at the ſides have mantles and vails. The elegant flowing robes that ſwept the ground which appear on theſe Lynne ladies, had not been adopted by lady Stapleton of Ingham, their contemporary. Her hanging ſleeves are alſo remarkably awkward, being ſo long and narrow; whereas thoſe of the abovementioned ladies are broader and ſhorter, and fall more conveniently behind the elbow.

Mr. Blomefield [4] gives an epitaph at Norwich for an *Aldreſs*, or alderman's lady, 1567, but does not mention her habit.

[1] *In the habit of the times* is a phraſe frequent in Mr. Bridges and other church noters — without defining the *times*.
[2] Bridges, Northamptonſh. I. 369, 370. [3] Pl. XLIV. [4] II. 595.

Mr.

Mr. Strutt is of opinion, that the chief distinction between married and unmarried ladies appears to be an additional robe over the gown, which hangs down not unlike the sacerdotal robe of a priest. If he means the mantle, it is common to married and single women; and I have given instances where it is omitted on the former in French monuments. This distinction has not occured to me; nor is it illustrated by him by any example. He adds, Robert de Brunne, in his illustration of Peter Langtoft's Chronicle [1], describing the flight of the empress Maud from Oxford, in the reign of Stephen, says, she got forth

Withouten kirtelle ore kemse, save koverchief alle bare vis.

i. e. without a kirtle or petticoat over her shift, and only the koverchief or veil over her head. Mr. Hearne tells us *kemse* is the ὑποκαμισιον, or ὑποχίτων, the *shift* or *smock* [2], but must here denote a white garment over the queen's, like the *camisia* of the Latins; and καμισιον or χίτων, of the Greeks, signifying a priest's white garment or surplice. Robert Brunne had not so much delicacy or tenderness for the ladies who run over the frozen Thames ten miles to Wallingford in a cold night, as the rest of the old historians, who say the Queen and her retinue cloathed themselves in white sheets or white linen cloth, or *albæ vestes*.

Female statues, whether cumbent or standing, hold the cordon on the breast in the left hand [3]; so all the figures on the side of Crouchback's tomb, Pl. XXV. the right being filled with a sceptre. The right hands of the husband and wife are frequently joined: as Richard II. and his queen; Henry Beaufort earl of Somerset and lady, at Wimborn minster; Sir Robert Gousel and lady, at Hoveringham, c. Nottingham; Sir Thomas and lady Boteler, in brasses at Warrington [4], Sir John Harsick and lady, and many more.

Precious stones were a considerable part of female ornament. Isabel countess of Warwick gave to the monks of Tewksbury, "so that they grucht not with her burial there, and what else she had appointed to be done about the same," her great *templys* with the *baleys* [5], sold to the utmost. These were jewels hung to the foreheads of ladies by bodkins thrust into their hair [6]. Eleanor queen of Henry III. set up in the feretory of St. Edward at Westminster the image of the Blessed Virgin Mary; and the king caused Edward Fitz Odo, keeper of his works at Westminster, to place upon her forehead for ornament an emerald and a ruby taken out of the rings which the bishop of Chichester had left him for a legacy [7].

Gloves [8] seem to have been no part of female dress till after the Reformation, unless they are held by female figures, on the tombs of John of Eltham

[1] P. 121.

[2] Smocca is the oldest name in our language for a linen covering, whether of a priest or woman. That it was a part of female dress early in the fifteenth century, and consequently not novel, appears from the penance imposed by archbishop Islip on Elizabeth de Juliers countess of Kent, for breaking her vow of chastity, and marrying a second husband: that she should once a week eat only bread and a mess of pottage, *wearing no smok*; and especially in the absence of her husband. She died 1411. Dugd. II. 94, 95. ex Reg. Islip. See the Carpenter's wife's in Chaucer, I. 3238.

[3] Several kings, and other men, in Montfaucon, hold their cordons in their left hand.

[4] Pennant, Voyage to the Hebrides, p. 9.

[5] Q. Balls or ballass, which last name is given to the rubies in the inestimable collar of Henry VIII. See Walp. Paint. II. 72.

[6] Dugd. Warw. 413. Walp. I. 40.

[7] Walp. I. 10. ex Dart. I. 16.

[8] If one did not see the rude Tartars and Samoiedes covering their hands against the cold with something like gloves, not divided into fingers, one would be led to think that they were first introduced into Europe by the Christian bishops and emperors. Casaubon has proved, on Athenæus, XII. 2. that the antients knew of no such covering for the hands. See Du Cange, in v. *Chirotheca*. The Roman de la Rose describes the hands of *Oyseuse* as guarded from the bushes by white gloves, but he does not say of what material, though most probably of leather:

Et pour mieux garder ses mains blanches,
De haller elle eut unge gans blancs. l. 575.

Robert Thornton before mentioned in the reign of Edward IV. seems to have short gloves on.

and

and Aymer de Valence, and on the hands of a lady in Worcester cathedral. They were worn by kings, nobles, and prelates, and were a costly article of drefs, and richly decorated, being fometimes, particularly thofe of bifhops, adorned with precious ftones [1]. But the hands of the fair were loaded with as many rings as the ladies of Indoftan wear on their fingers and toes. The fleeves were lengthened mitten fafhion to the knuckles, as we fee in the Turkifh and Ruffian female dreffes, but no more of the hand was concealed. I am not clear whether thefe mittens were not fometimes diftinct from the fleeve, like modern ones. They appear of one piece with the fleeve on ladies Harficke and Stapleton, 1365. 1384. and a lady at Enfon, Suffolk, of the 15th century. They come from under the fleeves of the wife of Henry of Nottingham, at Holm, Norfolk, in the reign of Henry IV. and of Cecilia de Kerdefton, 1391; and are buttoned on the Elnftow abbefs; and they feem to be diftinct from the fleeve on Maud de Cobham, Lady Burgate, 1409, Frances Poynings, in St. Helen's, Bifhopfgate, and the abbefs at Goring, and on Idlenefs in the Romaunt of the Rofe before cited [2].

At the fale of the earl of Arran's goods, April 6, 1759, the gloves given by Henry VIII. to Sir Anthony Denny were fold for £. 38. 17*s.* thofe given by James I. to his fon Edward Denny for £22. 4*s.* the mittens given by Queen Elizabeth to Sir Edward Denny's lady for £25. 4*s.* the fcarf given by Charles I. to one of the family for ten guineas: all which were bought for Sir Thomas Denny of Ireland, who was defcended in a direct line from the great Sir Anthony Denny, one of the executors of the will of Henry VIII. who had a particular efteem for him. Sir Thomas died at the caftle of Tralee, 1761; and by his death an eftate of £4000 *per annum* defcended to his eldeft fon Sir William Denny.

Thefe may be fuppofed fome of the oldeft gloves extant. Of others in fucceeding reigns fee Thorefby's Ducatus Leodienfis, p. 481.

The oldeft monument of an *Abbefs* I have feen is at Romfey: a marble figure with a lion at her feet, under a rich arch, which has no relation to her; the figure being, as I recollect, dug up in the choir. Perhaps there may be another at Worcefter. Leland mentions the habit of a *vowefs*, i. e. nun, as *votarift* in *Comus* [3] in palmer's weed is a pilgrim.

The firft drefs of an abbefs is fuggefted by Mr. Walpole in his marriage of Henry VI. though I think on uncertain ground. I doubt it for this reafon, becaufe the king was married at *Southwick*, which was a priory of Auftin canons, and at Tichfield was a Premonftratenfian abbey, confequently no Englifh abbefs could have affifted on the occafion, for there was no nunnery at Southampton, nor at any place nearer than Winchefter, to Portchefter, where fhe landed [4]. The marriage is reprefented as celebrated before the church door, which, though the general practice, was hardly obferved even by this confcientious prince. This circumftance barely corroborates the defign of the picture.

I fhall engrave two abbeffes from Elnftow, c. Bedford, and a third from Goring in Oxfordfhire, which efcaped induftrious Hearne when he took church-notes there. There are two more in Denham and Ifleworth churches, c. Middlefex, not fo remarkable, and a fixth in the church of Clerkenwell in London.

[1] Rot. Pip. 53 Henry III. 1267. is an entry "de ii paribus chirothecarum cum *lapidibus*," Warton's Hift. of Englifh Poetry, I. 181. where a pair of gloves are mentioned on a lady's hands in Romance.

[2] Thus tranflated by Chaucer:

And for to keepe her hondes faire
Of gloves white fhe had a paire.

[3] I. 189. [4] Carte, II. 725.

The Elnſtow abbeſſes have wimples finely plaited, and coming up over the chin; and on one of them it covers the ſides of the face, like a hood: both have the mantle. The abbeſs at Goring, in the 15th century, has very little of the appearance of a religious; her mantle reſembles thoſe of lay ladies; her gown is buttoned in front down to the toes; ſhe wears the mitten ſleeves buttoned; her headdreſs is reticulated and ſtudded, and her treſſes fall looſe on her ſhoulders; at her feet is a dog of the maſtiff kind. One of the abbeſſes of Elnſtow holds a fine croſier, but theſe of Syon at Denham and Iſleworth dying after the diſſolution have no marks of their dignity, except that the firſt has the ring on the fore-finger of her right hand; but all except her at Goring have the veil.

Chaucer deſcribes his prioreſs,

> Ful ſemely hire *wimple yprinched* was,
> Ful fetiſe was hire *cloke*, as I was ware.
> Of ſmale corall aboute hire arm ſhe bare
> A pair of bedes *gauded*[1] all with grene;
> And thereon hong a broche of gold ful ſhene,
> On which was firſt ywritten a *crowned* A.[2]
> And after, *Amor vincit omnia*.

Mr. Blomefield gives two inſcriptions in braſs for nuns (Sanctæ Moniales) in Hilburgh church, but without dates or figures[3].

Mr. Bridges deſcribes a nun in a black and white habit at Ruſhton, 1567.[4] and another, 1577, at Wollaſton[5].

Iſabel d'Alencon daughter of Charles de Valois count d'Alencon, who died 1346, on her monument on the church of St. Louis de Poiſſy, where ſhe was a nun, has the mantle, gown girted round her waiſt, the wimple over her cheſt, and from it an apron, and on her head a veil or flowing hood.

The cloiſter of Portroyal des champs between Verſailles and Chevreuſe, now diſſolved, abounded with monuments of abbeſſes of the Ciſtertian order, who, agreeable to St. Bernard's rule, wore no *croſſe*; neither did the laſt abbeſs; and there were in this houſe religious women conſecrated by a biſhop, two of which were repreſented on the ſame tomb with a kind of maniple[6].

The ſituation of the nunnery of Montmartre, founded by Adelaid wife of Louis le Gros, 1133, on the top of an high hill, made it ſo cold that the abbeſs Heliſenda, 1231, ordained, that they ſhould have an allowance of three ſols apiece on All Saints day, to buy them *furred boots*[7]. Weever[8] has a curious circumſtance about taking a nun out of a nunnery, and making her reſume a ſecular habit. "I find, ſays he, inter Brevia regis, E. III. a. r. 24, that William Fox, parſon of Lee near Gainſboro', John Fox, and Thomas of Lingeſton, friers minors of that convent in Lincoln, were indited before Gilbert Umfrevill and other Juſtices, in partibus de Lindeſey, apud Twhancaſter die Sabbati poſt

[1] *gaudes*, trinkets, gawdies; ſo Philippa counteſs of Maien bequeathes a pair of rings, the *gaudes* of red croſſes enamelled. Royal Wills, 130. And Eleanor Bohun ducheſs of Glouceſter, a pair of pater noſters of coral of fifty large beads, with five gaudes of gold "en manere des longets, ſwages, et ponſonez." Ib. 180. Some were ſilver gilt, and ſome had mottoes over them.

[2] The initial of *Ave*, as a crowned M. ſo common on church porches and windows, was of *Maria*?

[3] III. 438. [4] Northamptonſh. II. 102. [5] II. 72.

[6] Moleon, Voyage Lit. 234.

[7] Gallia Chriſtiana vii. 615. Lebeuf Dioc. de Paris, II. 110. We have ſeen *ſhort boots* among female apparel before.

[8] P. 72.

festum

festum S'ci Joh'nis Baptiste, in the said year, for that they came to Bradholme, a nunnery in the county of Nottingham, 18 kal. Feb. and then and there *rapuerunt et abduxerunt inde contra pacem Domini regis quandam monialem nomine Margaretam de Everingham sororem dicte domus*, exeuntes eam habitu religionis, et induentes eam roba viridi seculari, *ac etiam diversa bona ad valorem 40 solid.*" The nuns who professed chastity wore black; the seculars colours: *viridis* is *varius* in the old books. Bracton, l. 111. See Jacob's *viridis rosa* [1].

At the interment of queen Jane it is said that the ladies left off their bonets, and took [for mourning] white kerchers to apparel their heads, called *Paris hoods*, with white kerchers coming over their shoulders [2].

Silk, we are told by Mr. Camden [3], was first brought into use among us in the reign of Henry II. *bombycina* made by silk worms, which first came out of Greece into Sicily, and then into other parts of Christendom; for *sericum*, which was a down kembed off from the tree among the *Seres* in the East Indies, as *byssus* was a plant or kind of silk grass, as they now call it, was unknown. "There was also, adds he, a costly stuffe at these times here in England, called in Latin *Aurifrisium*: what it was named in English I know not, neither do imagine it *auriphrigium*, and to signify embroidery with gold, as *Opera Phrygia* were embroideries. Whatever it was, much desired it was by the popes, and highly esteemed in Italy." Du Cange has clearly shewn that *Aurifrasium*, *Aurifrigia*, *Aurifrisca*, *Aurifrisum*, *Aurifres*, *Orfreys*, *Orfroy*, *Orfrais* (for by all these names it is called in antient writings) means a *gold fringe*; but he confines it I think too closely to ecclesiastical vestments. "Limbus acu pictus auro plerumque argentove "distinctus qui ad vestes sacras assuitur." It was very broad on the copes, set crosswise on the chasubles, brought from the shoulders behind and before in the tunics, on the albs only before and behind the lower edge and at the extremities of the sleeves, and in that part of the garment which went over the head. Frederic bishop of Strasburg excommunicated those priests who wore on their habits double fringes, commonly called *Bortum*, a corruption for *Bordum* from *Borde*, a border. The Benedictine editors of this most excellent Glossary add, that *Aurifrigium* is synonymous with "*Opus Phrygium* auratis filis intextum;" and so the Roman de la Rose describes the rich gown of *Lyesse* or *Gladness*.

Et un chappeau d'Orfrays eut neuf,
Le plus beau fut de dix et neuf:
Jamais nul jour vu je n'avoye
Chapeau se bien ouvre de soye.
D'une sainture moult doree,
Fut elle sur son corps paree [4].

Of Orfrais fresh was her garland;
I which seene have a thousand,
Saw never ywis no garland yet
So well wrought of silk as it;
And in an ovir gilt samite
Clad she was by grete delite [5],

[1] Dr. Taylor's MS. penes me.
[2] M. 6. p. 1. MS in Coll. Arm.
[3] Remains, p. 232.
[4] l. 872—877.
[5] Chaucer's Translation.

Another

Another lady reprefenting Riches wore a beautiful purple gown embroidered with figures of Emperors and Kings.

> Pourtraictes y furent d'Orfroys
> Hyftoyres d'Empereurs et Roys [1].

Thus in Chaucer's tranflation:

> With Orfreis laced was every dele,
> And purtraied in the ribanings
> Of dukes ftories and of kings.

Oyfenfe

> D'Orfraiz eut ung chappel mignot
> Qu'oncques nulle pucelle n'ot
> Ne plus coint ne plus defguysè,
> Ne l'auroye a droit devisè,
> Ung chappel de rofes tout frais
> Eut deffus ce chappel d'orfrais [2].

Thus tranflated by our countryman;

> And of fair Orfrais had fhe eke
> A chapelet fo femely on
> Ne never wered maide upon;
> And faire above that chapelet
> A rofe garland had fhe fet.

Thefe *aurifrigia* were fometimes of *opus Cyprenfe* [3]; and garters are embroidered of filk and Cyprus gold [4]. *Cyprus* was a thin tranfparent texture like gaufe or lawn; and hence Milton's ftole of *Cyprus lawn* [5]; fo that they fhould feem like our modern gauze trimmings. It is alfo applied to crape, and then is black, for widow's weeds: and fometimes Cyprus is a *fhroud.*

A fringe, or perhaps only a broad hem, appears on the tunic of William de Valence, earl of Pembroke, 1296.[6] A fringe or furr to the mantle of William de Hatfield, fecond fon of Edward III. at York [7]. A double fringe is not uncommon on the monuments of our prelates. Chefubles with fringes are among prefents to churches and to religious houfes [8].

Samit, or as the Latin writers call it, *Samittum*, *Samitium*, *Scyamitum*, *Xamitum*, or *Exametum*, is defined *Pannus holofericus*, and taken for *Silk* in general [9], as *Satinus* is defined *pannus fericus* rafus.

" Silk manufactures were introduced from the Eaft into Italy before 1130 [10]. The crufades much improved the commerce of the Italian ftates with the Eaft in this article, and produced new artificers of their own. *Diaper* occurs among the rich filks and ftuffs in the Roman de la Rofe [11].

> Samites, *dyaprès*, camelets.

[1] Ib. l. 1070. [2] Ib. l. 564. 568. [3] See Charpentier in voc. & aut. ibi citati.

[4] Pro opere in MCLII gart. operat. de feric. & *auro de Cipre*, Comp. Rob. Rollefton. cuft. magnæ garder. 9 Hen. V. Anftis' Black Book of the Garter, p. 171. note *b*. The materials there faid to be ufed in the compofition of a garter are *Tartrin*, *aurum de Cipre*, filk, *corde*, *buker* [q. bukram], *pakfil* [packthread], and *fil*, or thread. Ib. *Tartrin* fhould feem to be filk from Tartary or China. See Du Cange in voc.

[5] Il Penferofo, l. 35. and Warton on it, p. 66, 67.

[6] Pl. XXVII. [7] Drake, 491.

[8] Papa dono dedit ecclefiæ Ortanæ unam *planetam* de examito rubro cum aurifrigio decenter ornatum. Du Cange, v. *Examitum*.

[9] Du Cange in vocibus.

[10] Giannone Iftoria de Napoli, XI. 7. [11] l. 21867.

where

where it fems to fignify *damafk*. I find it alfo in the Roman d'Alexandre written about 1200 [1].

Dyapres d'Antioch, famis de Romaine.

Here is alfo a proof that the Afiatic ftuffs were at that time famous; and probably *Romanie* is *Romania*. The word often occurs in old accounts of rich ecclefiaftical veftments. In Dugdale's Monafticon [2] we have "*fandalia* cum caligis de rubro fameto *diafperato* brendata cum imaginibus regum [3]. This rich pattern of fhoes and boots muft be added to thofe before mentioned, p. clvii. and clxiv.

The Carpenter's young wife in Chaucer [4] wore a *feint* (*ceinture*, girdle) *barred* all of *filk*.

A *barme cloth* [5], eke as white as morwe [6] milk,
Upon her *lendes* [7] ful of many a gore.

In the fifteenth century fatin was fo common that it was worn in all proceffions. Thus at the receiving of Henry VI. into Paris, a. r. 10. the provoft met him with a great company all clothed in red fattin with blue hoods: the provoft of the merchants and fheriffs of the town received him with a rich canopy of blue velvet richly embroidered with fleurs de lis of gold [8].

Sattin, in Beaumont and Fletcher's time, was become fo common, that a lady, in one of their plays [9], is introduced faying

That fourteen yards of fattin give to my woman;
I do not like the colour, 'tis too civil.

In the reign of Edward I. the general wearing of furr on garments began to be ufed, whereas before thofe ornaments were confined to the coronation robes of kings and creation robes of nobles [10]. It was forbidden to proftitutes by a ftatute 27 Edward III. [11] It was firft called *Vares* from the Pontic moufe, which Scaliger on Ariftotle fays is brown with a white belly; and by Benjamin of Tudela is called *Veergares* or *Vairs gris*. Hence *pelles variorum* for *vairorum* and *pelles variae*. The council of Saltzburg, 1386, forbid it the clergy, except dignitaries [12]. Montfaucon, as we have feen, gives female habits faced with it [13]. The furrs of fables, ermines, foxes, &c. were ufed about the fame time, thus enumerated by Guifeppe Barbaro in his travels to the Don, p. 456. "*Sibelinos* [14], *Armelinos*, *Doffos*, *Vares*, vulpes, et id genus animalium alia illi offerentes." The Roman de la Rofe, fpeaking of Avarice, fays,

Au manteau n'avoit *penne vaire* [15]

i. e. Peliffe ou peau fine du fourrure fine et precieuse pour doubler les habits. Gloffaire.

[1] MS. Bodl. fol. 1. b. col. 2. [2] III. 314. 321.
[3] Warton, Hift. of Englifh Poetry, I. 177. n.
[4] I. 3235—6—7. [5] Apron or *lap-cloth*, from barm, lap. [6] morning. [7] loins.
[8] Hall's Chron. f. cxvi. b.
[9] Woman's Prize, Act. III. Sc. II. V. VIII. p. 221. where *civil* may mean fit only for citizens.
[10] Strutt, II. 83. [11] Stowe, 254.
[12] Du Cange and Charpentier in voce *Vares*.
[13] Particularly II. xvii. 2, 3. Blanche of Caftile wife of Charles VIII. 1100. whofe mantle is "doublé de *vair renverfe*; doublure que nous verrons fouvent dans le fuite," p. 119. This is exactly like *Vair* in Heraldry.
[14] A fuit of fables was the richeft drefs that could be worn in Denmark. Steevens on that famous paffage in Hamlet. [15] L. 222.

Again, l. 5500.

Le roy a ſa penne vaire

Again, Auſſi tres bien ſe Dieu me garde
Me garantit et corps & teſte
Par vent, par pluye, & par tempeſte,
Fourrée d'aigneaulx ſur gros bureaux
Comme pers fourré d'eſcureaux.
Mes deniers ce me ſemble pers
Quant j'ai pour vous robes de pers,
De camelot, ou de brunette,
De vert, ou d'eſcarlate achette,
Et de *vair* & de gris la fourre[1].

Miniver, which occurs in old wills, &c. is *Menue vair, minutus varius*, in oppoſition, I ſuppoſe, to the furrs of larger animals.

John de Montfort duke of Bretagne and his dutcheſs both wear fur, 1341.[2]

The old portrait of queen Edyve, in Canterbury cathedral library, engraved in Haſted's Kent, I. 464. repreſents her in a ſurcot and long ſleeves, all ſtudded, and the ſurcot faced with ermine, and a mantle lined with ermine; ſhe has a double cordon, and the veil headdreſs, ſurmounted by a crown. Lady Tiptoft, in Enfield church, has a ſurcot of ermine, with a kind of flap or ſhort apron of the ſame to it before.

That valuable furs were not unknown in the time of Henry III. appears from the order to his taylor, to make two cloaks for the king and two for the queen againſt Chriſtmas day, to be furred *cum ermino*, and "ſupertunicæ de *minuto vario*[3]; and two robes "cum *aurifraxis ſemilatis* et varii coloris[4]." There was a further order to make three robes *de quintiſis*[5], viz. one of the beſt violet coloured *ſamit* embroidered round with three little leopards in front and three behind, and two more of the beſt cloth that could be got[6].

William de Hatfield ſecond ſon of Edward III. on his monument at York is repreſented in a mantle fringed or furred, a cloſe coat embroidered, with long cloſe ſleeves, his hoſe and breeches of one piece, his ſhoes embroidered, and a ducal coronet on his head[7].

In the more antient colleges of our univerſities the annual expences for furring the robes or liveries of the fellows appear to have been very conſiderable. Milton[8] talks of the,

Budge doctors of the Stoic *fur*.

Explaining, ſays Mr. Warton[9], the obſolete word by a very aukward tautology. Stowe[10] derives *Budge row* from *Budge*, furr, and ſkinners dwelling there. Dr. Hacomblen provoſt of King's College, Cambridge, 1528, has the cape of his doctor's robe covered or lined with a rich heavy fur on his figure in braſs in his college chapel. Richard Peyton, at Iſleham, 1574, has a long gown lined throughout with fur.

[1] l. 9495—9504. [2] Montf. II. xlv. 256. [3] Clauſ. 36 Hen. III. m. 30. [4] Ib.
[5] See *cointyſes*, p. clxxxix. cxci.
[6] Gowns were furred *cum beſtis* de erm. & erm. *miner*. Record before cited from Anſlis, 9 Hen. V. We have there alſo *minev*. men groff. & men. pur.
[7] Drake, 491. [8] Comus, l. 707. [9] P. 219.
[10] Survey of London, ed. 1618. p. 455.

Robert

Robert the third of the name, earl of Dreux and Braine, who died 1232, is reprefented on his tomb of what the French call *pierre plate*, in the abbey church of St. Ived de Braine, has a mantle lined with ermine; fo has the wife of Robert de Dreux lord of Beu, about the fame time, in the fame church. The mantles of two nuns of St. Louis de Poiffy, 1344. 1371. in their conventual church, are lined or faced in like manner.

Two figures on the fame tomb, beautifully enamelled of Alice countefs of Bretagne, 1221, and Joland de Bretagne her daughter, 1272. in the church of Yved de Braine, have their mantles faced with vair, white on a blue ground, like their arms.

In the fourteenth century fur appears very frequent on the ladies gowns, at their wrift, like a long ruffle turned back, alfo about their necks, and as a fringe or hem.

Mede in Piers Plowman is thus defcribed [1]:

I was ware of a woman worthlyich clothed,
Purfiled with *pelure* the fineft upon erthe,
Crowned with a crowne, the king hath no better;
Fetiflich her fingers were fretted with golde wier;
And thereon red rubies as rede as any glede,
And diamonds of dereft price and double maner faphirs,
Orientales & Ewages venemis to deftroye:
Her robe was full rich of red fcarlet engrained,
With ribandes of red gold, and of rich ftones;
Her arrayne ravifhed, fuch riches faw I never.

Knyghton defcribing the drefs of the women of fafhion at public diverfions in his time, A. D. 1348. fays [2], "Thefe tournaments are attended by many ladies of the firft rank and greateft beauty, but not always of the moft unblemifht reputation. They are dreft in party-coloured tunics, half of one colour and half of another; their liripipes, or tippets, are very fhort, their caps remarkably little, and wrapt about their heads with cords; their girdles and pouches ornamented with gold and filver, and they wear fhort fwords, called *daggers*, before a little below their waifts. They are mounted on the fineft horfes with the richeft furniture: and in this attire they ride about from place to place in queft of tournaments; thus fpending their fortunes, and not unfrequently ruining their reputations.

The wife of Bath's

—covrechiefs weren ful fine of ground,
I dorfte fwere they weyeden a pound,
That on the Sonday were upon hire hede;
Hire hofen weren of fine fcarlet rede,
Ful ftreite yteyed, and fhooen ful moift [3] and newe,
Ywimpled wel, and on her hedde an hat
As brode as is a bokeler or a targe;
A fote mantel about hir hippes large [4].

Of the lady's trains, fays Chaucer,

It is full fayre to ben ycleped Madam,
And for to gon to vigils all before,
And have a mantel reallich [5] ybore.

[1] Paffus fecundus.
[2] col. 2597.
[3] frefh, oppofed to ftale.
[4] l. 458. 472.
[5] royally.

The

The magnificent and coftly dreffes of the barons and knights who attended the marriage of Alexander III. king of Scotland to Margaret eldeft daughter of Henry III. at York, 1251. are thus defcribed by Matthew Paris[1], who was prefent at the folemnity: "It would raife the fpirit and indignation of my readers if I attempted to defcribe the wantonnefs, pride, and vanity, which the nobles difplayed on this occafion in the richnefs and variety of their dreffes, and the many fantaftical ornaments with which they were adorned. To mention only one particular: the king of England was attended on the day of the marriage by 1000 knights, uniformly dreft in filk robes, which we call *Cointifes*; and the next day thefe knights appeared in new dreffes no lefs fplendid and expenfive."

The duke of Gloucefter met Henry the Sixth's queen, Margaret, 1444, on Blackheath, with 500 men in one livery. The other lords and eftates had great retinues of men in fundry liveries, with the fleeves broidered, and fome beaten with goldfmiths works, in moft coftly manner[2].

The preaching of a Cordelier juft returned from Jerufalem, at Paris, 1429. had fuch an effect on his audience that the gentlemen burnt all their gaming tables, cards, dice, billiards, and bowls; and the ladies their headdreffes, which the chronicler who tells this ftory called *bourreaux truffes*, the leather and whale-bone boddices *(pieces de cuir & de baleines)* their horns and trains (leurs *cornes*, leurs *queues*[3].

During the 15th and the middle of the 16th century plated armour kept its ground on the figures of men of all ranks above that of merchants or burgeffes, who were fuppofed of too peaceful a difpofition and too deeply engaged in commercial purfuits to buckle it on. The fafhion of it grew more fantaftic and fhewy from about the middle of the 15th to the middle of the 16th century. In the beginning of the 17th, during the reign of James I. who wifhed neither to difturb the peace of Europe, nor to be interrupted in his own repofe, it was exchanged for doublets and trunk hofe, but refumed in the reign of his fon, as if preparatory to the troubles that were to enfue, and maintained its ground on monuments to the clofe of the laft century, and the long fword was worn under the doublet, with the knee and fhoe ftrings.

I obferve fome clumfy varieties in kneepieces and other parts of armour in the 15th century, which will be noted in their proper place, together with trunk hofe plated in front. A knight at   has a tabard of arms over his plated armour, his head with flowing hair refts on a cufhion, and he holds up his hands in front fpread. The coats were fhorter, the mantles or cloaks lined with fur throughout, and had long hanging fleeves, fometimes adorned with crofs feams or facings, as Richard Peyton of Ifleham 1514, or with two openings for the arms at different intervals; the hofe and breeches of one piece, the latter frequently paned in whole or in half, and trunk or ftrait; ruffs and clofe caps were worn by men in the 16th and 17th century, the hair clofe cropt or ftrait; beards and whifkers. Eldred the navigator has a fhort cuff open and buttoned as in modern times, and a clofe cap or coif, a very fhort coat tied round him with a bow-knot, a piked beard and whifkers, and large ruff. Thomas Barwick phyfician at Bury, who died 1590, has on his monument at Farnham All Saints, a clofe coif, long fleeves, moderate ruff, and a coat buttoned from his chin.

[1] P. 829   [2] Fabian fub anno.
[3] Journal of the reign of Charles VII. in Lebeuf, Hift. du Dioc. de Paris, III. 23.

In

The attitude began to change in the 16th century: John Brooke and John Borrell, ferjeants at arms, at Broxbourne, appear in profile, as walking: the former has his head on a helmet, yet turns both face and feet to his lady, and ten years after it became almoft the univerfal fafhion for the figures both in brafs and ftone to kneel fronting each other to a *prie dieu* or defk. Sir Clement Higham, in Barrow church, Suffolk, has a fon in a fhroud kneeling behind him. The profile attitude continued as late as brafs plates. We fee it in the reign of James I. and there are inftances of men praying ftanding in profile; fometimes the helmet is thrown on the ground at the party's knees, and the gauntlets hung on the front of the defk. On a brafs in Barwell church, Leicefterfhire, engraved for the appendix to Mr. Nichols's "Hiftory of Hinckley," Mrs. Torkfey and her 5 daughters are kneeling to a defk, before which is a pulpit with her hufband in it, who died in 1613. An infant in a fhroud lies between her defk and the pulpit.

In the reign of Edward IV. female apparel affumed a more coftly form. The firft wife of Thomas Payton, at Ifelham, is habited in the richeft flowered filk [1], and a fancy necklace of precious ftones; her veil flies behind her head, but fhews very little hair, and in the coif under the veil is an infcription, which feems *lorde jefu, mercy!* On her wrifts fhe has fomething like the ftiff turned back ruffle of fucceeding times: her feet are concealed under the folds of her robe. The fecond wife, who appears older, has the fame kind of headdrefs, the fame necklace and ruffles; but thefe laft are of fur with which her breaft and fhoulders are covered, and her robe trimmed at bottom. Both thefe ladies have very flender fhapes, and are girded with broad belt-like girdles. The drefs of the French ladies was very different at this time, and had lefs departed from the antient fafhion [2]. The furcoat was not left off in 1481. [3]

In the middle of the 15th century female drefs made great approaches to that worn in the fucceeding one; the long fleeves were left off entirely, the mantle exchanged for a flowing gown, tightened more indeed round the waift, but training in the fkirts like modern drefs. The headdrefs floated more at eafe with veil-like lappets ftretched on wires, and fupported by a ftiffened cawl; or if at all confined it was in the pediment form before mentioned, p. clxxv. of which we have innumerable inftances on braffes. A lady at Eafton in Suffolk retains the long mitten fleeves, with a tighter gown, which feems to reach only to the knees, and fhew a petticoat; her girdle drops fo low that her purfe is at her knees. This is one of the laft inftances of a cufhion under the head. The wife of Thomas Broke ferjeant at arms to Henry VIII. 1518, in Broxborne church, has the pediment headdrefs with very long lappets before and behind, while other ladies have only the lappets in front, and a kind of hood or clofe veil behind. She has alfo a belt reaching to her feet. About 1546 we come to ruffs round the neck and wrifts, puffed fleeves with oiellet holes, large falling hoods and jewels in front, ftiff ftays, laced apron, long petticoats, as Benet wife of Richard Dering, 1546.

[1] Such I fuppofe as Stowe defcribing Sheriff Lion's gown, 1381. (fee p. 137.) calls "*branched* damafk wrought with the likenefs of flowers," like Milton's *flowery-kirtled* Naides (Comus, 254.) See alfo Mary of Burgundy, Montf. IV. vi.

[2] See Montf. III. p. lir. lxvi.

[3] Ib. IV. vi.

In the reign of Elizabeth and James I. the ſtay or boddice was not ſo ſtraitly laced, the ſleeves at the ſhoulders were ſet in with raiſed and puffed work, the gown and petticoat and apron were diſtinct, the ruff confined to the neck, but enlarged [1]. In James's reign the women wore heavy ſhoes like men's, and high-crowned hats with ribbands or bands. Even the youngeſt daughters retain the mother's habit, but ſometimes have a kind of fly cap. Such a cap is worn by Mary Payton of Iſelham, about the end of the ſixteenth century. She has a ſtanding cape to her gown, a ruff round her neck, her ſleeves tied with ribbands from the ſhoulder to the wriſt; a kind of fringed ſaſh tied round her waiſt, and her gown opening in front diſcovers a rich embroidered petticoat. Radcliffe wife to Thomas Wingfield of Eaſton, Suffolk, 1607, has a cloſe cap, hair drawn up high and ſtiff in front, ſtanding ruff, pufft ſleeves, with falling laced ruffles, very narrow pointed boddice, gown puckerd up over fardingale, and ſhewing a rich embroidered petticoat. Elizabeth lady Culpeper, in Ardingley church, Suſſex, 1633, has an almoſt Vandyck headdreſs, a mantle wrapt round her, puſt and corded ſleeves, with pinked ruffles, a falling band or ruff, and an embroidered petticoat. A young lady of this family, in the ſame church, 1634, is dreſt ſomewhat like her, except the mantle, and has a taſſel to her girdle. In the middle of this century we ſee the veil falling over a black hood tied under the chin, and over the neck and ſhoulders a ſquare white kerchief, as on the monument of John Oneby and wife in Hinckley church, engraved in Mr. Nichols's Hiſtory of that town, pl. VI. and worn both by the mother and daughters. The huſband, who was a barriſter of Gray's Inn and ſteward of the court of records at Leiceſter, is in the dreſs of his profeſſion, with a coif and large band.

Dr. Henry, who has given a ſhort view of the dreſs of each reign at the end of his hiſtory of each reign, is rather too tender of his contemporaries, when he ſays, "Upon the whole, I am fully perſuaded, that we have no good reaſon to pay any compliments to our anceſtors of this period at the expence of our contemporaries, either for the frugality, elegance, or decency of their dreſs."

[1] In France at this time the ſleeve was long, to the wriſt, and puffed at the ſhoulders, the gown ſometimes open in front, ſometimes faſtened with bows: the ruff ſmall; the gloves ſhort early in the ſixteenth century; ſee alſo later Catharine of Medicis, Elizabeth daughter of Henry II. Margaret daughter of Francis I. (Montf. V. pl. v. IX. XI. XII.) Margaret de Bourbon has a tucker without a kerchief; Diane de France, natural daughter of Henry II. has a handſome laced kerchief and larger ruff. Ib. pl. XII. 5, 6. The kerchief of Elizabeth queen of Charles IX. is of fur, Ib. pl. XXIV. Magdalen de Corbie, ſo late as 1562, has the old-faſhioned cloſe ſleeve buttoned at the ſides, and iſſuing out of larger, and terminating in a kind of ruffle. Ib. XV. 2. The hair of Frances princeſs of Conde, pl. XXVII. is divided at top mitre-faſhion. That great piece of ſtuff, as Montfaucon calls it, (V. p. 63) riſing up over the ſhoulders, at the back of the neck and head, appears in moſt of the portraits of Catharine de Medicis. Ruffles appear as early as 1503. and long furr cuffs, pl. XXVII.

APPEN-

APPENDIX.

COPY and Tranſlation of the DUTCH INSCRIPTION at the back

Int Jaer dniſzſt vyſhondert en XXIII' op ten XXIX dach *in*
December ſoe hebben adriaen adriaenſſzende Jonc vrauw
paeſchine van den ſteyne gefon*deert bennen* deſz *kerk* op
Suncte Cornelis ouctaer eene *eenige miſſe* daechs de
Welke de kerckm'rs angenomen *bebben* te doen doene en
Tonderhoudene. te begginnene de *daege*miſſe altyt nader
Clock ſlach van thien nurn daer den prieſter vooren hebben
Zal vit poont g's vlaems t ſiaers jn vier termine den coſter dieter
Voorlt miſſe luiden ſal de groote ſcelle V. ſſ. ge t ſiaers op ſinte aechte
Dach els men huer beyder jaergetyde doet oft des ander
Daechs daerna jndien zy op eenen ſondach com't ende op
Gheenen dach anders ſoe zullen de voorn kerckm'rs of *die*
Beſitters ſyn ſal t ſavens ter vigelie ent ſmerghens ter miſſe
Doen brengben ben gracht pelle en ſaerge ende daer updoen
Stellen VIII bernende ſtallichten van waſſe ende de vier
Kerckm'rs de iii' heleghegheeſtm'rs endeken en beleeders buyſor
Van Sinte Cornelis ouctaer zullen come zitten ten grave ter
Vygelie van ix leſſen en ter miſſe van requiem die deroorn'
Bezitters doen ſinghen zullen mette volle' chore met andoenders
En providerders leverendaer toe dat offerliecht daer de volle
Choer de kerckm'rs helegheeſtm'rs deken en baleedets van de
*Clock*enluiders huere huyſiranwe de priſter bezitter van dezer
Miſſe coſter coſtriſſen ende bodel mede zullen gaen offeren
Singhende onder de offtraude de Sequentie Dies ire dies illa, *&c.*
Daer vooren de voorn bezitters t goets ghehouden zullen zynte
Betalen jnde vigelie den deke iiij g' elck canoinck, vice paſtoer,
Coraelmeeſtar ij ge elcken capelaen ende mercenarius .I. g' ende
Elck chorael xii te ende des anderdaechs jn de miſſe dieſgelyke
Wel inſlaende zoe en zal niement van hemluiden hierafgauder
Dan die p'nt zyn van beghinſel van den dienſt tot eynde noch
Zullen zy betalen den prieſter die de miſſe voerſz ſinghenzal vi g'
De endoenders elcxii g' die providierder ii g' de coſter ii g' de
Coſtriſſen t ſamen vi g' voor t decken en' de kaerſen t ontſteken

This ſeems to be a contract in the Dutch language for an annual maſs. The parts defaced are filled up by conjecture, as may be ſeen by the words in *Italics*; only as the words *eenwig* [eternal, perpetual], and *eenig* [ſingle], begin both with *ee*, and the reſt of the word is effaced, this word is therefore very dubious; but fortunately in the ſenſe it makes no difference; for if a ſingle

of the brass plate in Norton Disney church, mentioned p. cxxii.

In the year thousand five hundred and XVIII on the XXIX day *in*
December so have Adrian Adriaensſ. and young Lady
Paesschine Van Den Staine founded within this church on
Saint Cornelis altar a *single mass daily*
which the churchmasters have accepted to cause to be performed
and continued to begin the daymass always after the clock
has struck the hour of ten, for which the priest is to have
VII pound gr. Flemish a year, in four termes; the sexton, who
at the foresaid mass shall ring the large bell, V gr. a year on Saint Agatha's
day, when both are yearly paid; or on the following
day, if this day comes on a Sunday, and on
no other day; so shall the before-mentioned churchmasters, or he
who shall be possessor, in the evening at the vigils, and in the morning at
Mass, *cause to be brought* the grave cloth and serge, and thereon cause
to be put VIII burning torches of wax, and the four
Churchmasters, the III Holy Ghostmasters, and the dean and the wife of the
Director of Saint Cornelis altar, shall come and sit at the grave at
Vigils of IX lessons and at the mass of requiem, which the foresaid
Possessors shall cause to be sung with the full quire with affectors
and providers furnishing thereunto the oblation light wherewith the
full quire, the churchmasters, the Holy Ghostmasters, the dean, and the directors
of the bellringers, their wives, the priest-possessor of this mass,
The sexton, sextonesses, and beadle, shall go and offer,
Singing, whilst offering, the Sequences Dies iræ Dies illa &c.
Wherefore the foresaid possessors shall be obliged
to pay at the vigils to the dean IIII groats, to every canon, vicepastor,
Choralmaster, II groats; to ev'ry chaplain and mercenary I groat; and
to ev'ry choralis XII . . .; and the day following, at the mass, the same;
Being it well understood, that nobody of them shall profit hereof
unless they be present from the beginning of the service to the end.
Likewise they shall pay to the priest who shall sing the foresaid mass
VI groats, the affectors each II groats, the provider II groats, the sexton II groats,
the sextonesses together VI groats for covering and lighting the candles.

or *eenige* mass is always annually performed, it becomes an *eenwige* or perpetual mass. To keep the closer to the original, the translation is made very verbal, as may be seen in the word *kerkmeester*, here translated *churchmaster*; *churchwarden* would have been more modern, but not so near to the original.

T A B L E.

XIth CENTURY.

1065	EDWARD the CONFESSOR,	*Westminster,*	1
1074	Editha his Queen,	———	8
1069	Archbishop Stigand,	*Winchester,*	—
1073	Bishop Leofric,	*Exeter,*	—
1084	—— Arfast,	*Thetford,*	—
1089	William Warren, Earl of Surry,	*Lewes,*	—
1081	Gundreda his Countess,	———	—
1085	Abbot Vitalis,	*Westminster,*	10
1092	Bishop Remigius,	*Lincoln,*	11
1059	—— Dudo,	*Wells,*	—
1088	—— Giso,	———	—
1089	WILLIAM the CONQUEROR,	*Caen,*	—
1086	Maud his Queen,	———	13
992	Bishop Oswald,	*Worcester,*	—
1095	—— Wulstan,	———	—
1099	—— Osmund,	*Salisbury,*	—
——	—— Raynelm,	*Hereford,*	—
1080	Richard, son of the Conqueror,	*Winchester,*	14
1090	Constance, daughter of the Conqueror,	*St. Melaine,*	—

XIIth CENTURY.

1100	WILLIAM RUFUS,	*Winchester,*	15
——	Ingelrica,	*Hatfield Peverel,*	16
——	Juga Baynard,	*Dunmow,*	—
1107	Robert Fitz Haimon,	*Tewkesbury,*	—
1108	Bishop Gundulf,	*Rochester,*	17
1115	—— Raynelm,	*Hereford,*	—
1119	—— Theulphus,	———	18
——	—— Losinga,	*Norwich,*	—
1122	—— Blowet,	*Lincoln,*	—
1125	Abbot John,	*Peterborough,*	19
——	Edith D'Oilli,	*Osney,*	—
1134	Robert Curthose,	*Gloucester,*	—
1135	HENRY the FIRST,	*Reading,*	20
1139	Bishop Roger,	*Salisbury,*	—
1147	Robert, Earl of Gloucester,	*Bristol,*	23
1148	Gilbert de Clare, Earl of Pembroke,	*Tintern,*	—
——	Bishop Betune,	*Hereford,*	—
——	Geoffrey de Magnaville,	*The Temple,*	—
1150	Bishop Chichester,	*Exeter,*	24
1155	Henry of Huntingdon,	*Lincoln,*	—
——	Abbot Martin,	*Peterborough,*	—
1159	—— Waldevus,	*Mailros,*	—
1160	—— Blois,	*Westminster,*	25
——	Archbishop Theobald,	*Canterbury,*	—
1167	Bishop Melun,	*Hereford,*	27
——	Empress Maud,	*Rouen,*	—
1170	Robert Fitz Harding,	*Bristol,*	—
1174	Bishop Blois,	*Winchester,*	—
1176	Abbot Laurentius,	*Westminster,*	—
1178	Richard de Lucie,	*Lesnes,*	27
1171	Archbishop Roger,	*York,*	—
1182	Prince HENRY, son of Henry II.	*Rouen,*	29
1184	Abbot Crispin,	*Westminster,*	—
1189	HENRY the SECOND,	*Font Evraud,*	—
——	Bishop Toclive,	*Winchester,*	—
1191	—— John,	*Exeter,*	—
1197	—— Longchamp,	*Ely,*	—
1198	—— de Constantiis,	*Worcester,*	—
——	Walter } Fitzwalters,	*Dunmow,*	31
——	Matilda, }		
1199	Abbot Andrew,	*Peterborough,*	—
——	Bishop Vere,	*Hereford,*	—
——	RICHARD the FIRST,	*Font Evraud,*	32
——	St. Cleres,	*Danbury,*	—

XIIIth CEN-

XIIIth CENTURY.

1200	St. Hugh,	*Lincoln,*	33
1201	Bishop Bleys,	——	36
1202	Abbot Alan,	*Tewkesbury,*	—
1203	Sir Hugh Bardolf,	*Banham,*	—
1205	Archbishop Walter,	*Canterbury,*	*35
1206	Bishop Marshall,	*Exeter,*	—
——	—— Blesensis,	*Lincoln,*	*36
1215	—— Bruse,	*Hereford,*	—
——	Alberic de Vere,	*Earl's Colne,*	—
1225	Prior Philip,	*Christchurch, Oxon.*	—
1219	William Marshall, Earl of Pembroke,	*the Temple,*	37
1219	Bishop Mapenore,	*Hereford,*	39
1221	Robert de Vere,	*Hatfield Broad Oak,*	—
1222	Abbot Humez,	*Westminster,*	—
1223	William de Tracy,	*Morthoe,*	—
1226	William Longespe, Earl of Sarum,	*Salisbury,*	41
——	John Lord Montacute,	——	—
1227	Robert Lord Ross,	*the Temple,*	—
1228	Archbishop Langton,	*Canterbury,*	42
1228	Bishop Fauconbrigge,	*Old St. Paul's,*	—
1229	—— Jorwerth,	*St. David's,*	—
1249	—— Anselm,	——	—
1230	Isabel, Countess of Cornwall and Gloucester,	*Beaulieu,*	—
1231	William Marshall,	*the Temple,*	43
1237	Bishop Poore	*Salisbury,*	—
1240	Llewellin, Prince of Wales,	*Llanrust,*	—
1241	Bishop Niger,	*Old St. Paul's,*	44
——	Lord Berkeley,	*Bristol,*	—
1243	Thomas Berkeley,	——	—
1246	Abbot Berking,	*Westminster,*	—
1247	Bishop Bingham,	*Salisbury,*	—
1250	—— Wendover,	*Westminster,*	—
1251	Robert and Ralph Neville,	*Coverham,*	45
1252	Sir Henry de Bathe,	*Christchurch, Oxon.*	—
——	Blanche, Queen of France,	*Pontoise,*	46
1253	Abbot Robert,	*Tewkesbury,*	—
1254	Bishop Northwold,	*Ely,*	—
——	—— Grostete,	*Lincoln,*	47
1257	Roger de Weseham,	*Litchfield,*	49
1255	Archbishop Gray,	*York,*	—
1256	Bishop Kilkenny,	*Ely,*	—
——	—— York,	*Salisbury,*	—
1257	Children of Henry III. }	*Westminster,*	—
1282	Children of Edward I. }		
1256	William Plantagenet, }	*the Temple,*	—
1241	Gilbert Marshall, }		
1258	Archbishop Sewal,	*York,*	52
——	Isabel, Countess of Athol,	*Canterbury,*	—
——	Abbot Crokesley,	*Westminster,*	—
1261	Bishop Ethelmar,	*Winchester,*	53
1262	Abbot John de Caleto,	*Peterborough,*	—
1263	Bishop Bridport,	*Salisbury,*	—
——	Hugh de Vere earl of Oxford,	*Earl's Colne,*	54
1262	Bishop Button,	*Wells,*	—
12 5	Simon de Montfort, Earl of Leicester,	*Evesham,*	55
129[illegible]	Bishop Aquablanc,	*Hereford,*	56
1270	—— de la Wyle,	*Salisbury,*	57
——	Sir Fulk de Kerdeston,	*Repeham,*	—
1272	Henry the Third,	*Westminster,*	—
1274	Bishop Button,	*Wells,*	58
1277	—— Merton,	*Rochester,*	59
1279	—— Gravesend,	*Lincoln,*	60
1280	—— Bronscomb,	*Exeter,*	61
——	—— Chishull,	*Old St. Paul's,*	—
1282	Nicholas de Ry,	*Gosberton,*	—
——	Bishop Cantilupe,	*Hereford,*	62
1286	Prior Paris,	*Peterborough,*	—
——	Prior Cliffe,	——	—
1295	Prior Basing,	*Winchester,*	—
1289	Bishop Wykehampton,	*Salisbury,*	63
1290	Eleanor, Queen of Edward I.	*Westminster,*	—
——	Eleanor, Mother of Edward I.	*Ambresbury,*	66
1293	Bishop de la Corner, }	*Salisbury,*	67
1291	—— Longespe, }		

1292 Archbishop

1292	Archbishop Peckham,	*Canterbury,*	—
1293	Agatha de Narborough	*Norborough,*	—
—	Aveline, Countess of Lancaster,	*Westminster,*	—
1295	Robert Vere, Earl of Oxford,	*Earl's Coln,*	68
—	Urien de St. Piere,	*St. Pierr,*	—
1296	Edmond, Earl of Lancaster,	*Westminster,*	—
1298	Bishop de Luda,	*Ely,*	77
—	Sir Robert Shurland,	*Minstre,*	—
—	Elias de Bekingham,	*Boteham,*	78
—	Ralph de Hengham,	*Old St. Paul's,*	—
—	Alban,	*Much Hadham,*	—
—	William de Valence, Earl of Pembroke,	*Westminster,*	—

XIVth CENTURY.

1300	Ela Longespe,	*Osency,*	79
1301	Bishop Gifford,	*Worcester,*	—
1302	—— March,	*Wells,*	80
1303	Archbishop Corbridge,	*Southwell,*	—
1304	John Warren, Earl of Surry,	*Lewes,*	—
1305	Dean Husee,	*Wells,*	81
—	Henry Lacy, Earl of Lincoln,	*Old St. Paul's,*	—
1306	Edward the First,	*Westminster,*	—
1307	Bishop Bitton,	*Exeter,*	—
1308	Canon De la Barr,	*Hereford,*	82
1309	Bishop Haselshaw,	*Wells,*	—
1311	Sir Robert Du Bois,	*Fersfield,*	—
1316	Bishop Swinfield,	*Hereford,*	83
1319	—— Dalderby,	*Lincoln,*	—
1320	Dean Aquablanc,	*Hereford,*	84
1321	Bishop Langton,	*Litchfield,*	—
1243	—— Pateshull,	————	85
1323	Aymer de Valence, Earl of Pembroke,	*Westminster,*	—
—	John Benstead,	*Bovingdon,*	91
1325	Adam de Frampton,	*Wiberton,*	88
—	Sir John de Freville,	*Little Shelford,*	89
1326	Bishop Stapeldon,	*Exeter,*	90
	Hugh le Despencer, jun.	*Tewkesbury,*	—
1327	Edward the Second,	*Gloucester,*	92
—	Archbishop Reynolds,	*Canterbury,*	—
1329	Bishop Mortival,	*Salisbury,*	—
—	Abbot John,	*Tewkesbury,*	—
1332	Abbot Knowle,	*Bristol,*	93
1333	Emma de Mountalt,	*Stradset,*	—
—	Abbot Curtlington,	*Westminster,*	—
—	Archbishop Mepham,	*Canterbury,*	—
—	Abbess Juan,	*Romsey,*	94
1334	John of Eltham,	*Westminster,*	—
1337	Bishop Hotham,	*Ely,*	95
—	William Grandison,	*St. Mary Ottery,*	—
1340	William of Wyndsor, }	*Westminster,*	96
—	Blanch de la Tour, }		
1342	Abbot Meutemore,	*St. Alban's,*	—
1343	Bishop Burghersh,	*Lincoln,*	—
—	—— Thomas Charlton,	*Hereford,*	—
1345	Henry, Earl of Lancaster,	*Leicester,*	97
1346	Sir Humphrey Littlebury,	*Holbeche,*	—
1345	Bishop Aungerville,	*Durham,*	98
1347	—— Gower,	*St. David's,*	—
—	Sir Hugh Hastings,	*Elsing,*	—
1348	Archbishop Stratford,	*Canterbury,*	101
1349	——— Bradwardin	————	—
—	Abbot Sutton,	*Dorchester,*	—
—	Robert Egglesfield,	*Queen's Coll. Oxon.*	102
1351	William de Rothwell,	*Rothwell,*	103
1352	Bishop Hethe,	*Rochester,*	—
—	William de Bois,	*Fersfield,*	104
1354	Elizabeth Lady Montacute,	*Christchurch, Oxon.*	105
—	John } Cobham,	*Cobham,*	—
—	Joan } Cobham,		106
—	Agnes } Cobham,		—
—	Maud } Cobham,		107
—	Cecilia Kerdeston,	*Repeham,*	—
1354	Robert de Hungerford,	*Hungerford,*	—
1356	Bartholomew Lord Burghersh,	*Lincoln,*	108
1358	Isabel, Queen of Edward II.	*Grey Friers, London,*	109

1360 Henry,

1360	Henry, Duke of Lancaster,	*Leicester,*	—
—	Bishop Trilleck,	*Hereford,*	—
1361	John Lord Welles,	*Lincoln,*	111
—	Philip Peletot	*Watton,*	113
—	Robert de Bokking,	*Starsted Mountfitchet,*	—
—	Robert de Buers,	*Acton,*	—
—	Ralph } Lord Neville,	*Durham,*	114
—	John, }		
—	Thomas Lord Berkeley,	*Berkeley,*	—
1358	Sir John Beauchamp,	*Old St. Paul's,*	—
1363	Bishop Applebee,	*Carlisle,*	115
1396	—— Welton,	——	—
1364	Robert Braunche,	*Lynne,*	—
1365	Sir John Maltravers,	*Lechiot Maltravers,*	117
—	Sir Miles } Stapylton,	*Ingham,*	119
1422	Sir Bryan, }		
—	Sir Oliver Ingham,	——	120
14.0	Sir Roger de Bois,	——	—
1366	Archbishop Islip,	*Canterbury,*	121
—	Sir Walter Malebysse,	*Acaster Mallebis,* 122,	177
1367	William de la Pole,	*Hull,*	—
—	Thomas Cobham,	*Cobham,*	—
1369	Bishop Louis Charlton,	*Hereford,*	123
—	Philippa, Queen of Edward III.	*Westminster,*	—
1368	Lionel, Duke of Clarence,	——	125
1370	Sir John de Erpingham,	*Erpingham,*	126
—	John Evesham,	*Worcester,*	—
1370	Thomas Beauchamp, Earl of Warwick,	*Warwick,*	127
1371	Thomas Vere, Earl of Oxford,	*Vendosme,*	129
1:51	Guy de Beauchamp,	*Earl's Coln,*	130
1372	Nicholas Lord Cantilupe,	*Lincoln,*	—
—	Edward, eldest son of the Black Prince,	*King's Langley,*	131
—	John de Bicobury,	*Shillingford,*	—
—	Joan Wynston,	*Nutton,*	—
1374	Archbishop Wittlesey,	*Canterbury,*	—
1375	Bishop Wyvill,	*Salisbury,*	132
—	Edward Lord Despencer,	*Tewkesbury,*	133
1376	Archbishop Langham,	*Westminster,*	134
1375	Joan, Countess of Athol,	*Westminster,*	135
—	Sir Richard Pembridge,	*Hereford,*	—
1376	EDWARD the BLACK PRINCE,	*Canterbury,*	136
—	Robert Attelath,	*Lynne,*	138
1377	EDWARD III.	*Westminster,*	139
—	Hugh Courtney first Earl of Devonshire,	*Exeter,*	24
—	Sir John de Creke,	*Westley Waterless,*	—
1362	Robert } de Ufford, Earl of Suffolk,	*Campasse,*	143
1381	William }		
—	Markenfield,	*Ripon,*	—
—	Richard Lions,	*London,*	144
—	Bishop Hatfield,	*Durham,*	—
1383	Joan, wife of the Black Prince,	*Stamford,*	145
1384	Sir John Harsick,	*Harsick,*	146
—	William Dybbys,	*Campden,*	147
—	Philippa de Beauchamp,	*Nettlen,*	—
	Abbots Birchester, Bebington and Mershton,	*Chester,*	—
1385	Margaret de Cobham,	*Cobham,*	—
1386	Nicholas Litlington, abbot of Westminster,	*Westminster,*	148
1420	William Colchester, abbot of Westminster,	——	149
1386	William Estfield,	*Tickhill,*	—
1388	Sir Simon Burley,	*Old St. Pauls,*	—
1389	Michael de la Pole, Earl of Suffolk,	*Wingfield,*	150
1390	William West,	*Sudborough,*	151
1391	Margaret lady Willughby,	*Spilsby,*	—
—	Guy de Brien,	*Tewkesbury,*	—
—	Robert Swynborne,	*Little Horsley,*	152
1392	Henry de Cobham,	*Cobham,*	—
—	John Harold, dean of Hereford,	*Hereford,*	—
1394	Sir John Hawkwood,	*Sible Hedingham,*	153
1395	John Waltham, bishop of Salisbury,	*Westminster,*	154
—	Lady Mohun,	*Canterbury,*	—
1396	Thomas de la More, abbot of St. Albans,	*St. Albans,*	—
—	Archbishop Courtney,	*Canterbury,*	—
—	Sir John Golofre,	*Westminster,*	155
1397	Archbishop Waldby,	——	156
—	Thomas of Woodstock, Duke of Gloucester,	——	—
—	Thomas Holand, Earl of Kent,	——	157

1398 Sir

Additional Monuments not exactly ascertained.

Bishop

	Biſhop Harewell, —— Ergum, King INA.	*Wells,*	199
	Biſhop Brithwy,	*Glaſſenbury,*	—
	Lacy,	*Heukſtridge,*	—
	St. Quintin,	*Hinton St. George,*	200
	Templar,	*Exeter,*	201
	Monuments at	*Kingſweer and Ilfracombe,*	—
	———	*Winchester,*	—
	Draitons,	*Dorcheſter,*	—
1387	Sir Robert de Grey,	*Rotherfield Grey,*	202
1291	Biſhop Inglethorpe,	*Rocheſter,*	—
1214	—— Glanville,	———	203
	Sir Roger de Northwold,	*Minſtre,*	—
	Sir John de Gonſhal,	*Aſh,*	—
	Lancrock,	—	204
	Baz,	*Ickham,*	—
	John and Mariote de Crepe,	*Stroud,*	—
1375	Peter de Lacy,	*Northfleet,*	—
	Abbot,	*St. Alban's,*	205
1335	Abbot Wallingford,	———	206
	Hermits Roger and Sigar,	———	—
	Abbots,	———	207
1500	Richard Standen,	———	—
	Bartholomew Halley,	———	—
	Robert Beauner,	———	—
	John de la Lee,	*Albury,*	208
	Monument at	*Royſton,*	—
	———		
	Robert de Gravele, Walter de Molington,	*Watton,*	209
	Grey or Freville,	*Little Mundane,*	210
	Monument at	*King's Langley,*	—
	———	*Eaſtwic,*	211
	Sir Walter de Patteſhull,	*Tolleſhunt Knights,*	—
	Richard Montfichet,	*Stanſted Mountfichet,*	—
	Monuments at	*Tuddington,*	212
	Walter Roloun, Nicholas Roland,	*Cople,*	—
	Monuments at	*Tempsford,*	—
	John Coveſgrave,	*Eton Socon,*	—
1339	Sir William Bernak,	*Hetherſet,*	214
1372	Joan Wynſton,	*Nelton,*	215
	Cecilia Kerdeſton,	*Reepham,*	—
	Henry de Nottingham,	*Holm,*	—
1373	Ralph de Shelton,	*Shelton,*	—
	Braſs figure at	*Gorleſton,*	216
	Monument at	*Stonham Aſpal,*	—
	Cloptons	*Long Melford,*	—
	Lionel, duke of Clarence,	*Clare,*	—
1317	Robert de Ufford,	*Rendleſham,*	217
	John Wingfield, Another, William de Boville,	*Letheringham,*	218
	Eſmound de Brundiſh,	*Brundiſh,*	—
	Trumpington,	*Trumpington,*	219
	Chambrelan,	*Landbeach,*	220
	Monuments at	*Ely,*	—
	Burghs,	*Burgh green,*	221
1255	Biſhop Everdon,	*the Temple,*	—
	Sir Nicholas de Styvecle,	*Great Stukeley,*	—
	Monument in	*Sandleford chapel,*	222

CENTURY

CENTURY XI.

A

Death came dryvynge after, and all to duſt paſhed
Kings & Kayſers, Knightes & Popes,
Learned ne lewed, he ne let no man ſtande
That he hitte even he never ſtode after.
Many a lovely lady & lemmans of Knightes
Swoned & ſwelted for ſorrow of Deathe's dintes.

PIERS PLOWMAN.

C E N T U R Y XI.

THE tomb of EDWARD THE CONFESSOR, the laſt of the Saxon line, may fairly be ſaid to be the firſt of Norman work among us. His original one before the high altar [1] was too inauſpicious to his ſucceſſor to let it remain long. Wolſtan, biſhop of Worceſter, a great favourite of king Edward, refuſed to reſign his ſee to any other than the prince who placed him in it. He went to his benefactor's tomb, and ſtruck it with his ſtaff, which immediately adhered to it, ſo that it could not be plucked away by any prayers or hand but Wolſtan's [2]. 1065

The Conqueror, on his firſt coming to London, paid a viſit to this tomb, and made an offering of two palls to lay over it. He not long after altered the tomb, and built a more curious one of ſtone, ſaid to be very coſtly [3].

In his charter to Weſtminſter Abbey, by which he gave them other lands in exchange for Windſor, which the Confeſſor had given them, after a gift of £100. of ſilver to complete the building of the Abbey, he adds, "Ob reverentiam "nimii amoris quem ego in ipſum inclitum regem Edwardum habueram tumbum "ejus & reginæ juxta eum poſitæ ex auro & argento fabrili opere artificiosè de"coris mirifice operiri feci [4]." This was the leaſt reſpect he could ſhew to the memory of a prince whoſe pious chaſtity had left the ſucceſſion open to him.

The coffin of the Confeſſor was firſt opened 36 years after his death, when Gilbert Criſpin was abbot, 1101, and found perfectly incorrupt, the joints flexible and ſound, the fleſh whiter than ſnow, and the beard of the ſame colour. Gundulf, biſhop of Rocheſter, would fain have got a hair of it, but it would not ſtir. I ſhall tranſcribe Alured abbot of Rievaulx's account of this firſt tranſlation, as he calls it. "Accedunt ad tumulum ſancti viri qui ad "hoc fuerunt invitati, ſullatoque lapide quo ſarcoſagum claudebatur, tanta odoris "fragrantia omnium narihus, ut et eccleſia repleretur, & in ſepulchro aromata "ſcaturire putarentur. Primum deinde pallium quo ſacratiſſima membra fue-

[1] Widmore's Hiſt. of Weſtminſter Abbey, p. 15.
[2] Dart's Antiq. of Weſtminſter Abbey, I. 52. & aut. ibi cit.
[3] Allred Rieval de vita Edw. p. 408.
[4] Walpole's Anecd. of Painting, I. 19.

"runt

"runt involuta priſtinam venuſtatem & integritatem reſervaſſe conſpiciunt. Spe "deinde gloriæ potioris animati extracto pallio cætera ornamenta veſteſque con- "ſiderant, & omnia ſolida invenerunt & integra. Producunt brachia, plicant "digitos, articulos explorant, & omnia ſana, omnia flexibilia, & antiquo repe- "riuntur vigore firmiſſima. Inveſtigant poſtremo carnis integritatem pariter & "colorem, quæ vitro purior nive candidior futuræ reſurrectionis gloriam præ- "ferebat. At cum deſideratam faciem ejus attingere omnes pariter timuiſſent, "præfatus epiſcopus Roffenſis teſtimonio conſcientiæ vel amoris factus audacior, "ſudario quo caput ſanctiſſimum tegebatur manum injecit, & a parte inferiori "diſcendens barbam beata canicie niveam fide plenus extraxit, eam ac ſi viveret "mento firmius inhærere præſentiens. Delectatus miraculo & deſiderio igni- "tus pilum unum extrahere, ſibique ſervare conatur; ſed hæſit firmius, nec ſe- "quitur voluntatem effectus.—Itaque retento pallio quo ſanctiſſima ejus membra "fuerant involuta, aliud æque precioſum apponunt, diligenterque curatam glebam "illam dulciſſimam ſuo recondunt in thalamo [1]."

Miracles multiplying at the tomb, abbot Gervaſe de Blois, about 1158, applied to pope Innocent II. to get Edward canonized. His want of ſucceſs did not diſcourage the next abbot Laurence, who, in a ſermon, publicly called upon Henry II. and his ſubjects to ſecond his wiſhes. Such an application could not fail of ſucceſs. Pope Alexander III. iſſued an order for the canonization of the "glorious king Edward." Henry II. at the inſtigation of Becket (who little ſuſpected how ſoon it would be his turn to be martyred and ſainted) prepared an higher tomb and rich ſeretory, into which his reliques were tranſlated 1163 [2], 77 years after his burial. This ſolemn ceremony was performed at midnight; and, upon opening his coffin, his body was found uncorrupted: for which reaſon Flete, the hiſtorian of this abbey, ſays, *precioſiſſimum incorrupti corporis ſui theſaurum in hoc ſacro monaſterio reponi mandavit.* The habit in which he was dreſt was taken off, and likewiſe the ring which he had given to St. John the Evangeliſt diſguiſed as a beggar, and which the apoſtle had returned him by certain pilgrims from the Holy Land. Of the burial clothes (*tres panni*) abbot Laurence made three embroidered copes (*capas brudatas*). The body was arrayed (as it appeared, if the late diſcovery by Charles Taylour, who drew out of the coffin pieces of gold-coloured and flowered ſilk and linen, were true) *veſtimento boloſerico* as uſual, depoſited in a cheſt of oak, and removed into the aforeſaid ſeretory.

From this time the royal tomb became a ſacred ſhrine. When Henry III. rebuilt the church, he erected, in a chapel dedicated to St. Edward, an higher tomb, in which it is ſaid he incloſed the two former ſeretories, (though Mr. Dart doubts this) and placed over him a third of gold and precious ſtones. In this ſhrine his body was lodged 1269 [3], the king himſelf, his two ſons and brother, and the chief nobility, aſſiſting to carry it; and in or near it was placed in a gold cup the heart of Henry, ſon of Richard, king of the Romans, ſlain at Viterbo [4]. This ſhrine Mr. Widmore, from Wykes, ſays, was made 1269 [5]. Mr. Widmore adds, and after him Sir Joſeph Ayloffe [6], that Henry had before made one, 1241; but that was not ſufficiently ſumptuous, or not conveniently ſituated, or it might be new made for the ſake of the Moſaic-work, then probably firſt introduced into England from Rome. Mr. Vertue did not know of the ſhrine made 1241, but refers 1269 to that of Pietro Cavallini, who, he ſuppoſes, was commemorated on it in an inſcription to the following effect, not noticed by Camden in his account of the monuments here, 1600, 1603, 1606. Great part of it was remaining in Keep's time, who ſays the other was of a late hand [7].

[1] P. 408, 409.
[2] Bromton & Matthew of Weſtminſter. "Præſente rege Henrico qui hæc procuraverat." Mat. Par. 99. See the Ceremony in Taylor, 29—31.
[3] Dart, ubi ſup. In a coffin of pure gold. Weever, 455.
[4] Wikes, 88. Ann. Waverl. 225. and Widmore, p. 75.
[5] 1166, Knighton, col. 2438.
[6] Account of the Weſtminſter Monuments, p. 14.
[7] P. 138.

Anno

Anno milleno Domini cum feptuageno
Et bis centeno, cum completo quafi deno,
Hoc opus eft factum, quod " Petrus duxit in actum
" Romanus civis," homo, caufam nofcere fi vis,
Rex fuit Henricus fancti prefentis amicus.

Mr. Vertue adds, the words marked by inverted commas only remained in April 1741; and in June following they were picked out and erafed.

The cavities of them in the cement are ftill very apparent; and at the eaft end, or head of the fhrine, I read, Apr. 14, 1781, the following words:

——uxit in actum Romanus civis ho.——

They are cut in the moft antient fimple Gothic letters of this century, without abbreviation:

No more of this original infcription is now to be difcovered. A coat of plaifter has been laid over it on the north and fouth fides, and at the ends of the eaft fide, which has totally concealed it; and on this coat coloured black has been written in gold capitals the following infcription in Richard the Second's time [1]:

O Omnibus infignis O virtutum laudibus O heros fanctus Edwar O dus.

Eaft fide:

co [here follows the infcription in Gothic letters] die.

North fide:

O moriens 1063 fu O per æthera fcandit O furfum corda.

The rounds in both infcriptions are in relief, and formerly contained mofaic-work. At the head and end of this fecond infcription are thefe figles, which to better myftagogues than myfelf may unravel the whole. The firft is moft unfaithfully given, the other totally omitted, in Vertue's and Dart's plates.

It is controverted whether the fhrine was erected by the king or his chancellor Ware, who was chofen abbot of this houfe 1260, 43 Hen. III. and went to Rome for his confecration the fame year. There it has been fuppofed he met with Cavallini, then in high fafhion, having juft finifhed, 1256, at the expence of Giacomo Giovanni Capocci and his wife, in the church of St. Maria Maggiore, an elegant fhrine of St. Simplicius and Fauftina, which, on the new paving the

[1] Mr. Dart is miftaken in fuppofing the infcription of Richard II's time to have been put on when the old one, which was inlaid, was worn away. We have feen many letters of it remain fo lately as 1741. But perhaps the greater part were picked out much fooner.

church

church 1768, was brought over to England, and is now at Strawberry-hill, set with stones in mosaic-work, and supported with wreathed columns.

Ware was sent to Rome by Henry III. 1267, to procure workmen for his new building. Mr. Dart [1] remarks a material difference between the work of the shrine, and that of the pavement of the Confessor's chapel and the high altar: that of the shrine being of a thin mosaic, like the tomb of Henry III.

The conformity between the shrine and the tomb is most striking, whether we observe the stile of the design or the inlaying: the capitals of the pillars at the corners of Henry III's. tomb and those of the niches of the Confessor's are the same: the porphyry is of the same polish.

The artist brought over by the abbot executed the singularly rich, but now miserably neglected, pavement of the high altar at Westminster; on the north side of which the abbot had a monument with this inscription, alluding to this pavement;

> Abbas Ricardus de Ware qui requiescit
> Hic, portat lapides quos hic portavit ab urbe.

Ware died 1283.

The first invention of mosaic-work has been generally ascribed to Giotto, whose birth is dated 1276, and his death 1336, at the age of 60.

When Giotto is celebrated as the inventor of the art of working in mosaic, it must be understood of his executing elegant figures in it: for the general practice of this art had been long before him revived in Europe. In 977 the best artists were brought from Constantinople to Venice for rebuilding the church of St. Mark, which was ornamented with several works in mosaic [2]. The great dome at Pisa, in which were the like works, was begun in 1016; and in 1225 a heaven in mosaic was begun at St. John Baptist's church at Florence [3]. Besides St. Peter's at Rome, pope Innocent III. restored in 1200 some mosaics then decayed [4].

We have no reason to be surprized that there were able artists skilled in this manner of working so early as the reign of Henry III. and among them a Roman citizen named Peter, who should, on account of their merit, be invited by this magnificent monarch to adorn his grand and costly cathedral dedicated to St. Peter.

Andrea Tassi acquired great reputation by his works at Florence, particularly a large figure of Christ seven cubits long, which was much celebrated. He died 1294, aged 81.

Gaddo Gaddi, of Florence, worked with reputation both in Rome and Florence in mosaic-work. He died 1312, aged 73. These were both earlier than Giotto, Cavallini's master.

It is extraordinary what confusion we find in authors about Pietro Cavallini. Mr. Vertue [5] endeavours to prove, that the shrine of the Confessor, and the tomb of Henry I. who died 1272, were executed by this artist, who, he adds, made the shrine for the Capocci 1256, and died, according to Vasari and his epitaph at Rome, 1364, at the age of 85. By this last date, Cavallini could not have been born till 1279. Vasari says, Cavallini was born when Giotto restored painting to life, assisted him in his famous Bark of St. Peter (which was finished in 1319) and died at the age of 85. He does not ascertain the year of his death, nor does Baldinucci give the dates of his birth or death (contrary to his usual custom) but contents himself with telling us, that he flourished about 1310, and is of opinion that he drew towards the end of his life in 1372 [6]. He was of Rome, and was buried there in the church of St. Paul without the walls [7]. P.

[1] II. 24. [2] Ridolfi, Part I. p. 12. [3] Cinelli, Bellezze de Firenze, p. 27.
[4] Bonanni Hist. Templi Vaticani, p. 33. [5] Archaeol. I. 33. [6] Decen. I. Sec. II. p. 6, 7.
[7] Vasari. I cannot find any account of his monument in travellers.

Resta puts the birth and death of Giotto 1276—1336, of Pietro Cavallini 1304—1379, but these last dates are erroneous. Pietro Cavallini was born in 1279, and died 1364 [1].

The name of *Petrus Romanus Civis*, has led Vertue strangely astray. We do not find, indeed, any other Peter, a Roman. The probability seems to be, that this Peter was some workman sent either by Taffi or Gaddi to execute their designs. If any weight could be given to the accuracy of expression in monkish Latin rhymes, *duxit in actum* would seem to mean, *carried into execution*; but the writers of these jingles always sacrificed meaning to sound, so that no argument can fairly be drawn from their expressions.

It is not to be doubted, but the artist, whoever he was, executed both the shrine of the Confessor and the pavement at the same time, if he did not stay here till the death of Henry III. or perhaps returned again to do the monument. I am inclined to think from the words *cum completo quasi deno*, the date of the inscription of the shrine is to be translated 1280 instead of 1270, and then he may well have executed all three together; and there will be no improbability in Mr. Walpole's giving him the honour of designing the Eleanor crosses. Mr. Vertue adds, the design of Sebert's shrine on the south side of the altar, and the paintings over the shrine; and Sir Joseph Ayloffe, the monument of Aveline, countess of Lancaster. But admitting the objections above stated to Cavallini being the artist, not only the merit of these works, but that of the invention of working in Mosaic-work will be taken from him.

Mr. Talman drew the shrine of the Confessor, when nearer its original state, and the Society of Antiquaries employed Vertue to engrave his drawing.

On the north and south sides of the lower story, which is solid, are three niches or arches, and another at the east end not half the depth of the others; the back of each is inlaid with mosaic in as many different patterns; the little wreathed pillars inlaid with beautiful coloured mosaic, some of which is still in high preservation; Mr. Dart seems mistaken, when he supposed these niches to be intended for the sick and infirm to repose in.

On this basement or pedestal is a fertory or frame of wainscot, which Mr. Dart supposes of original erection, and to have been formerly covered with plates of metal; I rather think it was painted in pannels with figures of saints. It consists of two stories, very neat and regular, said in time past to have been curiously plated with gold, and adorned with precious stones, but Mr. Dart says it does not seem ever to have been covered over head. Great part of what are called precious stones is still there; for on the pilasters between the arches is a kind of Mosaic-work of stained glass [2], a customary ornament at that time, as appears by the tomb of Edmund Crouchback on the north side of the altar, which is inlaid after the same manner [3]. In the spandrils, the glass in one single place seems to cover colours, and shew them through. The frame was originally terminated at the top by a third story or pediment, as appears by Sandford's and Vertue's print, and that in the octavo account of the abbey 1722; but that upper frame is now sunk in. Over all was the curious one mentioned by Paris [4].

Mr. Dart was of opinion, from the difference of workmanship, that the shrine was built or repaired at different times. The pillars at the East end are very unlike each other [5], one having a Doric capital, the other a rich wreath of vine-leaves wretchedly expressed in the plate, and both stand on the base of the tomb: the pillars at the West end have no capitals, and their bases are buried in the earth. This last circumstance he accounts for, by observing, that under

[1] See Pilkington's Dictionary, articles, Taffi, Gaddi, Giotto, Cavallini.
[2] Dart II. 22. [3] See the Antiquary Society's print. [4] Dart Ib.
[5] These differences in the pillars are expressed in Vertue's print, but not in Dart's, though he gives the same side.

the coronation-chair the floor is paved with tiles different from the Mosaic pavement, in which place he inclined to think were steps to descend under the tomb, where very probably the enshrined body of the saint lay. The custom of enshrining, he says, was very different; sometimes the coffin was placed level with the surface of the earth, sometimes upon it, and sometimes *in altum*. The first was for men of exemplary piety and mortification, which was the case of this saint: the second for men of more early example, and was first a custom, as in the case of St. Cuthbert before he was sainted, and others, but afterwards allowed as a favour to saints of the second rank: the elevated body was usually for martyrs. Upon the most attentive examination, and the intermixture of red tiles with the pavement, I am inclined to think the same part of mosaic pavement was originally laid on such tiles. They now appear not only through several round holes, whence the mosaic has been removed, and where one might suspect them of being inserted by way of repair, but in other parts where they seem coæval with it. So that whether there was or was not a way at the back of the high altar under the coronation chair, by which to descend into the Confessor's vault, it was probably once covered, as well as the whole floor of this chapel with mosaic, which is broken into only by the tombs of the dutchess of Gloucester, John Waltham, bishop of Salisbury, 1395, and another older at the head, ascribed by Dart to Richard de Wendover, bishop of Rochester, 1250. Though I do not think Mr. Dart has accounted for this variation of the pillars at the West end, I cannot substitute a better hypothesis. I once conceived, from the plain face of the lower part of the shrine here, and rich inlaying of the upper, there might have been an altar against this end; but this is contradicted by the mosaic-work continuing close up to the shrine here, unless we suppose it removed hither at the dissolution. It is astonishing to observe on what a hard stone this beautiful and rich mosaic has been inlaid in rounds, lozenges, serpentine wreaths, and other forms.

Within this shrine lay the coffin, of firm strong wood, bound about with iron. The boards of this coffin being broken after the coronation of James II. and a hole of about 6 inches by 4 made in it, opposite to the right breast of the corpse, Mr. Taylor, or Mr. Keepe, on Saint Barnaby's day, 1685, after morning service, accompanied by two friends who had been viewing the tombs, examined the place by the help of a ladder. He put his hand into the hole, and turning the bones, drew from under the shoulder-bones a crucifix richly enamelled and gilt, affixed to a gold chain two feet long, which he shewed to his friends; but fearing to take them away without the knowledge of the bishop of Rochester then dean, and not being able to obtain access to him, he acquainted one of the choir with the discovery, and shewed him the things. This person advised him to take charge of them till he could see the dean. He did so for near a month, when he shewed them to the archbishop of York, Dr. Dolben, who introduced him with them to archbishop Sancroft. After this the discoverer had drawings made of them, and they were shewn to Sir William Dugdale, who promised to write some observations on them. The dean of Westminster at last saw them, and the finder had the satisfaction of depositing them in the royal hands. In consequence of this, the coffin was secured in a new one of two inch planks, fastened together with iron wedges.

The chain is described as being 24 inches long, of pure gold; the links oblong, and curiously wrought. The upper part to lie in the nape of the neck, was joined by a locket, composed of a large knob of massy gold of the size of a milled shilling, and half an inch thick. Round this went a wire, on which half a dozen little gold beads finely wrought hung loose. On each side of the locket were set two large square red stones, supposed rubies, and from it, fixed to two gold rings, the chain descended, and meeting below, past through a square piece of gold made hollow for the purpose, wrought into several angles, and painted

painted of different colours, refembling fo many precious ftones. To this was joined the crucifix, to be taken off at pleafure by a fcrew. It was in fhape like a crofs humettè flory or botonè; the upright part four inches, the tranfverfe fcarce three: all the ends neatly turned, and the botons enamelled with figures. The crofs had enamelled on it the figure of Chrift crucified, and an eye above cafting a ray on him: on the reverfe, a Benedictine monk, and on each fide of him thefe Roman capitals.

On the right limb, on the left,

(A)
Z A X
A

P
A C
H

The crofs was hollow, opening by a fcrew, as if to inclofe fome relique. The difcoverer drew the head to the hole, and found it very found and firm; the upper and nether jaws whole, and full of teeth; a lift of gold about an inch broad, like a coronet, furrounding the temples. There was alfo in the coffin white linen and gold coloured flowered filk, that looked indifferently frefh, but on a touch fell to pieces.

The author of this difcovery quotes Ailred abbot of Rievaulx's life of St. Edward p. 402, as faying, that after his death, " his body was wafhed, and embalmed with fweet fcenting odors and aromatick fpices, wrapped in white and precious linen, and thofe covered with rich and coftly veftments; *a coronet on his head, a crucifix on his breaft, and other regal enfigns of majefty.*" But all Ailred fays is, " Parantur regales exequiæ, preciofis lintheis & optimis palliis corpus involvitur." Hoveden (p. 256.) fays, he was buried the next day after his deceafe.

Such is the ftory told in the quarto pamphlet printed 1688, and figned Cha. Taylor. The truth of this difcovery was queftioned by Mr. Talman, who drew the fhrine, fince engraved by Vertue for the Society of Antiquaries, and in 1722 could find no traces of the coffin having been opened [1]. But this is not extraordinary, fince the writer exprefsly fays it was new cafed immediately after. Hearne, in a MS. note in my copy of this tract, fays, *Cha. Taylor* was an affumed name for *Henry Keepe*, the author of the firft Englifh account of the Weftminfter monuments. Mr. Dart [2] calls him *Young*, and fays it was H. Keepe who turned papift under James II. Who the writer was, and whatever credit is due to his narrative, we have already feen he is very little to be trufted in his extracts from the old hiftorians who relate the feveral tranflations of the Confeffor's body.

Mr. Le Neve imagined that what Taylor found was part of the jewels offered at this fhrine by Alphonfo the Third, fon of Edward I. with the golden coronet of Llewellyn, prince of Wales. But it is very unlikely fuch offerings fhould get within the coffin. At the fame time I am not without my doubts, that the crucifix and chain were not depofited with the body originally, or at any fubfequent tranflation.

I fhall juft add, that the prefent ftory among the Vergers is, that the difcoverer found with the chain a fceptre three feet long, which, after fhewing to one of his friends in Tothill-ftreet, was fhewn to the archbifhop, and by him to the king, who, when he abdicated the throne, carried it away, and prefented it to the pope, among whofe regalia it is ftill to be feen. If any more ftrefs could be laid on the oral than the printed ftory, one would fufpect, that the Confeffor was buried like Edward I. with his fceptre, &c. in his hands; and that by the decay of the coffin fome fuch paraphernalia came to light.

Within the wooden coffin ftrongly bounded with iron in the middle of the fhrine the body is ftill fuppofed to be lodged [3]. By a meafurement which I

[1] Antiquary Society's minutes. [2] II. 15.
[3] Antiq. of Weftm. I. 174. ditto by J. C. 154. Keepe, 138.

took

took of it April 14, 1781, it appears to be feven feet fix inches long, by two feet one inch wide at the head, and twenty-two inches at the feet, and twenty-two inches deep. It lies within the ftone-work at the depth of about fifteen inches from the top of the fide arches, and five from the ftone-work at each fide.

1074. The Confeffor's *virgin* wife EDITHA, daughter of earl Godwin, who furvived him fix years, and died 1074, was buried on the north fide of his tomb, but has no diftinct memorial. The words before cited from the Conqueror's charter feem to imply that fhe and her hufband had one common tomb.

1069. The celebrated archbifhop STIGAND died in prifon at *Winchefter*, and was buried there. Bifhop Fox lodged his remains in the fame leaden cheft with Wina, firft bifhop of Winchefter, with this fhort infcription:

Hic jacet Stigandus.

They were diflodged 1647 [1], and are now in another leaden cheft on the wall of the choir, without any diftinct memorial.

1073. The monument of LEOFRIC, firft bifhop of *Exeter*, who died 1073, and was buried in what was then the cemetery, but fince, by the addition of buildings, made the fouth tranfept of his cathedral, has been long fince demolifhed. That erected by the dean and chapter, 1568 [2], is in the ftyle of the age in which it was erected; an altar-tomb under an elliptic arch garretted at top, fpringing from grouped pillars, having the fame above their capitals. The firft border under the table is adorned with angels, the fecond with quatrefoils and little arches, and the lowermoft with plain compartments. On the upper border is this infcription in gold letters:

Leofric, the fyrst bishoppe of Exeter, lyeth here.

1084. The monument of ARFAST, firft bifhop of *Thetford*, who died 1084, is gone with the cathedral in which he was buried.

1089. No better fate has attended that of WILLIAM WARREN, earl of SURREY, who died 1089, and was buried in the Chapter-houfe at *Lewes*. His epitaph preferved in Dugdale [3] from the abbey regifter is as follows;

Hic, Guillielme comes, locus eft laudis tibi fomes,
Hujus fundator & largus fedis amator.
Ifte tuum funus decorat, placuit quia munus
Pauperibus Chrifti quod prompta mente dedifti.
Ille tuos cineres fervat Pancratius heres,
Sanctorum caftris qui te fociabit in aftris.
Optime Pancrati, fer opem te glorificanti;
Daque poli fedem talem tibi qui dedit ædem.

1051. But that of his countefs GUNDREDA, who died before him in child-bed [4] at Caftle Acre, May 27, 1085, has been recovered by a fortunate accident. This coffin-fafhioned tomb ftone of black marble, 5 feet 5 inches long to the break, 2 feet broad at head, and 22 inches at foot, was accidentally difcovered by Wm. Burrell, Efq. fixed over the tomb of Edward Shirley, Efq. who died Mar. 16, 1550, and was fon of John Shirley of Isfield, clerk of the kitchen to Henry VII. and cofferer to Henry VIII. fome of which family probably removed it from the monaftery foon after the diffolution into Isfield church, feven miles from Lewes.

[1] Godwin, 213. [2] Le Neve's Fasti 80. [3] Bar. I. 74. [4] Viperius cruciata, Lewes reg.

It

It was removed from thence 1774, at Mr. Burrell's coſt, to St. John Baptiſt's Southover church by Lewes, as neareſt to its original ſpot, which it was to have a ſecond time covered, could it have been determined in the ruins of the abbey. It is now incloſed within a pew, and this inſcription over it;

Within this pew ſtands the tomb-ſtone
of GUNDRAD, daughter of William the
Conqueror, and wife of William the firſt
Earl of Warren, which having been depoſited
over her remains in the Chapter-houſe
of Lewes priory, and lately diſcovered
in Isfield church, was removed
to this place at the expence
of William Burrell, Eſq.
A. D. 1774.

An elevation of its modern front was engraved with the ſtone itſelf for Mr. Watſon's Hiſtory of the Earls of Warren. The latter makes a head-piece to this century.

The form of the letters anſwers to thoſe on the tombs of biſhop Roger at Saliſbury, William Deincourt at Lincoln, between 1087 and 1100, Ilbert de Chaz at Monkton Farley, and that of Hilperic at Cologne [a]. One may account for the intermixture of the Saxon and Roman capitals here, by ſuppoſing the C maintained its ground with the Saxon names and orthography longer in theſe ſouthern countries. The ſigle ∽ occurs on our coins as late as the three firſt Edwards.

The inſcription is in leonine verſe, and contains a turn of ſentiment unuſual in monkiſh epitaphs.

Stirps, Gundreda, ducum, decus evi, nobile germen,
Intulit eccleſiis Anglorum balſama morum:
Mar[tis *or* tha] - - - - - - - -
- - - v.t miſeris, fuit ex pietate Maria.
Pars obiit Marthe, ſupereſt pars magna Marie.
O pie Pancrati, teſtis pietatis & equi,
Te facit heredem, tu clemens ſuſcipe matrem.
Sexta kalendarum Junii lux obvia carnis
Ifregit alabaſtu - - - - - - - -

The firſt line comprizes her illuſtrious deſcent more comprehenſively than biſhop Roger's. The ſecond alludes to her merit in firſt introducing into England the Cluniac order, a reform and perfecting of the Benedictine, and this is the *balſama morum*. Then follows a beautiful alluſion to the characters of the two ſiſters, Martha and Mary, in the Goſpel, with the happy application of the contraſt between them. The poet, concealing the blameable part of Martha's attachment to the world, ingeniouſly repreſents her worldly-mindedneſs as directed to and governed by the beſt views, thoſe of providing for the neceſſaries of life, and relieving the diſtreſſed. Enough remains of the third line to ſhew that the compariſon begins here, that the firſt word is the name of Martha, and that her example was followed by Gundreda in charitable diſtributions, while in her devotion ſhe copied the example of her other ſiſter, who ſat at Jeſus's feet attentive to his doctrine.

The corporal part, in which this good lady reſembled Martha, came to the end of all fleſh. The *pars magna Marie*, which I underſtand as ſynonymous with the *better part*, i. e. the ſoul, ſurvives. The addreſs to St. Pancratius is peculiarly happy. He was the patron of the new foundation, and of the old church which preceded

[a] Montf. I. 175.

it. The endowments of this houſe were very conſiderable; fourteen churches and chapels in Yorkſhire, beſides large poſſeſſions in Suſſex, and the church before of wood was rebuilt of ſtone. The revenue at the Diſſolution amounted to between £900. and £1000. a year. As the counteſs died in child-bed, and the mother only is recommended to the regards of the ſaint, it is probable the infant ſurvived. The ſeventh line fixes her death to the *ſixth* calends of June with Dugdale and Sanford, though an antient record ſeen by Le Neve[1] makes it the *eighth* calends. Notwithſtanding the harſhneſs of the conſtruction, I cannot underſtand *obvia* in the ſenſe of *hoſtilis*. Theſe two lines do not rhyme together. The compariſon with the two ſiſters holds very conſiſtently with ſtyling this good princeſs's devotions the breaking the alabaſter box of her fleſh and body, in alluſion to the alabaſter box of precious ointment with which Mary, the ſiſter of Lazarus, anointed the feet of Jeſus preparatory to his death; and with this the *balſama morum* correſpond. *Iſregit* wants, indeed, the mark of the N over it, and makes the verſe hobble; but there is a ſimilar omiſſion over *herede* in the ſecond line, where it is indiſpenſable; and inſtances of ſuch hobbling are not unfrequent.

Ordericus Vitalis is guilty of two miſtakes about this lady. He makes her ſurvive her huſband, which is expreſsly contradicted both by the regiſter of Lewes abbey and the earl's charter to it[2]; and he calls her daughter of Gherbod, a Fleming, to whom the Conqueror had given the city and earldom of Cheſter[3]; in which he is copied by Du Cheſne[4], Imhof[5], and Dugdale[6]. Milles[7] and Sandford[8] make her the Conqueror's fifth daughter. The ledger book of Lewes abbey[9] calls her daughter of Queen Matilda mother of Henry I. conſequently ſhe was daughter of the Conqueror.

1085. The monument of VITALIS, twenty-firſt abbot of *Weſtminſter*, and ſecond after the Conqueſt, who was elected 1076, and died 1082; (though Widmore puts his death 1085) is ſuppoſed to be ſtill ſubſiſting in the ſouth cloiſter there, miſtaken for that of *Laurentius*, another abbot. But ſince Flete deſcribes it as being "a ſmall one of *white marble* at the feet of *Gervaſius's*;" and Sporley, as "of white marble, plain, almoſt even with the pavement," I do not ſee how one of theſe three figures of abbots now there, and which are of *grey* or *blue* marble, can be aſcribed to him; much leſs one *with braſſes* deſcribed by Keepe. Theſe three figures are probably of this or the next century, and being without mitres, muſt precede *Laurence*, who procured the mitre for this houſe[10]; but I doubt they have loſt all the criteria for aſſigning them to their owners. See Widmore, p. 20. Dart's Appendix to Vol. II. p. 11. Mr. Dart's print is much too flattering. Mr. Baſire's here annexed is a faithful repreſentation of their preſent ſtate. The middlemoſt, which is alſo the rudeſt, being in ſo low relief as to be hollowed in the ſtone, and incloſed in a border, and without a mitre, which was granted afterwards, is now inſcribed GILBERTUS CRISPINUS, who immediately ſucceeded Vitalis, and died 1117, as Widmore, but as the preſent inſcription 1114. Widmore gives the middlemoſt to *Gervaſius*, who died 1160, but Dart denies it.

Vitalis's epitaph now gone, though the poetry be mean enough, is yet, ſays Mr. Widmore, better than thoſe of ſome of his ſucceſſors. It was this:

A vita nomen qui traxit, morte vocante,
Abbas Vitalis tranſiit, hicque jacet.

[1] MS. note in Dugdale's Baronage in my poſſeſſion.
[2] Mon. Aug. I. 616.
[3] P. 522. a. c.
[4] Tab. Geneal. com. Warr. & Surr. p. 1083.
[5] P. 2. Tab. XVIII.
[6] Bar. I. 74.
[7] Cat. of Honor. 62.
[8] P. 12.
[9] Mon. Ang. II. 909. in addit. ad tom I.
[10] The ſecond is dated 1176, conſequently the mitred one cannot be Vitalis as now inſcribed. Dart gives it to Humez, who died 1222. Add. Epit.

VITALIS ABBAS
1082
GISLEBERTVS CRISPINVS ABBAS
1114
LAVRENTIVS ABBAS
1176

Gilbert's epitaph was gone in Flete's time. Sir Joseph Ayloffe assured me there never were any inscriptions on the sides of these tombs, as I had conceived there might have been, like that on the sides of bishop Roger's at Salisbury.

On the north side of the altar at *Lincoln*, is a rich canopy monument of six arches with purfled pediments, buttresses, and finials; and at the head and feet within are double pannels of rich diversified foliage. In the south front of the lowermost of the two tombs covered by it are two quatrefoils in circles; a third replaced with a black marble table, with this modern epitaph, erected by bishop Fuller: 1092.

HUJUS FUNDATOR TEMPLI REMIGIUS URNA
HAC JACET ATQUE BREVI: SIT SATIS APTA VIRO!
SI TAMEN INGENTI TRIBUES ÆQUALE SEPULCHRUM
EJUS PAR MENTI, MENS EA QUANTA FUIT!
SIT TUMULUS TEMPLUM QUOD STRUXERAT IPSE, MINORE
NEC POSSIT TUMULO, AVT NOBILIORE TEGI.

The south front of the easternmost tomb has three knights in mail and surcoats, sitting and reclining their heads and arms on blank shields, an unusual decoration; and on the north front are two figures writing. The first of these tombs belongs to bishop REMIGIUS, who having translated the see from Dorchester hither, began to build this church 1088, and left it unfinished at his death, 1092. Both he and his successor Bloet, who finished the church, and died 1122, are said by Willis [1] to have been buried in the church of Remigius's building; the first in the choir, the other in the north transept, and both to have had contiguous monuments, or as he calls them *chapels*, on the north side of the choir. It seems probable, that the present monuments ascribed to both were erected over their remains within the old choir, when it was rebuilt by bishop Alexander in the reign of Henry I. and Stephen. This choir was continued further east about the close of Henry III's. reign, and the screen, rood-loft, and stalls, made in that of Edward II [2]. To some of these periods may these monuments be ascribed. They can therefore be mentioned here only by anticipation, being the work of the succeeding century. For this remark I am indebted to Mr. Essex's intimate acquaintance with every part of this cathedral. The knights on the front of this monument may denote the soldiers placed to guard our Lord's sepulchre; as on a tomb in the north side of the altar at Northwold, in Norfolk, where are three armed men between three trees, all in a reclining posture. These sepulchres were always erected on the north side of the altar. Thomas Fienes, lord Dacre, by his will, 1531, bequeathed his body to be buried on the north side the altar at Hurstmonceaux, and ordered, that a tomb should be made for placing there the sepulchre of our lord. Sir Henry Colet wills to be buried at Stepney, at the sepulchre before St. Dunstan, and his monument is still to be seen on the north side of the church [3].

The last of the monuments on the south side without the choir at *Wells* is by 1059.
Godwin [4] referred to bishop DUDO, who died 1059; and that on the north 1088.
side to his successor GISO, who died 1088 [5].

Though the CONQUEROR had no grave or monument in England, the circumstances that attended his death are connected with the present subject. He had no sooner breathed his last at the abbey of St. Gervase, on a hill out of Rouen to the west, than all his domestics not only forsook him, but plundered his apart- 1089.

[1] Cathedrals, II. 46. [2] See Arch. IV. 150—156. [3] Blomfield's Norfolk, I. 517, 518. [4] P. 365. [5] Ib. 366.

ments so completely, that his corpse was left naked, and he would have wanted a grave, had it not been for the more grateful clergy and the archbishop of Rouen, who ordered the body to be conveyed to Caen, and one Herluin, a gentleman of the place (*pagensis eques*) from pure goodness of heart (*naturali bonitate*) took upon himself the care of the funeral, provided the proper persons (*pollinctores & vespiliones*) and hired a carriage to convey it to the river, and thence quite to Caen. There the abbot and convent, attended by crouds of clergy and laity, came out to meet it. But as they were proceeding to pay the proper honours, they were alarmed by a sudden fire which broke out in a house, and destroyed great part of the city. The distracted people went to give the necessary assistance, and left the monks, with a few bishops and abbots, to go on with the service; which being finished, and the *sarcophagus* laid in the ground, the body still lying on the bier, Gilbert, bishop of Evreux, pronounced a long panegyric on the deceased; and, in conclusion, called on the audience to pray for his soul. On a sudden starts up from the croud Ascelin Fitz-Arthur, and demands a compensation for the ground they stood on, which he said William had forcibly taken from his father to found his abbey on it; and in God's name forbids the burying him on his property, or covering him with his turf. The bishops and nobles having satisfied themselves about the truth of his demand, were obliged to pay him immediately sixty shillings for the grave, and promise an equivalent for the rest of the ground, which they afterwards gave him. They then proceeded to the interment: but in laying the body in the sarcophagus, it was found to have been made so small by the ignorance of the mason, that they were forced to press the corpse with such violence, that the fat belly burst, and diffused an intolerable stench, which all the smoke of the censers and other spices could not overcome. The priests were glad to hurry over the service, and make the best of their of their way home in no small fright [r].

William Rufus erected to his father's memory a costly monument, executed by the goldsmith Otho, to whom he caused to be delivered a great quantity of gold, silver, and precious stones; and the following epitaph, composed by Thomas, archbishop of York, was put on it in gold letters [s].

Qui rexit rigidos Northmanos, atque Britanos
  Audacter vicit, fortiter obtinuit,
Et Cenomanenses virtute coercuit enses,
  Imperiique sui legibus applicuit;
Rex magnus parva jacet hic GULIELMUS in urna:
  Sufficit & magno parva domus domino.
Ter septem gradibus se volverat atque duobus
  Virginis in gremio Phœbus, & hic obiit.

In 1522, Peter de Marigny, bishop of Castres, and abbot of St. Stephen at Caen, at the sollicitation of a great cardinal, an archbishop, and an Italian bishop, desirous to see the remains of the Conqueror, opened his tomb, and found the body in the original situation. The abbot caused a painting to be taken of it on wood just as it appeared. But in 1562, the Hugonots, not content with destroying this painting, demolished the tombs of the Conqueror and his wife, with their effigies in relief to the life, and broke in pieces with their daggers the Conqueror's *biere* made of *pierre de volderil*, and supported on three little white pilasters. They expected to have met with some treasure, but found only his

[r] Porro dum corpus in sarcofagum mitteretur, & violenter, quia vas per imprudentiam cæmentariorum breve structum erat, complicaretur, pinguissimus venter crepuit, & intolerabilis fœtor circumstantes personas & reliquum vulgus implevit. Fumus thuris aliorumque aromatum de thuribulis copiose ascendebat; sed teterrimum putorem excludere non prævalebat. Sacerdotes itaque festinabant exequias perficere, & ad atum sua cum pavore mappalia repetere. Ord. Vit. 663.

[s] Versus hujusmodi ex auro inserti sunt. Ord. Vit. Ib. *Pencilled* in letters of gold upon his tomb. Sandford, p. 6. Rather *inlaid*, as on the Confessor's shrine.

bones, ſtill joined together, and covered with red taffety. Thoſe of the arms and legs were thought longer than thoſe of the talleſt men of the preſent age. One of theſe ſacrilegious wretches, named Francis de Gray de Bourg l' Abbe, gave them to Dom Michael de Comalle, religious and bailiff of the abbey, who kept them in his chamber, till Admiral Coligny and his *reiſtres* ruined and deſtroyed every thing there[1].

The Conqueror's wife MAUD was buried, 1086, between the choir and altar, 1086.
in the nunnery of the Holy Trinity, which ſhe had founded at Caen. A tomb of gold and jewels was erected over her, and this epitaph[2]:

Egregie pulchri tegit hæc ſtructura ſepulchri
Moribus inſignem, germen regale, MATHILDEM.
Dux Flandrita pater, huic extitit Hadala mater;
Francorum gentis Roberti filia regis,
Et ſoror Henrici regali ſede potiti,
Regi magnifico Willermo juncta marito,
Præſentem ſedem, præſentem fecit & ædem,
Tam multis terris quam multis rebus honeſtis,
A ſe ditatam, ſe procurante dicatam.
Hæc conſolatrix miſerum, pietatis amatrix,
Bonis diſperſis pauper ſibi, dives egenis.
Sic infinitæ petiit conſortia vitæ,
In prima menſis poſt primam luce Novembris.

The monuments of biſhops OSWALD and WOLSTAN at *Worceſter*, under the 992.
window of the Lady Chapel (miſcalled by Dr. Thomas, biſhops *de Conſtantiis* and 1095.
Gifford, who lived one and two centuries later) are very much in the ſtyle of thoſe of Roger and the other biſhop at Sarum; the ſame attitude and the ſame foliage under their heads, as under the latter. It is remarkable, that both the Worceſter biſhops hold a mere baculus, or ſtaff[3], inſtead of a croſier (though both Thomas and Green call them croſiers[4]) and have a roſe on their breaſt. Oſwald died 992; Wolſtan, 1095. The monument in the Lady Chapel, miſcalled *Wolſtan's*, is more probably biſhop *Gifford's*, who died 1301: the altar part of it is adorned with ſix figures of apoſtles ſitting in quatrefoils; and on it lies a figure in pontificalibus, the hands elevated, but not joined. At the head is a rich canopy, on which ſit angels.

That of OSMUND, biſhop of *Sarum*, in the midſt of the Lady Chapel there, 1099.
is a plain coffin-faſhioned ſtone inſcribed in modern characters ANNO MXCIX, yet ſaid to have been brought from the old church. The Sarum Obituary ſays, he lies *inter capellas Salve Regina & S. Stephani*[5].

The tomb in *Hereford* cathedral, on the north wall, a little above Stainſbury's 1099.
chapel, commonly given to biſhop RAYNELM, is by Godwin[6] aſſigned to Robert *Loſinga*, the firſt biſhop of this ſee after the Conqueſt, who rebuilt this church, and died 1095. I ſhall in the next century give my reaſons for differing from this opinion.

[1] Meulan's Hiſt. gen. de Norm. Rouen, 1631, fol. p. 239, 240. [2] Ord. Vit. VII. 648.

[3] It is remarkable, that the ſtaff of the antient archbiſhops of Rouen, like thoſe of other antient biſhops and abbots, is not *bent*, as we ſee it on their monuments within the laſt three centuries. It was only tipt by a ball *(pomme)* ſomething like the top of a cane. Afterwards it was made like a ſhepherd's crook; and at laſt the end was curved *(recourbé)* as at preſent. Moleon, Voy. Liturgique de France, p. 171.

[4] Green's Hiſt. of Worc. 74, Thomas's Antiq. of Worc. 39. [5] Tanner Bib. Brit. 565. [6] P. 481.

RICHARD, ſecond ſon of the Conqueror, who came to an untimely death as he was hunting in the New Foreſt, was buried in the ſouth aile of the choir at *Wincheſter*, where is an altar tomb ſet in the wall, under a ſmall Gothic canopy, on which is this inſcription, in Roman-Saxon capitals.

Hic jacet Ricardus Willi ſenioris regis fil. et Beorn. Dux.

On the ledge above, in the ſame letters:

Intus eſt corpus Richardi Willhelmi
Conqeſtoris filii et Bernie ducis.

William of Malmſbury[1] ſays it was reported, that this young prince, who had a ſpirit above his years and delicate perſon, was ſtruck by a blaſt of foul air as he was hunting in the New Foreſt. Gemericenſis[2] only ſays he died of a wound received by the blow of a tree, of which he lingered a ſhort time. Ordericus Vitalis[3], that as he was purſuing his game full ſpeed a hazel branch bruiſed him againſt the pummel of the ſaddle, and gave him a mortal wound, of which he died within the week, univerſally regretted. Thomas Rudbourne[4] ſays, he died ſuddenly. The ſhort Chronicle of Glouceſter Abbey, in Mon. Ang. I. 994, puts his death 1080, and his burial in that church. He certainly does not witneſs a charter of his uncle Robert earl of Morton to St. Michael's mount in Normandy, which Mr. Haberlin refers to 1076[5].

Sandford deſcribes his monument as two black marble ſtones, inlaid into the new work built by biſhop Fox, one of which ſtands edgeways in the wall, and the other lies flat, containing an epitaph on the verge thereof in Saxon letters, ſignifying the perſon therein interred to be duke of Bernay in Normandy[6].

1090. CONSTANCE, ſecond daughter of the Conqueror, wife of Alan Fergant duke of Bretagne, died 1090, and was buried at *St. Mclaine*. Her corps was found 1672, under the Tower. It had been wrapt in leather, of which only the fragments remained, as alſo thoſe of a coarſe woollen cloth, with her ſcull and other bones, and a leaden croſs, whereon were engraved her name, date of her death, and the name of her father and huſband[7]. Alan died 1119, and was buried in Redon abbey[8].

William's four other daughters were, *Cecily* abbeſs of Holy Trinity, Caen, where ſhe died and was buried 1127[9]: *Adeliza*, a nun, betrothed to Harold king of England, but died before marriage, before 1066[10]: *Adela* or *Alice*, wife of Stephen earl of Blois: *Agatha*, betrothed firſt to Harold, after to Alphonſus, king of Galicia, but died before marriage, agreeable to her prayer for pure virginity; buried in St. Mary's church at Bayeux[11].

[1] Richardus magnanimo parenti ſpem laudis alebat puer delicatus, & ut id ætatulæ puſio altum quid ſpirans: ſed tantam primævi floris indolem mors acerba cito depaſta corripit. Tradunt cervos in nova foreſta terebrantem tabidi aeris nebula morbum incurriſſe. III. p. 61. b.

[2] Iſtu arboris male evitatæ ægrotans, poſt paululum hominem exuit. viii. c. 9. p. 296.

[3] Dum prope Guentam in nova foreſta venaretur, & quandam feram caballo currente pertinaciter inſequeretur ad ſellæ clitellam valido corili ramo admodum conſtrictus eſt, & lethaliter læſus. Dehinc eadem hebdomada penitens & abſolutus, atque ſacro viatico communitus eſt: nec multo poſt cum magno multorum luctu in Anglis defunctus eſt. V. p. 573. Idem, p. 781 & Chron. Tinmouth ap. Lel. Coll. I. p. ii. p. 315.

[4] Ap. Lel. Coll. I. II. 417.

[5] Familia Aug. Will. Conq. Gotting. 1745. 4°. p. 7.

[6] P. 8. [7] Lobineau, I. 104. II. 353. [8] Ib. I. 118. [9] Ord. Vit. 549. Sandford.

[10] Ord. Vit. 185. 492. 573. [11] Ib. 573.

CEN-

CENTURY XII.

Ye pallid ſpirits, and ye aſhie ghoſts,
Which joining in the brightneſs of your day,
Brought forth theſe ſigns of your preſumptuous boaſts,
Which now their duſty reliques do bewray,
   Tell me, ye ſpirits, (ſith the darkſom river
   Of Styx, not paſſable to ſouls returning,
   Encloſing you in thrice three wards for ever,
   Do not reſtrain your images ſtill mourning),
Tell me, then (for perhaps ſome one of you
Yet here above him ſecretly doth hide)
Do ye not feel your torments to accrue
When ye ſometimes behold the ruined pride
Of theſe old Gothic works, built with your hands,
Now to become nought elſe but heaped ſands.

SPENSER, Ruines of Rome.

p. 14.

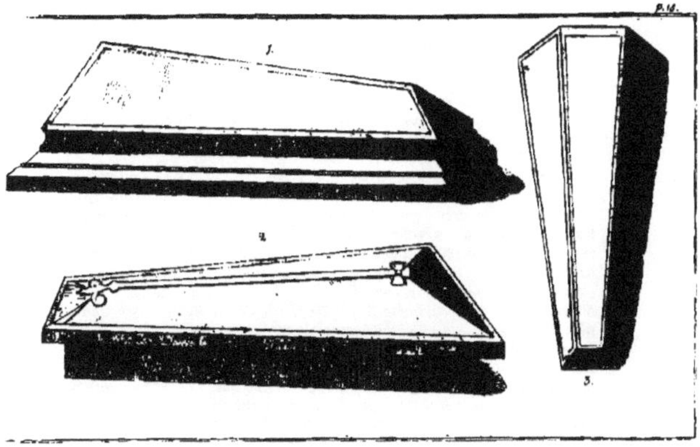

C E N T U R Y XII.

OF the twelfth century the moſt antient monument is perhaps that aſcribed to WILLIAM RUFUS, in the middle of the choir of *Wincheſter*. Whoever at- 1100. tends to the ſlovenly, haſty, contemptuous manner, in which this wretched prince was conveyed to his grave [1], will not be ſurprized at the plainneſs of his tomb, which is only a common ſarcophagus of grey marble, with a cover *en dos d'ane*. This being broken open by the Parliamentarians in the civil war was robbed of ſome pieces of cloth of gold, a ring ſet with rubies, ſaid to be worth £ 500. and a ſmall ſilver *chalice* [2]: circumſtances which would rather induce one to ſuſpect that this was the tomb of ſome religious perſon [3] than of a king, eſpecially if it be further conſidered, that the bones of William Rufus had already been lodged by biſhop Fox, at the Reformation, in the cathedral, in one of the cheſts on the ſide of the choir, along with thoſe of king Canute and other Saxon kings and illuſtrious perſons, who had been depoſited in the Sanctum Sanctorum, or, as Rudburne calls it, *The Holie Hole* [4], behind the altar [5]. Hence

[1] Mortuo rege plures optimatum ad lares ſuos de ſaltu manicaverunt, & enorta futuras motiones quas timebant res ſuas ordinaverunt. Clientuli quidem cruentatum regem vilibus utcunque pannis operuerunt, & veluti ferocem aprum venabulis confoſſum de ſaltu ad urbem Guentanam detulerunt. Clerici autem & monachi & cives duntaxat, egeni cum viduis & mendicis, obviam proceſſerunt, & pro reverentia regiæ dignitatis in veteri monaſterio Sti. Petri celeriter tumulaverunt. Porro eccleſiaſtici, doctores & prælati, ſordidam ejus vitam & tetrum finem conſiderantes tunc judicare auſi ſunt, & eccleſiaſtica velut biothanatum abſolutione indignum cenſuerunt quem vitales auras carpentem ſalubriter a nequitia caſtigare nequiverunt. Signa etiam pro illo in quibuſdam eccleſiis non ſonuerunt, quæ pro infimis pauperibus & mulierculis crebro diutiſſime pulſata ſunt. De ingenti ærario ubi plures nummorum acervi de laboribus miſerorum congeſti ſunt eleemoſynæ pro anima cupidi quondam poſſeſſoris nullæ in opibus erogatæ ſunt. Ord, Vit. 8, p. 782. Langtoft, by an evident miſtake in the writing or print, ſays,

At *Weſtmynſtre* is he laid, in St. Peter kirke,
In a tomb purtraid, the biſhop did it wirke.

For,

At *Wincheſtre* is, &c.

[2] Sandf. 13. [3] Biſhop Blois, who died 1171, was buried before the high altar in his church, according to ſome, but perhaps at Clugni. See Peter abbot of Clugni's letter to him. Ep. iv. 23. Richardſon ad Godw. 216. 1.
[4] Q. If not a corruption of the *Holie of Holies*. [5] Hiſt. Maj. Wint. Ang. Sac. I. 207. Hiſt. of Winch. I. 40. 49.

it

it is that we find no monument for Canute; but on the screen behind the high altar are niches and pedestals for the statues of all the kings and holy men deposited in this grand repository, with their names inscribed on them.

INGELRICA, wife of Ranulph de Peverell, mistress to the Conqueror, who had by her William de Peverell of Nottingham, and foundress of *Hatfield Peverel* priory, Essex, has a better monument of the same date. Her figure, cut in stone, with a lion at her feet, is said to lie in one of the north windows of the priory church. I confess myself almost inclined against the opinion of my late ingenious friend who drew the monument, to refer it to some religious, and that what she holds in her hands, commonly supposed a heart, is a chalice, were I not aware that Leland expressly says Edith D'Oilley, foundress of Oseney, had a heart in her hand on the north side of the high altar there [1]. The figure might *possibly* have been at first placed as it now stands. It is raised six or seven feet from the ground, and there might be an altar beneath for masses. The window I should think is not older than the reign of Edward III. Most probably the figure lay on the ground, and was removed to the window when that part of the aile was pewed. Both the figure and window are drawn on a scale of one inch to a foot. See Pl. II. The shields were intended to be put up in the window by Mr. Wright the proprietor of the estate and patron of the church. They are the arms of all the possessors since the dissolution. On the left hand those of *Giles Leigh*, to whom it was granted by Henry VIII. 1537. On the right the same impaled by those of *John Allen* who married Margaret eldest daughter of Leigh, and succeeded to his estate on his death the following year [2]. In the centre are the arms of *John Wright*, esquire [3], who rebuilt the priory-house on another spot, and repaired the church about 20 years ago, and since procured the curacy to be augmented to a vicarage.

The tomb given to the foundress of *Dunmow* priory, Essex, JUGA BAYNARD, who died in the beginning of this century, is a coffin of grey marble, the cover *en dos d'ane*, with a cross fleury on the ridge, in the South wall of the present chancel, originally the nave; from which circumstance, though the ancient tradition of the place is against me, I should, were it not that Leland describes such a cross on the tomb of Henry D'Oilli, son of the foundress, at Oseney [4], rather ascribe this tomb to some prior. See the plate at the head of this century, fig. 2.

1107. ROBERT FITZ HAIMON, of the blood of duke Rollo, nephew to William the Conqueror [5], who founded *Tewkesbury* abbey 1102, died 1107, and was buried in the chapter-house there, was removed, with his wife, by abbot Parker, 1397 [6], into a chapel of free-stone, beautifully carved, with a border of oak-leaves round it, and a gilt fascia of roses, having letters now almost vanished, probably the inscription given by Rudder [7], and at the corners angels hold scrolls inscribed, *Requiet hic dulcis manna*, and other sentences too high and indistinct to be read. The inscription before referred to was

In ista capella jacet Dn'us Robertus Filius Haimonis.

Leland [8] gives it *in camera sacelli*,

Hic jacet Robertus filius Haymonis hujus loci fundator.

[1] It. II. 19. 21. [2] Morant's Essex, II. 131.
[3] Mr. Wright has here the three fine busts in terra cotta of *Henry* VII. *Henry* VIII. when a boy, and bishop *Fisher*, from the Holbein chamber in the gate last taken down at Whitehall.
[4] It. II. 21. [5] Lel. It. vi. 96. [6] Willis, Mit. Ab. p. 185.
[7] Gloc. p. 746. [8] Ubi sup. p. 96.

Within

The Monument of Robert FITZHAMON, 1107.
erected in Tewksbury church 1397.

Within this chapel is an altar tomb of ſpeckled marble, having on the ſouth ſide five niches, and one at the feet: thoſe on the north gone. On the ſlab was inlaid his figure in braſs, with a pointed helmet, long ſword, lion at the feet, under a canopy, above which were two ſhields, and at the ſides a braſs ledge; all gone. On the eaſt wall of this chapel are indiſtinct traces of painting of a battle. Two knights in it have on their ſurcoats Az. bears' heads muzzled, creſcents, and bezants. Another knight has a ſword and ſhield, and by him is an angel, and over him a little ſavage. I am not certain whether there are not two rows of three figures in compartments. The ſtone roof of the chapel is compoſed of beautiful fan work, of the age of Henry IV or V. This monument is deſcribed here by way of anticipation, being two centuries later.

Robert Fitz Haimon was the chief actor in the conqueſt of Glamorganſhire. Mabel his eldeſt daughter married Robert earl of Glouceſter, natural ſon to Henry I. who became patron of this abbey in right of his wife, and from them an heir female carried it to the family of Clare, who were created earls of Glouceſter, and from them it paſt through the Diſpenſers, Beauchamps, Nevills, &c. till the diſſolution. Jeſtin, ſon of Gurgunt, lord of Glamorganſhire, being unable to defend himſelf againſt the invaſion of Rhys ap Theodore prince of South Wales, ſent one Enion his ſervant to Robert Fitz Haimon then knight of the privy chamber to Rufus, 1091, with promiſe of large reward for his aſſiſtance. Robert having retained twelve knights, marched into Wales, ſlew Rhys and his ſon Conan; but Jeſtin breaking his word with them, they turned their victorious arms againſt him, and having defeated and ſlain him, divided his territories among them, giving his ſon and friends a ſmall part [1]. He adhered to Robert Curthoſe againſt William Rufus [2], whoſe death was revealed to him in a viſion [3], and died of a wound by a ſpear at the ſiege of Faleiſe in Normandy, 7 Hen I [4]. His body was brought over and buried in the Chapter-houſe at Tewkſbury, which church and tower he rebuilt [5]; whence it was removed betwixt two pillars on the ſouth ſide of the choir, where a daily maſs was ſung for him. He married Sibill daughter of Roger de Montgomery earl of Shrewſbury, by whom he left four daughters [6].

Gundulph, biſhop of Rocheſter, who died 1107, was buried before the high altar of his cathedral, *in baſilica ſedis ſuæ* [7]; *ante altare crucifixi eccleſiæ* [8] *quam ipſe conſtruxerat*; probably on the ſouth ſide, near to the confeſſionary, in a cheſt without any effigies [9]. Whether his remains are interred in the antient large ſtone cheſt of gray marble covered by a ſlab of the ſame, ſtill remaining on the ſouth ſide of the high altar within the rails is not certain [10]. It does not ſeem to admit of a doubt, that the former was the place of interment, if we believe the contemporary author of his life in Wharton. But it would be committing too great an anachroniſm in the æra of monuments to ſuppoſe that his was the braſsleſs ſlab which had the figure of a biſhop, under a rich canopy, with four ſhields, and a ledge with four rondeaux at its corners, and two in the middle of each ſide, now lying before the ſteps of the altar, or that other braſsleſs ſlab with a canopy at the foot of the ſteps of the altar. 1107.

The monkiſh hiſtorian ſays, the biſhop's body and hands which had always been black in his life time, after his death turned ſuddenly white. While he was *in extremis* the monks laid him on a board [11], on his hair cloth, near the

[1] Powel's Hiſt. of Wales, p. 124. [2] Malmſb. p. 68. [3] Mat. Paris, A. D. 1100, p. 53.
[4] Malmſb. p. 89. [5] Mon. Ang. I. 155. [6] Ord. Vit. p. 578. Mon. Ang ubi ſup.
[7] Wharton, Ang. Sac. I. 406. [8] Ib. II. 291. [9] Willis, p. 287. Hiſt. of Roch. p. 121. [10] Hiſt. of Roch. 65.
[11] Tabula de more percuſſa.

When a religious of the abbey of Cluny dies, they waſh him at preſent *on a table* in the very place where he died. An old ſtone lavatory uſed on theſe occaſions is preſerved in a chapel there; it is ſix or ſeven feet long, ſeven or eight inches deep, with a ſtone pillow of the ſame piece with the trough, and a hole at the feet end to let off the water. There are ſimilar ones in the cathedrals of Lyons and Rouen, and in the hoſpital in Cluny in the middle of the hall of the ſick poor. That in the ſecond church of Cluny ſerves now only to lay the body in after it is dreſt, till the proceſſion and ſervice begins. It was formerly in a hollow in the ground, on the left hand of the door of the great infirmary without. Moleon, Voy. Liturgique, p. 151, 152.

chapel infirmary, and after he breathed his last they carried him washed and cloathed in pontificalibus into the church of St. Andrew [1], and laid him before his altar.

1115. Pl. III. In the north aile of the choir at *Hereford*, under a pointed arch, with a border of nailhead quatrefoils, a mitred head in point, and two in caps at the bases, is a handsome figure of bishop RAINELM; his right hand gloved blessing; in his left a crosier, the top broken off; at his feet a bracket. He died 1115. The inscription painted over him for a long time gave it to bishop Lozing, to whom Godwin [2] and Leland [3] had assigned it, and to whom it is now fixed, by the name of Robert. It was repaired 1768. Over it is painted,

Dn's Robertus de Lotharinga epus' Heref. ob. A. D. 1095.

Bishop Godwin's reason for transferring this tomb from *Rainelm* to *Lozinga* is, that the figure on this holds in its hand a church, as if alluding to him as founder of the church. It is true Losinga began to rebuild it, on the model of that erected at Aix la Chapelle by Charlemagne, and at the same time that Remigius began that at Lincoln. But it is no less true that he lived to finish only the nave, and left the rest to his successor; and that Rainelm erected the tower, with the spire and two transepts. The church which he holds in his hand exhibits the structure thus completed; and I have engraved it, that my readers may judge for themselves, whether this monument belongs to Losinga or Rainelm, and whether the figure of the church refers to the beginner or finisher thereof.

Willis [4], after saying that Losinga was buried "on the south side of the high "altar" (instead of which, in strictness he should have said, in the south aile of the choir) but by mistake of the painter is "called Rainelm," presently after says, that Rainelm was buried "under an arch on the outside the *south* aile" (he should have said *north*) opposite to the choir, by mistake painted Losinga.

Godwin [5] buries THEULPHUS, bishop of *Worcester*, who died 1115, in the nave at the entrance of the choir, under a stone whereon were to be seen the figures of two bishops, representing himself and his predecessor Samson. These appear in no late accounts of this cathedral. Two bishops on the same slab are not uncommon on the French monuments.

1119. HERBEBT DE LOZINGA, who transferred the see from Thetford to *Norwich*, 1094, and died 1119, was buried in his own cathedral, before the high altar, under a tomb about an ell high. When the pulpit in the late civil wars was placed at the pillar where now bishop Overall's monument is, and the aldermen's seats were fixed at the east end and the mayor's seat in the middle at the high altar, the height of the tomb being an hindrance to the people it was pulled down. It had, many years before, lost its inscription, which may be seen in Weever. The tomb continued demolished till 1682, when the present altar tomb, inclosed with iron rails, in the middle of the choir near the steps of the altar, was erected by the dean and chapter, adorned with their arms and those of the see on the sides and ends, and on the top an inscription said to be drawn up by Dr. Prideaux, which may be seen in Blomfield, II. 334.

In the north aile of the choir of *Hereford*, under a pointed arch is the figure of bishop CLYVE pontifically habited, the top of his crozier broken off, and over him this inscription.

Dn's Godfridus de Clyve ep. Hereford. ob. A. 1119,

1122. ROBERT BLOET, bishop of *Lincoln*, who died 1122, was buried in the north transept of his church, but had a chapel on the north side the choir, where it now remains at the head of Remigius, as already described, p. 11. with three

[1] The Cathedral. [2] P. 481. He adds bishop Clyve lies a little above his predecessor Robert.
[3] II. VIII. 6b. *In bor. sala* ... *beri* Robert de Loreine *episcopi Herefordensis*. He calls him *de Loreine* because he was a Lorrainer. [4] Survey of Hereford Cathedral, p. 512 [5] P. 456.

soldiers

Pl. III * p. 18

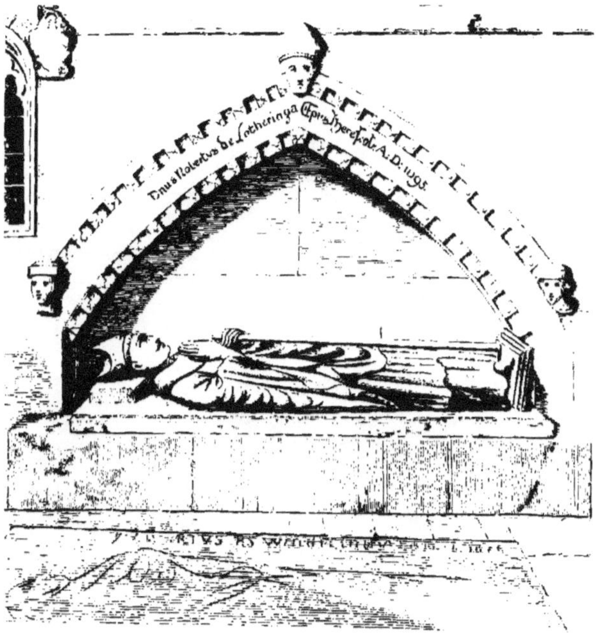
Dnus Robertus de Lotheringa Epus Heref. ob. A.D. 1095

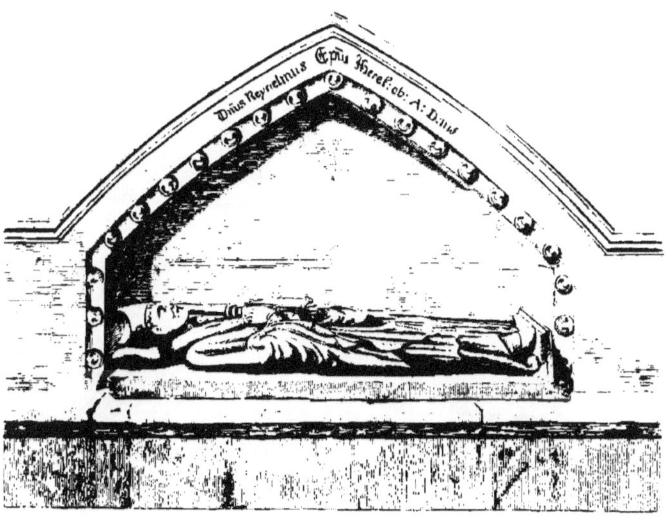
Dñus Reynelmus Epūs Heref: ob: A: D. 1115

Hos tres abbates quorum est prior abbas **Johannes**
Alter **Martinus**, **Andreas** *ultimus, unus*
Hic claudit tumulus; pro clausis ergo rogemus

1125

Fig. 1

1153

Fig. 2

1199

Fig. 3

Fig. 4

In a Chapel in y. [illegible]

Fig. 5

As they lie 1782:
3 is John
4 .. Martin
1 .. Andrew
5 in Chapel of S. transept
2 [illegible] in the chapel of d°

foldiers fleeping on its fouth front. His portrait whole length *in pontificalibus* painted on the weft wall of the north tranfept is the only memorial of him now over the place of his actual interment.

JOHN abbot of *Peterborough*, who died 1125, had a monument in the cloifter there, with his figure in relief in a rich robe; in his right hand his ftaff piercing a dragon under his feet, in his left a book: two angels fupport his head. This monument is at prefent in the fouth aile of the church. See plate III. 1125.

EDITH, wife of Robert D'OILEY, foundrefs of *Ofeney*, who died temp. Hen. I. had on the north fide of the high altar there a ftone figure in the habit of a vowefs, holding a heart in her hand, and on the wall of the arch over the tomb was painted the hiftory of her coming to Ofeney, Radulph, her confeffor, waiting on her, and the chattering of the pies[1]. Her fon Henry was buried in the middle of the prefbytery, under a flat marble, whereupon was a crofs fleuri.

The figure of ROBERT CURTHOSE or COURTOIS, eldeft fon of the Conqueror, 1134.
in a chapel in the north aile of the choir at *Gloucefter*, might pafs for one of the firft genuine monuments of this age. It is certainly a curiofity in its kind; and its materials befpeak its antiquity. It is made of Irifh oak, in armour, and crofs-legged[2], lying on a tomb of the fame material, and covered by a grating of wire. Tradition fays it was broken in pieces in the civil war, but Sir Hugh Tracey of Stanway bought the fragments, joined them together, and reftored them to their place at the Reftoration. Leland[3], however, fays, this image was made long fince this prince's death, which happened in 1134.

Inftances of fepulchral effigies made of wood are not uncommon among us. I have feen one of a knight unknown in *Buers* church, Suffolk; one in *Meffing* church, Effex, called *William de Meffing*, its founder; and two in *Danbury* church in the fame county; a fifth crofs-legged, at *Abergavenny*; and a fixth in the fame attitude in St. Mary Overy's church in *Southwark*. William Valence earl of Pembroke, at *Weftminfter*, has both altar-tomb and figure of wood; and William Longefpee, earl of Sarum, who died 1226, has a ftone effigy lying on a wooden tomb at *Salifbury*. But there appears no reafon for putting off a prince of the blood with fo cheap a memorial, unlefs from the hard condition to which his brother's injuftice reduced him. His eldeft fon WILLIAM, earl of FLANDERS, has a handfomer monument in St. Bertin's church at St. Omer's, engraved by Sandford[4] from Vredius[5] with an efcarboucle[6] on his fhield, and a very fingular helmet.

Robert is habited in a hauberk and gorget of mail, a coronet of oak leaves and fleurs de lis alternately; his right hand croffes his body to draw his fword, which is pendant from his left fide, and held in his left hand. On his breaft are three lions paffant guardant. The flab of the tomb is adorned with a light border of leaves and flowers. On the fide are 1. The Confeffor's arms. 2. G. a lion rampant, O. 3. O. wings, or, as Sandford, three birds flying . . . . . 4. Per pale O and . . . a fpread eagle S. beakt G. impaling G. three fleurs de lis O. At the head an efcarboucle; the fhield at feet broke out. Sandford fays this laft was the arms of France and England quarterly, which fhew the efcochcons to have

[1] Lel. It. II. 19. 21.

[2] Mr. Lethieullier, (Archaeol. II. 291.) obferves, that this Robert was not of the order of Knights Templars, in allufion to which fo many figures are fuppofed to be crofs-legged: but he forgot that Robert was a leader in the firft crufade, 1095. See Malmfbury, P. 64. b. Probably the other inftances Mr. L. mentions were at leaft of perfons who had taken this vow, if they did not actually fulfill it.

[3] It. IV. 172. [4] P. 17. [5] Sigilla Com. Flandriae.

[6] This efcarboucle, which Sandford feems to call Gironne of eight pieces O and Az. an inefcocheon G. was the reputed arms of the Forrefters and firft earls of Flanders; which Sandford well confutes: But quaere if William had it not from his father on whofe tomb we fee it.

been

been painted ſince the reign of Henry IV. He calls the reſt the arms of ſeveral of the *Worthies*. But whence he got his *lion ſitting in a chair, and holding a pole ax* for the ſecond coat I cannot conceive, ſince they are plainly as above given, taken by me, July 27, 1781. He ſays that Robert was buried in the *choir* of St. Peter's church at Glouceſter, *before the high altar:* but neither Ordericus Vitalis [1], nor Gulielmus Gemiticenſis, whom he cites, ſay more than that he was buried in that church. Leland [2] ſays he is buried in the *Preſbytery*.

1135. The corpſe of HENRY I. was removed from Chateau Lyon, or the royal palace of St. Denys in the Foreſt of Lyon [3] where he died [4], to St. Mary's abbey at Rouen. The next night the fat carcaſe was opened in the archbiſhop's chamber, by a ſkillful perſon, and embalmed [5]. His bowels [6], brains, and eyes, were carried in an urn to the town of St. Ermentrude, and buried in St. Mary de la Pre church, which had been begun by his mother, but finiſhed by him. His body, after having been gaſht with knives, and ſprinkled plentifully with ſalt, was ſewed up in bulls' hides, to avoid the ſtench, which was ſo great as to affect the aſſiſtants, and the perſon who was hired at a great price to cleave his head with an ax, in order to extract the infected brain, though his own head was wrapt round with linen clothes, died of the ſtench. This, ſays Hoveden, was the laſt of many who owed their death to king Henry. While the corpſe waited at Caen all the ſalt and leather envelope could not prevent a black ſtinking matter from ouſing through, which was received in veſſels ſet under the bier, and thrown away. Robert de Sigillo biſhop of London, Robert de Vere, John Algaſa, and others, both clergy and laity, conducted the bier *(feretrum)* through Pont Audomar and Bonanville, to Caen, where it was kept in the choir of St. Stephen near a month, waiting for a wind to bring it to England. After Chriſtmas it was conducted from thence by the monks, and honourably enterred by the king his ſucceſſor, the biſhops and nobles, in *Reading* abbey [7]. Dr. Stukeley [8] ſuppoſed the chapel of that houſe was remaining 1721. a large ſhell 16 yards by 28, with five lancet ſemicircular windows towards the eaſt, and three windows over three weſt doors. Sir Henry Englefield takes this for the hall, 42 feet by 79, and ſuppoſes the church intirely deſtroyed [9].

1139. I flattered myſelf I had, by a plauſible conjecture at leaſt, aſcertained one of
Pl. IV. the three tombs of biſhops under the ſouth arches of the nave of *Saliſbury*
Fig. 1. cathedral, to ROGER third biſhop of that ſee after its removal from Sherborne

[1] P. 893. [2] VIII. b. 75.

[3] Ord. Vit. p. 901. If we believe Robert of Glouceſter, the King had recourſe to the amuſement of the chace to relieve the diſtreſs of his mind for ſome quarrel between his beloved daughter Maud and her ſecond huſband Geffrey earl of Anjou.

> "The kyng hyre fader was old man and drou to feblèſſe
> And the anguyſſe of his doghter hyre dyde more deſtreſſe,
> And ſkelde hym wel the more, ſo yt febla he was.
> So yt he wende an honteth aday to abbe ſolas." P. 442.

[4] Gemetic. p. 309.

[5] Ibi noctu a perito carnifice in archipræſulis conclavi pingue cadaver apertum eſt, et balſamo ſuaveolenti conditum eſt. Inteſtina vero ejus Ermentrudis ad villam in vaſe delata ſunt. Ord. Vit. 901.

[6] The heart, tongue, and bowels of this prince were buried before the high altar at that time (for it has been ſince removed) of the priory of Bonnes Nouvelles, or de Preez, at Rouen. (Deſc. de haut. Norm. II. 51.)

> Kyng Henry brayn and gottes and eyen ybured were
> At Reynys in Normandye, and ſuthe the bones lie here,
> Wel yſeld & yſode to the abbeye of Redyng,
> And yburede ys there vayre ynon, as wel to an kyng.
> Rob. of Gloc. p. 446. Hoveden, 276. a.

[7] Corpus cultellis circumquaque diſſecatum & ſic multo ſale aſperſum coriis taurinis reconditum eſt & conſutum, cauſa fœtoris evitandi, qui multus & infinitus jam circumſtantes inficiebat, unde & ipſe qui magno pretio conductus ſecuri caput ejus diffiderat ut fœtidiſſimum cerebrum extraheret, quamvis linteaminibus caput ſuum obvolviſſet mortuus tamen ea cauſa pretio male gaviſus eſt: hic eſt ultimus e multis quos rex Henricus occidit. Inde vero corpus regium Cadomum ſui deportaverunt, ubi dum diu in eccleſia poſitum in qua pater ejus ſepultus erat, quamvis multo ſale repletum eſſet & multis coriis reconditum tamen continue ex corpore niger humor & horribilis coria pertranſiens decurrebat, & vaſis ſuppoſitis ſub feretro ſuſceptus a miniſtris horrore fatiſcentibus abjiciebatur.

[8] Itin. Cur. I. p. 59. [9] Archæol. VI. p. 62.

to

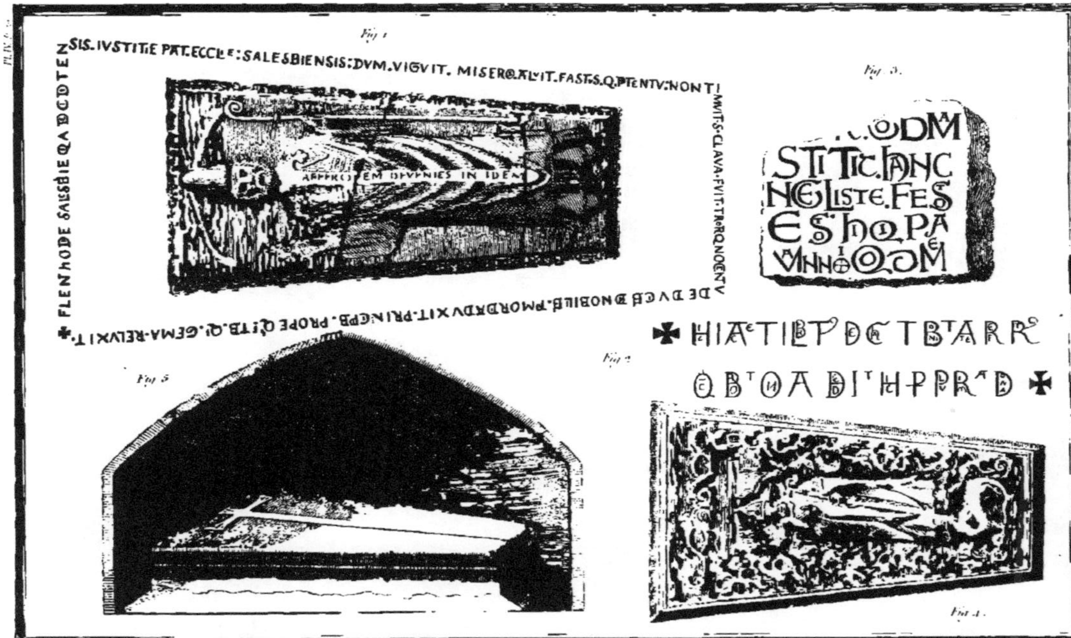
FLENHODE SALESBIE QA DCDTENSIS. IVSTITIE PAT. ECCLE: SALESBIENSIS: DVM. VIGVIT. MISER@ ALVIT. FAST. S. Q. PTENTV: NONTIMVIT. S. CLAVA. FVIT. TR@ Q NOCENTV
DE DVCE DNOBILE. PMORDAD VXIT. PRINCPB. PROPE Q. ITB. Q. GEMA. RELVXIT.
AFFKCT EM DEVENIES IN IDEM
STITIC. ANC
NE LISTE. FES
E S HQ PA
VNNO QOM
HIATILBP DE TBTARR
QBTOA DITHPPRTD

to Old Sarum. That it belongs to one of the prelates who ſat at the latter place, and whoſe tombs were brought from thence on the removal to Saliſbury, is clear from the evidence of Leland, though he miſtakes the north for the ſouth aile [1]. The inſcription on the pall is given by that induſtrious antiquary, and it is probable that round the edge was never raiſed above the pavement, till I procured it to be raiſed 1770, and the pavement diſpoſed round it in ſuch a manner that it can in future receive no injury nor eſcape the notice of the curious. William de Wenda, who wrote the account of the building of the preſent church, mentions the removal of only three biſhops from Old Sarum, 1226, Oſmund, Roger, and Joceline. The monument of Oſmund the firſt biſhop is well known to be in the Lady Chapel; Herman anſwers to none of the characters in the epitaph. Theſe three are the only biſhops of Old Sarum that could be buried here: the fourth and fifth were tranſlated to Canterbury, and the ſixth and laſt was buried at Wilton. Of all who filled the now ſee, except one or two of leſs note in the 13th Century, the monuments are well known in and about the choir, as will be hereafter ſhewn in their order.

I conceived the various traits of the epitaph to be deciſive in favour of biſhop Roger. His great influence with his ſovereign Henry I. and his reciprocal mutual eſteem for him I traced in the words *Principibus gemma reluxit:* his adminiſtration of juſtice as chancellor and regent of the kingdom intitled him to the name of *Enſis Juſtitiæ*, as did his munificence to his infant church to that of *Pater eccleſiæ Saleſburienſis.* His impregnable fortifications, as well as his irreproachable conduct made that *non timuit faſtus potentum*; as his high rank in the ſtate made him *clava terrorque nocentum.* By his great wealth diſpoſed on religious foundations *miſeros aluit*; and if we conſider the ſad reverſe of his fortune in the ſucceeding reign, *dum viguit* is not without its meaning. The words inſcribed on his pall more ſtrongly mark the diſtreſſes of his declining age. *Affer opem, devenies in idem*, is an earneſt addreſs to the ſympathy of the ſpectators, warning them, at the ſame time, of the uncertainty of human events. The concluſion *Prope que tibi qui gemma reluxit* ſeems an addreſs to the church, reminding her of the luſtre he reflected on her while he preſided as biſhop in her former ſituation at Old Sarum. My only difficulty was about the words *de ducibus de nobilibus primordia duxit.* He may have been the younger ſon of ſome noble family in Normandy, which the maker of the epitaph may have known from ſome evidences not noticed by general hiſtory; or it may have been introduced merely to eke out the line and the verſe. Gervaſe de Blois, Stephen's baſtard, abbot of Weſtminſter, 1160, is ſtyled in his epitaph *de regum genere.*

Theſe ideas I had communicated to the Society of Antiquaries, who thought them worthy of a place in the ſecond volume of the Archæologia, p. 188, &c. It has lately been ſuggeſted to me by a learned member of the church of Exeter that the laſt words of the epitaph ſhould rather be read,

Prope quos tumbo quaſi or *quoque gemma reluxit.*

referring to ſome memorials of noble or royal perſons interred in this church. Such, ſays he, may lead to a diſcovery of this biſhop, whom Mr. Gough, on very inſufficient grounds, ſuppoſes to be biſhop Roger, who ſat from 1101 to 1139. He then proceeds to quote a paſſage from the Continuation of Trivet's Annals, that in February, 1309, the water roſe ſo high as to come up to the feet of the kings which ſtand at the weſt door of the choir here, ſo that maſs could not be

[1] It. III. 64.

said for two days [1]. He adds, William Longsword, son of Henry II. died 1226, and is buried in Salisbury cathedral. His son Nicholas, bishop of Salisbury died 1296 [2], and is buried near his father, says Godwin, at the entrance of St. Mary's chapel, under a large marble tomb, adorned with brass plates, and with the arms of his family.

Nothing gives me greater pleasure than to have the best founded opinions controverted in pursuit of truth; but though I offer mine only as a plausible conjecture, and profess myself at a loss as to the meaning of the words in question, I cannot adopt the proposed reading for the following reasons. There are not more noble personages buried in Salisbury than in our other cathedrals, and there are no royal ones. There are not now any figures of kings on the screen of the choir, only twelve arches stopt up; and it seems a very forced allusion to refer to such statues, which, like the portraits in windows, are frequently the invention of the artist, and not historical memorials, much less sepulchral monuments. The reference must have been to figures erected, or persons buried in the old cathedral; for that the monument is of that æra must be admitted from Leland's testimony, to whichever of the bishops of Old Sarum we refer it, and it does not appear that any royal bodies lay in that church, though the monuments of Longespee and the other earl of Salisbury might be brought from thence. Bishop Longespee's tomb, stript of its brasses, remains to this day in the place assigned it by Godwin, and we cannot suppose the reference reached from the nave thither.

There is a striking conformity between the figure of this bishop and that of Leodegaire on a bas-relief in Montfaucon's Monumens, I. pl. XXXI. p. 348. The latter lived in the middle of the seventh century. The monument at Salisbury is of blue speckled marble, with the figure habited *in pontificalibus*, his right hand lifted up to give the blessing, his left holding the crosier. The inscription is cut on the perpendicular edge or side all round in large capitals, and continued on the front of the robe. The letters are of a form which appears to have been in use among the Romans. On an altar dedicated to Mercury, found at Middleby in Scotland, and whose æra is by baron Clerk fixed to the reign of Julian, we see several letters included in larger ones. But they are more common in the Gothic ages, as has been shewn before on the article of letters used in epitaphs among us.

None of the antient historians who mention the death of bishop Roger tell us where he was buried. Dr. Richardson [3] says he was buried in his own church. Browne Willis, in his short account of the church at the end of his Mitred Abbies, only says he was removed hither; but neither of these writers produce their authorities. Mr. Price says, he was placed in the wall of the north aile of the present church, in an arch made for the purpose, by tradition. The tomb shewn for his by the vergers is that in the north wall of the presbytery, which I think belongs to bishop Mortival, who died 1329, or perhaps to some intermediate prelate. Pl. IV. f. 5.

If it be objected, that the three old monuments of bishops now in the nave, added to Osmund's in the Lady-chapel, make more than Wenda expressly says were brought from Old Sarum, and that therefore one of them must be given to some prelate of the new see; I submit to any impartial critic in these matters, whether any of them suit with the style of the 13th century.

I foresee but one more person to whom this monument may suit, and that is *Osmund*, who was of Norman extraction, enobled and invested with the same

[1] A. 1309. 16 kal. Feb. Inundatio aquarum qualis non visa fuit multis annis antea. Ita quod in ecclesia cathedrali Sarum aqua illa regum pedes qui ad ostium chori occidentale astant attingebat: unde per duos dies non cantabatur missa in eadem. Continuatio Triveti, ed. Hall. 1722. p. 7.

[2] Triveti Ann.

[3] Note on his life in Godwin.

high office, and honoured with his confidence, by William I. as Roger was by Henry I. but if it can be rendered probable that the monks of Salifbury, when they placed his remains in the Lady chapel, threw this venerable tomb into the nave, or if it can be proved that it was the practice thus to feparate the corps and the monument, I confent to this transfer, and admit, that as Lady chapels are of later date, the corps might be afterwards moved into it, and that the ftone now there is a bare memorial erected after the diffolution; but ftill I think, he would have been lodged originally in a more diftinguifhed place.

The other antient unaffigned tomb in the nave is engraved pl. IV. f. 4. It may belong to bifhop *Herman* or *Joceline*.

ROBERT earl of GLOUCESTER, natural fon of Henry I. who died 1147, was 1147.
buried in the middle of the choir of St. James's church, *Briftol*, "in a fepulcher "of grey marble [1], fet upon fix pillars of a fmall height [2]." In his tomb was found a writing containing the time of his death and what he was, which a brewer in Briftol had [3].

GILBERT DE CLARE earl of PEMBROKE, who died 1148, 14 Stephen, was 1148.
buried in *Tyntern* abbey, Glamorganfhire, which his brother Walter had firft founded. When the late duke of Beaufort had the fcite of this fine church cleared, to be preferved in a manner worthy himfelf and it, they found a figure of a knight in free-ftone, in complete mail; his right hand [4] croffes his breaft to his fhield, which is on his left arm; a dagger in his belt, and encircling around his flat round helmet; his croffed legs, with the dog or lion at his feet, were broken off, and kept in private hands. The tomb appears to have been very little raifed from the floor, and to have been divided into two compartments lengthwife, without admitting a figure on either hand. A beautiful moulding of flowers and leaves runs round it. Being opened at the time of its difcovery, it was found to contain the bones of more than two perfons. The tradition of the place afcribes this to *Strongbow*, fon of Gilbert, Conqueror of Ireland. But he is exprefsly faid by Leland [5], to have been buried 1176, in the Chapter-houfe at Gloucefter, with this infcription;

Hic jacet Ricardus Strongbow filius Gilberti comitis de Pembroke.

Above bifhop Melun's monument at *Hereford* is a fimilar one for bifhop 1148.
BETUNE. Over it,

D'nus Robertus de Betun epus Herefordenfis.

In the *Temple* church, *London*, is the figure of GEOFREY DE MAGNAVILLE, firft earl of ESSEX, fo created by Stephen, A. D. 1148. He is reprefented in mail with a furcoat, and round helmet flatted on the top, the nofe-piece of which very much refembles that worn by Raoul de Beaumont, who lived 1210, in Montfaucon [6], who calls it a bar of iron to defend the nofe from fwords. His head refts on a cufhion placed lozenge fafhion, his right hand on his breaft, a long fword at his right fide, and on his left arm a long pointed fhield, charged with

[1] Dugd. I. 535. fays a green jafper ftone, from Lel. It. 6. 155. b. [2] Lel. It. 7. 68. b. [3] Ib.

[4] Mr. Grofe fays, his right hand, which is fhewn, has five fingers and a thumb; a peculiarity which I confefs efcaped me, when I viewed it 1761: nor does it appear in the drawing fent to the compiler of the Antiquarian Repertory, v. I. p. 112. I am therefore almoft tempted to fufpect my good friend was mifled by a figure of a brafs hand grafping a fpear eight feet long, cut in ftone over the door of a neighbouring cottage, formerly taken from another tomb in this church, in which was found a body intire, with leather bufkins and buttons on the coat, which all crumbled away on touching. There is fomething in this laft carving like the hilt of a fword, which may be miftaken for the fixth finger.

[5] Ib. IV. 172. [6] Monumens II. Pl. XIV. 7. p. 113.

an

an eſcarboucle on a diapered field. The chronicle of Walden-abbey [1], which he founded, ſays, after his creation he augmented his family arms, which were quarterly A. and G. with an *eſcarboucle: poſtquam gladio comitis accinctus erat arma progenitorum cum Carbunculo nobilitavit.* This is the firſt inſtance of arms on a ſepulchral figure among us. They obtained in France 40 years before.

This noble earl, driven to deſpair by the confiſcation of his eſtates by king Stephen, indulged in every act of violence, and making an attack on the caſtle of Burwell, received his death's wound, and was carried off by the Templars, who, as he died under ſentence of excommunication, declined giving him Chriſtian burial, but wrapping his body up in lead *(canali incluſum plumbeo)* hung it on a crooked tree *(torva arbore)* in the orchard of the Old Temple, London. William, prior of Walden, having obtained abſolution for him of the pope, made application for his body, in order to bury it at Walden; upon which the Templars took it down, and depoſited it in a mean manner, in the cemetery of the New Temple [2]. They probably afterwards gave him more honourable ſepulture in the porch before the weſt door of the church [3]. See pl. V. fig. 1.

1150. Robert Chichester biſhop of *Exeter*, who died 1150, was buried on the ſouth ſide of the high altar of his church [4]. Godwin [5] aſcribes to him a tomb of a biſhop, contiguous to which, and oppoſite to the door leading to the biſhop's palace, is the monument of a knight of the ſame family, as appears by the arms on his ſhield. Leland [6] places the latter tomb in the ſouth aile of the choir.

1155. A blue ſtone, with uncial letters, in the ſouth aile of *Lincoln* choir, may be that aſſigned by Willis in his plan to Henry of Huntingdon, who is ſuppoſed to have died after the year 1150.

1159. Martin abbot of *Peterborough*, who died 1155, had a monument in the cloiſter there, with his figure holding a croſier and book, treading on a double dragon, who bites the pillars of the flowered arch of his canopy. See Pl. III. fig. 2. It is now in the ſouth aile of the cathedral.

Waldevus, ſecond abbot of *Mailros*, who died 1159, lies on the ſouth ſide of the high altar there, under a tomb of beautiful blue marble, engraved in the frontiſpiece to this century, fig. 3. He was ſon of Simon de St. Liz, and canonized by Pope Alexander III. His body being found uncorrupted twelve years after his death, this poliſhed marble was put over him. The cover being raiſed by one of the lay brethren, when they were preparing to lay his ſucceſſor William the 7th abbot by his ſide 1206, 48 years after his death, there iſſued from the tomb an extraordinary fragrance, and on applying a candle the corps was ſeen entire, and all the veſtments were found as freſh and entire as at firſt [7]. On opening this tomb a third time (1240) the body was found crumbled to duſt [*incineratum*], except a few ſmall bones which were carried off by the aſſiſtants [8].

[1] Mon. Ang. I. 449. [2] Ib. 450. [3] Ib. 448. This is the circular part of the church in which his figure now lies.
[4] So biſhop Lyttelton, in his obſervations on the cathedral of Exeter, MS. pen. Soc. Ant. [5] P. 408. [6] It. III. 32.
[7] Fordun Scotichr. viii. c. 66. Hoc anno, qui eſt quadrageſimus octavus a deceſſu Sti. Walthevi, hic Willelmus abbas ſeptimus poſt eum moritur, & ut juxta corpus ejus tumularetur proviſum eſt, tamquam alter Walthevus vitæ ſanctitate. Cum vero cæmentarii tumulum tanti viri in loco præfato ad dextram ejus conderent, incitantibus quibuſdam monachis, frater Robertus latomus innatus quaſi & valde formidoloſus operculum marmoreum tumbae Sti. Walthevi paululum ſublevabat, & ecce ſuaviſſimi odoris fragrantia evaporans illico ſe infundit naribus ac ſi monumentum repletum fuiſſet aromatibus. Et quia noctis crepuſculum aderat accenſa candela per aperturam intromiſſa idem frater ac ceteri circumſtantes introſpiciunt, & corpus ſanctum integrum, & omnia ejus indumenta incorrupta cum integritate & venuſtate priſtina reperiunt, ibi ſex monachi & totidem converſi, qui pia ac devota indagine ſed præſumptuoſa domicilium illud virtutum virginitatis balſamo delibutum conſpexerunt.
[8] Chron. Mailros, p. 205.

Gervase

PLATE I.

Geffrey de Magnaville first E. of Essex. — W.m Marshall E. of Pembroke — Robert Ros — W.m Plantagenet fifth son of Hen. III.

Gervase de Blois, natural fon of king Stephen, and abbot of Weftminfter, 1160.
was depofed, and buried 1160, according to Flete, under a little plain black marble flab, in the fouth cloifter, at the feet of abbot Humez; (not under the great fmooth one, commonly called *Long Meg of Weftminfter*, which Keep miftakes for it;) and had this epitaph [1],

> De regum genere pater hic Gervafius ecce
> Monftrat defunctus mors rapit omne genus.

The beginning of which refembles bifhop Roger's at Sarum. Matthew Paris fays [2], he was *clarior genere quam moribus*, and charges him with mif-fpending the revenues of his church. Mr. Widmore affigns the middlemoft of the three ftones now in the cloifter to him; but Dart denies it. Sandford gives the epitaph in the Gothic capitals [3].

In the fouth wall of Trinity, or Becket's, chapel, at *Canterbury*, oppofite the 1160.
tomb of the Black Prince, "we fee one of a fingular form, fo unlike all the "monuments fince the Conqueft that I have met with the defcriptions of, that "I fhould look on it as a piece of Saxon antiquity rather than Norman: per"haps brought hither to be preferved as fuch after this chapel was built. It "was defigned to ftand clofe to a wall, but is not fo here. It is fhewn as the "tomb of archbifhop Theobald [who died 1160], but there is very little rea"fon to think it fo. It has been conjectured to be that of St. Anfelm; but of "this there is no probability. His remains were depofited in the old chapel at "firft dedicated to St. Peter and St. Paul, but from his being entombed there "called St Anfelm's chapel to this day. This chapel efcaped the fire, and here "it is probable his bones refted till the demolition of Becket's fhrine, when it is "much more reafonable to believe his remains fhared the fame fate, than that "the commiffioners for deftroying all remains of fuperftition here would re"move his bones from the chapel where they had been worfhipped to a more "honourable place. St. Anfelm being a native of Piedmont, in king George "the Second's reign the king of Sardinia defired to have his remains fent over "to him, and his ambaffador had fucceeded fo far as to obtain leave and "authority to have a fearch made for the purpofe. A perfon commiffioned to "make this fearch applied to a member of this cathedral, whom he thought "beft able to affift in his enquiry, and inform him whether this tomb might "not probably contain the remains of that prelate; but was fo fully convinced "by him that all fearch after any fuch relics would be fruitlefs, that the monu"ment was left entire, and the defign laid afide. The writer of this account "gives this from his own knowledge [4]."

After fuch authority as is here adduced it would be prefumption in me to fuggeft a conjecture, that from the form of the monument, refembling a fhrine, and the four heads on it in high relief, two mitred, one fhorn, and the fourth covered with a cap, it may have been the depofitary of the reliques of fome prelate who filled this fee in the Saxon times. Godwin [5] adopts the tradition that gives it to Theobald. "Sepultus fertur (fays he) ab auftrali parte facelli quod "D. Thomæ dicitur; tumulum vidimus marmoreum fatis elegantius fere *ad* "*tecti formam faftigiatum*."

As it may feem a little extraordinary that archbifhop Becket had no other tomb than his fhrine, I fhall beg leave to tranfcribe a little more from Mr. Goftling. In a MS order of chapter appropriating the vaults to the prebendaries among Mr. Somner's collections the firft prebendary is to have the vault

[1] Dart. II. xiv. Widmore, p. 26.
[2] Vit. Ab. St. Alb. p. 73.
[3] P. 44.
[4] Goftling's Canterb. p. 268, 269.
[5] P. 71.

called *Bishop Becket's tomb under* our Lady's chapel. Mr. Somner corrects this *above* our Lady's chapel. Mr. Gostling observes, that the assassins threatning to return, and cast his body out a prey to birds and beasts, the monks buried him privately next day, in the vault *under the east end of the church*, and in a *new sarcophagus* of marble. Without stopping to account for those threats, this hasty burial, and this new marble tomb procured on a sudden, Mr. Gostling conceives he was laid in a common grave. This grave he thinks was opened in archdeacon Batteley's time, who had a stone in the undercroft taken up, under which was found a grave, with no remains of corps or coffin, but all perfectly clean, the earth having probably been disposed of, as an invaluable relic. Mr. Gostling goes on to conjecture that the circular tower added to the east end of Trinity chapel, and to this day called *Becket's crown*, was erected in honour of him, the ground room designed for a chapel to be dedicated to him, and an altar to be prepared there, for the reception of his relics, when it should be thought proper to remove them thither: that this should be called the *tomb* of St. Thomas, rather than his chapel, by way of distinction; for other churches might soon have chapels or altars to him, but his tomb was only to be found here: that therefore this place was called his tomb even when it was carrying up, and communicated its name to the adjoining vault, through which was the way to it, as his shrine did that of the martyr, to the whole church not long after: that over this chapel should be one of our Lady, perhaps in allusion to his having invoked her with his last breath. That there was such a chapel in this tower appears from the place and dimensions of an altar to be seen in the pavement, and from the steps up to it, and that it was dedicated to the Virgin Mary appears from a figure of her still in the window over it. If it be objected, that no signs of a tomb appear in the place which Mr. Gostling proposes to call by that name, he answers, that the votaries becoming too numerous for this chapel to contain them, the monks translated the body to the more capacious one of the Trinity, where the shrine could be seen on all sides. Gervase says, Becket was buried in a little chapel added at the outside of the circular wall at the east end of the church, in which he was particularly fond of performing his devotions. An anonymous correspondent of Mr. Gostling's has also accounted for the delay of translating 36 years, from 1184 to 1220, that the monks waited till they had an archbishop so zealously attached to their interests, and so obsequious to the Pope, as to consent to give up the profits of this shrine to them from the see. This archbishop they found in Stephen Langton [1]. The chapel at the east end called *Becket's crown* was begun about this time, but left unfinished at the dissolution, till a citizen of Canterbury gave £ 100, 1748, to complete and bring it to its present figure [2]. Erasmus describes the shrine as a coffin of wood covering another of gold (i. e. plated with gold, or gilded metal) [3], and drawn up from it by pullies and ropes. "The shrine (says Stow) was builded about a man's "height, all of stone, then upward of timber plain, within which was a chest "of iron, containing the bones of Thomas Becket, scull and all, with the wound "of his death, and the piece cut out of his scull laid in the same wound [4]. The "timber

[1] Godwin (p. 77.) insinuates, that the body was not taken out of the *subterraneous crypt* where it was first buried till its translation and enshrinement in the east part of the church.

[2] Gostling, ib. 121, 122.

[3] Sub capsa ex auro purissimo fabrefacta & lapidibus pretiosis innumerabilibus, margaritis nitentibus velut porta Jerusalem, & gemmis coruscantibus ornata, ac etiam imperiali diademate coronata. Symeon. 6.

[4] He should have added the point of Sir William Tracl the fourth assassin's sword, which broke off against the pavement, after cutting off the top of his scull, so that the brain came out.

In thulke fede the verthe smot, yt the other adde er ydo.
And the point of is sverd bree in the marbreston a tuo.
Zat thulk point at Canterbury the monckes lateth wite
Vor honor of the holi man yt therewith was ismite.
With the [illegible] stroke he smot al of ys fenil, & eke the crowne
That the [illegible] al abrod in the pavimente ther donne. (Robert of Glouc. p. 476.)

"In

" timber work of this ſhrine on the outſide was covered with plates of gold, da-
" maſked with gold wire, which ground of gold was again covered with jewels
" of gold, as rings, 10 or 12 cramped with gold wire into the ſaid ground of
" gold, many of thoſe rings having ſtones in them, broches, images, angels,
" precious ſtones, and great pearls; the ſpoil of which ſhrine in gold and
" precious ſtones, filled two great cheſts, one of which ſix or ſeven ſtrong men
" could do no more than convey out of the church at once; all which was
" taken to the king's uſe, and the bones of St. Thomas, by command of the
" lord Cromwell, were then and there burned to aſhes, in September, 1538.
" 30 Hen. VIII [1]." The figure of this ſhrine, engraved by Vaughan in the Monaſticon [2], from a Cotton MS. and copied by Dart, allowing for bad drawing, may bear ſome reſemblance to that of the Confeſſor, ſuppoſing the arches below to be drawn out of proportion. "All above the ſtone work was wood. The *Clinodia* [3] were ſet with gold and jewels, covered with gold plates, and bound with gilt bands, like bracelets, ſet with jewels, adorned with figures of Genii and rings to the number of about ten or twelve, forming a golden circle. Theſe ſacred ſpoils filled two large cheſts, which ſix or eight of the ſtrongeſt men could hardly carry out of the church. A rich jewel, with an angel carved on it [4] [probably an antique gem with a victory], which had been offered by the king of France, Henry VIII. had ſet in a ring, which he wore on his thumb. The iron cheſt below contained the bones; ſcull, and broken part of the latter, which occaſioned his death. The three bouquets on the top of the ſhrine were gilt, and weighed two of them ſixty ounces, the middlemoſt eighty ounces [5]."

In the ſouth aile of the choir at *Hereford*, under a pointed arch, with two borders of lilies, and a biſhop's head in the point, and two at the baſes, is the figure, pontifically habited, of biſhop Melun, who died 1167. Above is painted; 1167.

D'nus Robertus de Melun, epus Herefordenſis,
Obiit A. 1167.

The empreſs Maud, mother of Henry II. was buried, according to Hoveden [6], at *Rouen*, in the abbey, or rather priory, of St. Mary de Pré, or des bonnes nouvelles. But the Chronicle of Bec ſays, in that abbey before the high altar, where her corps was found 1282, *ante ſedem majoris altaris*, done up in an ox's hide, and that in 1421, the Engliſh, in plundering the monaſtery, laid open the tomb of the empreſs, which is in the middle of the choir. Laſtly, in repairing this altar, February, 1684, they found her bones directly under the lamp which burns before the hoſt, and taking them up, incloſed them in a wooden cheſt, with leaden plates. A copper tomb was made, to perpetuate her memory, and the bones were depoſited in the ſame place the 22d of December following [7]. 1167.

In alluſion to this circumſtance the portrait of Becket in the windows of Trinity chapel, Oxford, has a ſword's point ſticking in his ſcull. Edmund Grime, who was croſs-bearer to Becket, and had his arm almoſt cut off in defending him, and wrote his life, ſays, Hugh the ſubdeacon, who had joined himſelf to the aſſaſſins at Canterbury, ſcooped out his brains with the point of a ſword, and ſcattered them over the pavement. Lyttelton's Hiſt. of Henry II. IV. 361. Eraſmus ſaw the ſtatues of the three aſſaſſins over the ſouth porch of the cathedral, and under them their names, *Tuſc*, *Fuſci*, *Berri*. We muſt ſuppoſe he overlooked the fourth figure (for there are four empty niches), and gave a foreign ſound to the names of *Tracy*, *Fitz Urſe*, and *Briton*. Patrick's note in loc.

[1] Chron. p. 576. Ed. Howes. Goſling, p. 278. 279.
[2] I. 21.
[3] *Clenodium* or *clinodium*, a trinket or jewel, *bijou*. Du Cange.
[4] *Gemmam inſignem una cum angelo eam indigitante.* This is what Stowe, p. 155, calls "that renowned precious ſtone that was called the *Regall of France*, which Henry VIII. put into a ring which he wore on his thumb.
[5] The Latin account, at the ſide of Vaughan's plate.
[6] Ann. p. ii. 289. b.
[7] Deſcript. de la haute Normandie, II. p. 52.

Robert

1170. ROBERT FITZ HARDYNG, who founded the Auſtin Monaſtery at *Briſtol* and died 1170, has on the ſouth ſide of the beautiful Lady chapel in that cathedral, under a canopy, an altar tomb, with his figure in compleat armour, and a lion at his feet, and that of his wife EVA by him. At their feet is a ſhield, with their arms projecting from the wall, and at their head a modern inſcription, probably put up when the whole was repaired, 1742.

1171. HENRY DE BLOIS, brother to king Stephen, who died biſhop of Wincheſter 1171, was buried before the high altar of his church. Some have ſuppoſed this the church of Clugni; but on new paving the choir at Wincheſter, about 25 years ago, they diſcovered, cloſe on the right hand of Rufus's tomb, almoſt by the biſhop's throne, juſt below the ſurface, a ſtone coffin, containing an entire ſkeleton, which ſome imagined the body of Canute; but others, more juſtly that of this prelate. It was wrapt in a brown and gold mantle, with traces of gold round the temples; a wooden croſs about two yards long and of the ſize of a common walking ſtick lay by its ſide, and a large gold ring with a ſtone of great value, which was lodged in the treaſury.

1176. Five years after comes the laſt of the three abbots of Weſtminſter before mentioned, LAURENTIUS, whoſe name is now cut over an unmitred figure, contrary to what one would expect for the man who procured the mitre for this houſe. This figure ſhews a ſimple religious; it never had any thing abbatial about it, though Keepe[1] deſcribes it as having mitre, ring, and paſtoral ſtaff. See plate I. The form of the ſtone is uncommon, and I do not recollect another inſtance. Mr. Widmore[2] has appropriated this to Vitalis; Dart[3], from the mitre, gives the tomb inſcribed Vitalis to a later abbot (Humez, 1222), but it is moſt likely that his tomb was miſplaced or broken at the rebuilding of the church by Henry III. The epitaph preſerved and once, ſays Mr. Dart, cut in the ſtone ledge of it, was as follows:

> Clauditur hoc tumulo vir quondam clarus in orbe,
>   Quo præclarus erat hic locus, eſt, & erit.
> Pro meritis vitæ dedit illa laurea nomen,
>   Detur ei vitæ laurea pro meritis.

1178. RICHARD DE LUCIE, chief juſtice of England, who firſt planned the juſtices of aſſize throughout the realm, was buried 1178, in the abbey of *Leſnes*, which he founded 1177. In Weever's time ſome workmen digging for ſtones on the ſite of the church, found ſeveral ſtone coffins, and a handſome freeſtone effigy of an armed knight, his ſword hanging at his ſide in a broad belt, on which were engraved many fleurs de lis[4], lying on a flat marble, which lay as a lid to a tomb of white ſmooth hewn aſhler ſtone, in which wrapt in a ſheet of lead lay his dry body, whole and undisjointed, having on its head ſomething like hair[5]. Sir John Hippiſley, the owner, covered it up, and planted on it a bay tree, flouriſhing 1753. His ſon Geoffry, biſhop of Wincheſter who died 1204, was alſo buried here, being a benefactor.

1181. Archbiſhop ROGER's is the oldeſt monument in the cathedral at *York*. It is wrought in the north wall of the nave, under a ſurbaſt or elliptical arch, ſurrounded by a faſcia of very rude oak leaves, projecting in the middle, with an angel or

[1] P. 180. [2] P. 19. [3] II. xix. but p. xi he acknowledges his miſtake.

[4] Weever ſuppoſed the fleurs de lis a rebus of the name of *Lucy*; but beſides that this would be founded only on the corruption of *flower de luce*, this ornament is not unfrequent on belts and in the diapering of ſhields.

[5] They found other ſuch ſtatues of men and one of a woman, with many grave-ſtones and bones. Weev. 777. Stukeley, Arch. I. 47. Haſted. I. 202.

View of the Monument of Robert Fitz Harding who died 1170
and his Lady in the N. side of Bristol Cathedral

figure in relief. The front of the tomb is composed of pierced quatrefoils; through which, Mr. Drake[1] says, may be felt with a stick his leaden coffin, which seems also to have been laid in the wall. He died 1181.

1182. HENRY son of Henry II. who died 1182, has a tomb on the south side of the altar at *Rouen*, with his figure, royally robed and crowned (he having been crowned in his father's life time) a sceptre surmounted by a bouquet in his left, his right on his breast, a long belt, and his mantle fastened on his breast by a fibula[2]. He was first buried at *Mans*, but soon after, by his father's command enforcing his own bequest, at Rouen[3].

1184. Mr. Dart[4] ascribes to GILBERT CRISPIN, abbot of Westminster, who died 1184, the middlemost figure in the south cloister, at the feet of Vitalis, which he observes has no mitre, that being acquired afterwards, by Laurence, between 1160 and 1176; but Mr. Widmore thinks his gravestone is not remaining. It was of black marble, and had this epitaph not legible in Flete's time:

> Hic pater insignis, genus altum, virgo, senexque,
> Gisleberte, jaces; lux, via, duxque tuis.
> Mitis eras, justus, prudens, fortis, moderatus;
> Doctus quadrivio, nec minus in trivio;
> Sic tamen ornatus nece sexta luce Decembris
> Spiramen cœlo reddis, & ossa solo.

Flete says it was *in eadem tumba marmorea sculptum*. Widmore, *round* the tomb. Petrus Blesensis gives him and Geffrey abbot of Croyland this common character. "Ambos Franciæ genitos & nutritos, ambos in septem liberalibus artibus "insignes doctores, sensu celebres, senio reverendos[5]."

1189. HENRY II. who died 1189, and was buried at *Fontevraud*, had a monument there in the style of the time. It is a figure without a beard or whiskers, royally robed and crowned. His mantle is now Azure, his surcoat red embroidered with flowers and lozenges, and his mattress with crosses and lozenges, a cushion under his head. On the back of each hand a jewel, which Montfaucon[6] knew not what to make of, and which appears in Dr. Stukeley's print of king John's effigy[7]. This figure, with those of his queen, his son Richard I. and Isabel wife of king John, were removed from their original tombs, and laid together on one altar-tomb, under a magnificent arch, highly ornamented with emblematic figures and festoons, &c. by the abbess of Fontevraud, daughter of Henry IV. of France, 1638, who sent Sandford a drawing of it by her own *scenographer*,—to whom it does no credit.

The manner of this king's burial was as follows. He was cloathed in royal robes, a crown of gold on his head, gloves[8] on his hands, boots of gilt wrought work, and spurs on his legs[9], a great ring on his finger, his sceptre in his hand, his sword by his side, and his face uncovered[10]. In this manner we may suppose succeeding kings were buried, and their effigies on the tombs copied from it. Edward I. was found in nearly the same circumstances, and Henry III's statue answers to this idea. The four figures singly are engraved by Montfaucon.

[1] P. 481. [2] Montf. Mon. II. p. 114. pl. xv. 3. [3] Chron. Norman. p. 1004. Sandf. 67. [4] Append. xiii.
[5] Contin. Ingulphi, p. 130. [6] Mon. II. 114. pl. xv. 1. [7] Itin. I. pl. xviii.
[8] Sandf. 64, calls them *white*, but the original gives no colour.
[9] Calceamenta auro texta in pedibus et calcaria. M. Par. boots of gilt *leather* and *gilt* spurs. Sandford.
[10] Math. Paris, p. 151. Sandf. 71.

His epitaph infcribed on his tomb is thus given by Matthew Paris, the third line alluding to a common faying of his, that "the whole world was not fufficient "for a great prince[1];" and the laft to the dying words of Severus to his urn: "Thou wilt hold the man whom the whole world could not contain[2]."

Rex Henricus eram, mihi plurima regna fubegi,
Multiplicique modo, duxque comefque fui.
Cui fatis ad votum non effent omnia terræ
Climata terra modo fufficit octo pedum.
Qui legis hæc penfa difcrimina mortis, & in me
Humanæ fpeculum conditionis habe.
Sufficit hic tumulus cui non fufficerat orbis.

At the corners of the tomb the abbefs placed two modern kneeling ftatues of white marble, of Joan queen of Sicily, third and youngeft daughter of Henry II. who died 1195, and of her fon by her fecond hufband Raymond, earl of Touloufe; who both had tombs and figures in this church[3].

1189. On the north wall of the Prefbytery at *Winchefter* is this Infcription for bifhop TOCLIVE:

Præfulis egregii paufant hic membra Ricardi
Toclive, cui fummi gaudia funto poli.
Obiit Anno 1189.[4]

1191. In the fouth wall of the fouth tranfept at *Exeter* is an altar tomb, with quatrefoils at the fides and ends, and a black marble flab, the brafs gone. This is the place affigned by Leland[5] to bifhop JOHN. If this means John who was promoted from the chantérfhip of this church 1186, and died 1191, I doubt a monument adorned with braffes does not fuit this early period. No other bifhop of this name was before Leland's time buried here.

1197. The heart of WILLIAM LONGCHAMP, fourth bifhop of Ely, who died 1197, and was buried abroad, was depofited in a little marble tomb near the altar of St. Martin in his cathedral[6]. He gained the confidence of Richard I. who promoted him to the higheft dignities in the ftate.

1198. Under an arch on the north-weft fide of the choir at *Worcefter* is a defaced monument of a bifhop, lying on a double cufhion, and at his feet two lions. JOHN DE CONSTANTIIS, who died 1198, was buried on the north fide of the altar, in or near this fpot. Gifford, in the next century, erected himfelf a handfome tomb in the fame place, *juxta magnum altare a dextra parte*, fays his will; but by order of the archbifhop of Canterbury, January, 1302, John's remains were replaced here, and Gifford was entombed on the oppofite fide of the altar[7].

1198. In the fouth wall of *Little Dunmow* church, Effex, is an altar tomb of alabafter, with the figures of a knight in armour, his helmet under his head[8], his hair cut round; his feet with the lion at them broken off. His lady has the mitred head-drefs richly flowered, a rich ftomacher and necklace; and at her feet, which are wrapt in her robe, two dogs. On the north fide of the tomb are

[1] Quoniam fæpe vivens dixerat, univerfum orbem uni non fufficere pro voto principis, infcriptio illius tumuli talis fuit.
[2] Dio, lxxvi. 869.
[3] Sandford adds an 8th line,
Res brevis eft ampla cui fuit ampla brevis.
[4] Godwin, 217. Warton, 102.
[5] It. III. 32.
[6] Richardfon on Godw. p. 254. ex MS. Barlow. Bentham's Ely, p. 145.
[7] Green, p. 72.
[8] Q. if not the firft inftance of the helmet under the head.

fhields,

St. Cleres at Danbury. Fitz Walters at Dunmow.

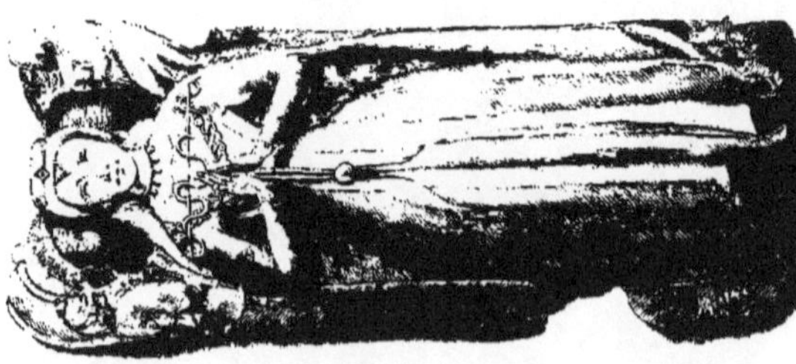

Monument of Matilda Fitzwalter, at Dunmow.

ſhields, alternately pendant and held by ſavages; *Fitzwalter* ſingle and impaling Vaire O. and Az. or G. and A. *Bohun*, or *Bohun* quartering Az. an inescocheon G. on a chevron 3 eſtoiles S. ſingle. and impaling *Bohun*. A Fitzwalter ſhield I reſcued from the head of a grave in the church-yard. The whole monument has ſuffered by removing from before the high altar, when the chancel was demoliſhed at the diſſolution. It is aſcribed to WALTER FITZWALTER, who died 1198, 10 R. I. and his ſecond wife MATILDA BOHUN.

His grandaughter MATILDA, who is ſaid to have been poiſoned by king John about the beginning of the next century for refuſing his ſolicitations and according to the Chronicle of Dunmow in the Monaſticon II. 76. was buried *inter duas columpnas in choro ex parte meridionali*, has now a monument overagainſt him. Her figure of alabaſter has on its head a covering like a woollen night-cap, a collar of SS. a necklace of pendants, falling from a rich embroidered neckerchief, a rich girdle, her ſleeves cloſe to her wriſt, and ſlit there. Her fingers ſtained with a red colour, which they pretend repreſents the effect of the poiſon, but more probably retaining traces of original painting, are loaded with rings, there being two on ſome of them; on her left little finger two together, on the third one, on the ſecond two ſeparate, on both thumbs one ſquare, and one on the middle, third, and little fingers of the right hand. Her face is round and full, but rather unmeaning. At her head two angels; at the ſide of her feet two dogs. This figure with its ſlab is now laid on a grey altar tomb, decorated with ſhields in quatrefoils parted by pairs of arches, and evidently of a more modern ſtyle. Though this ſituation above aſſigned will ſuit the preſent choir, it muſt be obſerved, that what now ſerves as choir is only the eaſt end of the ſouth aile, all the reſt being pulled down; ſo that the bodies to which theſe tombs originally belonged are probably in the ploughed field that now occupies the ſite of the choir.

I am indebted to the pencil of my ingenious and lamented friend Mr. Tyſon for the drawings of theſe monuments. Pl. VI. 1 & 2, & Pl. VII.

ANDREW, the third abbot, in the ſouth wall of the ſouth aile of the choir at 1199. *Peterborough*, has a rich Gothic canopy, and holds a book and a croſier piercing a dragon at his feet. Theſe three porphyry figures were brought from three arches of the chapter houſe now remaining in the ſouth wall of the cloiſters; and over them is written on the wall,

Hos tres abbates, quorum eſt prior abba *Johannes*;
Alter *Martinus*, *Andreas* ultimus, unus
Hic claudit tumulus; pro clauſis ergo rogemus.

Theſe three, buried in one grave, were John 18th abbot; who died 1125;
Martin 20th, 1155, and Andrew 23d, 1199 [1].
Below them lies a fourth, under an arch in the wall, without any animal.

In a chapel in the ſouth aile is a fifth abbot with book and croſier, piercing a double-headed dragon. This figure, which ſeems the oldeſt of the five, has not been aſſigned to any particular abbot. See plate III.

In the ſouth aile of the choir at *Hereford* biſhop VERE, third ſon of Aubrey 1199. de Vere, firſt earl of Oxford, who died 1199, has the ſame arch and figure as his predeceſſors *Clyve*, *Betune*, *Foliot*, and *Melun*, with this inſcription,

D'nus Gulielmus le Vere Epiſcopus Herefordenſis.
Obiit. A. 1199.

And the arms of *Vere*. This tomb is railed in.

[1] Willis, 488. Gunton, 37.

Bishop Godwin [1] justly observes, that these four monuments, with the figures on them, holding crosiers in their left hand, and blessing with the right, are so exactly alike that nothing but the place and rank distinguish them.

1199. RICHARD I. who died 1199, and was buried at the feet of his father, had a tomb at *Fontevraud*, with his figure in beard and whiskers, royally robed and crowned, his mantle adorned with flowers and lozenges (now as well as his tunic painted) and jewels on his hands, which are laid on his breast and belly [2]. This figure is now on the modern mausoleum. The same king has another figure on the tomb, in which his heart was interred at Rouen. It has no beard, and the crown is different; his right hand hangs down, his left holds a sceptre, surmounted by a bouquet; a fibula like that of Henry II. but longer, confines his robe on the breast; and a long studded belt is round his waist [3]. His bowels were buried at Chalons; Sandford [4] says, in disgrace of their unthankfulness, which if he means it as a reflexion on the bowels, i. e. the king himself, who behaved so very ungratefully to his father, the punishment should have been inflicted on his heart; if on the city of Chalons, it seems none; for bodies, hearts, and bowels, were, at that time of day, frequently buried in different places [5].

Two wooden figures of cross-legged knights, under arches in the north aile of *Danbury* church, Essex, are by Mr. Morant [6] referred to some of the ST. CLERE family, who had lands there from the reign of Stephen to that of Edward II, and probably founded this aile. The *Darcies*, to whom Weever [7], from the current tradition of the place, ascribes them, were not lords here till the end of the 15th century. They are engraved, Pl. VII. 3, 4. from drawings by Mr. Tyson, who much admired the elegance of their workmanship. There is a great resemblance between them and the monuments in the Temple church.

In opening a grave, October or November, 1779, near this spot, was found a leaden coffin, in which was enclosed a body, preserved in some sort of liquor. As far as the liquor covered it the body was well preserved: the hands were remarkably perfect, the nose decayed. This discovery led Mr. Tyson, who communicated it to me, to conclude with great probability that the above figures were not lids of coffins.

[1] P. 484. [2] Montf. II. 114. xv. 4. [3] Montf. II. 114. xv. 5. [4] P. 79.
[5] See his epitaph, Sandf. 79. [6] Hist. of Essex, II. 30. [7] P. 640.

Albericus de Vere, surnamed the Grim, first Earl of Oxford. 1194.

x 1653.

Scale of 3 feet.

CENT.

CENTURY XIII.

Ye heavenly ſpirits, whoſe aſhy cinders lie
Under deep ruines, with huge walls oppreſt,
But not your praiſe, the which ſhall never die
Through your fair verſes, ne in aſhes reſt:

If ſo be ſhrilling voice of wight alive
May reach from hence to depth of darkeſt hell,
Then let theſe deep abyſſes open rive,
That ye may underſtand my ſhrieking yell.

Thrice having ſeen, under the heaven's veil,
Your tombs devoted compaſs over all,
Thrice unto you with loud voice I appeal,
And for your antique Fury here do call.

SPENSER, Ruines of Rome.

P 33.

Bishop Peter Aquablanca 1268. 17, 8.

C E N T U R Y XIII.

THE XIIIth Century should open with St. Hugh the Burgundian, bishop of *Lincoln*, who had a magnificent shrine and silver chest, into which his reliques were translated by the kings of England and France, 1282, 5 John, behind the high altar of his cathedral. Only the traces of it remain in the pavement. It has been succeeded by a table monument, erected by bishop Fuller, between 1667 and 1675; with an inscription, which may be seen in Browne Willis' account of the cathedral [1]. The monument or shrine commonly ascribed to him, and engraved by Dr. Stukeley [2], was supposed by Mr. Lethieullier to be that of *Hugh*, a child, crucified and canonized 40 Henry III. I shall insert here his account at large, in a letter to Mr. Gale, printed in the Archæologia, I. 26. 1200.

" In looking over the several monuments within the cathedral of Lincoln I " took particular notice of the poor remains of one in the isle on the south side " the choir, which I recollected the author of the Itinerarium Curiosum had given " a draught of as entire (without mentioning from whence he had his authority), " and called it the shrine of St. Hugh the Burgundian, bishop of this see.

" The story of this bishop is well known. We are told, that in regard to his " sanctity he was carried to his grave on the shoulders of two kings: that he " was interred at the east end of this church, which he had built, and had a " shrine erected over his grave, which in the inventory of the riches of this " church (an original of which was shewn me in their archives) is said to have " been of gold, the marks of which still remain in the pavement and against " the pillar [3] where it stood, and in its place, bishop Fuller, a great restorer of " the antiquities of this church, placed a table tomb, with an inscription on it " that has frequently been published.

" Now I believe there is no instance of the same saint having two shrines " dedicated to him in the same church, and from what I have above said we may " therefore conclude, that the forementioned shrine in the south aisle never belong- " ed to St. Hugh the bishop; but some other saint must be looked for to hallow it.

[1] P 49. [2] It Cur. I. pl. xxix.

[3] This pillar is the first North Eastern one from the back of the high altar: but it may be doubted, whether the holes on the pavement, and marks of irons in the pillar, did not rather belong to another monument. It should seem that the shrine would occupy the centre of the area, or nearly the site of the tomb erected by Bishop Fuller.

" This

" This ſaint I think I may venture to affirm was a child named *Hugh*, who " was crucified by the Jews dwelling in the city, 40 Henry III. and whoſe " torments in the Chriſtian cauſe were in the zeal of that age thought ſufficient " to merit canonization. But before I attempt to prove that this ſhrine was " erected to this infant ſaint it ſeems neceſſary to produce ſome evidence that " ſuch an one ever exiſted: ſince M. Rapin, in his hiſtory of the reign of " Edward I. ſpeaking of the baniſhment of the Jews out of England by the fol- " lowing paſſage calls in queſtion the certainty of any ſuch crime having ever " been committed. As for the imputation, ſays he, of crucifying, from time " to time, Chriſtian children, one may almoſt be ſure that it was only a calum- " ny invented by their enemies. But to omit all the retailers of this ſtory, " which are many, I refer you at once to Matthew Paris, an hiſtorian of veracity " and credit, and who probably could not be impoſed upon in a fact he was con- " temporary with, it happening about five years before his death.

" That author has given us the ſtory in a very full manner, which I ſhall not " trouble you with repeating, but only obſerve, that he tells us the name of " the child was Hugh, and that the canons of Lincoln procured his body, and " buried it honourably in their cathedral [a].

" M. Paris's relation is fully confirmed by the two records you ſent me copies " of; the one being a commiſſion from the king to Simon Paſſelewe and William " de Leighton to ſeize to the king's uſe 'domos [b] quæ fuerunt Judæorum Linc. " ſuſpenſorum pro puero ibidem crucifixo,' and the other a pardon to one John

[a] I ſhall lay before the reader the original account at large.

" Anno quoque ſub eodem [1255] circa feſtum apoſtolorum Petri & Pauli Judæi Lincolniæ furati ſunt unum puerum Hugonem nomine, habentem ætate octo annos. Et cum ipſum in quodam conclavi ſecretiſſimo lacte & aliis puerilibus alimentis nutrirent, miſerunt ad omnes fere Angliæ civitates in quibus Judæi degebant, & convocaverunt de unaquaque civitate aliquos Judæorum, ut in contumeliam & opprobrium Jeſu Chriſti intereſſent ſacrificio ſuo Lincolniæ. Habebant enim, ut dicebant, quondam puerum abſconditum ad crucifigendum. Et convenerunt multi Lincolniæ. Et convenientes conſtituerunt unum Judæum Lincolnienſem pro judice tanquam pro Pilato; cujus judicio & omnium favore affectus eſt puer diverſis tormentis, verberatus eſt uſque ad cruorem & livorem, ſpinis coronatus, & ſputis & cachinnis laceſſitus. Et inſuper & ſingulis punctus cultellis qui dicitur *Anelatis* *, potatus felle, deriſus probris & blaſphemiis, & crebro ab iiſdem frendentibus Jeſus pſeudopropheta vocatus. Et poſtquam diverſimode illuſerant ei crucifixerunt: & lancea ad cor pupugerunt. Cum expiraſſet depoſuerunt corpus de cruce, & neſcitur qua ratione eviſcerarunt corpuſculum; dicitur autem quod ad magicas artes exercendas. Mater autem pueri filium ſuum abſentem per aliquot dies diligenter quæſivit, dictumque ei a vicinis quod ultimo viderunt puerum quem quæſivit ludentem cum pueris Judæorum ſibi coætaneis & domum Judæi cujuſdam intrantem. Intravit igitur mulier ſubito domum illam, & vidit corpus pueri in quondam puteum præcipitatum. Et caute convocatis civitatis ballivis inventum eſt corpus & extractum. Et factum eſt mirabile ſpectaculum in populo. Mulier autem mater pueri querula & clamoſa omnes cives in uno convenientes ad lachrymas & ſuſpiria provocavit. Erat autem ibidem dominus Johannes de Lexintona, vir quidem circumſpectus & diſcretus, inſuper eleganter literatus, qui ait, audivimus quandoque quod talia Judæi in opprobrium Jeſu Chriſti domini noſtri crucifixi non ſunt veriti attemptare. Et capto uno Judæo in cujus domum ſcilicet intravit puer ludens, & ideo aliis ſuſpectiore, ait illi, 'Miſer, neſcis 'quod te feſtinus manet interitus? Totum aurum Angliæ non ſufficeret ad ereptionem tuam aut redemptionem. Verun- 'tamen dicam tibi licet indigno qualiter poteris vitam tuam reſervare, & membra ne mutileris. Utrunque te ſalvabo, ſi 'quæcunque in hoc caſu acta ſunt ſine falſi ſtamine mihi pandere non formides.' Judæus igitur ille, cui nomen *Copinus*, ſe credens viam inveniſſe evaſionis reſpondit dicens, 'Domine Johannes, ſi dictis facta compenſas pandam tibi mirabilia.' Et animavit eum & ſtimulavit ad hoc domini Johannis induſtria. Et ait Judæus; 'Vera ſunt quæ dicunt Chriſtiani. Judæi 'fere quolibet anno unum puerum in injuriam & contumeliam Jeſu crucifigunt. Sed non quolibet anno comperitur. Oc- 'culte enim hoc faciunt & locis abſconditis & ſecretiſſimis. Hunc autem puerum, quem Hugonem vocat, immiſericordi- 'ter noſtri Judæi crucifixerunt, & cum obiiſſet, & mortuum vellent abſcondere non potuit obrui in terra nec abſcondi. Inutile 'enim reputabatur, corpus inſontis augurio; ad hoc enim eviſcerabatur, & cum mane putatur abſconditum reddidit illud terra, '& evomuit, & apparuit corpus aliquoties inhumatum ſupra terram; unde abhorruerunt Judæi. Tandem in puteum præci- 'pitatum eſt, nec adhuc tamen potuit occultari. Mater enim improba omnia perſcrutando tandem corpus inventum balli- 'vis intimavit.' Dominus autem Johannes tenuit Judæum vinculis mancipatum. Et cum hæc canonicis eccleſiæ Lincolnienſis cathedralis innotuiſſent petierunt corpuſculum ſibi dari. Et conceſſum eſt illis. Et cum ab infinitis ſatis conſideraretur, honorifice in eccleſia Lincolnienſi tanquam precioſus martyr humabatur. Sciendum quod Judæi tenuerunt puerum vivum per 10 dies, ut tot diebus paſtus lacte tormenta vivus multiformia toleraret. Cum rex rediiſſet de partibus borealibus Angliæ, & certificaretur de præmiſſis, increpavit dominum Johannem quod tam flagitioſo vitam & membra polliceretur, quod dare nequiverat: dignus enim erat blaſphemus ille & homicida mortis pœna multiformi. Et cum judicium reo immineret irremediabile, ait: " Imminet mihi mors mea, nec poteſt mihi dominus Johannes penitus ſuffragari. Nunc " dico vobis omnibus veritatem; hujus pueri de quo calumniantur Judæi mortis conſentiebant omnes fere Judæi " Angliæ, & cujuſlibet fere civitatis Angliæ in qua Judæi habitant quidam electi convocabantur ad illius pueri im- " molationem quaſi ad paſchale ſacrificium!" Et cum hæc dixiſſet ſimul cum aliis deliramentis, ligatus ad caudam equinam & tractus ad patibulum aereis cacodemonibus in corpore & anima præſentatur. Et alii Judæi hujus facinoris participes quater viginti & undecim in bigis Londinium ducti carcerali cuſtodiæ mancipantur. Qui ſi forte ab aliquibus Chriſtianis plangebantur ab emulis eorum *Caurſinis* † ſiccis lacrymis deplorabantur. Poſtea vero per inquiſitionem juſticiariorum domini regis perceptum fuit & inventum quod Judæi Angliæ communi conſilio puerum innocentem pluribus diebus flagellatum interemerunt crucifixum. Sed poſtea pro iniquitate illa mater dicti pueri contra ipſos de tali morte appellationem ſuam coram rege conſtanter proſequente Deus ultionum dominus dignam pro meritis reddidit retributionem: nam in die Sti Clementis 18 de ditioribus & majoribus civitatis Lincolnienſis fuerunt tracti, & ad furcas novas ad hoc ſpecialiter præparatas vento præſentati. Et in turri Londinenſi pluſquam viginti ter ad ſimile judicium in carcere ſunt reſervati." M. Paris, p. 912, 913. A. D. 1255.

[b] Part of the houſes ſo forfeited were purchaſed and appropriated to Welborne's Chantry. Reg. Decani & Capit. foundation of Welborne's chantry.

* *Anelace*, a kind of a knife or dagger worn at the girdle. See Tyrwhitt's Chaucer, ver. 359. and note.

† A ſet of foreign ſlippers and uſurers, with whoſe trade the Jews interfered.

" a con-

" a convert who had been condemned 'pro morte pueri nuper crucifixi apud " Lincoln dum prædictus Johannes fuit Judæus ejusdem civitatis.'

" As there is as good authority for the truth of this fact as can be brought for " any transaction in past ages, I am satisfied you will not require further proof[1].

" Upon a strict enquiry I was informed by one of the minor canons (a gen- " tleman who has a taste for these studies) that this was the tomb of the cru- " cified child; and as a farther proof, the verger shewed me a statue of a boy, " made of free-stone, painted, about twenty inches high, which by tradition " they affirm was removed from the said tomb or shrine. I have inclosed a " slight sketch of it[2], by which you will observe the marks of crucifixion in the " hands and feet, and the wound made on the right side, from whence blood " is painted in the original as issuing: the left hand is on the breast, but the " right held up, with the two fingers extended in the usual posture of bene- " diction; which attitude, I apprehend, denotes his being a saint, as the " wounds do his being a martyr[3]. The head is broken off, probably at the time " when the statues in this church underwent that fate.

" In the draught of this shrine given in the Itinerarium the figure of the boy " is not expressed. That draught I have reason to believe was copied from a book " of drawings of all the monuments in this cathedral, taken by order of Sir " William Dugdale before they were destroyed in the late civil wars, which book " is now in lord Hatton's library; but the statue of the boy I apprehend was re- " moved by an order from Henry VIII. for taking away all causes of superstition " or idolatry.

" The materials this was made of were not worth transferring to the Exchequer " (whither the shrines of St. Hugh and John Dalderby were sent, the one being " gold, the other silver). But this figure was set in a by place just behind the high " altar, where we found it covered with dust and obscurity. As there is no danger " of superstition in this age, I could wish it were replaced in its proper station[4].

" Give me leave further to observe, that I think this a very remarkable mo- " nument, and strong proof of a piece of our English history, which by the passage " in Rapin is rendered very dubious; and since this fact at Lincoln is so well at- " tested, there is the less reason to doubt the other stories of the same kind which " are recorded in different historians, and are collected together by Mr. Prynne, in " his "Demurrer to the Jews."

" Mr. Willis, to whom I have communicated the purport of this long epistle, " sends me word he is entirely of my opinion, and extremely pleased to have his " error in calling it the shrine of St. Hugh the bishop corrected."

The monument has suffered much damage since the draught was taken which Dr. Stukeley has engraved. The pediment and two pillars which projected from its front are gone, as are the three short arches on which they rested, and which there appear adorned with four shields, bearing the arms of England single and impaling Old France alternately. All that now remains is the back part of this shrine or tomb; on each side of which are two or three arches, within which have been painted shields of arms now defaced.

This second application of the monument in question must give way to a third hypothesis.

This was the place of an image of the Virgin Mary. It appears from the Dean and Chapter's books, 21 June, 1533, "Decanus et Capitulum concesserunt con-

[1] "I shall beg leave only to add the testimony of our English Homer.

O yonge Hewe of Lyncoln, slayne also
With cursyd Jewes, as it is notable;
For it is but a litel while ago;
Pray eke for us, we synful folk unstable,
That of his mercy God be merciable
On us! his grete mercy multiply,
For the reverence of his mother Mary! Chaucer: Prioress's Tale."

[2] This sketch does not appear in the Society's archives.

[3] The posture of the hands, so different from the attitude of a crucifix, proves it could not be an image of our Saviour.

[4] In the late repair of this beautiful church this mutilated statue was thrown away, among other lumber.

"fratri

"fratri suo Christophero Massingberd cancellario maximum lapidem marmoreum "coram *imagine beatæ M. V. in insula australi dicta ecclesia* cath. Linc. in quo "nulla apparet scriptura seu sculptura, ita quod ipse cancellarius cum ab hac luce "migraverit bene et libere possit et valeat sub eodem lapide sepeliri.

1201. WILLIAM DE BLEYS, bishop of *Lincoln*, called by Leland *William de Montibus*, who died 1201, after having filled the see two years from his consecration, was buried in the upper North transept of his cathedral. Of his body on its removal a century after its inhumation, in order to rebuild or improve this part of the church, we have the following account from Schawk, who was register at the time. "Will's de Bloynes, vir literatus et benignus, cujus memoriam be-"nedictione cedit a nonnullis. Nam circa 100 annos a corporis sui humacione "effluxis, cum corpus suum a loco in quo jacebat humatus amotum fuisset prætextu "pulchrioris fabricæ [1] faciendæ inventum fuit integrum, et vinum in calice cum "quo humatum fuerat recens, ut videbatur, et purum [2]."

1202. Pl. IX. ALAN, abbot of *Tewkesbury*, canon of Beneventum, and five years a novice and sacristan of Christ-church, Canterbury, 1179, a great favourer of Becket, and stout opposer of Baldwin archbishop of Canterbury, for which reason that prelate got him removed to this abbey 1186 or 7, where he sat 18 years, and died 1202, has, in the south aile of the choir of his church in the south wall, near the vestry, a blue speckled slab, with a cross on it, and this inscription, ✠ ALANVS ÆBI. under a demi-quatrefoil arch. He is said to have been a man of great wit, learning, and piety, and wrote a life of Becket, the acts of Clarendon, Epistles to Henry II. &c.

1203. X. & Pl. XI. In the north aile of the chancel at *Banham*, Norfolk, under an arch in the wall terminating in a bouquet, and remarkable for its extraordinary simplicity, lies an oak figure of a knight in plaited armour, and surcoat, and round helmet, his head on a cushion; his right hand lies by his side, his left lifted up. A large cinquefoil under his left arm bespeaks him to be Sir HUGH BARDOLPH, knight, who had a monument here, and died 1203 [3]. See Pl. X. & XI. an exact representation of this figure, from a beautiful drawing communicated by Mr. Kerrich, Fellow of Magdalen College, Cambridge; with the following description of it.

"The Effigy itself is a cumbent statue of wood, cut out of the same piece of oak with the board on which it lies; but some of the smaller, and more saliant parts, were made separately, and are fastened to the rest with wooden pins [4]. The whole is hollow and is open at the bottom. It was originally painted all over, but is now almost bare. From the little paint remaining we may gather that his armour was mail, which did not cover the head, but at the height of the mouth was laced with a red lace to a light head-piece, which has a kind of crest or sharp eminence running over it from behind forwards. From what remains on the left arm, there may be some reason to think it was not covered with mail, but narrow plates like those in the seal of king Edward II, but there is so little left, that this is very uncertain; but whatever this part of the armour consisted of, it certainly covered his fingers quite to the ends, and was not divided for each finger. The mailles on the legs seem not to be plain circular rings as usual, but formed into square figures; but this too on account of the very little paint remaining may be questioned [5]. The sword which was placed very forward is now gone; it was fastened to the figure, and was not of the same piece with it. The sword belt was of a yellowish colour, flowered with green and red; the girdle nearly like it; the surcoat, which is scarce longer than the coat of mail, is divided before about four inches be-

[1] Agreement between Dean and Chapter, and Richard Stowe, 1306, to keep up *novum opus*, in arch. eccl. Linc.

[2] Lib. Cratim, fol. 135.

[3] Blomfield's History of Norfolk, I. 140.

[4] As the whole of the right arm, and cubit of the left, several small pieces in the folds of the surcoat on the right side towards the bottom, and one large one on the outside of the left knee, which last seems to have been supplied long after the figure was made.

[5] There are lines cut into the wood in all the parts of the figure which were covered with mail; these seem to have determined the form of mailles, and I have therefore attended to the number of them in my drawings.

low

Pl. X. XI. p. 34.

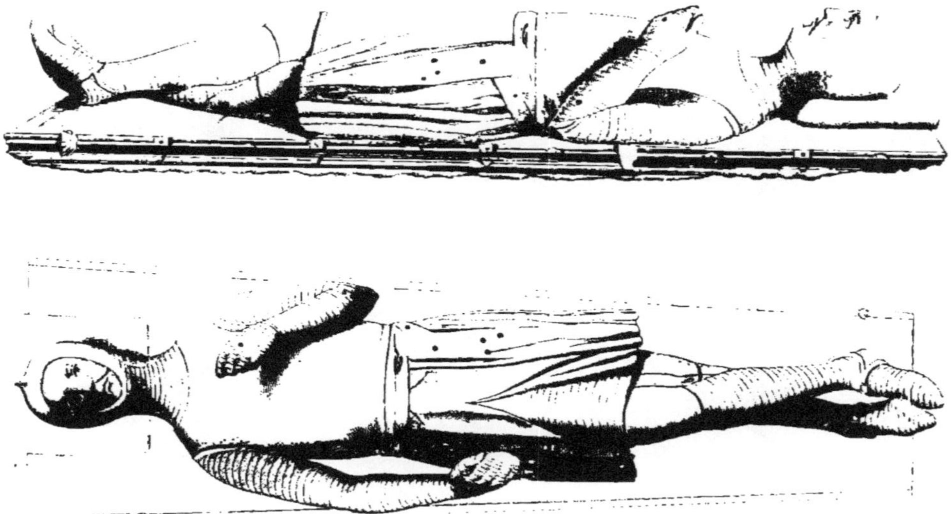

S.r Hugh Bardolph. 1203.

low the girdle; it was of a deep brownish crimson colour, flowered with yellow. On his knees are plates, which lie over the mail of the legs. There are two large holes in the cubit of the left arm, from whence we may conclude he bore a shield upon it. In his right hand he held something, perhaps a sword. The spurs were gilt, the necks of them are lost, and were not of the same piece with the figure. The spur-leathers buckled upon the top of the instep, and were very gayly painted with green, red, yellow and black. His head rests upon a pillow, of the same colour, and flowered nearly in the same manner, with his girdle. The board, or bed, if you please, on which the figure lies, was green and flowered. There have been upon the edge of this board, on each side six roses (or, as Mr. Blomefield calls them, cinquefoils) and five small shields for arms; but there remain at present only one of the roses entire, which is under the right arm of the figure, and half of another near the feet on the other side, and only one of the shields.

"The paint is water colours, laid upon a very thick ground of whiting, which in several places, as the mailles for instance, is raised into a kind of relievo, so as to be quite rough to the touch; and, before this was applied, the wood, in some parts at least, was covered with linen cloth, but certainly not all over. The colour of the lace, or ribband, which fastens the mail to the helmet, is exceedingly vivid, which perhaps is owing in some measure to the being laid upon gold. The colours of the surcoat are laid in the same manner.

"Upon digging we found almost immediately below the surface of the ground, before the monument, a bed of flint stones laid in very strong mortar, about nine inches thick, near eight feet long, and three wide. We broke through this, and went to the depth of six feet, but could find no coffin, nor any remains of a body, and came then to strata of earth which seemed never to have been disturbed.

"Query, If the body of the person to whom this monument belongs was really buried here, is it not probable we should have found it in the wall itself immediately under the Effigy."

Under the north window of the south aile at *Canterbury*, east from the song 1205.
school, is the tomb of archbishop HUBERT WALTER, who died 1205. His statue, lying on it defaced, is *in pontificalibus*, his hands joined, a dog at his feet. His robe was once neatly painted with the armorial bearings of his family, but time and white-wash prevent these remains from being discoverable [1]. The tomb must have been more perfect when drawn for Dart, who has engraved it p. 131, or it is supplied from fancy. He represents it lying on an altar tomb with nine pointed arches; but as the figure is much shorter than the tomb, they probably were not *intended* for each other. Godwin says he is reported to be buried in the wall. He saw his epitaph, but heard it was afterwards some how or other defaced [2]. Giraldus Cambrensis [3], his contemporary, gives him this great character: "Principis erat frenum & tyrannidis obstaculum; populi pax & solatium; majorum pariter & minorum suis diebus contra publicæ potestatis oppressiones in necessitate refugium."

Bishop MARSHALL, who filled the see of *Exeter* from 1193 to 1206, and is 1206.
supposed to have built the choir of his cathedral as it now appears, has a monument on the north side of the high altar. The figure lies *in pontificalibus*, the two least fingers of his left hand bent, the others extended as giving the benediction: in his right hand a crosier, at his feet a horned lizard or dragon: at the corner of the arch over his head angels in several niches; on each side the tomb six figures in quatrefoils, three monks on the north side, a bishop on the south side; and in one quatrefoil two figures together. Above, a lion rampant, which Izaacke makes his arms [4].

The improvement or variation between this tomb and bishop Roger's is, the *altar* tomb decorated with figures, and the *coat of arms*. It is not however improbable, that Roger had a sarcophagus either above or under ground; I rather

[1] Gostling, p. 252. [2] Godwin, p 83. [3] De jure & statu eccl. Menev. & Gemma Eccles. Dist. 2. c. 36. [4] P. 5.

think the latter; and that if not left behind at Old Sarum it lies under the raised base at Salisbury.

1206. The only memorial of WILLIAM BLESENSIS bishop of *Lincoln*, who died 1206, and was buried with his three successive predecessors, in the Upper or Lesser North transept of his cathedral, is a whole length figure of him, painted with three more of them on the west wall of this transept. There lie below, in the middle of the floor, close and parallel to each other, three plain blue stones coffin-fashioned, and a fourth decorated with massive figures in alto releivo of persons with various symbols, sitting on branches of a tree, on whose top seems to be the Deity. Among these figures one plainly appears to hold a harp.

The Ichnographies of this cathedral, in Dugdale's Monasticon[1], and Willis, ascribe one of these four stones to bishop *Walter de Constantiis*. But besides that the date of his death in these plans is confounded with that of Blesensis, he enjoyed this dignity but one year, being translated to the archbishopric of Rouen 1184[2].

On the north side of the choir[3] at *Hereford* is the figure of a bishop pontifically habited; his right-hand giving the benediction, in his left a crosier and embattled tower of two stories. On the wall over him is painted this inscription, *D'ns Egidius de Bruse Epus Hers.*
Ob. A. D. 1215.

This is the monument of GILES BRUCE, or BREOSE, bishop of Hereford, from 1199 to 1215. He was son of William Breose baron Brecknock, and for adhering to the barons against king John, was obliged to fly his country, but having afterwards recovered the king's favour, died at Gloucester Nov. 17, 1215, on his way home, leaving his ample fortune to his brother Reginald, who married the daughter of Llewellin prince of North Wales. From the tower in his hand Godwin conjectures he built the west-tower of his cathedral[4].

1215. Fig. 3, 4. Pl. IX. are supposed to have been the figures of ALBERIC DE VERE, third of that Christian name, and second earl of Oxford, and his Lady, on their monument at *Earl's Colne* priory in Essex. They were made of wood, and painted, but being totally destroyed 1736, are here engraved from drawings taken by Daniel King 1653, which were the property of Lord Fairfax, afterwards of Mr. Lethieullier, and now of the Hon. Horace Walpole, to whose polite and liberal spirit of communication I am indebted for many other drawings with which this work is embellished. Mr. Lethieullier, whose judicious remarks accompany all the drawings that were his property, was induced by the material of which these figures were made to assign them to this earl of Oxford, who died without issue 16 John, 1215. Whom he married does not appear from Dugdale. Alberic succeeded his father Alberic, who was made earl of Oxford by the empress Maud, and confirmed in that dignity by her son Henry II. His brother Robert has a monument at Hatfield Broad-oak, before described, engraved in plate VIII.

1225. Pl. XII. In the north aile of *Christ-church*, Oxford, is a tomb generally ascribed to PHILIP third prior of St. Fridiswide, who finished the present church, erected the beautiful shrine of the patroness still remaining two arches above him, into which he translated her remains 1180, and wrote an account of her life and miracles. He died before 1225, but in what year is uncertain. Bishop Tanner and Wood[5] make him flourish 1180, Bishop Kennet[6] and Wood, in another work[7], 1189. Browne Willis[8] makes him die 1190, and ascribes this monument also to *Guymund*, the first prior, by whose care this house was re-established 1111, and the present church began to be built, and who died 1149.

In this diversity of opinions we may suppose the monument to have been erected to one or other of these priors in a late period, to which Mr. Lethieullier, whose drawing is here copied, assigns it.

[1] III. 25. [2] Godwin, p. 287. or, as Mr. Willis indeterminately expresses it, under an arch in the south aile.
[3] Survey of Hereford, p. 513. [4] P. 414. [5] MS alia. [6] Paroch. Antiq. p. 144.
[7] Hist. & Ant. Ox. I. 53. [8] Cath. of Oxf. p. 410.

Pl. IX. p. 36.

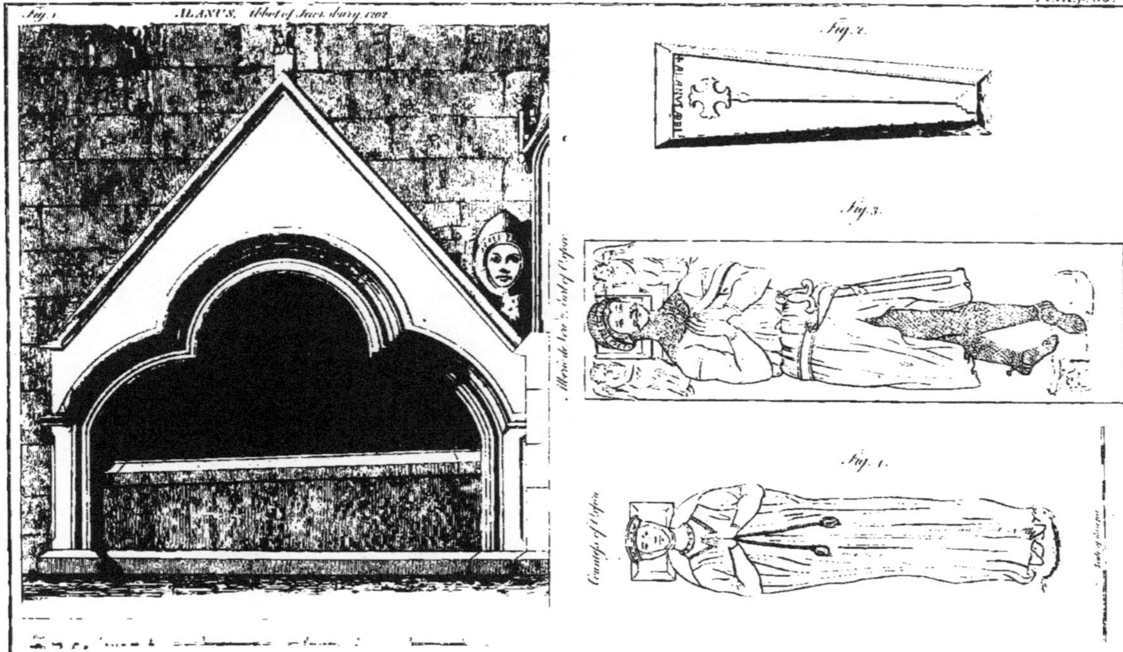
Fig. 1.
Fig. 2.
Fig. 3.
Fig. 4.
Alberic de Vere 2. Earl of Oxford
Countess of Oxford

PHILIP, 3d Prior of St Frideswide in Christ Church Oxford

Bishop POORE in Salisbury cathedral 1237

King JOHN died 1216, and his monument in the choir at *Worcester* is probably of his own age, and the oldest of our Kings in England, if we except that ascribed to Rufus. He was buried here by his own desire in his will, in a monk's cowl. His effigies is royally apparelled. Within his crown was JOHANNES REX ANGLIÆ, now entirely defaced. In his right hand was a sceptre, now broken; in his left a sword reversed, and piercing a lion at his feet. On each side of his head, instead of the usual accompaniments of angels, are two Bishops *in pontificalibus*, as Dr. Thomas [1] says, and as Dr. Stukeley has drawn them [2], *censing* him, but as Thomas has engraved it, *holding their crosiers*. These are supposed to be the bishops Oswald and Wulstan, patrons of the church, whose monuments now lie in Lady-chapel, though mistaken for two other bishops [3]. The royal body is supposed to lie under Lady-chapel, in a stone vault, in a strong chest, in which, upon opening, was found a leaden coffin, but without any marks or inscription. The tomb above ground being also opened was found quite empty [4]. The Annals of Worcester published by Mr. Wharton [5] expresly say, he was buried *coram magno altari inter S. S. Oswaldum et Wulstanum*. The then choir was afterwards converted into the Lady-chapel; and when the high altar was placed where the communion table now stands, and the floor of the new choir had gained a considerable elevation by a subterraneous vault made underneath, the king's tomb, now hidden from view, was taken down, and erected before the new high altar, and between the shrines here, as it had hitherto stood between the sepulchres of these two bishops [6]. On its sides in quatrefoils are the arms of England, three lions passant guardant. Stukeley [7], on what authority I know not, supposes the image lay on the ground, in the Lady chapel, on a stone now between bishops Oswald and Wolstan, though since elevated on a tomb in the choir. Dr. Nash thinks the body was left in the choir, when on its being ruined the tomb was brought forward. Sandford pronounces the figures of the king and bishops, all of one stone, to be as old as the time of Henry III. but the altar-tomb on which it is placed is certainly of modern fabrick [8]. 1216.

One of the figures in the *Temple* church belongs to WILLIAM MARSHALL, earl 1219.
of PEMBROKE [9], whose arms per pale O. and V. a lion rampant G. armed and Pl. V.
langued G. are on the shield. It is a knight in mail with a surcoat, his helmet fig. 2.
more completely rounded than the adjoining one, and the cushion as in all the rest, and under Longespee's at Sarum, laid straiter under his head. He is drawing his short dagger or broken sword with his right hand, and on his left arm has a short pointed shield. Below his knees are bands or garters, as if to separate the cuisses from the greaves; his legs are crossed, and under his feet is a lion couchant.

Our William was descended from the antient family of that name, who held the office of marshal of England, and of whom Sir William Dugdale [10] has given a succession of seven descents from the time of Henry III. to Edward II. He was son of John, who lived in the reign of Stephen, and brother of John, who held the above high office in the reigns of Henry II. and Richard I. and died without issue in the latter. The first account of William is 28 Henry II. when Henry son of that prince, who had behaved himself rebelliously against his father, lying on his death-bed, with great penitence delivered to him, as to his most intimate friend, his cross to carry to Jerusalem [11]. He obtained from Richard I. on his first coming to England after his father's death, Isabel daughter and heir of Richard earl of Pembroke [12] in marriage, and with her that earldom, and by that title he assisted at Richard's coronation [13]. When that prince went to

[1] P. 35. [2] Itin. I. xviii. He has represented the figure amazingly rude. [3] See before, p. 30.
[4] Green's Survey of Worcester, p. 40. 67. [5] Angl. Sac. I. 483. [6] Green, p. 38. [7] P. 65.
[8] P. 85. [9] Weever, p. 442. [10] Bar. I. 599. [11] Hoved. p. 354. Dugd. ib. & aut. ibi citati.
[12] Dugdale after Bromton, p. 1155. and Hoveden, 373. says only of *Strigul*; but this was Richard de Clare, surnamed Strongbow, second earl of Pembroke, which title pass'd with his daughter to her husband. See Camden in Pembrokesh. p. 513. M. Paris also calls our William earl of Pembroke, as well as his son William.
[13] Hoved. p. 354. Bromt. p. 1158.

the Holy Land he gave him a ſhare in the government[1], and he engaged himſelf for the king's performance of his engagement with the king of France to undertake the cruſade[2]. He was ſheriff of Lincolnſhire from the 2d to the 6th of this reign, and of Suſſex during the whole, as alſo 1 Joh. and of Glouceſterſhire the ſame year, till the eighth. Upon John's acceſſion he was ſent before him from Normandy to keep the peace till his arrival[3]. He obtained of the king a grant of the whole province of Leinſter in Ireland, beſides the government of ſeveral caſtles in Wales, and on the borders[4]; and he was ſent to receive the demands of the malcontent barons at Brackley, 17 Joh[5]. He ſupported Henry III. againſt the partiſans of the Dauphin, amongſt whom was his own ſon[6], and defeated them at Lincoln, which they had laid ſiege to[7]. He then beleaguered London, and reduced it to the utmoſt diſtreſs; and by his prudent conduct a peace was ſoon after brought about, 2 Henry III[8]. The laſt public office which he filled was that of ſheriff of Eſſex and Hertfordſhire[9]. He founded Cartmele priory, Lancaſhire, and three more in Ireland, and began a Ciſtertian foundation at Dowyſken in the county of Kilkenny[10], and was a benefactor to ſeveral others both there and in England. He died advanced in years at his manor of Caverſham near Reading, 3 Henry III. 1219. His body was carried firſt to Reading-abbey, then to Weſtminſter, and laſt to this church, where it was ſolemnly interred on Aſcenſion-day, 27 cal. April[11]. This epitaph, expreſſive of his character, was made for him:

> Sum quem Saturnum ſibi ſenſit Hybernia, Solem
> Anglia, Mercurium Normannia, Gallia Martem[12].

"Fuit enim," ſays Matthew Paris, "Hybernorum nocivus edomitor, Anglis honor & gloria, Normanniæ negotiator, qui in ea multa comparavit, Gallicis bellicoſus & miles invincibilis." The ſame writer, juſt before, alluding to the ſhare he had in ſettling the young king on his throne calls him, "Rector Regni[13]."

He married to his ſecond wife, 5 Joh. Alice, daughter of Baldwin de Bethune earl of Albemarle; and left by his firſt wife five ſons, William, Richard, Gilbert, Walter, and Anſelm, who all ſucceeded one another in his lands and honours, and died without iſſue; and five daughters, married to ſome of our principal nobility, to whoſe heirs the inheritance at length deſcended. By his ſecond wife he had one daughter, who died without iſſue. The title borne by this earl and his deſcendents was earl of Pembroke and marſhall of England, lord of Longuevile in Normandy, of Leinſter in Ireland, and of Chepſtow, Striguil, and Caerwent, in Wales[14].

[1] Hoved. p. 375.

[2] Ib. 376. He obtained for his ſhare of the lands of Walter Giffard earl of Buckinghamſhire the chief ſeat of the barony in Normandy in right of his wife. Dugd. ib. 600, ex rot. Selden Titles of Honour, p. 719.

[3] Hoved. p. 450. [4] Dugd. Bar. I. 601. [5] M. Paris, p. 254. [6] Ib. p. 192. [7] Ib. p. 295.

[8] Ib. p. 298, 299. [9] Dugd. ubi ſup. [10] Ib. Mon. Hib. p. 177.

[11] MS. in Bib. Bodl. cited by Dugdale.

[12] For this epitaph Camden (p. 513.) cites Rodburne's Annals; but it is not in the printed copy in Wharton's Ang. Sac. I. 242. Weever applies to this earl the other epitaph, which Camden (Midx. 307.) ſays was in his time to be read "*on the ſide* of his tomb."

"*Miles eram Martis, Mars multos vicerat armis.*"

[13] The young king remained in his care after his coronation. M. Paris, 289. The author of a Life of Frideſwide, in Leland Coll. I. 261. has it "rector regis & regni," and a certain writer cited by Dugdale from Lel. ib. II. 737. which paſſage I cannot find, calls him "miles ſtrenuiſſimus ac per orbem nominatiſſimus, Governour both of the realm and the king's perſon, a man of ſuch worthineſs, both in ſtoutneſs of ſtomach and martial knowledge, as England had few then that might be compared with him." Hollinſhed, p. 292. His brother Henry was dean of York and biſhop of Exeter. See his monument deſcribed, p. 36.

[14] Inq. de hundr. de Norf. in bag of quo warrantos in the talley court of the Exchequer, cited by Le Neve, MS. n. in Dugd. Bar. pen. me. in which record he is called, "Mareſcallus Angliæ et Comes de Penbroc." Dugdale does not give us the date of his advancement to this earldom, only to that of Strigul. But ſee Camden, as before quoted. Milles ſays he was, in right of his wife, created earl of Pembroke by king John, at his coronation, though before this time he was entitled and called earl marſhall and earl of Pembroke, temp. H. II. and R. I. as appears by many deeds which he witneſſes by that title, and among the reſt, in the confirmation of a charter to Langley church, 8 R. I. Cat. of Honor, p. 1084. Vincent on Brook, p. 413.

In

Monument of ROBERT DE VERE, 3d Earl of Oxford 1221.

In the north aile of the choir at *Hereford* we have, under a pointed arch, 1219.
Bishop MAPENORE, *in pontificalibus* and colours. Over him is painted,

D'ns Hugo de Mapenore Eps Hereford
Obiit A. 1219.

On the north side of the altar, within the rails at *Hatfield Broad-oak*, c. Essex, 1221.
lies the effigies in freestone of ROBERT DE VERE, third earl of OXFORD. It is in Pl. VIII.
good preservation, except the features; in a round helmet, in mail and a surcoat, cross legged, the right hand drawing the sword, on the left arm the shield fastened also by a belt over the shoulder, and having on it, in a field of fleurs de lis in lozenges or diaper work, on the upper half the Vere mullet: the lower half of the shield is adorned with squares of quatrefoils in rounds with flowers between them. The head rests on two cushions supported by angels; two more angels kneel at desks with books at his feet. This figure was originally in a chapel on the South side of the church, of which a piece of wall remains. Weever gives the inscription as follows.

Sire Robert De Veer le primier count de
Oxenford le tierz git ici. Dieu de lame si lui
plest face merci. ki pur lalme priera XL
jors de pardon avera. ✠ Pater noster, &c.

Dr. Ducarel in 1738 gave the Society of Antiquaries an account of the inscription, which is probably the same cut in relief in capitals on the ledge of the slab, of which remains only *Sire* .... *er* ... and some more letters too imperfect to be read. See plate VIII.

Morant[1] gravely calls this an effigy of *wood*, which he must have had from hear-say, or his own mistake; for neither Weever nor Salmon led him into it. Not this earl, but *Aubrey* de Vere founded the priory here[2].

HUMEZ the last Norman abbot of Westminster, who died 1222, is supposed 1222.
to be buried under the westernmost of the three tombs in the cloister there, generally ascribed to Vitalis. His image on it is in pontificals; and this was the inscription *round the ledge* in Saxon characters[3].

Ortus ab Humeto Willielmus hic, venerando
Prefuit iste loco, nunc tumulatus humo.

See it engraved Pl. I.

WILLIAM DE TRACY, one of the murderers of Becket, has been generally 1223.
supposed, on the authority of Mr. Risdon[4], to have built an aile in the church at *Mortboe*, Devon, and to have therein an altar-tomb about two feet high, with his figure engraven on a grey slab of Purbeck marble, 7 feet by 3, and 7 inches thick, and this inscription:

SYRE [Guillau]ME DE TRACY [gist icy, Diu de son al]ME EYT MERCY.

On the upper end of this tomb is carved in releif the crucifixion with the virgin and St. John, and on the north side some Gothic arches, and these three

[1] P. 506. [2] Tan. I, 27. [3] Dart. XIX. [4] P. 116.

coats:

coats: 1. Az. 3 lions paſſant guardant, Arg. 2. Arg. 3. two bars, G. Az. a ſaltire, Or. The firſt of theſe is the coat of *William Camville*, formerly patron of this church: the ſecond that of the *Martins*, formerly lords of Barnſtaple, who had lands in this neighbourhood: the third that of the *St. Albins*, who had alſo eſtates in the adjoining pariſh of Georgeham.

The figure on the ſlab is plainly that of a prieſt in his ſacerdotal habit, holding a chalice between his hands, as if in the act of conſecration.

Biſhop Stapledon's Regiſter, though it does not contain the year of his inſtitution, fixes the date of his death in the following terms, "*Anno* 1322, 16 *Dec. Thomas Robertus præſentat. ad eccleſ. de Morboe vacantem per mortem* Wilhelmi de Traci *die Dominic. primo poſt nativ. Virginis per mortem Will. de Campvill.*"

The æra of the prieſt is therefore 140 years later than that of the knight.

It does not appear by the epiſcopal regiſters, that the Tracies were ever patrons of Morthoe, except in the following inſtances.

"Anno 1257. Cal. Junii, John Allworthy, preſented by Henry de Traci, guardian of the lands and heirs of Ralph de Brag [1].

Anno 1275. Thomas Capellanus was preſented to this rectory by Philip de Weſton [2].

In 1330, Feb. 5. Henry de La Mace was preſented to this rectory by William de Camville [3].

In 1381, Richard Hopkins was preſented by the Dean and Chapter of Exeter, who are ſtill patrons [4].

It is probable that the ſtone with the inſcription to William de Traci did not originally belong to the altar tomb on which it now lies; but by the arms ſeems rather to have been erected for the patron *William de Camville*, it being unuſual in thoſe days to raiſe ſo handſome a monument for a prieſt, eſpecially as the altar tomb and ſlab are of very different materials, and the benefice itſelf is of very inconſiderable value. It is alſo probable the monument of *Traci* originally lay on the ground, and that when this monument was broken open, as it was, according to Riſdon, in the laſt century, this purbeck ſlab was placed upon the altar tomb, though it did not at firſt belong to it.

The Devonſhire Antiquaries aſſert, that Sir *William de Tracy* retired to this place after he had murdered Becket. But this tradition ſeems to reſt upon no better authority than the miſrepreſentation of the inſcription here given, and becauſe the family of Traci poſſeſſed the fourth part of a fee in Wollacombe, within this pariſh, which is ſtill called after their name. But the Tracies held many poſſeſſions in this county, as Bovey Traci, Nymett Traci, Bedford Traci, &c. William de Traci held the honor of Barnſtaple, in the beginning of Henry the Second's reign. King John granted the barony of Barnſtaple to Henry de Traci, in the 15th of his reign, and the family ſeem to have been poſſeſſed of it in the reign of Henry III.

I am indebted to the friendſhip of the preſent Dean of Exeter for the above obſervations, which aſcertain the monument in queſtion.

I ſhall digreſs no farther on this ſubject than to obſerve of Sir William de Traci, that four years after the murder of Becket he had the title of Steward, i. e. Juſtice of Normandy, which he held but two years. He was in arms againſt king John in the laſt year of his reign, and his eſtate was confiſcated: but on his return to his allegiance, 2 Henry III. it was reſtored. He was living 7 Henry III [5]. conſequently died about or after 1223, having ſurvived Becket upwards of 57 years.

[1] Reg. Broneſcombe. [2] Ib. [3] Reg. Grandiſon. [4] Ib. [5] Dugd. Bar. I. 611.

On

Pl. XIII p. 41

Fig. 1.

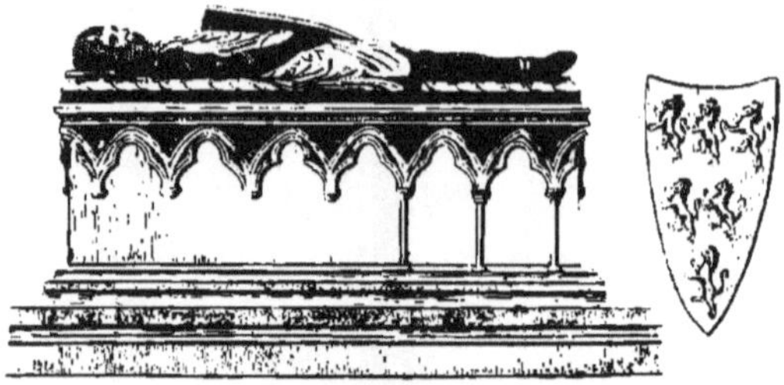

Fig. 2.

Fig. 3.

On the north fide of the Lady-chapel at *Salifbury* is an altar tomb of *wood*, 1226.
with fix demiquatrefoil niches in relief in front, and a flab ornamented with a Pl. XIII.
border of leaves, like thofe on the tomb of an abbefs at Romfey, and on it a fig. 2.
ftone figure of a knight in mail, with a round helmet fomewhat flatted at top, and covering his mouth as one of the Temple knights; his fpurs with rowels, his fhoes piked; his face turned to the right, and on his fhield Az. 5 lions rampant, but not on his furcoat, as faid by Sandford [1]. This monument belongs to WILLIAM LONGESPE, Earl of Sarum, natural fon of Henry II. by fair Rofamund, fuppofed to be poifoned, and brought hither from Old Sarum. Sandford has engraved this, and fays the figure is of *grey marble*. Both it and the tomb have been painted blue, and the back of the niches adorned with two patterns of mofaic; but the arms in front are now gone. They were his own, which he took after his wife's father William de Eureux, or Fitz Paine earl of Salifbury, and thofe of England alternately. A portrait of Rofamund on board, formerly in the hands of Mr. Lutton, private fecretary to James II. afterwards of Mr. Weft, and fhewn at the Society of Antiquaries 1743, had a rib-bone nailed behind it, faid to be this William's. The monument is engraved Pl. IX. fig. 1.

Below this is another monument belonging to JOHN Lord MONTACUTE, Pl. XIII.
younger fon of William firft earl of Salifbury of that family: an altar tomb, fig. 2.
with a knight in a pointed helmet of mail, gauntlets, fword, piked fhoes, a lion at his feet, and under his head a helmet with a griffin for creft. At the fides of the tomb in quatrefoils, Az. 3 fufils in a border, impaling a fpread eagle, *Monthermur*; and the fufils in a border ingrailed quartering the fpread eagle; and two fhields defaced.

The moft elegant of all the figures in the *Temple* church reprefents a comely 1227.
young knight, in mail, and a flowing mantle, with a kind of cowl; his hair Pl. V.
neatly curled at the fides, his crown appears fhaven. His hands are ele- fig. 3.
vated in a praying pofture, and on his left arm is a fhort pointed fhield charged with three waterbougets. He has at his left fide a long fword, and the armour of his legs, which are croffed, has a ridge or feam up the front continued over the knee, and forming a kind of garter below the knee: at his feet a lion. The arms befpeak this knight to be one of the family of Ros or Rous, and Weever has confirmed this application by the following fragment of an infcription infculped upon one of thefe crofs-legged monuments, as he found it among the collections of one ftudious in antiquities in Sir Robert Cotton's library.

Hic requiefcit —— R—— Ep—— quondam vifitator generalis ordinis militie Templi in Anglia & Francia & in Italia.

This, from the pedigree of the lords Ros, he proved to have belonged to one ROBERT, a Templar, who died about the year 1245, and gave to the Templars his manor of Ribfton. Sir William Dugdale [2] informs us, that Robert, fecond of the family of Ros of Hamlake, in the reign of Henry II. was a fpecial benefactor of the Templars, as appears by his grants recited in the Monafticon [3], among which occurs Ribftane (in the Weft Riding of Yorkfhire) where they founded a Preceptory. But Bifhop Tanner fhews that Sir William miftook this Robert for his namefake and grandfon the fecond Lord Ros, furnamed *Furfan*, who incurred the difpleafure of Richard I. for what offence is not faid, and afterwards of John for a while. About the 14th of that reign he took upon him the habit of religion for a fhort time, and afterwards was fheriff of Cumberland, and governor of Carlifle. He was as

[1] P. 115, and the Hift. of Salifb. p. 91. [2] Bar. I. 545. [3] II 551. 557.

fickle in his adherence to John, and was one of the chief who undertook to compel his obſervance of the great charter. But he was more faithful to his ſon. Sir William refers this monument to this Ros, who at the cloſe of his life took upon him this order, and died in their habit, and was buried in their church 1227, 11 Henry III.

1228. The large ſtone coffin of archbiſhop LANGTON, who died 1228, is remarkable for its elegant ſhape, yet has on it in relief a very rude croſs, which Dart calls patee, though it is rather fleury. It ſtands in St. Michael's chapel at *Canterbury*, half within the thickneſs of the wall, under an arch now cloſed up; but whether it was altogether within or without the firſt chapel on this ſite does not appear[1].

1228. Biſhop FAUCONBRIGGE, in old *St. Paul's*, has a figure like the Saliſbury and Worceſter biſhops of this time, with the pillars of the arch ſomewhat like Marſhall's at Exeter; the ledge of the altar like that of Longeſpe, and quatrefoils at the ſides. He died 1228.

Biſhop WENGHAM, at his feet, in the ſame church, has a ſimilar figure. He died 1262.

Both theſe monuments are engraved in Dugdale's Hiſtory of this church[2].

1229. On the north ſide of the choir at *St. David's* is the figure *in pontificalibus* of biſhop JORWERTH, who died 1229, and that of his ſucceſſor ANSELM, who died 1249.

Pl. XIV. fig. 1. In the middle of *Beaulieu* church, Hants, is a long blue flag, with a braſsleſs figure under a canopy, and an inſcription round the ledge, each letter in a ſingle ſquare. This ſtone was found in a field near the Duke of Montague's houſe on the ſite of the abbey-church, and is ſuppoſed to have belonged to ISABEL, Counteſs of Cornwall and Glouceſter, third daughter of William Marſhall earl of Pembroke, widow of Gilbert de Clare, and afterwards, 1230, firſt wife of Richard Plantagenet, ſecond ſon of king John, earl of Cornwall, and king of the Romans, who married a ſecond wife 1243. It muſt be confeſſed, there is nothing but the circumſtance of her being buried here to fix this ſtone to her, unleſs it ſhould be ſomething like a coronet over the head of the figure. Mr. John Bridges ſhewed the Society of Antiquaries, 172½, a drawing of it, copied here, Pl. XIV. fig. 1. Her heart was ſent in a ſilver cup to Tewkſbury, where her brother was abbot, to be buried before the high altar[3].

1231. Pl. V. f. 4. The next figure but one to that of the earl of Pembroke before deſcribed in the *Temple* church, is a croſs-legged knight, in mail, with a ſurcoat, his helmet round, ſurmounted with a kind of round cap, and the mouth-piece up, his hands folded on his breaſt, his ſhield long and pointed, and now plain; a very long ſword at his right ſide; the belt from which his ſhield hangs ſtudded with quatrefoils, and that of his ſword with lozenges. This may be for WILLIAM MARSHALL, eldeſt ſon of the foregoing earl William.

He was among the barons who rebelled againſt John, but made his ſubmiſſion to Henry III. All that hiſtory records of him is, that he defeated Llewellin Prince of Wales in a pitcht battle, 1222[4], and contributed much to keep the Iriſh in obedience. He founded the houſe of Friars Preachers at Kilkenny. He

[1] Dart. 134 Goſtl. 142. [2] P. 81. [3] Sandford, p. 96, 97. [4] Dugd. I. 603. Mat. Par. p. 317.

married

Pl. XIV N°42.

Fig 2

Fig 3

Fig 4

Fig 1

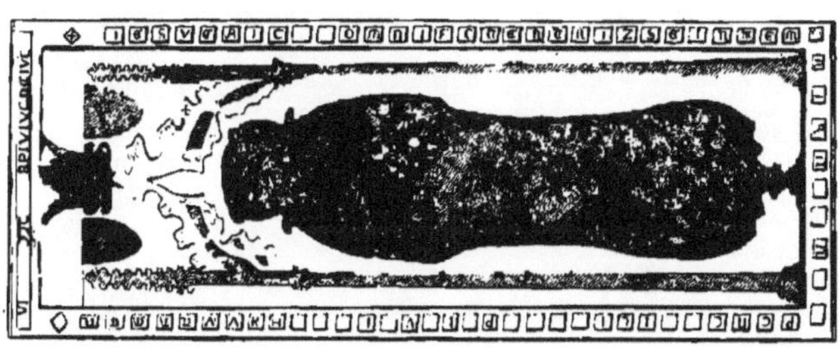

married Eleanor[1] fecond daughter of king John, who was at firft highly difpleafed with the match, and dying without iffue, April 6, 1231. 15 Henry III. was buried in this church, 18 Cal. Maii, near the grave of his father[2]. In the annals of Waverley is this epitaph for him, whether put on his tomb is not eafy to fay; as we meet with many epitaphs for the fame perfon in monkifh chronicles, compofed by the compilers, or handed about:

Militis iftius mortem dolet Anglia: ridet
Wallia, viventis bella minafque timens.

Mr. Price (in additional obfervations printed from his MS. at the end of the quarto defcription of Salifbury 1774) fays, at *Salifbury* bifhop POORE has by tradition a monument on the north fide of the altar, though he was buried at Tarrant Monkton, Dorfet. His effigy *in pontificalibus*, his right hand holding a crofier, his left on his breaft, lies on a flab, with a flowered border, under a canopy of three arches, whofe fine flowered ftone roof has been fupplied by a plain ceiling of rough deal. See Pl. XIII. fig. 3. engraved from a fketch by John Carter, 1780. Pl. XIV. fig. 2. exhibits the fame monument as it was about 1736. 1237.

This worthy prelate, after he had transferred the fee from Old to New Sarum, and began the noble ftructure which we now fee there, was tranflated to Durham 1228, and, after having difcharged a heavy debt contracted by his predeceffor there, died 1237, at Tarent Monkton in Dorfetfhire, where he was born and where he founded a nunnery, in whofe church his heart was buried[3]. Matthew Paris gives him the character of great fanctity of life and deep learning; and adds, that when he perceived his diffolution drawing near he preached a folemn farewel fermon to his people, and after a proper difpofition of his worldly effects, met death with firm compofure.

LHEWELLIN the Great, prince of Wales, who died 1240, was buried in *Conway* abbey, of his own founding, from whence, at the diffolution, his coffin was removed into a ftable among the ruins, and thence to the beautiful chapel adjoining to *Llanrwft* church, built by Inigo Jones for Sir Richard Wynne, bart. of Gwedir, who was lineally defcended from that prince, as is fet forth at large in a long infcription there. The coffin is of dark brown marble or granite, feven feet long in the clear, and four inches thick: the fides adorned with whole and half quatrefoils in relief. At the head within is the following infcription in Roman capitals on a brafs plate, 1240.

"This is the coffin of Leolinus Magnus, prince of Wales, who was buried in "the abbey of Conway, and upon the diffolution removed thence."

It is etched by Mofes Griffith in the fourth of his fupplemental plates to Mr. Pennant's Tour in Wales.

I would juft obferve here, that the ftatue over the Welfh gate at Shrewfbury commonly afcribed to this prince really reprefents Edward I. who conquered Wales, and the arms of England and of Shrewfbury are on the fame fide of the gate.

ROGER NIGER, bifhop of London, who died 1241, had only a plain farcophagus, covered *en dos d'ane*, without figures or ornaments[4]. Somewhat fimilar coffins, but both alike ornamented with arches, contained the remains of the king Sebba and Erkenwald there[5]. 1241.

[1] She at firft made a vow of chaftity; but feven years after his death remarried Simon de Montfort, earl of Leicefter, and was buried at Montarges in France. Weever. Milles, p. 135. Sandford, p. 93.
[2] Dugd. Bar. I. 603. ex MS. Bodl. Ann. Waverl. p. 193. Ed. Gale.
[3] Godw. de Præf. ed. Richardf. p. 740.
[4] Dugd. St. Paul's, p. 86.
[5] Ib. p 91.

In

In the wall of the fouth aile of the choir at *Briftol*, formerly opening into the veftry, is an altar tomb for a lord BERKELEY, his arms painted on the arch. Quære, if THOMAS the fecond lord, whofe wife JANE was buried in the arch between the veftry and the fouth aile [1].

1243. Below him, under another arch, an armed figure of THOMAS BERKELEY who died 1243, and was grandfon of Robert, the fecond lord Berkeley [2]. His arms on his fhield.

1246. The tomb of abbot BERKYNG, who died 1246, ftood before the high altar of the Lady chapel at *Weftminfter*, but was taken down in the following century by abbot Colchefter, and a flat ftone laid in its place, which when Henry VII. built his chapel, was removed to the area at the foot of the fteps, where it ftill continues, being a large grey ftone, robbed of its brafs ledge and figure of a mitred abbot, and the traces fo worn, that only two rofes at the Weft corners are difcernable. The infcription given by Dart [3] was as follows:

> Ricardus Barkyng prior eft, poft inclytus abbas;
> Henrici regis prudens fuit ille minifter.
> Hujus erat prima laus, infula rebus opima,
> Altera laus æque Thorp [4] cenfus, Ocham decimæque,
> Tertia Mortone caftrum fimili ratione,
> Et regis quarta de multis commoda charta.
> Clementis fefto mundo migravit ab ifto
> M. Domini C. bis XL. fextoque fub anno.
> Cui detur venia parte pia virgo Maria.

He was privy counfellor, chief baron of the exchequer, and one of the lords juftices of the kingdom during Henry III's Welfh wars. His being abbot of this rich houfe was his firft praife: his fecond and third were, that he affigned the manor of Thorpe [4] for the expences of the convent and the church of Ockham (I fuppofe the vicarage of Okcham, c. Rutland [6]) for his table [7]. He purchafed of the Foliot family the caftle of Moreton Foliot, half the manor of Langdon, with the chapel there, and half the foreft towards the manor of Morton [5].

1247. ROBERT BINGHAM, bifhop of *Salifbury*, who died 1247, lies on the north fide of the chancel there, under a moft elegant arch, on which fit ten angels, furmounted by a rich bouquet, and fided by four rich pointed arches, whofe finials are deftroyed. In the centre of the embatled wall of the choir here is fome rich open work of three ftories diminifhing. The flab was inlaid in brafs, with a crofs fleure charged with fome figure, and four lozenges; all gone. See Pl. XV.

1250. Mr. Dart [8] affigns a grey marble flab between the gates of Henry V's chapel and the Confeffor's fhrine, with the bare traces of a crofs, two fhields at top (once brafs) and a worn ledge of letters, once in high relief, but not now legible, to ROGER DE WENDOVER, bifhop of Rochefter, who died 1250, and was buried here by the king's exprefs command, though Weever [9] mentions, from tradition, his portraiture in the wall of Bromley church.

[1] Dugd. Bar. I. 355. [2] Dugd. Bar. I. 353. [3] XXI.
[4] William the Conqueror granted Sac, &c. to Thorp. Dart. I. 21.
[5] Dart. I. 27. [6] Ecton, p. 319. [7] Dart. Ib. [8] II. 40. [9] P. 338.

Pl. XV.

BRISTOL

Jane wife of — Thomas 2nd Lord Berkeley — Maurice Berkeley 1326 — Thomas Berkeley 1243

Of the two figures dug up in building some offices to Mr. Wray Atkinson's 1251.
house at *Coverham* abbey, in the North riding of Yorkshire, one may be that of Pl.XIV.
the founder RALPH FITZROBERT, lord of Middleham, who died 1251, after having fig. 2.
transferred this religious foundation from Swaynaby. The other may represent 3.
WALKRAN eldest son of Helewise[1], the original foundress, or her father RANULPH DE GLANVILLE, a baron and chief justice of England in the reigns of Henry II. and Richard I[2]. who died 1189. 1 Richard I. at the siege of Acon; or her grandson RALPH, who died 1270, and was buried in the choir here[3].

Mr. Topham, who has examined them more than once, and has collected materials for an history of Coverham, inclines to assign them to the NEVILLES, of whom ROBERT married the great-granddaughter of the foundress and representative of her family, and being surprised by some of her friends in an intrigue with a lady of Craven, was so severely handled by them, that he died of the wound 1271, and was buried in the chapter-house at Coverham, near the foundress's tomb[4].

RALPH, son of this Robert, was in his youth passionately fond of hunting; and once in a sally of jollity, when he presented the annual stag by which he held Baby and other manors of the prior of Durham, insisted that himself, with his own friends and servants, should be feasted with it instead of the prior and his domestics, contrary to the established custom by which the lord partook of the dinner only by special invitation, and his servants, on bringing the stag into the hall, had only a breakfast. This Ralph is said to have neglected his own affairs to converse with the canons of Coverham and Merton, and he had the reputation of a weak[3] and vicious man. He died 1331, and was buried in the choir of Coverham, near the high altar[4].

It may be no unreasonable conjecture, that the stag-chace on the monument, Pl. XIV. fig. 2. (though since Mr. Buck drew it all these appendages have been destroyed), assigns it to this young sportsman, who was a considerable benefactor to his monkish friends here, who may have decorated his tomb with his appendages.

Fig. 3. may be the monument of his father. There is no small conformity between the two monuments.

It is impossible to ascertain either with precision: but I have engraved both, from drawings by the late Mr. Buck, which may at least serve to shew the severe undeserving censure of them by Mr. Maude, in his account of his abbey under Mr. Grose's print of it, that "they are in a style almost *too rude* for the *grossest* period of the Gothic ages." On the contrary the design and ornaments of both are rather superior to the generality of this century, which yet was no barbarous æra of statuary.

The tomb under the west arch of the north aile of the choir at *Christ Church*, 1252.
Oxford, for Sir HENRY DE BATHE, justiciary of England, t. H. III. who died 1252. Pl.XIV.
has his figure in armour, with whiskers, with a gorget of mail, the helmet fig. 4.
pointed terminating in a nob, and under it another with a bull's head; on his breast 3 gerbes O. at his feet a hound collared. In quatrefoils on the front of the tomb are these five coats; a chevron between three greyhounds rampant S. impaling an escocheon G. in a border of roses O. 2. The first impaling nebule . . . . . and G. 3. The first single, and impaling 4. O. three piles, G. a can-

[1] Her bones were removed from Swaynebey, and buried in the Chapter-house at Coverham. Mon. Ang. II 648.
[2] Dugd. Orig. Jurid. Chron. ser. p. 4.
[3] Observat. in Regist. Hon. de Richmond, p. 235. [4] Dugd. Bar. I. 293.
[3] *Ex sapientioribus in rebus mundanis haud aestimaretur*, Regist. de Richm. p. 36. [4] Dugd. Bar. I. 292.

ton, Erm. and also 5. G. three lucies hauriant A. At the head a fess between three gerbes O. impaling the chevron and greyhounds. In a window above is the chevron between three greyhounds.

1252. BLANCHE, grandaughter of Henry II[1], and Queen of Lewis VIII. of France died 1252. Just before her death she became a nun at *Pontoise*, which she had founded, and to which church she bequeathed her body. "Facta est sanctimo-"nialis professa velata ante mortem, & supra velum apposita est corona, & vestita "est reginaliter, & sic sepulta est, ut decuit, redimita[2]." I mention this princess only as an example of the ceremonial used at the funeral of a royal religious.

1253. On the south side of the south aile of the choir at *Tewksbury* is a freestone altar-tomb, with 4 quatrefoils on each side. In the spandrils are the cypher here engraved, and a chevron between 3 escallops. In one shield, a Palmer's staff passes through the point of the chevron, or as B. Willis[3], over all in pale. He ascribes this monument, which the tradition of the place gives to abbot ROBERT FORTYNGTON, to ROBERT, who died abbot here 1253. But he mistakes when he talks of "his effigies carved in full proportion" on it.

p.46.

1254. HUGH NORTHWOLD, bishop of Ely, who died 1254, has a very ornamented monument there, not faithfully represented in Pl. XV. of Mr. Bentham's well-written history of that church, where it is thus described, p. 148. "It is a raised "monument of grey marble, with his effigies curiously carved in his episcopal "habit, and as it were enthroned or installed: at the head were angels support-"ing a crown of glory: on the sides of the stall were carved, on the right hand, "a king, an abbot, and a monk. On the left St. Etheldreda, an abbess crowned, "and a nun, and at the foot the story of St. Edmund's martyrdom, alluding to "the founding of the church of Ely in his time, and to St. Edmund's abbey, "over which he presided. This monument, which stood close by St. Etheldreda's "shrine, behind the high altar, was probably removed when that was demolished, "and the effigies being casually laid on bishop Barnet's tomb, has by the incurious "been taken for that bishop." To illustrate this description I would observe, that of the figures on the right side, the king, holding in his right hand a ragged staff, in his left a globe, treading on a serpent, probably refers to Henry III. the abbot or rather the bishop, holding in his right hand a rich flowered cross, in his left a church, to Northwold himself when abbot here, as also the figure of the monk broken in the middle, but having under his back at the bottom of his arch a twisted cockatrice: the bishop's right foot treads on a lion looking up, and his left on the breast of a dragon, whose head is defaced. The three figures on the left side represent St. Etheldreda, in three different characters; as abbess, holding in her left hand a church, in her right a crosier; as queen, crowned, her left hand on her breast, her right holding up her robe; and as a nun, her

[1] Henault (I. 210.) makes her daughter of Alphonso IX. king of Castile: and says, her sister Berengaria was wife of Alphonso king of Leon: whereas she was daughter of Alphonso VIII. king of Castile, and her sister Berengaria married Alphonso IX. king of Leon, who was in right of his wife king of Castile. Sandf. 70.

[2] Math. Paris, p. 859. [3] Mit. Ab. I. p. 177.

left

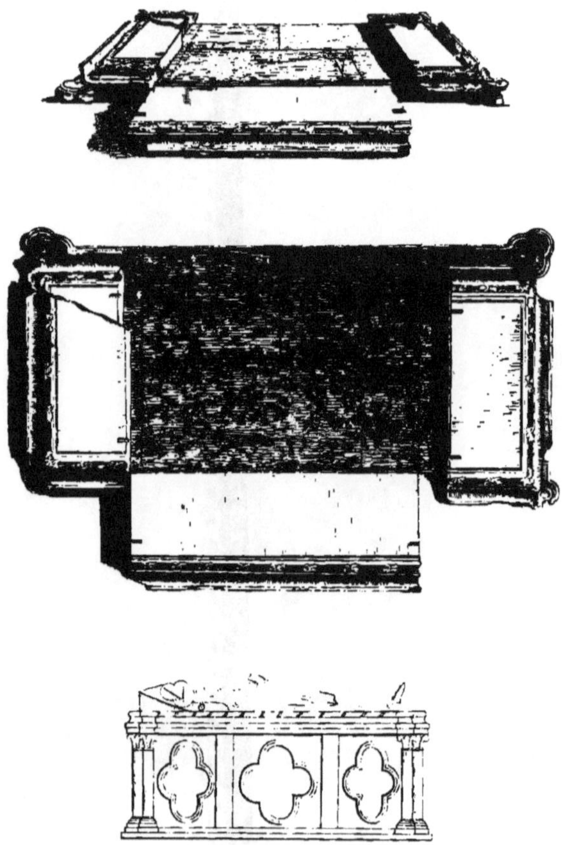

Bishop Grosteste, 1254

left hand holding up her robe, in her right a globe. I ſhall only add, that the pillars of the niche (which Mr. Bentham calls, I think improperly, a *ſtall)* are of richer and more Grecian work than uſual, and that over the head of the king at the right ſide one ſees a building, alluding to the magnificent preſbytery here, begun by this prelate 1235, and finiſhed two years before his death.

Godwin[1] deſcribes Biſhop GROSTHEAD's as a "goodly tomb of marble, with 1254. Pl. XVI.
"an image of braſs over it." Dugdale ſays, "at the ſouth end of the aile, going "into the reveſtrie is an antient tomb, called Groſthead's; at the feet a chapel, "made ſouth, to another of the ſame faſhion, both ſemicircular." It appears to have been an altar tomb, with a border of foliage round the table, which was ſupported by circular pillars at the corners, but now lies broken and diſordered on the floor. See Plate XVI. So imperfect is the memorial of this great prelate, a proteſtant in popiſh times, whoſe ſuperior judgement ſtruggled hard to break the ice of reformation in the 13th century. He died in his palace at Bugden, Oct. 9, 1253[2].

Matthew Paris is laviſh of encomiums on this conſcientious intrepid Prelate, who ſpoke his mind both to the King and the Pope. He calls him, "Domini "Papæ et Regis redargutor manifeſtus, prælatorum correptor, monachorum "corrector, preſbyterorum director, clericorum inſtructor, ſcholarium ſuſtentator, populi prædicator, incontinentum perſecutor, ſcripturarum ſedulus perſcrutator diverſarum, Romanorum malleus et contemptor[3]." Epithets that might ſupply the place of any modern epitaph. No one has yet done juſtice to his life[4]; for the hiſtory of which, and of the times he lived in, a period of forty years of the reign of Henry III. my learned and induſtrious friend Mr. Pegge has collected the beſt materials, whenever his own inclination and the public voice ſhall bring them forth.

After the biſhop had reſted in his grave exactly 529 years and one month, the hand of inquiſitive curioſity (*abſit invidia ſacrilegii*) availing itſelf of the new paving of the cathedral, and the friendſhip of the preſent Præcentor, expoſed his venerable remains to view. After removing a ſolid heap of earth and rude ſtones, to the depth of near 18 inches, the maſons ſtruck on the freeſtone-lid of a coffin, in which had been hollowed a cavity for the face, and which not being cemented was eaſily removed, and diſcovered a ſheet of lead, raiſed up over the face, and laid on four looſe iron bars, over a freeſtone-coffin, 23 inches wide at top, diminiſhing to 11½, 13¾ deep, 2½ thick. In this the body of the prelate had been depoſited in pickle, a ſmall quantity of which was remaining under the back, in the middle of the coffin. The corpſe was reduced to a ſkeleton; the bones were fallen together, but none of them abſolutely periſhed. The head reclined to the left ſhoulder; the under jaw, in which all the teeth were complete, was totally fallen; three fore teeth of the upper jaw were gone. Under the right ſide of the head were a chalice and patten of latten compreſſed together, by which compreſſion the head had probably reclined to the left. No liquor appeared in the chalice. The left arm lay acroſs the belly; the right was fallen aſide. The marks of the ſlipper ſoles were viſible againſt the foot of the coffin. The thigh-bone meaſured 16 inches. Acroſs the body, from the right ſhoulder to the left foot lay a croſier of red wood, whoſe middle part was entirely decayed: the top, which lay flat on the bottom of the coffin, was carved into the rude form of a lamb's head, at the bottom of

[1] P. 240. [2] Ang. Sac. II. p. 341. ex Ann. Lanercoſt. See alſo Ann. Burton, p. 328.
[3] See a noble character of him Ann. Lanercoſt ubi ſup.
[4] He has not even a place in the Biographia Britannica. Mr. Wharton only wiſhed to have found an old MS. life of him in ſome library; for want of which he printed a meagre rhyming legend, by a monk of Bardney. Dr. Knight's performance eſcaped the ſtricteſt reſearches of the late Dr. Maſon, and the late Biſhop of Lincoln. Hearne ſays Wood left a life of him, ſtill in the Aſhmolean Muſeum. Ann. Dunſtaple, I. 299. n.

whoſe

whofe neck was a horn or ivory fillet: two rings of horn of the different diameters went round the crofier-top at different intervals; and where it was fitted to the ftaff there was a brafs plate, fitted on with leather, and charged with this infcription in two lines,

✠ PER BACVLI FORMAM X
PRELATI DISCITO NORMAM.

The point of the crofier was fhod with a pointed metal ferule armed with a knob, and from it iffued a tranfverfe piece of metal, alfo knobbed, as a ftop to keep it fteady at the foot. Thefe metal ornaments were repofited in the veftry, and the wooden fragments replaced in the coffin. A ring of gilt metal, with a very fmall blue ftone fet in it, was found to have fallen off the fingers.

After a careful examination by the Precentor, Mr. Sympfon, Mr. Bradley, the organift, and one or two more members of the church, thefe refpectable remains were carefully covered up again, and as the furface of the coffin is confiderably below the level of the new pavement it may be prefumed they will reft undifturbed to the end of time—to that period in which all who have enlifted under the banners of Truth, Liberty, and Virtue, fhall fhare with this worthy prelate the great reward; as far beyond the empty wifh of the people, and the univerfity of Oxford, that he might be canonized, as his virtues tranfcended the fuperftition of his contemporaries.

Thefe remains could not however efcape the penetration of the Prefident of the Royal Society, to gratify which they were again opened about a month after their firft uncovering. Sir Jofeph Banks took out a fmall portion of the liquor in which the body was originally laid.

Camden [1] fays, the bifhop commanded this only to be engraven over his tomb,

Quis fim nofce cupis! caro putrida, nil nifi vermis:
Quifquis es hoc de me tibi fit fcire fatis.

But upon his death this was written,

Rex dolet, ac regnum gemit, & flet Anglia tota,
Plebs plangit, gemitus ingeminare juvat.
Quippe Groftedus, *fpeculum virtutis, afylum*
Juftitiæ, Regis anchora, morte jacet.
Non poterit tamen ille mori cui fama perorat,
Laus loquitur, redolet fructus, abundat honor;
Unde dolens triftatur homo, canit angelus unde,
Unde ferenantur fidera pallet humus [2].

D'Alderby, the fourth of his fucceffors, was buried, in the fame manner, in the lower fouth tranfept, as appeared on new paving it this fpring. The place of his fhrine may be diftinguifhed againft the Weft wall of the tranfept.

Between bifhop Grofthead's tomb and the fouth wall was buried his intimate and learned friend *Adam de Marifco*, chief of the Francifcans, who died of grief for his lofs prefently after him the fame year [3].

[1] Remains, p. 373.
[2] Part of thefe lines, with fome alterations, are in the monk of Bardeney's Life of him, Angl. Sacr. I. 340.
[3] Ann. de Lanercoft, ubi fup.

Pl. XVIII. p. 19.

Monument of Henry III.ds Children.

ROGER DE WESEHAM, another of his friends and favourites, *vir omni laude* 1257.
digniſſimus[1], died 1257, and was buried in his own cathedral at *Lichfield*, in a wooden chapel (*ſub oratorio ligneo*) over againſt canon Radcliffe's monument[2]. But of theſe two monuments not the leaſt traces remain.

Archbiſhop GREY's monument at *York*, in the ſouth end of the tranſept erected 1255.
by him, is a curious piece of work of grey marble. His figure, pontifically habited and gloved, piercing a ſnake with his croſier wrapt in his mantle, lies under a very plain arch, with round pillars finely foliated. On the pediment of this arch ſtand angels cenſing him; under his feet two human figures trod on by him writh themſelves, while a dragon bites the end of the croſier. The canopy above conſiſts of three arches, and the pediment part of three or more ſuch ſhorter with their proper pediments, the buſts on the tops of whoſe pillars totally miſrepreſented in Mr. Drake's print are really the uſual figures. In this upper ſtory it was pretended the biſhop dying excommunicate was lodged, till Mr. Drake had it opened for near a yard, and found it ſolid. There was no epitaph on this tomb.

KILKENNY, ſucceſſor of Hugh Northwold, at *Ely*, has a plain monument; only 1256.
his figure, in purbeck marble, ſomewhat like the biſhops at Sarum and Worceſter; on his breaſt a lozenge. In the ſpandrils of the canopy angels hovering with cenſers[3]: which in Mr. Bentham's print are made fleurons. At his feet a bending canopy of five arches. This cenotaph in fact covers only his heart, his body being buried in Spain, where he died 1256[4].

WILLIAM of YORK, biſhop of *Saliſbury*, lies oppoſite to his predeceſſor Bing- 1256.
ham, on the ſouth ſide of the choir, under a flowered arch of another form, ſurmounted by a rich bouquet, and ſided by purfled finials. The black ſlab had nothing on it.

The next monument of this time is one erected in Weſtminſter abbey for four 1257.
infant children of Henry III. RICHARD, JOHN, and HENRY, his third, fourth, Pl. XVIII.
and fifth ſons, and his youngeſt daughter KATHARINE. It is formed of Moſaic, the ſides in plain pannels, the top of the table inlaid in circles, and other irregular figures, with a border of teſſelæ in front; and is fixed in the aile, in the wall between the chapels of St. Benedict and St. Edmund. Over this tomb, on the maſonry in the upper arch are faint traces of painting, now almoſt ſcratched out, repreſenting a church in perſpective, an embattled wall ſeen through the arches, and in the pavement in front ſingle fleurs de lis O. and lions rampant S. or Az. Under the proper arch or canopy of the tomb were painted four figures[5], two and two, kneeling oppoſite to each other, of whom faint traces are yet viſible. But on the cloſeſt inſpection, May 27, 1782, I muſt acknowledge myſelf unable to determine whom they repreſent, as the figures to the left appear ſurrounded with nimbi, and thoſe oppoſite to them to be in armour. Over this laſt arch are broken traces of a few capital letters. This tomb is covered with a wooden lid for the accommodation of the vergers as a deſk. Mr. Dart having engraved it very inaccurately, the whole, with the arch over it, is here given, Pl. XVIII.

It appears by records in the Tower, that on the death of the princeſs Catharine 1257, under the age of five years[6], the king her father ordered a ſump-

[1] Matt. Par. 190.   [2] Whitelocke in Ang. Sac. I. 447.
[3] Nothing ſo common as theſe, or ſo often miſtaken. In the windows of Stapleford church near Hertford Salmon calls them *fiſhing-nets*.
[4] Hiſt. of Ely, pl. xvi. p. 149.
[5] Keepe ſays, they are the effigies of four children painted *in plano*, p. 56.
[6] Matthew Paris ſays, ſhe was dumb and helpleſs, but very pretty, (*muta et inutilis*, ſed facie pulcherrima); and that the queen her mother was inconſolable for her death. P. 948.

tuous monument to be here erected to her, and commanded his treasurer and chamberlain of the exchequer to deliver to master Simon de Wells five marks and a half for his expences in going to London for a certain brass image to set on her tomb, and returning home again [1]. And on this tomb was likewise placed a silver image, for which William de Glocester the king's silversmith had 70 marks [2]. For this Mr. Dart quotes Strype.

Two artists in stone and silver applied to Henry III. to make a figure for his daughter. He gave the preference to the last, and paid premiums to such candidates as came out of the country: a proof our artists were not so despicable at this æra as is generally supposed. The monument of Henry II. at Fontevraud was made by English artists, who had safe conducts to carry it over.

Five children of Edward I. viz. JOHN his eldest, ALPHONSUS his third son, BERENGARIA and ALICE his fourth and fifth, and ELEANOR his tenth daughter, are said to be buried here, and to them Mr. Dart refers the painting of two boys and two girls abovementioned; but unless we suppose them added to Henry III's children, the tomb suits best with the age of the latter.

Alphonsus died 1214, highly regretted by the kingdom for his great beauty and valour [3].

It appears that Richard son of Henry III. and Alphonsus son of Edward I. were buried, the first on the South side of St. Edward's shrine, the other on the South side of the choir; but whether the children of these kings had one common place of sepulture is not expressed, though it may be presumed.

1256. Among the figures in the *Temple* church is a stone coffin *en dos d'ane*, the
Pl. V. ridges and angles of its cover forming a kind of cross, whose top terminates in
fig. 5. a trefoil, and the foot rests on a bull's head, or perhaps a ram's, referring to the holy lamb; and from the middle of the shaft issue two fleurets or leaves. This may be the monument of WILLIAM PLANTAGENET, fifth son of Henry III. who died in his infancy, and was buried here according to Weever [4], about 1256 [5]. His father intended to be buried there himself. See Dugd. Mon. Aug. II. 531.

Pl. XIX. The five figures in the north groupe of this church being absolutely unascertained, I can only presume them to be of the same century, and subjoin their descriptions.

Camden and Weever ascribe one of them to GILBERT MARSHALL, third son of the first William, who on the death of his brothers succeeded to the whole of the paternal inheritance. 19 Henry III. he took the cross with Richard earl of Cornwall, in order to go to the Holy Land [6], which was delayed only by his difference with the king [7]. He was a firm adherent to Richard earl of Cornwall, who at length procured his reconciliation with the king. He married, 1235, Margaret [8] sister of Alexander king of Scotland, and after her death Maud de Lanvaley, without the king's licence [9]. He lost his life at a tournament at Ware [10], 1241, being run away with by a mettlesome Italian horse, whom he could not check,

[1] Rymer, I. 41.

[2] This record has given rise to the tradition of the vergers, that three silver images were affixt over the tomb by the irons now remaining.

[3] Ann. de Dunstaple, p. 507. where he is called son and heir. The Annals of Waverly, p. 238. call him "filius primogenitus" of Edward I.

[4] P. 443. [5] Miller, p. 145. Sandford, p. 91, 93.

[6] Powel's Hist. of Wales. p. 295. [7] M. Paris, p. 516. [8] *femina elegantissima*. Math. Par.

[9] Dugdale seems to date his two marriages wrong; for he quotes Rot. Fin 14 Hen. III. for his second marriage; yet makes his first take place 1235, 19 Henry III. M. Paris, p. 565, mentions that with Margaret under the year 1236, but it is most probable, from the above circumstances, that it was the second match.

[10] About a bowshot from Hertford. M. Paris, calls the sport *torneamentum quod vulgariter appellatur*. It was a name given to disguise the sport, which the king had expressly forbidden. See Ib. p. 572. and Du Cange in voce.

the

Monuments in the Temple Church London

the reins breaking at the bit; the heat, the duft, and a full ftomach (for the combatants dined before the exercife) rendered him incapable of keeping his feat, and his foot hanging in the ftirop he was dragged a confiderable way, and taken up for dead. He was conveyed to the friery at Hertford, where he expired in the evening 5 cal. Jul. Upon opening his body his liver was found mortified by the bruifes he had received. His bowels were buried before the high altar of our Lady church there, and his corps conveyed next day to the Temple, and there depofited near his father and brother. Matthew Paris afcribes all the extraordinary parade which coft this unfortunate earl his life to an effort of figuring as a knight of great prowefs; a character he was never trained to, having been bred to the church, till, by the death of his brother, the fucceffion devolved to him. He adds [1], that the earl affifted at this tournament without the king's leave, who made this a pretence to withhold his eftate from his brother Walter for a while. This antient and noble family became extinct about ten years after, by the death of Walter and Anfelm, the laft furviving fon of earl William.

In the prefent ftate of thefe monuments it is almoft impoffible to afcertain the property of more than one of the Marefchall family. If it be objected, that the figure affigned to the father may rather, on account of its youthful appearance, belong to one of the fons, I fhall not contend for fo controvertible an opinion. One conjecture however I may propofe, which is, that the two figures whofe belts have the fame ornaments were of the fame family.

Mr. Lethieullier [2], who afcribes three of thefe figures to the earls of Pembroke, takes it for granted, "none of them were of the order of Templars." It is only a vulgar error to fuppofe every figure whofe legs are croffed was actually of that order. But that two at leaft of the three Pembrokes were, or meant to be, Crufaders, and confequently had taken the vow, their hiftory plainly fhews; and it is highly probable the infection of the times reached the other, as a perfon of a diftinguifhed family. Yet to make up the eleven defcribed here by Stowe, they muft all be confidered as crofs-legged. I fhall juft obferve, that Magnaville, William Marfhall, jun. and the laft figure in the other groupe have their legs croffed in an unufual manner. They lie on their backs, and yet crofs their legs as if they lay on their fides. So were thofe of Henry Laci earl of Lincoln, 1312, in old St. Paul's.

The fpurs of all are remarkably fhort, and feem rather ftraps without rowels. Not above two or three have the long pointed fhoe, and two have their furcoats exactly reaching to the knee, whereas the other are of different lengths, and fall more eafily.

I have dwelt only on thofe perfonages who are exprefsly pointed out by Camden, Stowe, and Weever, and by the more antient hiftorians. Weever informs us, that fepulture in this church was much affected by Henry III. and his nobility. Stowe has determined that four of the crofs-legged figures belong to the three earls of Pembroke and Robert Ros: "and thefe are all, fays he, that I can remember to have read of." The later furveys of London content themfelves with copying Stowe and Weever.

However deficient our notices are to whom thefe feveral antient monuments belong, we have at leaft light enough to pronounce that they do not belong either to "Dunwallo and other Britifh kings," as tradition reports to Weever, nor to thofe "kings of Denmark who reigned in England," as Hentzner mifunderftood.

[1] P. 572. [2] Archæol. II. p. 291.

Feb. 25, 1718. It was unanimoufly agreed at the Society of Antiquaries to take a drawing of the Knights Templars, and the tomb of the patriarch in the Temple-church, and the infcription over the door, and Mr. Director (Talman) was ordered to employ Seigner Grifoni about that work, who was chofen by the Society when they fhall have occafion for drawings [1]. Mr. Lethieullier informed the Society, 1736, that he had, for his own private curiofity, caufed drawings of thefe tombs to be taken, which were then in his hands.

I cannot conclude this article without recording an anecdote communicated to me on good authority, that application was made, by a Hertfordfhire baronet, for fome of thefe crofs-legged knights to grace his new-erected parochial chapel: but the fociety of Benchers difcovered their good fenfe, as well as regard to antiquity, by refufing their compliance.

Similar to thefe is the figure of Sir JAMES BEAUCHAMP in the north aile of the choir at *Worcefter*. It is in mail, with a round helmet and furcoat, drawing his fword with his right hand, his left under a long pointed fhield: his legs croffed as thofe above noticed, and at his feet a lion. Thomas [2] feems to give the left hand a glove of mail, and make the other bare.

1258. The tomb at *York* of Archbifhop SEWAL, who died 1258, is the firft inftance of a table monument, without an altar tomb. It refts on twelve arches, and on the flab, which diminifhes by five mouldings, is a crofs florée in relief [3].

1258. ISABEL countefs of ATHOL, wife of David de Strabolgy earl of Athol, and fecond daughter of Richard de Dover, natural fon of king John by Rohes his wife daughter of Robert de Dover, baron of Chilham [4], has an altar tomb in the undercroft at *Canterbury*; the fides adorned with three fhields in quatrefoils, two charged with three cinquefoils, the middlemoft with a trivet. Her figure is very delicate, dreffed in a mantle and petticoat, her head-drefs finely plaited and veiled, fupported by angels, her hands joined, a dog at her feet, the face of the arch annulated, in the centre above a rofe [5].

1258. CROCKESLEY or CROSSLEY, abbot of Weftminfter, who died 1258, and was buried, according to Flete, in the old chapel of St. Edmund, which he had himfelf built, near the north door, and on the taking that down being ruinous, removed to the adjoining chapel of St. Nicholas, under a little plain ftone before the middle altar, was again difturbed in the reign of Henry VI. at which time the whole convent faw his corpfe firm and frefh in the veftment in which he faid mafs in a ftone coffin. This coffin Dart [6] thinks was laid on Flaccet's tomb in St. John Baptift's chapel, and in it was faid by Keepe to have been lately found a body, though Dart could find only the disjoined boards of an inward coffin, which he looks upon as a proof of its antiquity. It has been afcribed to Bohun earl of Hereford and Milling bifhop of Hereford, but againft this he alleges its form, and that ftone coffins were rarely or never in ufe in the 14th century [7]. All that can be faid is, it is the coffin of a religious, and it now lies on the tomb of abbot Flaccet.

His epitaph was only thefe two obfcure lines,

Jam Wintona polis de Richardo
Mortis amara dedit, at locus ifte capit.

[1] Stukeley's Copy of the Minutes. [2] P. 422. [3] Drake, p. 429.
[4] Sandf. p. 96. [5] See the print in Dart, p. 90. [6] XXIV. [7] I. 191.

He was archdeacon of Weſtminſter, and owed his advancement to the favour of Henry III. which he ſoon loſt by his ill conduct in his monaſtery, and recovered it only by his concurrence with unpopular public meaſures. He died of poiſon at Wincheſter: and is characterized by Matthew Paris as a handſome man and good orator, who ſpared no pains or expence to ſerve the king, both at home and abroad. 1261.

" Under the ſtairs leading up to the organ in *Wincheſter* cathedral there is a
" buſt (by tradition) of ETHELMARUS, the biſhop, who died A. C. 1261, who
" nevertheleſs ſeems to have been interred in another place; for I find his heart
" was buried in the South wall of the preſbytery, where this monument is ſtill
" viſible.

" *Obiit anno Domini* 1261
" *Corpus* ETHELMARI *cujus cor nunc tenet iſtud*
" *Saxum Pariſiis morte datur tumulo* [1]."

Godwin [2] confirms this laſt deſtination. The only reaſon therefore for introducing this monument here is to refute the erroneous appropriation of this buſt, which is in fact a mutilated figure of an old knight, under which is a ſhield charged with Barry of 18.

JOHN DE CALETO, abbot of *Peterborough*, who died 1262, was buried before 1262.
the altar of St. Andrew, at the eaſt end of the ſouth aile of the choir, near the ſhrine of St. Tibba, commonly called the Queen of Scot's tomb. He was elected abbot 1249, and appointed treaſurer of England 1260 [3]. He built the Infirmary, and gave a great bell to the church, which was in being till 1711, inſcribed, *Jon de* Caux *abbas Oſwaldo conſecrat hoc vas.* His grave was opened in February, 1742, for the interment of Mrs. Fuller, and his remains carefully re-entombed. On raiſing the earth where he was buried they found two pieces of braſs: one an Ave Maria piece, with a croſs flory in a ſquare; the other a man ſitting at a table, with a caſe of printing types, which he was ſetting: the 4 in the alphabet is Roman. The laſt piece could hardly be contemporary with John de Caleto [4]. The monument or ſhrine before which he was buried was removed on the late repair of the cathedral, 1782, into the Dean's garden, where it is raiſed on pedeſtals, *to ſerve as a ſummer-houſe.*

Biſhop BRIDPORT lies in St. Mary Magdalen's, or the firſt chapel in the ſouth 1263.
tranſept at *Saliſbury.* His effigy is pontifically habited: his croſier a rich one; Pl. XVII
angels ſupported his head; on the ſide of the tomb are eight niches [5]. The arch over him is a ſurbaſt one: the outer moulding charged with birds holding ſcrolls, inſcribed, **honor Deo et glia**, and lilies alternately. In the South ſpandrils the arms of the ſee, and two chevronels G. indented. See Pl. XVII. On the other France and England quarterly, and a croſs flory between five martlets. This prelate died 1263, having filled this ſee ſeven years. The preſent church was dedicated under his adminiſtration by archbiſhop Boniface.

Among Daniel King's drawings of the Vere monuments before mentioned, p. 36, was one repreſenting the fragment of a very antient figure, and the effigy of a lady. Theſe are both ſaid to have been of alabaſter, and therefore

[1] Gale's Wincheſter, p. 24, 25.
[2] P. 221.
[3] Dugd. Orig. Jurid. calls him J. de *Crakeale.*
[4] T. Neve, in the Spalding Society's minutes.
[5] Price ſays this tomb "was wrought as a model of the outſide of the tower by tradition." Additional Remarks at end of the ſecond edition of his Obſervations on the Deſcription of Saliſbury. 1774. 4°. p. 139. He muſt mean of the archwork.

Mr. Lethieullier imagines them to be later than those in wood (engraved Pl. IX. fig. 2, 3.) and appropriates them to HUGH DE VERE earl of OXFORD and his countess HAWISE, daughter of Saer, earl of Winchester, 46 Henry III. He was only son to earl Robert buried at Hatfield-Broadoak, and nephew to earl Alberic before-mentioned, and died 1263. The principal event in his life was, that he subscribed the barons' letter of complaint to the Pope, 30 Henry III[a].

Weever[b] says the following inscription was on his tomb:

"Hic jacent Hugo de Vere, ejus nominis primus, comes Oxoniæ quartus, mag-"nus camerarius Anglie, filius & hæres Roberti comitis, & Hawisia uxor ejus, "filia Saeri de Quinci comitis Wintone; qui quidem Hugo obiit 1263. Quorum "animabus propitietur altissimus."

These seem to be the alabaster figures described as lying 1746 in an old summer-house in the South East corner of Mr. Wale's garden at Colne priory: the lower part of one of which is in armour from waist to mid thigh, and as much of a female trunk. Many pieces of marble and alabaster lay scattered about, and others were cut into chimney pieces for every room in the house. The foundations were discernable in dry weather. In digging up the foundation of the old conventual church were found stone coffins, bones, and many coins: an old piece of lead, circular, with a loop, or hole, which seemed appendant to a parchment, and had a rose, circumscribed THOME ROTHYNG, probably from that person's coffin.

Mr. King made a drawing of three views of a colossal free-stone figure, called by tradition GRIMEVERY, the first of the family of the Veres. This Mr. Lethieullier apprehends to be a mistake, for the following reasons: Albericus, the first of the family, settled indeed at Earl's Colne, where he died, and was buried, in the time of William the Conqueror, an age prior to the erecting any such monuments; and as he was the founder of their monastery, and himself shorn a monk therein, there is no reason to expect a representation of him in the habit and attitude of a soldier. He was therefore rather inclined to believe this monument was intended for ALBERICUS, the third of that family, but first earl of Oxford; from whence perhaps arose the tradition of his being the first of this family. This earl was an eminent soldier in the reigns of Stephen and Henry III. and dying 6 Richard I. 1194. was interred in this priory. Mr. Lethieullier adds, he had met with some other figures of like colossal proportions, which there is good reason to imagine were of that age. We have therefore subjoined the plate to the end of the preceding century. It was totally destroyed when Mr. Lethieullier visited the spot 1736.

These monuments, with that of earl Alberic and lady, were in the chapel at Colne priory in Essex, which had been founded by earl Alberic in the beginning of the reign of Henry I. but on its demolition were entirely destroyed. Others of the same family were removed into the parish church, where they are still preserved, and will be mentioned in their order.

1264. In digging a grave in the middle of the Lady chapel at *Wells*, 1727, was found about 20 inches under the pavement a free-stone coffin, containing the bones of a bishop, with a large gold ring set with a stone on his finger, and a small silver cup full of liquor, which was thrown in the dirt before any person of curiosity came; it was covered with a small silver paten somewhat rusty. All these things were preserved by archdeacon Archer. This was generally sup-

[a] Dugd. Bar. I. 191. [b] P. 615.

posed

posed the body of BUTTON, first bishop of that see of that name[1], who, according to Godwin[2], was buried *in tumulo marmoreo*, in this spot. The inattention of the labourers made them probably fancy there was liquor in the cup, which I believe is not usual, though chalices and patens are frequent in the graves of religious of rank, nor is it probable the vessels were of any better metal than latton, as those in bishop Grosthead's tomb. Nothing is more common than the mistake. Thus the prelatical rings, and the regal scepters, buried with the respective parties are, with the highest degree of improbability, conceived to be of gold or silver, when, at most, they are only gilded or silvered over. This bishop died 1264. Thomas Button, one of his family, afterwards bishop of Exeter, gave to the church of Wells, for this bishop's soul, the bell which used to ring for service in bishop Godwin's time, as the inscription on it set forth[3].

SIMON DE MONTFORT, earl of Leicester, being slain at the battle of Evesham, 1265.
his head, hands, feet, and privities[3] cut off on the field by Roger Mortimer[4], and the former sent to Wigmore castle[5], by leave of the King the trunk was carried away on a weak old ladder, covered with a torn cloth, to the abbey-church of Evesham, and, wrapt in a sheet, committed to the earth, before the lower step of the high altar there, with his eldest son Henry and Hugh lord Despencer, who fell with him[6]. But shortly after, some of the monks alledging that he died excommunicate and attainted of treason, and therefore did not deserve Christian burial, they took up his corps, and buried it in a remote place, known to few[7].

One of his hands being carried into Cheshire by the servant of one of the king's party, was, at the elevation of the host in the parish church, miraculously lifted up higher than the heads of all the assistants, notwithstanding it had been sewed up in a bag, and kept in the bearer's bosom[8]. One of his feet was carried by John de Vesey, the founder, to Alnwic abbey, where continuing several months uncorrupted, the monks made for it a silver shoe[9]. It had a wound between the little and the third toe, made either by a knife or sword, in the mangling of the body. The distant sight of this foot wrought instant cures. A canon of Alnwic, who swore the earl was a traitor, lost first his eyes, and then his life. "Think," cries out the monk of Mailros, who relates this story, "what "will be the glory of this foot at its rejunction to Simon's body after the general "judgement, from the comparison of this foot before that great event, which displayed such healing powers through the silver shoe, out of which went invisible "virtue to heal the sick." The other foot was sent, as a mark of contempt, by the victor to Llewellin prince of Wales, who had formed an alliance with this earl, and married his daughter. Though it is not to be doubted that this also was endowed with a power of working miracles, they were not sufficiently authenticated to be recorded. His other hand was preserved with great reverence at Evesham, where it may fairly be presumed to have wrought miracles; "for GOD, continues my author, does not so justify one part of a man by these "powers as to leave another part without the same." This chronicler, in his

[1] Letter to Hearne, Pref. to Adam de Domerham, p. 27. [2] P. 373.
[3] *Testiculos abscissos appenderbant ex utraque parte nasi.* Lib. Guildhall, MS. The man who cut them off was discovered two years after in the river Tay, and his body being taken up, there were found two frightful *scrabones*, (q. crayfish) fastened on his belly, so that they could scarce be pulled off. Chron. Mailros, 230.
[4] *Contra disciplinam ordinis militaris.* M. Paris. Sir William Maltravers did this, according to Robert of Glocester, p. 560.
[5] On the point of a spear. Wikes, 71.
[6] Ann. Waverley, 220. Matt. Paris says prince Edward assisted at the funeral of young Henry, whom his father stood godfather to, and for whom he himself had a great regard. This misled Dr. Nash (I. 413) to say the *king* assisted solemnly at the earl's funeral.
[7] Dugd. Bar. I. 758. ex MS. in Bib. Bod. "Simonis cadaver extumulatum in loco remotissimo projectum fuit qui locus nisi paucissimis est cognitus. MS. Cotton, Tib. A. IX. but discovered by miracles.
[8] Chron. Mailros, 231. [9] *Ca[illegible]amentum de argento purissimo.*

 enthu-

enthusiasm for the earl, compares him with his namesake Simon Peter, celebrates his exemplary vigilance and habit of rising at midnight, his abstinence, and his moderation in dress, always wearing haircloth next his skin, and over it at home a *russet* habit [1]; and in public, *blovet* or *burnet* [2]; and his constant language was, that he would not desert the just defence of England, which he had undertaken for GOD's sake, through the love of life, or the fear of death; but would die for it. Justly therefore did the religious prefer his shrine to the Holy Land: and his favourites the friars minors celebrated his life and miracles, and composed a service for him, which, during the life of Edward, could not be generally introduced into the church.

Matthew Paris [3] and the author of the Annals of Waverly [4] pretend, that at the instant of his death there happened extraordinary thunder and lightning, and general darkdarkness. "Sicque labores finivit suos vir ille magnificus Simon comes, "qui non solum sua sed se impendit pro oppressione pauperum, affectione justitiæ, "& regni jure. Fuerat utique literarum scientia commendabilis, officiis divinis "assidue interesse gaudens, frugalitati deditus, cuisamiliare fuit in noctibus vigi-"lare amplius quam dormire: constans fuit in verbo, severus in vultu, maxime "fidus in orationibus religiosorum, ecclesiasticis magnam semper impendens re-"verentiam." These are the words of Matthew Paris, who adds, that he had a high opinion of Bishop Grosteste. "Ipsius consilio tractabat ardua, tentabat du-"bia, finivit inchoata, ea maxime per quæ meritum sibi succrescere æstimabat; that the bishop promised him the crown of martyrdom for his defence of the church, and foretold that both he and his son would die the same day in the cause of justice and truth. His professions of religion (for he and all his army received the sacrament before they took the field [5]) and his opposition to the king's oppressive measures made him the idol of the monks and the populace. Tyrrel says [6] he had seen at the end of a MS. in the public library at Cambridge certain prayers directed to him as a saint, with many rhyming verses in his praise, and the pope was obliged to repress these extravagances. He certainly was possessed of noble qualities; but amid the prejudices of antient writers in his favor, and the violent declamations of the moderns against him, it is not easy to decide whether ambition or the public good was the motive of his opposition to his sovereign, who had been his benefactor, and whose sister he had married. The Chronicler of Mailros appeals to heaven for the justice of his cause, and the miracles wrought at the tomb of his associate Hugh Despencer, who was chief justice of England; and the Chronicler of Waverley scruples not to call his death a glorious martyrdom for his country, and the good of the kingdom and the church; while Carte condemns him as a traitor [7]: and Tyrrel says, he and his family perished, and came to nought in a few years. Knighton [8] says, he reproached his sons for having brought him to his end by their pride and presumption. Mr. Philips, owner of the site of Evesham-abbey, digging a foundation for a wall between the church-yard and his garden, found the skeleton of a man in armour, probably one of the heroes that fell in this battle. He scrupulously left it untoucht, and built the wall upon it [9].

1268. In the north transept at *Hereford* is the monument of bishop PETER DE EQUEBLANK, who died 1268. His figure *in pontificalibus* lies on a low altar tomb under a canopy. At his head a flat canopy, resting on three heads,

[1] Amictu Russeti. [2] *bloveti vel burnet.* [3] P. 998.
[4] P. 220. [5] Chron. de Mailros, p. 231. [6] II. 1052. [7] II. 158. [8] Col. 2453. Hollinsh. 270.
[9] Nash, I. 410.

which

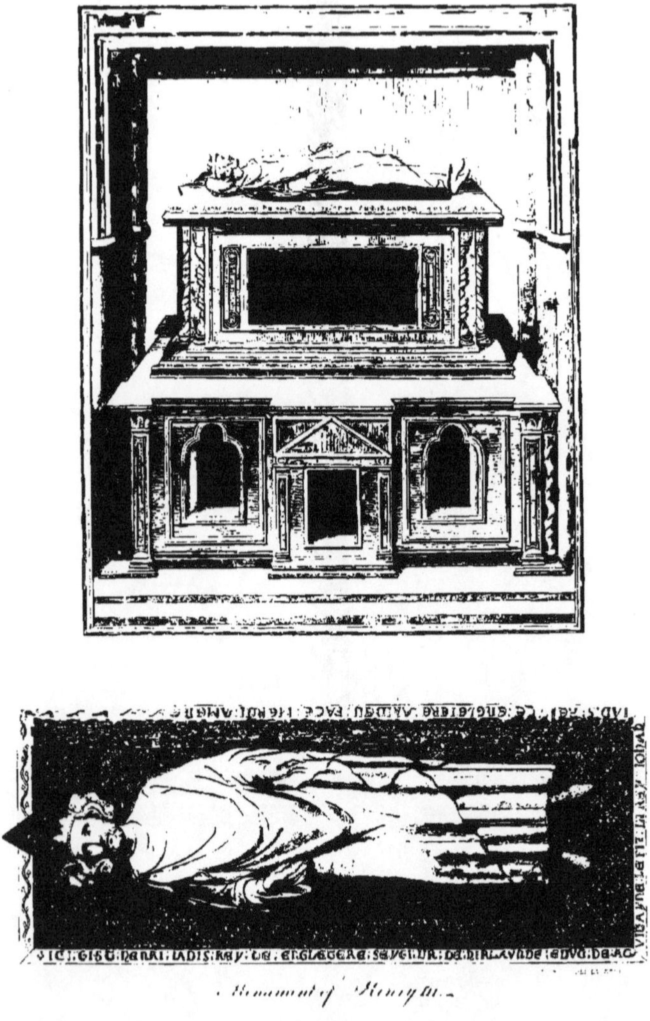

Monument of Henry III.

Pl. XI p. 5

North view of the Tomb of Henry III.

Portrait of Henry III. from his Monument

which are also down the sides, and three under arches at his feet. Over his head is painted on the wall,

D'ns Petrus de Aquablanca epus Heref.
Obiit A. D. 1268.

His heart was buried in a monastery of his founding at Aigues belles in Savoy, whereof he seems to have been a native.

In the middlemost chapel of the north transept at *Salisbury*, on the south side 1270.
of the chapel under a surbast arch, the spandrils open, lies a bishop *in pontificalibus* mitred: in his right hand a crosier piercing a beast; another beast at his left foot. This is the monument of WALTER DE LA WYLE, who died 1270.

"Under an enarched monument raised against the north wall of the chan- 1270.
cel at *Repeham* in the county of Norfolk lies a knight templar of the *Kerdeston* family, in armour, with his hands and legs crossed: on the basis of the monument are the effigies of six boys and four girls: on the side of the canopy work are the arms of Kerdeston, but no inscription remains. This knight lies on stone-work carved as a rock, with a lion at his feet; and probably represents Sir FULK DE KERDESTON, or, as some say, Sir THOMAS, who died in 1270 [1]."

We come now to the most magnificent and costly monument of this century, 1272.
that of HENRY III. in *Westminster* abbey, which if not actually the work of Cavallini, Pl. XX. XXI. XXII.
was probably executed from a design of his, and with materials brought from Rome, where Edward I. was the year after his father's death. [2] *Magnifico et sublimi sepulchro, quod rex Edwardus filius jaspidibus ophiticis, &c. quæ e* Gallia *attulerat plurimum ornavit* [3]. Leland, or the chronicle cited by him [4], says it was erected in the 8th year of Edward I. which is 1280. The side and end pannels are of porphyry, highly polished in frames of gold and scarlet. It stands on an ascent of three steps, and under it are three *ambries* or *lockers*, lined with the same Mosaic [5]. We may observe a great conformity between this tomb and the Confessor's in the form of the wreathed pillars and their capitals, and the contour of some parts of the inlaid work; though the palm of elegance must be given to the *shrine* [6]. The monument of this king's children, before described, p. 49, is composed of the same materials. The table of the royal tomb is of copper, diapered, and enamelled with flowers and lions in lozenges. The king's figure is of cast brass, once gilt, laid exactly in the attitude in which the body of Edward I. was found on opening his tomb in 1774, and I think there can be little reason to doubt that his own body would be found in the same situation in the altar-tomb on which the figure lies. The drapery is the same in which Edward I. was found to be vested, except that the fibula is double on the effigy, which was single on the royal mantle. Time has robbed Henry's statue of his two sceptres, which were actually existing in the tomb of his son, and one of which, in proof of Mr. Dart's accuracy, he has restored in his draught, though wanting fifty years before when Sandford wrote. Since that time the lion at his feet, and the canopy over the king's head, reaching down to his feet, are also gone, and only the marks of the fastenings left. But I shall decline a further description of this monument, which is so faithfully represented with the effigies and portrait distinct by Mr. Basire. Dart says he had a cast with one eye, so as to hide part of the ball and pupil. An

[1] Blomf. Norf. IV. 405. [2] Archæol. I. 34. [3] Camden's Westminster.

[4] Collectanea, II. 369. "Anno octavo sui regni Edwardus I. ex Gallis advexit porphyreticum marmor, ex quo sepulchrum patris ornavit." He adds, "Ex crustis & reliquiis prophyretici marmoris facta sunt ibidem pulcherrima pavimenta tessellata illa."

[5] Dart, II. 34.

[6] On viewing the same April 11, 1783, I found the pillar at the South East angle had been removed since I examined it April 14, 1781.

old MS. in proſe, aſcribed by Hearne to Robert of Glouceſter, thus deſcribes his perſon: "This kyng was but of mene ſtature, his other eyelede hangyd ſo "myche adown yt hit heled [covered] half the blake of his eye [1]." So Matt. Paris [2], and the Chronicle of Tinmouth, cited by Leland [3], "Erat autem ſtature "mediocris, compacti corporis, alterius oculi palpebra dimiſſiore ita ut partem "nigredinis alterius oculi palpebra celaret." This circumſtance is not expreſſed on the figure.

The inſcriptions given by Mr. Camden on this tomb are as follow:

On the north ſide towards the area in gilt letters:
Tertius Henricus eſt templi conditor hujus.
DULCE BELLUM INEXPERTIS.

On a table ſometime hanging by:
Tertius Henricus jacet hic pietatis amicus;
Eccleſiam ſtravit iſtam quam poſt renovavit.
Reddet ei munus qui regnat trinus et unus.

Thus tranſlated by Fabian:
The friend of juſtice and alms-deed,
Henrie the Third whilome of England king,
Who this church brake [4] & after his meed
Again renewed unto his fair building,
Now reſteth here, which did ſo great a thing.
He yeeld his meed yt Lord of Deitie
That as one GOD raignes in perſons three.

Mr. Vertue ſays, part of the laſt Latin inſcription, which was written in gilt capitals, was legible 1741 [5]. So it ſtill is.

Round the verge of the table is this inſcription emboſt in Saxon capitals,

ICI : GIST : HENRI . IADIS : REY : DE : ANGLETERE : SEYGNVR :
DE : HIRLAVNDE : E : DVC : DE : AQVITAYGNE : LE : FIZ : LI : REY : IOHAN :
IADIS : REY : DE : ANGLETERE : A : KI : DEU : FACE : MERCI : AMEN.

This prince fell ill at St. Edmund's Bury, on his return from Norwich, and died at Weſtminſter, 1272. 16 kal. Dec. aged 65; and the Sunday following, on the feaſt of St. Edmund the King, he was buried magnificently in this church, his body dreſſed in his royal robes, with his crown on his head, and all the nobility, the Templars (who Camden ſays wanted to have buried him in their church [6]) carrying the body; which ſhow was ſo magnificent that he was ſhewn more magnificent (ſays Wykes [7]) when dead than he appeared when living. His body was buried *before the high altar*; but his heart he gave order ſhould be buried at Fontevraud [8], which accordingly was delivered to the abbeſs of that place by the abbot of Weſtminſter, on the Monday next before the feaſt of St. Lucia the Virgin, in the preſence of many of the nobility, 20 Edward I [9].

1274. In the ſouth aile of the choir at *Wells*, on an altar-tomb, is the figure of Biſhop BUTTON, ſecond of that name, with a lion at his feet.

[1] P. 521. [2] P. 1009. [3] Coll. I. 177. Hollinſhed, I. 276.
[4] i. e. pulled down. [5] Archæol. I. 34.
[6] Qui corpus regium ſibi vendicabant. Ubi ſupra. [7] Chron. p. 98. Ann. Waverl. p. 226. Walſingham, p. 1.
[8] Mat. Weſtm. [9] Dart, Ib. Sandf. p. 91.

WALTER DE MERTON, chancellor of England under Henry III. and Edward I. bifhop of Rochefter from 1274 to 1279, the munificent founder of Merton-college at Oxford, which he began at Merton, in Surrey, 1264; but before his appointment to the fee of Rochefter transferred it to Oxford 1270; died 1277. The beautiful alabafter monument which we now fee on the north fide of St. William's chapel at the north end of the crofs aile in his cathedral, was erected to his memory at the procurement of Sir Henry Saville, knight, warden of Merton-college, who caufed the old marble one to be pulled down. The figure of the bifhop habited *in pontificalibus*, his hands elevated and joined, lies on an altar tomb, on the front of which is the following infcription in two tablets, in Roman capitals. 1277.

" Waltero de Merton, cancellario
Angliæ fub Henrico tertio; epifcopo
Roffenfi fub Edwardo primo: reg unius
Exemplo, omnium quotquot extant
Collegiorum fundatori; maximorum
Europæ totius ingeniorum fœlicifſimo
parenti; Cuftps & fcholares domus
fcholarium de Merton in univerfitate
Oxon. communibus collegii impenfis,
Debitum pietatis monumentum pofuere
Anno Domini 1598. Henrico
Savile cuftode."

Obiit in vigilia Simonis & Judæ anno
Domini 1277 Edwardi primo quinto.
Inchoaverat collegium Maldoniæ in agro
Surr. A° Domini 1264, Henrici tertii
Quadragefimo octavo, cui dein falubri
Confilio Oxonium 1270 tranflato
Extrema manus faelicifſimis, ut credi
Par eft, aufpiciis acceffit A° 1274 ipfis
Kalendis Augufti A° regni regis Edwardi
Primi fecundo.

Magne fenex titulis, mufarum fede facrata
Major Mertonidum maxime progenie;
Hæc tibi gratantes poft fecula fera nepotes
En votiva locant marmora, fancte parens.

On another tablet, under the arch, this infcription, expreffing a later repair after the civil war:

Hunc tumulum fanaticorum rabie
(Quæ durante nupero plufquam civili
Bello prout in ipfa templa fic et in
Herorum fanctorumque reliquias ibidem
Pie reconditas immaniter fæviebat)
Deformatum atque fere deletum cuftos
Et fcholares domus fcholarium de
Merton in academia Oxonienfi pro
Sua ergo fundatorem pietate &
Gratitudine redintegrabant.
Anno Dom. 1662 cuftode
D'no Thoma Clayton equite.

This

This tomb was cleaned and repaired once more 1770, by the college, and the whitewashing all taken off.

At the back, over the figure, are these arms:

O. 3 chevronels G. *Walter de Merton* and his college.

Arg. on a saltire G. an escallop O. See of *Rochester*.

Between them hangs a purse, denoting his office of Lord Chancellor.

This monument, which is a much better imitation of Gothic than that of Leofric bishop of Exeter erected about the same time, was engraved very indifferently by John Bayley, at the expence of the warden and fellows of Merton, 1768. In the first impressions the bishop's arms were debruised by a cross patee fitche, and the same without the cross given instead of the arms of the see. The tablet and inscription between them was also omitted. This was afterwards corrected, and the tablet inserted over the bishop's head, and his arms over his feet: those of his see omitted.

Adjoining to this monument is a large chest of Petworth marble much defaced, the sides and top decorated with antient ornaments, but no traces of an inscription, which is all that remains of St. William's shrine, that brought such considerable emolument to the monks of this priory. This charitable saint was a Scotch baker, who in his way to the Holy Land was murdered by his own servant between Canterbury and Rochester. Laurence de St. Martin, bishop of Rochester, and predecessor of Merton, wanting a pretence to recover his church from the dilapidations committed by Simon de Montfort earl of Leicester and his party, obtained his canonization of the pope 1266, and a great resort of votaries soon attended at his tomb.

Bishop St. Martin died 1274. and was buried on the north side of the high altar, in his cathedral, where his effigy, *in pontificalibus*, remains on an altar-tomb.

1279. Bishop Gravesend, who died 1279, had his figure inlaid in brass, now gone, on a stone in the upper lesser transept of his cathedral, at *Lincoln*, under which is to be read this inscription in old square characters.

Ego Richardus quondam episcopus Lincolniensis credo quod redemtor meus vivit et in novissimo die de terra resurrecturus sum et rursum circumdabor pelle mea, et in carne mea videbo Deum salvatorem meum.

p. 60.

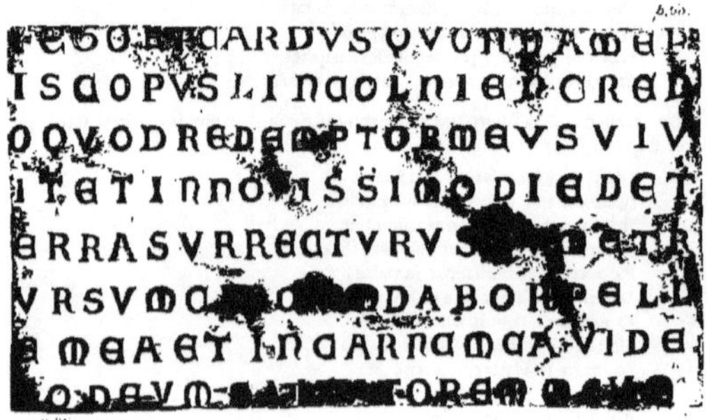

Anc.t Monuments of Bishops in Rochetter cathedral. Pl. XXII* p. 8.

Laurence de St. Martin 1274

In the north wall of the chapel, at the end of the ſouth aile at *Exeter*, under a ſurbaſt arch, on an altar tomb lies biſhop BROWNSCOMB, who died 1280. At his head a pointed-arch flowered canopy; at his feet a lion. On the ledge is painted this inſcription, the words in Roman ſupplied from Izaacke, and Leland, It. III. 32.

Olim ſincerus pater *omni dignus amore*
Primus Walterus magno jacet hic *in honore.*
Edidit hic plura digniſſima laude ſtatuta,
Quæ tanquam jura ſervant hic nunc omnia tuta.
Atque *hoc collegium quod Glaſney*[a] *plebs vocat omnis*
Condidit egregium pro voce data *ſibi ſompnis.*
Quot loca conſtruxit? pietatis quot bona fecit,
Quam ſanctam duxit vitam, vox dicere quæ ſit.
Laudibus immenſis jubilat gens Exonienſis,
Et chorus & turbæ, quod notus in hac fuit urbe.
Plus ſi ſcire velis, feſtum ſtatuit Gabrielis[b].
Gaudeat in celis igitur pater ille fidelis.

O. on a chevron S. 3 cinquefoils O. between 2 keys craſt in chief, and a ſword of the ſecond. *Brownſcomb.* Angels hold G. a chevron O. between 2 keys and ſword; probably the ſame coat partly craſt and indiſtinct.
Az. a croſs patonce between 4 martlets O. *Saxon kings.*
O. a ſpread eagle with two heads, G.
. . . . a buck's head caboſt, G.
Three Apoſtles painted, and under them texts from their epiſtles.

Jacob.	*Jobe's.*	*Judas.*
Vita veſtra	*Vitam habetis*	*Ecce ve-*
vapor eſt ad	*eternam qui*	*nit d'ns*
modicum [parens]	*creditis in*	*face . . .*
& exterminabitur.	*noie filii*	*judicium*
c. Jacobi 4°.	*dei. t. canonica Jobis 5°.*	. . . . .

Of the ſame date was biſhop CHISHULL's monument in Old St. Paul's, but 1280. much plainer, being only an unornamented ſtone cheſt, with pointed arches [Q. of a chapel] reared upon it.

In *Gosberton* church in the county of Lincoln, in the North aile of the chancel, now a ſchool, is an alabaſter figure of a knight in a pointed helmet, gorget, and coat of mail, a lion at his feet. On the ſide of the tomb three rows of ten quatrefoils in circles. In the centre a large quatrefoil in a lozenge ſided by two blank ſhields. On the baſe remained, 1782, in old capitals, only—" *us filius ejus. pro animabus propitietur Deus. Amen.* Hi" 1282.
Mr. Ray, vicar of Surfleet, copied it in 1740.

HIC JACET NICOLAVS REY
MILES ET EDMVNDVS FILIVS
EIVS
ANIMABVS PROPITIETVR DEVS. AMEN.

Maurice Johnſon referred it to NICHOLAS DE RYE, ſheriff of the county 5 & 6 Edward I. 1278, who died 1279 or 1280, having obtained a weekly market for his manor of Goſberkirk [c].

[a] Or *Penryn*, in Cornwall, which he was warned in a dream to found. Godwin, 405.
[b] He left an eſtate to ſupport this feſtival. Ib.
[c] Dugd. Bar. I. 110. ex Rot. Pip. de iiſdem annis. Cart. 9 E. I. n. 17. Spalding Society's minutes.

1281. In the middle of the east end of the north transept at *Hereford*, stands the shrine or tomb of Bishop CANTILUPE, patron of that church, where he sat from 1275 to 1282. He died at Civita Vecchia, 1282, in his way to Rome, with a complaint against archbishop Peckham, concerning the rights of his church. His *flesh* was honourably buried at Rome in St. Severus' church [1]. His heart at *Ashridge*, and his *bones* here, where they wrought so many miracles that the register of the church makes them amount to 420 cures of various diseases [2]. His tomb of red stone is altar-fashioned, with a large canopy of six pointed arches over it. His figure, and an inscription on the verge and at the feet, all in brass, have been torn off. In the six arches on each side the tomb are six knights in mail with swords and shields, treading on lions, griffins, and lions with double tails. Over these figures six more arches. The flowers and foliage in every spandril different.

1286. In the north transept at *Peterborough* was [1760] a raised coffin-formed stone, with a cross inscribed

Hic jacet Willh*elmus Parys, quondam* prior Burgi *cujus anime propitietur Deus. Amen. Pater noster. Amen.*

The Italics supplied from Browne Willis, 486. PARYS was prior 1286.

Round two others,

Hic William natus Pighteste quiescit humatus.
*Facta prior*atus claustro rexit monachatus.
Sit prece salvatus Petri, *celoq. locatus.*

The second line I can only understand to mean that he governed the actions of his priorship by the severity of monkery.

Such has been the progress of improvement in this church within these few years, that I could find neither of these tombs 1782.

The next now turned out under the great West porch has a cross, and this inscription in Gothic capitals,

Cristus *Rogeri Clyff* dignetur misereri
In Burgo natiq. prioris et hic tumulati.

Clyff died . . . .

In the South transept of *Winchester* cathedral is a coffin-fashioned tomb of grey marble, having on the lid a cross florè of this shape and round the ledge in deep cut letters this inscription.

Hic jacet Willielmus de Basyng, quondam prior istius ecclesiæ, cujus animæ propitietur Deus. & qui pro anima ejus oraverit tres annos & quinquaginta dies indulgentiæ percipiet.

[1] Godwin. Lel. III. p. 89.
[2] Rudder's Glocestershire, p. 747.

Pl. XXII. p. 85

Monument of Eleanor Queen of Edward I. 1290

Portrait of Queen Eleanor from her Monument

p. 13.

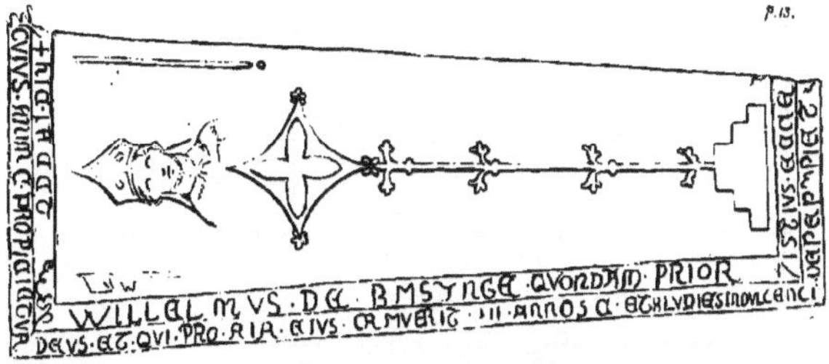

Willis, and the Historians of Winchester, refer it to the second prior, of the name of WILLIAM DE BASING, who died 1295. His predecessor of both his names, who died 1284, is supposed to lie at his right hand in a plain tomb of the same materials without crosier or inscription.

The plain altar-tomb in the south wall of the Lady-chapel, *Salisbury*, under an arch opening into Beauchamp's chapel, adorned with shields in quatrefoils, which some plans assign to bishop WIKEHAMPTON, who died in 1289, is by Mr. Lethieullier more probably ascribed to some of bishop BEAUCHAMP's family, of whom hereafter. It is not unlikely that the mistake arose from Leland's [1] placing bishop Wikehampton at the right hand of bishop Longespee. It is most probable he means that both Wikehampton and Brandeston (who died 1287) were covered by marble slabs. 1284.

The church of *Westminster* received additional embellishment 1290 from the tomb of queen ELEANOR, consort of Edward I. Her figure is of copper gilt, on a tablet of the same. Her left hand laid lightly on her breast holds her collar; while her right falls gracefully on her drapery, and perhaps held her sceptre. Her head is adorned with a coronet of fleurs-de-lis and trefoils, under which her hair falls in ringlets down her neck. Her drapery consists of a close mantle, the latter spreading from her shoulders, and meeting again about her gown and knees, overruns her feet. Under her head are two cushions enamelled with lions and castles, and at her feet two lions, one of which has been almost covered by the building of Henry V's chapel. Over her head a canopy nich of the same metal, the corner part of which has been torn away, as appears by two holes remaining in the table. 1290. Pl. XXII. XXIII.

Sandford says, that her statue on her cross at Waltham resembled this. It is certainly a delicate figure of a beautiful lady.

The tomb is of Sussex marble, charged with the arms of England, Castile and Leon quarterly, and Ponthieu [2], each twice repeated, hanging from oak leaves, in demiquatrefoil arches, whose pediments and fynials are lightly frosted and terminated with foliage. The same style of ornament appears to the shields on the tomb and the cross.

[1] Itin. III. 63.
[2] On the south side England, Castile and Leon, Ponthieu, each twice. At the head England. On the north side Ponthieu, Castile and Leon. England, Ponthieu, Castile and Leon. England.

3 On

On the edge of the copper table, which is enamelled with lions, and the arms of England and Castile in lozenges, is this inscription, in capitals of the time,

ICI GYST ALIANOR JADIS REYNE DE ENGLETERE FEMME AL RE EDEWARD FIZ LE R . . . . .
OVNTIE. DEL ALME DE LI DEV PUR SA PITE EYT MERCI[1].

Over all is a wooden canopy, the ceiling of 14 compartments. On the north side was painted a sepulchre, with two monks at the feet, and at the head an armed knight and the Virgin Mary; the tomb and figures in robes and armour at its head, two or three just visible; the figures at feet, one with a scroll, just visible; the rest hid by the monument of Esther de la Tour de Governet. Over it, on the lower ledge of the tomb, in modern black capitals, this line, now entirely defaced, except the words in Roman and the date.

Regina Alionora, consors Edvardi primi fuit Alianora, 1298. *Disce* mori.

Camden and Weever add two long rhyming epitaphs, in Latin and English, which were probably painted or inscribed on appendant tablets.

This princess was only child to Ferdinand III. king of Castile, by his second wife daughter of John earl of Ponthieu, and paternal sister to Alphonso his successor in the crown of Castile. She was married to Edward I. when prince, and only fifteen years old, at Bures in Spain, 1254, 39 Henry III. was crowned with him, and lived 36 years the partner of his troubles and expeditions even into the Holy Land. The story of her saving his life by sucking the poison out of the wound given him by a Saracen assassin is first quoted by Camden[2], from Roderic archbishop of Toledo, who, as himself tells us, wrote his history in 1243, which was twenty years before this event happened; nor could bishop Tanner find it in that history.

Hemingford[3] expressly says, that the grand master of the temple immediately sent the prince plenty of precious drugs to stop the progress of the poison; but a mortification being apprehended an English physician undertook to cut out the bad flesh, in the presence of the nobility and the princess, who, not being able to stand the operation, the prince ordered Edmund and John de Vesey to lead her out, who told her it was better she should weep than all England. Wikes[4] only says he was healed *by the grace of Christ*. Edward's affection for his consort wants no embellishment or inducement of this sort. The monuments erected by him to her memory, on the places where her corpse rested in its progress from Herdby in Lincolnshire to Westminster, no less than thirteen in number, of which only three now remain, are so many memorials of conjugal love unparalleled in any other kingdom[5]. He had by her seventeen children, five sons and twelve daughters. He remained a widower nine years, after which, in 1299, he took to his second wife Margaret sister of Philip Le Bel, and eldest daughter of Philip le Hardi king of France, with whom he lived eight years, and by whom he had three children. She survived him ten years, and dying 1317, was buried in the Grey Friars of her own foundation at London. This heroic prince is celebrated by all historians as a pattern of chastity; and it is remarkable that we find no natural children of his on record.

[1] Dart omits the last line. [2] Britannia, Middlesex.

[3] P. 591. dedit ei preciosa quæque libere ne infusum venenum noceret, & ne in interiora ascenderet.

[4] P. 97.

[5] In omni loco & villa quibus corpus pausaverit jussit rex crucem cum tabulatu erigi ad reginæ memoriam ut a transeuntibus pro ejus anima deprecatur, in qua cruce fecit imaginem reginæ depingi. Walsingh. Ypod. Neustriæ, p. 477. Hist. p. 55. Hemingford, p. 11. mentions only those at Charing and Westminster. He adds, 'that the king every 'Wednesday for a whole year "*ad quemcunque locum se diverteret*," gave a penny apiece to all the poor that came 'for it; and at the end of the year settled a certain revenue on the abbey at Westminster, to celebrate her anniversary, and distribute the like dole thereon.'

The

The king returned back in great grief from his expedition into Scotland, to accompany the funeral of his beloved consort.

When the corpse reached St. Alban's it was met at the town's end by St. Michael's church by the whole convent, in their copes, who conducted it to the high altar, where they attended it the whole night, celebrating the proper offices. From thence it moved to town, where the king, nobles, and bishops met it, and after embalment it was deposited in the church of Westminster with all due reverence and honor.

Our old historians do not deal in characters; but Walsingham [1] says of this princess, "Fuerat hæc regina dicta Alienora, soror Aldefonsi regis Castilie, nobilis "genere, sed *multo nobilior morum gravitate.*" And elsewhere [2] he says, the king lamented her loss as long as he lived, ordaining perpetual masses and alms for her soul in divers parts of the kingdom; for she was a woman of great piety, moderation, and tenderness, fond of the English, and as it were the pillar of the realm. In her time foreigners did not pester England, nor were the subjects opprest by the king's officers, if the least complaint came by any means to her ears. She administered comfort to the distrest every where, as her rank enabled, and reconciled to the best of her power all who were at variance.

The two epitaphs before mentioned celebrate the political advantages of her alliance with Edward, and conclude with saying that she was *consilio prudens, pia.*

It has been generally supposed that the place where she died, of a slow fever [3], was in Lincolnshire. Wikes says at *Grantham.* Bishop Gibson placed it near Bolingbroke, and at the head of the river Witham [4]. Walsingham [5] expressly puts it at Herdeby *juxta Lincolniam.* It is in the parish of North Clifton, on the Trent, in Nottinghamshire, five miles from Lincoln, where was a villa [6], and chapel of ease to that parish, which is one of the prebends of Lincoln. The king founded a chauntry in Herdby chapel, which her son afterwards removed into Lincoln cathedral [7], where her bowels were buried under the East

[1] Ypod. Neustr. p. 477.

[2] "Fuerat nempe mulier pia, modesta, misericors, Anglicorum amatrix omnium, & velut columna totius regni. Cujus temporibus alienigenæ Angliam non gravabant, incolæ nullatenus per regales opprimebantur si ad aures ejus vel minima querela oppressionis aliqualiter pervenisset. Tristes ubique prout dignitas sua permittebat consolabatur, & discordes ad concordiam quantum potuit reducebat." Hist. Angl. p. 54.

[3] *Modicæ febris igniculo contabescens.* Wikes, p. 121. *Corporis gravi infirmitate correpta.* Trivet, p. 268.

She died 5 kal. Dec. 1290. M. West.n. 381. Weever 464. Sanford 129. 4 kal. Dec. Wikes, 121. Lel. Col. I. 461. Carte II. 208. Rymer II. 498.

[4] Britannia in Lincolnshire.

[5] Hist. Ang. p. 54. Ypod. Neustr. 477. In the latter place it is misprinted Herdeley.

[6] Sandford, p. 29. says, "she died in the house of one William Weston, at Hereby, c. Nott."

[7] Pat. 19 E. I.

"Rex venerandæ religionis viro abbati Cluniscensi salutem & dilectionem in Christo sinceram. Deus omnium condi-"tor & creator, qui cœlesti profunditate consilii ordinat, vocat, disponit, & revocat subjectas suæ providentiæ creaturas, "serenissimam consortem nostram Alienoram quondam reginam Angliæ ex regali ortam progenie 4 kal. Decembris de "præsenti sæculo (quod vobis non sine multa mentis amaritudine nunciamus) sicut sibi placuit avocavit. Cum itaque "dictam consortem nostram, quam vivam care dileximus, mortuam non desinamus amare, ac opus sanctum & salubre "juxta divinæ scripturæ sententiam censetur pro defunctis ut a peccatorum solvantur nexibus exorare, paternam carita-"tem vestram affectionis precibus duximus exorandam & instancius implorandam, quatenus ipsius consortis nostræ exe-"quias communi devotione solempniter provocantes animam ejus cum decantatione missarum & aliis ecclesiasticis sacra-"mentis Deo vivo qui aufert spiritum principum specialiter recommendatis; adjuvantes eandem, ac etiam facientes a "prioribus, monachis, clericis, & aliis vestris subditis in sacramentorum suffragiis, eleemosynis, cæterisque operibus cari-"tatis salubriter adjuvari; ut si quid maculæ non purgatæ in ipsa forsan oblivionis defectu vel alio modo remansit per "utilia orationum vestrarum præsidia juxta divinæ misericordiæ plenitudinem abstergatur. Quæsumus igitur ut de "missarum & aliorum suffragiorum hujusmodi numero quæ pro præfata consorte nostra decreveritis facienda per vestras "literas nos curetis reddere certiores, ut ex hoc scire possumus ad quales quantasque grates & gratias ob præmissa "devotioni vestræ teneri merito debeamus. Dat. ap Asherugge 4 die Januarii."

"Cantaria pro anima Alianoræ quondam reginæ Angliæ consortis illustrissimi domini Edwardi regis Angliæ in capella de Herdeby in parochia prebendæ de Clifton com. Nott. et Ebor. dioc. ubi præfata d'na regina diem clausit extremum, de uno capellano presentando quocies vacaverit per decanum & capitulum Lincoln D'no Archiep'o Ebor. vel ejus vicesgerentis qui quidem capellanus percipiet annis singulis centum solidos per manus prebendarii de Clifton, qui recipiet de co's annis singulis decem marcas, & inveniet eidem capellano panem, vinum, calicem, missale, luminaria, vestimenta, & cætera ornamenta altari necessaria, necnon & hospitium conveniens atque locum; & sustentabit suis sumptibus præmissa. Dat. 12 kal. Junii, A. D. 1293." Liber de ordinand. cantar. fol. 1, 2. and f. 148, a. "Postea vero, sc. die Mercurii in septimana Paschæ A. D. 1310. hæc cantaria translata fuit et ordinata in ecclesia cathedrali Lincoln ad altare s'ci Jon'is ubi viscera præfatæ reginæ jacent humata." Ex antiquo reg'ro A. primus notato in archives Dec. & Capit. Linc. F. 32. b.—N. B. Hæc cantaria ordinata fuit per Dec. & Cap. eo quod rex Edw' I. non solum dedit eis c marcas argenti ut prefatur, sed etiam concessit manerium de Nevenby libere possidendum, statuto de terris in mortuam manum non ponendis non obstante." This payment of ten marks is to this day made by the Dean and Chapter to the curate of Herdeby chapel.

window under a sumptuous marble cenotaph, or altar monument, whereon was a queen's effigy, at full length, of gilded brass, according to bishop Sanderson's account printed in Peck's Desiderata Curiosa VIII. 1. "This tomb stood close "with the feet to the wall, and North to the tomb of — — On the "marble on the South were 3 escutcheons." Mr. Peck rightly apprehended these escocheons were, 1. England, 2. Castile and Leon quarterly, 3. Ponthieu. This inscription was on the edge, inlaid in brass:

✠ HIC : SVNT : SEPVLTA : VICERA : ALIANORE : QVONDAM : REGINE : VXORIS : REGIS : EDVARDI ; FILII : REGIS : HENRICI ; CVJVS : ANIME : PROPICIETVR : DEVS : AMEN : ✠ PATER : NOSTER.

So it remained 1641.

It shared the fate of many others in the civil war; but there still remains a beautiful fragment of the chapel in which it stood, at the East end of the choir. The position assigned it in the plan prefixed to Browne Willis' account of this cathedral is on the South side of what is there called Robert Lord Badlesmere's tomb. It is described there p. 6. as having "her effigies in brass, exactly like that on her monument in Westminster-abbey. See the draught of it in Sandford, and the inscription in the same author [*] There are no traces left in the pavement on this spot of any monument having stood here, except a sort of rise or foot pace in front of the Badlesmere tomb, which, from the tooling off of a corner, seems to have been carried higher there; but if it had been raised, it must have entirely hid the arms on that monument, which certainly must have been open, at least at its first putting up. Almost close adjoining to this projecting kind of foot-pace (not vastly unlike the bench kind of seat carried along the other monument, and indeed the church itself) are two recent gravestones of 1757 and 1759. If the Queen's tomb had remained so late as bishop Reynolds's time, at whose expence Willis's ichnography is said to have been taken, it must have existed within the memory of some persons now living.

The king gave the dean and chapter 100 marcs more to support this chantry, whereby they purchased the manor of Navenby, a market town near Lincoln; which maner is still enjoyed by the Dean and Chapter of Lincoln.

Her heart was buried in the church of the Friars Preachers at London [z].

The crosses erected to her memory were at *Herdby*, *Lincoln*, *Newark*, *Leicester*, *Geddington*, *Northampton*, *Stoney Stratford*, *Dunstaple*, *St. Alban's*, *Waltham*, *Cheapside*, *Charing*, and by *Westminster*. Peck adds three more, at *Grantham*, *Stamford*, and *Woburne* [a]. Of these now remain only those at *Northampton*, *Geddington*, and *Waltham*. How this latter place came to be a station between St. Alban's and London is not easy to conceive; but the cross actually existing puts it out of doubt that it was so.

ELEANOR, mother of Edward I. died the same year, on Midsummer-day, at Ambresbury, where she had lived a nun nineteen years. Her son being in Scotland, she was kept unburied till the Lady-day following, "*myrrha tamen et aromaticis pretiosis linita magnifice ut decuit et peruncta.*" She was then buried with due pomp, her son assisting, in *Ambresbury* monastry church. Her heart in the church of the Friars minors, at London [b].

[z] Walsingham, Hist. Angl. 551. Wikes, 123.

[a] "Grantham and Stamford were stages. Mr. Howgrave says there was a Queen's cross at Stamford; and the like is affirmed of Grantham, and that it stood in the open place in the London road; and I saw a stone carved with foliage work, and said to be part of it, and I believe it, seeming of that sort of work. If so, then Newark and Leicester must be left out, and they travelled with the Queen's corpse by way of Oundle to Geddington from Stamford. I suppose the present London road from Stamford being unpassable, or not having at that time royal seats, manors, or abbies, by the way sufficient to entertain the cavalcade. Mr. Peck, in his Stamford Annals, asserts Grantham and Stamford to be two of the stages, and where crosses were erected; no doubt that at Grantham stood in the open London road, before my neighbour Hacket's house, called Peterchurch-hill, and the people have some memory of it. Camden, who doubtless had seen them, in his Remains, p. 116, inserts Grantham and Stamford." Mr. Peck puts in Woburne, between Dunstable and St. Albans, on what authority I know not. Geddington was a manor of the king's. (V. Reg. honoris Richmond, p. 180.) Stukeley It. Cur. I. 34. 36. 2d edit.

[b] Ann. Waverl. p. 242. Wikes, 123.

Tradition buries WILLIAM DE LA CORNER, bishop of *Salisbury*, who died 1290, in the middle of the choir, nearly under the eagle. 1290.

In the door-way of the Lady-chapel at *Salisbury*, and under its screen, is a monstrous blue slab of two stones 16 feet 8 inches long [1] by 7 feet 8 inches broad, full of traces of brass canopy work, which seems to have belonged to bishop NICHOLAS DE LONGESPEE, son of the earl before mentioned, p. 41, who died 1297. It is thus described by Godwin [2]: "Prope patrem jacet sepultus "juxta ingressum capellæ B. Mariæ saxo ingenti marmoreo contextus, laminis "æreis & familiæ suæ insignibus affabrè ornato." Leland [3], without fixing the spot where it is, gives the following inscription on it, or rather perhaps account of it. 1291.

"*Sub hoc lapide marmoreo desuper insculpto humatum est corpus reverendi patris* "*Nicolai Longespe, quondam Sarum episcopi, qui plurima huic contulit ecclesie, et* "*obiit* 18 *mens. Maii, A. D.* 1291 [4]. *ex cujus parte australi jacet Robertus Wic*-"*hamton, ex parte boreali Henricus Brandesburn requiescit.*"

The monument of archbishop PECKHAM, who died 1292, and was buried in the north transept of the nave at *Canterbury*, is another instance of correspondence in style with those of Edmund Crouchback and Valence. The altar-tomb is adorned with the images of nine bishops, in their habits, with crosiers and mitres, and the pillars of the arch with eight more; the arch is radiated like that of Valence, and the moulding both of arch and pediment foliaged, and in the pediment a rich rose in a sexfoil and circle. The figure of the archbishop is of oak, *in pontificalibus*, on a slab of oak, very sound, though almost 500 years old, if originally made for this tomb, which, says Mr. Gostling [5], some have doubted. I know not on what authority, since other oak figures occur in churches, and those of simple knights would scarce be received. 1292.

In *Narburgh* church, Norfolk, is a half statue of a lady, a foot long, her head dress antique, and her hands holding a heart on her breast. Inscription 1293.

DOMINA : ALATDA : A : NARBOROVGH.

A MS. account temp. Eliz. mentions her 1293 [6].

Next follows the elegant monument of AVELINE countess of LANCASTER, wife of Edmund Crouchback, on the North side of the choir at Westminster. Mr. Dart, for reasons best known to himself, has thought fit to engrave only the altar part of it, which is the most inconsiderable part; and Sandford, with Hollar's assistance, has not done the rest justice. The figure of the Countess, worthy a Grecian sculptor, and the finishing of the arch above, with its foliage, and enamelled blazonry, were reserved for the hand of Mr. Basire; and I congratulate the Society of Antiquaries on the fortunate opportunity of having this perfect model of monumental architecture taken before it was closed up again. It is with the utmost reluctance I cast this reflection on the members of the chapter at Westminster in 1776. It had been shut up from the area by the tomb of bishop Duppa, 1662; which gave place, 1772, to that of Lord Ligonier; where the chubby muse of modern history, surrounded with drum, blunderbuss, and thunder, and leaning against a pyramid, hung round with

[1] Hearne describes a slab 9 feet long at Aldworth, Berks, which he refers to the time of Edward III. Roper's Mora, p. 248. [2] Ed. Richards. p. 347. [3] It. III. 63.
[4] A mistake for 1297. All after the date, though given in Hearne as part of the epitaph, seems rather to be the words of Leland.
[5] P. 120. [6] Blomf. Norf. III. 470.

medallions

medallions of three Georges, his Lordship's masters, holds forth his victories on a scroll, and has his head in a rondeau at her feet.

1295. Pl. XXIV. On the north side of the chancel at *Earl's Colne*, c. Essex, is an altar-tomb of freestone, embattled, the table of grey marble. In double compartments in front are the apostles; St. Peter only distinguishable at the head, the other defaced, perhaps St. Paul and St. Thomas. A freestone figure in armour, cross-legged, once, as well as the whole monument, richly painted and gilded, his arms broken, lies on the tomb; a round helmet on his head, under which are remains of angels: at his feet a boar, very well preserved. Between each pair of apostles a three-sided tabernacle, with purfled frontoons, and in the spandrils shields and birds.

This is the monument of ROBERT VERE, fifth earl of Oxford, who married Alice daughter of Gilbert de Samford, and died 24 Edward I.

The workmanship of the tomb far excells those of his predecessors. Monuments in many churches in England began about this to be made more splendid than those of the foregoing ages. That noble one erected by Edward I. to his father in Westminster-abbey might perhaps be one cause of introducing this taste.

The arms on this tomb ascertain the true owner. They are as follow:

At the head 3 lions. *England.*

O. a lion rampant G. *Isabella* heiress to Walter de *Bolebec*, grandmother to this earl.

At the feet *Vere*, single.

Arg. 3 fesses wavey. *Alice* daughter and heiress to Gilbert de *Samford*, and wife to this earl.

On the South side Q. *Samford.*

G. a lion rampant O. as at the head.

Vere.

Two fesses G. and 5 torteaux in chief.

Vere, with a label of five points, probably the bearing of his eldest son.

Vere, in a border engrailed S. This was the coat of *Hugh* his second son, as on his seal to the baron's letter to the pope.

The arms on the North side, now fixed against the wall, were exactly the same as on the South. They are all taken from a MS. description, accompanying Daniel King's draught, made 1653, and now in Mr. Walpole's possession, by whose favour it is here exhibited, Pl. XXIV, and under it a sketch of the same monument, taken by Mr. Tyson, 176 .

This tomb was removed, at the dissolution, from the priory chapel, into the parish church, and placed in the middle of the chancel, but was a second time finally removed as it now stands against the North wall of the chancel.

1295. The monument of URIEN DE ST. PIERE, who died 1295, 23 Edward I. was discovered 1765, on removing some rubbish in the church-yard, near *St. Pere*, the seat of Morgan Lewis, Esq. in Monmouthshire, on the Severn, a little South of Chepstow. It is a coffin-fashioned stone, with a cross in releif and by its side a long sword. Round the ledge is cut this inscription in Saxon capitals.

ICI GIT LE CORS V DE SENE PERE
PREEZ PVR LI EN BONE MANERE
DE IESV PVR SA PAISVN
DE PDECEZ LI DONC PARDVN. AMEN. RP.

So

Pl. XXIV. p. 60.

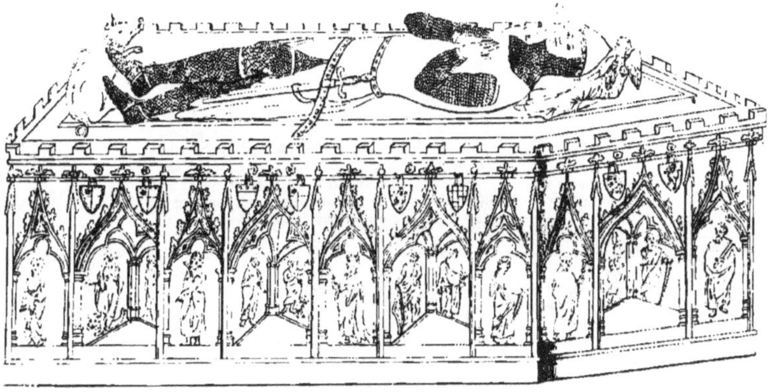

S.E. View

Pl. XXV. p. 60

N. Side.

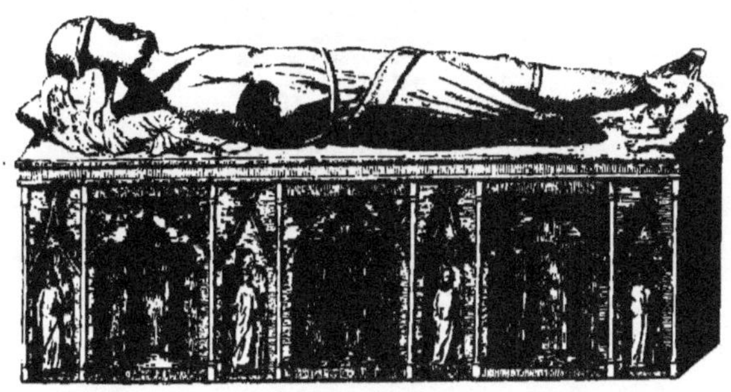

Monument of ROBERT VERE, fifth Earl of Oxford.

1296.

So it is given by Mr. Strange [1]. But the firſt word in the third line, PE, is probably miſcopied for kE. In PDCCEZ the D may be added by miſtake, for ſome ſcratch or mark, or a miſ-ſpelling of the ſtone-cutter, and in that line DONC is probably DONE. The two laſt letters, if intended for *Priez*, are much out of place. Q. If not rather miſcopied for P. N. *Pater Noſter*; which words alone, or with *Ave*, are no unuſual concluſion of old epitaphs. The blank after the V ſeems to have afforded room for VR or VRIEN. SENE may rather be SENC.

The party whoſe remains were covered by this ſtone was a knight, who lived in the reign of king Henry III. and left behind him at his death by his wife Margaret a ſon of his own name 16 years of age. He alſo was a knight, and had iſſue John de St. Pere, who ſucceeded his father 8 Edward III. and was the laſt heir male of his family. His ſiſter and heireſs Iſabel married Sir Walter de Cokeſey, knight, who died 30 Edward III. and ſhe died 6 Henry IV.

Mr. Pegge, to whom a neat drawing of this and another ſtone found with it was ſent by Mr. Perry of Liverpoole, which he inſerted in the Gentleman's Magazine for 1765, Vol. XXXV. p. 72, ſuppoſed the other ſtone, adorned with a croſs fleuré held by a hand, and having birds and beaſts at its ſides, covered Margaret. There being no criteria to aſſiſt us in aſſigning it, it may as well have belonged to any other perſon; for the 10 pellets at the top, which my worthy friend ſuppoſed alluded to her huſband's arms, are very doubtful.

The huſband of Aveline, EDMUND earl of LANCASTER, ſecond ſon of king 1296.
Henry III. born, as Matthew Paris [2] 1245, as Wykes [3] 1244, vulgarly called *Crouchback* [4], q. d. *Croſtback*, from his having been ſigned with the croſs for a cruſade, 54 Henry III [5], has a no leſs ſplendid tomb than that of his conſort from which it is ſeparated only by that of Aymer de Valence earl of Pembroke, who lies at her feet. In this monument I know not which moſt to admire; the free-ſtone figure of the earl in armour laid on one ſide towards the choir, with a round helmet, coat of mail, and ſurcoat, hands joined, long ſword, hilt and ſhield gone, legs croſſed, and butting againſt a lion [6], his head ſupported by angels; the elegant little ſtatues at the ſides, ten on each, repreſenting his alliances, or the airy triple canopy, with all its finials, froſtings, ſtatues, enamelling, emblazonry, and other elegant decorations, and above all, the bold beautiful relief in a trefoil in the larger pediment of the earl on horſeback, habited as hereafter, holding his ſhield, his horſe trapped armorially.

The canopy of ſtone over this tomb conſiſts of three trefoil pointed arches, one in the centre, and one leſſer on each ſide of it. Each of theſe arches is ſurmounted by a double pediment, ſeparated from the arches by a pilaſter, which ſlopes back in three ſeveral ſtories, and is painted white, chequered with double red lines, in every other ſquare of which is a red cinquefoil (the

[1] Archæol. V. p. 76, 77
[2] P. 635. [3] P. 45.
[4] Not as Vincent contends from his figure, and that the epithet of *Gibboſus* is given him in all records. The defect in his ſhape is expreſsly denied by Harding, c. 147. and one may juſtly doubt the inſertion of ſobriquets in public records. Sandford, p. 103. ſays he had this name from the *bowing of his back*; but preſently adds, "Others ſay he was ſo denominated from his wearing a croſs (anciently called a *crouch*) upon his back, which was uſually worn by ſuch as vowed voyages to Jeruſalem, as he had done 54 Henry III. grounding their conceits upon the word *crouch* (the wooden ſupporter of impotent and lame men, made like a croſs at the top) further confirming their opinion from the name of *Crouched-friars*, that wore a croſs upon their garments, and bore the croſs for the badge and arms of their houſe."
[5] Pat. 54 Hen. III. m 8. when Wykes (Chron. 86.) ſays, 107 perſons *caractere crucis humeros ſuos adornabant*. See Dugd. I. 473. Knighton, 2438.
[6] Not *cur*, as in Dart's Print.

two uppermoſt ſlopes ſerving as a baſe to a pointed flowered niche) and terminates in a rich purfled finial. The mouldings at the four angles, or weatherings, of the leſſer pediments, as well as the two of the greater, are decorated with bunches of oak leaves, and from among thoſe of the centre pediment project four brackets, which originally ſupported as many angels, whole length, in a ſtanding poſture, as expreſſed in Sandford's print. Each pediment terminates in a bouquet of oak leaves. The ground of the large pediments is painted of a dark blue ſprinkled with golden fleurs de lis. The ſpandrils and interſtices have alſo been painted with plain grounds, or foliage, and the arch work of the pilaſters inlaid with pieces of blue and red ſtained glaſs, ſet in ſo firm a cement that it is not eaſy to diſlodge the ſmalleſt piece without cracking it. Within the point of the leſſer pediments are carved in high relief a bunch of oak leaves iſſuing from a ſtalk, and a head of an animal ſurrounded by foliage, bearing ſome diſtant reſemblance to the modern cherub with ſix wings. The inſide or cieling of the canopy was a ſky with ſtars, in gold, on a blue ground, by time changed into a dull red; and within the leaves of the trefoil of the arch were painted the vine tendrils and elegant foliage as on Aveline's monument.

The inſide of the weatherings of all the ſix pediments are painted and gilt in diſtemper, with coats of arms, in oblong ſquares, thoſe on the centre or large pediment, which has nineteen on each ſide, being divided by a red ſquare charged with a ſixfoil. They ſeem to have been the arms principally of the royal houſes to which the earl was allied, as thoſe on the leſſer pediments are of the principal nobility of the time when he lived, who were probably his particular friends, and accompanied him in the wars. On the Weſt or right ſide of the centre pediment, beginning at the bottom, and going upwards to the finial, are the following coats.

1. G a feſs between 6 croſs croſslets Or. *Beauchamp* earl of *Warwick*.
2. O. 3 bendlets Az. a bordure G. *Ponthieu*. The arms of the Counteſs of *Ponthieu*, mother of queen Eleanor, Crouchback's ſiſter-in-law.
3. O. a lion rampant Az. *Redvers* earl of *Devon*, the family of the mother of *Aveline de Fortibus*, his firſt Counteſs.
4. A. a lion G. quartering S. a lion rampant O.
5. as 2. *Ponthieu*.
6. O. a ſpread eagle S. *Frederick II. Emperor of Germany*, who married *Iſabel* daughter of king *John*, Crouchback's aunt.
7. O 4 paletts G. *Eleanor of Provence*, Crouchback's mother.
8. 3 lions of England with a bendlet Az. *The arms uſed by John firſt ſon of Henry II. afterwards king*. Mr. Brooke rather takes this coat to be that of *Henry of Monmouth*, Crouchback's ſecond ſon, afterwards earl of Lancaſter, who probably might erect the monument.
9. Quarterly of 4, 1 & 4 G. a caſtle Or. 2 & 3 A. a lion rampant P. *Caſtile* quartering *Leon*.
10. 3 lions. *England*, with a label of 5 points, Az. each charged with 3 fleurs de lis Or. *Crouchback's* own arms.
11. O. a Lion rampant S.
12. *Crouchback*, as before.
13. *Germany*, as before.
14. *England*.
15. *Ponthieu*.
16. *Caſtile* and *Leon*.
17. Az. ſemee of fleurs-de-lis Or. *Old France*.
18. *England*.
19. *Old France*.

On

On the East or left side, beginning at the bottom, and going upwards to the finial.

1 & 4 *Ponthieu*, as 5 on the West.
2. O. a lion rampant Az. *Redvers.*
3. The 4 lions rampant quarterly as 4 on the West.
5. *Germany.*
6. *Provence.*
7. *Henry of Monmouth.*
8. *Castile* and *Leon.*
9. *England* under a label of 5. *Crouchback.*
10. O. the lion rampant G. as before.
11. *England* with the label of 5. *Crouchback.*
12. *Germany.*
13. *England.*
14. O. 4 pallets in a border G. *Provence*; the bordure probably added on account of that family being a younger branch of the house of *Arragon.*
15. as 1. *Ponthieu.*
16. Quarterly, the 4 lions rampant, as before.
17. *England.*
18. *Old France.*
19. *England.*

On the innermost weatherings of the lesser Eastern pediment from the bottom to the finial, the oblong shields are divided by Sable squares charg'd with cinquefoils Or. peirc'd.

1. O. 2 bends G. Baron *Sudley.*
2. O. a lion rampant B. Baron *Percy.*
3. O. 2 bars G. in chief 3 torteaux. Baron *Wake.*
4. Quarterly A. & G. in 2d & 3d fretty O. over all a bendlett S. *Despencer*, earl of *Winchester.*
5. O. a lion rampant Az. *Redvers.*
6. Quarterly O. and G. *Mandeville* earl of *Essex.*
7. O. 3 chevrons G. *Clare* earl of *Gloucester.*
8. A. a lion rampant G. crowned Or, in a bordure S. bezantè. *Richard* Earl of *Cornwall*, *Crouchback's* uncle.
9. *England.*

Returning down the opposite weathering, from the finial.

1. *Mandeville.*
2. Chequè O. & Az. Earl *Warren.*
3. O. a lion rampant Az. *Redvers* earl of *Devon.*
4. G. a fess between 10 cross crosslets O. *Beauchamp* earl of *Warwick.*
5. O. a cross G. *Bigot* earl of *Norfolk.*
6. G. a lion rampant O. *Fitz-Alan* earl of *Arundel.*
7. Lord *Wake.*
8. G. a fess between 6 martlets O. *Beauchamp* baron of *Powick.*
9. O. a fess between 2 chevrons G. Baron *Fitz-Walter.*

On the outermost Eastern weatherings of this pediment, 8 on a side.

1. *Germany.*
2. Or. a maunch G. *Hastings* earl of *Pembroke.*

3. O. lion rampant, Az. *Redvers.*
4. A. a bend between 6 martletts G. Lord *Furnival.*
5. Quarterly, per fefs indented A. and G. Baron *Fitz-Warine.*
6. O. 3 barrs G. The coat of *Alice* de *Romely*, Lady of *Skipton caſtle*, &c. co. *Ebor*. See Dugd. Bar. vol. I. p. 89. *Aveline de Fortibus*, the earl's firſt wife, was coheir-general to this lady, and as ſuch inherited that caſtle, and other fair poſſeſſions.
7. *Furnival.*
8. Broken, but apparently has been a faltire between 12 croſs crofslets G.

Returning down on the correſpondent or outermoſt weſtern weathering from the finial.

1. *Arragon*, or *Provence*, as before.
2. G. a feſs dancettè between 6 billets O. Lord *Beauchamp* of *Holt.*
3. Barry Nebulè O. & G. Lord *Lovell.*
4. Bendy of 6 O. & S.
5. *Redvers.*
6. *Hastings* earl of *Pembroke.*
7. *Fitzwalter.*
8. Lord *Sudley.*

The innermoſt weathering of the weſtern leſſer pediment is painted with the ſame arms exactly, placed in the ſame order as thoſe in the eaſtern leſſer pediment; but thoſe on the outermoſt differ, and are as follow, beginning at the bottom on the right-hand, and going up to the finial.

1. Lord *Lovell.*
2. *Redvers.*
3. *Fitz-Walter.*
4. Gironny of 12 O. & S. *Roan* or *Raan*
5. *Hastings*, earl of *Pembroke.*
6. *Sudley.*
7. O. a cheveron G. Lord *Stafford.*
8. *Germany.*

On the ſame weathering, going down the weſtern ſide of this pediment.

1. *Mandeville* earl of *Eſſex.*
2. *Beauchamp* of *Holt.*
3. Barry of 8 O. & G. *Alice de Romely*, as before.
4. A. fretty & on a chief S. 3 bezants. Baron *St. Amand.*
5. *Wake.*
6. *Hastings.*
7. *Sudley.*
8. Barry nebulè Or. & S. *Blount.*

All theſe ſhields appear to have been repeated on the South ſide.

The figure of the earl on the front of the pediment is a moſt beautiful and high finiſhed relief, and repreſents him on horſeback, armed in mail, and a ſurcoat, on the front and back of which are painted his arms; his helmet round and cloſe up to his chin; his face animated and eyes open, expreſſing devotion, perhaps alluding to the Cruſade he had juſt undertaken, his hands covered with mail elevated, his ſhield adorned with his arms hung round his neck, his ſcabbord alſo richly ornamented. His horſe in a ſtanding poſture, beautifully

beautifully dappled with brown and white ſpots under the belly, his face turned outwards, has the bridle on his neck, and is completely covered from head to foot, having the earl's arms on his caparison and on the back part of the ſaddle.

The ſouthern ſide of the tomb given by Sandford is now cloſed up with the wainſcot of the choir, but the figures, arms over them, thoſe on the weatherings, and the relief of the earl on horſeback, appear juſt the ſame as thoſe on the north ſide, except that when they were viewed by Mr. Brooke, May 19th, 1783, the whole had much more the appearance of damage and decay than the north ſide. This ſide is here engraved, Pl. XXV. XXVI.

The ſhields over the little figures on the ſouth face of the tomb preſerved in Hollar's print of it in Sandford will aſſiſt in aſcertaining the perſons they repreſent. They are, beginning from the Weſt, and two over each figure, in the ſpandrils of its arch, as follow.

1. *England* ſingle. King *Henry* III.
2. *England* under a label of 5 points. *Crouchback.*

3. Quarterly, *Caſtile* and *Leon.*
4. *Leon* ſingle.
} Queen *Eleanor.*

5. Semé of fleurs de lis, under a label of 3 points, G. charged with as many caſtles. *Artois*; for *Blanch*, Crouchback's ſecond wife, queen of *Navarre*, counteſs palatine of *Compeigne* and *Brie.*
6. *England.*

7. A lion rampant in a bordure bezanté. Earl of *Cornwall.*
8. 4 pallets. *Provence.*

9. A croſs patonce vairè. *Aveline* daughter of *William de Fortibus*, Crouchback's firſt wife.
10. *England* under a label of 5 points, Az. each charged with three fleurs de lis, Or. *Crouchback.*

11. Paly of 6 a bend vairè.
12. A ſpread eagle. *Frederick* II. emperor of *Germany.*

13. Barry of 8, A & G. 10 martlets, S. *Chaworth.*
14. *England*, under the former label.

15. *England* debruiſed by a bend. *Henry of Monmouth*, the earl's ſecond ſon.
16. *Caſtile* and *Leon.*

17. Three bendletts within a bordure. *Ponthieu.*
18. *Leon.*

19. *Provence.*
20. Paly of 6, a bend vairè as 10. In Hollar's plate the bend appears charged with 3 eagletts.

The ſhields on the North ſide are as follows, 20 by pairs over images.

1. Paly of 6 A. and G. a bend
2. 2 O. 4 pallets G. *Provence.*
} a King; ſceptre in right hand, left on breaſt.

3. O. A lion rampant. Az. a Queen, holding a ſceptre in her left hand, her right on her breaſt. Probably *Joan* Queen of *Caſtile*, Counteſs of *Ponthieu*, mother of Queen *Eleanor*, wife of *Edward* I.
4. O. 3 bendletts Az. within a bordure G. *Ponthieu.*

5. Quarterly *Caſtile* & *Leon.*
6. *England*, 3 Lions paſſant guardant, O.
} a Queen, holding a ſceptre in her left hand, her right on her breaſt.

Queen *Eleanor*, wife of Edward I.

7. *England*, with a label of 5. *Crouchback.*
8. Barrè A. and G. 8 Martlets S. *Chaworth.*
} an old King; in his right hand gloves; in left a ſceptre.

Henry of *Monmouth* earl of *Lancaſter*, and *Maud Chaworth* his wife.

{9. G. a ſpread Eagle O. } a Queen, holding a ſceptre in her right hand,
{10. As 1. } her left on her breaſt.

Query, if not *Beatrix*, Queen of *Sicily*, wife of *Charles* King of *Sicily*, daughter of Raymond, Earl of *Provence*, father of *Henry* III's Queen.

{11. *England*, with a label of 5 points. } an old King bearded, his right hand
{12. A croſs patonce vaire. *Fortibus*. } gloved, lifted up; in his left a ſceptre.

Crouchback and his firſt wife *Aveline de Fortibus*.

{13. O 4 pallets G. *Provence*. } a Queen, holding a
{14. A a lion rampant G. within a border S. bezantée. } ſceptre in right hand, left on cordon.

Sanchia of *Provence* wife of *Richard* King of the *Romans*, Earl of *Cornwall*.

{15. G. 3 lions paſſant guardant O. a label of 5. *Crouchback*. } a Queen, with a ſceptre in her right hand,
{16. *Old France* under a label of 5 O. } her left pointing to the former figure.

Blanch Queen of *Navarre*, ſecond wife of *Crouchback*.

{17. O. a lion rampant Az. *Redvers* earl of *Devon*. } a Queen as the laſt. *Eleanor*
{18. Quarterly *Caſtile* and *Leon*. } wife of *Edward* I.

{19. *England*, under a label. } a King; ſceptre in his left hand, his right
{20. *England*, plain. } on his breaſt.

The figures by the arms appear the ſame on both ſides of the tomb, only the arms are inverted in their order, and probably were deſigned to repreſent the various crowned heads to whom the Earl was related. But the arms over ſome of them do not ſeem to bear relation to the figures underneath, who appear by their crowns, ſceptres, and robes of gold, to have been all intended for royal perſonages.

On the belt of the earl's ſword were various arms enamelled.

On the baſe of this tomb next the area are the remains of paintings much defaced, exhibiting ten knights in ſurcoats of arms and croſs belted, with banners, repreſenting perhaps his expedition into the Holy land, the number ſuiting Matthew Paris's account, that there went the Earl, his brother Edward, afterwards king, four earls, and four barons; of which may be diſcovered, *Roger* lord *Clifford*, in a ſurcoat chequé, O and Az. charged with a ſeſs G. The Annals of Waverley, 1270, mention *William de Valence* and *Thomas de Clare*, but the colors on the ſurcoats are loſt, and it is with difficulty one can trace any remains of their figures, which before the laſt coronation were viſible. Such havoc does the public uſe of this venerable pile make of its monuments in modern times.

Theſe knights Mr. Brooke and myſelf juſt brought to light by the ſpunge, July 3, 1777. All hold banners; the firſt from the Eaſt has on his breaſt a ſaltire Argent, the fourth chequé, the fifth a lion rampant; the 6th chequé O. and Az. over all a ſeſs. Their helmets of mail are all viſible, and ſome ſwords and feet.

Theſe figures have been engraved by Mr. Carter in his 5th number of Antiquities, illuſtrated with a verboſe detail by Mr. Hawkins, who ſuppoſes that the firſt and third figures, bearing croſſes on their breaſts, repreſent the princes Edward and Edmund, denoting the ſervice they were engaged in, and that the ſecond bore the arms of the earls of Provence; but unfortunately Mr. Hawkins forgets that theſe bearings were arms, not badges; and that the arms of *Veſey*, are O a croſs S. We need not ſeek for the bearers of theſe coats out of our own country. Knighton (col. 2438) names among the aſſociates of prince Edward in this expedition John de Bretagne, John de Veſey, Thomas de Clare, Roger de

 Clyfford,

Clyfford, Thomas de Grantson, Robert le Brus, John de Verdon, and many others. Mr. Brooke takes the second figure, with the arms paley and a bend, to be *Grandison*. We have the arms of *Vesey*, *Clifford*, (Chequé O. and Az. a fess G.) *Bruce*, O. a saltire and chief G. on a canton a Lion rampant.

The ridiculous grant of the kingdom of Sicily [1] to this prince by pope Innocent IV. produced the greatest events, in their consequence, that ever appeared in our annals. Amongst others, the association of the barons against Henry III. the appointing conservators of the peace in the several counties, and the settling the democratical part of our constitution on a permanent basis, by Simon Montfort earl of Leicester, whilst the king was his prisoner. Three popes practised on the weakness of our Henry to extort immense sums of money from his subjects for ten years together, from 1253, when Innocent IV. made the grant which Urban IV. revoked 1263, at which time the king, prisoner to Leicester, renounced it in form. But he made ample amends to his son for the loss of that kingdom, conferring on him the forfeited titles of Leicester and Derby, with that of Compeigne, and the stewardship of England, as well as by procuring the rich inheritance of William de Fortibus earl of Albemarle and Holderness, and his second wife Isabel daughter of Baldwin de Redvers earl of Devon, by the marriage of their only daughter and heiress Aveline, 1269. These vast possessions laid the foundation of the greatness of the house of Lancaster, which afterwards ascended the throne of England; and thus, in the person of prince Edmund, were originally founded the great contentions which long subsisted between the houses of York and Lancaster.

Edmund died in his 51st year, of vexation at the desertion of his troops for want of pay [2], at Bayonne, 1296, on an expedition into Gascoigne. He married, 4 Edward I. to his second wife Blanche [3] queen of Navarre, countess of Compeigne and Brie, daughter of Robert earl of Artois, brother to St. Lewis, king of France, and widow of Henry king of Navarre, who died 1274, and by her had three sons [4]. No epitaph is given for him.

The arms on this tomb are much the same as those on Aveline's, and from the style of the ornaments and paintings it may be concluded they were both executed by the same artist.

In *St. Edmund's* chapel, *Westminster*, is an altar-tomb of free stone for 1296.
WILLIAM DE VALENCE, earl of Pembroke, so named from the place of his birth, Pl.
son of Hugh le Brune earl of March, by Isabel widow of king John, father of XXVII.
Aymer de Valence, and half-brother of Henry III. who died 1296, having married Joan daughter of Warine de Montchency. His mother was Isabel, daughter of Aymer earl of Angoulesme, third wife of king John, and her arms Lozengé O and G are on this tomb. The two fronts of the lower altar, in which, from the expression in the second line of the epitaph, one may conclude the body lies, are adorned with quatrefoils in squares, and in four larger starred quatrefoils are these shields; *England* twice, and twice *Valence* impaling *Claremont*, viz. Barry A. and Az. 12 martlets G. impaling G semee of trefoils 2 fishes indorsed Or. These

[1] The original gold matrix of the seal, or *aurea bulla*, which Innocent gave Edmund licence to make and use, and which is expressly referred to in the prince's letter to his new subjects, dated 1261, printed in Rymer's Fœdera, I. 720, is in the possession of Mr. Astle, who has illustrated it in a dissertation inserted in Archæol. IV. 195—211. Whether the piece of gold with the same impression treated of by Mr. Pegge in the same vol. p. 190—194, was a coin or a seal remains still open to discussion.

[2] Walsingham, Ypod. Neustr. p. 483. Matth. Westm. p. 428.

[3] Dugd. Bar. I. 779. Tillet, p. 107. She is miscalled by some historians *Joan*.

[4] Sandford, p. 105. Lel. Collect. I. 739. Claus. 26 Edward I. m. 7. His eldest son and successor Thomas was beheaded at Pontefract in the reign of Edward II. and his second son Henry, successor to his brother, died 1345, and was buried in his collegiate church at Leicester, which, with his monument, was destroyed at the dissolution.

two coats being dimidiated, as was antiently ufual, make but one fifh, and 6 martlets; and the coat is otherwife confufed. It was this earl's fon that married to his firft wife Beatrix daughter of Raoul de Claremont feigneur de Nefle, and conftable of France; but it was ufual formerly for the erector of a tomb to place his own arms thereon.

On a wainfcot cheft above lies the wooden figure, covered with gilt copper, in a round helmet with a ftudded fillet, and compleat mail, the furcoat fprinkled with fix fmall metal enamelled fhields, four loft and one left on the breaft, and another on the fhoulder, all charged with the arms of Valence, as is the large fhield on his left arm, the coat on which is barry A. and Az. curioufly diapered; over all an orle of martlets G. The helmet had a flowered fillet fet with ftones, now pickt out. The belt is finely enamelled with the coat of arms. A lion lies at his feet. His hands are joined and elevated. The wrift and elbow bands have flowerings; the fword and fhield are at the left fide, the hilt of the former gone, the edges of the latter ferrated and enamelled. The fafcia of the cheft is an enamelled plate, as is the cufhion under the head, which is richly ornamented with rows of quatrefoils and efcutcheons alternately, charged with the fingle coats of *England*, G. 3 lions paffant guardant Or. and *Valence*. The cheft was formerly plated with copper, of which only a little now remains on the edge, and had round it thirty fmall images, twelve on a fide and three at each end [1], now all gone, with the niches. The infcription in Saxon capitals [2] was as follows, on the inner edge of the tomb:

Anglia tota doles moritur quia regia proles,
Qua florere foles, quem continet infima moles.
Gulielmus nomen infigne Valentia prebet,
Celfum cognomen nam tale dari fibi debet;
Qui valuit validus, vincens virtute, valore,
Et placuit placidus, fenfu morumque vigore,
Dapfilis et habilis, immotus prælia fectans,
Utilis ac humilis, devotus premia fpectans.
Milleque trecentis cum quatuor inde retentis
In Maii menfe hunc mors proprio ferit enfe.
Quique legis hic repete quam fit vita plena timore,
Meque lege te moriturum & nefcius hore.
O clemens Chrifte, celos intret precor ifte,
Nil videat trifte, quia pertulit omnibus hifce.

This perfon, with his brother and fifter, being much oppreffed by the king of France, was fent for to England 1247 by Henry III. who procured for him an advantageous match, and knighted him publicly at Weftminfter, and four years after granted to him the caftle and town of Hertford. Having, by thefe and many other expreffions of royal favour, drawn on himfelf the jealoufy of the Englifh, and a conteft enfuing between the king and his barons, he withdrew to France 42 Henry III. from whence the king brought him back about three years after, and created him earl of Pembroke, for fo he is ftyled by Matthew Paris [3], in his account of the battle of Lewes, from which Valence being a principal commander on the king's fide, after his mafter and his fon was taken prifoner, efcaped into France. Prince Edward getting out of Windfor caftle, he fent him a fupply of troops, and was inftrumental to the victory of Evefham. He

[1] So Dart. I. 119. But there were 13 on each fide, and four at each end.
[2] Dart. Ib. He had another, and much more memorable epitaph, in profe, St. Lo Kniveton, MS. note on Vincent on Brooke, pen. me. p. 418.
[3] P. 995.

had

had now confiderable grants of property in Wales, and laboured hard to baftardize his wife's brother's only daughter, that he might enjoy her eftate. He died, according to Matthew of Weftminfter [1], Stowe [2], Hardyng [3], Dugdale [4], and Carte [5], May 13, 1296; the latter author fays he was flain by the French at Bayonne. Knighton [6] puts the fight at Bayonne between the Englifh under John Lacy earl of Lincoln and the French the following year. His epitaph as given both by Camden and Weever [7] exprefsly dates his death 1296. For the prayers of all devout people offered up for his foul at his tomb was granted indulgence for the term of 100 days [8].

WILLIAM DE LUDA, bifhop of *Ely*, died 1298, and his monument in the fouth fide of the prefbytery, near the antient high altar of his own church, though of fmaller proportions in breadth, bears great refemblance to that of Edmund Crouchback. In the nitches at the fides are two figures of Mathew and Luke, with the lion and bull, to which correfponded two on the other fide, now hid by the ftalls of the new altar. In the pediment the Virgin and Chrift. A brafslefs flab lies level on the floor, on which are traces of the brafs infcription, which efcaped Mr. Bentham [9]. 1298.

. . . . DE LVDA : QVOND. . . . .
. . . . IVS : ECLESIE : CVIVS : ANIME : PRO. . . . .

This flab and bifhop Gray's are plainly taken off their altar tombs, and laid flat.

Sir ROBERT SHURLAND, who was lord warden of the cinque ports, and with Edward I. in the 28th year of his reign at the fiege of Caerlavarock, where he received the honour of knighthood, has in the South wall of the South or high chancel of *Minftre* church, *Shepey*, a monument, under an arch enriched with quatrefoil work, with his figure in armour, in alabafter, crofs-legged, a round helmet, and another under his head, his fhield on his left arm, and fword on fame fide; an armed page and lion at his feet, and a horfe's head, as if rifing out of the waves, at his right fide below. This head (which Mr. Hafted [10] fays *feems either part of the marble* on which it lies, or at leaft to have *been firmly fixed to it when the tomb was put up*; or, as Mr. Grofe [11], "emerging out of the waves "of the fea, as in the action of fwimming,") being alfo on the weathercock of the tower, is probably the family creft. Various traditions, not worth repeating, are told of it: "the vulgar," as Philipot [12] quaintly expreffes it, "having digged "out of his vault many wild legends and romances;" for which he thus accounts; that Sir Robert had from his fovereign a grant of liberties among which was wreck of fea for his manor at Eaftchurch adjoining. The extent of this royalty is efteemed to reach as far into the fea at ebb-tide as a man could ride in and touch any thing with the point of his lance. But this fuperftructure built on the horfe's head is as little capable of fupport as the vulgar tradition derived from it.

Sir Robert's only daughter and heirefs Margaret married William Cheney, whofe lineal defcendant Sir John Cheney, adhering to the earl of Richmond before his acceffion to the crown, had fummons to parliament among the barons of this realm 3, 7, and 11 of Henry VII. and dying fome time after was buried under a handfome monument in Beauchamp's chapel on the South fide of Lady-chapel at Salifbury. Thither the fame vulgar tradition has followed this heir

[1] P. 405. [2] P. 207. [3] Ch. 151. [4] Bar. II. 776. [5] Carte, II. 261.
[6] P. 2509. [7] P. 476. [8] Dart. I. 120. [9] Hift. of Ely, p. 151. II. 17.
[10] Hift. of Kent, II. 653. 661. [11] Account under his view of Minftre Church. [12] Kent, p. 182.

of the Shurland possessions. The vergers pretend that it being foretold to Sir John that his horse would be his death, he caused him to be killed, and standing by as the animal was in the agonies of death, he received from it a blow on his leg or foot, which occasioned his death; and they attempt to illustrate their error by the leaves carved under the soles of the knight's feet.

A stone in the nave at *Bottesham*, c. Cambridge, has this inscription for ELIAS DE BEKINGHAM, one of the justices itinerant, who died after 27 Edward I.

HIC : JACET : ELIAS : DE : BEKINGHAM : QVONDAM :
JVSTICIARIVS : DOMINI : REGIS : ANGLIE : CVIVS : ANIME :
PROPICIETVR : DEVS.

The brass figure is torn off[1].

It is not improbable that he was of the family of Bekingham of Bekingham, c. Nottingham, where they had lands from 12 Edward I. to 18 Richard II[2]. Elias de Beckingham was party to a fine for lands in Stoke by Newark in the same country 27 Edward I[3]. He and John de Mettingham alone escaped being included in the severe punishment inflicted on Ralph de Hengham and his brethren for corruption, 16 Edward I. 1288[4]. Whether he died in this or the succeeding century is not known.

RALPH DE HENGHAM had, in the North wall of the choir in Old *St. Paul's*, a tomb, with his figure on it, habited in a gown and coif, under a canopy standing on a lion; the table adorned with lambs and mullets. Whether this figure was inlaid in brass, or cut in, Dugdale[5] does not say; probably the former. The inscription round the ledge, in Gothic capitals, was as follows:

PER VERSVS PATET HOS ANGLORVM QVOD IACET HIC FLOS
LEGVM QVI TVTA DICTAVIT VERA STATVTA
EX HENGHAM DICTVS RADVLPHVS VIR BENEDICTVS.

In the chancel at *Much Hadham*, c. Herts, is a large fair grey slab, whereon was once inlaid in brass a cross florè erected on a dog or lion, and on the ledge round it this inscription in Gothic capitals:

HIC JACET : SIMON : FLAMBARD : QVON
DAM : RECTOR : HVIVS : ECLESIE.

The first rector in Newcourt[6] is Robert de Ros, in the time of Bishop Gravesend, between 1280 and 1303; the next Henry de Iddesworth, 1332. Whether FLAMBARD was rector before or after Ros is uncertain. There was one Simon Flambard, knight of the shire, 3 Edward III. who Dr. Salmon[7] thinks was probably father of this rector.

ALBAN, who is commemorated in the following inscription on a brass in a blue slab, to the North of the foregoing, may fill up the vacancies in Newcourt's history[8].

Priez pur lalme Alban psone de hadhm.

Of these two, Dr. Salmon observes Flambard's must be the oldest, by the way of writing; and both are older than the register, which has in the first place Robert de Ros, and next Henry de Idesworth, 1332.

[1] Blomf. Coll. Cantab. p. 32. Rymer's Fœd. 20 Edw. I. Dugdale's Orig. Judic. Chron. Ser. p. 28, 29. Records, &c. Citat. [illegible] p. 55[illegible] 563, 564, 565, 566, 577, 578, 581.
[2] Thoroton, p. 411, 443. [3] Ib. 175. [4] Blomf. Norf. I. 680. [5] St. Paul's, p. 101.
[6] Repert. I. 831. [7] Herts, 278. [8] Ib.

CENTURY

www.ingramcontent.com/pod-product-compliance
Lightning Source LLC
Chambersburg PA
CBHW030903270326
41929CB00008B/558